DOING SPORT PSYCHOLOGY

Mark B. Andersen, Editor
Victoria University, Melbourne, Australia

Human Kinetics

Library of Congress Cataloging-in-Publication Data

Doing sport psychology / Mark B. Andersen, editor.
p. cm.
Includes bibliographical references and index.
ISBN 0-7360-0086-0
1. Sports--Psychological aspects. I. Andersen, Mark B., 1951-

GV706.4 .D65 2000
796'.01--dc21

00-033451

ISBN-10: 0-7360-0086-0
ISBN-13: 978-0-7360-0086-4

Acquisitions Editors: Amy Pickering and Linda Bump, PhD; **Developmental Editor:** Patricia A. Norris, PhD; **Assistant Editor:** John Wentworth; **Copyeditor:** Lisa Morgan; **Proofreader:** Sarah Wiseman; **Indexer:** Gerry Lynn Messner; **Graphic Designer:** Nancy Rasmus; **Graphic Artist:** Dawn Sills; **Cover Designer:** Jack W. Davis; **Printer:** United Graphics

Printed in the United States of America 10 9 8 7 6

Human Kinetics
Web site: www.HumanKinetics.com

United States: Human Kinetics, P.O. Box 5076, Champaign, IL 61825-5076
800-747-4457
e-mail: humank@hkusa.com

Canada: Human Kinetics, 475 Devonshire Road, Unit 100, Windsor, ON N8Y 2L5
800-465-7301 (in Canada only)
e-mail: orders@hkcanada.com

Europe: Human Kinetics, 107 Bradford Road, Stanningley
Leeds LS28 6AT, United Kingdom
+44 (0) 113 255 5665
e-mail: hk@hkeurope.com

Australia: Human Kinetics, 57A Price Avenue, Lower Mitcham, South Australia 5062
08 8372 0999
e-mail: info@hkaustralia.com

New Zealand: Human Kinetics, Division of Sports Distributors NZ Ltd.
P.O. Box 300 226 Albany, North Shore City, Auckland
0064 9 448 1207
e-mail: info@humankinetics.co.nz

For Robert Kaplan, Lee Sechrest, Jean Williams, and Deborah Brogan—
a bloke couldn't ask for better mentors.

CONTENTS

ACKNOWLEDGMENTS

First, I would like to thank the School of Human Movement, Recreation, and Performance at Victoria University for giving me time to hang this albatross. Also, a big thanks to the people at Human Kinetics—Rainer Martens, Steve Pope, Linda Bump, Emily Holler, and Pat Norris for all their help. Dr. Harriet Speed (what a great name for a sport psychologist) has my gratitude for all her moral support, and Jeff Simons gets special thanks, not only for writing a terrific chapter but also for jumping into the role of being my meta-supervisor and sage council. Finally, along with thanks to all the contributing authors, much appreciation goes to those "gradual" students in our applied psychology program (they gradually get their degrees): Jenny Ealey, Simon Lloyd, Matt Queree, Jacqui Louder, Peter Kello, Janine Don, Shayne Hanks, and Matt McGregor. They were the first "public" for this book, and their comments and feedback have helped make it a better piece of work.

PREFACE

Mark B. Andersen
Victoria University

WHY ANOTHER APPLIED SPORT PSYCHOLOGY BOOK?

Relaxation, imagery, goal setting, self-talk—these are the workhorses in the applied sport psychology canon, and the applied texts describing and outlining the use of these mental skills in the service of performance enhancement are legion (e.g., Gauron, 1984; Harris & Harris 1984; Murphy, 1995; Syer & Connolly, 1984; Williams, 1998). So, is there a need for another applied sport psychology text? The answer to that question, in what must be a prime example of equivocation, is yes and no. Why yes and why no would depend on what sorts of issues and questions the author(s) of such a new applied text would attempt to address. So how does this book address new issues and questions, and how will it be useful to students, supervisors, and practitioners?

The first question, which lies at the core of the format of this book, is, How can doing sport psychology service best be illustrated? Instead of writing about *what* should be done (relaxation, goal setting), what is needed are examples of *how* service delivery is accomplished. The best way to provide a window into what occurs is to have extensive examples of conversations (and inductions) between sport psychologists and athletes and coaches. Examples that give students, practitioners, and instructors actual voices from documented encounters can bring service delivery alive. Real-life conversations, along with commentary and interpretations, allow students and practitioners to hear what applied sport psychology in action sounds like. Next to actually delivering service or participating in a live role-play, the encounters between sport psychologists and athletes on these printed pages are about as close as one can get to real experience.

The questions, How do we do sport psychology? and, How do we do it well? are asked regularly by most students and many practitioners. These are the process questions of our practice. Interestingly, sport psychologists often, when consulting on goal setting, place great emphasis on process goals with more limited attention to outcome goals. Many researchers and applied authors, however, when writing about sport psychology services, place great emphasis on the outcome of interventions and service delivery (e.g., improved performance), and very little, if any, emphasis on the process of working with athletes (e.g., how athletes and sport psychologists talk to each other). My prejudice is that if we take care of, and understand, the process of service delivery, then the athlete's (and sport psychologist's) desired outcomes may be more likely to eventuate.

And that brings us to the book you are holding, *Doing Sport Psychology.* It is a book devoted, in large part, to revealing and understanding process. I have shamelessly borrowed the title from the classic clinical text *Doing Psychotherapy* by Michael Franz Basch (1980). In my master's and doctoral training I used a variety of counseling and psychotherapy texts. Although most of the texts were interesting and helpful, they were more about models and what should occur in counseling and psychotherapy rather than how one puts models into the actual words, action, and process of psychotherapy. Then I started training in psychodynamic psychotherapy with Deborah Brogan, MD, and my beginning text was Basch's. It was a revelation. Before me was a fascinating model of psychotherapy with long transcripts of therapist-client conversations coupled with in-depth analyses and dynamic interpretations of the psychotherapy encounters. Next to actually doing psychodynamic psychotherapy and going through the supervision of that therapy, reading *Doing Psychotherapy* taught me, as we say in Australia, "heaps" about the process of service delivery. During that time in my education I thought that training in sport psychology could use the equivalent of *Doing Psychotherapy.* That was the beginning of this book's gestation. My goals here are not to produce a psychodynamic sport psychology text; far from it. I don't think Oedipus or castration anxiety are mentioned even once (some core process issues from psychodynamic theory, however, such as analyses of the relationships between athletes and sport psychologists, will be prominent features). Rather, I wanted to take *Doing Psychotherapy* as a model for this book and with each chapter present various theoretical orientations and models of service delivery coupled with conversations and interventions illustrating what sport psychology services sound like. Along with the dialogues, in-depth commentaries, interpretations, and athlete case analyses, the authors will also explore sport psychologist-athlete interactions and the developing working relationships in the practice of applied sport psychology. I hope this approach will help the reader consider the complexities of what we do when we work with athletes, how we go about understanding the people we serve, and how we understand ourselves in the process of delivering service.

ORGANIZATION OF THE BOOK

Sport psychology service delivery does not have a unitary model, and I have assembled a group of practitioners who represent the wealth and diversity of viewpoints on working with athletes. The authors come from exercise science/coaching (e.g., Jeff Simons, Vance Tammen); counseling psychology (e.g., Trent Petrie, Karen Cogan, Al Petitpas); and clinical psychology backgrounds (e.g., Kate Hays, Sean McCann). The models the authors use to guide practice have coaching, cognitive-behavioral, rational-emotive, performance enhancement, developmental, and psychodynamic roots.

In some of the case studies, the clients are actually amalgamations of athletes constructed for illustrative purposes. All of the cases, however, are based on real encounters. For the cases that are based on single athletes, names, personal details, situations, and sometimes even the sports have been changed to protect confidentiality.

The book is divided into five broad sections. Part I: Getting Started contains three chapters and covers three broad approaches to service delivery. These chapters provide three different viewpoints or orientations to service delivery and serve to illustrate how models of service actually guide practice in general, and getting started with service in particular. There is no singular model of where to start and how to proceed in sport psychology, but each of these chapters could serve as a foundation for practice. In chapter 1, I start the book off where all good stories start, and that is at the beginning, looking at first encounters, intake sessions, and the development of working alliances between sport psychologists and athletes. In chapter 2, Burt Giges reframes sport psychology interventions and describes his work in removing psychological barriers to optimal performance. Al Petitpas addresses, in chapter 3, his approach to working with athletes in general and the issues of managing the stressors athletes have both on and off the playing field in particular.

Part II: From the Applied Sport Psychology Canon covers the more traditional aspects of sport psychology service delivery such as goal setting, relaxation, imagery, and self-talk. These techniques and interventions are the mainstays of sport psychology and performance enhancement service delivery. Many applied sport psychology texts have covered similar ground in terms of the broad topics. The difference in these chapters is that the focus is not so much on what to deliver, but on how to deliver the service. The chapters in this section were developed because so much of sport psychology service centers around these cognitive-behavioral interventions. These interventions, however, are quite complex, require a significant amount of training to master, and are not as easy to deliver effectively as some past texts seem to imply. I hope the chapters in Part II help the reader develop a strong sense of the power of these techniques and the responsibilities that accompany them.

In chapter 4, Clay Sherman and Artur Poczwardowski offer a look at relaxation techniques and their complexities. Clark Perry and Herb Marsh, in chapter 5, discuss working with an Australian Institute of Sport athlete on what she says to herself and how self-talk and self-concept are intertwined, and Jeff Simons reports on how he uses imagery with international track and field athletes in chapter 6. Then, in chapter 7, Daryl Marchant discusses team goal setting based on his years of working with a professional Australian Rules football team.

In Part III: Beyond Performance Enhancement: Working With and Working Through, the focus moves away from traditional sport psychology services into the realm of counseling and clinical psychological issues with athletes. Again, the focus is, what do clinical and counseling sessions with athletes sound like, what is happening in such sessions, where are the sport psychologist and athlete headed, and how do they get to where they are aiming when dealing with sensitive problems? Sport psychologists constantly come up against clinical and personal counseling issues in service delivery. Often after five or six performance enhancement sessions, the athlete gets up the nerve to talk about feeling blue or drinking too much or having panic attacks. Clinical issues also affect performance, and any practicing sport psychologist, sooner or later, is going to run into clients similar to the fascinating athletes in these chapters.

Beginning this section, Karen Cogan (chapter 8) reports on her emotionally taxing but rewarding work with an athlete who is depressed. Trent Petrie and Roberta Sherman (chapter 9) discuss their cognitive-behavioral approach to working with an athlete who has an eating disorder. In chapter 10, Steve Barney and I present a difficult and challenging case from Steve's predoctoral service delivery experiences with the way an athlete approaches, avoids, and begins to come to terms with personal issues of deep loss.

Part IV: The Study of Service: From Supervision to Complex Delivery is what I would have to call a *synthetic* section, and it is where we examine practice and process at a more complex level. The major emphasis is on the supervision of working with athletes and the professional development of the sport psychologist as reflected in supervisory sessions and the analysis of multifaceted cases. The chapters progress from a prime focus on supervision through to descriptions of complex delivery with supervision as a leitmotif. Complex cases and supervision are grouped here to illustrate the depth and richness of sport psychology in some of its more advanced forms.

Chapter 11 is the odd-one-out chapter in the book in that it does not contain any dialogue. Judy Van Raalte's and my prejudice is that supervision is one of the most important services sport psychologists deliver and receive, and it is nearly impossible to discuss it too much. It is a new topic in applied sport psychology, and we know of no major text in the field that offers more than a few sentences (if that) on service delivery supervision (there is one full page on supervision of counseling in a recent sports medicine text; Ray & Wiese-Bjornstahl, 1999). So we decided that supervision would need a full introductory chapter before presenting a case study. The following chapter 12, written with Greg Harris, is dedicated to a year-long case study of the supervision of a neophyte sport psychology practitioner. Vance Tammen, in chapter 13, describes his experiences coming out of an exercise science department and landing his first internship at the United States Olympic Training Center in Colorado Springs and how his supervision was a key facet of his learning experience. This chapter was written specifically for graduate students just starting out and captures the Alice-Through-the-Looking-Glass atmosphere of a beginning sport psychologist working for the first time at a national sport center. Moving on to complex delivery, in chapter 14, Frances Price and I discuss the many ways she worked with a professional American football player (e.g., consultation one-on-one, over the phone, through e-mail, through transcontinental travel). Underlying all the complex delivery is the theme of understanding the dynamic quality of the relationship with the help of supervision.

Part V: Branching Out: Other Practitioners, Other Settings takes the delivery of service into areas beyond sport and illustrates practice in the hands of other professionals (coaches, physical therapists, career counselors) and with other clients (performing artists). This section shows the applicability of many of the skills sport psychologists teach and how those skills can be used by other professionals to enhance their services. Before branching away from traditional practitioners, this section starts out with Sean McCann, the head of sport psychology at the United States Olympic Committee, who in chapter 15 tells the story of service delivery in a setting that is truly *other*—the Olympic Games. Greg Kolt (chapter 16), who is both a psychologist and a physical therapist (being an Aussie, his title is actually *physiotherapist*) writes about combining psychology and physical therapy when working with injured athletes undergoing rehabilitation. Britt Brewer takes a spin on sport psychology service delivery in chapter 17 with his experiences as a cross country coach helping athletes with the mental aspects of running. In chapter 18, David Lavallee and I write about another type of branching out, through helping athletes with the transitions they experience in their lives and in their sports when they retire from sport careers. Kate Hays takes us out of sport and pushes service delivery into the arts. In chapter 19, she applies performance psychology to her work with a musician. Finally, Shane Murphy, one of the most sagacious sport psychologists I know, offers, in the afterword, a few comments on "what it's all about."

I have enjoyed working with all the authors in this book; they have taught me heaps about doing sport psychology. I believe their contributions will help many beginning and seasoned sport psychologists see and understand themselves and the athletes they work with in new and fascinating ways. I hope you enjoy their efforts.

REFERENCES

Basch, M.F. (1980). *Doing psychotherapy.* New York: Basic Books.

Gauron, E.F. (1984). *Mental training for peak performance.* Lansing, NY: Sport Science.

Harris, D.V., & Harris, B.L. (1984). *Sports psychology: Mental skills for physical people.* Champaign, IL: Leisure Press.

Murphy, S.M. (Ed.). (1995). *Sport psychology interventions.* Champaign, IL: Human Kinetics.

Ray, R., & Wiese-Bjornstahl, D.M. (Eds.). (1999). *Counseling in sports medicine.* Champaign, IL: Human Kinetics.

Syer, J., & Connolly, C. (1984). *Sporting body, sporting mind: An athlete's guide to mental training.* Cambridge, UK: Cambridge University Press.

Williams, J.M. (Ed.). (1998). *Applied sport psychology: Personal growth to peak performance* (3rd ed.). Mountain View, CA: Mayfield.

INTRODUCTION

Mark B. Andersen
Victoria University

SOME BASIC QUESTIONS ABOUT SERVICE

What are some of the questions about applied sport psychology service that still need answers? At an elementary level, this is where a journalist might be useful. The classic questions put forward and drilled into every beginning student in Introduction to Journalism 101 classes are What? Where? When? Why? Who? and How? and many applied sport psychology texts answer, or attempt to answer, some, but not all of them. As an overview of how the authors in *Doing Sport Psychology* address them, a quick roll call of those questions seems appropriate for this introductory note.

What?

This question has two basic subquestions: What is sport psychology? And, What do sport psychologists do? Definitions of sport psychology range from the generic and extremely broad *the study of the psychological aspects of sport* to the rather narrow *the study of psychological principles aimed at enhancing sport performance* and everything in between. Which definition one espouses will have a profound influence on the second question of what sport psychologists do. If one believes that sport psychology is solely performance enhancement, then what one does will most likely be limited to those workhorses mentioned in the opening sentence of the preface (e.g., relaxation, imagery). If, however, one believes that sport psychology concerns any aspect of psychology and sport and also involves the psychological training, treatment, and care of athletes and coaches in and out of sport (e.g., Andersen, 1992; Balague, 1999; Murphy, 1995), then what one does, or might do, covers a much broader range of academic investigation and applied practice. This book will not be a forum for a debate concerning the scope of discipline or the scope of practice. As can be seen from the table of contents, the definition and scope of the practice of sport psychology in this book leans much more toward the broad end of the spectrum. Thus, what appears in the following chapters is a view of service that encompasses any aspects of performers' and athletes' worlds that may be useful in helping them become more competent in their sports, their performances, and their life endeavors. Just as some chapters in the book are dedicated to helping athletes improve, there are also chapters specifically designed to help sport psychologists become more competent at what they do. The chapters on supervision, for example, were designed to illustrate models and theories about this vital service for the growth and development of practitioners.

Where?

Where does one engage in sport psychology services, or performance enhancement training, or whatever we want to call it? In the sport psychologist's office? On the sidelines? In the training room? By the discus cage? In a motel room before an away game? On an airplane? At the training table? In the hospital after a serious injury? The question of *where* has many answers, and those answers depend on individual sport psychologists' models of service delivery and boundaries of practice. Applied sport psychology as a field probably contains very little that would be new under the general applied psychology sun. Where we practice, however, and questions about when we practice are probably more different and varied than in most other applied psychological services. Traditional *where* boundaries for many applied psychologists may not extend beyond the consulting room. For some other applied psychologists, such as organizational psychologists, community psychologists, and social workers, the *where* might also include on-site and home visits. For sport psychologists, traditional applied psychology boundaries would leave one bereft of important data (e.g., behavior at competitions), and often, working with athletes is done in a wide variety of settings and on the run. As Ken Ravizza said:

> The ideal situation is to be in your office and have the athlete come in, and you've got two hours together, and you really get into it. But a lot of work is when you're traveling with a team. It's in a hotel lobby, it's on a bus, it's 5 minutes here, 6 minutes there, and in these little blocks of time you can do a lot (Simons & Andersen, 1995, p. 459).

The question, Where? has many answers and will arise often in this book, as in Jeff Simons' chapter on imagery with track and field athletes.

When?

The question of *when* is inextricably tied to the previous question of *where*. When is the most appropriate time for sport psychology interventions and services? Or maybe we should really ask at which times (preseason, midseason, precompetition, during competition) and in what situations (team selection, a playoff game) are which interventions or services most appropriate? Questions of when and where will feature prominently throughout this book, but probably nowhere more strikingly than in Sean McCann's chapter on sport psychology services at one of the pinnacles of world sport, the Olympic Games.

Why?

The questions of the *why* in sport psychology services have some decidedly different levels. On the surface, the question of why we deliver sport psychology services and interventions seems obvious—to help improve athletes' performance, or possibly to increase athletes' satisfaction with what they do in sport, or to help athletes feel better about themselves, or to improve communication between athletes and coaches. There are myriad reasons for delivering services, but they all come down to two words: getting better. We are all in the improvement game. Whether we define sport psychology services as solely performance enhancement training (e.g., Rotella, 1992) or as encompassing the psychological health of the athlete in and out of sport (e.g., Balague, 1999), the goals are the same: helping athletes get better and become more competent in what they do in their sports and in what they do in their lives.

The next level of *why* questions concerns why we use the techniques and services we do. Why do we use those standard sport psychology cognitive-behavioral techniques mentioned at the beginning of the preface? Obviously, because we think they work; we think they help athletes get better. The question at this level is, If those techniques we use do work, why do they work? For example, Davis (1991) found that after a stress management program was introduced to swimmers and football players, there was a dramatic reduction in injuries for both teams. Why? Why does teaching a distance runner how to relax improve her performance? There is a large worldwide community of academic/research sport psychologists seeking answers to whether certain techniques really work, and a smaller, but still global, community seeking to understand the mechanisms underlying the effectiveness of those techniques.

Unfortunately, there is a bit of positivistic or classic scientific method naïveté behind the question, Why does it work? I am not scoffing at scientific method here; I am one of the scientific method's biggest fans. I want cancer and AIDS researchers to be well-grounded in scientific method. I want any surgeon who cuts into me to be well-versed in what passes for knowledge in science (and being subclinically obsessive-compulsive about surgical procedure would also be reassuring). It is just that, traditionally, the burden of proof and the evidence for the effectiveness of the techniques sport psychologists use stem from models in science that pay maximal attention to the intervention (treatment) and minimal attention to the human deliverer of that intervention. For example, contributors to journals such as the *Journal of Sport and Exercise Psychology* and *The Sport Psychologist* are admonished by reviewers and editors to provide evidence that designs and analyses of intervention studies show that the effectiveness of the techniques used are not "just" placebo effects, the results of attention, or the sport psychologist's personality. Relaxation and imagery, however, are not delivered in a vacuum.

In a scientifically heretical sense there really are no placebo effects. There are only treatments that work (more or less) for some people and treatments that don't. If an imagery technique helps improve an athlete's performance, and part of the propellant behind that improvement is the quality of the relationship (and trust) the athlete has with his sport psychologist (see Petitpas, Danish, & Giges, 1999), then that is no argument against the effectiveness of imagery. The question is not whether imagery works or doesn't work. The question is, which interventions, delivered to which athletes, under which circumstances, and in which relational contexts, appear to help athletes become more competent (i.e., get better) at what they do? A large portion of the answer to *why it works* is contained in the personality of the sport psychologist and the quality of the working alliance that develops with the athlete. And that is what a significant portion of this book is about. The examination of the personal attributes of the sport psychologist and the study of the quality, context, and relationship facets of service delivery is what will help us better understand, to paraphrase Ken Ravizza, what we bring to the dance: what we do with athletes, how we affect them, how we understand them, and how they influence us.

In psychotherapy outcome research, there is an ongoing discussion of approaches to examining the efficacy and the effectiveness of treatments or interventions. Efficacy, Chambless and Hollon (1998) would argue, "is best demonstrated in randomized clinical trials (RCTs)—group designs in which patients are randomly assigned to the treatment of interest or one or more comparison conditions" (p. 7). The rigidity of efficacy research has been challenged by many as being divorced from actual clinical practice (e.g., Goldfried & Wolfe, 1998). The question of treatment effectiveness—that is, whether the interventions actually work in the real world of practice—points out the difference between the strong internal validity of some RCT research and the external validity of proving whether or not a treatment is effective in the field. RCT research, in general, does not reflect field practice. Real clients are not randomly assigned to treatments. Interventions are often formulated and delivered in a highly idiosyncratic manner, and complex interactions (psychologist characteristics × client characteristics × presenting concern × social [coach, team, family] situations) are the norm. *Doing Sport Psychology* is about what practitioners have found to be helpful out there on the playing fields, and it focuses more on the effectiveness side of the ongoing debate in treatment outcome research.

Another, more fundamental, answer to the question of why we deliver sport psychology services concerns the models and theories sport psychologists hold on such basic questions as, Why do people develop counterproductive or maladaptive behavior (or thinking)? How and why do people change behavior? and, Why does what we do help initiate and maintain change of behavior? In the chapters ahead, the authors will describe the models and theories behind their service delivery, answering the question of why they do what they do. The dialogues and commentary in each chapter will be devoted to illustrating how theories and models of service delivery and change of behavior are reflected in actual practice.

Who?

The *who* question is really two rather large questions: (a) Who receives applied sport psychology services? and (b) Who delivers such services? The answer to the first question appears to be, on the surface, an easy one—athletes and coaches. That answer, however, begins to appear facile when complex cases, such as athletes with eating disorders, muddy the waters about who the client is. Is the athlete with eating and weight control concerns the client? Or should the focus of intervention be the coach, the sports medicine team, the intercollegiate athletics administration, the team itself, or the family of the athlete? This *who* question cogently illustrates that few problems are simple and that when difficulties are closely and meticulously examined, they become even more complex and convoluted. *Who is the client?* is being asked more often and explored in greater depth in the recent applied sport and exercise psychology literature (e.g., Heyman & Andersen, 1998; Perna et al., 1995), and even though much of this book is about one-on-one service with clearly defined clients, the chapter on a coach using sport psychology and the chapters on supervision explore, in part, that important service delivery question.

The second *who* question, that of who delivers sport psychology services, is one that has sparked much, and at times acrimonious, debate. This question of who can, or should, do sport psychology never seems to go away. It has been debated repeatedly at American Psychological Association (APA) Division 47 and Association for the Advancement of Applied Sport Psychology (AAASP) meetings for years. It also seems to crop up about every six to eight months on the Internet newsgroup SPORTPSY. The best answer I have come across is that regardless of what you call yourself and regardless of what department you received your degree from, you practice what you know how to do; and, with appropriate supervision, you practice what you are learning how to do.The crucial issue is this: Do people know what they know and what they don't know? In other words, do people know their own limits and boundaries of competence? Competencies are what limit service delivery, not degrees and departmental names. Burt Giges (in Simons & Andersen, 1995) summed up and transcended the issue of who can do what beautifully:

> What we know, and what we do, need not be limited by what we call ourselves. Is helping someone learn a new behavior, change a belief, or change thinking considered education, counseling, or therapy? I believe it is a part of each and all three, therefore it can be done by an educator, counselor, or therapist who has acquired the necessary knowledge, skill, and experience to do so.

In all the chapters that follow, the authors will illustrate what they know and how they put what they know into action. In some chapters (e.g., chapter 13 by Vance Tammen), the reader will find examples of authors pushing the limits of what they know and using supervision to expand their knowledge and their scope of service. The question of who can do sport psychology will not appear in this text. It is a naive and alienating question from the field's infancy. We already have a relatively simple, but thoroughly adequate, answer.

How?

Of all the questions an Introduction to Journalism student might ask, the one that has had the least attention, or at most, limited attention, is *how?* How does one actually go about the process of doing sport psychology? The many volumes on applied sport psychology contain descriptions of the *what* of sport psychology in terms of imagery scripts, relaxation scripts, goal-setting protocols, and so forth, but there is precious little on how to *do,* or deliver, those services. There have been notable exceptions, such as Ken Ravizza's guide to what to do to gain entry for consulting (Ravizza, 1988). In addressing the *how* question, for example, most of us have read (and delivered) relaxation scripts, but a relaxation exercise is not just a relaxation exercise. Relaxation probably officially starts when the sport psychologist says, "Today, I'd like us to work on some relaxation exercises." But what went before this suggestion was probably rapport building and establishing trust that developed to the point where the sport psychologist felt the athlete was ready to explore the quite powerful realm of relaxation, and that too is part of the gestalt of relaxation. What follows, or should follow, after the suggestion of trying some relaxation exercises, is a rather complex interchange that involves an understandable rationale, anticipatory guidance, suggestions for having a good experience, demonstration of the tensing-relaxing involved, caveats about strange sensations, inquiries about questions the athlete might have, and all this occurs before the sport psychologist begins with, "Sit back comfortably and take a nice, deep breath . . ." The debriefing and feedback after the first session and the development of the relaxation experience through the following sessions only adds to the complexity of doing relaxation (see the Sherman and Poczwardowski chapter in this book for more details). Relaxation is only one small piece of working with athletes, yet really good examples of doing relaxation, or any other sport psychology interventions, such as imagery, are rare.

How do we do sport psychology? How do we understand athletes? How do we understand ourselves in relational context? How do we make mistakes? The answers are at the core of every chapter in this book. I hope that through our efforts to answer these and other questions we can help current and future sport psychologists get better at what they do, ultimately helping athletes get better, too.

SOME FINAL WORDS

The conversational style of this book is intentional, because that is what we do in service delivery—we have conversations. Although the style may be somewhat relaxed, this book is designed for master's and doctoral graduate students studying applied sport and exercise psychology; supervisors of sport psychology practica and internships; academics; and practitioners and clinicians who work with athletes, coaches, and performers of all kinds. This book is also for those in the field of sport psychology service delivery who have ever asked themselves questions such as, Am I missing something here? What the hell is going on with this athlete? What do I say now? and, Why is this working so well? The authors in this book may not have all the answers for you, but they will let you know how they have answered questions such as these and many others. And most important, the authors will attempt to answer those central *how* questions such as, How is it done? How does it sound? How do we proceed? and, How are we doing?

REFERENCES

Andersen, M.B. (1992). Sport psychology and procrustean categories: An appeal for synthesis and expansion of service. *Association for the Advancement of Applied Sport Psychology Newsletter, 7* (3), 8-9, 15.

Balague, G. (1999). Understanding identity, value, and meaning when working with elite athletes. *The Sport Psychologist, 13,* 89-98.

Chambless, D.L., & Hollon, S.D. (1998). Defining empirically supported therapies. *Journal of Consulting and Clinical Psychology, 66,* 7-18.

Davis, J.O. (1991). Sport injuries and stress management. *The Sport Psychologist, 5,* 175-182.

Goldfried, M.R., & Wolfe, B.E. (1998). Toward a more clinically valid approach to therapy research. *Journal of Consulting and Clinical Psychology, 66,* 143-150.

Heyman, S.R., & Andersen, M.B. (1998). When to refer athletes for counseling or psychotherapy. In J. M. Williams (Ed.), *Applied sport psychology: Personal growth to peak performance* (3rd ed., pp. 359-371). Mountain View, CA: Mayfield.

Murphy, S.M. (Ed.). (1995). *Sport psychology interventions.* Champaign, IL: Human Kinetics.

Perna, F., Neyer, M., Murphy, S.M., Ogilvie, B.C., Murphy, A. (1995). Consulting with sport organizations: A cognitive-behavioral approach. In S. M. Murphy (Ed.), *Sport psychology interventions* (pp. 235-252). Champaign, IL: Human Kinetics.

Petitpas, A.J., Danish, S.J., & Giges, B. (1999). The sport psychologist-athlete relationship: Implications for training. *The Sport Psychologist, 13.*

Ravizza, K. (1988). Gaining entry with athletic personnel for season-long consulting. *The Sport Psychologist, 2,* 243-254.

Rotella, R. (1992). Sport psychology: Staying focused on a common and shared mission for a bright future. *Association for the Advancement of Applied Sport Psychology Newsletter, 7* (3), 8-9.

Simons, J.P., & Andersen, M.B. (1995). The development of consulting practice in applied sport psychology: Some personal perspectives. *The Sport Psychologist, 9,* 449-468.

PART I

GETTING STARTED

CHAPTER 1

BEGINNINGS: INTAKES AND THE INITIATION OF RELATIONSHIPS

Mark B. Andersen
Victoria University

Athlete meets sport psychologist: What happens? Before we answer that question, we need to look at the situations, environments, and referral processes that help bring an athlete (or coach, or athletic trainer) and a sport psychologist together for the first time face to face. In many of the applied psychology professions, the pathways to psychologists and clients meeting each other are fairly limited. A self-initiated phone call to a psychologist's office and an appointment made with a receptionist; a prescreening interview with an HMO psychology technician; a referral from a physician, school counselor, or social worker; and a few other routes are the primary avenues for referral to psychologists. The meeting places for such referrals are often formal office settings.

The pathways to athletes and sport psychologists talking to each other, however, can be formal, casual, a few words in passing, the result of time and familiarity, a coach or athletic trainer referral, or the result of teaching a university course on sport psychology. When I was a full-time practitioner in an intercollegiate athletics department, I started working relationships with athletes from a huge variety of happenstances, and the relationships varied from long-term encounters that moved into psychotherapeutic realms, to group discussions, to hallway chats, to many hours spent on the pool deck, the track, and the golf course, to athletes just dropping in to say hello (the geography of my office was perfect, being near the locker rooms and on the main hallway that led out to the playing fields). In contrast, the way I started counseling relationships, on the other side of campus, with regular students at the University Health Center, was that their names appeared on my schedule of appointments, and we met in my Student Mental Health office and began from there.

By clinical, and most counseling psychology standards, the initiation of helping relationships in sport psychology, and the delivery of service, is admittedly loose. And so it should be. This is not a criticism of sport psychology and sport psychologists, but rather, a recognition that how and where sport psychologists operate probably represents greater variety and latitude than more traditional psychological helping professions. Seeing, meeting, and engaging athletes and coaches in such a wide variety of situations and environments actually means that we might have to pay even greater attention to our roles and our boundaries than a psychologist working in a managed health care clinic from 9 to 5 would. The formal clinic setting supplies more structure than hanging out at the tennis courts does.

In reference to beginning relationships, the topic of *hanging out* is near and dear to many sport psychologists I know. The following scenario is a common one for beginning sport psychologists: A coach contacts a sport psychology faculty member of a university psychology or exercise science department and wants some sport psychology. Never mind that occasionally they are not really sure what that entails; nonetheless, they know they want *some* service. The faculty member offers to the coach an advanced sport psychology graduate student to deliver some group presentations, attend practices and games, and be available for one-on-one sessions (many sport psychologists who have recently come out of North American and Australian programs will easily identify with this scenario). And then what happens? Usually, the student delivers some group presentations, maybe once a week (must not intrude too much into practice time), on relaxation, goal setting, imagery, and so forth. The student spends the rest of the time observing practice, maybe helping drag hurdles onto the track or videotaping divers, but generally they *hang out*. Hanging out is not doing nothing. We often tell our students that hanging out is part of the process of entrance into service delivery, that they are becoming part of the scene, part of the furniture, and that their being there is helping the athletes become comfortable with their presence. Our overly eager students, who really, really want to help athletes, initially have a great deal of trouble doing what they believe is nothing. Learning to hang out is a first, and often difficult, lesson to grasp.

Burt Giges, author of chapter 2, tells a story of working with a track and field team, and for the first year his main duties involved hauling hurdles back and forth onto the track and filling water bottles. Burt became an expert at hanging out. Once one has hung out enough (one month, two months, six months), the hopeful sport psychologist may be so lucky as to have an athlete come up and say, "Hey, how's it going? Do you think we could have some time to talk?"

OK, here it is. The sport psychologist has been put in the game. Now what happens? Up to this point, what theories and models have guided the sport psychologist's behavior? I would guess primarily social psychology models and learning theory (getting used to a new member of the team). Now, however, begins a new helping relationship, and what models are going to guide the sport psychologist through a first one-on-one session?

GETTING STARTED

In the applied sport psychology literature, Taylor and Schneider (1992) have provided a guide for athlete intake interviews, which covers a combination of sport psychology and clinical concerns, called the Sport-Clinical Intake Protocol (SCIP). This protocol is a valuable resource, especially for those who routinely do clinical work with athletes. It is, however, a rather comprehensive intake that covers ground many athletes might consider odd. Probing about clinical issues may alienate some athletes, and when starting out with an athlete, in most cases, it is probably wisest to follow the athlete rather than follow a protocol. The SCIP is a useful tool that I use in graduate seminars to illustrate the range of potential issues athletes may bring when they come to see a sport psychologist, but I will not be using it in this chapter. I will, however, illustrate two protocols for keeping case notes at the end of the chapter.

Regardless of the model or the theory a sport psychologist is using to guide the one-on-one intake interview, understand the athlete, and form a basis for interventions, intake interviews are all about getting athletes to tell their stories. The rational-emotive–trained sport psychologist will be interested in the stories primarily as a source of information about adaptive and maladaptive thinking processes (see Ellis, 1994). Client-centered practitioners will listen to personal accounts with an ear for detecting discrepancies between where athletes are and where they would like to be (real versus ideal self; Rogers, 1957, 1961). Behaviorists (Wolpe, 1973) will listen to stories for what they say about athlete associations (e.g., "I always get nervous in that stadium"), classical and operant conditioning histories, and current contingencies of reinforcement (e.g., what is maintaining current behavior). Family systems approaches (e.g., Hellstedt, 1987, 1995; Stainback & La Marche, 1998) will concern issues such as family homeostasis (the family can also be the team), patterns of communication, hierarchies, and the balance of power. Psychodynamically oriented sport psychologists (not too many of those types around; see Andersen & Williams-Rice [1996], Giges [1998], and Strean & Strean, [1998]) will be interested in stories about early experience, family involvement in the athlete's sport participation, relationships with coaches and teammates, and how those stories might reveal something about the nascent relationship developing between the athlete and the sport psychologist. What we do with the stories we hear, how we interpret them, and where we decide to go with the athlete in terms of interventions or treatment plans will be determined by the models we choose. But the bottom line is helping athletes tell their stories. Without the stories, we have nowhere to go.

How do we get them to talk? By being receptive, engaging, genuine, encouraging, nonjudgmental, truly interested, and by giving them helpful nudges and probing questions. It is not an easy task. To illustrate the point, here is an example, with commentary, of how the beginning of a first session can go wrong (and later, how it can go right).

Sport Psych (SP): Welcome, Sue; I'm Jim. Why don't you come in and have a seat.

S: Thanks.

SP: So what brings you in to see me today?

What has happened here in the first 15 seconds of this initial session? The athlete has been welcomed, and there is a comfortable informality, with the sport psychologist introducing himself by his first name. Introductions and first impressions are important, and the sport psychologist is letting the athlete know that the distance between them may not be as great as the athlete might have imagined. I always start out with first names when meeting athletes and avoid titles such as *doctor*. Starting with first names may help start the rapport-building process, a process that may lead to the athlete later calling the sport psychologist by a folksy title such as Doc (see chapter 10 in this volume), a nickname denoting respect, familiarity, and yes, even affection. But the point here is that the use of a title is left to the athlete; thus, the title (or lack of one) serves closeness and rapport, and is not imposed on the relationship by the sport psychologist.

The sport psychologist's line "So what brings you in to see me today?" on first glance seems like a good one to start the ball rolling and help the athlete begin to talk about herself. But in a subtle sense, this is a suboptimal opening line that could cause a bit of shift of focus from the athlete to the sport psychologist. The question might be perceived as "Why do you need to talk to ME?" or it might reflect the sport psychologist's own needs. Why would the sport psychologist bring the session back to himself? We do not know, but this is a point for speculation and a good starting place for a discussion of the motives of psychologists in sport psychology settings. The examples the authors use in the chapters in this book are designed for discussion, speculation, and alternative interpretations. One of the main goals of this book is to provide a source of classroom (and supervision session) discussions and debate. I hope this intake interview example can serve such a goal and purpose.

With this opening question, for example, some explanations for the sport psychologist's behavior might include (a) the sport psychologist sees himself as the agent of change, that HE will be the one to help the athlete; (b) the sport psychologist needs the athlete to see him as someone who can fix things; (c) the sport psychologist has a power motive and needs to play the doctor (even though he dispensed with the title) to the athlete's patient; and (d) the sport psychologist's narcissistic needs are being met through the objectification of the athlete and through the focus on the psychologist as the center of service delivery. These explanations for a toss-away opening question have gotten progressively pathological, and one might wonder if this is making too much of the use of the first person singular objective pronoun. Well, yes and no. Yes, in the sense that "So what brings you in to see me today?" seems a harmless and innocent enough opening line. And no, in the sense that this line has potential educational value and can serve as a rich source of argument and speculation about motives for involvement in sport psychology service delivery. Examining and speculating on others' motives for being in the field can only help us examine our own motives for involvement in working with athletes. What do we get out of athletes coming to see us? That one question could easily fuel a full afternoon of a graduate student seminar. Now let's go back and start that conversation again.

SP: Welcome, Sue; I'm Jim. Why don't you come in and have a seat.

S: Thanks.

SP: So what brings you here today?

S: [speaking rather flatly] I don't know. The coach just said I had to come see you.

One of my rather uninhibited students called this the "Oh, shit!" line, and I think that fits quite well. What does this response evoke in the sport psychologist? Questions start coming up such as, What the hell am I going to do now? and, Does she feel coerced and angry about being here? Is she embarrassed about seeing a psychologist? Is her 'flatness' a warning sign of unhappiness, or is she just bored? Is she actually relieved to be able to talk to someone, but just can't get started? Or, Is this simply a case of what you see is what you get, and she just doesn't have a clue as to why the coach has sent her? So where does the psychologist go from here?

SP: So what brings you here today?

S: [speaking rather flatly] I don't know. The coach just said I had to come see you.

SP: Can't you think of any reason why the coach wanted you to come here today?

Where did this questionable response come from? The sport psychologist has violated what should probably be a cardinal rule in beginning interviews, and that is *Don't make the client take a quiz right off the bat.* Such quizzing of athletes has the potential to put them on the defensive. I have often heard beginning sport psychologists ask athletes questions such as, "So what do you know about sport psychology?" The goal of such a question is to get a feeling for the athlete's knowledge, but because the sport psychologist is obviously the expert in the field, asking athletes what they know is sort of like giving them a test (or, at least, it can be perceived that way). In an intake interview we need to ask questions that we know athletes can answer easily (e.g., How did you get into diving?), questions that get them rolling in telling their stories—not questions that put them on the spot. Our sport psychologist in this example, however, has not only asked a quiz question. His negative phrasing of the question (i.e., "Can't you . . .") has an overly challenging sound to it. Maybe the sport psychologist is a bit frustrated. He does not know what to do or where to go with this athlete. His feeling of impotence at not knowing what to do may have led to a somewhat hostile response, not directed inward at himself but directed outward at the athlete. The question has become, "Can't you think of a reason you are here [you dummy]?" The "you dummy" is actually a projection of his own feeling of incompetence onto the athlete. He is putting the athlete on the spot precisely because the athlete has put him, professionally, on the spot. This psychologist, when met with a professionally challenging situation, responded aggressively (although probably unintentionally). Why did this occur? Insecurities about his knowledge? A need to feel competent and in control? Any answer here would be highly speculative, but speculation and discussion are what I hope the material in this book stimulates. This practitioner-athlete interchange is another good place to start a discussion about sport psychologist personal characteristics and how they may help or interfere with service delivery. A question that has never shown up in articles on service delivery or in conference presentations is what to do when the sport psychologist's own problems interfere with service. This is a tremendous topic to discuss with graduate students, but, unfortunately, a debate about what to do with impaired sport psychologists is beyond the scope of this book (see Andersen, Van Raalte, & Brewer, in press). That aside, how might an athlete respond to the sport psychologist's poorly posed question?

SP: Can't you think of any reason why the coach wanted you to come here?

S: No, I can't.

End of story. The sport psychologist's aggressiveness has evoked massive resistance in the athlete, and this encounter is moving close to being irreparable. We need to take a step back and start over. What would be a more salubrious response from the psychologist when faced with this rather taciturn, and possibly unmotivated, athlete?

SP: So what brings you here today?

S: [speaking rather flatly] I don't know. The coach just said I had to come see you.

SP: Hmmm . . . I don't know why the coach wanted you to come here either, but let's not worry about that now. My job here is to talk to athletes about how things are going for them and see if there are ways we can work together to make their athletic involvement more enjoyable and to help with some of the mental aspects of training and competition. What I usually like to do first is hear about you, how you got into diving, what in diving really makes you happy, what's a pain in the butt, how things are going with teammates and coaches, and so forth. And everything we talk about is just between you and me. Nothing we say to each other has to go outside this room unless you want it to. Later, I'd like to tell you a bit about some of the work I've done with other athletes so you can get a feel for what we do around here. How does that sound?

S: That sounds OK.

SP: Why don't you tell me how you first got into diving.

S: All right. Well, actually I started out in gymnastics. That was when we lived in California . . . .

And they're off. The sport psychologist responded to the diver's bewilderment by expressing that he too was bewildered. The message was *we're both in the same boat, here*. This response is probably a relief to the athlete, who may have had fantasies of the coach talking to the sport psychologist and saying all sorts of negative things about her. In order to allay anxiety further, the sport psychologist neatly dismisses the concerns and motivations of the coach. The coach, up to this point, was the unseen third party in the room, but now the coach is put on the back burner. The sport psychologist then begins to explain some rules about their encounter. The most important aspect of his speech is explaining that his job is to find a *we*. He has established that it is a cooperative effort. First, the diver will tell him stories, and then he will tell her the story of his sport psychology work with athletes. There is also a pleasant bit of conspiratorial cooperation going on in that this is also a special relationship, one that is just between the two of them. The psychologist has let the athlete know that she is the central focus and that he wants to work with her. The athlete has come into the office of someone who has no agenda other than to form a working alliance with her. This sets her free to talk about herself, and it looks like the start of a mutually rewarding relationship.

All that out of one minute of a sport psychology encounter? Well, maybe this analysis was a bit of an overanalysis, but beginnings are auspicious times, and it is probably difficult to say too much about them. A central question in search of an answer in an intake interview is, Can we work together? This question supersedes questions of theoretical orientation and any potential interventions. The answer to this question will depend on what the athlete and the sport psychologist bring to the relationship they are about to start (e.g., personalities, histories, interpersonal styles). If the sport psychologist has a strong straightforward, take-charge, directive type of personality and style and the athlete operates well under clear-cut direction and enjoys order, log keeping, and charting progress, then the dyad developing could become a strong working alliance that will be beneficial for the athlete and satisfying for both parties. If, however, the athlete is resistant to authority figures and is a bit of a rebel, then the working alliance between the no-nonsense psychologist and the athlete may not develop as strongly, or indeed, may not develop at all.

To some extent, how the working alliance forms is a question of match. On the side of the sport psychologist it is seriously a question of personality. Sport psychology service delivery is not a relaxation technique or a guided imagery exercise. Those interventions are tools, albeit important tools, but tools nonetheless. The study of service delivery, in this book, will focus on the delivery of the service and the tools used (but not so much the tools per se). The study of delivery is the study of process. In other words, how do we go about the process of introducing ourselves, finding out about the athlete's stories, developing working relationships and hypotheses about what may help the athlete, setting up, introducing, and delivering psychoeducational interventions (e.g., the tool of relaxation), and evaluating the effectiveness of our work with athletes?

Our personalities are the main tools of our profession and they lie at the center of the process of service delivery. If a sport psychologist is genuine, caring, has positive regard, is relatively free of narcissistic needs, truly sees sport psychology as service to others, and is fascinated by the variety of human behavior and human relationships, then the sport psychologist probably has a pretty damned good tool to work with (i.e., him- or herself). If a sport psychologist is needy, wants to be accepted by coaches and athletes, overidentifies with clients, empathizes with athletes to the point of boundary blurring, and really *needs* to be seen as a good sport psychologist, then her need mocks her gear. An even more troublesome example would be the sport psychologist who has visions of fame, desires to work with high-profile athletes, is primarily interested in status, and sees athletes as a route to recognition. Such narcissistic needs may lead him to subtle (dependency fostering) and not-so-subtle (outright exploitative) behaviors that ultimately influence the core relationship that is the focus of this book: the working alliance.

One of the core processes of forming that working alliance is the telling of, and the listening to, stories. The tools the sport psychologist uses in evoking, listening to, responding to, and interpreting athletes' stories are her personality and the theoretical orientation she brings to the encounter.

TELLING STORIES

Earlier, the one-minute dialogue of an opening intake interview showed how the process of establishing a working alliance could start out poorly or positively. I would like to continue with the diver (actually a conglomerated case out of my own files, and I will be the SP from now on) and explore how the sport psychologist (now on the right track, I hope) helps the athlete tell her story. Before we begin I will discuss theoretical frameworks, because they guide what the sport psychologist is looking for, and they form a foundation for understanding the athlete's world, how the athlete fits (or does not fit) into the world she describes, and where the points of intervention can be made most effectively.

To borrow from the classic dream analysis of Freud (1955/1900), I use the concepts of *manifest* and *latent* content as a way to conceptualize the distinction between the two approaches I usually take for working with and understanding an athlete. The manifest approach (what is there, the athlete's apparent story, the presenting problem) comes directly from cognitive-behavioral counseling and psychotherapy. To understand the manifest concerns of athletes ("I get nervous before I dive," "The coach doesn't seem to want to help me"), I examine their stories for information as to how their thinking about themselves, competition, coaches, teammates, parents, and their goals influences, for good or ill, the quality of their experiences in and out of sport. I also look for behaviors that are healthy and behaviors that are counterproductive and the contingencies of reinforcement that are maintaining those behaviors. A close examination of thinking and behavior will give me an idea of where to intervene in order to break some cycles of faulty thinking and maladaptive behavior, often with those techniques so solidly associated with sport psychology interventions (e.g., cognitive restructuring, desensitization, relaxation, mental rehearsal).

The manifest approach to service delivery forms the field of endeavor (behaviors and thinking) for the working alliance to play out its labor. The latent approach I take has its roots in psychodynamic theory, and I use it to understand why the thinking and the behavior of the athlete are the way they are, how they are rooted in past relationships and early experiences, and how the athlete is relating to me in the working alliance. The core of the latent approach is listening for information about past and current relationships (with parents, coaches, teammates) and how those relationships are working, or not working, for the athlete. The core of psychodynamic theory is that past patterns of relationships with significant others have a profound impact on current relationships and functioning. For instance, in the foregoing example where the athlete has trouble with authority figures, that problem with authority may have stemmed from conflict with an oppressive parental figure in the past. Such past conflicts are likely to play themselves out with current authority figures (e.g., coaches, teachers, sport psychologists). I may not try and interpret for an athlete that the trouble he is having with a coach reflects his conflicts with his father. Rather, I use that information as a tool for my understanding of the athlete, not (usually) as a source of intervention strategies. Occasionally, however, a dynamically oriented athlete comes into my office and wants to talk about his parents or childhood, and then I move directly into a more dynamic mode. Hamilton (1997), in her work with performing artists, takes a similar combination of cognitive-behavioral interventions coupled with psychodynamic examination of athletes' lives. Central to studying athlete relationships with parents, coaches, and sport psychologists are the dynamic concepts of transference and countertransference.

Transference and countertransference have been mentioned briefly in the sport psychology literature (Andersen & Williams-Rice, 1996; Yambor & Connoly, 1991), and recently they have received more attention (Strean & Strean, 1998). In the most simple psychotherapy terms, *transference* is when clients begin to respond to therapists in ways either similar to how they have responded to significant others in the past (e.g., parents) or in ways they would like to respond to fantasized figures (e.g., the good father they never had). Transference phenomena occur not only in relationships with psychotherapists, but are also ubiquitous in sport. The coach as mother or father figure (Henschen, 1991), conflicts with the coach being similar to conflicts at home, and romantic attachments to coaches form the bases of stories many of us have heard from athletes.

Countertransference is when similar transferring of past responses, perceptions, and behaviors occurs on the part of the therapist and is directed toward the client. There are misperceptions that transference and countertransference are necessarily negative phenomena that interfere with therapeutic interventions and that they should be avoided. It is true that transference and countertransference can have negative influences on relationships between sport psychologists and athletes, but a distinction should be made between positive and negative transference and countertransference.

Take the following example. An athlete likes her sport psychologist, enjoys meeting with her, feels better from the caring and the attention, works hard at her mental imagery (in part to please and repay the sport psychologist for all her good work), emerges from the relationship feeling better about herself and her sport, and ends up having better interactions with her coach. The athlete has learned mental and communication skills and has been exposed to a healthy model of human behavior and interaction (i.e., the sport psychologist) that she has taken to heart as witnessed by her better communication with her coach. Her transference to her sport psychologist, and her good feelings for her, have fueled the positive changes that she has experienced. The transference has been a helpful one. The countertransference from the psychologist was also most likely strong and positive.

To give a personal example of countertransference, I was the child in the middle, between two sisters, and for whatever reasons I felt it was my job to look after, protect, and defend my sisters. I also recall often wanting a little brother to tease, protect, and have look up to me. I found when I started my counseling and psychotherapy practica, and later when doing sport psychology with collegiate athletes, that particularly among those clients and athletes near my age or younger, I would get these feelings of wanting to protect them and keep them from harm. I also recognized a need to have athletes look up to me (a big-brother syndrome?). I found that among athletes, I would take particular, and personal, interest in their successes, and those feelings were definitely tinged by pride and could easily have sounded like "Hey, that's my little sister" or "That's my baby brother." Such countertransference could lead to helping too much, doing too much for the athlete, or problem solving for the athlete when one's job is to help athletes problem-solve for themselves. Through supervision (see chapters 11 & 12), I learned to recognize those positive (good sibling feelings) and negative (narcissistic need to be admired) countertransference responses, keep them in check, and thus, make sure my behaviors were directed at helping athletes become more competent and independent. Transference and countertransference are powerful phenomena. Learning about them helps sport psychologists understand what is occurring in service delivery and how the personalities and past histories of psychologists and athletes are part of the whole process. Understanding dynamic issues helps us examine ourselves in relationship and appreciate or watch out for what we "bring to the dance" (to quote Ken Ravizza; Simons & Andersen, 1995), to make sure we are serving the athlete and not serving our own needs and wants.

I think I have left Sue, the diver, alone long enough. With the background in manifest (cognitive-behavioral) and latent (psychodynamic) formulations of athlete and psychologist behavior, we can return to the initial interview with Sue.

> S: I gave up on gymnastics when I was 14. To tell you the truth, I hated it. I had made it to the state level of competition, but I was always injured in some way. And the coach! Boy, was she a pain. I think maybe she had a few problems. Anyway, it was kind of tough quitting because I liked all the girls.

Sue quieted down and it looked like she was wistfully remembering some of the missed good times in her gymnastics past. I stayed quiet, waiting for her to either talk about some of the sadness of leaving her first sport, or go on to another topic. Probably one of the most common difficulties of beginning sport psychologists is learning to be quiet. In close to 100% of neophyte sport psychologists (me, most definitely included), intake interviews become data-gathering missions. The sport psychologist has an agenda, there are several questions to be answered (e.g., past history, parental involvement, presenting problem, relationships with coach), and any moment there is silence, it is time to move on to the next question. Having structure for an intake interview is nice and comforting, especially for a beginner, and a difficult lesson to learn is to follow the athlete, not the prepared list of questions. The goal of an intake interview is not to get the sport psychologist's agenda of questions answered. It is to get the athlete to tell her story, not to construct the story for her. But we want to help, and sometimes we just try too hard. The athlete has the story within her, and in a Socratic way, we need to be midwives. Learning to be quiet can help the story develop. In this case with Sue, I waited for awhile, and then she went on:

S: My mom was kind of upset with me, but Dad . . . he's such a "dad," said "whatever you want to do, sweetie." I think Mom was thinking about college scholarships. I always loved to watch diving, and my brother is a really great swimmer so I had been to swimming and diving meets for years, and I knew I could do diving well what with all the gymnastics and trampoline work I had done. It was a natural for me. So anyway, I was good at it, got the scholarship Mom was hoping for, and here I am [freshman at university, halfway through her first collegiate diving season].

Here Sue stopped and looked up at me with a sort of "now what?" expression. Some of the family dynamics were beginning to emerge, and she seemed to be able to talk about her family in a forthright and candid manner, so I did not suspect that her family was a significant part of why the coach had sent her. I filed the family information for later reference: mom, possibly concerned about education, finances, and success; a father who loves and dotes on his little girl; and an admired brother, possibly one she also tries to compete with. But, there was much more story to be told, and she needed a little help to continue to tell it.

To fill out a cognitive-behavioral picture, I often ask athletes questions dealing with what it is about the sport and competition that they really like and enjoy. The answers to such questions often reveal the reinforcing aspects of their sport involvement and also touch on achievement and goal-directed behavior.

SP: You have been in diving for about five years [she's 19], got your scholarship, and here you are. So let me know a little bit more about diving for you. What about diving do you really like? What do you get out of it?

S: Hmmm . . . That's a good question. I think I really love nailing a dive, you know, a great hurdle, perfect take-off, quick rotation, and a rip entrance. Nothing feels better than that, like you know you have done a great job. I also really like the guys and gals on the team. They're fun to work out with, and we do stuff together after practice. They kind of became family when I got here [she came on scholarship from another state].

SP: Sounds like you really enjoy doing something excellently, and you have people around you who also make diving fun.

S: Exactly. I have three more years here after this season and I would really like to get a lot better.

SP: You seem dedicated to improving your diving, and maybe we can work together to help you get better. But before we talk about that I'd like to turn that question I asked you around. What is it about diving that you don't like, that's a pain?

S: Nobody has ever asked me that. I am not really sure.

SP: Maybe think about some aspect of diving that makes you uncomfortable.

S: Well, I kind of have a love-hate relationship with competition . . .

SP: I think I understand what you are saying, but tell me what that "love-hate" means for you.

S: I really love performing well, nailing dives in competition, and scoring well, but sometimes—what am I saying, "sometimes?"—almost all the time, I get the jitters, you know, real nervous, feel almost sick, and just want it to be all over with. Sometimes I dive through it and do well, but other times I really suck. Just thinking about it now makes me feel a little weird.

SP: Weird? How so?

S: I am just sitting here and I feel kind of nervous and anxious.

SP: You know, just recalling past nerve-wracking experiences is often enough in itself to bring back those unpleasant feelings. I know I can make myself nervous just by thinking about my last major competition.

S: Kind of strange how strong memory can be, isn't it?

SP: Memory is powerful stuff. Do you think some of the things we're talking about right now might be why the coach wanted you to come in and have a chat?

S: I don't know. . . . Could you help with competition jitters?

This brief interchange contains a great deal of information about the athlete and about the growing relationship. The question of what is reinforcing about diving for Sue has revealed a deep love of performing well along with the sport meeting some social and affiliation needs. The coach has not been mentioned yet, and I am keeping questions about the relationship with the coach ready. I have found, in all the years of working with athletes, that difficulties and communication problems with the coach are some of the most common presenting concerns in service delivery.

After reflecting for her her joy in performing well and the social aspects of diving, Sue said, "Exactly." She knew she had been understood, and she went on to comment that she wanted "to get a lot better." As stated in the introduction, that is the job of sport psychologists—helping people get better. The sport psychologist and the athlete are moving toward shared goals, although the athlete may not know that yet. I am saying to myself, "Yes! She is starting to take me where she wants to go, toward excellence," and I make the suggestion that we could possibly work together, and that I am willing to help her move toward her goal of getting better.

Turning around the "what makes you happy?" question to its opposite often begins to reveal the stumbling blocks, the conditioned negative reactions, and the punishments that may stand in the way of improvement. Discussing the negative aspects of sport and competition can be a bit threatening, and in Sue's case there seemed to be some trepidation, and even confusion, about approaching the subject. I softened the question, rephrasing it as things "that make you uncomfortable." Her comment on a love-hate relationship with competition was just about perfect, and I knew what she meant, but I wanted her to elaborate on what she had said so she could hear it for herself. In our need to help athletes, we may end up formulating their problems for them. This "helpful" process seems suboptimal. A cardinal rule to remember is to let the story emerge from the athlete; don't tell the story for her.

Sue reported a powerful stress and anxiety response, one so strong that reflecting on the past experience brought about a minor version of the response itself. I tried to normalize that current nervous feeling. If this were psychotherapy, I might have taken a different tack and explored her current feelings and thoughts as she is becoming nervous and anxious, but this was not psychotherapy, and she had not come for the treatment of an anxiety or stress disorder. She came at the request of her coach. Doing psychotherapy and doing sport psychology have much in common, and there are many times when the distinctions become blurred. I generally think of psychotherapy as having a focus on some relatively pervasive problem or pathology (e.g., depression, borderline personality disorder, agoraphobia) that has been identified and is the target of the work. Psychotherapy seems more involved in helping the dysfunctional become functional, whereas much of sport psychology service seems directed at already high-functioning people, helping them get better at what they are quite competently doing already.

After her statement about being anxious, I then made a self-disclosure about also feeling nervous when thinking about competition. What purpose did that serve? First, I was trying to validate her current state: she felt "weird" just thinking about competition. Again, this was more normalizing, but with the addition of the sport psychologist's experience. Her nervousness and anxiety in many of her competitions were dysfunctional, sources of worry, and barriers to excellence. I let her know that those responses were also part of my competitive history to help further the connections we were making with each other.

When practicum students and interns ask me about whether it is good or not to self-disclose, I usually answer that they are asking the wrong question. What they are asking requires a dichotomous answer (yes or no), and there is no such simple answer. The question I want students to ask themselves is, Who is being served by my behavior? The answer to that question will guide the student into whether the self-disclosure is appropriate or not. If the self-disclosure is in the service of the working alliance, helps further the relationship between the sport psychologist and the athlete, or lets the athlete know that she is not alone in her experience, then the answer is obvious. If self-disclosure is in the service of the sport psychologist's need to identify with the athlete, to make the athlete more interested in the sport psychologist, or to bring the focus of the session back to the sport psychologist and serve his narcissistic needs, then the answer of whether or not to self-disclose is again quite obvious. There are few better lessons acquired in applied sport psychology than learning to ask oneself, when in doubt about one's behavior or about what to do, Who is being served by what I am doing? It is comforting to avoid relativity and shades of gray in answering this question. If the answer is not "the athlete," then the answer is wrong.

With her line "Kind of strange how strong memory can be, isn't it?" Sue made an acknowledgment that we shared a similar experience and was asking me to join her in talking about that shared experience (i.e., when she engages me with "isn't it?"). This interchange was a good sign; the working alliance was becoming a two-way street. I believed at this point she was ready to hear a suggestion as to why she might be here. She was still hesitant (i.e., she said "I don't know" to the suggestion) and possibly resistant, but she also wanted to know if I could help. At this point we had reached the second major landmark of the intake interview. The first occurred with the establishment of the rules (telling stories) and agreeing to talk. The current landmark is the request for help. Sometimes both these landmarks occur within the first 30 seconds of the intake, as when the athlete says, "I gotta talk to you about some trouble I am having on the field, and I want to know if you think you can help me." Most intakes do not take off that fast, and some intakes never get farther than the agreement to talk, ending the first session (one hopes) with an agreement to talk some more at a later time.

SP: Well, helping athletes with competition jitters is one of the things we specialize in around here. I think we might be able to decrease some of that nervousness. Let's look a little closer at those jitters right now. If we can get a really good picture of when, and how, and where they happen, we may be able to figure out how to tackle them. I'd like you to think back to a time when those jitters were really bad, and they had a big impact on how you dove.

S: That's easy, that would be three weeks ago when we had the meet against State. It was awful.

SP: Good! [She looks at me oddly.] . . . Not that it was awful, but that we have a recent example to work with.

S: [She smiles, understanding my bungled communication.] Oh yeah, it was a mess of a meet. My brother was there, and it was so embarrassing.

SP: Let's go over that whole day, OK? I want you to think back and tell me about how the day started, what you did before the meet, how you were feeling just before competition, and then describe the competition dive by dive.

S: OK. . . . The day started out great. I got a good night's sleep and had a light breakfast.

What we were doing here was starting another part of the intake process, the assessment phase, where the athlete, with prompting and probing questions from the sport psychologist, begins to tell the story about what seems to be the presenting problem, her debilitating competition anxiety. There are many other paths an intake interview can take (see Taylor & Schnieder, 1992), and this apparent problem may not be the main issue with her sport (Henschen, 1998), but I am going with this anxiety concern for now. I could have put this anxiety topic on hold and gone on to ask questions about her relationship with her new coach (she is a freshman), how she has settled into her new school, academic pressures, previous exposure to sport psychology techniques, and so forth. And all those topics are important and probably should be covered at some time, but as I mentioned before, I wanted to try to follow the athlete. It seemed she wanted some help with her competition jitters, so I was moving in the direction of getting as much detail on her competition anxiety as possible in order to figure out her triggers, conditioned responses, and how she thinks about competition (and her jitters). This cognitive-behavioral information would allow me to make an assessment as to which interventions might be most helpful to her. I noticed that her brother had come back into the scene. So my first thoughts about her admiring and maybe being in competition with him seemed to be holding up. I decided to leave her brother alone for the time being, but would ask about him later if she did not mention him again. From what she said, her competition anxiety happened whether a family member was present or not, but maybe her brother being there exacerbated the stress response.

I asked about the whole day of the poor performance to get a feel for how she prepares for competition, any routines she has for the day or precompetition, and any turning points in how she was feeling and thinking. Even though she does not appear to have any routines for competition day, everything seemed to be OK. That is, until she got to the pool, and then her anxiety (jitters) started to show up.

S: I don't know what happens; when I walk into the locker room I am fine, but as soon as I step out on the pool deck, I get nervous. I am nervous before every meet, but that one with State was a real doozy. Who is the first person I see out there, but Patricia Z. God; she looked great, and her suit was fantastic. As we say in diving, she probably would get an extra half point just for putting on her suit, she looked that good. She's a great diver on top of all that, and I had this sinking feeling that I could not really compete against her that day. And that's when I started feeling really shitty.

SP: So what happened to you? How shitty did it get? [As a general policy, I don't use colorful Anglo-Saxon expressions until my clients do.]

S: The jitters just got worse, and I felt sick, and I looked at my body and said, Why can't my body look like hers? I think my boobs are too big for the rest of me. Anyway, my warm-up was so-so, and my competition diving stank. Do you want me to go through each dive?

Well, here's an awkward moment. What do I say to her comment about her body? Saying "your boobs look just fine," I think, would be out of the question. But what does her saying something so frank indicate about the relationship? Sometimes clients say things to shock psychologists, as a sort of test, to see if the psychologist is still with them or is still accepting of them even when they are shocking. Sue, however, did not have any *did that shock you?* expression on her face and went on to tell her story as if nothing special had been said. I took this as a good sign (along with her feeling comfortable using scatological language with me earlier) indicating that she felt she could say anything. I let the comment go, but filed it for later reference (possible body image concerns). We then went through all her dives, how she felt somatically, what she was thinking, and what was going on during the long periods between dives. We also examined her interactions with her teammates and her coach during this time. Finally, I asked her to talk about what she was thinking and feeling later that day after the meet was over and she was back in her dorm room. Her stories revealed substantial cognitive and somatic anxiety throughout the competition, and paradoxically, some resignation at the end of her competition that corresponded to her nailing her last two dives. It was, unfortunately, too little too late, and she came in eighth.

The end-stage of the intake interview begins with me retelling the athlete's story so I can be sure I have got it right, and I can let the athlete know, once again, that she has been heard. I use this retelling as a prelude to an outline of a preliminary plan for future work together and to provide an opportunity for the athlete to add anything to her story.

SP: Well, Sue, let's kind of wrap this up for today and see where we are. You have told me quite a bit about your diving, and it seems that one of the things that gets in the way of your diving up to the level you know you can is that you get nervous, the jitters as you call them. They make you tense and make it difficult to get that powerful, but elegant, combination you need to really nail the dives the way you want. From what you were saying, it looks like those jitters are also connected in some way to what you are saying to yourself before and during competition, like when you saw Patricia at that meet against State and said to yourself, God, she looks great; she'll get an extra half point just for being in that suit, I am never going to beat her; and then you got even more nervous and jittery and your diving went downhill. It also seems your nervousness doesn't really begin until you walk into the pool area. The really interesting part is that when your performance has gone to hell, and there's no way to place well, you nail your last dives. Do I have the whole picture here?

S: That's about it in a nutshell. I guess the coach was right sending me here, I am screwed up. [She laughs, a bit nervously.]

With such a strong and negative self-appraisal, I would normally want to explore what she meant by being "screwed up," but, as I said, this is not psychotherapy. I think I know what she means, and her negative self-evaluation seems more tied to her diving than to her sense of who she is. I decide to do some reframing of her picture of herself as a diver.

SP: Well, that would make just about everybody else in diving screwed up, too. Everyone gets nervous and jittery and talks bad to themselves at some time in their careers. Competition is nerve-wracking. I have worked with several athletes here on similar reactions to competition. I remember helping a track and field athlete who had nerves, jitters, and negative thoughts before every meet, and he got so hyper that he threw up before his races. After working together with him for a couple months, he stopped getting sick before races. He was still a bit nervous, but he got it down to being "good nervous," as he called it. I think we can work on your jitters like we worked on his. And I think there is a real good lesson about negative thoughts in that bad meet you had. When everything was over, and you knew you couldn't place well, all the pressure was off, and you went out there and *just dove,* with no negative thoughts or jitters, because there was nothing to lose. That might be something to work toward: learning how to just dive without the interference of bad thinking and nervousness.

What I was trying to do here was let Sue know that getting nervous is a universal phenomenon and that she is not "screwed up." I gave the example of the track athlete to further normalize getting nervous, give her an example of someone who was worse off than she (it is often nice to know that someone else has a bigger problem), and let her know that the nervousness can be handled if we work together. Also, her story about nailing the last dives "when it was too late" let me reinterpret that situation, which was futile in her view, in a very positive light. My story telling and reinterpretation seemed to have worked, because she appeared ready to start work.

S: So what did you do with the track guy, and can we do the same stuff?

SP: Where I was thinking we would start, and where we started with the runner, was a sort of two-pronged attack. First we would work on the jitters by learning some major relaxation techniques that you could practice at home and some quick relaxation skills you could take to the pool with you to help you calm down on competition days. Also, we would start to work on your thinking and see if we could replace those negative thoughts you have with some more positive ones, because your negative thoughts seem to add to your nervousness.

S: OK; so when do we start?

SP: How about we set up an appointment the next time you can make it in, and we can start on some relaxation then? For now, what I would like you to do is a little homework. Do you have a training log with your workouts in it? [It is surprising how many collegiate athletes don't.]

S: Sure, all the dives I do every day I keep in a notebook along with my other workouts.

SP: Great! What I would like you to do between now and when we meet next time is add to that training log and keep a record of your thoughts during practice. Every 15 minutes or so during practice, just stop for a minute and ask yourself, Now what have I been thinking? Just note it mentally, both the good and the bad thoughts, and after practice, when you have time, write down the thoughts you remember. I want you to do this so we can get a handle on what it is you are saying to yourself—sometimes it's kind of embarrassing, but don't worry about that—so we can know what sort of thoughts to attack and try to change.

S: Sure, that will be easy, you should hear what I say to myself sometimes when I blow a dive.

SP: Exactly, that's what we want a record of. I also want to talk to you about working with me and starting this mental training for diving. To me, it's just like physical training, and there has to be a commitment and a time investment, or it just isn't going to work. Just like your diving won't get any better if you don't practice. So to start with I'd like you to dedicate a good 20 minutes a day to relaxation, about five days a week, and probably 5 to 10 minutes a day keeping a log of your thoughts. How does that sound? [I was winding down the session with a request for commitment, probably unnecessary in Sue's case, but I like to put my expectations out on the table and obtain agreement.]

S: I can do that. Could we meet again on Thursday at this time?

SP: That will fit in my schedule; I'll put you in. Now before you go, are there any questions you would like to ask me about anything we've covered today?

S: I just wondered how you decided to become a sport psychologist.

Now here's a direct request for the sport psychologist to self-disclose. I do not try to avoid answering these questions for a variety of reasons. A question such as this one illustrates substantial progress in the development of the working alliance. Sue has spent close to an hour talking about herself. I have done some moderate self-disclosure and have told her a few stories about my work, but with this question, Sue is asking for more personal information about me. Her request probably stems from a sense of wanting to balance the relationship. I now know a lot about her, so she wants to know more about me. When athletes ask me direct personal questions, I try to answer them in a way that sheds light on what we are doing together, helps further the working alliance, and satisfies the athletes' natural curiosity (a curiosity that indicates the athlete is beginning to become invested in the relationship).

SP: Well, for many years two big loves of mine have been psychology and sport. When I thought about what I wanted to do "when I grew up," I knew I needed a job where going to work felt like going "out to play." I am fascinated by sport and fascinated by human behavior, so what a great combination to become a sport psychologist. Talking to athletes like you may be my job, but it is also what I love to do.

S: Cool.

I am doing a few related things here. First, I am telling the truth (always good to do with athletes) and not trying to avoid the question, but I am not going into elaborate detail and serving my own narcissistic needs. I am also giving Sue what I think will answer her curiosity. My response serves the working alliance in that it lets Sue know, even more strongly than I had voiced before, that I am committed to the work we do together. My answer to her question supplies Sue with a bit more balance, in that the message is: I too get a lot out of working with athletes, and talking to you is something I really enjoy. In the give-and-take of sport psychology service delivery, it is sometimes helpful to let athletes know that the sport psychologist is also gaining something. Doing sport psychology is pleasurable.

Sue's response of "cool" probably indicates that her curiosity was satisfied and that she liked the brief story about my investment in my work. In Sue's eyes, I guess I was "cool" now. We then wound up the session.

SP: So work on that thought log, and we'll begin some relaxation training on Thursday. And remember, we can talk about anything you want in here; this is your time, and it's all between you and me. I look forward to working with you, and I'll see you on Thursday.

S: OK; thanks, Doc. I'll see ya.

Sue and I had set up a plan, and from all indications it looked like she would be a hard-working client. In a first conversation with an athlete, it is difficult, and probably unnecessary, to jump right into mental training. First contacts are times to get to know each other, figure out what the athlete's story is, build rapport, and look for evidence that the working alliance is beginning to form. With Sue, evidence of the forming alliance and the comfort level have appeared at several points: early, when she asked me if I could help with the jitters; when she was quite blunt about how she saw her body; at other times along the way, when she asked for personal information about me; and at the end, when she called me "Doc."

Finally, I reminded Sue that this is a special relationship, and that the door is open to discuss whatever she wants. My final comment about looking forward to working with her served the purpose of again letting Sue know I expect that this relationship and work together are going to be enjoyable, and that I am invested in the process.

Sue and I had started to work on the cognitive-behavioral aspects of her diving, and she was enthusiastic about getting started. Dynamically, the relationship seemed to be going nicely, too. There appeared to be positive transference and countertransference going on. I was not sure what the basis for her transference was, but I strongly suspected there was some "older brother" stuff happening. As for me, I really liked her. I liked how open she was, and how refreshingly blunt and unself-conscious she was in our interactions. I was hooked into the working alliance, and I hoped she was, too.

Every intake is different, and a whole section of this book could be dedicated to intakes, but I hope the process is apparent from the example of Sue. Intakes are a process of building rapport, telling stories, and establishing working alliances. When we sit down with athletes, we need to listen for evidence that these processes are in place; that what we are saying and how we are reacting to the athlete are in the service of the working alliance. Are our story retellings and plans of action in congruence with what the athlete can hear and with what the athlete can use? Intakes form the foundation for later work. Sue came back that Thursday, and we worked for two more years together. Sometimes athletes do not come back after the first session. Why that happens is often mysterious, but a close examination of what occurred in the intake process may reveal why the alliance never really formed. Intakes are endlessly fascinating; I hope this one was informative, educational, and entertaining.

NEW BEGINNINGS

Every session with a new athlete starts the intake process all over again. The dance of the intake with Sue moved from mystery to shared mystery (about coach motives) to telling stories. The relationship evolved to a request for help and some self-disclosure by the psychologist. As the working alliance unfolded, Sue and I became more and more comfortable with each other, and we had laid the foundation for a long-term relationship. Not all intakes are so easy. Sometimes it takes weeks to get as far as Sue and I did; sometimes it takes only minutes. When I think of starting up with a new athlete, and especially with a new team, I think of Miranda in *The Tempest:* "O brave new world/That has such people in't!"

REFERENCES

Andersen, M.B., Van Raalte, J.L., & Brewer, B.W. (in press). When sport psychology consultants and graduate students are impaired: Ethical and legal issues in training and supervision. *Journal of Applied Sport Psychology, 12.*

Andersen, M.B., & Williams-Rice, B.T. (1996). Supervision in the education and training of sport psychology service providers. *The Sport Psychologist, 10,* 278-290.

Ellis, A. (1994). The sport of avoiding sports and exercise: A rational-emotive behavior therapy perspective. *The Sport Psychologist, 8,* 248-261.

Freud, S. (1955). *The interpretation of dreams* (J. Strachey, Trans.). New York: Norton. (Original work published in 1900).

Giges, B. (1998). Psychodynamic concepts in sport psychology: Comment on Strean and Strean. *The Sport Psychologist, 12,* 223-227.

Hamilton, L.H. (1997). *The person behind the mask: A guide to performing arts psychology.* Greenwich, CT: Ablex.

Hellstedt, J.C. (1987). The coach/parent/athlete relationship. *The Sport Psychologist, 1,* 151-160.

Hellstedt, J.C. (1995). Invisible players: A family systems model. In S. M. Murphy (Ed.), *Sport psychology interventions* (pp. 117-147). Champaign, IL: Human Kinetics.

Henschen, K. P. (1991). Critical issues involving male consultants and female athletes. *The Sport Psychologist, 5,* 313-321.

Henschen, K.P. (1998). The issue behind the issue. In M. A. Thompson, R. A. Vernacchia, & W. E. Moore (Eds.), *Case studies in sport psychology: An educational approach* (pp. 27-34). Dubuque, IA: Kendall/Hunt.

Rogers, C.R. (1957). Training individuals to engage in the therapeutic process. In C. R. Strother (Ed.), *Psychology and mental health.* Washington, DC: American Psychological Association.

Rogers, C.R. (1961). On becoming a person. Boston: Houghton Mifflin.

Simons, J.P., & Andersen, M.B. (1995). The development of consulting practice in applied sport psychology: Some personal perspectives. *The Sport Psychologist, 9,* 449-468.

Stainback, R.D., & La Marche, J.A. (1998). Family systems issues affecting athletic performance in youth. In K. F. Hays (Ed.), *Integrating exercise, sports, movement, and mind: Therapeutic unity* (pp. 5-20). New York: Haworth Press.

Strean, W.B., & Strean, H.S. (1998). Applying psychodynamic concepts to sport psychology practice. *The Sport Psychologist, 12,* 208-222.

Taylor, J. & Schneider, B.A. (1992). The sport-clinical intake protocol: A comprehensive interviewing instrument for applied sport psychology. *Professional Psychology: Research and Practice, 23,* 318-325.

Wolpe, J. (1973). *The practice of behavior therapy* (2nd ed.). New York: Pergamon.

Yambor, J., & Connoly, D. (1991). Issues confronting female sport psychology consultants working with male student-athletes. *The Sport Psychologist, 5,* 304-312.

APPENDIX

Keeping Records

Record keeping in applied sport psychology practice serves several purposes. The act of writing down case notes gives the practitioner some time (and some psychological distance) to reflect on the session and think about what the important issues were. Case records also act as refresher notes to go over before the next meeting with the athlete or team. Keeping records is part of staying in compliance with ethical (and legal) codes. For example, in the American Psychological Association's Ethical Principles of Psychologists and Code of Conduct, sections 1.24, 5.04, 5.09, and 5.10 all deal with some aspect of keeping records.

In medical and psychological record keeping the most common format is called SOAP, each letter standing for a part of the record. The S (subjective) stands for the client's stated views, perceptions, needs, discomforts, or problems—how the client sees the situation. The O (objective) represents the sport psychologist's observations about the client during the meeting. ("Objective" has always seemed a misnomer to me, given the subjective nature of all human observations.) The A (assessment) is the sport psychologist's picture of what is going on with the client (a synthesis of S and O), and P represents the plan of action that the athlete and the sport psychologist have agreed to embark upon.

For an intake session, as in the one depicted in this chapter, the progress notes will most likely be substantially longer than the usual notes for a tenth session. In the following example from one of my sport psychology interns (names, places, dates, etc. have all been changed), all of the parts of the SOAP format are present even though they are not labeled with letters.

Intake Summary

Name: Juliette O.

Age: 18

Sport: Cross Country

Date: September 3, 1992

Intern: Ignatius J. Reilly, MA

Reason for Referral: Juliette was self-referred for concerns related to low self-confidence and subpar athletic performance.

Background: Juliette is an 18-year-old freshman from Lima, Ohio. She is currently living in a dormitory on campus. Her roommate is also an athlete on the cross country team.

Juliette reported that she is adjusting fairly well to the academic demands that have been placed upon her. She said she was a "B" student in high school. Juliette stated that, in terms of social contact, she "mostly hangs out with athletes."

Juliette was not invited to the preseason cross country camp in the mountains, which she had been expecting to attend. She expressed anger and disappointment at having been left off the list of those who could attend the camp. She said that because she did not go to camp, she entered the season feeling alienated from the team. Juliette indicated that these feelings have abated somewhat as she has gotten to know other team members. Nonetheless, the team's level of "closeness" has fallen short of her expectations.

In the first meet, Juliette's performance was noticeably below both her expectations and her high school performance level. She said that the meet was a letdown for her (because of the relative lack of fanfare associated with a small college cross country meet) and noted that she had little energy during the race. Juliette suspected that she may have warmed up too much before the race, and added that the team was "training through" the meet.

Juliette stated that her major problem is low self-confidence. She said she frequently doubts herself and gives up on herself, both in practice and in meets. She expressed satisfaction with only two races in her whole career. Juliette indicated that before races she tries to convince herself that she can run well. She listens to music, thinks of strategy, and has positive images, but when she begins to fall off the pace during a race, she uses negative self-talk. Juliette said that she has historically done better in unimportant meets than in important meets. She said her performance "bombs" when she is most confident before the race. She reported that she cannot remember ever having self-confidence for any lasting period of time. She did not attribute her lack of self-confidence to any environmental factor (e.g., parents, coaches).

Juliette assessed her strengths as being a nice, cheerful person who tries hard. She could not identify any sport-specific assets. Juliette said her main weaknesses are a negative attitude, a lack of self-confidence, and a poor latter stage of the race in cross country.

Impressions: Consistent with her statements, Juliette appears to lack self-confidence, especially with regard to her sport involvement. Her low self-efficacy seems to be compounded and reinforced by negative self-talk. She is disappointed by her cross country performance to date and is unsure of what she can do to improve. In our discussion of using psychological skills, Juliette demonstrated motivation to work on developing those skills for her sport.

Recommendations: At the end of the intake session, Juliette agreed, and was encouraged, to document her cognitions associated with running. She was instructed to identify the antecedents, content, and consequences of her self-talk (particularly negative self-statements), and to keep track of them in a logbook. This procedure will serve for further assessment of Juliette's sport-related cognitions and their relation to her athletic performance.

A second appointment was made for the following week. Future interventions could include goal assessment and cognitive restructuring for her athletic-related negative self-talk.

______________________ ______________________

Intern Supervisor

Note

The foregoing example is from the files of a thorough and conscientious student, and I encourage my students to keep such records early in their work with athletes. Recording notes of this length is a time-consuming, but valuable, exercise for students finding their way around the world of service delivery. The act of writing down cases in detail helps students really think about their encounters and formulations of clients' situations. As service continues with an athlete, progress notes usually become shorter (unless a crisis occurs). The notes on Juliette, after three months of service, were about a quarter of the length of the intake summary.

Keeping adequate progress notes in this age of accountability, litigation, responsibility, and professionalism is (no hyperbole intended) imperative. Good notes help us deliver good service and remind us of where our athletes have been and where they are headed. Case notes also become valuable resources when one sits down and begins to write a chapter for a book such as *Doing Sport Psychology.*

CHAPTER 2

REMOVING PSYCHOLOGICAL BARRIERS: CLEARING THE WAY

Burt Giges
Springfield College and Westchester Track Club

In sport psychology, performance enhancement generally refers to helping athletes improve, using a variety of methods or techniques referred to as *psychological skills training* or *mental training*. These techniques include goal setting, relaxation, imagery, self-talk, concentration, and others (Cox, 1994; Nideffer, 1985; Orlick, 1986; Van Raalte & Brewer, 1996; Weinberg & Gould, 1995; Williams, 1998). In this chapter, I will describe an alternative approach to performance enhancement that identifies and aims to remove psychological barriers to performance excellence (Giges, 1997). This approach represents a synthesis of different disciplines learned in the course of my professional development. To give in-depth meaning to this synthesis, I will summarize my philosophical perspective and identify the guiding principles and focus in my work. Examples of the method, selected from dialogues with athletes and graduate students, will then be presented.

PHILOSOPHICAL PERSPECTIVE

What we do as practitioners comes in large part from our training. From my medical research background, I learned the importance of careful observation and evaluation—to inquire how something worked and what happened that made a difference. From psychoanalytic theory, I gained an understanding of the principle that all behavior has meaning, that past events and unconscious processes influence present functioning, and that the working alliance between the practitioner and the client occupies a central role (Greenson, 1967; Munroe, 1955). From gestalt therapy, I developed an appreciation of the significance of awareness, responsibility, and present experience—how the athlete is functioning in the here and now (Perls, 1969). From transactional analysis, I discovered the child and parent within and their influence on internal dialogue and on communication (Berne, 1961). Cognitive therapy taught me to emphasize thinking as the major determinant of feelings and behavior (Beck, 1967), and I regard feelings (affect) as the important mediator between thinking and behavior (Giges, 1995).

Although originally trained as a clinician, I gradually became more of an educator working with a growth and development model (Erikson, 1950; Danish, Petitpas, & Hale, 1992), in which problems are viewed as the result of learning, rather than with the medical model of psychotherapy. The growth model came into prominence as part of the human potential movement in the 1960s, from the seminal work of Abraham Maslow (1954) and other founding contributors to humanistic psychology (e.g., Carl Rogers, Gordon Allport, James Bugental). The growth model includes focusing on developing one's potential, giving prominence to here-and-now experience, encouraging risk-taking behavior, and highlighting choices and responsibility. A basic assumption of the model, as applied in sport psychology, is that athletes inherently have the capacity for functioning optimally and would be able to do so if nothing were in the way. Removing psychological barriers is an approach that helps release potential and can be seen as "clearing the way." The medical model, in contrast, implies that problems are a result of sickness or disease and that something is wrong with the patient. Helping the patient, therefore, would require interventions by an expert to correct or alleviate the defect or illness.

For me, the greatest challenge in working in sport psychology was the shift from the clinical perspective to the educational one. The most useful idea in making this transition was the concept of psychological barriers to optimal functioning rather than the emphasis on deficits and illness (Giges, 1996a). With this change, concentrating on the present became more important than the past and opened new possibilities for effective interventions. I had learned from my training that for significant change to occur, it was necessary to have long-term contact. As I began to explore alternatives, I found this idea too restrictive. Working with an athlete about performance is not the same as psychodynamic psychotherapy (Giges, 1996b). In the process of removing psychological barriers, transference, resistance, and early childhood experiences (classic psychoanalytic concerns) are not usually the focus of the work (Giges, 1998). Present functioning and here-and-now experience are the starting points of intervention.

GUIDING PRINCIPLES

In the process of synthesizing the several influences on my present work, there are three guiding principles that help me integrate the concepts and apply them in consultation with athletes: (a) examining present psychological experience, (b) listening carefully to the athlete's language, and (c) using "entry points" to help remove psychological barriers.

Psychological Experience

Past negative experiences (a psychodynamic factor) might recede into the background of our inner world (a gestalt therapy concept), were it not for present thinking patterns that keep them in the foreground (a cognitive therapy principle). For example, past parental ridicule of a young athlete's performance can exert a detrimental influence if the athlete continues an internal dialogue of self-ridicule in the present. This dialogue, which began in the past, now takes place in the present between the critical parent and the child within (a transactional analysis concept) and represents a psychological barrier to optimal functioning. I have found that focusing on removing such present barriers, in this case self-ridicule, has been an effective method in helping athletes improve their performance.

Present psychological experience includes thoughts, feelings, needs, wants, and behavior. Each of these, in turn, consists of many specifics. Thoughts include ideas, opinions, judgments, decisions, and speculations, as well as memories of past experience. Feelings represent the emotional part of an experience, such as fear, anger, sadness, joy, shame, guilt, and embarrassment. Needs are the basic elements of psychological growth, and are broad and enduring (Maslow, 1954). Some examples are the need for safety and security, for self-worth and self-acceptance, and for autonomy and mastery (Maslow, 1962). Others are the needs for belonging, meaning, and purpose (Frankl, 1992) and for intimacy and relationship (Erikson, 1950). Wants pertain to issues of striving or desire and are the specific ways to meet underlying needs. For example, wanting to do well in competition would help meet the needs for mastery or for self-acceptance. Behavior is the physical bridge between our inner experience and the outer world and between ourselves and others. Fully understanding an athlete's experience, therefore, involves knowing something about each component of psychological experience and may be accomplished by exploring feelings when thoughts are described, inquiring about thoughts after feelings are expressed, and in both instances listening for the athlete's wants.

Listening

Words can be clues to inner experience, revealing hidden thoughts, feelings, or wants. We can, therefore, use words in much the same way as we use nonverbal messages, such as voice tone, rate and volume of speech, facial expressions, and body positions or movements, to help understand athletes. Words, however, not only express experience, they also contribute to it, operating as a feedback loop. An example would be athletes who call themselves "losers." They not only reveal their dissatisfaction and unhappiness, they also reinforce their sense of impotence and undermine their self-confidence. Words that are not spoken can be as meaningful as those that are. A useful clue to something that is avoided is the unanswered question. Not answering a question may indicate an underlying fear, guilt, embarrassment, shame, or other unpleasant feeling or thought.

Entry Points

In describing their experiences, athletes will often say something that the consultant hears as an opportunity for more in-depth exploration. These entry points are openings that can be used to help increase athletes' understanding of their experience, such as an unexpressed feeling, an unrecognized want, or an underlying judgment. They allow the consultant to follow the athlete's discussion, then lead her or him into unexplored areas. For example, if an athlete is describing performance and mentions that he or she does better in practice than in competition, this would be an opportunity to explore the significance of that experience more fully.

REMOVING PSYCHOLOGICAL BARRIERS

Danish, Petitpas, and Hale (1992) have described various roadblocks athletes may encounter in reaching their goals. They stated that "these individuals had to overcome their roadblocks before they were able to work toward their goals. For many, removing the roadblocks became a goal in itself." (p. 409). The process of removing psychological barriers, which is analogous to overcoming roadblocks, involves identifying them, exploring their meaning, and initiating a change that will decrease their impact on athletes.

Identifying Barriers

Psychological barriers include those aspects of athletes' experiences that interfere with the ability to use the talent or skills they have. The barriers may be categorized into the three familiar groups—cognitive, affective, and behavioral, and the one less-familiar group—conative (pertaining to issues of striving and desire; i.e., wants). Cognitive barriers include self-criticism, self-doubt, low self-confidence, low self-esteem, unrealistic expectations, and negative thinking patterns. These barriers can be detected in the language used by the athlete, or in facial expressions or gestures. For example, athletes calling themselves "stupid" can undermine self-confidence. Affective barriers might be embarrassment, guilt, shame, anxiety, anger, sadness, disappointment, or hurt feelings. If not directly expressed by the athlete, these feelings often reveal themselves in voice tone, rate of speech, or in bodily gestures or positions. Behavioral barriers could be overtraining, pushing too hard, impulsiveness, giving up, communicating poorly, or other self-defeating behaviors. Examples of conative barriers are low motivation, loss of interest, and conflicting wants between sport and other interests or between what the athlete wants and what others want. In the course of identifying which barriers are interfering with performance, it is important to be as specific as possible. For example, if an athlete is vague in describing an upset, helping remove that upset may require knowing whether the upset feelings are sadness, anger, fear, shame, or some combination of several feelings. Specificity is preparation for the next step, and that is examining the meaning given to the identified barrier.

Exploring the Meaning

In the process of removing a psychological barrier, it is often necessary to examine the meaning given to it in some detail. This examination could begin, for example, with the question, "What would it mean for you to perform poorly?" Examining meaning also involves (a) describing the content of the barrier (e.g., "I'll never be able to do it," "I'm not good enough"); (b) determining how much power or intensity it has, its impact (e.g., how much of a grip it has on the athlete, how strongly it is believed); (c) considering the context (e.g., whether it is part of a larger issue, such as entitlement, assertiveness, or self-concept); and (d) if necessary, identifying its origin, such as when, how, or where it began, or who might have believed it in the past. This last step may be useful if the previous information is not sufficient to make an effective intervention.

Initiating Change

Having some understanding of the meaning given to the barrier paves the way for initiating a change in that meaning, so as to diminish its impact on the athlete. The purpose of this change is to help athletes alter the habitual patterns that lead to distressful feelings or troublesome behavior. The entry points previously mentioned can be used to create a shift in the athlete's experience. Examples of ways to initiate change include (a) exploring behavioral options; (b) helping the athlete recognize "all or none" thinking; (c) identifying the athlete's pessimistic anticipations, such as "what if . . . "; and (d) comparing reality and fantasy (i.e., the actual experience with ideas about the experience). These examples are not, of course, unique to this approach. Whatever changes are initiated usually require practice and persistence in order to be maintained and strengthened. As will be shown, however, some shifts in experience can occur relatively rapidly and can be of lasting benefit.

CASE ILLUSTRATIONS

The following are illustrations of removing psychological barriers, drawn from sessions conducted either in an office setting or from workshops in sport psychology. As stated in the introduction, sport psychology services are delivered in a variety of settings. Besides holding sessions in my office and conducting workshops, I also deliver service at the sporting venues during practice and competition. Office settings allow for maximum uninterrupted privacy, and at times that is exactly what the athlete needs. Field settings allow for interventions in the real world and are the time for putting what was discussed in the office into practice (literally).

In the Office

The duration of a first session is usually about an hour and a half, and subsequent sessions often last at least an hour. The four examples selected in this section illustrate several psychological barriers commonly seen in consultation with athletes.

An Anxious Young Athlete S is a high school junior and a member of the swim team. His mother called to ask if I would see him because he was unhappy about his swimming. I saw him for three sessions of 60 to 90 minutes' duration. The following excerpts were taken from each session and were selected to illustrate the problem, how it was approached, and the result.

Session I

B: Your mom told me on the phone you were unhappy about your swimming.

S: Yeah.

B: Would you tell me more about it?

S: I haven't been doing too well.

B: In what way?

S: My times are terrible.

B: Would you fill me in on the details?

S: Whatever I race.

B: What do you mean?

S: It doesn't matter whether it's the 100, the 200, or the 400.

B: Is this happening just in competition?

S: I don't know . . . I guess. I do better in practice.

His response is an example of an entry point—an opportunity to go beneath the surface for a clue in identifying the barrier or perhaps removing it. I note that his answers are quite short, and then he waits for the next question. He may be guarded because he feels unsafe or is concerned about how he will sound, or possibly he is demonstrating a passive compliance. At this point I'm not sure if I will be able to help him alter his pattern and become more active in the session.

B: What's different about practice?

S: I don't know.

This "unknowing" is a common first response to questions. It often says more about a reluctance or even a disinclination to think about an answer rather than a lack of information. So I persist.

B: Can you recall a recent practice?

S: . . . Yeah.

B: Would you describe it to me?

S: What do you want me to say?

His response cautions me not to make indefinite requests. To answer his question with a specific instruction might continue his pattern of short replies followed by waiting for the next question, and not being actively engaged. An unstructured reply, such as, "Whatever you want," invites another "I don't know what to tell you." So I decide to change from a question to a more structured intervention, a guided fantasy, which can be particularly useful in working with what someone remembers or anticipates. Its value is in stimulating the thoughts, feelings, or desires that are part of the event, thereby bringing past or future experience into the present.

B: I would like to ask you to try something using your imagination. Would that be all right?

S: Sure.

B: Okay, would you close your eyes for a few moments? . . . Now imagine yourself at practice. Can you do that?

S: Yeah . . . I'm seeing myself at the school pool.

B: What's happening?

S: Well, it's noisy.

B: Go on.

S: It smells of chlorine.

Although he's not really talking about swimming yet, he is giving olfactory and auditory confirmation of his imagery, and this response is an indication that he is becoming involved in the process.

B: What's in your head?

Usually I would ask, "What are you thinking?," but it seemed better to be concrete with S because of his previous responses.

S: I'm getting ready.

B: How are you doing that?

S: I'm looking at where I'll dive in.

B: What's going on in your body?

Usually, I would ask "What are you feeling?" but the concrete questions seemed to be working.

S: I feel loose, ready to go.

B: Okay, now would you please come back to the room and open your eyes. . . . What did you notice?

S: What do you mean?

B: How were you feeling?

S: I wasn't under any pressure.

B: How come?

S: Well, nobody was expecting anything. I hate it when that happens.

B: What makes pressure bad?

S: I get so tense and anxious. I can't concentrate when that happens. I get afraid I'll do too much, you know, go out too hard, and then not have anything left at the end.

His short responses are changing. Without my having done anything direct to help him change his way of answering questions, he has became more open about expressing himself. This change may represent a beginning trust. The idea of others' expectations may be a clue to removing the barrier of pressure. He may also have a strong internal critic. I continue in the direction of exploring the effect of others' expectations.

B: Let's do another one, okay?

S: Another what?

B: Another imagery with your eyes closed.

S: Okay.

The working alliance is forming; the athlete is engaging in the process, and a *we* is being established (i.e., "Let's do another one"). As the *we* develops, the dialogue becomes more of a two-way conversation with both the athlete and consultant engaged in examining his performance.

B: Close your eyes again. This time imagine you're at a swim meet.

S: Yeah.

B: Tell me what's going on.

S: Okay. I'm at the start of the 100, my first event. . . . I'm very jittery. . . . All I can think about is not letting the coach and my folks down. . . . I'm hoping I don't go out too fast. . . . I wish nobody knew me here. I can't stand people expecting me to do things.

B: Let yourself imagine that nobody knows you.

S: Okay.

B: What are you feeling?

S: I don't know . . . I guess I don't feel as much pressure [opens his eyes]. Boy, I wish that would happen at a meet.

B: When is your next meet coming up?

S: Actually, I have one coming up this weekend.

B: Do you suppose you could pretend that you don't know anybody when you're there?

S: I could try. Do you think that will help?

B: I think it's worth a try. You might not feel as much pressure.

The psychological barriers at this point were his anxiety and his concern about not living up to others' expectations. It might become necessary to address this latter barrier first before his anxiety can be decreased.

Session II

B: Hi, how did it go?

S: Well, I did pretty well in the first race. Then I did poorly.

B: Let's start with your telling me about the first race.

S: I wasn't too anxious at the start. I was thinking about not going out too fast, and I was able to pace myself during the race so I had something left at the end.

B: Did you pretend you didn't know anybody?

S: Not when I was at the start. I did that before the race.

B: What happened after the first race? [In the meet he had four races.]

S: I was afraid I did too much, that I wouldn't have anything left for the other races. Well, in the next race I did poorly, and then I started to lose confidence. So I thought I better hold back until the last race.

B: What happens when you lose confidence?

S: I get more nervous. Then I get angry at myself for not doing well.

B: What do you say to yourself when you get angry?

S: You're a screw-up! You're no damned good!

There were several barriers to his performing well: his thought that he has to do well, his worry about not living up to others' expectations, his anxiety, his low self-confidence, and his anger. This combination adds to the likelihood of him having a strong internal critic. What helped me decide which to explore was noticing that he was tentative and almost apologetic in talking about most of these issues. In contrast, when expressing his anger, he came alive and seemed more powerful. Therefore, I decided to use that strength to help change his experience of not swimming well. This change was accomplished by leaving the anger unchallenged and helping him shift its target. The goal was for the anger to become an ally rather than a barrier.

B: So let me go over what you've told me. When you get anxious you swim poorly. Then you lose confidence. Then you get more anxious, swim poorly again, and get angry at yourself.

S: Yeah, it sounds kind of stupid when I hear you repeat it.

If he had demonstrated more interest in self-examination, I might have commented on his self-critical remark and discussed the effect it could have on his self-confidence. In this situation, I decided to focus directly on his performance.

B: I think you can put the anger to better use.

S: What do you mean?

B: Imagine that the anger is raw energy that's available to you before a race.

S: Yeah?

B: Maybe you could use it to help you.

S: How?

B: The way some athletes psych themselves up at the start of a race.

S: Like, Damn it, go! You can do it! [said with emphasis]

B: How does that feel?

S: Great!

B: Would you be willing to do that at your next race?

S: Sure.

Between sessions, his mother called to tell me he had a very good meet, which he believed was the result of his sessions. I was not clear about why she called but decided to wait until his next session rather than go into it with her. I did, however, feel some immediate relief that he had a good meet. The relief I felt was related to my concern about the effectiveness of the previous sessions.

Session III

S: [smiling] I had a great meet!

B: I'd like to hear about it.

S: Well, I used the "You can do it!" and had a good first race.

B: How were you able to keep it going?

S: I felt confident, stronger. I kept using "You can do it!" and took two to eight seconds off all four races. That's never happened to me before in one meet. I felt great!

Toward the end of his third session, we discussed other aspects of his life—his schoolwork, social life, relationships with his parents, and plans for the future. He felt very satisfied about his visits, and quite comfortable ending them. He thanked me and said he'd be back if he ever needed it again. I heard a year later that he had used what he learned on several occasions and that he had continued to improve. If he had come for therapy, we could have dealt with his low self-esteem, his self-criticism, his need to please, his fear of letting people down, and his fear of failure. In the presence of these problems, it would have been easy to focus on the underlying issues. That was not, however, why he came. It is still a bit of a surprise to me that focusing on performance concerns can suffice in the face of several intrapsychic issues.

An Angry Amateur Athlete G is a businessman and a very competitive athlete to whom sports have been important all his life. He came to see me because he had become enormously frustrated with his golf game. He previously had been a swimmer, tennis player, runner, and skier. An excerpt from the first session follows.

G: I'm ashamed to be here—a grown man acting like a baby.

This comment already reveals a harsh internal critic and strong disapproval of his display of intense emotion.

B: What do you mean?

G: Well, when I play well there is nothing in the world that's better—not even a woman. But when I don't, I get crazy.

B: In what way?

G: I can't seem to play a single game without getting so frustrated that I throw the damn golf balls into the woods, and it's even gotten worse; I've broken golf clubs after really bad shots.

Before going further with the problem, I wanted to get a broader picture of his life as a golfer to explore whatever strengths he might have that would help him confront the problem.

B: Tell me more about yourself as a golfer.

G: Well, about six years ago I came back to playing golf after years doing other sports. It's a stupid game, but I love it—and I hate it. I was able to lower my handicap to twelve, not only by playing a lot but also by studying the game, reading about golf technique, about the pros and the games they played. I took lots of lessons, and I bought the best clubs.

He seemed to take pride in being a student of the game, and I saw this as a possible entry point for removing barriers. I returned to the present.

B: What's been happening more recently?

G: I've been playing lousy golf. It began by my getting upset after a few bad shots, then my handicap started creeping up. First I just got angry, then things got out of control. How could I behave this way? It's stupid! The last thing I want is to be like my father on the golf course. He was a lousy player and used to go nuts when he played.

Several barriers can already be identified in this first interview: his anger at hitting poor shots, his self-criticism for playing the "stupid game," his shame at losing control, his fear of being like his father, his uncontrollable behavior, and his judgment of himself when he plays poorly. There are, therefore, many possible approaches to helping him. He could be taught relaxation techniques, better pre-shot routines, or imagery to visualize the path of the ball. Helping him manage his anger would appear to be important as well. He could explore why his game has changed, what else is going on in his life, or how his relationship with his father may be affecting his game. Discussing how his self-esteem seems tied to his golf score might help him be less driven. Each of these might lead him to a better experience with his golf game. Because he took pride in being a student of the game, using this strength might be a way to make a shift in his perspective. Instead of criticizing himself for poor performance, he might then appreciate himself for his ability to learn. I believed that with more self-appreciation he would be able to decrease the influence of his psychological barriers.

B: Let me go back to something you said before. As you were telling me about your studying the game and learning more about strategies and techniques, you seemed proud of your ability to learn. Is that true?

G: Yeah! Whenever I do something difficult, I love to research it, study it, learn everything I can about it. I feel great when I'm really into that.

B: Maybe you can use that in your golf game.

G: Well, I've already done that.

B: I mean in the game.

G: I don't understand.

B: Okay, how do you know when you haven't hit the ball right?

G: [with a puzzled expression] Obviously, it either hooks [goes left] or slices [goes right].

B: How can you tell?

G: All I have to do is watch the ball!

B: So the ball tells you when you didn't hit it right.

G: Sure.

B: In a way, that ball is your teacher. It lets you know that some adjustment needs to be made in the way you're hitting it.

G: I never thought of it that way.

B: Now if you want to apply what the ball taught you, you'll obviously need your clubs.

G: Of course.

B: So they could be your allies.

G: Wow! All this time I've been throwing away my teachers and busting my buddies [laughing]!

At this point, there is a shift in his perspective and he can laugh at himself. The next questions are intended to reinforce his new experience by helping him describe his reaction in more detail.

B: What do you feel right now?

G: I feel good. I'm even a little excited.

B: What would you like right now?

G: I'd like to get out on the course and see what happens.

B: What do you think might happen?

G: Right at this moment, I don't think I'd throw my teacher away or break my friends. But I don't know for sure. I've been doing this sort of thing for quite a while. Can it just change?

B: It might. We'll see.

In the next session, he said he played poorly but he did not "get crazy." He did have the urge to throw a golf ball and break a club, but he did neither. He was also surprised to feel some enjoyment about being a student of the game even though he did not play well. The following weekend he played "so-so," and again did not lose control. After that, he played "okay" in some games, and was able to manage his upset when he did not. He called a few months later and reported that there had been no recurrence of his problem behavior, and that the urges to throw golf balls and break clubs had subsided. The work on his performance difficulties was helpful, even in the presence of a multitude of other psychological issues (Giges, 1998). Although I have seen this relatively simple reframing intervention work many times, I continue to be somewhat surprised when it happens and wonder how long the good result will last.

An Elite Athlete L is a middle-distance runner whom I had known for about a year through my weekly attendance at track practice before she came to see me. In local and regional races she usually expected to finish in the top three. The coach suggested she talk with me because she had recently been dropping out of races before the finish.

B: The coach told me it was his suggestion that we talk.

L: Yeah, and I thought it was a good idea, too. In fact, I'm kind of relieved he did.

B: Tell me more about it.

L: I'm not racing well.

B: How so?

L: I've dropped out of a few races before finishing.

B: Is that a new experience?

L: Yeah, I've never done that—until recently.

B: What do you think is going on?

L: I don't know. I've tried to figure it out, but nothing seems to fit. I'm in good physical shape. Training has been going well. I'm enjoying running. I really don't have a clue.

B: Anything outside of running causing you trouble?

L: Not really. My boyfriend and I have been fighting lately, but that started after my dropping out. I think I'm taking it out on him. I'm feeling kind of down and discouraged, and it makes me irritable.

Here was an opportunity to explore her "down" feelings in more depth. Because this session was not psychotherapy, I decided not to unless it became important in helping her remove the psychological barriers to her performance.

B: Tell me about the last time it happened.

L: Well, just last week again, in the mile. I was running well and feeling strong. I was leading for most of the race. Then someone passed me near the end of the race, and I just quit.

B: What happened?

L: I don't know.

At this point, I thought the question/answer approach might not be the most effective way to identify the barrier. Her last comment about someone passing her seemed like an entry point, and I decided to follow it.

B: Would you be willing to go back to that race and tell it to me as if it's happening right now?

L: OK.

B: Would you close your eyes? . . . Now go back to last week's race, and picture yourself before the race.

L: I'm there.

B: Tell me what's going on for you.

L: I'm a little nervous. I know a couple of the runners, and one of them is pretty good. I've beaten her in the past, and that helps my confidence.

B: OK, take me through the race.

This comment is asking the athlete to help me understand her experience—it is part of building the working alliance.

L: Well, I decide to go out fast and take the lead. I figure I can put some pressure on the others that way. . . . I'm not going too far ahead, and I'm still leading the pack after the first lap. . . . I feel strong, so I pick up the pace a little, and at the half I've increased my lead. . . . In the third lap I'm getting a little tight, and the runner I told you about is closing the gap. . . . At the three-quarter mark, she is almost up to me. . . . As we go down the back stretch, she pulls even, is right on my shoulder, and on the turn she goes past me. . . . I'm slowing down. . . . I can't seem to run any more. . . . [She looks puzzled.]

B: Hold it right there. What just happened?

L: [long pause . . . eyes still closed] I feel so ashamed!

Shame can be a substantial barrier. It is a powerful emotion with deep-seated roots. Because this is not psychotherapy, I am reluctant to explore it with her more deeply. It would change the original purpose in her coming, and probably involve a longer period of time than dealing with her performance problem. It might, however, become necessary. I decided to ask her about it, without intending a deep exploration.

B: Is this something you've felt before?

L: [eyes open] Not since I was a little girl.

I am treading on thin ice here. Discussing a childhood memory of a significant emotional experience brings me back to when I was a psychoanalytic psychotherapist. Yet something inside me says, Go ahead. Just because it feels similar doesn't make it the same. I will try to stay focused on her performance issue.

B: Was that situation also about your performance in sport?

L: As a matter of fact it was. I was just a kid, and we were playing soccer. I was one of the fastest kids on the team, so when I got out ahead, nobody could catch me. I was going for the goal with the ball when I tripped and fell. My father, who always came to our games, yelled at me about how clumsy I was, in front of everybody. I was so ashamed! He was always doing something like that. I felt like nothing.

The therapist in me was certainly tempted to look further into her past and present relationship with her father, its connection to her self-worth, and its implications for her sport performance. It was something I would not be doing unless it was at her request (Giges, 1995).

L: So what do I do about that now?

B: Is there something you want to do about it?

L: No. It's past and I'm done with it. Or at least I thought I was done with it. Do you think it has something to do with my dropping out of races?

B: Maybe—but sometimes becoming aware of something from the past is enough to change its influence on us. Let's see what happens. Would you close your eyes again, and go back to last week's race? Describe the race again.

I was interested in seeing whether that emotional connection to the past would have any effect on her description of the race. She began to describe it in the same way until the final lap.

L: . . . As we're going down the backstretch, she's pulling even. She's passing me [pauses] . . .

B: What's happening?

L: [eyes still closed] Well, it didn't really happen this way, but I'm still running. Around the turn, she pulls ahead, and I'm right behind her. Down the stretch, she pulls away and wins, and I finish second [opens her eyes].

B: What seemed to be the difference between the two descriptions?

L: This time I didn't feel that overpowering shame. I just kept racing. I wish that were real.

B: Even though that was a fantasy, you might be able to make it real in your next race.

L: I hope so.

In the four years that I continued to see L race, dropping out did not recur. What accounted for the change is not exactly clear. One possibility is that the fantasy experience was like hypnosis, and the result resembled post-hypnotic suggestion. Another is that she formed a positive transference with her new father (me) and continued to try to please "him" by not dropping out. A third possibility is that her shame was reconnected to its origin, and, therefore, had less impact on her present experience. Each of these, as well as others, may have contributed to what was a significant and lasting effect. During the session, what had seemed like therapy remained focused on her sport performance.

A Changing Competitor P is a young adult tennis player who graduated from college two years before he came to see me. He was unhappy about the way he was currently playing. Excerpts from two of his sessions are described.

Session I

P: I'm very frustrated about my playing. I just haven't been doing well this past year. I can't seem to concentrate or stay focused during my matches.

B: What do you think is going on?

P: I've been getting injured a lot lately. Nothing major, but I'm afraid to go all out. I'm not playing up to my ability, and I'm not enjoying it any more.

B: Is that the situation in all your matches?

P: Actually, the more competitive it gets, the worse it is. If I win, I think, I should have beaten him by more. If I lose, I think, I didn't play as well as I should have. Then I get angry at myself.

B: Any ideas about why this is happening?

P: I don't really know. One thing I've been noticing is that I'm starting to worry that I won't look good. Lately I seem to be more caught up in looking good than in playing good.

A few barriers can already be identified: difficulty concentrating and staying focused, distraction by thoughts about how he looks when he's playing, and holding back because of fear of injury. His comment about looking good stands out, suggests a strong internal critic, and may be a useful entry point. It also indicates a capacity for insight that augurs well for our work together.

B: Who watches you when you play?

P: It doesn't seem to make any difference. Sometimes my parents come to a match, sometimes they don't. Sometimes I don't really know anybody in the stands, and I'm still worried about how I'll look.

B: What do you think about that?

P: What do you mean?

B: Got any ideas about worrying how you look even when nobody you know is in the stands?

P: I guess I'm the one that's looking.

This last comment again shows some ability for self-reflection and may provide a clue about which barrier to address. I explore his comment a bit further.

B: What do you notice when you see yourself playing?

P: It seems like I'm not really into it. I don't have the drive I used to have.

B: What's your reaction to that?

P: Maybe it means I'm lazy. Maybe I've become a loser.

His self-criticism is more apparent. It is not surprising, therefore, that he would expect criticism from others, especially because the source of his internal critic was from others (i.e., his parents). In his situation, reassurance with a statement of affirmation would probably have little effect. Because his agenda is performance improvement, it also did not seem appropriate to explore the origins of his self-criticism. Starting where his attention is focused (i.e., the critical audience), I tested the possibility of shifting his negative expectations to a positive experience.

B: Who in your life is most accepting of you . . . someone who appreciates you for yourself, not just for what you achieve?

P: I don't know . . . I do have three great friends that I'm very close with. No matter how bad I play, they still want to go out with me and have fun.

B: Would they judge you as lazy or a loser?

P: Never in a million years!

The relationship he has with these friends might be able to influence his negative view of himself enough to lessen its impact on his performance.

B: Are you up for doing something different right now?

P: What do you mean?

B: Instead of me asking you more questions, how about if I guide you through an imaginary scenario?

P: That's fine with me.

B: So, would you close your eyes now? . . . Recall the match that you recently played. . . . Before the match starts, imagine that your three friends are in the stands. . . . Can you do that?

P: Yeah, I can see them right at mid-court grinning at me.

B: Now allow their feelings and thoughts about you to be with you as you begin to play the match. . . . Describe what's happening.

P: I'm kind of smiling inside. . . . I feel nice. As I'm starting to play I notice my legs don't feel as heavy as they did in the real match. . . . I'm a little faster on my feet. . . . I'm beginning to make points I didn't make before. . . . I seem to be playing better.

His imagery continued in a positive frame of mind, and at the end he described feeling warm and confident.

Before the next visit, he was to play in another tournament.

Session II

B: How'd it go?

P: Well, I played OK, but I lost.

B: What else happened?

P: I was surprised, but I noticed I wasn't as worried about how I looked. I still didn't play with the intensity I had in college.

B: What do you think about that?

P: Well, one thing I realized was that playing tennis was not as important to me as it used to be.

B: Is that OK with you?

P: I guess so, because what's really important to me right now is going to med school. The only reason I played this last tournament was because I had signed up for it a while back.

B: It's good to realize that. Does that create any problem for you?

P: Well, I'm worried that I'll be letting my parents down. They put so much into my playing.

B: How do your folks feel about you going to med school?

P: Oh, they're very happy about it.

B: Do you think they would be upset if you gave more importance to med school than to tennis?

P: No way! . . . I guess I'm not really letting them down. . . . I'm moving up.

B: You also sound as though you're more accepting of the change you're making.

P: Yeah, I feel good about it.

In this instance, the performance problems resulted in part from a changing interest (from tennis to medical school), which created the psychological barriers of guilt and fear about not living up to the expectations of others. Guided fantasy can be a useful intervention because it allows the athlete to re-create a past situation that was unpleasant or upsetting and alter the experience or the outcome. This alteration can be accomplished by a change in perspective, in feelings, or in attitude, and followed by a change in behavior.

From Workshops in Sport Psychology

The first example in this section was selected from a university workshop on "Psychological Barriers to Excellence in Sport Performance," in which, after I gave a lecture on this topic, one of the graduate students in sport psychology volunteered to work on an important performance issue. The workshop participants were current and former graduate students and members of the faculty; all agreed that the contents of the interview would remain confidential.

A Student/Dancer/Teacher D is a lifelong dancer who became interested in teaching and helping others to dance. Recognizing that psychological factors were important in performance, she decided to study sport psychology.

B: Where would you like to begin?

D: I have a performance problem, and I feel stuck right now. Dancing is something I've been able to do all my life, and technically there shouldn't be anything holding back my performance now.

B: What do you mean there shouldn't be anything holding back your performance?

D: I was hit by a car almost three years ago, but I didn't have any broken bones or anything like that. I was told I could go back to class and work the way I had been working. But I couldn't do it. Something occurred during the warm-up, while we were on the floor. I started feeling strange.

B: Strange in what way?

D: Physically, something didn't feel right on the left side of my neck. I wasn't sure what was going on. I got scared and started to hold back. I felt like I was going to fall. I thought I couldn't hold my balance on my left side. The next morning I had such a severe pain I went to the E.R. The doctors thought it was a migraine, but I never had one before.

B: What happened after that?

D: Well, since that experience I haven't gone back to jazz class. I went to a couple of ballet classes, but I didn't do any jumps, and the turns have me terrified. I don't know if I'm holding myself back or if there is a legitimate cause. I'm too chicken to try it.

The intensity of the fear did not appear to be fully explained by the physical injury. I believed there was an important psychological cause of such anxiety, namely a threat to D's identity as a dancer. Because dancers do not hold back, her holding back meant to her that she was not a dancer. So I began with her judgment that holding herself back was not a "legitimate cause" for her behavior.

B: Does that imply that if you're holding yourself back, it's not legitimate?

D: I would hate to think that I'm afraid of something I've done all my life.

B: Let's suppose both are true—you have what you call a legitimate cause and you are holding yourself back. Since you mentioned before that you are afraid, which of these do you want to focus on now?

D: I think I'm afraid I'm going to wind up back in the E.R. But the thing is I can't even bring myself to try it—any turns or leaps.

A physical cause seemed less likely to me at this point. If fear were the main psychological barrier, there are different ways to approach trying to lessen its grip on her: (a) explore why she's afraid; (b) use imagery to decrease the impact of the fear; (c) do a relaxation exercise; or (d) experiment with doing what she fears in small increments, as in desensitization techniques. Her emphasis on not being able to try turns or leaps led me to start with the last one.

B: Would you be interested in trying a turn or leap now?

D: I'm not sure, because after this much time, I'm afraid I've even lost the technique.

Because her reluctance was expressed by another fear, I decided to postpone any direct experiment with jumping or turning.

B: So, in addition to your fear of injuring yourself, there is also a fear that you won't know how to do it. Is that correct?

D: And the really big one is I don't want to look stupid, especially after the career I had before.

At this point, I decided to do more preparation before encouraging her to take any risks. Because there is evidence of significant self-criticism, I began to address this barrier of judgment against herself.

B: What would looking stupid consist of?

D: I guess people who knew what I've done in the past would see me working at a much lower level.

B: And they would say that's stupid?

D: No. Well, maybe stupid is the wrong word.

B: It may not be the wrong word; it may be your own thought. So what would be stupid about your performing at a lower level from your point of view?

D: It would be embarrassing.

B: Because . . .

D: Well, because of the level I was at before.

B: You were at a much higher level, sustained an injury followed by severe pain, and now perform at a lower level. What is embarrassing about that?

D: If I do a turn, I might fall out of it, or it might not look as clean as it used to, or I won't spot it correctly. If I'm demonstrating in the jazz workshop I'm doing, and I'm holding back, I don't want my students to think I can't do it.

B: What do you imagine they would think?

D: Something like, Why isn't she doing it? Why isn't she showing us?

B: How do you think they would answer those questions?

D: Some of them know about the accident, and some of them don't.

B: What might those who don't know about it be thinking?

D: I've never thought about that.

B: Well, would you think about it now?

D: They might think I'm not good enough.

B: Do you have any clues that they do think that?

The issue of low self-worth would be important to pursue in depth if this were psychotherapy. It cannot be avoided, however, in exploring the performance barrier.

D: No, none at all.

B: But you think they would?

D: Right now, yeah.

B: So, whether they actually do or not, you think they do?

D: I guess so.

In working with barriers such as low self-esteem, low self-confidence, or low self-worth, it is important to clarify the basis for these ideas as specifically as possible.

B: In what way do you think you're not good enough?

D: Oh, there's a laundry list of ways.

B: Tell me what they are.

D: Double turns, chain turns across the floor, grand jeté, which is a huge split leap in the air, rapid jumps, doing a layout, which requires arching the back, keeping the leg high, and leading with it.

She is quite specific about which techniques she fears. It began to sound as if she wanted to do these movements so badly she could almost "taste" it. I decided to press a little.

B: What seems to be in the way?

D: I'm afraid I'll fall.

B: And if you fell?

D: That's not an acceptable option.

B: To whom?

D: To me.

B: What makes falling unacceptable?

L: I've never done it before. I've never fallen out of a turn or a jump, or from a layout.

Here is an example of an unanswered question mentioned previously in the Listening section. What is avoided is not clear, so I ask again.

B: And what makes it unacceptable?

D: I was really good at it. I don't like the idea of not being really good.

B: I realize that you have never fallen before, and that you don't like the idea of not being really good, but what is it that makes falling unacceptable?

D: The feeling that I'd get from falling. I'm not even sure what that would be, but just the idea of it gives me the creeps. Based on what I've done in front of an audience in the past, it's way below the level I know I'm capable of.

B: And therefore . . .

D: And that . . . it's just . . . I can't . . . I guess I can't accept the idea that I'm less than I was.

B: And if that's true, what makes that so difficult for you?

D: What I was . . . meant the world to me.

B: So if you're not at that level, then . . . ?

D: I guess part of me feels that I'm no longer a dancer.

B: And if that's true, then . . . ?

D: It's kind of like something in me died. It gets me emotional.

B: What kind of emotion?

D: Loss . . . big loss . . . knowing I could do it. . . . I was secure doing it. I got paying jobs doing it. I knew I was better than most other people doing it. I wish I had it back . . . the people I worked with, the experiences I had. It was so much fun. It wasn't work. I wish I had it all back.

B: It sounds like it was more than just fun. It sounds very important to you.

D: It was pretty much my whole life!

Certainly D's identity is significantly involved with being a dancer. The idea of no longer being one is frightening for her to anticipate. Because this was a workshop interview, I wasn't sure that a significant beginning could be made toward changing her perspective and removing the barriers. I decided to explore this possibility with her.

B: What's your reaction to hearing yourself say that?

D: I never talked much about it, but I always saw myself as a dancer. I didn't feel a need to talk about it. I just did it. People would ask, "What do you do?" and I'd always answer, "I do shows" or "I go to class." I always felt, no matter what, I had a chance to get better, because I knew I was good. I knew I was a dancer. And it was more than that . . . it was being a performer . . . you could dress up, become someone else . . . you could do anything.

She began to be more animated. I could really sense how much it meant to her, and this strengthened my resolve to do what I could for her in this situation.

B: How is it different now?

D: I haven't been back in the studio. I grew up in the studio. From the time I was able to walk, I always danced. By the time I was five years old, there wasn't a week in my life when I wasn't in the studio for at least one class. And by the time I was in high school, I was at the studio five to seven days a week. If I wasn't taking a class or teaching a class, I was at the desk. I can't tell you what the smell of rosin does. You know, you combine rosin, sweat, and humidity, and that's life.

B: I have a sense of what it meant to you, and what it still means to you. What feelings do you get with not performing at the level you used to?

D: I'm angry.

B: At?

D: At the fact that I can't do it.

B: And at whom are you angry?

D: I'm very angry at the people who caused the accident that did this to me.

B: Is there any anger at yourself?

D: Yeah. It's the "what if" thing. If I hadn't gone to get a bagel and tea, if I hadn't been standing on the corner, if I hadn't crossed the street, this never would have happened.

B: That may be true. If it is true, how would that make you angry at yourself?

D: I should've stayed inside stretching, getting ready for class. I should have been doing something different. I should've been getting the music ready. I should've been working on the last sixteen counts of the combination. If I had done something different, then I could still be doing what I love more than anything.

Self-blame and more self-disapproval make it difficult for her to forgive herself.

B: If you should have been doing all those things and weren't, does that say anything about you?

D: It says I wasn't being as responsible as I should have been for class. And because I made the decision I did, I'm not what I used to be.

B: If you're not the dancer you used to be, what does that say about you?

D: I keep thinking that maybe my talent was all in my head.

B: That you never were what you thought you were?

D: Yeah, because I can't get it back!

B: So if you can't get it back, it means you never had it?

D: Well, I know I had the experiences; and I know I had the feedback. But since some of the best stuff I did is not on film, I don't really know for sure.

The dialogue that begins with "what if" illustrates the tenacity of negative thinking, even leading her to doubt her own experience. I decided to introduce a lighter note to see how much of a hold this self-doubt had on her.

B: Well, at least you never fell.

D: No, I never fell. . . . Wait, I take that back. I did fall once, but it was absolutely nothing I did. Someone washed the floor in the studio, and this is something you never do because when you wash a wooden dance floor, it's like an ice skating rink—very slick. When I went into a move, my foot slipped out from under me because of the floor. But that was the only time ever.

Her comment about that being the only time she ever fell suggests a lot of control, a great deal of caution, or difficulty remembering what might threaten her image of herself.

B: Were you angry at yourself for falling?

D: Actually, I was laughing because we all knew the floor had been washed, and were taking really good care not to fall. The way it happened looked really comical.

In discussing her present experience, it became apparent that she had given up trying to come back. I believe this was partly from the fears she described, partly from her pessimism about the outcome, and mainly from the threat to her identity as a dancer. She no longer did even gentle practicing when she was by herself. I was quite moved in hearing this and decided to try to help her clear the way to begin doing so by providing an opportunity and direct physical support.

B: Would you be willing to do some practice jumps right now?

D: [laughs] Well, OK . . .

B: Come, let's work together on this. I'll hold your hand while you take a practice jump.

What followed was a first jump with her holding my hand, then several off-balance jumps by herself. I noticed that she began her jumps without getting ready and suggested that she get set before jumping. During the jumps she had some shortness of breath and felt anxious. After encouraging deeper, slower breathing, I suggested that, in addition to getting set physically, she do something that represents getting set mentally as well. She then went over to the opposite wall and drew a spot to focus on. This was something she frequently did when jumping and was an indication of her focus in getting mentally ready to jump. She then performed several more jumps. We concluded the interview with her decision to continue the practice she had just begun. I asked her where she would be doing it, and when, and sensed her determination to do so. Several months later, she told me that her "life had gotten back on track," and she felt very satisfied with the work she had done in the interview. This example illustrates that even when important psychological issues exist and interfere with performance, these issues do not always require in-depth exploration in order for performance to improve.

Several factors might have contributed to the good result. Her volunteering in the workshop suggests that given the right conditions she was ready for change. During the interview, I was aware of a strong bond between us, working together to accomplish a difficult task, which I think was an important element in helping her overcome a barrier. This bond consisted of my being quite eager to help her, partly because we had gotten to know each other at sport psychology conferences for several years, and partly because I felt fatherly toward her. Her contribution to the bond was the considerable trust and respect that she felt toward me. My willingness to address her difficulty in physical as well as emotional ways (by holding her hand and supporting her first jump) must have been important to her, a woman who has danced all her life. For someone who is quite self-reliant, accepting help was difficult, and overcoming that difficulty was quite rewarding. I also think the presence of the "audience" worked in her favor, not only because she was a performer but also because this particular group was part of her support network (fellow students).

A Competitive Student T is a graduate student in sport psychology who volunteered in a seminar in sport psychology to discuss a problem he has been having in his tennis game. The seminar was an hour long and included 12 students and a faculty member. I was invited to present how I work with athletes who have some psychological difficulty with their performance.

B: How would you like to begin?

T: Well, I'm a tennis player, and I've played my roommate many, many times over the past few years . . . probably over 100 sets . . . and I've never beaten him.

B: What is your explanation of that?

Ordinarily, I would not start an interview with this question, but in this instance, I sensed T had spent a lot of time thinking about it and had a response ready to go.

T: Overall he is a better player than I am, and he started playing at a much younger age. In order to beat him, I have to play very well and he has to play just average, but I have never been able to put it all together. Several times I've come close, like 6-4, 7-5, but I can't seem to overcome all the factors. One particular incident stays with me, and is the primary reason for my volunteering in this session today.

B: I'd like to hear more about it.

T: A couple of months ago, we were playing just one set. I was playing great, and he was playing poorly. The next thing I know, I am up 5-0 and serving for the match [they played one-set matches]. Then things went downhill from there.

B: Describe what happened.

T: Well, at that point my play became very tentative, and my thoughts drifted away from the task.

B: What were your thoughts?

T: I began thinking about who I'd call when I won, and how great it would be to finally beat him. I had trouble concentrating on the match after that.

One barrier would be loss of concentration resulting from thinking about bragging after the match. It was important to get more specific information about how his performance was affected.

B: How did your performance change?

T: Well, I started to play "not to lose" and he seemed to sense this. As I became more distracted, his play gained momentum. I started hitting the ball short, and he consistently put the ball away. I also had several double faults. He very quickly evened the score at 5-5, and I was in shock.

B: What do you mean?

T: I couldn't believe how quickly the tables had turned . . . one moment I'm serving for the match, and a few minutes later I'm serving to just stay in the match. My head was filled with thoughts and concerns about losing the match after being up by five games.

B: What did you do then?

T: I tried to recycle several times and say, Let's go! to myself, but I got too caught up in the pace of his comeback. After being up, I let him dictate the rest of the match, and I didn't feel in control.

B: What interfered with you staying in control?

T: I lost confidence in myself, and I felt discouraged. I was unable to stay positive and was losing my incentive. Then my energy and enthusiasm started to go down.

Several additional barriers are present at this point, such as worry about losing, loss of confidence, loss of control, discouragement, and loss of incentive. Although any of these could have been pursued, they were described without much emotion. I was waiting to hear something that had more personal involvement to use as an entry point.

B: What might have helped pull you up in that situation?

T: I don't really know. I felt pretty alone out there.

His facial expression changed to a slight frown, suggesting that being alone might be an important issue for him. As I pictured him out there all alone, I imagined that he had difficulty supporting himself, being on his side, rooting for himself. Because focus on present experience is an important component of my working with athletes, I chose his feeling alone as an entry point.

B: What are you feeling right now?

T: I'm not sure . . . maybe I felt a little lonely when I said that.

B: Would you be willing to do something a bit different at this point?

T: Sure. What do you mean?

B: Instead of my asking you more questions right now, would it be OK if you closed your eyes? Now I'd like you to imagine that you're back in the situation you were just describing. Can you do that?

T: Yeah. I see him waiting for my next serve.

B: Let the match be at the point when the score is 5-5, and you are discouraged . . . losing energy . . . losing incentive . . . going down . . . feeling pretty alone out there. Are you there?

T: Yeah.

B: Now with that picture still in mind, imagine that you are also a cheerleader at the match, leading a cheer for you on the court.

T: Hmmm. . . . I don't know . . . I've never been much of the cheerleader type.

B: Well let's see how it goes. See if you can make up a cheer to encourage you on the court. . . . How would you like it to go?

T: How about "Go!"

B: Go whom?

T: Go T.

B: Now do that as a cheerleader.

T: Go T! [a little louder but without enthusiasm]

B: Notice the low energy in the cheer. Try this . . . turn to the group as if they are the stands, and lead them in the cheer . . . and stand as you lead them.

T: [to the group] OK guys, are you ready?

Group: Yeah!

T: [stands up hesitantly] We're going to cheer "Go T" . . . and raise your hands on "T" . . . like this. Ready . . . Go T!

Group: Go T! [with enthusiasm]

T: Nice job.

B: [to T] OK. Now do it again without holding back.

T: [standing] GO T!!!

Group: GO T!!! [very enthusiastically]

B: [to T] How did you do?

T: They did really well.

B: How did *you* do?

T: Pretty well, I guess.

B: Only pretty well?

T: I'm not sure. I'm not used to being a cheerleader for myself.

B: It seems difficult for you to root for yourself. Is that true?

T: I guess I've always been more comfortable telling others they did a good job than telling myself the same thing.

B: Is that something you would like to change?

T: I guess.

B: You sound uncertain.

T: Well, wouldn't that be boasting?

B: Some people might see it that way. Others might see it as you being on your own side. Would that be OK if it weren't at somebody's expense?

T: Yeah, that would be OK. In fact, I'm going to try it.

If this session were just the two of us, I might have explored further his difficulty being supportive to himself. Because it was a time-limited demonstration, I asked if it would be OK if we stopped here and he agreed. Months later, the idea of being his own cheerleader was still with him. The purpose of performance enhancement is usually improvement in some objective, quantitative result, such as running faster, hitting the ball further, jumping higher, throwing further, or shooting more accurately. It can also be improvement in the subjective, qualitative experience of performing, such as more enjoyment, increased motivation, better attitude, or more satisfaction. In this interview, the latter type of benefit, improved self-support, might have been initiated.

SUMMARY

My approach to the process of removing psychological barriers in sport performance includes theory and techniques drawn from psychoanalytic psychotherapy, gestalt therapy, transactional analysis, and cognitive therapy. Each of these approaches contributes an essential component to my work with athletes. From psychoanalytic theory the component is that all behavior has meaning; from gestalt therapy it is a focus on the here and now; from transactional analysis comes the concept of the internal child and parent; and from cognitive therapy the principle that thinking is the major determinant of feelings. These several theories exert their influence on my work, which is grounded in humanistic psychology—in particular, a growth model of human development.

Some of the more common psychological barriers seen in sport performance are anxiety, low self-confidence, anger, self-criticism, low self-esteem, shame, loss of incentive, and difficulty staying focused. Each example in this chapter illustrates one or more of these barriers as well as the methods and rationale for the particular interventions. More specifically, guided fantasy is a major technique that plays a central role in removing psychological barriers. It is a means of reconstructing an athlete's experience to help remove or decrease the impact of the barrier and enable the athlete to move more easily into an effective mind-set for approaching competition.

REFERENCES

Beck, A.T. (1967). *Depression: Clinical, experimental, and theoretical aspects.* New York: Hoeber.

Berne, E. (1961). *Transactional analysis in psychotherapy.* New York: Grove Press.

Cox, R.H. (1994). *Sport psychology: Concepts and applications.* Dubuque, IA: Brown & Benchmark.

Danish, S.J., Petitpas, A.J., & Hale, B.D. (1992). A developmental-educational intervention model in sport psychology. *The Sport Psychologist, 6,* 403-415.

Erikson, E.H. (1950). *Childhood and society.* New York: W. W. Norton.

Frankl, V. (1992). *Man's search for meaning: An introduction to logotherapy.* Boston: Beacon Press.

Giges, B. (1995, September). *How people change.* Keynote address presented at the annual meeting of the Association for the Advancement of Applied Sport Psychology, New Orleans, LA.

Giges, B. (1996a, May). *Beyond psychopathology: An alternative to the medical model in sport.* Paper presented to the International Society for Sport Psychiatry at the annual meeting of the American Psychiatric Association, New York.

Giges, B. (1996b). Commentary. *Newsletter of the Association for the Advancement of Applied Sport Psychology, 11,* (3), 24, 27.

Giges, B. (1997, February). *Psychological barriers to excellence in sport performance.* Keynote address presented at the Southeastern Region Sport and Exercise Psychology Student Symposium, West Virginia University, Morgantown, WV.

Giges, B. (1998). Psychodynamic concepts in sport psychology: Comment on Strean and Strean. *The Sport Psychologist, 12,* 223-227.

Greenson, R.R. (1967). *Technique and practice of psychoanalysis.* New York: International Universities Press.

Maslow, A. (1954). *Motivation and personality.* New York: Harper & Row.

Maslow, A. (1962). *Toward a psychology of being.* Princeton, NJ: Van Nostrand.

Munroe, R.L. (1955). *Schools of psychoanalytic thought.* New York: Dryden Press.

Nideffer, R.M. (1985). *An athlete's guide to mental training.* Champaign, IL: Human Kinetics.

Orlick, T. (1986). *Psyching for sport: Mental training for athletes.* Champaign, IL: Human Kinetics.

Perls, F. (1969). *Gestalt therapy verbatim.* Lafayette, CA: Real People Press.

Van Raalte, J.L., & Brewer, B.W. (Eds.). (1996). *Exploring sport and exercise psychology.* Washington, DC: American Psychological Association.

Weinberg, R.S., & Gould, D. (1995). *Foundations of sport and exercise psychology.* Champaign, IL: Human Kinetics.

Williams, J.M. (Ed.). (1998). *Applied sport psychology: Personal growth to peak performance* (3rd ed.). Mountain View, CA: Mayfield.

CHAPTER 3

MANAGING STRESS ON AND OFF THE FIELD: THE LITTLEFOOT APPROACH TO LEARNED RESOURCEFULNESS

Albert J. Petitpas
Springfield College

My approach to doing sport psychology is rooted in a life development intervention (LDI) framework (Danish, Petitpas, & Hale, 1993). The LDI perspective assumes that continuous growth and change are natural aspects of human development. All of us face a number of events in our lives that force us to reevaluate our beliefs about ourselves and the world. These events can be normative and expected (e.g., moving from junior to senior high school) or paranormative and unexpected (e.g., incurring a season-ending injury). In the LDI model, any event that causes us to change our assumptions about ourselves or our environment and requires a change in our behavior and relationships is called a *transition* or *critical life event*. Unfortunately, most individuals and systems (e.g., families, teams, work units) resist change because it disrupts their routines and relationships (Watzlawick, Weakland, & Fisch, 1974).

The goal of the LDI approach is to enhance people's abilities to cope effectively with critical life events by enhancing their self-efficacy and helping them identify or develop a range of coping resources. By assisting people in setting goals, identifying coping skills that are already part of the repertoire, and acquiring new skills, the sport psychologist helps them learn how to anticipate, prepare for, and grow through critical life events. LDI is an education-oriented rather than pathology-oriented approach to helping. Therefore, the emphasis is on identifying strengths and building coping resources.

From a practitioner's perspective, the LDI approach has much in common with Meichenbaum's (1985) stress inoculation training. Both approaches espouse the virtues of what Meichenbaum termed *learned resourcefulness*. That is, instead of giving people a set of strategies to help them avoid stressful situations or critical life events, both approaches emphasize learning skills and changing attitudes that enable people to cope with stressful events directly.

Although my approach to doing sport psychology is clearly grounded in the LDI philosophy, I have developed a number of personal beliefs that guide the way I work with athletes. These beliefs come directly from my own sport psychology consulting experiences and from observations of graduate students working in our athletic counseling interview labs. These beliefs have been put together in what I developed, and call, the *Littlefoot* approach to counseling. In this chapter, I will describe the Littlefoot approach and illustrate how I use it in helping athletes enhance their athletic and personal development. In particular, I will outline the tenets of the Littlefoot approach and then provide samples of dialogues with athletes to illustrate how these beliefs and strategies are used to enhance the effectiveness of the athlete-practitioner relationship. I will then describe my work with an athlete who was having difficulty in managing stress during competitions.

THE LITTLEFOOT APPROACH TO SPORT PSYCHOLOGY INTERVENTIONS

The Littlefoot approach is a set of beliefs and guidelines that are concerned with the process of sport psychology consultations rather than the content of these interactions. These beliefs and guidelines assist me in understanding the dynamics of the athlete-practitioner relationship and provide a framework for evaluating the quality of the working alliance. Consistent with Bordin's (1979) original model, I believe that the quality of the working alliance is intimately tied to the practitioner's ability to get agreement on goals and tasks and to develop a collaborative relationship that is based on respect and trust. Research has shown that the working alliance is complex, changes over time, and may be viewed differently by clients and counselors (Sexton & Whiston, 1994). The quality of the client-counselor relationship, however, is the only variable that has consistently been shown to relate to successful counseling outcomes. By reviewing the principles of the Littlefoot model, I am better able to track the dynamics of the relationship and strengthen the working alliance.

In general, my work with athletes follows a traditional counseling framework: (a) build rapport, (b) define the problem, (c) set goals, (d) learn new skills, (e) test these skills in vivo, (f) evaluate level of goal attainment, and (g) end the relationship. Although there is a logical sequence to these components, they are not discreet stages and they frequently occur concurrently. I believe that this counseling framework outlines what I hope to do with clients. It does not, however, help me understand how I can better achieve my objectives. This is where I find the aspects of the Littlefoot approach so beneficial. The components of the Littlefoot approach are outlined in Table 3.1.

Table 3.1 The Littlefoot Approach to Athletic Counseling

- Understand the problem before you try to fix it
- Be inquisitive and avoid mind reading
- Pace before you lead
- Encourage but avoid discounting
- Listen for the "but"
- Put doubts in the doubts
- Athlete-clients will bring you back to where they believe they need to be
- Acknowledge the difficulty of the change process
- Plan for plateaus and setbacks
- Train for generalization

Understand the Problem Before You Try to Fix It

One of the common problems that I see when providing supervision to graduate students is that they attempt to provide quick solutions to athletes' situations before they understand the situations from the athletes' perspectives or what the athletes want from them. Consider the following exchange between a counselor (C) and a male golfer (A) who is having problems staying focused during important tournaments.

A: I don't know what happens. I get out there, and I get in brain lock. I can't focus, and I blow two or three shots in a row. The next thing I know, I'm out of contention.

C: Have you tried a pre-shot routine?

A: Well, I try to do the same stuff every time, but my mind just seems to go blank.

C: OK, it sounds like you lose focus because you are not going through the exact same routine before each shot.

A: Maybe, but it feels like something else is going on.

C: That might be true, but before we jump all over the place, let's start with the routine and see what happens.

In this exchange, the counselor has not taken the time to try to understand the problem from the athlete's perspective. Instead, the counselor immediately tries to fix the problem by suggesting a pre-shot routine. Although a pre-shot routine might prove to be a helpful strategy, the athlete is not likely to believe that the counselor understands what he is going through, and as a result, it is doubtful that he would invest sufficient time and energy into learning or using this new strategy.

I believe that the athlete is the expert on his or her own problem. I make an assumption that when people are having difficulties, the first thing they do is to try to fix the problems themselves. If this does not work, then they will typically go to their friends, coaches, or family for assistance. If they still cannot resolve the situation, then they seek out a sport psychologist or athletic counselor. Ironically, many of the problem situations that I deal with are the person's own attempt at self-cure that is no longer working. For example, a female basketball player in a shooting slump might try to focus on squaring up her shoulders and extending her arm on her follow-through. Unfortunately, this strategy might cause her to overemphasize mechanics and further erode her focus and concentration.

My first goal is to understand what the problem means to an athlete and how he or she has tried to correct it. I also try to learn what the athlete wants from me. Consider the following example of a male high school basketball player.

A: I feel like such a loser. All I had to do was dribble out the clock, but stupid me tries to throw a cross-court pass. The thing gets intercepted and we end up losing by one.

C: What happened then?

A: Well, the coach starts yelling, and I just wanted to bury my head somewhere.

C: What did you do?

A: I ran off the court with the other guys, and in the locker room the coach just blasted me, calling it the stupidest play he had ever seen in twenty years of coaching.

Based on what was said to this point in the interview, the counselor does not know what the athlete is feeling, thinking about, or how he is attempting to cope with the event. The counselor also does not know what kind of assistance the athlete is seeking. Does the player want reassurance that he is OK? Does he want help dealing with his feelings? Is he angry with the coach and looking for a place to vent his frustrations without jeopardizing his position on the team? These are just three of the many possibilities that come to mind. The key to understanding the situation from the athlete's perspective is to be patient and to listen well. The next two tenets of the Littlefoot approach address how to gain the athlete's perspective.

Be Inquisitive and Avoid Mind Reading

As a counselor, I do not assume that I know what an athlete is thinking or feeling. Instead, I verify my initial perceptions by using listening skills such as asking appropriate questions, reflecting feelings, and paraphrasing athletes' statements. As outlined in the *Columbo approach* identified by Meichenbaum (1985), I believe that the more inquisitive I am about athletes' situations, the more explicit they become in explaining their unique experiences. This process of inquiry not only allows me to gain a better understanding of an athlete's perceptions of the problem but often it facilitates the athlete's self-understanding as well. Although I refer to this approach as being inquisitive, care must be taken to avoid discounting an athlete's experiences or presenting oneself in a manner that would jeopardize one's credibility with the athlete. Some of the listening skills I have mentioned are illustrated in the following exchange that took place in an initial meeting with a female tennis player.

A: Well, I'm not sure why I wanted to talk with you.

C: OK! [silence.]

A: Well, I guess it's because I beat everyone I play against except Jane Doe. I know that I'm better than her, but I just play like crap against her.

C: What do you think happens?

A: I don't know. I guess I just get too pumped up and start pushing things instead of just playing my game.

C: What leads you to that conclusion?

A: I don't know, but it is the only explanation that I can come up with.

C: It doesn't sound like you are convinced. [silence]

A: Listen, the thought of losing to her just gets me ripped.

C: What do you mean?

A: You know. She thinks she is God's gift to the world, and she parades around the court like she's a queen or something.

C: I can only imagine what that must be like for you watching her.

A: You have no idea how angry I get. I just want to shove the tennis ball down her throat.

C: I wonder what you do with all that anger when you are playing her.

A: I never thought about it that way.

C: OK, so one thing worth exploring is what you do with your anger and how can you use it to advantage in your matches. What else have you thought about?

To this point in the example, I tried to understand the situation from the tennis player's perspective, using open-ended questions and reflective statements to encourage her to continue to elaborate on the situation. Although anger management appears to be a fruitful direction to pursue, I am still not sure what the problem is and, therefore, I will continue to work with the athlete in efforts to arrive at a mutually acceptable definition of the problem.

One of the check points that I use in evaluating my work is asking myself the question, Who is doing most of the work? As obvious as this next statement may sound, I have to remind myself on occasion that it is the athlete's problem and not my own. Therefore, the athlete should be working at least as hard as I am to come up with possible solutions to the situation at hand. It also means that it is the athlete's responsibility (with my assistance) to be able to explain the situation in a manner that I can understand. As part of the process of explaining the problems to me, athletes often gain additional insight about themselves and their reactions. The tennis player just described was able to see how anger might be having a negative influence on her play through the process of explaining her reactions to competing against Jane Doe.

Pace Before You Lead

Although the phrase *pace before you lead* originated from neurolinguistic programming (Lankton, 1980) I use it to help me focus on how athletes communicate their present concerns and priorities. *Pace before you lead* refers to matching or attending to the athlete's present focus before attempting to lead him or her in a new direction. For example, if a softball player is upset because she injured her ankle and lost her starting position, I would attend to her immediate feelings rather than try to get her to look at the situation differently. By so doing, I am in a better position to build a working alliance because I have demonstrated some understanding of her most pressing concerns. My belief is that if the softball player does not think that I understand what she is going through, then it is doubtful that I would be able to reframe the situation in a manner she would accept.

The notion *pace before you lead* brings up an important consideration in my work with athletes; namely, the timing of the intervention or strategy. As outlined previously, premature attempts at fixing problems or failure to attend to athletes' immediate concerns are likely to have a negative effect on the practitioner-athlete relationship. The importance of timing is also quite evident in the next tenet of the Littlefoot approach.

Encourage but Avoid Discounting

I believe that one of the most important aspects of the practitioner-athlete relationship is the encouragement that is provided by the helper, particularly when working with athlete-clients who are feeling down, helpless, or unlucky or who lack confidence in their abilities to overcome whatever is impeding their efforts to achieve their goals. These athletes have typically tried a number of strategies and talked with a number of people before seeking my services. Some of these athletes have no idea of what to expect from my services and others come in asking for a specific intervention (e.g., imagery, relaxation). In either of these situations, I strive to present myself as positive and optimistic, but at the same time I do not want to diminish the importance of the problem or misrepresent the amount of work that they may have to do to acquire the skills necessary to cope with their concerns.

I use the phrase *encourage but avoid discounting* to remind myself of the importance of building rapport before offering words or gestures of encouragement. In my experience, offering encouragement before an athlete believes that you understand what he or she is going through often discounts their feelings and impedes the development of a working alliance. In graduate training classes, I ask the group how they might feel if they were having a really bad day and someone they did not know well approached them and said, "Don't worry; everything will work out." The typical response from class participants is one of anger or frustration, because they believe that the person offering the words of support has no idea of what they are going through. A similar scenario can play out in the practitioner-athlete relationship, if the practitioner offers encouragement before an atmosphere of trust and respect has been established.

The tenets of the Littlefoot approach that I have outlined to this point are relevant particularly during the rapport-building, problem definition, and goal-setting phases of the practitioner-athlete relationship. These early phases are concerned primarily with challenging attitudes and setting the stage for the behavioral changes to come. I believe that it is much easier, however, to challenge someone's attitudes than it is to change his or her behaviors. Therefore, I do not find it unusual that many athlete-clients will experience doubts about or be reluctant to try new behaviors. The next two tenets of the Littlefoot approach are helpful to consider during the process of moving into the behavioral change phases of the helping relationship. These tenets are highly interrelated and will be discussed concurrently.

Listen for the "But" and Put Doubts in the Doubts

I find that many athlete-clients are skeptical about the efficacy of sport psychology interventions. For example, some athletes will question whether imagery can really accelerate their physical recovery or improve their game performance. Unfortunately, these doubts can either become major distractions or can restrict both the amount of effort that athletes put into acquiring new skills and their perseverance when learning new sport psychology strategies. Without confidence in the selected strategy or a sense of self-efficacy, it is questionable whether new skills can be mastered.

The doubts that I am describing can be observed in athlete-clients' verbal and nonverbal communications, their failure to do homework assignments, or their reluctance to engage in activities during sessions. Look for signs of doubts in the following exchange that took place between a graduate student counselor and a field hockey player who was given a homework assignment to practice with a guided imagery tape.

C: How did the mental rehearsal practice go?

A: It was OK, I guess.

C: What went well and what did not?

A: Well, to be honest, I just could not find a quiet place to practice. The whole dorm was a zoo this week.

C: How about early in the morning? I have some earphones you could use.

A: Thanks, but I'm just not a morning person.

C: Well, you can always use one of our interview lab rooms. They are open every night and available times are posted on each door.

A: I know, but it is tough to find open blocks of time in my schedule, and I hate coming across campus at night.

To this point in the exchange, it appears that the field hockey player is quick to find excuses for not completing her homework assignment. Although there may be legitimate reasons for her nonadherence, I follow the Rule of Thirds. That is, if something out of the ordinary happens three times, it is not an accident and should be discussed with the client. In the preceding example, the field hockey player continued to reject the counselor's suggestions. It would have been easy to get caught up in a "Yes, but" control battle, but the counselor recognized what was going on and decided to confront the athlete.

C: It appears that you are reluctant to try the homework assignment.

A: What do you mean?

C: I have offered several suggestions, and you don't seem interested in trying them.

A: No, that's not it [pause]. I don't know if I'm ready for that stuff.

C: Not ready or don't believe that it can help?

A: Well, I guess it's a little of both.

C: What do you mean?

A: You know, all this imagery stuff seems a little strange.

C: I'm confused. Earlier you described how you enjoyed replaying your best moves over and over again in your mind, and we talked about how you might be able to use this same technique to help improve your transition from offense to defense.

A: No, you're right. It just seems strange using it like this.

C: It may be like learning any new skill. It will feel uncomfortable at first, but after lots of practice it becomes your natural way of doing things.

A: You mean like changing your grip in golf or something.

C: Yes, something like that. The key is that you have enough faith or at least enough curiosity to give it your best shot. You need to find a strategy that you have confidence in. What do you think?

A: Do you really think the tapes will help me?

C: The more important question is, do you?

The counselor has begun the process of putting some doubts in the athlete's doubts about her ability to benefit from the proposed strategy. I have found that many of my athlete-clients go through a similar cognitive transition that begins with the thought, Maybe I can do this, and continues on until they have experienced the benefit of the new strategy often enough that they know they can do it. If athlete-clients continue to have doubts, or if they believe that other concerns are more pressing, they often let you know through the next tenet of the Littlefoot approach.

Athlete-Clients Will Bring You Back to Where They Believe They Need to Be

Earlier, I suggested that the word *but* is very important in the helping process and illustrated how "Yes, but . . . " exchanges often lead to control battles. Paying attention to an athlete-client's use of the word *but* can help to keep the focus of the interaction on the client's agenda as well. Because of the power differential that is often inherent in the practitioner-athlete relationship, many athletes will go along with where practitioners are leading them, even when they have more pressing concerns. If you listen carefully, however, the athlete will let you know that they have some doubts about where things are heading and they will try to lead you to the topics that they believe are most important. For example, I had the following conversation with a ski jumper, who had failed to qualify for the

Olympic Games after being a top performer on the national team for most of the year. He said he wanted to talk with me about whether or not to continue on the national team in hopes of making the next Olympic team.

A: Four years from now seems like such a long way off. I don't know if I have the energy to stick with it for that long.

C: How soon to do you have to make the decision?

A: Not for a while, and I'm still planning to compete in Japan or Europe after the Games. I don't know where they will send me.

C: So, at least you have some time before you have to decide.

A: Sure, but it doesn't make it any easier.

C: How are you planning to make the decision?

A: I don't know; talk to the coaches and see what happens, I guess.

C: It seems like there is a lot tied up in this decision besides the coaches' feedback.

A: Sure; family, career, relationships—everything gets put on hold for another four years, but I was *this* close [holding up his fingers] to making it.

Although the athlete presented concerns about making a decision about disengaging from sport, he appears to have a different agenda. I followed his lead and tried to get more information about his decision timeline (focus on content). He complied with my request; however, his use of "but" leads me to believe that he has some emotional energy still tied up in his failure to qualify this year.

C: I can only imagine what it must feel like to be so close to fulfilling your dream.

A: No one has a clue of what it was like. Everyone is being supportive [pause].

Although he stated that people were being supportive, his nonverbal behavior, the ironic flavor to his use of the term "supportive," and the pause caused me to believe that there was an unspoken *but*. I believe that what is said after the "but" is where athlete-clients believe they need to be. Therefore, I will typically follow up in the direction of the *but* even if the *but* is not stated.

C: I sense there is a *but* there.

A: What do you mean?

C: Everyone is being supportive, but . . .

A: Well, people tell me how proud I should be for coming so close. They have no idea how I hurt inside.

In this example, the ski jumper's surface presentation was focused on decision making. He had a lot of his identity tied up in being an Olympic athlete, however, and his failure to make the team this year was a devastating blow to his ego. Instead of letting others in on his emotional pain, he attempted to save face by putting on a brave front. Unfortunately, he was not sending off any signals that he needed emotional support and, as a result, his support system was not providing the type of support that he wanted in this situation. Although I followed his initial leads and focused on decision making, he quickly brought me back to the concerns that he believed were most important—his emotional reactions to not making the Olympic team.

The next few tenets of the Littlefoot approach are concerned with educating athlete-clients about the difficulties inherent in skill acquisition and helping them prepare for any obstacles to goal attainment. These tenets are educational in focus and occur concurrently with skill acquisition.

Acknowledge the Difficulty of the Change Process

I believe that changing established habits or adopting new behaviors is a difficult process that requires considerable time and energy. Without an understanding of what to expect, I find that some athlete-clients run into difficulties that they did not anticipate, become discouraged, and give up. In order to help them understand the change or skill acquisition process, I typically ask athletes to describe how they learned and eventually mastered a physical skill important to their sport. I then use their examples to illustrate how change or skill acquisition does not often take place in a straight line from point *A* to point *B*. Instead, there is typically a series of learning plateaus or setbacks that need to be addressed before mastery takes place. My goal is to provide enough information to help athlete-clients avoid the types of surprises or disappointments that often impede skill acquisition. Although people have argued that by acknowledging the difficulties of the change process I am giving clients excuses to fail, I would rather take that risk than have someone get blindsided by an unexpected plateau or setback.

Plan for Plateaus and Setbacks

I believe that plateaus and setbacks occur because something is getting in the way of goal attainment. These roadblocks usually fall into one of four categories: a lack of knowledge, a lack of skills, hesitancy to take risks, or a lack of social support (Danish, Petitpas, & Hale, 1993). For example, when working with injured athletes, I strive to make sure that they understand the reason for a particular treatment, the possible side effects or sensations they may experience, and the realistic markers of progress they can expect to achieve (Petitpas & Danish, 1995).

Without this knowledge, they can misinterpret pain signals or set themselves up for disappointments by setting unrealistic recovery target dates. I also want injured athlete-clients to understand that there is both a physical and an emotional recovery that takes place after a significant injury.

Once I believe that athlete-clients have sufficient knowledge, I assess what skills they have, what skills they are likely to need, and how will they use them to achieve their goals. If athletes have already had experience using specific psychological skills (e.g., goal setting, imagery), I will see if they can use these skills to achieve their new goals. If new skills are required, I will try to teach them using the model outlined by Danish and Hale (1983):

1. Describe the skill in behavioral terms.
2. Give a rationale for the skill.
3. Specify a skill-attainment level.
4. Demonstrate effective and ineffective uses of the skill.
5. Provide opportunities to practice the skill with supervision and feedback.
6. Assign homework to promote generalization of the skill.
7. Evaluate the skill-attainment level.

A hesitancy to take risks can show up as fear, anxiety, or even embarrassment. I have had athlete-clients who would not make phone calls as part of a career transition program because they felt "dumb just calling someone out of the clear blue." In my experience, the most difficult roadblock for athlete-clients is taking interpersonal risks. The thought of allowing themselves to be vulnerable by asking for help or talking about their fears is a risk that many athletes do not want to take.

The fourth roadblock is a lack of social support. There are several types of social support (e.g., informational, emotional, challenging, material), and athletes may not have sufficient access to the specific types of support that they need to address the problem at hand or to maintain a change effort. Although I have described these four roadblocks separately, they often occur concurrently and can be a major consideration in the helping relationship.

Train for Generalization

An important consideration in both the LDI and learned resourcefulness approaches is transferability of skills from one setting to another. In training for generalization, I want to ensure that athlete-clients are not only capable of demonstrating the desired behaviors with me but that they can also replicate the behavior in other situations. The more success athletes have in using a skill or behavior in various situations, the greater the likelihood that their mastery level and self-efficacy will also increase. A male athlete-client may be able to be assertive in his interactions with me, but if he is not capable of demonstrating these same behaviors in his relationships with peers, coaches, or teachers, it is doubtful that he will feel more interpersonally adept.

In training for generalization, I have athlete-clients practice skills in different domains. For example, if several athletes are working on focusing and concentration skills for their particular sport, I will also have them practice these skills in the classroom or during interactions with their peers. I believe that this extra practice not only facilitates skill acquisition but also promotes the importance of transferring skills from one domain to another.

Now that I have provided a brief description of the key tenets of the Littlefoot approach to learned resourcefulness, I will illustrate how I use them in my work with athlete-clients. The following excerpts of dialogue come from my work with an athlete who was having difficulty playing up to her potential during important competitions. I have changed the athlete's name and sport to ensure confidentiality.

MANAGING STRESS DURING COMPETITIONS

Ann is a 24-year-old professional golfer who was referred to me by her athletic trainer. Ann was not performing as well as she had during her first year on tour, particularly during major competitions or events held close to her home. Her athletic trainer noticed that Ann would frequently complain about a lot of small, nagging injuries on the days just prior to these events. The trainer, who had worked with Ann for several years, believed that Ann was putting extra pressure on herself and used the injuries as possible excuses for poor play in the event that she did not perform well. I had my first meeting with Ann on a Saturday after she had failed to make the cut the previous day.

A: Terry [the athletic trainer] said that you might be able to help me concentrate better. I've been so inconsistent this year. Yesterday, I ballooned up to a 78 and missed the cut.

C: Concentrate better?

A: Yeah; last year I could put four solid rounds together, no problem. This year I stink up the course at least one round.

C: And you believe that it is a lack of concentration.

A: Well, what else could it be? I know I have the skills. I proved that last year.

I sensed that I was getting off on the wrong foot with Ann. She seemed to be getting defensive. Therefore, I decided to slow down a bit and focus on building rapport as I tried to understand the problem from her perspective.

C: It sounds like you are really frustrated.

A: Not frustrated, just pissed at myself for screwing up so badly.

C: How so?

A: I'm better than this. I go out there and make a fool of myself in front of everybody I know.

C: And that just makes it worse.

A: You're damn right. It's amazing that I can hit it so pure during the practice rounds, and as soon as I get out there when it counts, I shit the bed.

C: Especially in front of people you know.

A: Yeah; that just makes it all the worse. Sometimes I think I would be better off playing in Europe or someplace else.

C: Help me understand how you are trying to deal with this.

A: God, I don't know. At first, I tried to ignore it and tried to focus on one shot at a time. I used to be able to do that, but now it seems when the money is on the line, I can't stay focused.

C: What else have you tried?

A: Everything.

C: I can only imagine that it feels like everything.

A: It sure does.

C: What other things?

A: Well, after my practice round, I would lie in bed and replay every shot or think about how I played each hole during last year's tournament [pause]. I also fooled around with my pre-shot routine.

C: How so?

A: Well, I tried to speed it up so I wouldn't think about things so much.

C: Things?

A: Yeah; like, What's wrong with me? or, Is today going to be my day?

C: OK, what happened when you sped up your routine?

A: It worked at first, but now I think it's screwing up my rhythm.

I continued to gather more information about how Ann was coping with the situation. Near the end of the contact, I summarized the key issues and sought Ann's agreement to work with me on helping her find some solutions.

C: Ann, it sounds like you are beating yourself up trying to find an answer. As I listen to you, it is obvious that you have the skills to make it big on the tour. You just need to get back on track, and you are struggling to find the key that will turn everything around. It also sounds like you can be quite tough on yourself, and this seems to only add to the pressure.

A: You're probably right. I'm just a different person this year.

C: I don't think you are a different person. You proved that you have the right stuff to make it, and your practice rounds are solid. It's just a matter of doing it when it counts.

A: Can you help me with that?

C: I've worked with several people in different sports who had similar concerns. Everyone is different, however, and what works for one does not necessarily work for everyone. You've got the physical talent. Maybe it's just a matter of adding the right mental skills. The key is that you have to feel comfortable with me and be willing to work just as hard on these mental skills as you do on the physical.

A: Whatever it takes.

C: OK; if you feel comfortable working with me, I suggest that we meet four or five times over the next three weeks. I would like to see if we can develop some skills that will allow you to handle any pressure that the tour can throw at you. I know that we have to move quickly because of your travel, but we can get up and running before the tour leaves the East. After that, we will have to keep it going by phone.

A: Sounds good, but do you really think you can help me?

Although Ann agreed to work with me, her last statement caused me to believe that she was full of doubts. I believed that her inability to play well in front of her friends or during major tournaments eroded her confidence and caused her to doubt her abilities. As her competition performance declined, she resorted to making changes in her swing, pre-shot routine, and tournament preparation. Unfortunately, each of these attempts at self-cure appeared only to exacerbate the problem. My goals for the first session were to validate her feelings, evaluate her coping strategies, build rapport, and get her agreement to work with me.

C: I can help you develop some skills, and I believe that the more coping skills you have, the better you will be in managing stress or distractions.

A: OK; let's give it a go.

After scheduling a series of appointments that would accommodate her travel schedule, I gave her a homework assignment to be prepared to talk about a time when she was successful in getting her game back under control during a tournament in which she had several bad shots in a row. Our second meeting took place the next day.

C: How is it going?

A: All right, I guess. I was trying to think about a time when I was able to pull it back together, but I just couldn't remember what I did. Maybe, I just focused better [pause]. I just don't know.

C: You sound pretty frustrated.

A: Sure am and I feel so stupid being here.

C: What do you mean?

A: This is all so dumb. Why can't I get a handle on this?

C: Maybe you are just trying too hard [pause]. Let's see if we can figure it out together. Take me through a specific event where you felt a lot of pressure.

A: That's easy. How about Friday?

C: OK; tell me what you did leading up to Friday's round.

A: Where do you want me to start?

C: How about Friday morning when you first started to think about the day's round?

A: Well, I was up by 5:30 and had my usual breakfast. I was checking the results sheet from Thursday to figure where I stood and what I had to shoot to make the cut [pause]. Now that I think of it, last year I would be thinking of what I had to do to win. Now I'm worried about the cut.

C: So one difference between when you were playing well and now is that before you were playing to win, as opposed to playing not to miss the cut. I think that is an important difference, and I'll come back to that. Tell me what you did next.

A: Well, I chatted with my host family for a while and then caught a van to the course. Once there, I started my normal routine. I checked in, went to the workout van and got stretched out, and then headed to the locker to grab my spikes. I then hooked up with my caddy and headed to the practice area. I putted some. Then I went and hit a few balls, and finished with some more putts.

C: What was going on inside you while you were going through your warm-up?

A: I heard that the first few groups were tearing it up, and I knew that I had to shoot a low number to play the weekend.

C: Did that get you pumped up?

A: No, I think it added to the pressure. Even when I was finishing up my last few warm-up putts, I was picturing myself with a five-footer to make the cut.

C: Just to help me understand, on a scale of 1 to 100, with 100 being the most pressure you ever experienced, how much pressure were you feeling?

A: I'd say about an 85.

C: Again, to help me understand you a little better, on the same scale, how much pressure do you have to have to be psyched enough to play at your best?

A: Probably about 55.

C: OK; if you can find a way to lower the pressure by 30 points, you would be at the right level of anxiety to play your best.

A: How do you do that?

C: There are a couple of ways to lower your anxiety. Some golfers use breathing. Others use self-talk, imagery, or refocusing strategies. Before we go there, however, it would be helpful for me to know when you first realized you were too anxious.

A: I could feel myself breathing.

C: Is that how you usually know when the pressure is on?

A: Yeah, I'd say so, most of the time. It feels like my heart is racing, and my breathing is trying to catch up.

C: When you first noticed your breathing, what happened next?

A: I started thinking, Here it goes again, and I kind of went into brain lock for a few holes. Next thing I knew, I'm 42 for the front.

C: It sounds pretty bad, but the good news is that you were able to recognize the early warning signs of too much pressure. Now the trick is to use that early warning as a signal for some corrective action. I'm not sure what is going on with you, but some of the other athletes I've worked with would go into panic mode at the first sign of pressure. After that it was nothing but downhill for them. They couldn't hit a good shot or make a putt if their life depended on it. Instead of thinking about the corrective action, they would dwell only on the negatives.

A: That sounds like me, too. As soon as I felt it coming, I knew it was not going to be my day.

During the remainder of this session, I continued to explore how Ann managed the stress of that specific tournament. In general, I tried to understand what she did before, during, and after the event. She explained that she had scrambled her way around the first few holes managing par. On the fourth hole, she managed to hit the green in regulation, but three-putted for bogey. On the way to the next tee, she could feel herself becoming "tight." The next thing she knew, she went bogey, double bogey, bogey. Although she played one over par the rest of the way in, she missed the cut by three strokes. Later that evening, she replayed her "bad holes" in her head and, in her words, "I beat myself up for a while."

Throughout the session, I not only tried to understand this event from her perspective but I also attempted to put some "doubts in her doubts" about her ability to manage stress. I did this by using stories about other athletes in order to normalize her reactions and by using scaling to help her differentiate between the anxiety necessary to get focused and the anxiety that was getting in the way of her performance. For example, Ann questioned her ability to manage her anxiety, but the use of scaling enabled her to believe that lowering her anxiety 30 points was a reasonable goal. At the end of the session, I summarized the main points of discussion and got Ann's agreement to develop strategies for before, during, and after events. I wanted to move Ann from her present state of helplessness to one of learned resourcefulness. To accomplish this goal, we discussed possible situations (e.g., logistics, weather, getting stuck in traffic on the way to the course, hitting a bad shot) that have caused her to become distracted in the past. We then formulated a strategy for each of these situations in order to get her to focus on a corrective action instead of allowing these distractions to erode her concentration.

Some of the strategies that Ann developed to use before competitions included time management and working with a mastery audiotape that I developed for her. During competitions, Ann learned how to use her awareness of changes in her breathing as a signal to use her refocusing strategy. The following exchange, which took place in our third meeting, illustrates how this refocusing strategy was developed. Ann had just described several of the situations that caused her to lose her focus during a recent event.

C: Ann, earlier you said that you could tell when you were getting overly nervous because your breathing changed.

A: Well, I don't know if it really changed, or I just became more aware of it, but I knew that something was different.

C: OK; what I would like to do is see if we can use your awareness of this change to your advantage. Instead of allowing your breathing to become a distraction, let's use it as a signal for a correction.

A: What do you mean?

C: Well, in the past, it sounded like when you became aware of changes in your breathing you became even more nervous or you focused so much on your breathing that it caused you to lose concentration. I've always believed that the best players in the world are those who can regain their focus quickest. The good news for you is that you know that you are breathing differently. It is your body's way of telling you that you need to make an adjustment. What do you think your body is saying to you?

A: It's telling me that I am too anxious.

C: So instead of being at 55, your anxiety is on its way to 85.

A: Yeah [pause]. So what you are saying is that I need to relax more.

C: Or maybe get yourself to that right level of anxiety so you can play your best. If you can use your awareness of your breathing as a signal to regulate your anxiety, you will be better able to keep yourself mentally ready to play your best golf.

The session continued by brainstorming several strategies that Ann could use. Eventually, Ann and I decided on a deep-breathing technique that she could add to her pre-shot routine when necessary. She would inhale on a count of four and exhale on a count of five. The counting helped her focus on her breathing and distracted much of Ann's negative thinking. As soon as Ann became aware of any changes in her breathing, she would use that awareness as a cue to "breath by the numbers until I'm cruising at 55."

Ann practiced the breathing exercise during practice rounds and in any situations where she felt herself getting too anxious or frustrated. For example, she got stuck in a major traffic jam on the way home after a grueling day of speaking engagements and clinics. She could feel herself getting very angry, so she practiced using breathing by the numbers in order to calm down. Ann also placed the number *55* on her golf bag and wrote it on the back of her golf glove. She did this to keep her new strategy fresh in her mind. The more success she had in getting herself refocused the more confident she became.

In the next session, Ann and I continued to practice her pre-event and competition refocusing strategies. We also looked at how she evaluated her performances after rounds or tournaments, because she had a tendency to focus only on her mistakes. With practice, she was able to evaluate her performances more dispassionately, and this strategy helped eliminate much of the negative self-talk that often dominated her post-round thinking.

After our initial six face-to-face meetings, Ann and I stayed in contact by phone and an occasional e-mail. Although she still had her ups and downs in future events, she told me that she felt more in control and she was able "to pull myself together before it was too late." She completed the year by making all but two cuts, and she had several strong finishes.

During the off-season, Ann and I met on four occasions for "booster sessions." Much of our discussions focused on the need to practice her stress management strategies in non-sport settings in order to promote generalization of learning. Ann appeared to get a lot of enjoyment when she was able to use her new skills in various settings, and I continually reinforced her efforts. Although Ann was not able to equal her rookie-year performance on the money list, she seemed pleased with her mental game, and she was looking forward to the start of the tour season. In my last conversation with Ann, she said, "I learned that I'm just like a car. I run most efficiently at 55, whether it's playing golf or just managing my life."

SUMMARY

In this chapter, I have described my approach to working with athletes who are having difficulty managing stress. Although my approach is rooted in a life developmental intervention framework (Danish, Petitpas, & Hale, 1993), I have also identified and applied a number of beliefs (the Littlefoot approach) that guide my interactions with athlete-clients. These beliefs help me understand the dynamics of the athlete-practitioner relationship that I believe are critical in fostering positive outcomes.

My approach is educational in nature and strives to identify clients' strengths and teach new skills. I believe that athlete-clients must trust and respect the practitioner if they are going to put forth the effort necessary to master new skills. Therefore, it is necessary to work hard at building rapport and understanding the problem from the athlete's perspective. It is also important, however, to pay considerable attention to the process of skill acquisition and generalization. My goal is to help athlete-clients move from a state of helplessness and doubt to one of learned resourcefulness. To acquire confidence in one's abilities and to master new skills, athletes must have frequent opportunities to practice these skills with feedback. As athletes have more success in using their skills in different situations, their ability to manage stress and their self-efficacy increases.

I hope the examples of my work presented in this chapter help readers understand some of the process concerns involved in athlete-practitioner interactions. I believe that the practitioner is the most important component of the helping relationship and not the specific techniques that he or she employs. Therefore, each practitioner has to understand the advantages and disadvantages of his or her own interactive style. In my opinion, self-understanding, the ability to build rapport, and appreciation of individual differences are the most important aspects of athletic counseling and sport psychology training.

REFERENCES

Bordin, E.S. (1979). The generalizability of the psychoanalytic concept of the working alliance. *Psychotherapy: Theory, Research, and Practice, 16,* 252-260.

Danish, S.J., & Hale, B. (1983). Teaching psychological skills to athletes and coaches. *Journal of Physical Education, Recreation, and Dance, 54* (8), 11-12, 80-81.

Danish, S.J., Petitpas, A.J., & Hale, B.D. (1993). Life developmental interventions for athletes: Life skills through sports. *The Counseling Psychologist, 21,* 352-385.

Lankton, S.R. (1980). *Practical magic: A translation of basic neuro-linguistic programming into clinical psychotherapy.* Cupertino, CA: Meta Publications.

Meichenbaum, D. (1985). *Stress inoculation training.* Elmford, NY: Pergamon Press.

Petitpas, A., & Danish, S.J. (1995). Caring for injured athletes. In S. M. Murphy (Ed.), *Sport psychology interventions* (pp. 255-282). Champaign, IL: Human Kinetics.

Sexton, T.S., & Whiston, S.C. (1994). The status of the counseling relationship: An empirical review, theoretical implications, and research directions. *The Counseling Psychologist, 22,* 6-78.

Watzlawick, P., Weakland, J., & Fisch, R. (1974). *Change: Principles of problem formation and problem resolution.* New York: Gardner Press.

PART II

FROM THE APPLIED SPORT PSYCHOLOGY CANON

CHAPTER 4

RELAX! . . . IT AIN'T EASY (OR IS IT?)

Clay P. Sherman
California State University, Fullerton
Artur Poczwardowski
St. Lawrence University

Part I of this book emphasized how important it is for sport psychologists to develop working alliances with their athlete-clients. This alliance, to a large degree, is the result of early rapport building, as the sport psychologist listens to athletes and helps them tell their stories. As the process unfolds, a reciprocal relationship often develops. The sport psychologist becomes a better helper from truly listening to and more completely understanding athletes' issues, and athletes feel understood as the sport psychologist helps them develop a deeper understanding of their own concerns. Thus, the athlete and the sport psychologist can work together to reach their mutual goals.

In this chapter, we will not discuss the formal aspects of the initial contact and interview (see chapter 1). Instead, we focus on the practical aspects of teaching one of the performance-enhancement techniques that the sport psychologist can use: relaxation. First, we discuss the theoretical bases for using relaxation, and then we provide dialogue between a collegiate Nordic (cross-country) ski racer and a sport psychologist. Interspersed with the dialogue is discussion related to the helping process and the choices the athlete and the sport psychologist have made in the service of performance enhancement. Finally, we turn our attention to providing the athlete with a didactic rationale for why we think relaxation will be helpful, and we discuss the process of teaching relaxation techniques (e.g., introduction, rationale, instruction, anticipatory guidance, caveats, passive-receptive attitudes, debriefing, and modification of inductions).

THEORETICAL FOUNDATIONS OF RELAXATION

Although relaxation can be used for different purposes, its most common application is to reduce stress. Stress, in several forms, is unavoidable—an everyday fact of life (Benson, 1975; Jacobson, 1962; Lazarus, 1966; Selye, 1974). Humans are subjected to physiological stressors (e.g., temporary and chronic illness, injury, physical training); social stressors (e.g., rejection from and disagreements with others, job demands, financial problems); environmental stressors (e.g., pollution, congestion, extreme climates); and mental/emotional stressors (e.g., thoughts and perceptions). Although it is what happens to us physiologically, socially, and environmentally that creates stress, it is our thoughts about or perceptions of each situation that are often responsible for magnifying, intensifying, or prolonging stress (Lazarus, 1966).

Situations in which performance is socially evaluated dramatically increase the amount and types of stress athletes feel. The relaxation response is an important tool athlete-clients can use to mediate or reduce stress in both socially evaluated situations and other life areas. It is important that sport psychologists understand the processes of both the stress response and the relaxation response in order to enhance their consulting effectiveness and to help athletes self-regulate in competitive settings. The purpose of this section is not to provide the in-depth background necessary for a practitioner's understanding of stress and relaxation. Instead, by discussing the theoretical background behind stress and relaxation and by providing references where appropriate, we are attempting to highlight the important issues related to stress management and self-regulation.

Stress is primarily mediated by two regulatory and control systems in the body: the nervous system and the endocrine system. Selye (1974) discussed stress as either a positive experience (eustress) or a negative one (distress). In both eustress and distress the physiological responses are similar. Baum, Gatchel, and Krantz (1996) discussed two separate but interacting systems responsible for these responses. The first is a result of sympathetic nervous system (SNS) activation. SNS stimulation causes the adrenal medullae to secrete catecholamines (epinephrine and norepinephrine) that stimulate a series of changes in the body. There are changes in blood pressure, respiration, and heart rate; in blood flow to skeletal muscles; in muscle tension; and in other bodily functions (e.g., decrease in digestive activity).The second system, under the influence of the hypothalamus and the pituitary gland secretes a hormone (adrenocorticotropic hormone, or ACTH) that stimulates the adrenal cortex to produce various corticosteroids, particularly cortisol. Although the exact role of cortisol in the stress response is not clear, it is likely that it is involved in facilitating rapid access to the body's fat and carbohydrate energy stores. These changes prepare the body for action when a person is faced with threats or danger (or with something more pleasurable, such as sexual arousal). Under ideal circumstances, the body reacts to the threat or danger and then returns to a homeostatic condition of low stress fairly quickly. Problems arise when people experience prolonged or chronic stress (distress) from real or imagined situations. Specifically, prolonged or frequent corticosteroid secretions can damage or decrease the efficiency of the body's immune, tissue growth and repair, reproductive, and digestive systems (Davis, Eshelman, & McKay, 1995).

Although the stress response served a purpose for early humans—who, as part of daily survival, needed quick bursts of energy to fight or flee—modern society and its social customs make either fighting or running away an often undesirable response. Although one could argue that our innate ability to prepare for and react to stress can prolong our lives (e.g., when faced with very real dangers such as a 1500-pound grizzly bear or a 250-pound linebacker), it is more likely that our ability to think clearly and react calmly will lead to consistently good decisions and positive results. A hiker encountering a 1500-pound grizzly might live if she is calm enough to recall her plan to slowly retreat and act unaggressively, and a quarterback reacting to a linebacker blitz may successfully find the outlet receiver if he remains relatively calm and poised. High levels of stress and arousal, however, can also facilitate performance (think of power lifters); it all depends on the demands of the task. The question becomes: Is one overaroused for the task at hand? If so, there is a countermeasure to hardwired (and learned) stress responsivity that facilitates the reduction of the stress response, and it is called *relaxation*.

In 1975, Benson described an innate response of the human body that is diametrically opposed to the fight-or-flight response. According to Benson, each of us has an inborn protective mechanism, called the *relaxation response,* to help shield us from the harmful effects of our bodies' reactions to fight-or-flight situations. This response is related to physiological changes such as significant decreases in oxygen consumption and carbon dioxide elimination, lowering of heart and respiratory rates, and decreases in arterial blood lactate concentration (Benson, 1983). Benson has also reported an increase in or "intensification of slow alpha-wave activity . . . [which characterizes a] wakeful hypometabolic state" (p. 282). Although the relaxation response is innate, eliciting it in times of stress often needs to be learned and practiced.

For thousands of years people have been trying to find ways to cope with the hardships of life. For example, Eastern religions (e.g., Hinduism, Buddhism) and their meditation practices can be viewed (in a rather naive way) by modern theorists and practitioners as relaxation strategies (Lichstein, 1988). In North America, relaxation's early introduction came through meditation centers (e.g., the Zen Center in San Francisco in 1909), and then it was carefully studied and popularized by Jacobson (through his progressive muscle relaxation techniques) beginning in 1912 (Lichstein, 1988). The efforts of Schultz and his disciple Luthe (e.g., Luthe, 1965) further stimulated clinical and theoretical interests in relaxation in the United States.

A systematic and scientifically grounded approach to dealing with stress was offered within behavior therapy. The term *behavior therapy* was first used by Skinner and

Lindsley in 1954 (as cited in Wolpe, 1973) but as a discipline was developed more completely by Wolpe (Poppen, 1998). This approach to behavior change used principles of learning (classical and operant conditioning) to weaken or eliminate nonadaptive behavior (e.g., anxiety) and strengthen or initiate adaptive behavior (e.g., coping skills, relaxation). A number of stress management approaches and techniques were developed by behavior therapists. Relaxation emerged as a powerful behavior therapy technique that helped patients and clients cope with stress, anxiety, and phobias.

Wolpe's *systematic desensitization* has been one of the most prominent behavioral applications using relaxation (Lehrer & Woolfolk, 1993). In his approach, Wolpe (1973) applied the principles of reciprocal inhibition he developed while working on experimental neurosis with animals. The process of reciprocal inhibition reverses the conditioned inhibition of adaptive responses (e.g., eating) caused by anxiety through a gradual exposure to less anxiety-provoking stimuli. Wolpe discovered that the autonomic sympathetic responses of cats to a certain set of stimuli interrupting their adaptive behavior (i.e., food consumption) were weakened through exposing the cats to food in less similar environments. In other words, reciprocal inhibition is a form of deconditioning of earlier learned (conditioned) unadaptive behavior.

These principles, when modified, set the foundation for systematic desensitization and were used in interventions with humans (Wolpe, 1973). Wolpe used systematic desensitization to teach clients how to relax by applying a modification of Jacobson's progressive muscle relaxation (PMR). PMR is used to train a client to elicit a relaxed state by developing sensitivity to muscular tension. The client does this by alternately contracting and relaxing skeletal muscles (Jacobson, 1962). After the client has learned to elicit a relaxed response using PMR, he or she (with assistance from the therapist) develops a list of situations that provoke anxiety (i.e., an anxiety hierarchy). These situations or items are then ranked from the least to the most anxiety provoking. Finally, the client imagines situations or items from the hierarchy in therapy during deep relaxation (relaxation serves as the reciprocal inhibitor) until feelings of anxiety and stress fade away. The client systematically works through each item on the hierarchical list in this fashion until he or she can imagine even the most anxiety-provoking items in the hierarchy without a stress response.

Other behavioral procedures beyond systematic desensitization and nonbehavioral techniques also proved to be effective tools for addressing self-regulation issues with clients. In their stress management textbook, Lehrer and Woolfolk (1993) presented a number of relaxation strategies and identified the need to carefully examine the nature of the client's presenting anxiety, tension problems, or both. For example, they reviewed the specific effects hypothesis proposed by Davidson and Schwartz (1976), which suggested that a treatment modality should match the nature of the symptoms. As a result of their review of the literature, Lehrer and Woolfolk confirmed the notion that behavioral techniques (e.g., systematic desensitization) would most effectively reduce behavioral symptoms (e.g., phobias); cognitive techniques (e.g., Ellis' rational-emotive behavior therapy; Ellis [1995]) would be best for treatment of cognitive symptoms (e.g., negative self-talk); and somatic treatment (e.g., progressive muscle relaxation) would be most appropriate to deal with somatic symptoms (e.g., tension headaches). However, the specific effects of different relaxation strategies on certain symptoms are, to some extent, based on a general relaxation response described by Benson (1975). In other words, any relaxation technique leads to a general relaxation response and to the specific modality-related outcomes. Furthermore, the effects of relaxation are enhanced by appropriate changes in the client's basic beliefs, values, and attitudes, as suggested by Smith's (1986, 1988) hierarchical model of relaxation therapies (cf. Lehrer & Woolfolk, 1993). Because every relaxation technique has its strengths and limitations, the consultant needs to assess the problem behavior carefully, conceptualize the issue at hand, and plan the intervention (e.g., an individualized combination of relaxation techniques) and evaluation strategies in order to use time and resources effectively. Lehrer and Woolfolk's review of research comparing different relaxation techniques (progressive muscle relaxation, autogenic training, hypnosis, biofeedback, meditation, breathing, music, exercise, and cognitive training) can be used as a fundamental reference to inform the consultant's decisions about which intervention to design for a given athlete.

A review of research using relaxation with athlete populations (Greenspan & Feltz, 1989; Meyers, Whelan, & Murphy, 1996; Vealey, 1994) provides evidence of the efficacy of relaxation for enhancing sport performance. Unfortunately, as a result of methodological concerns, many of the studies reviewed make it difficult to infer causality. In addition, many of the interventions studied in these reviews were multicomponent and included some form of relaxation training combined with other psychological skill training. Despite some of these concerns, there is good evidence that learning to relax can enhance performance or is part of an effective performance enhancement routine (e.g., Bakker & Kayser, 1994; Crocker, Alderman, & Smith, 1988; Hamilton & Fremouw, 1985; Meyers, Schleser, & Okwumabua, 1982; Wrisberg & Anshel, 1989; Zhang, Ma, Orlick, & Zitzelsberger, 1992).

Sport psychologists can teach relaxation in a way that helps athletes cope with stress and anxiety and builds the consultant-athlete alliance at the same time. Some researchers conceptualize relaxation training as a tool that can help build rapport (Henschen, 1995). For example, relaxation training is accompanied by an ongoing exchange of personal, but often safe to share, experiential content. The sport psychologist acts as a guide for athletes, leading them to pleasant relaxed states, and athletes are naturally appreciative of someone who helps them feel good. Also, a relaxed state may induce feelings of increased power, confidence, and self-control in some athletes. If relaxation is taught well, athletes may experience success fairly early in the consulting process. Consequently, feelings of control over their psychological state may be initiated and then nurtured throughout the entire consulting process. Relaxation also illustrates the psychophysiological unity of the human organism (e.g., how mental components affect sport/physical performance), a fact that athletes are not always immediately aware of. Ultimately, athletes are taught to view relaxation as one tool to regulate their activation level with the purpose of finding the optimal zone of arousal, and therefore enhance athletic performance (Hanin, 1980). Finally, relaxation is an altered state of consciousness (Unestahl, 1983, 1986) that an athlete can use as a foundation for learning and practicing other educational and psychological techniques aimed at performance enhancement (e.g., imagery, ideomotor training).

Williams and Harris (1998) offer several practical suggestions to increase the effectiveness of teaching relaxation. For example, they suggest that "the sport psychologist and/or coach should expose their athletes to a variety of relaxation techniques and convince them of the benefits that will result from practicing the techniques" (p. 221). In addition, they maintain that the sport psychology consultant should have a repertoire of relaxation techniques to meet the needs of different athletes. They provide a thorough overview of the two primary categories of relaxation techniques: muscle-to-mind and mind-to-muscle. These two labels, unfortunately, perpetuate dualistic thinking about relaxation. We would prefer to eliminate such mind/body dichotomies and view relaxation as having several paths. In the following section of this chapter, a technique from a primarily somatic path, and one from a primarily cognitive path, will be taught to a client. The remainder of this chapter examines the processes of doing relaxation in sport psychology service delivery settings.

DIALOGUE

Notes from an initial interview.

Amber is a 21-year-old collegiate cross-country skier. She is beginning her second season of university competition. She initially dropped in to see the sport psychologist after learning about the service from the athletic department. In the initial interview, Amber described herself as an ex-Alpine skier who started Nordic skiing after her second anterior cruciate ligament (ACL) reconstructive surgery. She is very enthusiastic about skating but is also a talented classic Nordic skier. (Nordic skating, or freestyle, is a style of cross-country skiing that became popular in the late 1970s and early 1980s. Today, World Cup competitions are split 50-50 between classic and skating races). When asked what she liked about skating, she called it a "rush unlike no other. The flats and the descents are awesome." She has "strong lungs and good, but not great, technique." She clarified this by stating that "some of my teammates have been skating for decades longer (smiling)." She learned "a ton" her first year and is technically a much better skier than last year. After some storytelling of past skiing experiences, Amber mentioned a recurring problem during races. She expressed feeling "frenzied" before races—even the simulated races run during practices. When asked what she meant by *frenzied,* she said her mind was "racing about, worrying about who else was there, whether my wax was right, whether I could stay with the leaders, etc." Once the race started she was usually "okay," but because she was worried and anxious before races, she often missed (or misunderstood) the prerace instructions given by officials or coaches. In addition, she mentioned that she had trouble pacing herself (despite her coach's instructions), often going out too fast and "blowing up." Amber was asked how other areas of her life were going and whether she felt frenzied at home, at work, or at school. She stated that she had "trouble taking tests in school" (getting nervous to the point that she forgot things she could remember right after the test) and often "got angry" with her boyfriend when he asked her to "do things I don't have time to do." Near the end of the session, the sport psychologist briefly summarized Amber's presenting concerns.

She feels frenzied before races, and as a result, gets distracted during prerace instructions and has difficulty pacing early in the race. She also has difficulty concentrating and struggles with remembering information when taking tests in school, and she gets angry with her boyfriend as a result of feeling overloaded with stuff to do. It seems that tension and worry are at the center of her less-than-optimal functioning.

The sport psychologist mentioned that he felt these issues were likely related to Amber's inability to control stress and reduce anxiety as the situation merited. Amber and the sport psychologist agreed that they could work together on some skills and strategies to deal effectively with the situations Amber had described, particularly those skills aimed at reducing the frenzied feelings. They agreed to meet once a week for following six weeks and then evaluate what had been accomplished to that point.

Session II

Sport Psychologist (SP): Hi Amber; come on in. Have a seat.

Amber: Hey. Thanks.

SP: So, how has your week been?

A: Not bad—same old, same old.

SP: Same old, same old? What do you mean?

A: Well, actually nothing has changed. I am struggling big time [silence and looking toward the ground].

Here the sport psychologist was not sure what "same old, same old" meant for Amber. By restating and asking for clarification, the sport psychologist discovers that "same old, same old" means that Amber feels she is getting nowhere, and she is struggling.

SP: What are you struggling with? What's going on?

A: I blew an exercise physiology test today [pause]. I know the stuff. At least I thought I did. I froze up and blanked.

SP: Well, how is your skiing going?

With this question, the sport psychologist has directed the athlete toward the sport domain. In doing so, he fails to take advantage of a client-initiated opportunity to learn more about freezing up in the academic domain. He also takes control of the direction of the session instead of letting the client express what is on her agenda. The athlete has presented a good opportunity for the sport psychologist to find out more about what it is like for her to freeze up and go blank. This information could be useful in helping the sport psychologist and the athlete develop strategies for relaxing under pressure, in sport and other life domains, and should be pursued. The reason that the sport psychologist shifted the conversation to the sport domain may have to do with where his comfort level is (i.e., in sport and not in academic pursuits). Thus, his actions serve himself much more than they do the athlete. The sport psychologist missed an opportunity and quite possibly communicated to the athlete that her worries over academic matters really did not interest him. Let's back up and try it again.

SP: That's frustrating when you know the stuff [pause]. What happens when you freeze up?

The sport psychologist reflectively expresses some empathy and then pauses for a moment to see if the client will continue on her own. After a few seconds or so, the sport psychologist helps the client express more about freezing up and what it is like for her.

A: I just can't remember. I get tense. I read a question or sentence, and I can't remember what I just read. So I read it again, and I can't believe I can't remember. Sometimes I go to another question and that can get me on track, but sometimes it's the same thing—no question and no memory. Then I start stressing, and even the easy questions get difficult. I can't organize my thoughts, and I start playing out all the consequences of failing the test while the minutes tick away.

SP: It sounds like a cycle that sometimes you can break out of, but other times not.

A: Exactly! Except I usually have problems. In fact, I am always worried I will have problems. Kind of like in skiing. When I used to race Alpine after my first ACL, I was always worried I would reinjure it, then it happened, bam! I blew it out again.

SP: Two ACLs, wow! What's it like?

Although the athlete may be very willing to share stories about the procedure, the anesthesiology, and the rehab, it would inappropriately detract from the important issues and not be an effective use of time. The sport psychologist is clearly leading the athlete off track, perhaps in an attempt to show empathy. The dialogue will not likely add any substance and will take the focus off the athlete's current issues. In effect, if the sport psychologist pursues this line of questioning, the focus of counseling will shift to a less productive track. A different approach is warranted.

SP: I've heard ACLs are difficult rehabs. I think recovering from two and competing in collegiate athletics attests to your discipline and commitment, which should give you great promise that you can tackle other obstacles in your life. [Pause; Amber seems a bit awkward.] Tell me about skiing this week.

A: Well, not much has happened. We travel tomorrow. I am already stressing.

SP: Stressing?

A: Yeah, you know, the butterflies, and I get distracted thinking about the race. I sit in class and play out all the negatives. We worked on pacing all week. I gotta get it right [pause].

SP: Why do you gotta get it right?

Here the sport psychologist has asked a question and challenged the athlete about her way of thinking. A therapist trained in rational-emotive behavior therapy (REBT) might pursue this line of inquiry, and the result could certainly be favorable. But with roughly 25 minutes left in the session, the sport psychologist has decided not to devote time (at this point) to discussing thought processes and irrational belief systems. Under ideal circumstances, the athlete and the sport psychologist would meet well before the season started and have time to work through some of the lengthier issues. The reality of the situation is that Amber will travel to compete in a race before the sport psychologist meets with her again. The sport psychologist has an opinion that Amber's nervousness (or butterflies), distractibility, and seemingly irrational beliefs are all interconnected issues resulting in what Amber terms "frenzy."

SP: Amber, what is it you would like to see happen as a result of our meetings? What is it specifically you would like us to focus on?

A: [pausing and thinking] Well, I would like to not stress so much. My boyfriend calls me a stress case. He says that's why I get headaches so much and my neck muscles are sore.

SP: Headaches and muscle soreness. How often do you get headaches?

A: Two or three times a week. My mom gets migraines.

At least three issues came up in the last two interactions that are significant. First, the athlete's headaches seem fairly serious and worth further investigation. A brief inquiry about medical evaluation is reasonable. Second, the athlete has brought up the boyfriend on at least two occasions (once previously, in the intake interview). The dynamics of this relationship may need to be explored further. Finally, a more thorough history taking related to the athlete's family and family dynamics may be useful. Because of the time limitation (less than half the session remaining) and a desire to provide the athlete with a practical skill she can use this week, the sport psychologist has decided to investigate the last two issues during the third session.

SP: Have you had a medical evaluation related to headaches?

A: No, should I? I mean I've read a few things.

SP: I think it would be a good idea. Would you like to schedule an appointment with one of the team physicians? I can make the appointment when we finish.

A: If you think it will help.

SP: I think it's a good idea to get a medical opinion with something like frequent headaches. So, you want to reduce your stress level and headaches and muscle soreness in the neck. There is a good chance these areas are at least partially related. Is there anything else?

A: [pausing, thinking] Well, like I said, I'd like to be less distracted when coaches or professors are talking to me.

SP: Like before races and during class and tests.

A: Yes.

SP: Are there any things or strategies you have tried to reduce stress when you feel like you're starting to get "frenzied?"

A: [pause, thinking] No, not really. I mean I normally just think about it.

Here the sport psychologist is interested in any strategies the athlete has used in the past. Sometimes athletes have learned coping strategies that can be modified or further developed in consultation sessions. In this case, the athlete indicates that she is not using any strategies.

SP: OK, I think together we can develop some skills that will help you in these areas. I want to pause for a moment and summarize what I have heard you say. Then I would like to discuss some possible strategies you can begin to use this week when you travel and compete. I am hearing some common themes between school and skiing. I believe there are three areas we can work on together that will help you in skiing and in school. The first is learning strategies to control stress and to relax. In fact, in a moment, I want to show you a very simple technique that may help you immediately. When you return next week, I'd like to spend more time here. Second, I'd like us to work together to develop some strategies to adjust the way you talk to yourself—really, the things you say to yourself. I think we can develop strategies for positive thinking and self-talk that eventually will take some of the pressure off of you. You seem to be a champion at worry and negative thinking. We might want to start retraining some of your thinking. Finally, I think we can work together, maybe including Sara from academic advising, to help develop time management strategies and perhaps look into test-taking strategies. In all, I think we can help you prepare and perform more consistently and feel less distracted. How does all that sound?

A: Sounds good. I am just not very confident that things will get much better.

SP: Well, to be real frank, they may not get better—at least not right away. I can't guarantee that they will. What I will offer is that if you believe in yourself, which I believe you do, and you commit to practice some of the techniques that we work on together, you will improve your ability to relax and focus, and as a result likely ski, study, and take tests better. The important thing to remember is that what we will work on together are skills, just like learning V1 or V2 when skating. With practice you get better.

After the sport psychologist helped the athlete articulate what she would like to work on, he made a decision to provide a plan of action based on the initial session and the information gathered up to that point. Because the athlete is competing in a couple days (before the next counseling session), the sport psychologist has decided to teach her a simple breathing strategy that she can use immediately. The technique is called *abdominal breathing*.

DIDACTIC RATIONALE AND TEACHING RELAXATION

SP: Amber, I'd like to talk about how useful relaxation is. Learning to relax has several benefits. One benefit is that relaxation can be used to reduce stress and tension. In fact, muscular tension is often a result of mental stress. Under stressful situations, like when you are taking a test or anticipating the start of a race, you are likely unnecessarily contracting unneeded muscles. This has a cumulative fatiguing effect. Sometimes this is called generalized muscle tension, meaning that you are contracting many muscles (in general most muscles), both agonist—the muscles required for whatever activity it is you are doing, and antagonist muscles—the opposing muscles. Are those familiar terms from anatomy and exercise physiology?

A: Yes.

SP: In effect, tension means wasted energy and early fatigue. The cool thing is, you can learn to do and say things that will reduce your stress and minimize some or much of your tension. I would guess that as a result of your worry before a race, your body is somewhat fatigued before you even start. Then you begin and go out a bit harder than you intended. The cumulative effect is what you termed "blowing up." In addition, there is a strong connection between stress and tension and concentration and ability to focus. When you are stressed or tense, you may be focusing on things other than the real task at hand. For example, when you need to be paying attention to your coach or the officials before a race, you are worrying about other things, like your competitors or your wax. Or, when you should be focusing entirely on a test question, you are worrying about what could happen if you do poorly on the exam. When you injured your knee the second time, you indicated you were worried about doing just that. It is not uncommon for athletes and other people to injure themselves either because they are distracted or because their bodies are tense. I believe our bodies have a natural protective mechanism that works best when we are loose and relaxed and free from distraction. Next session, I'd like you to take a simple written test that will help us identify the patterns you have for paying attention to things. This may give us some insight into how to better direct your attention or focus. What do you think about all of this? [pause] Can I clarify anything?

A: It all seems to be pretty logical. I mean it makes sense to me. You are right with my second blown knee. I was thinking about it happening, getting nervous, and then I fell, and it blew. I never thought about how that was connected to me being distracted. It totally makes sense.

SP: I am glad it is making sense. I'd like to spend a few minutes developing a breathing exercise that you can use this week, actually starting today. Like we just talked about, if you can reduce your stress level, muscular tension should diminish, and you will likely practice and perform better. Doing breathing exercises and becoming aware of your breathing are very effective ways to reduce stress and tension. Are you ready to try a breathing awareness exercise?

A: OK.

SP: The first thing we will develop is an awareness of your breathing patterns. The easiest way to do this is from a supine position, lying down on your back. That is what the pad is for along the side of the wall. Are you OK trying this lying down?

A: [She gets up and begins walking toward the mat.] I guess.

SP: I am just going to sit here and talk you through a simple exercise. You can close your eyes or leave them open, but it might be easier with your eyes closed. Either bend your knees or let your legs go straight, whatever is most comfortable. I'd like you to put your right hand on your abdomen, right at your waist, and your left hand on your chest, right at your sternum. Just breathing normally, simply notice how you breathe. As you inhale, which hand moves the most—the hand on your chest or the hand on your abdomen? Continue breathing for a while. It looks like your abdomen hand is moving. I would like you to exhale as fully as possible now, getting all the air out of your lungs. Good. Now inhale with a deep-belly or abdominal breath. Good, just keep breathing like that, trying to keep your chest hand still while the abdomen hand rises. Good. How does that feel?

A: Weird. I mean I feel weird lying here. It does feel good to take a deep breath.

Lying down in front of someone who is a relative stranger and closing one's eyes is not something one does everyday. That Amber feels "weird" is not all that surprising. She is putting herself in a vulnerable position. The sport psychologist assures Amber that the weirdness will fade.

SP: I think you will feel less weird the more you practice. Normally you can practice on your own wherever you are most comfortable. What do you mean it feels good to take a deep breath? What feels good about it?

A: I don't know, I guess it's just calm, like I am floating.

SP: It does help calm you down. In fact, deep-belly or diaphragmatic breathing is the one of the easiest and quickest ways to feel relaxed. As you exhale completely and your diaphragm contracts and expands [pause], you create a vacuum [pause] that draws air deep and fully into your lungs [pause]. Continue exhaling fully and then allow your stomach to rise as you inhale deeply. That's it [pause]. Make sure the hand on your chest stays still [pause]. Good. How are you doing?

A: I feel good.

SP: Good. I'd like you to just keep on breathing the way you are. Really think about exhaling completely and inhaling fully, allowing your stomach to rise. And Amber, just listen to the sound of my voice as you exhale completely, and inhale fully. Good. Now, I want you to notice how you feel right now. Are you calm and very relaxed?

A: Yes.

The athlete really does appear to be very relaxed. The sport psychologist gets a good feel for this by watching the athlete, counting her respirations, and listening to her tone of voice. The sport psychologist makes the decision to not do much more relaxation deepening for this first relaxation session, because the athlete looks and reports being calm and relaxed. A large part of learning to deliver relaxation inductions is working on one's voice. Some sport psychologists are gifted with what we call an *FM-radio voice,* sort of a resonant, mellifluous baritone. Many of us, though, have to spend a great deal of time working on developing a soothing, hypnotic tone with a gently undulating rhythm. We have heard some inductions delivered in a low register and in monotone. *Hypnotic* does not mean monotonous. Using one's voice as a verbal rocking chair or an oceanic wave slowly rising and falling will help the athlete enter the relaxed state. The sport psychologist working with Amber reminds her to "just listen to the sound of my voice," because his voice is an instrument he has trained for years to help people relax, and it is a very good instrument. Learning how to relax may be relatively easy. Learning to deliver relaxation isn't.

SP: [speech is slow and rhythmic] Notice how calm and relaxed you feel. I want to suggest to you that whenever you are feeling stressed or tense or disturbed in any way, you take a couple of deep and full abdominal breaths, just like you are now, except that you may be seated in a chair or standing on skis or whatever. By taking those breaths, you can feel just as relaxed as you do now. Just by taking a few deep abdominal breaths, you can feel more relaxed and more in control. More relaxed but also more alert and focused. Continue to exhale fully and breathe deeply. Good. You are breathing at a comfortable pace. In fact, because your body is so relaxed and you are exhaling so fully and inhaling completely, the number of respirations required to run your body has reduced. Good, your body is working very efficiently now. At any time and in any place, Amber, you can breathe and relax, just like this. I am going to pause for a moment now and just let you continue breathing and relaxing [pause for a minute]. OK, when you are ready to open your eyes, just let them open slowly. How are you doing?

A: Wow, your voice is great. I feel really good. Really relaxed. Kinda sleepy.

SP: You can use the exercise to relax so deeply that you fall asleep. Sometimes, especially at night, that may be your goal. But you can also use the exercise to relax and release stress and tension so you can concentrate and perform better. Amber, go ahead and stand up when you are ready, but do so slowly. I would like you to practice the same breathing pattern under a couple of other circumstances. First, while you are just standing here. Then, when you feel pretty comfortable with that, I want you to try imagining a stressful situation and see if you can remain calm while you breathe abdominally. How does that sound?

A: Kinda cool actually.

SP: Good. Now, in this standing position, continue to be aware of your breathing. Go ahead and place your hands the way you had they in the lying position [pause for about 10 seconds]. Which hand do you feel moving?

A: My right [on her stomach].

SP: Yes. Can you take a deeper breath and make your hand move even more? [She does this, deepening the abdominal breath.] How do you feel?

A: Good; a little light-headed.

SP: Really? OK, I'd like you to sit down in that chair for a moment. [Amber takes a seat.] I want to be sure you do not lose your balance. I may have asked you to stand too quickly. Just continue to breathe from your stomach and exhale completely. Have you ever gotten dizzy or fainted before?

A: No, I am fine. I just got a little head-rush.

SP: OK. Well, just continue to sit and breathe slowly and rhythmically [pause]. Remember, you will notice that you do not need to breathe as often because your body is becoming more efficient in taking in and using oxygen. How do you feel?

A: Better. Good.

SP: [pause] When you feel really comfortable and no dizziness or head-rush, go ahead and stand again. [She stands after about 20 seconds.] If you feel dizziness at any time in this session or anytime at all, be sure you take a seat or even lie down, OK?

A: OK.

SP: Good. As you continue to breath from your stomach I want you to remember how relaxed you were in the lying position—perhaps you feel as relaxed now? [pause]

A: I am still pretty relaxed.

SP: Good. It is the location and depth of your breathing that helps you relax. It really doesn't matter too much what position your body is in. Just continue to breathe from the stomach and do so very rhythmically [pause]. Good. Now, I want you to begin to imagine a stressful situation and see if you can remain calm. You are getting ready for a race. Perhaps you just pulled up in the van and you are getting your boots on [pause]. Now you're getting your equipment ready for a warm-up [pause]. How do you feel?

A: OK.

SP: Continue to breathe very rhythmically from your stomach. That's it. Now—you have completed your warm-up and are listening to the coaches discuss the course [pause]. You are breathing very rhythmically and look calm and relaxed. How do you feel?

A: OK; I feel those butterflies. That's weird.

SP: Butterflies where?

A: Oh, in my stomach like we talked about before.

SP: Gotcha. Some butterflies are OK. If you didn't have any, I might be worried. They mean you are getting ready to ski. It is when you start feeling frenzied and become unable to listen to instructions that we want to avoid. Keep breathing from your stomach, deeply and rhythmically [pause]. How do you feel?

A: Good, I guess. I still feel pretty relaxed.

SP: Good. Remember, with the breathing you are able to control your stress level a bit. With practice you will get better. Focusing on your breathing also helps you stay in the present. With every abdominal breath you will remember to stay in the present—the *right now!* You are still breathing rhythmically as you listen to your coaches. Now you are getting ready to go to the start. Three minutes before start time. Continue focusing on your breathing. Where are you breathing from and how are you breathing? [pause]

A: Umm . . . in my stomach. And, uh, deeply and rhythmically.

SP: Good. One minute before race time. Describe your race strategy for me.

A: Umm . . . I am breathing from my stomach, rhythmically. [Pause; Amber seems confused.]

SP: OK. Breathing to help you stay relaxed and focused on the present. Good. How are you going to go out?

A: Oh. Umm . . . I am going to pace myself. Coach always says for me to forget about the leaders and settle into a rhythm early. I am going to go hard for about 30 seconds and then settle into a steady rhythm.

SP: Good. Continue to breathe. Relaxed and steady. Do you think you can use this breathing technique when you begin to feel frenzied?

A: I think so.

SP: How do you feel now?

A: Good.

SP: We are about out of time. I want to continue working together on relaxation training next week. I would like to play out some other situations with you, like test taking. For the rest of this week, I have a very short audiotape I want to give you. It is a five-minute tape. I notice you have a Walkman—so you can play this tape at your convenience. This tape is designed to help you practice the breathing technique you learned and practiced today. Some people like the tape and others like to practice on their own. Still others do a little of both. I will leave it up to you. I would like you to practice the abdominal breathing at least three times a day until I see you next week. Is that doable?

A: I guess so. That's only 15 minutes.

SP: Yes. Do you have any questions for me?

A: Not really.

SP: OK. I have an open office hour for drop-in appointments from 8 to 9 A.M. every morning. If you have any questions, you can either call or drop by. Good skill at the races.

The first session included the initial contact and interview, history taking, starting a working alliance, conceptualizing the problem, and building rapport. In session two, the sport psychologist continued to build rapport and nurture the working alliance and also introduced and provided a rationale for relaxation, provided initial instructions and guidance, and presented a quick relaxation technique for the precompetitive environment. Session three will initially focus on a post-race debrief and discussion about how the breathing went for the athlete. In addition, as will soon be apparent in the dialogue, more attention will be given to helping the athlete develop a deepened state of relaxation.

Session III

SP: How are you, Amber?

A: Hi.

SP: How was your week?

A: OK. We were on the road; I saw my folks. Actually, they went to the race.

SP: How was that for you?

A: It was good to see them. I didn't have a very good race, though [silence].

SP: Tell me about it.

A: Well, I went down—right near the start as we were scrabbling for position. I wasn't sure what happened until I looked at the video afterward. A competitor stepped on the back of my ski and I lost my balance. I was OK and got right back up. I am used to falling [smiling]. After that I kinda lost focus and didn't think about anything but catching the group. I did, but I was spent. At least that's what coach said. I lost them the last 5K. Actually, my time was closer to the winner's than ever before. It was a flat, rolling course, which is good for me.

SP: Let me stop you for a second and make sure I understand. You went down near the start, got right back up and caught the pack but worked pretty hard to do that, and as a result lost the leaders the second 5K. Despite all that, you were closer to the leaders than ever before. Is that about right?

A: Yeah, that's right.

SP: What did your coach think about your performance?

A: He said I recovered well, [pause] and the fall was just bad luck.

SP: I obviously wasn't there, but it sounds to me like you had a good race, all things considered [pause].

Amber's judgment of not having a very good race, despite some indicators to the contrary, is perhaps another example of irrational thinking and may be closely connected to pressure and stress and the frenzied feelings Amber has been experiencing. The sport psychologist decides to address Amber's thought processes later in the session (or next session) after more information unfolds related to her use of the breathing technique.

SP: Were you able to use the abdominal breathing before the race?

A: Yes, but it didn't seem to work very well.

SP: I sort of thought that because you were just learning abdominal breathing it might not be effective. Why don't we try a different technique that is a bit more powerful?

The sport psychologist seems apprehensive and almost apologetic about the breathing not working. He is about to lose an opportunity to learn about Amber's experiences with relaxation in her performance setting, and he may unintentionally sabotage his own work by undervaluing the technique the athlete has learned. On the surface, his ambitious plan of equipping her with a bag of relaxation tricks seems reasonable. Such an approach can give a client more flexibility in terms of matching a technique with a particular symptom or situation. Nevertheless, an exploration of Amber's most recent experiences with self-regulation might provide him with insights into what works for her, and how, and what other techniques might be useful in the long term.

SP: Were you able to use the abdominal breathing?

A: I did it a few times, but it didn't seem to work very well [pause].

SP: Tell me about it.

A: Well, I was not as relaxed as I was in your office. In the van I listened [to the tape] on the headphones a bit, and a couple of times when I started to think about racing and was feeling nervous I was able to take a few breaths, and felt better, but before the race I was still pretty nervous.

SP: How did you feel after using the technique in the van?

A: Well, I don't know. I felt more relaxed; uh, the butterflies kinda went away.

SP: Anything else?

A: Not really [pauses, thinking]. Well, I was able to focus on my reading better. I noticed that I would start worrying about the race and I would totally not remember what I just read. If I took a couple of those abdominal breaths it kinda got me back on track with my reading—at least for a little while.

SP: Excellent! One of the major benefits of using centered breathing, other than helping you feel more relaxed, is that it can help you focus on what you need to be doing at that time. I call that "being in the moment." If you are trying to read and you are consumed with worry about a race, you are wasting time and energy. Just like if you are worrying about the wax on your skis or who is at the race when you are supposed to be listening to the coaches you are missing valuable information and wasting time and energy. Your success with relaxation in the van is an excellent start. Before the race when you felt nervous, did you use the breathing technique?

A: A couple of times, I think.

SP: You don't sound real sure.

A: Well, it was pretty busy. I know I did once after the warm-up [sounding frustrated].

SP: I sense some frustration in your voice. Would you tell me more about it?

A: Well, I felt a bit stressed-out right after the warm-up. So I thought of the breathing technique immediately. I started to breathe from my abdomen like I learned it here and practiced. But it wasn't the same feeling. Instead, my thoughts were still racing, and again I didn't register in my mind my coach telling me anything.

SP: It sounds like your breathing served you well while you were traveling to the race and reading. During the race, however, you were not able to control you arousal level—that is, you could not relax and focus on what you needed to. Is that right?

A: Yes.

SP: The fact that you remembered to use the technique is a good first step. Not only that, but you used it with success in at least one environment.

The sport psychologist decided to provide Amber with some positive reinforcement for the success she had and get her focusing on that success. Amber tends to be hard on herself and slow to recognize her achievements, as are many athletes. This pattern is another example of a maladaptive or irrational thought process, and the sport psychologist filed it away to address at a later time.

SP: Remember when you made the transition from Alpine to Nordic skiing—you had to learn elements of skating, and progressively you got better? You could use some techniques on the flats, with corduroy snow, but you had to learn to use others on icy, uneven terrain?

A: Yes, I see where you are going.

SP: Good, then you see that skills are developed over time and from simple to more complex situations?

A: Yes.

SP: And with practice and patience you will develop and enhance mental skills just like you developed and enhanced physical skills.

A: Yeah.

SP: My belief is that if we allow you to experience a deeper state of relaxation here and you practice achieving that state at home, you will have better control of how relaxed you are in many other situations—like before races. I would like to introduce you to another relaxation technique that will help you deepen the relaxed state you are able to elicit on your own. How does that sound?

A: Sounds good.

Just as with Jacobsonian relaxation, we like to prepare our clients for a good experience the first time they venture into the area of autogenic training. Introducing Amber to the first step of autogenic training (feelings of heaviness) went something like this:

SP: Amber, I'd like us to try another form of relaxation that you can practice at home and that can help you become quite relaxed. It comes from the field of hypnosis, but I hate to use that word because the word conjures the image of stage hypnotists and people clucking like chickens.

A: Yeah, I think those shows are rather rude.

SP: I am in complete agreement with you on that one, and that is not what hypnosis is about. Hypnosis for me is usually a nice state of relaxation where people are more receptive to some suggestions, and we use a version of it often when working with athletes. Hypnosis has the problem of a hypnotist and a subject, and some researchers several decades ago wanted to see if people could get into a relaxed hypnotic state by themselves. Thus, autogenics was born. The word *autogenics* just means *self-generated*. Another name for it is *self-hypnosis*. The first step in learning autogenics is to make suggestions to yourself that you are experiencing feelings of heaviness. I will repeat some phrases about heaviness in your limbs, and as I say them, you repeat them to yourself inside your head . . .

The sport psychologist has tried to place the upcoming autogenic training in a context that the athlete can feel comfortable with and to dispel myths the client may believe or negative preconceptions the client might have about hypnosis and autogenics. At this point, the sport psychologist will share with Amber some thoughts about what she might experience during this first session or what she may anticipate happening (anticipatory guidance). The sport psychologist will also try to maximize the possibility that the athlete will have a positive experience by discussing a desirable training attitude (passive-receptive), providing cautions or caveats about training, and teaching her how to terminate the session if need be.

SP: Your arms may not get heavy all at once, but many people experience their arms growing heavier even after we have left them and are working on the legs. Some people actually "lose" parts of their bodies. When I do this I lose my arms, and I don't really know where they are. If that happens, great. It's a good sign of relaxation. I'd also like to encourage you to remain what we call *passive-receptive* during relaxation training. This is the same as passively ignoring distracting thoughts when you are relaxing. Remember, we talked about not trying to think about nothing?

A: That sounds confusing. You mean letting my thoughts come and go and not thinking about some of them?

SP: Yes, that's what I mean. It is really hard to think about nothing. A better strategy is to just let any thoughts that enter your mind come and go, passively ignoring them [some call this passively attending]. With the breathing exercise, you were able to direct your attention to the location and rhythm of your breathing and let distracting thoughts come and go. With this current exercise [autogenic training], I want you to adopt a similar strategy; that is, to maintain a passive-receptive attitude. If you get heavy, great; if you don't get heavy, that's fine too. Don't try to force it; just let it come. Also, if you feel any strange sensations that are unpleasant or uncomfortable or make you feel uneasy with the exercises, just open your eyes. We can stop and talk about it. Although my experience is that most athletes really like autogenics and it helps them relax to a greater degree. I believe that as a result of the deeper level of relaxation you are able to achieve through this training, you will be able to better control the frenzied feelings and the distractions before a race. Learning autogenics may make the breathing exercises you have already learned more effective. How does all this sound?

A: Sounds good. I'm ready.

The sport psychologist, by discussing what the client might experience (anticipatory guidance) during autogenic training, by suggesting a passive-receptive attitude, and by providing cautions or caveats, is planting prehypnotic-like suggestions. The goal is to prepare the athlete for the very best experience possible.

SP: Are you comfortable lying down on the pad?

A: You bet! [Amber gets up, lies on her back in the comfortable position she learned earlier, and closes her eyes.]

SP: Good. You may shrug your shoulders and relax your neck muscles through a couple of neck rolls. Let's start with a couple of deep abdominal breaths—inhale 1, 2—exhale 1, 2, 3, 4 [repeated several times]. Inhale fully; exhale completely. As you are breathing, you might notice how you get calmer and calmer, more and more relaxed. As you continue to breathe, inhaling fully and exhaling completely, I want you to listen to the sound of my voice as you begin to feel more and more relaxed [pause]. Your mind and your body are intimately connected, so as I make a suggestion to you, you may either repeat the suggestions to yourself or just think about them, and your body will respond. As we discussed, just let it happen. As you practice, you will get better and better at doing this.

I want you to direct your attention to your right arm. Your right arm is feeling heavy now. Your right arm is feeling comfortably heavy now. And say to yourself, My right arm is heavy [repeated 7–10 times]. As your right arm gets heavier and heavier, Amber, it feels like it is sinking into the mat, getting more and more heavy—very heavy and very comfortable [pause]. Your arm is heavy now . . . comfortably sinking into the mat [pause]. Now, direct your attention from your right arm to your left arm. Your left arm is feeling some heaviness now . . .

These directions continue throughout the rest of the body: left arm, legs, hips and torso, and head. The sport psychologist maintains a calm and soothing tone of voice and periodically reminds Amber to breathe rhythmically and diaphragmatically.

SP: Now, I want to suggest to you that any time you choose, by taking a couple of deep abdominal breaths, you can return to the relaxed state you are in right now. By doing this, you will be able to focus your attention on the task at hand—whether it is preparing for a race, listening to instructions, taking a test, or going to sleep. As a result, you will be able to consistently perform at your potential for the task at hand [pause]. I am going to be quiet momentarily to allow you to just experience this relaxed state. I will speak to you in a couple of minutes.

A: [lying quietly, breathing deeply and slowly]

SP: [approximately three minutes later] OK, I want to suggest again that any time you choose, by taking a couple of deep abdominal breaths, you can return to the relaxed state you are in right now. Now we are going to slowly reverse the process and help you become more awake and alert and ready to take on the day with a renewed freshness and relaxed peace of mind. In a moment I'll start to count from one to five. As I count, you will feel more and more energy come to your body and become more and more alert. One, with each inhalation, you are feeling more and more awake—more and more fresh and alert—good. Two, continuing to breath a bit more rapidly and feeling more and more energy. Three, inhale and exhale, halfway here and more alert. Four, you are ready to open your eyes, feeling renewed and ready to complete any task. Five, you feel completely refreshed; energized, yet relaxed and comfortable. Go ahead and open your eyes [pause]. Good [pause]. How did it go?

A: I feel very relaxed. I really felt heavy and warm [pause]. I wish I could have stayed there longer.

SP: Tell me more about what you were experiencing.

A: [pause] That's pretty much it. I mean, I was relaxed.

SP: Did you feel any strange sensations in any parts of your body?

A: No, but I did kinda lose you a couple times. It was sort of like I heard your voice and knew you were there, but it was like far away, and I wasn't noticing what you were saying—just that you were there.

SP: Sort of like you heard my voice but weren't really hearing the content of what I said.

A: Yeah, that's how it was a few times. Weird, huh?

SP: Actually, that's a real good sign of deep relaxation. You were probably entering into a nice hypnotic-like state. Real good sign for your future work with this technique. Now what parts of your body got heavy?

A: Well, I did notice that my legs got very heavy; much more heavy than my arms. Kinda funny thinking about it now—with my arms I was really trying to get them heavy. Then I remembered the passive thing and just focused on my breathing and what you were saying.

SP: So you were able to just let it happen with the legs. And they got heavy.

A: Yeah, I guess.

SP: That's great! How about other parts of the body?

A: My neck and shoulders felt really relaxed when you were talking about making my head heavy.

SP: Good [pause]. Do you think our pace was about right? Could I have gone faster, or slowed it down?

A: Well, I thought the pace was good, but I wanted to relax a bit longer. When you left and came back, well, I wanted to continue just lying there relaxing, and you had me waking up.

SP: Good. I will remember that next time. Also, on the tape I send home with you, remember you can shut it off if you want to relax a bit longer. Of course, I recommend you do just that if you are using the tape to go to sleep.

Amber, I think this has been a very successful session. Your relaxation level has deepened, which no doubt will help you relax quickly with a couple of deep abdominal breaths; you have learned firsthand about remaining passive and receptive to relaxation; and I have learned more about you so we can tailor future sessions more to your needs. I think you have done a tremendous job. Your task or goal now should be to make autogenic training part of your life for the next couple of weeks. With practice you will continue to improve your ability to relax. Any thoughts or questions? [pause]

A: No, I can't think of anything.

SP: OK. Just to summarize, the idea with this session was to help you experience a deeper state of relaxation. As with the centered breathing, I will send a tape home with you. This tape is a bit longer, roughly 20 minutes. I would like you to practice this deeper relaxation once a day, five days a week. The last 2 to 3 minutes of the tape is designed to refresh and re-energize you. Like I said, if you are listening to the tape prior to going to bed, just turn the tape off before the energizing part. Under other circumstances, listen to the entire tape. It's fine if you want to listen to the tape before bed. I would like you to listen to it during the day as well and practice re-energizing, too. It's kind of like a 20-minute power nap, where you experience a deep state of relaxation and then refresh and recharge for the rest of the day. Just like with the breathing tape, the goal is for you to be able to self-relax; that is, practice autogenics on your own. So over the next month or so, we will slowly help you self-relax without the tape. Any questions?

A: No. Well, should I listen to the breathing tape, too?

SP: What do you think?

A: Well, I think it is helpful, too.

SP: You bet, then. I would like to see you work toward practicing the breathing exercises on your own, whenever you think you need them, but for this week, why don't you try to listen to both tapes at least once a day.

A: OK!

SP: See you next week, then.

Amber was an excellent student of autogenics and she progressed through the other autogenic stages rapidly (warmth, heartbeat, breathing, solar plexus, forehead). As Amber became more adept at deep relaxation, her use of breathing exercises to combat the stresses of competition and taking tests became more effective. As Amber learned relaxation, she also became more relaxed with the sport psychologist, and over time their sessions moved into realms of family, boyfriend, and Amber's sense of who she was.

Relaxation itself is a kind of metaphor for a lot of sport psychology service delivery, whether it is relaxing tense muscles, relaxing and letting go of irrational thought, or relaxing one's defenses and getting comfortable talking to the sport psychologist. Some of these relaxations may be relatively easy (relaxing muscles), whereas others may be more difficult (relaxing defenses).

CONCLUSIONS

There are a number of techniques from which a consultant and client may choose while improving self-regulatory skills for enhanced performance. This chapter focused on relaxation as a means of reducing anxiety, stress, and tension in order to maximize performance potential. In the process of designing and implementing relaxation training, the development of an athlete-consultant alliance serves as a foundation for effective work toward personal growth and development. In addition, a consultant may consider the following recommendations.

- Although telling someone to relax is easy, teaching relaxation is not. Teaching relaxation effectively requires the development of solid counseling and pedagogical skills along with a substantial amount of voice training.
- The relaxation technique selected should match the athlete's primary activation symptoms.
- An athlete's own self-regulatory skills (if any are present) can be used as a starting point for the intervention.
- The relaxation training can be used as a component of a broader sport psychology intervention aimed at performance enhancement and personal growth (and not as the only vehicle for a client's behavior change).

Amber's case is fairly typical. Performance enhancement was the first goal of service delivery, but as Amber learned how to relax (in many ways), her comfort with her sport psychologist grew and their sessions moved more into the intra- and interpersonal realms.

Doing relaxation comes in a multitude of forms, and in the hands (or maybe the larynx) of a master it looks easy. The skills needed for delivering relaxation inductions are many, and they are complex. We hope this chapter, with its small glimpse of the province of relaxation, offers students and practitioners a view of the intricacies involved. These techniques are powerful, as all practitioners who use relaxation on themselves (a practice we believe essential) know. We tell our athletes that relaxation is a skill that requires practice, and we tell our students delivering relaxation the same thing. Finally, we would like to say, Doing relaxation? It ain't easy.

REFERENCES

Bakker, F.C., & Kayser, C.S. (1994). Effect of a self-help mental training programme. *International Journal of Sport Psychology, 25,* 158-175.

Baum, A., Gatchel, R.J., & Krantz, D.S. (1996). *An introduction to health psychology* (3rd ed.). New York: McGraw-Hill.

Benson, H. (1975). *The relaxation response.* New York: William Morrow.

Benson, H. (1983). The relaxation response: Its subjective and objective historical precedents and physiology. *Trends in Neurosciences, 6,* 281-284.

Crocker, P.R.E., Alderman, R.B., & Smith, F.M.R. (1988). Cognitive-affective stress management training with high performance youth volleyball players: Effects on affect, cognition, and performance. *Journal of Sport and Exercise Psychology, 10,* 448-460.

Davidson, R.J., & Schwartz, G.E. (1976). Psychobiology of relaxation and related states. In D. Mostofsky (Ed.), *Behavior modification and control of physiological activity.* Engelwood Cliffs, NJ: Prentice-Hall.

Davis, M., Eshelman, E.R., & McKay, M. (1995). *The relaxation and stress reduction workbook* (4th ed.). Oakland, CA: New Harbinger.

Ellis, A. (1995). Rational emotive behavior therapy. In R.J. Corsini & D. Wedding (Eds.), *Current psychotherapies* (5th ed., pp. 162-196). Itasca, IL: F.E. Peacock.

Greenspan, M.J., & Feltz, D.L. (1989). Psychological interventions with athletes in competitive situations: A review. *The Sport Psychologist, 3,* 219-236.

Hamilton, S., & Fremouw, W. (1985). Cognitive-behavioral training for college free-throw performance. *Cognitive Therapy and Research, 9,* 479-483.

Hanin, Y.L. (1980). A study of anxiety in sports. In W.F. Straub (Ed.), *Sport psychology: An analysis of athlete behavior* (pp. 236-249). Ithaca, NY: Mouvement.

Henschen, K. (1995). Relaxation and performance. In K.P. Henschen & W.F. Straub (Eds.), *Sport psychology: An analysis of athlete behavior* (2nd ed., pp. 163-167). Longmeadow, MA: Mouvement.

Jacobson, E. (1962). *You must relax.* New York: McGraw-Hill.

Lazarus, R. (1966). *Psychological stress and the coping process.* New York: McGraw-Hill.

Lehrer, P.M., and Woolfolk, R.L. (Eds.). (1993). *Principles and practice of stress management* (2nd ed.). New York: Guilford Press.

Lichstein, K.L. (1988). *Clinical relaxation strategies.* New York: Wiley.

Luthe, W. (1965). *Autogenic training: International edition.* New York: Grune & Stratton.

Meyers, A., Schleser, R., & Okwumabua, T. (1982). A cognitive behavioral intervention for improving basketball performance. *Research Quarterly for Exercise and Sport,* 53, 344-347.

Meyers, A.W., Whelan, J.P., & Murphy, S.M. (1996). Cognitive behavioral strategies in athletic performance enhancement. In M. Hersen, R.M. Eisler, & P.M. Miller (Eds.), *Progress in behavior modification* (vol. 30, pp. 137-164). Pacific Grove, CA: Brooks/Cole.

Poppen, R. (1998). *Behavioral relaxation training and assessment* (2nd ed.). Thousand Oaks, CA: Sage.

Selye, H. (1974). *Stress without distress.* Philadelphia: Lippincott.

Smith, J.C. (1986). Meditation, biofeedback, and the relaxation controversy: A cognitive-behavioral perspective. *American Psychologist, 41,* 1007-1009.

Smith, J.C. (1988). Steps toward a cognitive-behavioral model of relaxation. *Biofeedback and Self-Regulation, 13,* 307-329.

Unestahl, L.E. (1983). Inner mental training for sport. In T. Orlick, J.T. Partington, & J.H. Salmela (Eds.), *Mental training for coaches and athletes* (pp. 135-140). Ottawa, Canada: Coaching Association of Canada.

Unestahl, L.E. (1986). Self-hypnosis. In J.M. Williams (Ed.), *Applied sport psychology: Personal growth to peak performance* 2nd ed., (pp. 285-300). Palo Alto, CA: Mayfield.

Vealey, R.S. (1994). Current status and prominent issues in sport psychology interventions. *Medicine and Science in Sports and Exercise, 26,* 495-502.

Williams, J.M., & Harris, D.V. (1998). Relaxation and energizing techniques for regulation of arousal. In J.M. Williams (Ed.), *Applied sport psychology: Personal growth to peak performance* (3rd ed., pp. 219-236). Mountain View, CA: Mayfield.

Wolpe, J. (1973). *The practice of behavior therapy* (2nd ed.). New York: Pergamon Press.

Wrisberg, C.A., & Anshel, M.H. (1989). The effects of cognitive strategies on the free throw shooting performance of young athletes. *The Sport Psychologist, 3,* 95-104.

Zhang, L., Ma, Q., Orlick, T., & Zitzelsberger, L. (1992). The effects of mental-imagery training on performance enhancement with 7–10-year-old children. *The Sport Psychologist, 6,* 230-241.

CHAPTER 5

LISTENING TO SELF-TALK, HEARING SELF-CONCEPT

Clark Perry, Jr.
Australian Institute of Sport
Herbert W. Marsh
University of Western Sydney

Developing a positive self-concept is seen as desirable in many disciplines, such as sport psychology, health, education, and clinical and social psychology. Self-concept is frequently posited as a mediating variable that facilitates the attainment of other desirable outcomes, such as increased physical activity, exercise adherence, or health-related physical fitness.

William James (1963/1890) is generally recognized as the first psychologist to develop a theory of self-concept. James developed four constructs related to self that are of particular importance: (a) the I (self-as-knower or active agent) and Me (self-as-known or the content of experience) distinction; (b) the multifaceted, hierarchical nature of self-concept "with the bodily Self at the bottom, the spiritual Self at the top, and the extracorporeal material selves and the various social selves between" (p. 313); (c) the social self, based on the recognition individuals receive from their peers, or a generalized (or potential) social self that represents the evaluations of a hypothetical higher authority, a future generation, or God; and (d) the definition of self-esteem as the ratio of success to pretensions and subjective importance so that a person must select carefully "the strongest, truest, deepest self . . . on which to stake his salvation" (p. 310).

James anticipated many subsequent developments in self-concept theories. His concept of social self highlighted the importance of the evaluations by specific and generalized others that was a central focus of symbolic interactionists such as Cooley (1902) and Mead (1925, 1934). The self-as-knower and self-as-known distinction appears in nearly all accounts of self-concept and corresponds approximately to the dynamic/process and structural/trait orientations that are currently popular in self-concept research (Bracken, 1992, 1996; Damon & Hart, 1988; Harter, 1985, 1990; Hattie, 1992; Marsh, 1986, 1987a, 1993; Marsh & Hattie, 1996; Oosterwegel & Oppenheimer, 1993; Shavelson & Marsh, 1986).

James' definition of self-esteem as a function of both accomplishments and aspirations, and also the subjective importance of actually working to accomplish one's goals, proved to have heuristic value in the development of self-concept theory. In addition, James' theory laid the foundation for the multifaceted hierarchical model of self-concept that is the major focus of this chapter (Marsh & Shavelson, 1985).

James further proposed that the best representation of a person's overall self-evaluation is an appropriately weighted average of self-evaluations in specific domains. Because a person cannot be all things, each individual judiciously self-appraises, so that "I, who for the time have staked my all on being a psychologist, am mortified if others know much more psychology than I. But I am contented to wallow in the grossest ignorance of Greek." (1963/1980, p. 310). Objective accomplishments are evaluated in relation to internal frames of reference so that "we have the paradox of a man shamed to death because he is only the second pugilist or the second oarsman in the world . . . Yonder puny fellow, however, whom everyone can beat, suffers no chagrin about it, for he has long ago abandoned the attempt to 'carry that line'" (p. 310). Putting these two ideas together, James concluded that our self-feeling "depends entirely on what we back ourselves to be and do" (p. 310). Apparently, the boxer's pugilistic competence contributes negatively to his esteem because he has a very high, unachieved ideal to be the best and because he judges this domain to be very meaningful. Unachieved ideals do not affect esteem in domains judged to be of little importance.

Carl Rogers (1951, 1977) further explored a model of self, and that model is reflected in his client-centered therapy. The central construct in Rogers' theory of personality is the self. The self consists of all the ideas, perceptions, and values that characterize "I" or "me"; it includes the awareness of "what I am" and "what I can do." This perceived self, in turn, influences both a person's perception of the world and his or her own behavior. According to Rogers, when one's perception of self does not match one's experiences or feelings, anxiety and dissonance will take place. That is, if how you consider yourself to be, cognitively, does not match with your experiences in life or your emotions and feelings, then it is likely to be a cause of distress.

Finally, Rogers postulated the ideal self, which is the kind of person that one would like to be. The closer the ideal self is to the real self, the more likely the person is to be in harmony and well adjusted. Conversely, when the real self does not meet the qualities of the ideal self, and the ideal self is the primary source of comparison and appraisal, difficulties in individual behaviors and emotions may arise. Therefore, two types of incongruence can develop: one, between the self and the experiences of reality; and two, between the self and the ideal self. Rogers (1950) has defined self-concept as "an organized configuration of perceptions of the self which are admissible to awareness" (p. 78). The *self-concept,* then, is the image that we have of ourselves, whereas *self-esteem* is the evaluation or feeling about that image. Because of the apparent inseparable nature of these two constructs they are, regrettably, used interchangeably in the literature, but we will maintain a distinction between the image one has of oneself and how one feels about it.

THE SHAVELSON MODEL

This chapter is a bit different from others in this book in that much of it is dedicated to a model (and to assessment) that is not commonly discussed in applied sport psychology circles. We believe this discussion will be informative and will also provide a solid foundation for understanding the work with the athlete illustrated in the case study.

Despite the rich beginnings provided by James and Rogers, self-concept theory, research, and measurement were slow to develop because of the dominance of behaviorism in the mid-1900s. During the past 25 years, however, there has been a resurgence in self-concept research. This resurgence is due in part to Shavelson, Hubner, and Stanton's (1976) critical review of the literature. They noted vital deficiencies in self-concept research, including inadequate definitions of the self-concept construct, few appropriate measurement instruments, and the lack of rigorous tests of alternative interpretations. They attempted to integrate features of various models of self-concept to form their working definition, which was then used to integrate empirical evidence.

According to their definition, self-concept is a person's self-perceptions, which are formed through experience with, and interpretations of, his or her environment. These perceptions are influenced, especially, by the evaluations of significant others, reinforcements, and the way people explain their own behaviors to themselves (i.e., their attributions or reasons for their behaviors). According to Shavelson et al., self-concept is not an entity within a person, but a hypothetical construct that is potentially useful in explaining and predicting how that person acts or will act. A person's self-perceptions influence the way he or she acts, and these acts in turn influence his or her self-perceptions. Consistent with this perspective, Shavelson et al. noted that self-concept is significant as both an outcome and as a mediating variable that helps to explain other outcomes. For example, they also distinguished between self-concepts based on a person's own self-perceptions and inferred self-concepts that are based on inferences by another person, noting that they would focus on the former. Shavelson et al. identified seven features that were critical to their definition of the self-concept construct:

1. It is organized or structured, in that people categorize the vast amount of information they have about themselves and relate these categories to one another.

2. It is multifaceted, and the particular facets reflect a self-referent category system adopted by a person and/or shared by a group.
3. It is hierarchical, with perceptions of personal behavior in specific situations at the base of the hierarchy, inferences about self in broader domains (e.g., social, physical, academic) at the middle of the hierarchy, and a global, general self-concept at the apex.
4. The general self-concept—the apex of the hierarchy—is stable, but as one descends the hierarchy, self-concept becomes increasingly situation specific and, as a consequence, less stable. There are reciprocal relations between self-concept at each level in that self-perceptions at the base of the hierarchy may be attenuated by conceptualizations at higher levels, and changes in general self-concept may require changes in many situation-specific instances.
5. Self-concept becomes increasingly multifaceted as a person moves from infancy to adulthood.
6. Self-concept has both a descriptive and an evaluative aspect such that people may describe themselves ("I am happy") and evaluate themselves ("I do well in mathematics"). Evaluations can be made against some absolute ideal (the four-minute mile); a personal, internal standard (a personal best); a relative standard based on comparisons with peers; or the expectations of significant others. People may assign different values (give more or less weight) to the various aspects in the hierarchical and multifaceted self-concept.
7. Self-concept can be differentiated from other constructs. Thus, for example, academic and physical self-concepts can be differentiated from other domains such as academic achievement and physical fitness, respectively.

Shavelson et al. (1976) also presented one possible representation of this hierarchical model, in which general self-concept appeared at the apex and was divided into academic and nonacademic self-concepts at the next level. Academic self-concept was further divided into self-concepts in particular subject areas (e.g., mathematics, English.). Nonacademic self-concept was divided into three areas: social self-concept, which was subdivided into relations with peers and with significant others; emotional self-concept; and physical self-concept, which was subdivided into physical ability and physical appearance.

At the time Shavelson et al. (1976) first developed their model, there was only modest support for the hypothesized domains, and no one instrument considered in their review was able to differentiate among even the broad academic, social, and physical domains. The Shavelson model provided a foundation for the development of new theory, measurement instruments, and research. Using this model and addressing developmental changes in self-concept throughout the life span, the Self Description Questionnaire (SDQ; Marsh & O'Neill, 1984; Marsh, 1990a) instruments were designed for preadolescent primary school students (SDQI), adolescent high school students (SDQII), and late adolescents and young adults (SDQIII). Reviews of subsequent SDQ research (Boyle, 1994; Byrne, 1984, 1986; Hattie, 1992; Marsh, 1990b, 1993; Marsh & Shavelson, 1985; Wylie, 1989) supported the multifaceted structure of self-concept and demonstrated that self-concept cannot be adequately understood if its multidimensionality is ignored. In practice, this means that people can have different self-concepts in different domains.

DISCREPANCY THEORY: ACTUAL AND IDEAL BODY IMAGE

As noted earlier, James (1890/1963) emphasized that "we have the paradox of a man shamed to death because he is only the second pugilist or the second oarsman in the world," leading him to conclude that objective accomplishments are evaluated in relation to an internal frame of reference. Following from James, discrepancy theory posits self-concept as a function of differences between self-perceived actual accomplishments and ideal standards, so that

- similar accomplishments lead to different self-evaluations, depending on ideal standards; and
- unrealistic ideals lead to poor self-concepts even when accomplishments are otherwise good.

Research by Marsh and Roche (1996) examining actual and ideal body image lends support for the discrepancy model. The findings revealed that low self-concepts may reflect poor actual self-perceptions and/or unrealistic ideal standards in relation to one's body image. That is, one's body image self-concept may be negatively influenced by an unrealistically high ideal, not necessarily by a poor actual self-perception. In practical terms, this means that when helping athletes with body image distortions, the sport psychologist must examine both the athletes' ideals and their actual appraisals.

INFLUENCE OF FRAME-OF-REFERENCE EFFECTS

People usually evaluate their accomplishments in relation to some standard or frame of reference. So, for example, even if several athletes have similar accomplishments, their sporting self-concepts will differ if they have different frames of reference. Following are descriptions of theoretical models and empirical support for two different frame-of-reference effects.

In the internal/external frame-of-reference (I/E) model, Marsh (1986) and others extended psychophysical and social contextual research to incorporate peoples' comparisons of their own ability levels in different domains. In the big-fish-little-pond effect (BFLPE), Marsh (1987b) proposed that self-concept is influenced substantially by the ability levels of others in the immediate context, in addition to one's own ability level.

Internal/External Frame-of-Reference (I/E) Model

The historical, theoretical underpinnings of this research (see Marsh, 1984a, 1990a, 1991, 1993; Marsh & Parker, 1984) are derived from research in psychophysical judgment (e.g., Helson, 1964; Marsh, 1974; Parducci, 1995), social judgment (e.g., Morse & Gergen, 1970; Sherif & Sherif, 1969; Upshaw, 1969), sociology (Alwin & Otto, 1977; Hyman, 1942; Meyer, 1970), social comparison theory (e.g., Festinger, 1954; Suls, 1977), and the theory of relative deprivation (Davis, 1966; Stouffer et al., 1949). The I/E model (Marsh, 1986; 1994; Marsh, Byrne, & Shavelson, 1988) was designed to explain why verbal and math self-concepts are so distinct. Verbal and mathematics achievements are highly correlated (correlations of .50 to .80); people who are good in one area tend to be good in the other. Verbal and math self-concepts, however, are nearly uncorrelated. People think of themselves as "math" persons or "verbal" persons. According to the I/E model, self-concepts are formed in relation to both external and internal comparisons or frames of reference:

- External Comparisons: According to this social comparison process, students compare their self-perceptions of their abilities in math and in reading with the perceived abilities of others in their frame of reference (e.g., other students in their classroom or year in school). They use these external, relativistic impressions as a basis for their self-concepts in each area.
- Internal Comparisons: According to this ipsative-like process, people compare their self-perceived abilities in math with their self-perceived abilities in English, and they use these internal, relativistic impressions as a second basis for arriving at their self-concepts in each area.

An external comparison process should lead to a positive correlation between verbal and math self-concepts (because the achievements are substantially correlated). Internal comparison processes should lead to a negative correlation between verbal and math self-concepts (because it is the difference between math and verbal skills that contributes to a higher self-concept in one area or the other). The joint operation of both processes, depending on their relative strength, should lead to the near-zero correlation between verbal and math self-concept that has been observed in empirical research.

To illustrate this model in a sporting context, consider two athletes: a weekend sports enthusiast who is best at golf (with a handicap of 10) and a professional tennis player who is also a good golfer (with a handicap of 2). Asked how good they are at golf, it would be reasonable for the professional tennis player to say "fairly good" (because she is so much better at tennis), whereas the weekend sports enthusiast might say "very good" (because golf is her best sport). Objectively, the professional tennis player is a better golfer, but if asked to complete self-concept of golf and tennis scales, the weekend sports enthusiast might have as high or even higher self-concept of golf than the professional athlete.

Big-Fish-Little-Pond Effect (BFLPE)

Marsh (1984a, 1984b; Marsh & Parker, 1984) proposed a frame-of-reference model called the big-fish-little-pond effect (BFLPE) to encapsulate external frame-of-reference effects. In this model, Marsh hypothesized that people compare their abilities with the abilities of their peers and use this social comparison impression as one basis for forming their own self-concepts. The BFLPE occurs when equally able people have lower self-concepts when they compare themselves to more able people and higher self-concepts when they compare themselves with less able people. For example, if an average-ability athlete were a member of highly talented team, his sporting abilities would be lower than the average of the other athletes on that team, and this discrepancy would lead to sporting self-concepts that were below average. Conversely, if the athlete were a member of a not-so-talented team, then his abilities would be above the average of the other athletes on the team, and that difference would lead to sporting self-concepts that were above average. Similarly, the sporting self-concepts of below-average and above-average athletes depend on their sporting abilities but also vary with type of teams or leagues in which they compete. According to the BFLPE model, sporting self-concept will be correlated positively with individual achievement (better athletes will have a higher sporting self-concept) but negatively related to team average achievement (the same athlete will have lower sporting self-concept on a team where the average ability is high).

The BFLPE may also have an effect on athletes who are selected for elite teams, camps, or residential training programs. Consider a capable athlete who has been evaluated as the top athlete throughout his early sporting career in his hometown or state. This athlete has now been identified as talented and brought into an elite nationwide program where he may be average or at a level below that of his teammates. As a result, it may have a detrimental effect on the athlete's sporting self-concept because he is no longer a big fish in a small pond (top of the state) but is in a large pond, full of even larger fish. The BFLPE is likely to be larger in highly competitive settings that use assessments that encourage athletes to compare their performance with other athletes. Research by Marsh and Peart (1988) suggested that BFLPE might be reduced if the emphasis and feedback is focused on cooperation as opposed to competition. Individual improvement becomes the measure of success when there is more emphasis on intra-competition (within each athlete) and less on inter-competition (between athletes).

BFLPE Contrast and Assimilation (Reflected Glory) Effects

The discussion regarding frame-of-reference effects cannot end here, because it appears that people can mediate the BFLPE through an assimilation effect; namely, *reflected glory*. For example, if students compare their own accomplishments with those of classmates in academically selective schools, then their academic self-concept should decline; a negative BFLPE or contrast effect (e.g., there are a lot of students better than I am, so I must not be as good as I thought). Alternatively, affect, identification, self-perceptions, and self-concept can be enhanced by membership in groups that are positively valued through the reflected glory of accomplishments or good qualities of other group members and should result in a positive BFLPE. There is ample evidence that people enjoy basking in the reflected glory of successful others by merely associating with distinguished people or joining highly valued social groups (Cialdini & Richardson, 1980; Snyder, Lassegard, & Ford, 1986; Tesser, 1988). Based partly on this theoretical perspective, Marsh (1984a, 1993 [also see Felson, 1984; Felson & Reed, 1986; Firebaugh, 1980]) argued that students in academically selective schools might have more positive academic self-concepts by virtue of being chosen to be in a highly selective educational program—an assimilation, reflected glory, identification, or labeling effect (e.g., if I am good enough to be in this selective school with all these other very smart students, then I must be very smart). A reflected glory effect would be particularly likely if the selection were highly valued and if the selection process were highly visible, with important implications.

There is considerable social comparison research (Buunk & Ybema, 1997) showing that people cope with stress either by choosing downward comparison targets that make them feel relatively better and protect their self-esteem (Lazarus & Folkman, 1984; Wills, 1981) or by choosing upward comparison targets for purposes of identification, fulfillment of aspirations, affiliation, and obtaining useful information or coping strategies (Buunk & Ybema, 1997; Taylor & Lobel, 1989). Thus, people prefer upward comparisons that facilitate identification with the comparison targets, but not when forced to contrast their own poorer attributes with the better attributes of those targets. Downward comparisons are preferable when they facilitate the contrast of one's own attributes with those of others who have poorer attributes, but not when one identifies with or perceives oneself (or is perceived by others) to be similar to the downward comparison targets.

Diener and Fujita (1997) referred to social comparison in school settings as a *situationally imposed* or *forced* comparison, as opposed to a more flexible situation in which people have considerable freedom to select or to construct a comparison target consciously so as to maximize various goals. They suggested that there is limited support for social comparison theory in this forced comparison setting but emphasized that school closely approximates a "total environment" (where the frame of reference affecting judgment is limited to the immediate context) implicit in the forced comparison. The school is a total environment in that there are so many inherent constraints and a natural emphasis on social comparison of achievement levels. Similarly, educational psychologists (Covington, 1992; Marsh, 1990a; 1993; Marshall & Weinstein, 1984; also see Goethals & Darley, 1987) emphasize the extreme salience of achievement as a reference point within a school setting, particularly when the outcome measure is academic self-concept.

Both the counterbalancing negative social comparison effects and the positive reflected glory effects are likely to influence self-concept so that the typically observed BFLPE is actually a net effect (Marsh, 1984a, 1993). An assimilation effect may operate even though the social comparison contrast effects overshadow it. McFarland and Buehler (1995) found that students from collectivist countries experienced significantly smaller BFLPEs than students from individualistic countries. They also noted an asymmetry such that individuals who value group membership can focus on their individual performances when they do well or on the performance of their group when they do poorly, thus allowing them to protect their self-concepts. Based on their findings, they proposed a revision to the BFLPE metaphor: "Although everyone feels good about being a big fish in a little pond, not everyone feels bad about being a little fish in a big pond" (p. 1068).

MEASURING SELF-CONCEPT

The self-concept facets proposed in the Shavelson et al. (1976) model, as well as their hypothesized structure, were heuristic and plausible, but they were not empirically validated by existing research. At the time, Shavelson et al. were unable to identify any instrument for measuring multiple facets of self-concept as posited in their model. In developing the SDQ, Marsh judged the Shavelson et al. model to offer the best available theoretical explanation of self-concept. Theory, model building, and instrument construction are inexorably intertwined, and the SDQ instruments are based on a strong empirical foundation and a solid theoretical model. There are eight SDQI (primary school students) factors (physical ability, physical appearance, peers, parents, reading, math, general school, and general self), whereas the SDQIII (late adolescents and young adults) divides the peers scale into same sex and opposite sex scales, and additional scales were constructed to represent emotional stability, problem solving, religion/spirituality, and honesty/dependability. Confirmatory factor analysis (using the Shavelson et al. model for the a priori factors) of the SDQs supported the assumption that self-concept is hierarchically ordered, but the particular form of this higher-order structure was more complicated than originally proposed. These findings led to the Marsh/Shavelson (1985) revision of the Shavelson et al. model in that there are two higher-order academic factors, math/academic and verbal/academic, instead of just one (see figure 5.1).

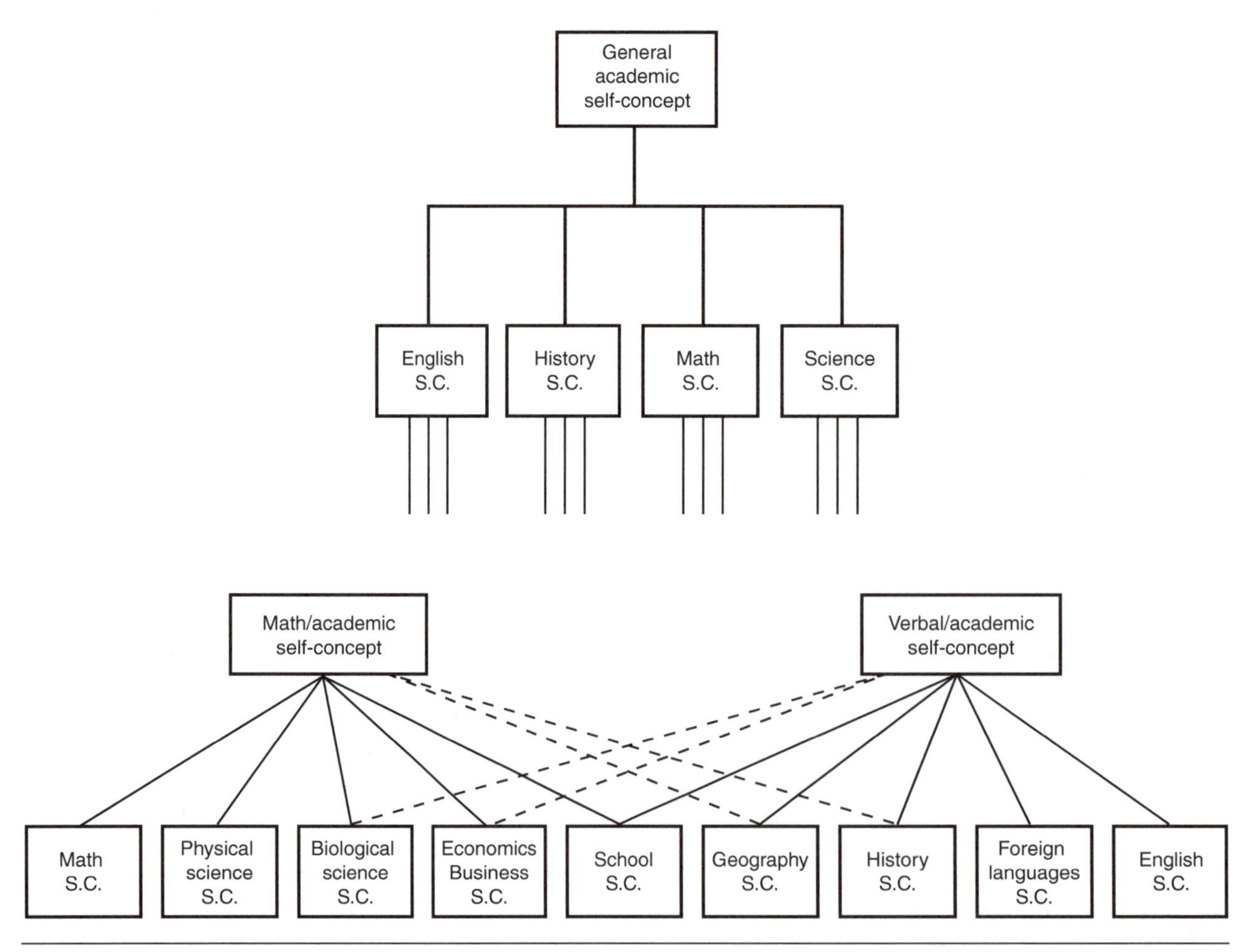

Figure 5.1 (Top) the academic portion of Shavelson, Hubner, and Stanton's (1976) original model and (bottom) an elaboration of Marsh and Shavelson's (1985) revision that includes a wider variety of specific academic facets (S. C. = self-concept). (From Marsh, Byrne, & Shavelson, 1988, pp. 366-380. Adapted with permission.)

Elite Athlete Self-Description Questionnaire

From an historical perspective, most self-concept instruments have either ignored physical self-concept or have treated it as a relatively unidimensional domain incorporating characteristics as diverse as fitness, health, appearance, grooming, sporting competence, body image, sexuality, and physical activity into a single score (Marsh et al., 1995). Disentangling this amalgamation of factors led to the development of the Physical Self-Description Questionnaire (PSDQ; see Marsh et al., 1994). The theoretical basis and design of the PSDQ follows SDQ research in that physical self is hierarchical and multifaceted. Current research and test development is extending the model to elite athletes with the introduction of the Elite Athlete Self-Description Questionnaire (EASDQ; Marsh, Hey, Roche, & Perry, 1997; Marsh, Hey, Johnson, & Perry, 1997). Results support the appropriateness of the EASDQ for diverse groups of elite athletes. More research is needed, however, relating EASDQ responses to external validity criteria like those used in PSDQ research and to criteria that are more specific to elite athletes (e.g., actual performance in competition).

Implicit Self-Valuation: The Self-Apperception Test

Although most of the recent research into self-concept has been based on sound methodology and measurement emphasizing the multidimensionality and hierarchical nature of the construct, little has been done in the theoretical distinction between its explicit (declarative) and implicit levels. Generally, self-concept measures use self-reports, which are vulnerable to self-presentation distortions and as result become explicit measures of self. One such potential source of distortion is social desirability, with responses being affected by socially accepted norms and a desire to project a certain image to the recipient of the test information. Addressing response bias, Greenwald and Banaji (1995) asserted that there is a clear need for sensitive indirect measures to assess individual differences in introspectively inaccessible implicit self-attitudes. Aidman (1999a, 1999b) has developed the Self-Apperception Test (SAT-2), an indirect measure, to examine self-concept based on Liggett's (1959) semi-projective test of self-esteem. The SAT-2 uses 10 computer-generated faces in a semantic differential format to represent a range of emotional expressions. People are asked to sort these faces from most liked to most disliked. The procedure is then repeated with the same faces, but people are instructed to rank the faces in order according to bipolar constructs such as happy/sad, capable/incapable, worthy/worthless, and strong/weak. The constructs used could be any characteristic or emotion that is under investigation by the test administrator. Finally, the faces are ranked in relation to one's self-concept, from most like myself to least like myself. Estimates of global self-worth, specific self-appraisals, and their respective importance (valency) estimates are determined by the correlations derived from this rank ordering of faces. Initial validation research indicated that the test has (a) reasonably ambiguous stimulus material, therefore minimizing social desirability distortions, (b) acceptable levels of internal consistency and re-test stability, and (c) promising validity characteristics (Aidman, 1999a). An example of the stimuli in the SAT-2 is presented in figure 5.2.

The SAT-2 has been shown to be of benefit in applied sport settings. Advantages of the SAT-2 are the short, 10-minute administration time and the apparent interest athletes have in completing this unique instrument. Perry (1999) used the instrument as part of the Australian swimming team's preparation for the 1998 World Swimming Championships. Swimmers completed the measure when they were selected for the team, six months prior to the championships. Individual feedback was provided to the swimmers to ascertain the accuracy of the information and to establish strengths and weaknesses in their self-concepts. This information provided an opportunity for the swimmers, coach, and psychologist to target intervention strategies in the lead-up to the competition. The SAT-2 was readministered two weeks prior to the

Figure 5.2 Schematic facial sketches from the Self-Apperception Test's stimulus set (Aidman, 1999a, 1999b). The majority of test takers tend to like *face A* and dislike *face C*. The preferences are usually divided on *face E* and seven other faces in the stimulus set Courtesy InterMind Consulting.

championships to evaluate the effectiveness of those intervention strategies. The psychologist used the tool as a means of reinforcing positive shifts in self-concept and identifying negative appraisals that could be corrected or managed in a relatively short period of time.

Psychometric instruments, if used judiciously, can enhance the sport psychologist's effectiveness in an applied setting. In the case example that will be presented, both the SAT-2 and the SDQ provided valuable information for the practitioner and the athlete.

A SWIMMER'S SELF-CONCEPT

The Australian Institute of Sport (AIS) is a residential training center for elite athletes ages 10 to 28 years. It houses 200 athletes across nine different sports. The athletes range in ability from developmental to Olympic level. An integral part of the AIS is the Sports Science and Sports Medicine Centre, which comprises the departments of Psychology, Medicine, Physiology/Biochemistry, Physiotherapy/Massage, Biomechanics, and Nutrition. The Centre uses a multidisciplinary approach to servicing coaches and athletes, where practitioners are assigned sports and work collaboratively with professionals in other disciplines to provide service.

The athlete in the following case is a composite illustrating characteristics and issues that are consistent with those of a number of athletes seen in the AIS psychology department over the past 18 years. Much of the dialogue in this case study is from actual conversations with a number of elite athletes from a variety of sports. This case is presented in a manner that demonstrates treatments or approaches that have worked along with interventions that have been less successful. Colleen (CM), a 19-year-old swimmer who has represented her country at major international competitions (world championships, Olympic Games), has come to see the sport psychologist, with whom she has a two-year history of on-again/off-again performance enhancement work. Generally, Colleen has been a successful swimmer, but of late she has been disappointed with her results. Medical and physiological tests have not revealed any evidence of overtraining to explain her performance decrement. Her coach claims that she is a perfectionist (in his mind a desirable trait) but at times she is unrealistic about her performances. Colleen has become more and more critical of herself and others and is quite self-deprecating in her words and actions. Her self-talk is substantially negative and appears almost apologetic to others in regard to her performances ("I can't believe I'm swimming this badly," "What's wrong with me?" "You were swimming better as an age-grouper!"). She has come to see the sport psychologist to learn some positive self-talk strategies, as her coach has stated that he is "sick of her negativity."

Sport Psychologist (SP): It's good to see you again, Colleen. How have you been?

Colleen (CM): Not too bad. I just wish that I was swimming better.

SP: What's been happening with your swimming?

CM: I've been working so hard, doing everything that the coach has asked, everything that you and I have worked on, but I'm not getting any faster!

Notice the comment, ". . . everything that you and I . . . " It shows that Colleen is feeling a certain amount of frustration, and the psychologist is part of it. She is disappointed and possibly angry with both her coach and her sport psychologist.

SP: It appears you're getting really frustrated by your progress. Where do you expect your performances to be?

CM: I'm not really sure, but they certainly should be better then they are!

SP: Can you identify what might be preventing you from improving?

CM: Well, the coach thinks that my negative attitude might have something to do with it.

SP: How so?

CM: Well, it is true that I can be really critical. I'm my own worst critic. If things don't go well I can beat myself up with the best of 'em.

SP: When you say "beat yourself up," I assume that you mean that you can be very hard on yourself. Can you give me an example?

CM: This afternoon was a good example. We were doing some sets that required maximum effort. I was swimming as fast as I could, but the times were so slow! The coach could tell that I was angry, but he kept saying that considering where we were in training those times were expected. Maybe he underestimates me.

SP: You were saying that the coach could tell that you were angry. How did you show that?

CM: It's pretty obvious when I'm swearing when he calls out the time. I'm the kind of person that can't hold it in. When I'm pissed off I think he should know it.

Interesting comment by Colleen. From past experience, the psychologist knows that she has perfectionistic tendencies. "When I'm pissed off I think he should know it" may be her projection of perfectionism onto the coach ("He should know everything about me without me telling him"). This comment may also reflect some sense of entitlement and may be something to visit later.

SP: I can see how it may be difficult to hold in your emotions when you are frustrated by your performances. Can you remember the types of things that you feel and say?

CM: I guess it starts when I see that the other swimmers, who shouldn't be beating me, are starting to pass me. My mind just kicks into overdrive then. I start thinking, What's wrong with me? I mean, I work so hard. I give up so much to do this. Honestly, I deserve more!

Here, Colleen's quandary is becoming clearer. She believes that when people work hard they deserve results; they are entitled to rewards. The psychologist will challenge this belief by exploring the relationship between hard work and performance.

SP: Well, Colleen, I've watched you train and compete for a couple of years now, and you are one of the hardest workers I've seen.

CM: Then tell me why I don't win more often.

SP: Have you thought that maybe you need to work smarter instead of harder?

CM: I'm not sure what that means.

SP: People can work very hard at doing the wrong things, and in the end not perform up to their expectations.

CM: Are you telling me that is what I do?

SP: Not necessarily. I'm merely asking whether you think that is a possibility in your case?

CM: Perhaps, but I only know one way. I was taught that good things come to those who work hard.

The concept of working smart, not just hard, is fundamental in the sport training process. Practicing bad techniques will bring about bad results. This is not limited to the physical or technical domain, but also applies to the mental side. Colleen's attitude is self-defeating. Her experience of anger is preventing her from realistically evaluating her training, and as a result, is negatively influencing performance. It will be important to explore the work ethic issue at a later date, as well as consult with the coach to ascertain whether the training program is fostering this attitude.

At this stage the psychologist has chosen to pursue the "giving up so much" element that Colleen mentioned earlier. Typically, athletes, who are so focused on the sporting aspect of their lives, do so in order to improve the quantity of time they can dedicate to that sport. But in the process, their quality of life is often diminished. Global self-concept evaluations become limited to performances in sport due, in part, to the huge amount of time invested in that domain (see chapter 18 for a discussion on identity and sport). Many perfectionists see their results as being quite dichotomous—success or failure—and without any balance to temper a global self-concept tied to being an athlete and to athletic performance, there are often quite dramatic swings in how athletes see and feel about themselves. The psychologist has a hunch that Colleen's perfectionism and exclusive athletic identity may be contributing to her frustration.

SP: Can we leave that discussion for a little later? I just would like you to accept that maybe there is another way to achieve results. Colleen, before you were saying that you've given up so much. What do you think that you've missed?

CM: I just look at my friends who aren't athletes. They're all either at university or have started a career. They seem to have boyfriends or girlfriends. If they feel like taking the afternoon off and just goofing around, they just do it. Their whole life just seems more relaxed. Not that I would want to be like that! I'm more dedicated, I know what I want, and I have to sacrifice to get it. In the end, when I have that medal hanging around my neck, it will all be worth it.

Colleen appears to be trying to convince herself that it will all be worth it. Again she demonstrates her focus on the outcome. There is real fragility in her perception of success. Notice her almost disdain for others who are "less dedicated." Her narcissistic view of how she is special ("I'm more dedicated") and how she is entitled ("I deserve more") continues to surface in her comments.

SP: Have you thought about what you would like to do after swimming?

CM: Not really. I figure that I'll get lots of offers after the Olympics. My manager says that with medals comes money. So if I rack up enough medals I shouldn't have to worry about my future.

At this stage there are a few issues that have arisen: (a) Colleen's anger (mostly directed internally) at her perceived lack of attainment; (b) her motivation, based largely on outcomes (i.e., medals); (c) her belief system that people should get rewards if they commit themselves; (d) her narcissistic world view; and (e) her one-dimensional approach to life—successful sport is the key to future happiness. The psychologist has decided to help Colleen examine her self-concept and its relationship to her apparent negative self-talk.

SP: Colleen, if I were to ask you, "Who is Colleen McGraw?" what would you say?

CM: Do you mean, like, what am I good at?

SP: Yes; that's part of it. Maybe if I put it a different way . . . how would someone who knew you very well describe you?

CM: Firstly, I was a very good swimmer, most of the time anyway. Eh . . . let's see . . . when I was really young I was pretty good at school, but as I became better at swimming and spent more time in training it became more difficult to get the best grades in the class.

SP: Would others consider you to be good academically?

CM: Maybe once upon a time. But all my friends have gone on to university, while I've concentrated on swimming. I wouldn't say that I'm academic.

SP: How else would this person describe you?

CM: I'd like to think that I am a good friend . . . besides that I'm not really sure.

SP: How about physically, how would they describe you?

CM: I'm strong . . . tall . . . fit.

The question the psychologist asked was "How would a person describe you?" Colleen's answer in the first person, "I was . . . ," is perhaps an example of her potential narcissism manifesting as a difficulty to understand someone else's point of view. Colleen probably does not meet all of the diagnostic criteria for narcissistic personality disorder, but she does have some of the features (e.g., grandiose thinking, need for admiration, feelings of entitlement, fantasies of fame, lack of empathy; American Psychiatric Association, *Diagnostic and Statistical Manual of Mental Disorders,* fourth edition, 1994).

SP: Are you attractive?

CM: Average, I guess. I wouldn't say that I'm anything special.

SP: Are you happy with who you are physically?

CM: Yeah; I like my body as a swimmer. I think that is one of my assets.

Colleen comments on her body as a swimmer. Is this the only way that she sees herself? The psychologist wants to know more about her self-concept in other areas.

SP: You say that you are happy with your body as a swimmer. As a woman, do you like your body?

This question is a bit of a reach. The psychologist has to be careful that he is not projecting his view of female athlete role conflict onto Colleen. Athletes must develop their bodies in order to exert force in their competitive environments. For most sports, that requires a physique that is strong, powerful, and lean. These concepts of force, power, and strength are atypical of the societal stereotype for women. In many cultures, women are regarded as submissive, nurturing, and demure. Women may perceive that these are desirable traits in attracting partners and establishing relationships. If the female athlete accepts this image of women, there is the potential for role conflict to develop. There are a number of possible explanations for Colleen's behavior: (a) she is in denial in regard to the swimmer/woman mismatch, (b) there is no issue for her because she truly recognizes and accepts or rejects the mismatch, or (c) her desire for recognition (medals) and her regret over "giving up so much" are central to the frustration and anger that she is experiencing in relation to her sport. The psychologist chooses to explore the dissonance angle and see how Colleen reacts.

CM: No, I wouldn't say that I do. I'm much bigger than most of my friends. When my hair was short, some people actually mistook me for a boy. That's one of the reasons why I grew my hair long. I certainly don't look like the girls in Baywatch.

SP: Do you sometimes wish that you did look like that?

CM: Sometimes, I guess. Mostly when I see my friends with boyfriends, I wonder if they would like me better if I looked more like them. But there is no way I could win medals in swimming if I looked like them.

This is the second time that Colleen has mentioned friends with boyfriends, perhaps enviously, but she immediately rationalizes her appearance with the desire for swimming medals. There appears to be substantial internal conflict regarding what she has given up and her desire for future success.

SP: Can you see how that might be confusing for you?

CM: Well, to be honest, I try not to think about it too much. If I worried about things like that, it would be too distracting, so it just makes me more determined to be better at swimming.

By now the psychologist should be getting a clearer clinical picture of Colleen's case. It is quite obvious that there is cognitive dissonance surrounding her image of herself as a swimmer and as a woman. Her perception of physical self is quite healthy, if not egocentric, as it relates to her swimming, but this is not congruent with her ideal for a female body that is attractive to potential mates. Recent research at the Australian Institute of Sport (Leahy, Harrigan, & Freeman, 1999) has revealed that elite female athletes who need to have a certain body type to excel at their sports experience significant body image anxiety because societal pressures require a very different body type to be consistent with gender expectations. It is possible that this anxiety is contributing to Colleen's emotional volatility and lackluster performance. Allison (1991), however, cautions the sport psychologist not to "suggest that the female athlete decline in performance is due to her inability to deal simultaneously with being a girl/woman and an athlete" (p. 58). She suggests that performance decreases are more likely to be related to a multitude of factors, and that to blame role conflict is problematic and much too simplistic. The psychologist needs to be mindful of the multidimensionality of the person and to treat the whole athlete within the system in which he or she operates.

It is also obvious that Colleen's physical self dominates her global self-concept. And to take that one step further, her physical self is dominated by her perceptions of herself as a swimmer (notice that she did not see herself as an athlete, but as a swimmer). Academically, Colleen's self-concept suffered as friends went on to university and she focused her energy on sport. Self-concept evolution is consistent with Marsh's frame-of-reference-effect models, discussed earlier. At this stage, it would be a good idea for the sport psychologist to administer a self-concept measure. This would establish a baseline for intervention as well as a point of reference he can use to develop strategies for improvement with Colleen. To measure and understand the contribution her physical self-concept is making to her global self-concept, as a multifaceted, hierarchical construct, the psychologist chose the SDQIII as well as the SAT-2.

SP: Colleen, I believe that a considerable amount of your frustration and subsequent disappointment in your performances may be related to how you see yourself as a swimmer and a person. I would like to use a couple of tools that will help us to gain a better understanding of these issues and perhaps assist us in monitoring your progress. The first, called the Self-Description Questionnaire, or SDQ, is a typical paper-and-pencil assessment instrument in which you'll respond to a series of statements. The second measure, the Self-Apperception Test, or SAT, is a bit different, in that there are no questions, papers, or pencils. It is administered on the computer and involves you sorting a series of faces according to how you perceive them. In both cases, it is important for you to know that there are no right or wrong answers, and I will not be comparing your answers to any one else's. All the information that we derive from these tools will be yours, and it will help me to help you achieve your goals. So what I'm basically saying is, be as candid and honest as possible. Are you happy to do these?

CM: Yeah, if you think that it can help. How long will they take?

SP: The SDQ will take you 15 to 20 minutes and the SAT around 5 or 10 minutes. In both cases you may take as much time as you need.

CM: I have some spare time now, if that's OK.

SP: Great; I'll get them organized for you.

Testing, in a practical sense, should be conducted to aid the therapeutic process. It has a place in educating both the client and therapist about the client's emotions, cognitions, and behaviors. It is not a panacea but an adjunct to therapy. Too often, testing is used much as a fisherman would cast out a net to haul in whatever catch was available. Just as instrument development needs to be theory driven, so too does therapeutic testing. The client needs to understand the rationale for testing. As a result, the information gathered from a willing participant becomes rich and valuable. Psychological testing depends on honest, candid responses to probing questions. Therefore, the client must see the merit in contributing to this process through legitimate introspection and projection.

The results of the testing revealed that Colleen's global self-concept is dominated by her appraisal of herself as physical. She scored relatively low on the domains of opposite sex, parents, reading, math, general school, emotional stability, and religion/spirituality. Colleen has a strong sense of self in problem solving, honesty/dependability, and same-sex relations. Her self-report on physical appearance and general self were moderate. Evaluation of her results on the SAT-2 were consistent with the SDQIII, lending support for the validity of the test results.

As the sport psychologist suspected through interviewing her, the psychometric assessment highlighted Colleen's view of herself primarily as a physical being. As such, she values herself on her ability to interact with her environment in a physical manner. That level of self-appraisal is subject to extreme variance, because she uses social comparisons in swimming to determine her level of worth.

SP: Hi Colleen; it's good to see you again.

CM: Hi Doc, it's good to see you as well. I'm anxious to see if those tests tell you that I'm nuts [nervous laugh].

It appears that the psychologist may not have prepared Colleen well enough for psychological testing. If she is showing some nervousness regarding the test results, it is possible that this anxiety may have created some response bias during the testing process. Often athletes feel that the test information is magically going to reveal some deep, dark, hidden secret that even they did not know. Seldom is this the case, because most testing is based on self-appraisal and subsequent self-report. The feedback from valid testing usually consolidates opinions that the athlete possesses but is presented in a manner she can more easily understood.

SP: [smile] I didn't think that we were trying to decide if you were "nuts." I'm not even sure what that really means, anyway. The testing that we did was to help us better understand the negative self-talk that you are having and to help you feel better about your swimming.

CM: I realized that. I was just having a bit of fun.

SP: I have the results right here. I'm excited by the information that we collected. It should really help us get to where we want to go [trying to stay upbeat, normalizing the results, and allaying her fears]. Should we have a look at them together?

CM: Sounds great.

SP: First of all, the SDQ tells us that you primarily think of yourself as a physical person. Does that sound reasonable?

CM: Yeah; like we discussed before, my physique and strength are my best attributes.

SP: And the testing information confirms that opinion. So, in essence, your global self-concept or overall worth is greatly influenced by your physical self-concept. When you are swimming well and performing well physically, everything is right with the world, so to speak, but when you don't perform as well as expected it has grave consequences on your overall sense of self-worth. Can you see how black and white that can be?

CM: But that's what I am, a swimmer. Why shouldn't it have, as you say, "grave consequences" on my overall self-worth? If I don't swim well, I don't feel very good about myself.

SP: Colleen, there is nothing wrong with being disappointed. As I've said before, you are one of the hardest workers I've seen in the pool, but the difficulty comes when you then place high expectations on yourself. You try so hard to succeed because being successful, especially physically successful, means so much to you that failure is not an option. Does that sound accurate?

CM: I've always viewed failure as something for losers. I'm not a loser! And, I don't want to be associated with people who are losers. That's the reason why I came to the Institute, to be around people like coach, yourself, and the other staff.

Here is another example of Colleen's narcissistic tendencies. She believes that she is unique and special, and she came to the Institute to be associated with similar types of professionals. Colleen's opinion of the Institute and its staff may also be a buffer for her self-concept, because it appears she may gain some reflected glory by being a scholarship holder at the Institute.

SP: Can you tell me how you define losing?

CM: People who don't achieve. People who are happy being second best. That's not for me!

Colleen's buttons have sure been pushed. She is becoming angry and defensive, so the psychologist knows he is hitting close to home. Colleen really measures her worth in a socially comparative manner. As regards frame-of-reference effects, and in particular the BFLPE, being at the Institute may have exacerbated Colleen's perfectionistic tendencies. Her frame of reference is external, and she is surrounded by perceived excellence. The key is to attempt to have Colleen see how limiting that view is and to expand her measure of success to controllable process goals.

SP: Colleen, this may sound like a silly question, but what do you mean by "second best"?

CM: Anyone who doesn't finish first, I guess. I thought that was why people swim at this level, to be the best.

SP: I believe that "being the best" is a strong source of motivation for many people, but it is not the only source of motivation. People are motivated by many different things, and we have to be careful not to project our opinions onto others. Can you remember back to when you first started swimming?

CM: Sure. It seems like so long ago. My parents got me into swimming when I could barely walk, and I've been a fish ever since.

SP: Were they fun times?

CM: Yeah! I would really look forward to going to the pool with all of my friends. I remember being so cold that my lips were blue, but I still wouldn't get out of the water, because I was having so much fun.

SP: Is it possible that the fun was something that kept you coming back again and again?

CM: Absolutely!

SP: Well, it's possible to still have fun as a motivator, even at the elite level. Many gold medal winners in various sports have said that they will continue to compete as long as they are having fun. The definition of fun, though, may be different for different people.

CM: Well, I think that's one big problem for me. I can't say that I am having a lot of fun lately.

Colleen has identified a problem, and therefore has taken the first step to change. Now is a good time to offer her a possible solution or to help her discover a solution for herself. At this stage, the psychologist will continue with the present flow and see what develops.

SP: I can see how it is difficult to have fun when you are getting messages from outside and inside, with your negative self-talk, that you are, in your words, "failing."

CM: [a bit teary eyed] But what do I do about it?

This is a critical moment. The psychologist has pushed a button that has evoked a strong reaction from Colleen. For her to admit that she is at a loss and show sadness demonstrates an apparent sign of weakness. Such an admission would not have been an easy thing for her to do. Colleen's perfectionism dominates her self-projection, and to lower her guard and expose vulnerability is a dramatic step. Given the nature of the therapeutic relationship and the psychologist's desire to help Colleen, it would be natural for him to want to come in at this point and rescue her. Such an action would be a mistake (see chapter 12 for a discussion on wanting to help and to "fix" things). The psychologist should help her understand this moment and not try to "fix" her emotions.

SP: That's a very good question. I can see in your eyes that where you are now is a big worry for you, but that's a good sign, too. It's like you see the problem, but just don't know how to get started. Now, perhaps we can find a way to get that spark back. Let's think of some ideas that we can try to make swimming more fun.

The psychologist has recognized that Colleen is emotional. He has identified this emotion as productive and not something shameful—a good step. He has also said that both parties will take part in this process of discovery.

CM: I really want to stop being so negative. I don't want to look at everything from the dark side. Do you know that I see just about everyone and everything as a challenge? I have such a difficult time relaxing.

SP: When you are so driven by outcomes, it is easy to understand why you view the world this way. What can we do to stop that negativity?

CM: That's a good question! This voice in my head needs to take a break. Do you have any suggestions on reducing the negative chatter?

SP: There are a few things that you can try. First, we need to work on helping you identify ways of achieving success, beyond conventional terms. Second, we need to build some strategies to identify and then change those negative thoughts. And last, we need to make sure that those negative thoughts don't become negative actions, bringing about negative consequences.

CM: It sounds like there might be hope for me yet.

It appears that the psychologist and Colleen have reached a level of agreement. Colleen recognizes that there are some issues that she needs to address if she is to become happy and productive in swimming. There is at least some degree of optimism in her last comment, and she is willing to have the psychologist assist her in this process.

In summary, Colleen appears to have a narcissistic view of her world; she becomes angry and frustrated when she does not achieve what she believes are her entitlements. Colleen sees a direct relationship between hard work and results but does not allow for normal, everyday variance to influence those results. She has a strong sense of control and need for achievement, measured by a social comparison. On the surface, there appears to be some body image dissonance. Her current body type is required for her to excel in her chosen sport, but may, in her mind, hinder her from attracting partners for a relationship. Colleen is also very outcome-focused and has little understanding of the need to balance that with process goals, thereby limiting her opportunities for success and subsequent enjoyment. Further limitations in Colleen's global self-concept make failure that much more unpalatable. The consequences of failure, even minor losses, become monumental and comprehensive.

From here it will be important to include the coach as part of the training process. With permission from Colleen, it would be advantageous to schedule a meeting with the psychologist, Colleen, and the coach. Discussion topics would be approved by Colleen prior to the meeting, but it would be important for the coach to understand the need to focus on process goals during training, helping Colleen set daily goals that would give her a sense of accomplishment. The coach probably already knows that something like the BFLPE may be at work within his squad and that it may have a negative effect on his other athletes. The psychologist can help the coach develop a training atmosphere that emphasizes individual accomplishments in order to minimize this frame-of-reference effect.

The coach can also play a significant role in helping Colleen recognize when she is exhibiting overt negative self-talk. With the coach's help, she can begin to manage the voice in her head, as opposed to being its victim, by using thought-stoppage and reframing techniques in practice. In addition, the coach, psychologist, physiologist, and biomechanist can help Colleen understand how to train smart, not just hard.

It is important for Colleen to expand the facets that contribute to her global self-concept in order to create more stability in her feelings of worth. She may want to look at enrolling in a course, taking up a hobby, learning to play a musical instrument, or getting a part-time job. Contrary to popular belief, if managed well, such activities do not detract from elite sport but contribute to performance by creating a much-needed life balance. The coach would also need to be part of this process, because time commitments often need to be coordinated.

Away from the pool, the psychologist and Colleen might explore her need for perfection and her feelings of entitlement. Why is she driven by this need to be the best? Is it for social acceptance? Perhaps self-acceptance? Why is it so difficult for her to show vulnerability? Is all of this part and parcel of a developing narcissistic personality disorder? Sperry (1995) described the narcissistic personality as quite common in Western cultures, particularly in the professions of law, medicine, entertainment, sports, and politics. He further proposed that narcissism may span a continuum from healthy (narcissistic personality style) to pathological (narcissistic personality disorder). Colleen probably lies somewhere between these extremes.

The preceding questions are the sorts of ideas the psychologist could consider during the therapeutic process. The other area that could be addressed is the body image dissonance and social displeasure. It is possible (and perhaps likely) that the psychologist is off base. Body image problems may be his issue, and he may be projecting this dissonance onto Colleen. As Allison (1991) warned, it is problematic, and too simplistic, to blame role conflict for performance decreases. Psychologists must always examine their own biases and any negative influences that these biases may have on service delivery. Negative countertransferential processes occur when the therapist's beliefs, prejudices, or biases are projected onto the client, therefore interfering with effective therapy. In this case, the psychologist's ability to identify Colleen's issues accurately may be clouded by previous experiences and prejudicial thinking about real or imagined females. That is not to say that countertransference is to be avoided; to the contrary, Bauer (1993) suggests that

> the presence of countertransference does not imply that the therapist is an immoral person or an inadequate clinician. As dynamic theory has evolved, therapists have realized that attempting to eliminate countertransference was not only impossible

but also unproductive for there is much to be learned about a patient by means of analyzing one's personal reaction to him. What is crucial is for countertransference to be explored and understood in order to increase the therapist's ability to intervene in a helpful manner. (p.79)

In Colleen's case, the psychologist should examine the role countertransference might be playing in his assessment of her body image dissonance. This dissonance might contribute to her general self-concept, or it might be a projection on the part of the psychologist. In either event, valuable information can be gathered by examining this relationship, and as Jung (1933) said, "You can exert no influence if you are not susceptible to influence" (p. 49).

Overt self-talk is often the window that allows us to see the effect self-concept has on our cognitions and behaviors. To fix self-talk merely through thought-stopping techniques, without addressing the underlying self-concept, would be like patching the crack in the roof when it is the foundation of the house that needs attention.

REFERENCES

Aidman, E.V. (1999a). *The Self-Apperception Test: A technical manual* (2nd ed.). Melbourne, Australia: InterMind Consulting.

Aidman, E.V. (1999b). Measuring individual differences in implicit self-concept: Initial validation of the Self-Apperception Test. *Personality and Individual Difference, 27,* 211-228.

Allison, M.T. (1991). Role conflict and the female athlete: Preoccupations with little grounding. *Journal of Applied Sport Psychology, 3,* 49-60.

Alwin, D.F., & Otto, L.B. (1977). High school context effects on aspirations. *Sociology of Education, 50,* 259-273.

American Psychiatric Association. (1994). *Diagnostic and statistical manual of mental disorders* (4th ed.). Washington, DC: Author.

Bauer, G.P. (1993). *The analysis of the transference in the here and now.* Northvale, NJ: Aronson.

Boyle, G.J. (1994). Self-description questionnaire II: A review. *Test Critiques, 10,* 632-643.

Bracken, B.A. (1992). *Multidimensional Self-Concept Scale.* Austin, TX: Pro-Ed.

Bracken, B.A. (1996). Clinical applications of a context-dependent, multidimensional model of self-concept. In B.A. Bracken (Ed.), *Handbook of self-concept* (pp. 463-503). New York: Wiley.

Buunk, B.P., and Ybema, J.F. (1997). Social comparisons and occupational stress: The identification-contrast model. In B.P. Buunk & F.X. Gibbons (Eds.), *Health, coping, and well-being: Perspectives from social comparison theory* (pp. 359-388). Mahwah, NJ: Erlbaum.

Byrne, B.M. (1984). The general/academic self-concept nomological network: A review of construct validation research. *Review of Educational Research, 54,* 427-456.

Byrne, B.M. (1986). Self-concept/academic achievement relations: An investigation of dimensionality, stability, and causality. *Canadian Journal of Behavioural Science, 18,* 173-186.

Cialdini, R.B., & Richardson, K.D. (1980). Two indirect tactics of image management: Basking and blasting. *Journal of Personality and Social Psychology, 39,* 406-415.

Cooley, C.H. (1902). *Human nature and the social order.* New York: Scribner.

Covington, M.V. (1992). *Making the grade: A self-worth perspective on motivation and school reform.* Cambridge University Press.

Damon, W., & Hart, D. (1988). *Self-understanding in childhood and adolescence.* New York: Cambridge University Press.

Davis, J.A. (1966). The campus as a frog pond: An application of theory of relative deprivation to career decisions for college men. *American Journal of Sociology, 72,* 17-31.

Diener, E., & Fujita, F. (1997). Social comparison and subjective well-being. In B.P. Buunk & F.X. Gibbons (Eds.), *Health, coping, and well-being: Perspectives from social comparison theory* (pp. 329-358). Mahwah, NJ: Erlbaum.

Felson, R.B. (1984). The effect of self-appraisals on ability of academic performance. *Journal of Personality and Social Psychology, 47,* 944-952.

Felson, R.B., & Reed, M.D. (1986). Reference groups and self-appraisals of academic ability and performance. *Social Psychology Quarterly, 49,* 103-109.

Festinger, L. (1954). A theory of social comparison processes. *Human Relations, 7,* 117-140.

Firebaugh, G. (1980). Groups as contexts and frog ponds. *New Directions for Methodology of Social and Behavioral Science, 6,* 43-52.

Goethals, G.R., & Darley, J.M. (1987). Social comparison theory: Self-evaluation and group life. In B. Mullen & G.R. Goethals (Eds.), *Theories of group behavior* (pp. 21-47). New York: Springer-Verlag.

Greenwald, A.G., & Banaji, R. (1995). Implicit social cognition: Attitudes, self- esteem, and stereotypes. *Psychological Review, 102,* 4-27.

Harter, S. (1985). *The Self-Perception Profile for Children.* Denver, CO: University of Denver.

Harter, S. (1990). Causes, correlates, and the functional role of global self-worth: A life-span perspective. In J. Kolligian & R. Sternberg (Eds.), *Perceptions of competence and incompetence across the life-span* (pp. 67-98). New Haven, CT: Yale University Press.

Hattie, J. (1992). *Self-concept.* Hillsdale, NJ: Erlbaum.
Helson, H. (1964). *Adaptation-level theory.* New York: Harper & Row.
Hyman, H. (1942). The psychology of subjective status. *Psychological Bulletin, 39,* 473-474.
James, W. (1963). *The principles of psychology.* New York: Holt, Rinehart & Winston. (Original work published in 1890)
Jung, C.G. (1933). *Modern man in search of a soul.* New York: Harvest Books.
Lazarus, R.S., & Folkman, S. (1984). *Stress, appraisal, and coping.* New York: Springer-Verlag.
Leahy, T., Harrigan, R., & Freeman, G. (1999, November). *Evaluation of a body image enhancement programme with elite female athletes.* Paper presented at the fifth IOC World Congress on Sport Sciences, Sydney, Australia.
Liggett, J. (1959) The paired use of projective stimuli. *British Journal of Psychology, 50,* 269-275.
Marsh, H.W. (1974). *Judgmental anchoring: Stimulus and response variables.* Unpublished doctoral dissertation. University of California, Los Angeles.
Marsh, H.W. (1984a). Self-concept: The application of a frame of reference model to explain paradoxical results. *Australian Journal of Education, 28,* 165-181.
Marsh, H.W. (1984b). Self-concept, social comparison, and ability grouping: A reply to Kulik and Kulik. *American Educational Research Journal, 21,* 799-806.
Marsh, H.W. (1986). Global self-esteem: Its relation to specific facets of self-concept and their importance. *Journal of Personality and Social Psychology, 51,* 1224-1236.
Marsh, H.W. (1987a). The hierarchical structure of self-concept and the application of hierarchical confirmatory factor analysis. *Journal of Educational Measurement, 24,* 17-19.
Marsh, H.W. (1987b). The big-fish-little-pond effect on academic self-concept. *Journal of Educational Psychology, 79,* 280-295.
Marsh, H.W. (1990a). A multidimensional, hierarchical self-concept: Theoretical and empirical justification. *Educational Psychology Review, 2,* 77-171.
Marsh, H.W. (1990b). The structure of academic self-concept: The Marsh/Shavelson model. *Journal of Educational Psychology, 82,* 623-636.
Marsh, H.W. (1991). The failure of high-ability high schools to deliver academic benefits: The importance of academic self-concept and educational aspirations. *American Educational Research Journal, 28,* 445-480.
Marsh, H.W. (1993). Academic self-concept: Theory, measurement, and research. In J. Suls (Ed.), *Psychological perspectives on the self* (vol. 4). Hillsdale, NJ: Erlbaum.
Marsh, H.W. (1994). The importance of being important: Theoretical models of relations between specific and global components of physical self-concept. *Journal of Sport and Exercise Psychology, 16,* 306-325.
Marsh, H.W., Byrne, B.M., & Shavelson, R. (1988). A multifaceted academic self-concept: Its hierarchical structure and its relation to academic achievement. *Journal of Educational Psychology, 80,* 366-380.
Marsh, H.W., & Hattie, J. (1996). Theoretical perspectives on the structure of self-concept. In B.A. Bracken (Ed.), *Handbook of self-concept* (pp. 38-90). New York: Wiley.
Marsh, H.W., Hey, J., Johnson, S., & Perry, C. (1997). Elite athlete self-description questionnaire: Hierarchical confirmatory factor analysis of responses by two distinct groups of elite athletes. *International Journal of Sport Psychology, 28,* 237-258.
Marsh, H.W., Hey, J., Roche, L.A., & Perry, C. (1997). The structure of physical self-concept: Elite athletes and physical education students. *Journal of Educational Psychology, 89,* 369-380.
Marsh, H.W., & O'Neill, R. (1984). Self-description questionnaire III (SDQ III): The construct validity of multidimensional self-concept ratings by late-adolescents. *Journal of Educational Measurement, 21,* 153-174.
Marsh, H.W., & Parker, J.W. (1984). Determinants of student self-concept: Is it better to be a relatively large fish in a small pond even if you don't learn to swim as well? *Journal of Personality and Social Psychology, 47,* 213-231.
Marsh, H.W., & Peart, N. (1988). Competitive and cooperative physical fitness training programs for girls: Effects on physical fitness and on multidimensional self-concepts. *Journal of Sport and Exercise Psychology, 10,* 390-407.
Marsh, H.W., Perry, C., Horsely, C., & Roche, L.A. (1995). Multidimensional self-concepts of elite athletes: How do they differ from the general population? *Journal of Sport and Exercise Psychology, 17,* 70-83.
Marsh, H.W., Richards, G.E., Johnson, S., Roche, L., & Tremayne, P. (1994). Physical Self-Description Questionnaire: Psychometric properties and a multitrait-multimethod analysis of relations to existing instruments. *Journal of Sport and Exercise Psychology, 16,* 270-305.
Marsh, H.W., & Roche, L.A. (1996). Predicting self-esteem from perceptions of actual and ideal ratings of body fatness: Is there only one ideal supermodel? *Research Quarterly for Exercise and Sport, 67,* 13-23.
Marsh, H.W., & Shavelson, R. (1985). Self-concept: Its multifaceted, hierarchical structure. *Educational Psychologist, 20,* 107-125.
Marshall, H.H., & Weinstein, R.S. (1984). Classroom factors affecting students' self-evaluations. *Review of Educational Research, 54,* 301-326.
McFarland, C., & Buehler, R. (1995). Collective self-esteem as a moderator of the frog-pond effect in reactions to performance feedback. *Journal of Personality and Social Psychology, 68,* 1055-1070.
Mead, G.H. (1925). The genesis of the self and social control. *International Journal of Ethics, 35,* 251-273.
Mead, G.H. (1934). *Mind, self, and society.* Chicago: University of Chicago Press.
Meyer, J.W. (1970). High school effects on college intentions. *American Journal of Sociology, 76,* 59-70.
Morse, S., & Gergen, K.J. (1970). Social comparison, self-consistency, and the concept of self. *Journal of Personality and Social Psychology, 16,* 148-156.
Oosterwegel, A., & Oppenheimer, L. (1993). *The self-system: Developmental changes between and within self-concepts.* Hillsdale, NJ: Erlbaum.

Parducci, A. (1995). *Happiness, pleasure, and judgment: The contextual theory and its applications.* Mahwah, NJ: Erlbaum.
Perry, C. (1999). *An investigation of the relationship between self-concept and elite swimming performances.* Unpublished doctoral dissertation, University of Western Sydney, Sydney, Australia.
Rogers, C.R. (1950). The significance of the self-regarding attitudes and perceptions. In M.L. Reymart (Ed.), *Feeling and emotion: The Moosehart symposium* (pp. 78-79). New York: McGraw-Hill.
Rogers, C.R. (1951). *Client-centered therapy.* Boston: Houghton Mifflin.
Rogers, C.R. (1977). *Carl Rogers on personal power.* New York: Delacorte Press.
Shavelson, R.J., Hubner, J.J., & Stanton, G.C. (1976). Validation of construct interpretations. *Review of Educational Research, 46,* 407-441.
Shavelson, R.J., & Marsh, H.W. (1986). On the structure of self-concept. In R. Schwarzer (Ed.), *Anxiety and cognition.* Hillsdale, NJ: Erlbaum.
Sherif, M., & Sherif, C.W. (1969). *Social psychology.* New York: Harper & Row.
Snyder, C.R., Lassegard, M., & Ford, C.E. (1986). Distancing after group success and failure: Basking in reflected glory and cutting off reflected failure. *Journal of Personality and Social Psychology, 51,* 382-388.
Sperry, L. (1995). *Handbook of diagnosis and treatment of the DSM-IV personality disorders.* Levittown, PA: Brunner/Mazel.
Stouffer, S.A., Suchman, E.A., DeVinney, L.C., Star, S.A., & Williams, R.M. (1949). *The American soldier: Adjustments during army life* (vol. 1). Princeton, NJ: Princeton University Press.
Suls, J.M. (1977). Social comparison theory and research: An overview from 1954. In J.M. Suls & R.L. Miller (Eds.), *Social comparison processes: Theoretical and empirical perspectives* (pp. 1-20). Washington, DC: Hemisphere.
Taylor, S.E., & Lobel, M. (1989). Social comparison activity under threat: Downward evaluation and upward contacts. *Psychological Review, 96,* 569-575.
Tesser, A. (1988). Toward a self-evaluation maintenance model of social behavior. *Advances in Experimental Social Psychology* (vol. 21, pp. 181-227).
Upshaw, H.S. (1969). The personal reference scale: An approach to social judgment. *Advances in Experimental Social Psychology* (vol. 4, pp. 315-370). San Diego, CA: Academic Press.
Wills, T.A. (1981). Downward comparison principals in social psychology. *Psychological Bulletin, 90,* 245-271.
Wylie, R.C. (1989). *Measures of self-concept.* Lincoln, NE: University of Nebraska Press.

CHAPTER 6

DOING IMAGERY IN THE FIELD

Jeff Simons
Optimal Performance Consulting

Imagery was the first topic in sport psychology that I explored to some depth. As an undergraduate setting my sights on graduate study in the field, I was attracted to the wholly psychological nature of mental imagery. Here was an obviously psychological aspect of human functioning that could have some sort of impact on sport performance. It was intriguing to think that an athlete might be able to learn through imagery alone, and that imagery might hold untapped potential for enhancing performance. At the end of the 1970s and into the early 1980s, a wave of sport psychology researchers were attempting to establish the effects of imagery on learning and performance unique from other mental and physical processes. Surely this mental activity could be a tool that would help validate the role of psychological factors in physical performance, and perhaps more important, give greater credence to sport psychology and sport psychologists.

Imagery once again excited me when I was introduced to the concept of psychological skills training (PST). According to PST approaches, imagery was one of the fundamental skills to be taught to all athletes. These fundamental skills would form the base of essential psychological knowledge that the modern athlete could put to use in the pursuit of excellence. Imagery skills, along with other mental skills such as goal setting, relaxation, and positive self-talk, began to define what applied sport psychology was and what sport psychologists did. Psychological skills promised to be a specialized area of knowledge apart from that held by coaches, biomechanists, exercise physiologists, and nutritionists. A sport psychologist would be needed, for instance, to provide talks on imagery, lead imagery sessions, and enhance imagery ability.

Taking the moderate but consistent support from the literature (e.g., Feltz & Landers, 1983), a multitude of anecdotal reports, and much optimistic (and perhaps wishful) thinking, a generation of sport psychologists have tucked imagery into their applied repertoire and have gone about spreading the word and extolling the importance of developing imagery skills. "Great performers, like the legendary Jack Nicklaus, report using imagery." "Work on developing vivid and controllable images." "Negative images are the result of untrained/unmanaged imagery skills." "Internal images are better than external images." "Practice, practice, practice." Written material and group presentations by sport psychology proponents have provided an abundance of declarative information on imagery.

Nearly every basic university course in sport psychology includes the topic of imagery (it is the module tucked somewhere between goal setting, relaxation, and positive self-talk). Unfortunately, most basic programs provide information about imagery, and they may even have imagery scripts, but there is little guidance in the process of introducing, developing, and using imagery. Athletes and coaches are typically left to figure out how to use the general information and how to adapt and apply imagery for their specific needs.

Athletes need to learn about their images and about how to develop applicable imagery skills. And there should be more sources of procedural knowledge available for sport psychologists—how imagery applies to performance. Procedural knowledge is more complex, because individuals and objectives differ, and because development of imagery skills does not follow a single linear sequence. Furthermore, there should be more recognition of the common problems that athletes have, such as incomplete images, interference by negative images, and difficulties in timing or flow of images. There is much room for greater discussion of the practical issues sport psychologists and their clients face when they use imagery as a performance tool. It is not enough for the sport psychologist to recite the value of imagery to athletes, or to supply athletes with imagery scripts, and then assume that sport psychology has provided a special skill to athletes.

Sport psychologists did not invent imagery. It is not a technique that some clever researcher or innovative practitioner developed. It does not belong to psychologists or to any science. Imagery alone is not an intervention. As I will show in my basic explanation to athletes, what we label *imagery* is our understanding of an ordinary mental function. I have been asked on a number of occasions whether or not I "believe in" imagery in the same manner I might be asked if I believe in intergalactic aliens or astrology. From a phenomenological perspective, there is no question that imagery exists and that it is used in mental processing. Researchers have yet to agree on the exact nature and function of imagery, but from a practitioner's point of view it is a natural human system serving memory, planning, learning, creating, and performing.

Imagery does have a long history in psychology and in the physical and mental health fields (Graham, 1995). Wundt (1896), using the technique of introspection to study the mind, considered imagery one of the functions of mind open to his methods of investigation. Freud's free association and dream analysis relied heavily on his and his patients' images (Freud 1965/1900), and imagery stands at the very heart of behavior therapy's influential systematic desensitization (Wolpe, 1973).

Because imagery appears integrally linked to perception and action, it has powerful potential to evoke understanding and change. The imagery system can be used to help a person meet some personal or performance goal, but it is most effective when it is used for a specific purpose. Sport psychologists and other professionals should not expect random or nondirected imagery to produce any specific performance results. Imagery techniques are simply tools that can be applied in coaching, counseling, and therapy to make use of the richness in imaginal processing.

I employ imagery techniques primarily for skill development, reinforcement of desired attitudes or philosophical perspectives, and mental preparation for competition. Imagery can also be used to help clients recall past experiences, learn relaxation techniques, build confidence, and desensitize anxiety reactions, but in my practice I do not often use it for such purposes. I will therefore focus the discussion in this chapter on my most common applications. To illustrate the process, I have chosen some cases of field-event athletes from athletics (as we call track and field sports in the British Commonwealth), which offer but a few examples of employing imagery with performers. Consequently, this is not an exhaustive description of imagery practice. There are ample approaches to and uses for imagery, and practitioners can be creative in applying imagery to address desired psychological states, learning, and performance. All the cases in this chapter are based on real athlete-clients, actual discussions, and events. Certain details have been changed to protect confidentiality, and some content has been modified to fit important ideas into the context of this chapter.

INITIAL IMAGERY SESSION: AN INTRODUCTION

It is not necessary to spend a great deal of time teaching about imagery at the outset. The concept that a full education phase must precede any training or practice phase is too rigid and unrealistic. Powerful teachable moments will arise with specific situations, needs, feedback, and experiences using the imagery. Assuming that one is applying the imagery to achieve some objective, there will be plenty of opportunities for discussion, clarification, and exploration of the process.

There are just a few concepts that I want to get across during initial discussions with athletes. I take a somewhat didactic approach in order to get through a reasonable amount of information, but I also encourage questions and discussion as we go along. I ask a few questions at the beginning or end of each point to check on comprehension and to develop a language for the athlete in relation to imagery. Beyond the main points that I want to convey, the initial discussion addresses whatever specific issues or questions the client presents, so individual sessions have differing content. Naturally, the level of presentation must be adjusted according to the athlete's age, education, and experience. The following is an example of a basic imagery introduction session with Michael, a university-educated discus thrower with whom I already had good rapport.

JS: We wanted to talk today about imagery and how you might use it to better understand and guide your performance. Let me start by asking you a question.

I want to get a relatively unbiased answer on the way that Michael processes information about his discus throw before I present much on imagery. If he naturally uses imagery to perform, then I will minimize discussion about verbal and analytical approaches and draw on his usual experiences to develop the imagery in a formal manner. If he engages in a great deal of analysis and verbal processing, then I will want to spend some time contrasting that with image processing.

JS: Discus is a technical event, so there is a tremendous amount of information that you have to deal with in preparing and performing each throw. How do you handle all the technical aspects of your throw?

Michael: Well, there are so many things to think about. I try to remind myself of what I'm supposed to do. But it's hard to remember everything. Coach tells me to focus on this part or that part, and sometimes I can get the one part, but usually I forget to think about some other important parts. After a throw, I often tell myself, You didn't do this right, or, Darn, I didn't remember that. But if I try to think of everything, I can't get my timing; there's no flow. Sometimes it's better if I don't think, you know, just throw.

JS: So, you try to talk yourself through your throw, but you find that hard?

M: Yeah. It's too much stuff. I can explain everything if I'm teaching a younger thrower, for example, but it's hard to remember it all and do it when I'm really throwing.

JS: You are bringing up a common problem that has to do with using descriptions—that is, words—to control your action. It's possible for you to guide your performance with words, but words are at least two steps removed from the perception and action that you actually experience.

Let me explain what I mean. A word is an abstract symbol meant to represent something else. The word *tree* is not a tree; it is an agreed-upon label for the actual thing. And the word, the symbol, is arbitrary. Different languages can have completely different words for the same thing. For example, *tree* in English, *arbre* in French, and so on. That is why one can say that a word is separate from the thing it refers to, the thing that we perceive or understand. When you think of a word, it has meaning only because you can relate the sound or group of letters to something you know through perception or experience.

To look at it the opposite way, it is often difficult to explain in words what you perceive. This is precisely because of the difficulty of expressing the complexity of experience in just a series of written or spoken symbols; that is, words. Words are just symbols that are meant to represent more complex things.

Here, I check to see if Michael understands the point about words. If not, I go back over the idea looking for a way to help him understand. Clarifying also gives him the chance to think about the information and put it into his own way of thinking. Michael was a highly intelligent young man who I had gotten to know well, and I was adjusting my communication to appeal to his intellect. I would not talk this way to a typical 14-year-old.

JS: Does that make sense?

M: Sure; words are just made up so we can communicate with each other. Language is the way of remembering facts and such, and telling each other information. It seems a little bit bizarre to think about it that way, but you're right, there is a complete difference between a description and what you do.

JS: Another way that we have of processing information is through images rather than words. Images are mental representations of what we perceive. They can remind us directly of something we perceived, what something looked like, sounded like, etc. Imagery is our most life-like memory of what we have experienced.

M: I think I see what you are getting at. Imagery is this special way of thinking without words.

JS: It is a different way of thinking, yes, but it is not special in the sense that it is an auxiliary to other forms of mental processing. Imagery is a basic memory system, one we use at least from birth. We are born with the ability to remember what we have seen, heard, tasted, touched, and smelled. Long before we can use language, we store information about what we perceive. We remember our experiences with these perception-like images. When you remember a sound, for example, it is most likely as an image. Do you have a doorbell at your place?

M: Uh huh.

JS: Think about the sound of your doorbell. Can you hear what it sounds like in your head?

M: Yeah [pauses]. It's silly, but yes, I really can.

JS: That's an auditory image. For every way of perceiving, there is a corresponding image. We can imagine sights, sounds, smells, tastes, and touch, as well as feelings of movement and emotional states. The term *visualization* is often used to describe techniques for imagining performance, but that is only one sense type. We can employ the other types of images as well. In fact, visual images are often less important than other sense images, especially kinesthetic, or movement images. Kinesthetic images can be the most important in physical performance, for obvious reasons.

M: Yeah, when I have the "feel" I know I can get into my throws. But I only get that sometimes. I don't think my "feel" images are very good, or at least they aren't usually complete, and I can't always get them. I'm not sure that I have very clear imagery of any sort. I don't think I'm very good at it.

JS: You aren't alone feeling that way. But everyone has used imagery extensively in early life. Children typically display excellent imagery skills. They naturally use images to remember things as well as to create their fantasy worlds. It's amazing, for example, how well children do with games such as "Concentration," where good imagery recall makes matching cards easy. Most people relate to the concept that infants must process information through imagery, and therefore that we all must have some natural capacity for it.

As children progress through school, they seem to use imagery progressively less. It may be because more and more emphasis is placed on other mental skills, particularly language and analytical thinking. Imagery abilities appear to atrophy into adolescence and adulthood for most people. But, just because there is less apparent skill doesn't mean that adults no longer have the potential capability. Basically they just lose the "fitness."

M: Use it or lose it.

JS: Exactly! OK, so I want to be clear on a couple of points. The first point to understand is that far from being some new or foreign technique, imagery is simply a type of mental processing that we all possess. You have it, I have it, everyone has the capability. The second point is that all our different ways of perceiving and feeling have corresponding images. So, Michael, do these points seem too vague, abstract, or unclear?

M: No, it makes sense. I guess I do have all kinds of images. I think I used to imagine all kinds of stuff when I was a kid.

JS: Do you remember your best throw this year? What was that like?

M: Sweet [pauses to reflect]. It just flowed . . . I was really "long" . . . like all this energy . . . and I could feel that I "hit it," you know? [pauses again] I know you want me to talk about the images. I've got a lot of them. It's hard to really describe, though.

JS: There may be more images than you might have thought?

M: Yeah, there is a lot there.

JS: Yet, as you said, they're hard to describe. Let me take that lead to talk a bit more about imagery. Images are perception-like and therefore rich with information. But that also makes them difficult to share with someone else. The saying *a picture is worth a thousand words* means that there is a lot of information that a perceived thing may hold, and it would take a great deal of effort to describe all that to another person through language. There is a clear difference between experiencing something and explaining it.

M: Absolutely! Like I keep telling coach that I need to see someone who actually moves through the middle of the ring the way he is telling me to. No matter how much detail he gives me in words, I'm not getting it. I can repeat back what he is explaining for me to do, but he says I'm not doing it. I need to see someone who does it, so maybe I can get it.

JS: You are describing the difference between image processing and verbal or analytical processing. Images allow the parallel, or simultaneous, processing of huge amounts of information. They can easily capture dynamic flow in events, like watching how a thrower moves through the circle. And you can replay it in the same brief time as the actual performance. Skilled movement is also a parallel processing event, with huge amounts of information going into the coordination of an action. Image processing and movement processing are much alike.

On the other hand, conscious analytic thought is done by serial processing, which requires each bit of information to be taken in sequence. Words and logical analysis have to be placed in a particular order to make sense. The necessity of processing all information in a single stream makes it much slower for the same amount of data. And as we already discussed, the words used to explain an action, for example, are somewhat lacking in the richness of the real thing. Both types of processing can be useful, but what do you think is going to help you most with your throwing?

M: Watching, observing, and imagining I think really give me more useful information. Descriptions help me, probably because I'm an analytical kind of person. I like to have everything explained and figured out. But when I just think of the throw . . . that is . . . I guess, just *imagine* it, I get more out of it. I think I need to see what I'm trying to do and imagine doing it so that I'm not trying to talk my way through it. That doesn't work anyway.

JS: So, you can see why images are so helpful for sport. First, they are the closest memory we have to perception and experience. They are rich in information used in performance. And, images allow the same parallel processing of complex information that is used in creating the movement.

You can make use of imagery in a number of ways. You can remember experiences and learn from them. You can recall good experiences and best performances and practice recreating the feeling. And you can imagine thinking, feeling, and acting in ways that you would like, even if you haven't done so before. For example, you can imagine what it would be like to have a certain attitude going into the ring, or what it would be like to use your desired technique, and those images can guide your performance. As we work on your imagery, we will explore all of these areas further.

From here, the session may take any number of directions. I typically let athletes lead with whatever observations or questions they might have. The following discussion with Michael is an example of additional dialogue that might take place in this initial imagery discussion.

M: What is the difference between imagery and subconscious? Do they differ? Where do they differ? Like, imagery is something that you've taken control of and you turn it into what you want? And subconsciously, if you want to make a move you just move without thinking? So is one a controlled movement and one just a movement that takes control of itself?

JS: Imagery is one way your mind processes information. It can happen at conscious or subconscious levels. The way we're talking about using it for our purpose is to set up imagery as a conscious plan. In time, these images can become more automatic. That is, your intention is expressed as an image, and you immediately carry it through.

In reactive situations, like adjusting your position during your turn through the discus circle, the perception of the need to do an action or adjust to the circumstances becomes an unconscious process. It is "perceive-do." The image of what you intend to do in an objective sense—for example, stay low through the middle—is the criterion against which the skilled actions take place. At a subconscious level, all the adjustments are taking place based on the intention in mind and the information that is perceived.

M: One of the difficulties I now have is that my technique is automatic, but it is not the technique I want. So, it's a real hard process for me to make one attempt go right. But, when I do get one right, I usually know it, and I can identify things like being relaxed, really doing the action in relaxed form. At the moment, just doing it and doing it right are two different things. How can the imagery help me with that?

JS: What we want to do is establish strong images of the form you want. Those images can serve as guides to your new actions. The images should be as rich as possible to help direct your attention. We want to include as much of the sensory experience of correct performance as possible. Because of the more direct connection of images to perception and action, using images will be far more effective than verbal instructions. If correct images dominate your attention during performance, we should see a shift in technique. Gradually, the new form will become automatic as the old form fades away into the background.

M: So this will be more than just sitting at home and imaging myself going through the motions? I will actually use this at the time of my performance?

JS: The imagery can prime you for the performance. The images set up the template for action. You then in essence ask your body to follow the pattern set forth in the imagery. The imagery becomes your intention for action. That is to say, rather than just doing whatever happens to come out of your body, you set up a clear intention with good images.

M: I can't yet keep myself straight during the middle of my turn through the circle, but I can imagine what that position might feel like.

JS: Use that as a guide. By setting forth the image of desired action, you give yourself a goal for movement. Mentally, it is analogous to the templates for drawing shapes that you may have used in school. It seems that strong images of what one is attempting to do pull the movements toward accomplishing that.

M: So what should I do first, image myself performing, or what?

JS: We will start by having you become more conscious of both your perceptions and your imagery reflecting those perceptions. We want to refresh your imagery abilities. The goal is to make them skilled once again, just as during your childhood. To begin, you can exercise your memory for what you perceive, what you experience.

Rather than just tell Michael what to pay attention to, I want to get him to become involved in thinking about the process of employing imagery.

JS: What are the images that are going to be important for your event?

M: As in what I need to image?

JS: Yes. Given the focus and action that you need in your event, what images would be important?

M: I need to transfer my body weight. I need to focus on that. Particularly at the start, because if I get that going, then the rest of the movement is pretty good. Then move to the middle and bend that right knee, turn and follow through over the right leg and complete the throw.

Michael is taking the question in a different way than I intended. I will use the technical description to draw out different sensory images.

JS: So, what are the important senses involved in that performance?

M: To move correctly. To get the sense of that right technique.

JS: How important is taste to your performance? How about smell? Hearing?

M: Not at all. Hearing, only if my coach is saying something to me [pauses]. Well, I suppose that wouldn't be a good idea during the throw. Just maybe the sound of moving through the circle [pauses to reflect again]. Not that much.

JS: Then, what senses are most important? How about visual?

M: Sight is important, because first of all if I look down, I'm going to throw bad. I've got to keep my head up. Where I look controls my head, and the head pretty much controls where the rest of your body is going to go.

JS: So you'll need to be aware of visual information.

M: Yes, but that wouldn't be the main part. It's definitely there, but not the most important. It's the balance, the moving, the feel of the throw. From start to finish, the movements.

JS: Spot on. That is the kinesthetic, or movement sense. The internal feel of the motion, the relative motions of your limbs and torso.

M: Balance, and weight shift, and the motion. And sense of quickness and the power transfer.

JS: So, what is the imagery that we need to work on?

M: Feel. The feeling of movement, the feeling of doing it.

JS: Yes, knowing what it feels like. The sense of relative movement, speed, balance, and power is going to be the most important.

M: Kinesthetic sense.

JS: We are going to start work on the skill of using kinesthetic imagery by heightening the experience of feeling the motion. You will want to practice paying attention to the sensory input of the internal feel so that it comes to have more meaning to you, so that you can remember it and use it. Because you also rely on visual cues, you can link what you see with the feel of the coordinated movement. The main point is to pay clearer attention to these important aspects of the throw.

M: And then it will get easier? Because I'm not sure how well I can do that right now. I know I can't do it very easily.

JS: The capacity is there. When you were young you probably used it constantly. It just needs some attention and practice, like any other underused skill.

M: It just seems a bit vague right now. Plus, I'm not exactly sure how to pay more attention to feel when I have so much else to do.

JS: There is no need to spend a great deal of time thinking about your awareness. Just remind yourself occasionally to *feel* and to *remember.* Also, determine some times when awareness of feel is the primary goal of the throwing attempt. When you pick up the discus, feel it in your hand. Be aware of the discus, your body movements, and the connections between yourself, the ground, your orientation in space, the air, and the entire flow. What is the feeling of being relaxed? What is the feeling when technique is correct? Reacquaint yourself with your senses and practice experiencing and remembering without analyzing.

Now I would like for Michael to rationalize, in his own words, why he might benefit from practicing awareness. Many athletes say they are already aware or think that awareness is easy and therefore not very important. Awareness can seem such a mundane thing, especially after all the discussion of rich complex images, parallel processing, and building intentions for desired performance. I want to emphasize the need for this first step through the athlete's recognition of its practical importance.

JS: So, why would I ask you to do this, to spend time just being more aware?

M: Well, as soon as I start to know the senses, I can work on knowing what is right. And just feeling the right motion, knowing it is right by the feel. Setting up the image of correct technique, knowing what that should feel like, and using that to set off the throw. Remember it, know it, then just do it.

JS: In doing so you will be in essence "speaking" in the language of your body, rather than in a language of abstract symbols; that is, words. Your body doesn't know English, but it knows perception and movement.

M: I need to get back in touch with that and use it!

JS: Now, I need to put in a word of caution, because when you get into this there are going to be times when you feel very awkward. Invariably, you will slip into analysis of what you are doing and that will interfere with both action and simple awareness. For instance, you may suddenly think, My elbow is there; is that where it should be? and so on, thereby throwing off the flow of the throw. It is like trying to snatch frames from a moving film. Or you may become so caught up in experiencing the throw that skilled motor control is compromised and you produce poor technique. You may do some pretty uncoordinated things.

These are normal difficulties. It takes time to be able to actively do and passively observe without interfering with the process. We'll play with these skills as we go along. In the meantime, take it all with an appreciation for the work in developing skills. And don't forget a sense of humor.

M: OK, I accept that it will take some time, but how will I see improvement?

JS: You will discover relatively soon that you can take a moment after a throw, remember what it felt like, and really "know" what happened. At least parts of it will be clear. And even though you may not be able to put it into words, you will find that you have a clear sense of "that's it!" or "that's not it." Your descriptions of that knowledge will require many words and probably some analogies, because as we said earlier, images contain rich and complex information.

M: Should I start describing my images? Should I write them down?

JS: The first thing to do is to simply start observing. For the next couple of weeks you are to work on experiencing what you are doing, without analyzing what you are perceiving. Become familiar with how you move and what sensory input accompanies your throw. In addition, any time that you approximate correct technique, stop for a moment afterward and recall the sensory experience. To help with this, we will ask your coach to give you a minute after each throw before giving you technical feedback.

M: What about when I make bad throws?

JS: Awareness of incorrect movement is still sensory awareness. Just observe, make a note of "wrong model," and let it go. Don't give it importance, which might strengthen its memory. Clear that recall from your mind, then take a moment and play through your best image of what you would like to do. Just play with that a little.

M: Well, this is going to give me a lot to work on. I'm actually looking forward to getting out to training and giving it a go.

JS: I look forward to our next meeting to find out how you went.

An initial session such as this one with Michael sets the base for developing an athlete's imagery skills. Even if there is no further work on imagery for a while, there is usually an improvement in the athlete's perceptual processing of sport information. I also find that athlete and coach typically engage in better communication about skills as they work to develop a way of discussing the athlete's perspective of movement. As image processing becomes familiar, it is easier to apply imagery for specific purposes in learning or preparation, as I will illustrate in the cases of Ann and Joe.

SKILL DEVELOPMENT

Imagery is an excellent tool for motor skill development. Imagery can facilitate the understanding, learning, and production of motor patterns because the perceptual experiences of action can be retained by imagery in much of their complexity. The key is to develop a close match between images and perceptual-motor elements of performance. Athletes then can use imagery to recall past experiences accurately and to mentally rehearse their best performances. They can also analyze images as feedback from performance attempts, and they can create images of desired actions to serve as intentions for future performance. The deliberate and conscious application of imagery to performance adds a rich dimension to the learning and performance process.

An example of developing imagery for skill development comes from the case of Ann, a high jumper who held the national record but had been stalled at the same level of performance for a couple of years. Ann met with me out of frustration over her lack of improvement. She was not clear on what she felt she needed but was curious whether we might discover some psychological aspect of her performance to pursue. Given her experience and level of achievement, I spent most of the session having her describe her objectives and goals, her training, and her competitive performances. At one point, I had her use imagery to recall some of her jumps. She was able to create some images but repeatedly made comments about the poor quality of her imagery. In particular, she found that she had no images of any kind from the moment of her final foot plant prior to takeoff until she was landing in the high-jump pit. Her weak and incomplete images, despite her considerable experience, led me to suggest that she might want to work on her imagery abilities.

Ann and I had another session where we discussed the basics of imagery, much like that described previously with Michael. She indicated that she found it hard to make adjustments according to her coach's instructions because she could not remember well what she had done nor imagine how to perform in the way her coach asked. It appeared that difficulties in making technical changes were a major factor in Ann's inability to improve her jumping. With a bit of guidance on my part, she came to the conclusion that developing her imagery could be of great benefit and was heartened to think that we had found something specific she could work on. Ann's coach, Kathy, was also eager to take part in the process, so we arranged to do an awareness session at the training track.

We met at the track during a normal training time. Kathy set aside the first half-hour of practice for me to guide the awareness exercises. Once Ann had done her basic warm-up, we began.

JS: The idea behind this awareness session is simply to pay attention to your experience of moving. There is not any one aspect that you have to attend to; just see what you notice by being aware. We're not trying to do anything precise, so don't worry about your form or anything. Now, let's start with a simple exercise that you do often, one that you know well and is easy.

It is best to work first on awareness with actions that are well learned and require little attention to be performed. If the movements are relatively automatic, then there is plenty of attentional capacity left over for conscious processing of the perceptual information (see Moran, 1996).

Kathy: Why don't we just do scissors jumps over a low bar? We do that all the time. I'll just set the bar here [places the high-jump bar around stomach level for Ann].

JS: OK. Ann, just do a couple of scissors jumps at your own pace. Pay attention to what you see, feel, and so on as you go through the run-up and jump over the bar and into the pit. Just observe as you do it. [Ann does a couple of scissors jumps.]

Ann: [stepping out of the pit after the second jump] I'm not sure what I'm supposed to pay attention to. What am I supposed to notice?

JS: Notice whatever you experience. Just pick something that you notice. It doesn't matter, you're just getting a feel for being more aware. Why don't you pay attention to the feeling of taking off and going over the bar this time? [Ann nods, walks away, and completes another jump at her own pace.]

A: Whoa! I was, like, floating. I lifted off and floated over the bar. I kind of kept my legs up a little longer to keep floating longer. I was feeling it.

JS: That's what this exercise is all about, noticing what your body experiences. Why don't you pay attention to watching the bar as you approach this time? See what it looks like. [Ann jogs back, pauses, then runs in and jumps.]

A: It was like the bar was just coming at me. I kind of played with it and pretended like I wasn't moving, but the pit was moving toward me. It was weird.

JS: Good; just play around a bit. Go do a few more jumps and observe whatever you want. Feel, see, hear the movement. [Ann bounds back and does a little dance before starting again. She does a couple of more jumps, obviously playing with her perceptions of movement. She then runs up, makes a clumsy jump at the bar, and crashes through it.]

K: What was that?!

A: [laughing] I think I forgot how to do the scissors. I got all crossed up.

JS: That's okay; it's pretty normal. You were probably paying so much attention to observing that you mixed up what you were doing. From time to time you may do some uncoordinated things. Just remind yourself of what action you are doing before you do it, then you can use the rest of your attention to observe.

We discussed a little more about the perceptions she was experiencing. Ann then performed a few more scissors jumps and shared some more of her observations. I suggested that she regularly use such awareness exercises during her training warm-ups. We then moved on to some formal jumping at an easy height. I asked Ann to continue her awareness, but also make technically good attempts in clearing the bar. On her first attempt, she knocked the bar off with her heel.

K: You've got to remember that little kick at the end! It is no use making a good jump if you get lazy and don't complete it. [Ann sits on the bag with an expression that says she has heard it all before.]

JS: [speaking privately to the coach] Kathy, that's not what we're here for right now. Let's not get technical. Remember, this part of the training session is just for Ann to build her awareness. Is that all right?

K: Yeah, right. Sorry; that's fine.

I try to minimize evaluation during the awareness exercises. The idea is to maximize the processing of perceptual information without all the interference possible from analysis, judgment, and concomitant thoughts and emotions. The purpose of the exercises is the experience of performance, not the development of motor skills.

JS: [Ann walks slowly over from the pit.] Forget about the technical stuff, Ann; it doesn't matter right now. How was your awareness in that jump?

A: Well, actually, I think I was a lot more aware. It wasn't a great jump, but I felt more in the run-up. And I felt kind of a "pop" up off my takeoff leg. I think I forgot some of my form because I was feeling myself sail over the bar.

JS: That's fine. Don't worry about missing some form details. The main thing is that you are more aware! Let's keep building your senses and make them an automatic part of your action.

A: I think I get what you mean more now that I've done some of it. I just need to do more of it.

JS: OK. I want to add one more thing today. I would like you to do a couple more easy jumps, concentrating on good form but continuing to be aware. After each jump, take a minute in the pit and try to recall the experience of that jump.

A: So, run through the jump I just did in my mind?

JS: Yes; see if you can recall that immediate experience.

A: OK. [She strolls back to her starting mark.]

JS: Kathy, it would be great if you could make sure that Ann has time to imagine what she has just done after most of her training jumps. That way she gets accustomed to actually processing the information. It should improve her understanding of her jumps and enhance her ability to use imagery.

K: Hey, I'm all for her becoming more aware of what she's doing! I find it so frustrating that she doesn't seem to know what she has done a lot of the time. It'd be so much easier to coach her if she had better recognition of her jumps.

JS: So, just hold off on your feedback until she has time to process the jump for herself.

K: Sounds good. That's easy enough to do. Well, I may have to write something down or look at the video to keep myself occupied, but I can do that. [Ann completes a jump, waits about 30 seconds in the pit, and then gets off the pads.]

A: Should I try to remember the jump with my eyes closed?

JS: Do it whatever way you'd like. What do you think is best for you?

A: I did it partially open, partially with them closed. I'm not sure what's best.

JS: Play around with it. Do both and eventually you'll settle on what you like best. Could you imagine what you just did?

A: A little, but not very well. I mean, it was all broken up. I got parts. I could feel a couple of things, and I saw a little bit. It wasn't flowing the whole way through the jump.

JS: That's fine. People have this idea that images have to be like going to the movies, in full color and sound and every detail clear. Our images usually aren't that way. Just use the images you do have. If you put them into practice regularly, you'll find that they improve considerably.

A: Cool. I do like the little bit I'm getting now. I'll keep working at it.

I left Ann and Kathy with the suggestion that Ann practice her awareness during her warm-up exercises and for at least a few jumps at each technical session. I asked that they limit the objective to simply developing awareness, giving Ann latitude to experiment and experience whatever she might discover. I reminded Ann to consider all her senses and to experience her images as richly as possible.

A couple of weeks later we met again at the track to work on Ann's imagery. Ann reported that she was feeling much more aware of her movements and that the images that she had after a jump were becoming fuller and clearer. Kathy noted that the training sessions were more positive than they had been for a while, and that they seemed to be making some progress on Ann's jumping. She felt that Ann was getting more of a feel for what she was doing. I suggested that it was time to develop an accurate match between what Ann imagined of a jump and the objective performance.

JS: Now that you're starting to get good images of what you're doing, we want to "calibrate" those images to the performance that we can evaluate from the outside. That is, we want to make sure that what you imagine represents what you actually did as accurately as possible.

K: So that it is not just a fantasy thing? So it's real?

JS: That's right. It doesn't do any good if what you imagine, Ann, bears little resemblance to reality. Fantasy imagery is fine for some purposes, but it does little to help skilled performance. You want to "know" what your body position was, for instance, based on your perceptions and images just as accurately as from feedback from Kathy or the video replay.

A: Well, my images are getting pretty good, but they're far from lifelike.

JS: Perfect clarity is not the important part. A person can have extremely vivid, lifelike images that are completely divorced from reality. The essential thing is to match the images you do have to the actual event. "This feeling means that particular position." "When I imagine seeing the bar from this angle, it means I had this trajectory in my run-up." We want that kind of accuracy, not that you have every possible detail in your imagery.

A: Still, that seems like a bit of work.

JS: It will take time. But, what else did you have planned for all your technical sessions, besides developing and grooving in your form? Calibrating your images is just part of the process. It doesn't require extra time, just better use of the time you will already spend on your jumping.

K: Right. Okay; what do we do?

JS: Well, it's a simple process really. On each jump there needs to be a comparison between what Ann perceives to have happened and some outside information source, usually video or coach feedback. Pick one particular aspect of the jump so that you don't create an overload trying to analyze everything.

A: We've been struggling with my takeoff mostly, so why don't we focus on that?

K: Yeah; I can't figure out how to get you to stay upright and not lean into the bar.

JS: Fine, as long as we keep our attention on calibrating Ann's images rather than the frustrations you two have been going through. [Ann goes through her normal warm-up for about 30 minutes, while Kathy and I talk about calibrating images.]

A: Now, what am I doing, again?

JS: Treat this essentially like any other technical session. The focus today is on your position at takeoff.

K: Use your regular approach, get a solid foot plant, and work on getting into the right position in your takeoff. Then just finish off the jump. [Kathy sets the bar at a moderate height.]

JS: After each jump, imagine your takeoff. Then describe what you noticed to Kathy, and we'll compare that to her view and the video. Start with just simple descriptions, like how solidly you planted your takeoff foot, the angle of your body, and maybe what happened to your shoulders or arms.

Ann then proceeded to take a few jumps and report on what she noticed. I had to remind both coach and athlete to keep their discussions simple for the moment, because they were both accustomed to detailed analyses. Ann was doing pretty well at reporting on some aspects of the jump, but she would draw blanks on other parts when Kathy asked about them. Each time she viewed the video replay, Ann noticed something else that occurred, such as arm motion or head tilt. Sometimes, she was then able to recall an image of those additional elements. They rapidly became immersed in the process, and I provided some encouragement and a few tips.

K: Can we put up the bar now? I want to get up to heights where Ann begins screwing up her takeoff.

A: Yeah; I've got to figure out what I'm doing when I try to jump high. I do get it right sometimes, though, Kathy.

K: Yeah, Yeah. That's what I keep reminding you. You just need to do it all the time.

JS: All right, break it up, you two [laughter]. Put the bar up. Ann, go for the clearance just as you would normally do it. Let's see if you can figure out what you are doing by recalling images after the jump. [Ann makes a couple of attempts where she runs through, not making a jump, because she does not feel comfortable with the approach. She eventually hits her marks correctly and gets good height, but knocks the bar off on her way up.]

JS: Don't worry about the miss. Just focus on your takeoff position.

A: I had a good takeoff position. My foot plant was on the mark, and I got good explosive lift. I had the right angle and everything, I think. I don't know; I just got to the bar too soon. Maybe my mark should be out further.

K: Your mark is fine. You just jump into the bar. Don't you feel it? You're creating an angle instead of going straight up.

A: [pauses for a few moments] You know what I think? When I go through it in my mind, I think as I take off I'm trying to get over the bar, to the other side. I'm going up at the angle I feel I need to do that. Yes, I get this image of trying to create the arc over the bar.

K: But the momentum from your run-up carries you across. You don't need to create that.

A: I know, I know, I'm supposed to create vertical lift. It's just that I need to arch over the bar to clear a good height. It's the arching up over the bar that gets that extra height. All the best jumpers get that.

JS: But what you see of a successful jump as an observer, what you are trying to reproduce, is not exactly what you feel and do as the performer.

A: But you said I needed to match my images to what we see on the video.

JS: Part of the artistry of sport performance is knowing what you need to make happen and what happens on its own. [pauses] Think about watching a jump on the video. When you watch yourself falling into the pit, how much energy do you imagine that you expend to make sure you fall all the way onto the pads?

A: Well, I don't have to put anything into it. Gravity does it automatically, if that's what you mean.

JS: And I bet that you can imagine the difference between the experience of falling versus leaping up at the same speed. Taking into consideration the way things operate in the world is part of the process of calibration.

Ann, Kathy, and I discussed a bit further the difference between the athlete's and the outside observer's perception of performance. I emphasized that imagery was a rich source of internal feedback, whereas external sources provided objective indicators of the movements produced and the results of the actions.

A: So, I'm supposed to understand what it is I do that produces the jump seen on the video?

JS: Yes, basically. That's why we spend so much time enhancing your awareness, internal perspective, and imagery. The feedback from the video is only useful if it gives you objective information about the jump that you can use to adjust your actions.

A: OK, so this is really about me learning about myself and what I do to jump well.

JS: That's what it's for, to give you control over your performance and give you better ability to make changes.

K: Ann, try this for me on the next attempt: at takeoff, think of popping straight up into the air as high as you can. Just straight up, to your full vertical leap. Once you've reached the top, then add your back arch and finish the jump.

A: Straight up? I'll crash the bar.

K: Straight up, that's all I care about. [Ann nods and jogs back to her starting mark. She concentrates, gathers herself, then moves through her run-up, hits her takeoff mark, explodes up, and at the last moment arches her back and sails a clear 10 cm over the bar.]

K: Yes!! That's it, that's it! Did you feel that? Did you get that one?

A: Yeah, kind of, but it didn't feel right.

K: What do you mean, it didn't feel right? It's exactly right.

A: But, it was really awkward, you know? It didn't feel natural.

Athletes often comment that a corrected action does not feel right. There is a commonly held belief that correct form should feel natural or otherwise comfortable and pleasing. Yet many sport skills consist of actions that are far from innate, easy, or comfortable on the first try.

JS: It just didn't feel like what you had become accustomed to doing, Ann. It doesn't feel natural because it's a different motor pattern; it's not automatic to you. What you are comfortable with is the motor pattern you have been doing regularly, not necessarily the correct one.

K: But that's the change we are looking for. And it's really not completely new for you, because that's the way you were jumping a couple of years ago when you had your best results.

A: It still doesn't feel quite right [pauses, then smiles]. But I did get some height, didn't I?

JS: Without a doubt. Now you'll want to get used to that new feeling so you can be comfortable with it and reproduce the form.

By the end of practice, Ann and Kathy were comfortable with the process of incorporating awareness and imagery into their technical session. I suggested that they might want to consider making this approach a regular part of their training. Without hesitation, both coach and athlete agreed that awareness and imagery would be integral to their program from now on. They felt that the process already had opened up new avenues for learning from which they could continually benefit. We all agreed that development of the imagery would take time and effort, but that we were happy to work on it.

A couple of weeks later, Ann and I met at my office. Our primary purpose was to discuss her progress with developing images of proper jumping form. Ann reported steady improvement in awareness of her body and her actions during her jumps. She also noted that she had become more aware of her posture while walking and sitting throughout the day, a beneficial side effect of her jumping awareness. Her physiotherapist commented that Ann seemed to have decreased the strain on her back and neck, which had likely been due to poor posture. Ann indicated that she was finding it easier to remember her jumps and was even able to recall some of her best past performances clearly with her imagery.

I specifically asked about her ability to image her jump from planting her takeoff foot through landing in the pit, something that less than two months earlier was a "blank" in her mind. Ann stated that she did not yet have a completely flowing image of the whole thing, but that she could definitely image all parts of the jump itself in various segments. We did a short guided imagery session where I had Ann imagine some of her best attempts, including some of her past competitive performances. Afterward, as we discussed her imagery, Ann became excited by an insight.

A: Wow, when I image my best jumps, particularly my record jumps, there's something special in my takeoff! It's not just the power of them, even though my fitness is a big part of it. But, it's the way I take off. I really keep my body straight, and I don't move my arms until I am finally heading over the bar.

I want to capture Ann's observation in a tangible form, one that she can use as a guide. Hopefully, her imagery will produce some useful keys.

JS: Focus on the sensations. What are you doing on those jumps?

A: [making gestures and body movements] I'm powering off the ground, and then I hold it, hold it till I get to the absolute peak height. Yes, I hold to the peak of the vertical jump. I wait until then to follow through with my arm leading the arc of my body over the bar.

JS: How do you get yourself to hold like that?

A: I think I'm just really committed to getting great vertical lift. I'm not worried about the bar. I don't have to think about what I do for the rest of the jump. All the rest of it just follows. I think it's when I trust my body to follow my arm and head over the bar. And I can do that, because even the last little flick of my heels is automatic when I do it right.

JS: So, how would you set yourself up to hold your position? How can you purposefully create that?

A: I guess I just need to tell myself to hold it straight . . . [pauses for a few moments]. You know, what it feels like, it's like being sucked up through a funnel! You know, a funnel that's upside down [motions to illustrate]. I hit my mark, and I get sucked up into the funnel. The funnel holds me straight up, vertically [mimics body movements]. Yeah, like the funnel doesn't let me move any other way until I burst out the top.

JS: Wow, that's a fantastic image! I can't say that I've ever actually been sucked up through a funnel, but it's easy to imagine what you are talking about. I kind of get the feeling.

A: And that's the way I feel when I'm really fit and jumping well. It's almost like I leave the ground without so much gravity, like I'm being pulled up off the ground.

JS: So, it's not just the position of going through the funnel, but also the sense of getting extra lift?

A: Yeah, that's it. I can even imagine it right now as we're talking about it. I am sucked up through the upside-down funnel.

JS: Do you think that you might be able to use that image to remind yourself when you are jumping?

A: It already feels like I know it. I can use it.

I then guided Ann through some imagery using the funnel metaphor. She found it helpful immediately and decided to use it as a guide in her training. Over the course of the season, both she and her coach felt that the imagery was of great assistance in Ann's development as a high jumper. She matched her former best achievements and looked to be on her way to future improvements.

The marriage of mental imagery and physical skills can form a common ground for athletes, coaches, and sport psychologists. Even with highly accomplished performers, there are often new and helpful uses that imagery can serve in the process of skill development. Most athletes discover that they have good images of their events once they make a concerted effort to bring them into use. As in the case of Ann, application of imagery can open up new dimensions to training, preparation, and competition that breathe fresh life into a sport career.

REINFORCING DESIRED ATTITUDES OR PERSPECTIVES

I often use imagery as a way of helping an athlete connect a positive attitude or frame of mind with performance. Imagery can be used for helping the athlete establish a personal philosophy for participation in sport. This frame of mind or philsophical approach with imagery is quite different from the skill-development use just described. The development of images allows the sport psychologist and athlete to explore the perspective from which the athlete would ideally address performance and to develop a broader philosophical understanding of what the activity might mean to the person. The images that are established serve as rich reminders of attitudes and personal meaning.

For example, one athlete with whom I worked for several years enjoyed a particular scenic point in the mountains. Often when this athlete was troubled by a decision or felt caught up in the stress of training and performance details, he would go to this favorite spot to regain perspective. With a 360-degree view and sometimes more than 100 miles visibility across mountaintops, gazing down through valleys of grass, rocks, and trees, he would feel connected to nature and life. His immediate difficulties or decisions would diminish in importance by comparison. The sweeping panorama provided a spiritual connection as well as a psychological clearing of thought. He felt calm, powerful, and in control. From this perspective, he found it easier to address questions that he had and to make decisions that seemed right for him.

The scenic location provided an ideal image for the athlete to recall at other times as well. For instance, we built this image into his pre-performance routines. He would find a quiet spot, relax himself physically, and then imagine himself at the mountaintop. He would recall the views and experience the power, the calm, and the sense of wholeness. From this emotional, spiritual perspective he would then turn his attention to the competition at hand: What needed to be done? How was he going to approach the performance? How was he going to deal with any adversity?

It was easy to develop the image, because it was a place the athlete loved and enjoyed thinking about. We spent a few sessions where we specifically formed, expanded, and enriched the image. Thereafter, we used it in conjunction with other sessions, usually at the end of a technical series of images and prior to returning to normal conscious attention. It was an enduring image in that he did not tire being reminded of the place. The imagery was useful because it easily conjured up strong positive emotional feelings and clear thinking.

So often, performers get caught up in the details and practicalities of training and competition. There are a multitude of demands in conditioning and skill training, technical and strategic issues, and the competitive events themselves. Then there are issues of achieving certain marks, qualification standards, rankings, medals, awards, financial rewards, or social status. It is not difficult for athletes to get so locked up in such issues that they lose a sense of perspective over the whole performance endeavor. They may lose touch with why sport is important and how it can have meaning to them. Having powerful reminders of a broader and more positive perspective can ground athletes in the midst of all the hubbub of their sports.

In discussions with athletes, I consistently look for opportunities to examine broader issues of perspective and meaning. Invariably there are certain philosophical points that individual athletes can connect with readily. Either these are points they express on their own or ones they quickly latch onto from various examples that I might mention. The power of viewing performance from the perspective of personal gains from participation is that it provides both motivation and stress relief. Motivation comes from the sense of challenge, adventure, accomplishment, and fun, whereas stress relief comes from throwing off irrelevant expectations and worrying less about immediate successes and failures in favor of focus on long-term development and appreciation of ongoing experience. The perspective reinforces the challenges rather than the dangers, and intrinsic worth rather than possible worthlessness from not meeting achievement expectations.

Images have a powerful way of reflecting perspective and philosophical concepts. They connect with the richness of experience and the complexity of beliefs and feelings. The images we develop may be literal, such as an experience of great performance, or they may be more metaphorical, such as feelings of connectedness induced by a striking scene in nature. We may develop emotionally charged images of inspiration, challenge, freedom, joy, or uniqueness, or images of calmness, acceptance, serenity, or satisfaction. Often they will contain a pleasing combination of feelings and beliefs. The most important aspects in developing such images are the meanings that the images hold for the athlete and the effect that they have on that person.

I have also used images in a similar way to create what I call a *power image*. The power image is one that evokes the specific attitude and action feeling that is desired in performance situations. Athletes develop the image during a calm time when it is easy for them to describe the way they would like to be. As a starting point, we reflect on past experiences of great performance states. We may pick a past event when the athlete has felt at his or her best, feeling in control, clear minded, confident, full of energy, fit/healthy, and balanced. The feelings are labeled with some sort of easily remembered cue, such as a word, an object, or a physical action. The cue is associated with images that express the richness of the performance state through a process much like classical conditioning. In an imagery session, the state is repeatedly experienced and associated with the cue. Examples of good cues are simple but personal words (e.g., *powerful, in control, alive*) or physical actions (e.g., clench and release fist, shrug and drop shoulders, breathe deeply with slow exhale).

Often, a metaphor provides a rich cue to the desired state. One long jumper I worked with imagined the feeling of being a cheetah laying in wait at the end of the runway, loose and conserving energy for the chase. He imagined building tremendous speed toward the pit, like the big cat setting off after a gazelle. Then, as he hit the board, it was like the cheetah launching itself far and high to reach the shoulder blades of the fast-moving prey. The great thing about this metaphorical image was the connection of qualities imagined in the cheetah, such as looseness, power, speed, grace, and single-minded purpose, to the performance that the athlete wanted to create. To the degree that a metaphor holds important meaning for the athlete, it can be a powerful cue for performance.

Whatever the cues, the idea is to stimulate recall of images that hold a composite of the attitudes, emotions, and physical readiness the athlete wants in competition. Practiced sufficiently, it becomes part of the athlete's mental skills toolbox. The athlete can use the power image to mentally prepare for performance or to help reestablish his or her preferred frame of mind during competition. It is then not necessary to depend on external conditions to create the desired attitude, and the athlete does not have to make something up on the spot. The desired mindset is readily available in the form of cued imagery.

Power images should be fascinating and attractive to the athlete. If they are engaging, athletes will more likely think to attend to them. To capture attention away from the immediate sources of threat and distractions, it is necessary that the image connects to perspective, philosophy, and performance states in which athletes truly believe. The beauty of the image is that it can be an easily recalled memory bringing with it reminders of the desired state of mind. Once athletes are reminded of this state, they are usually motivated to choose it in place of less helpful thinking, feeling, and actions.

DEVELOPING A MENTAL MODEL FOR COMPETITION

I have found that one of the most powerful ways to use imagery with athletes is in building mental models for performance. Developing and rehearsing images of ideal technique, attitudes, and emotional states can create a template for competitive performance. These models are different from achievement goals or affirmations in that they define the process of the performance itself.

An example comes from the case of a world-ranked javelin thrower, Joe, who had experienced great success at some international events and markedly poor performances at others. The expectations of others played a large part in his inconsistent results. When he felt pressure from others' high expectations, a collection of anxiety reactions hindered his performance. When the expectations were low, the atmosphere of a big event seemed to bring out his best performances. During several sessions focused on dealing with expectations and that coping with competitive anxiety, it became clear that he had no consistent mental preparation routine and was often at a loss to establish a useful focus once distracted or anxious at a competition. My observation was that the lack of a consistent performance focus was at least as much to blame for poor performance as were the pressure and corresponding anxiety responses.

We discussed the task of creating a template for performance, including both physical and psychological elements. He was excited by the prospect, especially with the idea of working on something positive, as opposed to the negatives of his anxiety experiences. We spent a little time identifying important aspects of his technical model and considering the keys to a great throw. We also talked about attitude and the frame of mind in which he liked to perform. From these initial discussions, I asked that he spend some time on his own thinking through his best performances and imagining throwing well, so that we could begin with what he already knew. We then met to work on his mental model of performance.

Joe: I've given this all a lot of thought, and really imagining my throwing, and feelings, and what I want to feel. You know, it's strange, but I realized that I don't get an image of the javelin. I mean, I can get a clear image of someone else throwing, and I can imagine myself on video throwing, but when I think of actually throwing, I can't see the javelin. I thought I could image pretty well, but maybe this is a problem.

Imagery is rarely as complete as people think it should be. It is common to hear about all sorts of imagery "problems." Usually, it is only necessary to provide some normalizing reassurance. In this case, Joe's difficulty in visualizing the javelin when imaging himself throwing is worth noting, because it likely relates to his information processing and, therefore, the mental model we wish to create. Given past descriptions of his images, it is most probable that his visual imagery is actually quite good. His comments are worth pursuing.

JS: Do you mean that as you mentally view yourself from the outside, like on videotape, you can't see yourself holding the javelin?

J: No, I can see that just fine. It's when I imagine myself in the process of throwing that I don't see it. I'm on the runway, and I'm throwing, but I can't see it.

JS: Well, what do you see of the javelin when you actually throw?

J: You mean when I'm actually doing it, like in competition?

JS: Yes. As you head down the runway, prepare to throw, and complete the throw, what do you see of the javelin?

J: When I'm throwing . . . oh, maybe just the tip. You might see the point in the run-up, and then after release. I get it. So, you're saying that when I'm imagining doing a throw I don't see the javelin because I don't really see it when I really throw.

JS: Right, you don't see much of the javelin until after you throw it. Other than keeping your head in position, basically watching where you are going on the runway, and generally looking out to the landing area, vision isn't involved much at all. And you certainly don't look at the javelin during the throwing action.

J: All right, that makes sense . . . [pauses to get started again]. Even though I've been thinking about it a lot, I'm still having trouble figuring out what I'm doing when I'm throwing well. But, maybe I've hit on something. There is something definitely different at my best comps, and when I'm throwing really well at any time. I think the word I'd use to describe how I feel when I throw well would be *aware*. I tend to have an amazing awareness of my body. On one hand it's almost as though I'm outside of myself and watching myself throw, but on the other hand it's not, because I don't see a visual picture of myself throwing. Wow, does that make any sense? Maybe if you think about it really hard [laughs].

Joe has again given clues that even though he may have perfectly good visual sense and imagery, it is probably not a crucial part of his throwing model. It is tempting to jump in and help him come to a conclusion on kinesthetic sense, but the process of discovery is moving along just fine on its own.

J: I think what happens is that I'm really aware of how I feel. When I think back on my great throws, I remember how they feel exceptionally well. I don't mean they feel exceptionally good—well, they do—but what I mean is that I have an exceptional memory of the feeling. I can close my eyes and actually feel the throw. Yes, that's it! The awareness that I have is definitely in relation to "feel." I remember it vividly because I am so aware of the feel when I'm doing it. Or, I throw well when I am concentrating on the feel, and the feeling makes me aware. I'm not sure what comes first, but it's all there.

Although it might be interesting to try to unravel the causal relationships in Joe's experience, there is little need to pursue it here. The difficulty in accurately ordering the phenomena might confuse the issue, and there is no reason to get into a philosophical exploration of experience. The significant thing is that Joe has recognized that he has a tremendous kinesthetic awareness of his actions during his best throws, and he has vivid images that he can easily recall from those throws. Now it is important to ascertain whether this kinesthetic awareness is indeed a feature unique to good throwing.

JS: And your disappointing competitions?

J: No feeling, no awareness, no concentration. Just anxious and distracted. Trying to force it, but not getting any feel. I try really hard, and I keep trying to think about my arm carry, and my hips, and where I plant my foot, and being active and dynamic and all that, but I can't keep the concentration. And I don't feel it.

JS: So this "feel" that you are describing should be a central part of the mental model we are building.

J: For sure. The question is, how can I get this feeling? [He pauses, thinking of the answer to his own question.] I honestly think that a big part of achieving it is improving my concentration. I just need to be able to concentrate, at least from the time that I get to my cross step, right before I throw. That's the stage where I turn and close my hips, keep a long arm, and then smash it all through. If I can concentrate and be aware of the feel, then I can do all of that. And all that equals a great throw. But a lot of times, even if I'm concentrating at the start, I forget by the time I'm ready to throw. I just don't concentrate very well.

JS: Concentration is simply the process of paying attention to something, without being distracted by something else. You just need to have something that captures your attention and helps you throw. That's what the mental model is for. We put in the elements that help you throw well, like the feel of that sequence of throwing actions you just stated, and you practice the model until it is easy to use in competition. Rather than waiting and hoping that you might get the feeling awareness, you train yourself to create it under whatever circumstances you encounter at competition.

J: Okay! I like that! Let's do the model.

We then spent time breaking down the skill from a technical, biomechanical standpoint to determine key elements of the throwing technique. Although this exercise was analytical, I made it clear that the mental model was to provide a descriptive or prescriptive technical guide for performance so that analysis would be minimized during the throw. Once we had listed a detailed flow of movements for the whole throwing process, Joe came up with a few cue words that he felt would remind him of the action. I emphasized that the descriptions and the cue words should stimulate images of the desired motions. As might be expected, there was a good match when the words evoked kinesthetic images (e.g., stretch, rotate). The final technical model was the imagery of correct throwing actions, with a few descriptors to help stimulate the imagery, guide technical focus, and keep awareness on kinesthetic feeling.

Joe was an accomplished and knowledgeable thrower, yet he still had his coach evaluate the technical content of the throwing model to make certain that it matched the form they were aiming to achieve. With less experienced athletes, it may be best to involve the coach from the beginning. Except for minor adjustments, Joe's technical model was just a reminder of skills he already possessed. The model, of course, is likely to be refined as the athlete works with it. For example, during the time he was preparing for the major event of that particular year, Joe made a number of changes to his cue words as he honed his images.

We did some guided imagery sessions using the technical model. Joe was readily able to imagine his ideal throw when encouraged to be aware of kinesthetic feel and when led by key movement descriptions and cue words. Once we were comfortable with the guided imagery process, I made a cassette tape of a technical imagery session. Joe began listening to the tape several times per week, particularly before technical training sessions.

The next step was to set the technical model within an emotional context. The objective was to create a mental model of action and attitude that would guide competitive performance. I usually begin by having athletes describe the psychological states that they believe help them perform well. We then consider the best performances that they have experienced in the past and begin to identify psychological elements to include in the overall performance model. Joe and I met for this purpose, and excerpts of our discussion follow.

JS: Joe, tell me how you want to be during competition. What attitude do you want to have, what emotions do you want to feel?

J: You mean besides my technical focus on my throw? My mental state?

JS: Yes. Describe your ideal mental performance state.

J: Well, I think that it is really important to be pretty hyped. You have to get fired up to be explosive, to accelerate into the foot plant and smash it all through. I try to get myself pumped before I start my run up.

JS: I see. So what is the attitude that you want to have?

J: I suppose "aggressive." I've got to look out to the mark [a spot marking the distance that Joe wants to throw] and just think of the power I've got to put into the javelin to make it fly there. I've got to get myself concentrating and gather up all my energy and make the throw explode.

As Joe continued, claiming that he wanted to be in a forceful, high-energy state during his competition, it struck me that he was describing correlates of his anxiety states and "choking" performances. I felt he was reporting an implicit belief in the need for pressure and intensity without considering whether or not it actually facilitated his throwing. I decided to challenge his suppositions by having him compare them to the psychological states that he actually had experienced at his best international competitions.

JS: OK, that's interesting. So, at the World Champs [his best international competition] you must have really gotten fired up. Tell me more about how you felt in that meet.

J: Well, that one was different. I was more relaxed. I mean, I was lucky because nobody thought I would do anything special. Most of the international competitors didn't know me, and there wasn't any pressure.

JS: How would you describe your attitude?

J: I was just calm, and I focused on getting a good throw. I was happy to be competing at that competition, and I just wanted to get the international experience. I was loose, and I knew that I was throwing pretty well. I just focused on my throwing, and it came out really good.

JS: But you would have thrown better if you had been more intense, under pressure, and fired up?

J: No. Hmm . . . no, because that's the way I was at [the Olympic Games]. And I choked. I don't even like thinking about it.

JS: Then let's think of something nicer. Think of all your best throws at major competitions. How would you describe your psychological state when you have been successful?

J: Actually, overall, my best competitions have been when I am more calm and relaxed and feeling more in control. I'm still motivated to throw well, but I'm not under so much pressure.

We continued to explore the attitudes and emotional feelings Joe had experienced in his past successful performances. We began to create a composite that might define a model for his desired performance state. During this process, Joe struck upon an image that seemed to encapsulate the state he wanted.

J: You know what I love best? I love coming out to training on summer evenings. You know, it's twilight and there is just that little cool change [in the temperature]. And the sun kind of makes the trees yellow-orange, and the grass looks really green. It just feels like the javelin flies out of my hand and sails forever. It's like gravity isn't as strong or something. And it is peaceful, and I really love to throw.

JS: That's great. I can imagine it there, as you describe it. How would you depict that mental state?

J: Fresh and loose. Happy and eager to throw. I feel like I belong, the field is mine. Yes, that's right, I belong and everything is fine. I don't have to make any certain distance or anything. It's just for me. I'm a thrower and I'm getting down to business. And it's just such a great thing to be able to do.

JS: How well do you think you would throw in a major competition if you had that frame of mind?

J: Oh, if I could be like that, and not panicked out and stuff, I figure it'd be awesome. I could really throw like that.

JS: Then you have found the match to your technical model.

We spent time further identifying the emotional and attitudinal components that Joe wanted for his performance model. Some exploratory imagery of his best competitions and the training scene helped refine the desired mental state. We also developed cue words and phrases that matched up with emotional images and could be used as simple reminders. The next step was to integrate the desired attitudes and emotional states with the technical model into the full performance model. Now when I guided Joe through his performance imagery, his desired attitudinal and emotional state served as the psychological context for his technical model. He would recall the mental state with cue words and images and then imagine executing his technical model within that perspective. Once we were satisfied with the content, I made a cassette tape of guided imagery. Joe used the tape to practice applying his whole mental model in preparation for the major international championship that year.

The mental model proved to be a valuable aspect of Joe's preparation. He listened to the tape regularly in the six weeks he was overseas before the championships. He became readily familiar with the feelings of belonging, calmness, control, and enjoyment, coupled with the execution of fine technique. Joe mentally rehearsed performing according to the mental model at the championships themselves. He listened to his tape the night before his final and found that he was able to sleep well in the confidence that he was well prepared. Even on the bus transporting the javelin competitors from the warm-up track to the competition venue, Joe again listened to his tape in order to block out the distraction of being confined with his edgy group and to remind himself of his desired focus (that was his last opportunity to listen to the tape, because competitors are not allowed to take any tape or CD player onto the field during the competition).

Joe's performance was outstanding. He won a championships medal with a personal-best throw. His consistency was excellent, producing the best series of six throws in the competition. Joe reported with particular pleasure that he was able to create the performance state defined by his mental model almost exactly. He felt entirely present in the moment. Joe felt that he belonged. He was calm, in control, and positively energized. He found it easy to lock into the feel of his throw and translate the power of his motion into the flight of the javelin. Joe was enormously pleased with his accomplishment and felt he had taken a decided victory over his past anxieties and inconsistency. Most important, he was certain that *he* had created the difference and felt confident that he had the strategies and skill to create it again in the future.

CONCLUDING THOUGHTS

I find the process of using imagery with athletes to be tremendously challenging and rewarding. There is no way that one person can share the exact perceptions and images of another. It usually takes much patience and probing to help athletes evoke and explore their imagery. It requires further work to develop ways to communicate with them about perceived and imagined experiences. But the process is endlessly fascinating. There is so much to learn from each athlete's unique experiences and particular perspectives. It is enthralling to observe athletes' development as they unite the images they have with their behavior in the field. The communication that evolves between the sport psychologist and the athlete in order to explore the complexity of perceptions, actions, and emotions contributes significantly to many other aspects of the professional interaction. For instance, if an athlete and I have spent time working closely together on imagery, it seems easier to come to understandings of personal issues. The precedence of exploring psychological states in depth is already set and is framed in a positive light.

Imagery is intriguing for its close relationship to perception and action. It is such a rich memory system, matching the complexity of information presented by the environment and contained in the execution of motor skills. Images bind personal thoughts and emotions to experience, and they have qualities far beyond simple stimulus/response propositions. The impact of metaphors attests to the meanings that images can convey. Imagery can be creative, allowing one to experience attitudes and actions mentally in ways that have not yet been encountered in real performance. When an athlete is capable of enacting imagined characteristics, those characteristics can serve as templates to guide new expressions in performance. For all these reasons, imagery is a valuable and exciting tool for sport psychology practice.

REFERENCES

Feltz, D.L., & Landers, D.M. (1983). The effects of mental practice on motor skill learning and performance: A meta-analysis. *Journal of Sport Psychology, 5,* 25-57.

Freud, S. (1965). *The interpretation of dreams* (J. Strachey, Trans.). New York: Basic Books. (Original published in 1900)

Graham, H. (1995). *Mental imagery in health care: An introduction to therapeutic practice.* London: Chapman & Hall.

Moran, A.P. (1996). *The psychology of concentration in sport performers: A cognitive analysis.* East Sussex, UK: Psychology Press.

Wolpe, J. (1973). *The practice of behavior therapy* (2nd ed.). New York: Pergamon Press.

Wundt, W. (1896). *Lectures on human and animal psychology.* New York: Sonnenschein.

CHAPTER 7

TARGETING FUTURES: GOAL SETTING FOR PROFESSIONAL SPORTS

Daryl B. Marchant
Victoria University

Given that goal setting is a mainstream sport psychology intervention, it is hardly surprising that many book chapters and journal articles have been published on the topic. Researchers frequently report on goal-setting outcomes (did the goal-setting program produce a significant improvement in performance?) but spend little time in discussing the process of goal setting. Journal space is limited and often precludes an extended description of what took place between the practitioner and client when working on goals. Process issues are wide ranging and include educating clients about goal setting, organizing goal-setting programs, carrying out face-to-face goal consultations, and handling goal failures. The first aim of this chapter is to present many of the subtleties of carrying out goal-setting consultations with professional athletes.

A number of excellent book chapters in applied sport psychology texts cover such issues as theories of goal setting, guidelines in setting goals, and potential problems in goal setting (e.g., Burton, 1993; Danish et al., 1992; Gould, 1998; Harris and Harris, 1984; Weinberg, 1996). I expect that the majority of applied practitioners are familiar with such texts and are well-versed in the principles of goal setting. A second aim of this chapter is to demonstrate that integrating the principles of goal setting into consultations is an important, but relatively small, part of making goal setting work with professional athletes. Having a sound working knowledge of the goal-setting literature and the mechanics of goal setting is essential and provides a solid foundation for setting goals with professional athletes. Goal setting is also about interpersonal skills, timing, creative thinking, and overcoming logistical limitations.

The third aim of this chapter is to provide an insider's viewpoint of working for a professional sporting organization. To achieve this aim, I provide a range of examples of goal setting with an Australian Rules football team over a one-year cycle using a diary approach. The diary is chronologically structured to emphasize the importance of planning and organization, and it is interspersed with narratives of individual consultations, comments, interpretations, and personal reflections. A working knowledge of Australian Rules football is not essential; the issues discussed here should have general application. The chapter is subdivided into two sections: the first relates to individual goal setting and the second to team goal setting. Other issues discussed in this chapter include planning, education, feedback, communication, using roving goals, triangular consensus, and flexibility.

Finally, my experiences, like those of many applied sport psychologists, are replete with successes and failures. I have attempted to present an authentic and open account of carrying out goal-setting work with professional football players. I encourage readers to examine the cases and issues presented, use what they find helpful, and learn from my mistakes.

INDIVIDUAL GOAL SETTING

Diary December 12

Themes: *Making the most of opportunities, dislike for written assignments, resistance*

I seize an unexpected opportunity to get the individual goal-setting program started by distributing individual goal-setting sheets while we travel by bus between the Australian Institute of Sport and an alpine training facility. This is early in the preseason period, approximately four months before the commencement of the official Australian Rules football season (March-September). The players are familiar with goal setting, having been required to complete individual goal sheets at the commencement of each of the past four seasons. My tenure at the club included the two previous seasons, and thus, much of my work in goal setting was refining what was already in place. I came to the camp prepared to distribute the goal-setting sheets when a suitable opportunity arose, knowing that the majority of players were familiar with the process and that minimal player briefing was necessary. Unfettered access to the entire list of 42 players is rare. I congratulate myself for being prepared and making the most of this unexpected opportunity. My briefing goes something like this:

> DM: This bus trip offers a perfect opportunity for you guys [players] to start thinking about your individual goals for the forthcoming season. As in previous years, you will receive a goal-setting sheet that has an information section, a preseason goals section, and an in-season goals section. I would like you to complete these sheets adding as much detail as possible about your plan for making these goals a reality. I've included a couple of examples to help you. Your goals may be fitness or skill oriented, tactical, or psychological—whichever you feel is important for you at this stage of your career. I will collect the completed sheets once we arrive at the alpine village, type them up, and return them to you as soon as possible. Are there any questions?

I anticipate getting virtually all the players to complete this first stage of their goal setting quickly and efficiently. At the end of the bus trip, I receive 24 of a possible 42 completed goal-setting sheets. Players offer various explanations for not completing the sheets (e.g., "I need time to think," "I'd rather do it with you personally," "I just wanted to relax on the bus"). The poor response rate is frustrating but should be balanced against my not giving them prior warning about doing their goals on the bus. I find myself consciously having to check the impulse to pester players into completing the goal-setting sheets. Despite the expectations of the organization, and my own, I prefer not to state explicitly that goal setting is compulsory. I view noncompliance as a form of resistance. Another, more subtle form of resistance is the athlete who does not take goal setting seriously by rushing through the process without due consideration. Noncompliance in a goal-setting exercise raises a red flag that should not be ignored. Potential reasons for noncompliance include a lack of knowledge about the fundamentals of goal setting (e.g., SMART goals—specific, measurable, achievable, realistic, and time phased); negative experiences with goal setting previously; inadequate literacy and writing skills; poor working relationship with the sport psychologist; and reluctance to share goals. Sport psychologists, especially those working with a large group of athletes, need to consider carefully, first, why noncompliance takes place, and second, what steps can be taken to reduce it. Sometimes a personal follow-up is needed to determine the reasons for noncompliance. Caution needs to be exercised, because players may be defensive about doing goal setting and may view this as checking up on them. The reluctance of some players to complete written work is symptomatic of the response of many professional athletes to assigned written work. Written work may be interpreted as homework and thus may evoke negative memories of school days, or it may be seen as a further impingement on their already busy lives. For this reason, I rarely use homework assignments or "canned" sport psychology material with Australian Rules players.

Diary December 21

Themes: *compliance and resistance, advantages of doing goal setting as a team sport psychologist, priorities and balance, professional guilt*

After making an announcement to the team that I had most, but not all, of the goal-setting sheets back, Brian approached me and requested that we complete his goals together. For individual goal-setting consultations, I come prepared with the player's goals from the previous season and any relevant results or statistics pertaining to those goals. I often review the goals at the start of a consultation, because this provides continuity and something tangible to discuss. Unachieved goals may remain important to the athlete, and successful past goals may still be priority areas. The consultation with Brian is held in the selection room that doubles as my office. This office, although not exclusively mine, is suitable because it is close to other player facilities and is generally quiet enough to conduct uninterrupted consultations and interventions where a quiet environment is essential (e.g., when using imagery or anxiety-management techniques).

B: Sorry for not completing the goal-setting sheet on the bus. I couldn't concentrate with so many other players around.

DM: That's OK; not everyone is ready to think through their goals at the same time. I have your goals here from last year. Perhaps we can start by briefly reviewing these and discussing whether any of these goals are still relevant for you.

B: Yes; well, last year things were going well. I was achieving my goals until I got injured, and then I kind of lost it a bit.

DM: Lost it a bit? How so?

B: I found it pretty frustrating after doing such a good preseason to lose a lot of that work. People kept saying my good form before the injury was due to the chick I was living with. Yeah, she was in training too, but I had made up my mind to have a really big preseason way before that. I lost a lot of fitness while I was out, and when I came back I struggled a bit. [Brian pauses; I keep quiet and wait from him to continue.] I kind of got negative and lost sight of my plans and goals while I was injured.

DM: Perhaps we could look at breaking the season into four-week blocks and set goals together once a month.

B: That would be good. . . . I much prefer to sit down and go through these goals together.

DM: What will be important for you over this first four-week block?

B: I still want to work on improving my kicking, but I want to wait till official training starts again [after the Christmas break] to get into this. Once the season starts, it's really hard to find the time to work on kicking.

DM: I realize kicking was an issue for you last year, but what specific subskills within kicking need the most work?

B: Mainly kicking on the run and being able to hit targets at top speed.

DM: What strategies can you use to improve this skill, and how can you measure your improvement?

B: I need to spend more special-skills sessions on kicking. Tony [assistant coach] has been really good; he has set up a video analysis of my action and given me feedback on what parts of my technique need work. Have you seen that kicking skills test with the circles he [Tony] uses to test our ability to hit targets on the run?

DM: Yes, I've seen the test; it's really game-specific the way Tony runs it. So, you're saying Tony is an important person in supporting you in this area? [Brian nods his head, and I continue.] That's terrific. What specifically will you do in the next four weeks to improve this skill?

This last part of the consultation reflects my desire to help Brian make the four-week kicking goal specific, process-based, and measurable. The rest of this consultation was spent on related issues, such as developing specific goals and targets, using imagery to supplement physical practice, finding a training partner with similar goals, discussing working with a coach to develop relevant kicking drills, and planning a retest for Brian on Tony's kicking test. After going through two other short-term goals, we concluded the consultation and made a time to meet the following week.

At the beginning of the consultation, Brian quickly moved from the specific question about last season's goals to the bigger issues of coping with injury, a relationship, and staying focused. Working through goals is often relatively nonthreatening for the athlete and can raise other issues beyond the boundaries of performance enhancement work. I could have explored the comment Brian made about the perception of others that he was playing well because of the influence of his new girlfriend, an athlete herself. When I started out in applied sport psychology, I probably would have responded directly to Brian by verbalizing my support for him and his interpretation of why he had such good form. On this occasion, I felt that a conversation about his relationship with his girlfriend would have been an unhelpful and perhaps complicated diversion.

Similarly, I chose not to explore directly Brian's comment about getting negative and losing sight of his plans and goal. When Brian talked about "losing it" when injured, I immediately realized I should have been more attuned to his situation and helped him adjust his goals accordingly much earlier. Now, six months later, he was in a more positive frame of mind, and I wanted to keep the consultation moving and focused on the forthcoming season. I was well aware of what went wrong for Brian the previous season and did not want to dredge all that up again. In hindsight, perhaps this was a mistake; Brian might have been signaling his desire to explore what went wrong in detail. Consultations with athletes are laden with opportunities to explore. By failing to examine an athlete's comment for latent meaning, or how he felt about last year's experiences, I might have missed something. Fortunately, Brian reacted positively to my suggestion that we set goals at four-week intervals as a means of providing better support for him when problems arise. As I learned early in my career, if I miss something athletes say that is important to them, the issue will almost certainly come up again later.

One clear advantage of being a team sport psychologist for several years is the time to build a fairly intimate knowledge, at least professionally, of the players. As team psychologist, I have the opportunity to interact with and observe my clients in a variety of contexts. Working with a team over an extended period in social and professional settings provides a continuity to the goal-setting process that fee-for-service consultancies often lack. For example, the club's welfare officer had previously told me that Brian did not have a lot of close friends and really responded to individual attention. Brian himself provided another insight into his preferences and needs when he stated, "I much prefer to sit down and go through these goals together." Here, Brian is implying that he is not resistant to working together; on the contrary, he wants the personal touch of face-to-face collaborative work. From my perspective, what started as passive resistance on the bus resulted in compliance when goal setting was reframed from an individual written task to a joint task.

I responded to Brian's request for help by committing myself to monthly goal-setting meetings. I believe I made the right decision to increase my contact time with Brian, and he responded positively in subsequent months in his training form, attitude (based on unsolicited comments by coaches), playing form, and enthusiasm for doing goal setting. Increasing contact time with an athlete may not always be the best course of action. In working with a squad of approximately 50 players and coaches, overcommitment can create problems. Goal setting is one of many responsibilities that a team sport psychologist performs. I have certainly found myself both investing too much time in some aspects of my program and concentrating on particular players at the expense of others. Similarly, maintaining a balanced workload as a team sport psychologist can be difficult, especially when the job is combined with other responsibilities (e.g., full-time university position, family, and other clients). An infinite number of issues can combine to make the management of a consultancy a very challenging task. Am I spending too much time on goal setting? How do I arrange my time to make the consultancy time effective? Does my commitment equal my capacity to successfully carry out the promised services? Do I prioritize my consultations when time is short? What needs of mine are being met by engaging in a consultancy? Countless such questions arise that I typically deal with in one of three ways: (a) carry out a periodic assessment of the consultancy or have the organization carry out an independent assessment, (b) consult with a mentor or professional supervisor to discuss specific problems as they arise, and (c) develop a network of other practicing applied sport practitioners to discuss general issues of consultancies.

Diary April 29

Themes: *goal failure, difficult client, personality types, suboptimal consulting*

A consultation with Andrew was initiated by one of the coaches, who asked me to speak with Andrew about his poor form. I then solicited a meeting with Andrew to talk about his goals and form. Following up on coach requests that I meet with a player, or sometimes setting up a meeting of my own volition are an accepted part of my role. Nevertheless, the dynamics of such meetings can be vastly different from the self-referred consultation. The player might be thinking, What have I done wrong that I have to see the sport psychologist? Or possibly, The coach has set this meeting up, so I'd better be there.

Andrew entered the room not saying much and demonstrating guarded body language

DM: Have a seat. How have things been going?

A: OK. [Pause; I allow time for Andrew to elaborate but he remains silent.]

DM: I was thinking now that we've played five games it would be a good time to sit down and review your goals and where you're at.

I choose not to mention that the coach has referred Andrew to me. I generally find that when players presume I have initiated the contact they are less likely to demonstrate passive-aggressive behavior. By showing his reluctance to meet with me and starting the consultation in a taciturn manner, Andrew is openly playing out his resistance. To me, this is preferable to the athlete who goes through the motions because he knows his coach has had a hand in bringing about the consultation. There are no pretensions or games, and the consultation can proceed with the player (possibly) feeling resistant, but at least not controlled or coerced.

A: I'm only just getting fully fit now after that hammy [hamstring tear].

DM: So, what are you working on at the moment?

A: Just getting my touch back and getting involved.

DM: Good; now, which of your goals are you working on at the moment?

A: Trying to improve my aerobic fitness to my target.

DM: Which is?

A: I can't remember exactly.

DM: How about your body fats? You were aiming for a total on eight sites of 50 mm.

A: Well, they are a bit high at the moment; about 65, I think. With the hammy problem it was difficult to get them down, but I'm trying.

DM: Good. In what ways are you trying to get them down?

The tone of this conversation, from my perspective, is direct, challenging, and a little confrontational. Andrew is not performing well and is clearly not achieving his goals. He is not being especially candid about admitting to his poor form and is a little elusive when I attempt to direct him toward discussing his goals specifically. The question about his specific target for aerobic fitness is aimed at checking how conversant he is with is own goals. In pursuing the body fats issue, I am assessing whether Andrew is serious about his goals and whether he is prepared to be honest with me. In my early days as a consultant, I was, at times, not challenging enough, perhaps being concerned that I would offend someone. With experience and confidence, I have become more direct with clients when I detect a discrepancy between what I am hearing from them and other sources of information. For example, Andrew stated that his body fat score was currently 65 mm, 15 above his goal of 50 mm. I already knew that his current body fat was actually 75 mm, not 65 mm as he suggested. There seemed little value in confronting him with this information, so I simply made a mental note of the inaccuracy. Although it is important for athletes to perceive the sport psychologist as supportive of their needs, one must be wary of being seen as naive or ingenuous.

There is much to be learned about athletes outside of face-to-face consultations. Information gathered in real-life settings or from psychometric tools is often useful in corroborating or challenging what I hear in consultations. At the time of meeting with Andrew, I knew that there was some talk among coaches, and especially among players, about Andrew's laziness. I frequently administer the 16 Personality Factor Questionnaire (16 PF) (Cattell, Cattell, and Cattell, 1994), and I was well aware that Andrew had scored low (2.5 on a 10-point scale) on self-control, the fifth of the global second-order factors. Andrew had also scored very low on the first-order factors—rule consciousness and perfectionism—both of which load on self-control.

Athletes like Andrew, who have low scores on self-control without associated positive features (such as high scores on reasoning and ego strength or low scores on liveliness) are, in my experience, difficult clients. This combination of scores indicates a person who is unconcerned about personal standards and has an underdeveloped conscience (Cattell, 1989). As an aside, the 16 PF is the only psychometric tool that I routinely administer to athletes. I use the 16 PF because it has strong psychometric properties and gives me an additional insight into the personality of athletes beyond other valuable sources of information (e.g., interview, observation, significant others, and face-to-face contact). Athletes who have the opposite of Andrew's 16 PF profile are often excellent goal setters who seem naturally inclined to follow classic goal-setting techniques. As Cattell suggested, these people (e.g., Brendan, in the following case) are persistent and conscientious and have strong willpower, despite being somewhat compulsive and rigid. These characteristics are generally helpful in attending to the mechanics of goal setting—keeping goals specific, measurable, time phased, and realistic.

The exchange with Andrew clearly demonstrates that goal setting will not work where there is not an open, honest, and mutually respectful working alliance, something that Andrew and I did not have. Putting time into developing quality relationships with clients is critical and in some respects is more important than many of the other professional skills we bring to a consultation. Compare Andrew with Brendan, who has the opposite 16 PF profile. Brendan sets his own process goals without the need for goal-setting training or assistance.

REVIEWING GOALS

DM: Since the season is almost half over, I thought we should sit down and review your goals. How many senior games have you played so far this year?

B: I've played in the Ansett Cup and 6 of the first 10 games.

DM: In monitoring your goals, how mindful are you of them?

B: I have my goals that I know are there and I'm always working on them. Some of them are difficult to measure, but they're important to me. I like to be organized, and I'm thinking that over the next month I'll spend two hours every Wednesday morning just specifically on my goals.

DM: Are you satisfied with the goals you chose back in December?

B: Generally, yes. I have a couple that are really central to the game plan that the coaches are big on anyway.

DM: Thanks. I like to ask these types of questions to assess how the goal-setting program is going. Let's work through your goals one by one and talk about how you've done on each of them. How about improved foot kicking? You talked last time about being conscious of holding your hands lower on the ball and dropping the ball lower to the ground.

B: Well, my kicking has been a whole lot better than last season, especially in the accuracy area. . . . Doing the extra work with Tony [assistant coach] has really helped in getting my technique sorted out, although I still need to keep working on it.

DM: How would you rate or assess your improvement?

B: I can't really measure it statistically, but I know I'm hitting more targets. . . . I don't worry if I can't measure all my goals, because it's nigh on impossible to fully address and monitor each of them.

DM: Yes, I agree. Now, how about those mental aspects, such as aggression, confidence, enthusiasm, and taking risks? Do I remember you saying that you wanted to transfer your ability to do these things at the reserve level to the senior level?

B: I'd say those last three areas have been fine. I would rate my aggression, though, as only being poor to moderate.

DM: How can you improve in this area over the last three months of the season?

B: To me, it's partly doing all those little physical things off the ball, like tackling hard, shepherding [i.e., blocking], and being prepared to make body contact if it helps the team. I've also got to talk more out there and make the most of situations when my opponent is down. A few weeks ago I had the perfect opportunity to let a [opposition] player really have it. He shirked a situation [i.e., avoided body contact], and instead of getting stuck into him and really nailing him, I let it go.

DM: So, you're saying aggression is both physical and verbal?

B: Yes, the two go together. Playing hard and having intensity sends a clear message to opponents. I don't want to back off in the verbal area because the two [physical and verbal] are all part of one package. By being more aggressive, I gain respect from teammates as well.

DM: What specifically are you aiming at doing in this aggression area in the coming month?

B: I want to win that weekly one percenter award [award that goes to the player with the highest number of physical contributions in that week's game]. I also want to move into the top five overall on the team for average one percenters per game.

DM: Where are you presently?

B: I'm averaging 35 points per game. I should be able to get over 40 points per game if I concentrate on this area more.

DM: OK; that is a clear goal and is measurable, but what practical things can you do to improve your physical aggression?

B: I guess I could spend some time watching some of those highlights videos of big hits and things, tackles and the sort of stuff we've used pre-match before.

DM: How about if I talk to the video guys and get them to run a copy off for you? If you're interested, we could do some imagery work like we have done before, but this time, the scripts could be tackling, chasing, bumping, and spoiling scenarios. What do you think?

B: Yes; that would be great. The only problem is time, but I'm sure I could manage to fit in at least one meeting [imagery intervention session] a week.

The session continued in this vein, talking about process goals and skill development (Brendan's physical aggression). We then discussed process and outcome goals for improving his verbal aggression.

Some athletes, such as Brendan, really respond well to the fundamentals of goal setting. Arguably, these people will set goals with or without a sport psychologist. I like to think that the structure and expertise I add is icing on the cake for these types of athletes. Not every goal an athlete sets is measurable. Physical fitness goals and some skill goals are generally easier to measure than those that are more abstract, such as mental and tactical goals.

One of the basic laws of goal setting is to make goals measurable. Although experts nearly always emphasize the importance of measuring goals, as Brendan states, "it is nigh on impossible to fully address and monitor each of them." With individual goals, I am prepared to let players set goals that are not easily measured as long as they have a process for turning the goal into reality. With Brendan, I chose to focus on what aggression meant for him and on ways to improve in this area rather than on measuring aggression with a questionnaire or rating scale.

Diary August 20

Themes: *goal for finals, setting realistic goals, competition goals, fluid goal setting*

I convened an educational session for a group of younger players to help them prepare for the upcoming series of finals matches. I asked Blair, a former champion player who had a reputation as a top performer in big games, to talk about issues such as anxiety, match preparation, self-talk, and goal setting. Blair's comments were helpful in showing how goal setting during matches can be a fluid process depending on what is required in different circumstances.

DM: To what extent have you used goal setting in finals matches?

B: On a number of occasions, especially when I had a job to do for the team.

DM: Can you describe for the players how you used goal setting in those matches?

B: Don't expect too much of yourself. You can have dreams that can turn into goals; you want to be the best player, or play well in the finals. I had dreams about being the Premiership captain. I went to bed saying, Don't dream it, I don't want to think about what's going to happen, too far away, and sometimes that is very hard. You really have to try and force yourself just to say, I don't want to be the best player on the ground, I just want to do my job—which is easier, because only one player can be the best player.

DM: So, you are saying to keep your goals realistic?

B: Exactly. The odds are against it [being best on the ground]. If that is what you're aiming for, you're probably not going to achieve it. You're already below the line, and already in a negative. Just aim to be as normal as possible, just to do your job and be a good team player. By doing the basics you'll probably achieve it and do better.

DM: How can these unrealistic expectations affect you?

B: Imagine it's quarter time, and you had these expectations to be one of the five best players on your team, and you aren't getting there. How much pressure is on you? The pressure of the game, the pressure of your family and friends, and then you've got this pressure to be the best player on the side. You don't need pressure. You just need to be normal.

DM: Can you give us an example of how you set goals and achieved them?

B: We were playing [opposition team]. I got put on [opposing player], who was actually cutting us up. Once I was

> given the task of playing on him, my first goal was to keep close personal contact to him on all occasions and not stop harassing him till I had seen him off the ground. The most important area of advice I can give you is to set yourself small goals [e.g., keep close contact], achieve them because they are possible to achieve, and then reward yourself. I was constantly talking to myself, saying, Gee, you know the ball came into [opposing player's] area and I stopped him from getting it. I've won the first battle. The ball came again and I stopped him again. All of a sudden, you start to feel good about yourself.

Goals can be self-defeating when they are unrealistic. Setting and achieving small goals often provide the impetus and confidence for taking on bigger and more challenging goals. Blair started with the small but achievable goals of keeping close personal contact with his opponent and stopping him from getting the ball on the next occasion it came into their area.

Blair also talked about how dreams can easily be confused with goals. Certainly dreams are important for all athletes (see Rotella, 1990, for a discussion on starting with a dream). Goal setting, however, is the down-to-earth reality of working dreams into something that is manageable and achievable. In this way dreams and goals can be complementary.

Hearing Blair talk about how he successfully used goals in competition made me aware that sometimes I have had football players focus on training and practice goals without necessarily helping them identify important match-day goals. Probably one of the best times to talk to professional football players about relevant match-day goals is the day preceding competition. At this stage, they usually know where they are playing, possible opponents, and team tactics. Furthermore, the day before competition is a rest day, and players have more free time to meet for consultations. Although goal setting can be done on match day, players are often locked into a busy routine or are otherwise physically and cognitively engaged.

TEAM GOAL SETTING

Diary January 7-20

Themes: *Organizational issues, aims, triangular consensus*

Making team goals work in a professional sports organization is an exercise in managing competing priorities and logistical issues. My approach to developing team goals is consultative. In the early part of the team goal-setting process, I am largely a facilitator. The initial aim is to help coaches and players take responsibility for setting relevant and important goals that follow the basic principles of goal setting. I call this three-way interaction between coaches, players, and the sport psychologist *triangular consensus*. In my experience, setting goals without an appropriate contribution from each person in the triad undermines the whole process.

All stakeholders in this process, however, are not equal. Football clubs often operate on an authoritarian, patriarchal model. I do, however, think that an opportunity needs to be given to coaches and players to contribute independently to the process. I have learned from previous experiences that doing team goals is a challenging task. I once tried to get a whole squad of 50 players involved in setting goals and soon found the process running out of my control.

I have tried various ways of initiating the setting of team goals, such as a more democratic approach. Involving all players and coaches sounds good in theory but does not always work in practice. Professional sports organizations do not always reflect trends in other business environments in terms of management structure and style. I have personally found the top-down approach of starting the goal-setting process (with the coaches) more successful that the bottom-up approach of starting with the players. In talking about operating standards, Ravizza (1990) referred to the concept of flexibility and being able to adjust to a situation. He stated, "In every situation there is an ideal way to do your job, and then there is reality" (p. 331).

My aim was to formulate goals that dovetailed with the priority areas of the coaches. I resolved to (a) include aspects of successful goals used previously, (b) have each coach and the fitness coordinator contribute one goal each (i.e., five goals), and (c) make sure the senior coach is comfortable with each goal. In so doing, I am attempting to help coaches take responsibility for the goal-setting process, recognizing that ultimately these goals cannot be successful unless the coaches reinforce them constantly.

I carried out discussions with the senior coach, three assistant coaches, and four senior players on where they think the team needs to improve for the forthcoming season. These discussions were with coaches and players individually and were largely informal. There are at least two advantages to such discussions. First, they elicit what key people think independent of each other, and second, they give me advance notice of issues that are likely to surface at an upcoming meeting with coaches. The following is an example of one of these conversations I had with a coach.

> DM: Hi, David. If you have a few minutes, I would like to talk to you about team goals for this season.
>
> D: Fine, come in [to his office] and have a seat.
>
> DM: I am just getting around to the coaches and a few of the senior players at the moment, trying to get a feel for areas

that are important for this season that may be useful as team goals. I'm intending to meet with all the coaches and a group of players in the next couple of weeks anyway, but first I want to talk to people one-on-one.

D: What sort of input do you want from me?

DM: Well, I want to know what, in your opinion, is vitally important this year.

D: There are a few areas. As you know, I have been spending a lot of time on developing key performance indicators (KPI). After each match, and even between quarters during a match, we should be able to assess how we compare to the opposition in the three KPI areas that I've identified. We can also give players individual feedback using a composite score for how they have performed in each of the three areas.

DM: So, perhaps we should be looking at target scores for the team in the three areas and translating them into overall season goals.

D: For sure; this would tie in with the feedback I'll be giving the players anyway. They [the players] are really excited about this; they are learning how this type of information is superior to the types of statistics that the papers publish.

DM: Good, because we need goals that everyone accepts and can relate to. Are the other coaches familiar with the system [KPIs] at this stage?

D: They are, but I want to spend more time with them on it, especially John [the senior coach], to make sure he understands the system fully.

DM: How about if you talk more about the three KPI areas at the meeting with the coaches on team goals, and in the meantime, we can both put some thought into making specific goals relating to them?

During this time, I asked myself the common questions of goal setting, including, Are the goals measurable? For example: Can we get statistics on how we are doing on match days and on a weekly basis for comparison with other clubs? Are the goals specific enough? Clearly, all clubs aim to win the Premiership, and stating an obvious goal such as that is relatively meaningless. Is the goal too specific? Goals can be broken down into smaller and smaller components. Consequently, it can become increasingly difficult to keep the goals relevant to the unstated goal of winning the Premiership. Can adequate feedback be provided?

Diary: January 21

I was given 30 minutes in a coaches' meeting to outline my plan for team goal setting.

Here is a portion of the dialogue from the start and middle sections of this meeting.

DM: The main aim of this meeting is to discuss potential team goals for the coming season. I suggest that each of you contribute one or two ideas you consider really important. After we have come up with some concrete ideas, I'll then hold a meeting with a representative group of players to get some input from them. We then need a process for agreeing on these goals collectively [triangular consensus].

Senior coach (SN): Once you have had the two meetings [present meeting and meeting with the players], give me a copy of what is planned before you go any further.

DM: OK; that should be within a couple of weeks. Ideally, these team goals should be set in place by the end of January [2-3 months before the regular season starts). Once you [John] are comfortable with the goals, I might run a session with all the players and yourselves [coaches] together to make sure everyone is on the same wavelength. What do you think?

DM: [fifteen minutes later, after three possible goals have been discussed] What else is important?

Assistant coach (AC): I think we really need to look closely at off-field behavior. I mean, we don't have a really clear discipline policy, and last year some guys were letting the club down with unprofessional conduct.

DM: What sorts of things do you mean?

AC: Being late for training, not taking every opportunity to do the extra skill sessions . . . not looking after soft-tissue injuries properly, sometimes not wearing club apparel for media interviews, and getting into the night-club scene too often. Look, most guys are really good, but we don't do ourselves any favors by letting some guys get away with unprofessional behavior. If we propose this as a team goal, I'm sure 95% of the players will support it. This way they are accountable for their behavior. Unprofessional conduct just isn't acceptable at this level.

DM: If this were a team goal, how could we go about monitoring it?

AC: For a start, we could improve our recordkeeping of attendance at extra skill sessions and also punctuality generally. We don't want to be like the military, but we have to improve in this area. I guess we would need to check last year's records before setting targets for this year.

Ten minutes of discussion followed on professional behavior, the impending introduction by the club of a new discipline policy, and the merits of developing a team goal in this area.

In the following week, I called a group of eight senior players together to discuss the proposed goals from their perspective. The following is an excerpt from this meeting.

DM: I had a meeting with the coaches last week, and they came up with some ideas on team goals for next season. Prior to this, I had talked with a few of you guys and the coaches informally about possible priority areas. I'll start by reviewing the ideas that the coaches generated; then we can talk about adding or subtracting from these. I would also like to hear your thoughts on practical strategies for reinforcing these goals.

Player 1 (P1): [after reviewing potential goals suggested by the coaches] With the first goal that John [senior coach] has suggested [outscoring opposition teams in the last five minutes of each quarter], can you give us an idea of how we went last year?

DM: Yes, I checked this with the club statisticians. Apparently, we kicked about 360 points compared to 440 points by opposing sides.

P2: What should we be aiming at?

P1: At the very least we should be aiming to outscore them [opponents].

DM: Supposing this ends up being a team goal for this year; what can we do to make sure we improve in this area?

P3: Perhaps Neil [the team "runner"] should come out and remind us at the 25-minute mark. [The "runner" in Australian Rules football is a nonplayer who is the only person sanctioned to deliver messages from the coaches to the players during play.]

P2: He probably wouldn't have time to get around to everyone. Wouldn't it be better if he went out to a key player in the back half, forward half, and centerline? They would be responsible for reminding the other guys in their area with a signal or something.

DM: It would need to be a signal that is not obvious to other teams.

P4: You [DM] could give us feedback at halftime and after each game on this as well.

DM: I would probably make up a chart that could be updated each week that would show our progress in this [last five minutes of quarters] area. Have you guys got any other ideas on steps that could be taken to improve in this area?

The eight players were very positive about the proposed goals but suggested that we have a "roving goal" that changes every month and comes from the players. The roving goal seemed an excellent idea, because it provided a degree of flexibility in the goals program, and it was a goal that was completely player driven. A second meeting was held with the coaching staff to present the goals in flow chart form and outline the process details and possible feedback mechanisms. We finally agreed on six team goals and put them in place. I then convened a meeting with all players and coaches to present the goals, to discuss how the goals would be monitored on a week-to-week basis, and to answer player questions or queries. The box below shows the collectively generated team goals without going into specific details of each.

Finally, in this instance it was important to start the process of setting goals well in advance of the forthcoming season. The consultative model that I have described takes time. Coaches and players are more generous with their time during this preseason period and thus are more likely to engage psychologically in the goal-setting process.

MONITORING TEAM GOALS: MARCH TO SEPTEMBER

Themes: Feedback, roving goals, awards, process mechanisms

Once the season started, I gave specific feedback on each of the goals on a weekly basis. I provided expeditious feedback, in the form of color graphs, of the team's progress toward each goal. I posted these graphs on the Monday following each of the 23 games played, pinning them to a designated notice board placed in a position accessible to only the players. Each of the coaches, the fitness coordinator, and the football manager also received copies of the graphs. Depending on the type of goal, I used line graphs, bar charts, and percentage graphs. Graphs are useful in conveying a large amount of information in an interesting and efficient manner. I rarely change the format of these graphs once the season has started, because players and coaches get comfortable with the style of graphs used to present the relevant information.

Figure 7.1 is an example of the visual feedback I used in conjunction with goal five (goal kicking conversion percentages on set shots) over the previous two seasons. In figure 7.1, the improvement in set shot conversion percentage is clearly shown for seasons 1997 and 1998 in comparison with the 1996 season, when no specific goal

Team Goals

1. Match-related goal (concerning outscoring opponent over the last five minutes of quarters). Proposed by the senior coach.
2. Match-related goal (concerning KPIs—key performance indicators). Proposed by first assistant coach.
3. Fitness-related goal (concerning player skinfolds). Proposed by fitness coordinator.
4. General goal relating to professional conduct. Proposed by second assistant coach and team manager.
5. Match-related goal (concerning setting goal conversion rates). Continuation of successful goal from the previous year. Proposed by sport psychologist.
6. Roving goals changing monthly. Proposed by a subgroup of players.

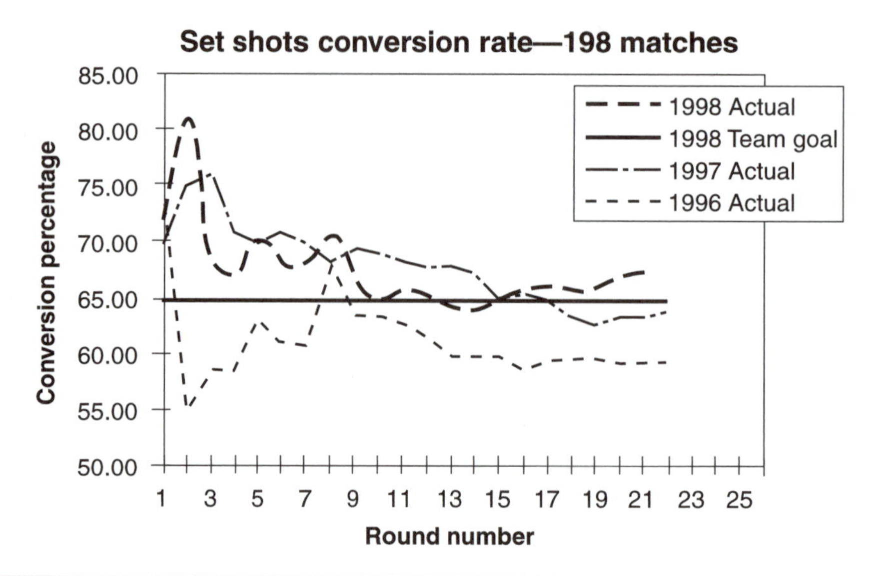

Figure 7.1 Visual feedback.

was set. Please note that the figure shows a decrease in conversion rate over the course of the season in each of the three seasons (1996-1998). This is normal in Australian Rules and is related to playing conditions and weather (rather than the goal-setting program). In setting the goal of 65%, we (players, coaches, and myself) were mindful that good playing conditions in the early part of the season would temporarily inflate the conversion rate. Australian Rules football is a winter game, and as weather and playing fields deteriorate over a season, so do conversion rates. When I asked one player if these graphs were useful, he said, "The team goals feedback sheets and graphs are really good; most of the guys read them."

A consistent feature of the goal-setting literature in sport is the importance of identifying strategies to turn goals into reality. Where possible, I used graphs that showed the team's progress toward a goal. I also gave players individual feedback on their personal contributions toward the team goal. I found that players were more likely to take notice of tables and graphs that gave them individual feedback on their contributions toward a team goal. I also used flow charts to develop strategies relating to each of the six team goals; this approach is similar to using goal ladders to help athletes develop a step-by-step approach to goal setting. For example, we used a number of strategies in relation to team goal five, the set shots conversion rate.

1. Coaches developed a detailed protocol for regular goal kickers to practice their goal kicking. During goal-kicking training, each of the fifteen players involved took the same number of shots from the same positions with the outcome of each shot being recorded. This tactic helped in making direct comparisons between players and tracking patterns of missed shots, such as players who predominantly missed to one side. These sessions were structured to replicate match demands (e.g., having teammates deliberately use distracting tactics). As with actual competition, I graphed and posted the results of these sessions.
2. We encouraged players to develop a pre-kick routine and to implement this routine in practice and matches.
3. A biomechanical assessment of each player's kicking style was carried out in the preseason. Coaches then met with players to assess their kicking technique using videotape equipment.
4. Regular weekly feedback was provided to each player on his cumulative conversion rate in both practice and competition.
5. In addressing the players, the senior coach made frequent references to the importance of maintaining a high conversion rate.

The subgroup of eight players who participated in the development of the team goals also suggested that regular verbal feedback on goal progress was needed throughout the season. I addressed the whole squad of players and coaches briefly every second month. This allowed me to review goal progress to date, monitor goal familiarity (i.e., how conversant players were with the goals), set new roving goals, and field general questions.

At about the midpoint of the season, the senior coach became aware that our team was underperforming in the efforts part of goal two. In Australian rules football, *efforts* refers to chasing opponents when the opposition has control of the ball, tackling opponents, sheperding (blocking), spoiling marking (catching) attempts, and smothers (blocking kicks off the boot). As a result, we made efforts a roving goal and focused heavily on giving players additional feedback in this area. On match days, I posted specific individual feedback to players by first getting halftime statistics from the club statisticians on efforts and writing these up quickly on a whiteboard for players to see during the break. During the following weeks, the coach asked me to provide him with updated averages for each player in the efforts area. We used a weekly award that a sponsor had donated for the player who accumulated the highest statistics in this area.

In my experience, the team goals that have worked best have been underpinned by a number of reinforcing strategies. I guess the real challenge for applied sport psychologists is to find an array of reinforcers that ultimately converge on a particular team goal. For example, including a tangible award was helpful in recognizing the contribution of players in an area that was not particularly visible (total efforts), at least to the ordinary fan or to the media. The players who won these awards were nearly always the workers of the team and not the stars.

The team made the finals (i.e., playoffs) but was knocked out in the first round and finished 8th in the competition of 16 teams. At the conclusion of the season, I reviewed the goals in my yearly report to the senior coach, the chief executive, and the football manager. A brief overview of the outcome for each of the six goals follows.

Goal 1 (outscoring opposition in the last five minutes of quarters) was achieved (543 points scored by our club compared to 454 points scored by opposition teams).

Goal 2 (top four in the league in the three key performance indicators) was subdivided into three components:

Goal 2a (increasing "one percenters") was not achieved—13th in the league.

Goal 2b (increase in going after the "hard ball") was achieved—3rd in the league.

Goal 2c (improved general field kicking delivery)was achieved—3rd in the league.

Goal 3 (body fats average across the squad below 56 mm) was achieved.

Goal 4 (improve professionalism) was achieved. For example, the attendance register showed a significant reduction in arriving late for training (60% improvement) and more attendance (30%) improvement at extra skill sessions.

Goal 5 (top four in conversion rate for set shots above 65%) was achieved. The team finished second in the league in conversion rate for set shots with a season average of 68.1%.

Roving goals: Two of the four roving goals were achieved (increased efforts, increased field assertiveness). The other two roving goals were rather poorly formulated and difficult to measure.

CONCLUSION

My main aim in writing this chapter was to present applied goal setting as a dynamic and creative enterprise. My intention was also to interweave some of the traditional fundamentals of goal setting with ideas about the interplay between personality traits and goal setting, triangular consensus, and roving goals that, although not documented in the goal-setting literature to date, are readily recognized by experienced applied practitioners. Finally, the material presented here is edited and condensed, yet I hope that I have still conveyed the reality of goal setting as being a dynamic and imperfect intervention.

REFERENCES

Burton, D. (1993). Goal setting in sport. In R.N. Singer, M. Murphey, & L.K. Tennant (Eds.), *Handbook of research on sport psychology* (pp. 467-491). New York: Macmillan.

Cattell, H.B. (1989). *The 16 PF: Personality in depth.* Champaign, IL: Institute for Personality and Ability Testing.

Cattell, R.B., Cattell, A.K., & Cattell, H.B. (1994). *Sixteen Personality Factor Questionnaire (16 PF)* (5th ed.). Champaign, IL: Institute for Personality and Ability Testing.

Danish, S.J., Mash, J.M, Howard, C.W., Curl, S.J., Meyer. A.L., Owens, S.S., & Kendall, K. (1992). *Going for the goal leader manual.* Richmond, VA: Virginia Commonwealth University.

Gould, D. (1998). Goal setting for peak performance. In J.M. Williams (Ed.), *Applied sport psychology: Personal growth to peak performance* (3rd ed., pp. 182-196). Mountain View, CA: Mayfield.

Harris, D.V., & Harris, B.L. (1984). *The athlete's guide to sport psychology: Mental skills for physical people.* Champaign, IL: Human Kinetics.

Ravizza, K. (1990). Sportpsych consultation issues in professional baseball. *The Sport Psychologist, 4,* 330-340.

Rotella, R.J. (1990). Providing sport psychology consulting services to professional athletes. *The Sport Psychologist, 4,* 409-417.

Weinberg, R.S. (1996). Goal setting in sport and exercise: Research to practice. In J.L. Van Raalte & B.W. Brewer (Eds.), *Exploring sport and exercise psychology* (pp. 3-24). Washington, DC: American Psychological Association.

PART III

BEYOND PERFORMANCE ENHANCEMENT: WORKING WITH AND WORKING THROUGH

CHAPTER 8

THE SADNESS IN SPORT: WORKING WITH A DEPRESSED AND SUICIDAL ATHLETE

Karen D. Cogan
University of North Texas

It was the Olympic trials, and Dan, a swimmer, had trained for this event for years. At the age of 23, he felt this was his last chance to make the Olympic team before he moved on with his life, and he was completely focused on getting a spot. His training had gone well in the past few months, and he felt as ready as he had ever been. He reviewed what he needed to do mentally as he stepped into starting position. Then the race was beginning; he was in the water moving as fast as he could. As he came to the finish, he touched the side of the pool and turned around to see his time. He could not believe it; he had just missed making the team. At first he was in shock. All the time and training and planning and hoping, and this was the end. He pulled himself out of the pool and left. He could not stand to be around people at that point. For the next week Dan was listless and slept a lot. He was despondent and had little appetite. He did not want to talk to anybody or do anything. He felt depressed.

At first thought, an athlete's depression might not seem like a sport psychology issue. But significant mood alteration, especially if it is a clinically diagnosable depression, affects many parts of an athlete's life, including sport performance. In some cases, an athlete may suffer from depressed mood or even a diagnosable depression but prefer not to address it in a sport psychology setting. A sport psychology consultant can be sensitive to the athlete's preferences and work on what the athlete chooses. In many cases, however, when it is a central issue for an athlete, it is impossible not to deal with it and treat it. If we are concerned about a holistic approach to treating an athlete, then we want to recognize the possibility of depression and the need for treatment. If, in a sport psychology consulting situation, it is determined that treatment for depression is needed, and the consultant is not trained to treat depression, then a referral to a competent psychotherapist (or psychiatrist if medication is indicated) is necessary for the athlete's well-being.

WHAT IS DEPRESSION?

A sense of depression can be experienced at many levels; it is helpful to view depression on a continuum from mild to severe. Depression is almost the common cold of clinical psychology and is such an everyday word in conversations that people use it to identify a variety of levels of feeling down or sad. A brief clarification of the difference between depressed mood and clinical depression will help readers understand this chapter.

Most everyone experiences depressed mood because of periodic or occasional mood fluctuations or events such as disappointments or losses. Such a depressed mood does not necessarily require medical or therapeutic intervention. When a depressed mood escalates and remains, then is it possible to have a clinical depression. Clinical depression has specific diagnostic criteria that a person must meet to be diagnosed with a major depressive episode.

According to the DSM-IV (American Psychiatric Association, 1994), depression can be characterized by many of the following: (a) depressed mood, (b) diminished interest or pleasure in most activities most of the time, (c) significant weight loss or weight gain or decrease or increase in appetite, (d) sleep disturbances (insomnia or hypersomnia), (e) psychomotor agitation or retardation, (f) fatigue or loss of energy, (g) feelings of worthlessness or excessive guilt, (h) diminished ability to concentrate, and (i) recurrent thoughts of death or suicidal ideation. For a diagnosis of depression, at least five of the preceding symptoms must be present during a two-week period, and at least one symptom must be either (a) depressed mood or (b) loss of interest or pleasure. The symptoms cause significant impairment in social, occupational, or other important areas of functioning, such as sport participation. These symptoms also can be the results of other physical or medical conditions that may need to be ruled out. For a diagnosis of depression, however, the symptoms just mentioned must not be the result of substance abuse, medication, or medical (physical) condition.

On occasion, an athlete may experience some depressive symptoms, but not for the duration or to the intensity required for a diagnosis of major depression. In such cases, other diagnoses (e.g., adjustment disorder with depressed [or anxious] mood, bereavement) may be more appropriate. Sometimes athletes develop subthreshold characteristics of depression and may exhibit maladaptive coping behavior (e.g., self-medication with alcohol) following injury. Such self-defeating behavior needs attention, and athletes with subthreshold depression or adjustment disorders with mood disturbance would certainly benefit from clinical interventions.

An athlete can experience depression for a variety of reasons. For some, there is a biological component or chemical imbalance that results in depression. A biological etiology is likely if there is a family history of depression. Often there is some event (or combination of events), or trigger, that results in feelings of depression. The event might be unrelated to sport (e.g., chronic family conflicts, traumatic life events such as an assault) or might directly involve sport (consistent poor performance, inability to meet a very important goal, severe injury, pressures to perform). Not every athlete who experiences a difficult event, or series of events, will develop a diagnosable depression, but when there have been ongoing stressors or difficulties, or when athletes present with many of the DSM-IV symptoms, depression should be considered.

In Dan's case, as outlined at the beginning of the chapter, the question becomes: Is he really depressed in the clinical sense? He certainly has had a major disappointment and understandably is experiencing sadness and depressed mood. But a diagnosis of depression depends on the degree and duration of symptoms. After one week he could not be diagnosed with depression and may be experiencing an expected depressed mood because of serious disappointment and feelings of loss. If his condition continued for at least two weeks, and he met the DSM-IV criteria, then he could be diagnosed as clinically depressed.

How would the presence of depressive symptoms affect an athlete in training and competition? Athletes who have difficulty getting up in the morning, have no appetite and no energy, and cannot concentrate will not be performing up to their potential. They could even be at risk for sustaining an injury (e.g., because of attentional deficits). Sport psychology consultants can be most helpful to athletes if they can identify depression and help the athletes get the appropriate treatment. If sport psychology consultants are focused only on performance issues, then they might assume that an athlete's lethargy and diminished concentration can be treated with energizing strategies or focusing techniques. An athlete who is clinically depressed will be unlikely to respond well to those techniques until the depression has been treated. Treating the depression may restore energy and concentration abilities, and thus, further interventions may not be necessary.

THEORETICAL AND THERAPY PERSPECTIVES ON TREATING DEPRESSION

Depression has been conceptualized in many different systems of psychology, but an in-depth exploration of the many theories of depression is beyond the scope of this chapter. Instead, I will provide brief outlines of relevant portions of theories that I use in treating depression. These outlines are not intended to be complete overviews of any of the following orientations.

Cognitive and Cognitive-Behavioral Therapies

Cognitive and cognitive-behavioral therapies have at their core the examination of cognitive processes and their impact on behavior. These therapies focus on how thoughts and information processing can become distorted and lead to maladaptive emotions and behaviors (Carson, Butcher, and Mineka, 1998). Beck's cognitive model indicates that depression occurs because of negative misinterpretations of experience (Hollon & Beck, 1978). These misinterpretations result in a negative view of oneself, one's world, and one's future. Beck and colleagues identified a variety of thought distortions that contribute to how people maladaptively process information.

Ellis, the founder of rational-emotive behavior therapy, provided another model that helps us understand how emotions and thoughts are connected (Ellis, 1973). He labeled it the ABC model, where *A* is an external event or situation to which a person is exposed, *B* is the belief or thought that the person has in respect to *A,* and *C* is the emotion that results. For instance, athletes might interpret a poor performance in a variety of ways. One athlete might focus on a series of errors as the cause of a loss and view himself as incompetent and lacking. This line of thinking is likely to result in a depressed mood that, with enough repetition, could become clinical depression. Another athlete might use her errors as learning tools and guides for future improvements. Although the athlete might be momentarily disappointed, she also can maintain positive attitudes and develop goals as she goes back into training. Depressed people often think of themselves as helpless and believe that life is not worthwhile. Cognitive therapists hold that people can alter their thinking and interpretations and consequently gain control of their emotions. The goal of therapy, then, is to confront distorted perceptions and irrational cognitions and shift a person's thinking into a more positive realm.

Behavioral models and therapies can be combined with cognitive treatments to help heal depression. Because thinking and feeling do not function independently of behavior, it is important to examine and encourage behavioral change as well. Depressed people are often lethargic and inactive, and they feel ineffective in their world. Sometimes "depressed behaviors" (e.g., staying in bed) have been reinforced and are difficult to extinguish. For example, a person who is sad and inactive may not be expected to perform household chores, and thus, someone else performs the onerous daily tasks for her. Part of behavior therapy, therefore, focuses on replacing the inactive behaviors with more active ones and reinforcing activity rather than lethargy. Some of the therapeutic benefits that depressed people gain from starting to exercise may be due more to them taking up an activity than to the exercise per se.

Psychoanalytic/Psychodynamic Theory

Although Freud and psychoanalytic theory have received criticism for being the products of their time and place and having an overemphasis on sex, Freud's formulation of the etiology of depression is often useful. He conceptualized depression as aggression turned inward (Freud, 1953/1917). That is, when aggressive impulses are inhibited or frustrated (e.g., against an abusive parent), their focus may turn against self (e.g., self-hatred, feelings of worthlessness, self-denigration). Freud's conceptualization of depression is particularly useful for women who are often prone to inhibit anger and partially explains why women are more likely than men to be diagnosed with depression. A higher rate of depression makes sense given women's socialization processes (e.g., messages that "nice girls" do not get angry). When working with depression, it is useful to ask about unexpressed anger and to look for any connection between the depression and frustration or inhibited aggression. Although athletes may be unaware of unexpressed anger at first, as therapy progresses they are likely to become more aware of those impulses.

Crisis Intervention Issues

When a client becomes extremely depressed, the possibility of suicidal ideation and suicidal intent must be considered. It is important to ask about suicide potential as a standard part of a depression assessment. Often clients will not mention suicidal thoughts without prompting because they feel ashamed or are generally uncomfortable with talking about death or suicide. Once the subject is broached, many clients are relieved that they can talk about such thoughts without being judged and that someone understands enough about their pain to ask the questions other people avoid.

If the potential for suicide is great, the therapist may need to shift to crisis management mode and gather information in an efficient yet sensitive manner. It is helpful to get an understanding of the stressors that have contributed to the crisis state. It also is important to ask if the client has a suicide plan, and if so, get details (see also chapter 10). If it seems likely that a client will inflict self-harm, then hospitalization or other immediate interventions (e.g., a halfway house) are necessary. More often, though, a client has merely thought about suicide as an escape and does not intend to carry out any self-harm.

Implications for Treatment

When people are depressed, they often feel they have no control. They are unable to get out of bed, do not want to eat, and have no energy. They generally cannot get themselves going. They often feel they are ineffective in their lives. They feel helpless and allow life to take them wherever it may. Athletes may be dragging themselves to practice because they have to but are not able to do much else.

One important step in combating major depression is to help athletes take charge of their lives. Sometimes the last thing they want is to be active or to train, and often they feel unable to do even minor things for themselves. It is best to begin with something small, such as getting out of bed, getting dressed, or finding an activity they enjoy (or used to enjoy). Just as with goal setting, an athlete uses short-term goals to reach a larger, long-term goal. Eventually it becomes easier for an athlete to be active and take control.

Depression and Student-Athletes

Some researchers have suggested that student-athletes experience more stressors than non-athletes because of the multiple roles they balance (Bergandi & Wittig, 1984; Parham, 1993; Pinkerton, Hinz, & Barrow, 1989). Even though they experience more stress, student-athletes are less likely to use counseling services. Athletes may believe that they should be strong enough to cope independently and may not want to acknowledge any psychological concerns. Acknowledging the need for help with depression may be very difficult for an athlete. In addition, taking medications, which often are indicated for depression, may be undesirable because of adverse side effects, subsequent performance effects, or concerns about drug testing. A sport psychology consultant must be aware of these additional issues when treating a depressed student athlete.

I do not use any one theory exclusively in treating depressed athletes. I examine the athlete's issues and use parts of cognitive-behavioral, psychodynamic, and crisis intervention models as appropriate. I might even incorporate intervention strategies based on other theories when needed. For example, I might adopt a feminist perspective in which I work to reduce the power differential in the therapeutic relationship, empowering the client to take action, make necessary changes, and address the issues at the root of the depression. This approach is often useful when dealing with clients who are in (or have been in) abusive relationships.

The ultimate goal is efficient treatment, and sometimes the best approach is not always one that follows a theory. For instance, when a client is showing little improvement, I may adopt a paradoxical approach and comment, "It seems like you are not really ready to get past the depression." I may even add, "Maybe you just need to be depressed a little while longer." Sometimes clients do not know if I am serious or not. I am careful about employing this approach and use it only when I have a substantial relationship with a client and do not see the person as a danger to self or others. I also sometimes incorporate humor into the "paradoxical" discussion as we examine what it would be like to remain depressed.

When depression is severe, treating its symptoms becomes a central issue in therapy. Sometimes sport issues take a back seat except to determine how sport may be a source of the depression. Especially in crisis situations, sport may only be peripherally involved in the moment. When examining the bigger picture, however, there are often more connections to sport. In addition to the previously mentioned implications for treatment, the athletes I work with recognize that I have knowledge of sport and a sporting background, so trust is enhanced and work can proceed more smoothly.

CASE EXAMPLE

This example is based in part on a real case, but names, identifying information, and specific events have been changed. Because this is a real case, the transcripts of sessions do not necessarily represent "perfect" therapy, if such a thing even exists. I am not a perfect therapist. I have good insights at times, but I occasionally get lost and stumble around. Being human, not knowing what to do, and being confused about what the athlete is trying to tell me (and letting the athlete know that) are all actually part of developing a trusting, caring, and honest relationship with an athlete.

Background Information

Jill, a lean 19-year-old Caucasian tennis player, was beginning her second year on an NCAA Division 1A team. She was recruited by several top schools because of her outstanding performance in high school and was expected to lead the team to a high ranking and possibly a conference championship title. Her performances during her first year, however, were mediocre by her own standards, and she reported that the coach was disappointed in her. She discussed at length her feelings of depression and lack of motivation to improve.

Jill was born and raised in the southern United States with a brother who is two years younger than she is. Her parents have been married for 22 years and own a small business. Most of her family memories from her childhood are negative, and she firmly believes that both of her parents have psychological problems. She mentioned that her father was emotionally distant and unpredictable. Although he never physically harmed her, she remembers a time when he tied up and threatened to kill her mother. Her mother verbally and physically abused Jill and her brother. Her mother is also extremely intrusive in Jill's life and allows her little privacy. Her mother always demands to know where Jill goes, what she does in training every day, and who her friends are. She often walks in on Jill without knocking when Jill is showering or changing and comments on whether Jill has gained or lost weight. Her parents have few friends and depend highly on each other but are not happily married. Jill feels they continue to be married purely because a divorce would be costly and they do not know any other way to live.

Jill's parents were extremely proud when she was offered a scholarship to attend a prestigious local university. They wanted her to go to a college near their home, but Jill wanted to go away. She could not get into the distant school, however, and accepted the scholarship close to home.

Jill recently recognized that her parents only gave her affection and attention when she performed well in matches. She felt that they were living vicariously through her because her parents had few of their own accomplishments. If she made errors or lost, they were critical and psychologically abusive. For example, during her first year, she had tendinitis and had been out of practice for several weeks prior to a tournament. She did not feel physically prepared to play but had not informed her coaches about her discomfort. She discussed her hesitancy with her mom, but her mom insisted that she go anyway. She immediately lost the first two matches, and her mom left in the middle of the second match as Jill was losing. When Jill went back to the hotel room, her mom had her bags packed and was ready to leave. She did not say a word to Jill.

A few weeks later, at her parents' house, Jill attempted suicide by overdosing on some pain medication she was using (this was, in part, a fairly angry and aggressive act directed at her parents in their own home). She reported that she really wanted to die but did not know enough about how much medication to take. Her parents found her passed out and rushed her to the emergency room, where she had her stomach pumped. She remembers the sequence of events as being "surreal" and traumatic. Her parents commanded all the attention in the hospital and afterward, because they "freaked out."

Jill's feelings about her parents and tennis continued to become more negative. Everything for her parents revolved around tennis, and Jill was feeling smothered by their presence. She would have preferred that they stay out of her tennis career and allow her to monitor her performance and make her own choices. Now she feels she is not performing well because of parental pressures, even though she has tremendous potential, and she is concerned that her depression is becoming worse.

Initial Interview

Note: During the initial phone contact, I get some background history about the athlete's concern(s), discuss confidentiality and fees, insurance, and my policies such that the initial interview begins with the athlete's issues and finding a focus. I establish initial rapport on the phone by talking, asking questions, and offering support so that the first session can move smoothly. Jill was hesitant about counseling at first. She canceled her first appointment saying she felt better and did not need counseling. Then she decided she could benefit from counseling and rescheduled.

KC: Hello, Jill. It's good to meet you. Please come in and have a seat.

J: Thank you.

KC: I know you said you have been feeling depressed, so we can talk about that today. And I'll also be asking you some more general questions about your background so that I can better understand the issues you are facing. If you have any questions of me, you can ask them as well. Then we can decide how best to work on your concerns. How does that sound?

J: That's good. So you are a sport psychologist?

KC: Yes, that's right.

J: Were you an athlete?

KC: Yes; I was a gymnast and competed in college.

J: Oh, good, so you'll understand [shows obvious relief]. You know what it is like to train with a bunch of other girls all having mood swings at the same time . . . and dealing with parents too. I talked to another counselor before, and she didn't understand anything about tennis or athletes. Do you know a lot about tennis?

KC: I know some, but I might also need you to teach me and help me understand what is has been like for you.

J: OK.

Many counselors in training are taught to be cautious about sharing too much personal information, but self-disclosure can be used effectively and therapeutically. I knew that Jill was hesitant about coming to counseling in the first place. She needed to feel comfortable with me and to begin trusting me. Knowing that I had been a collegiate athlete, even though the sport was different, was comforting to her. Therefore, I tend to answer questions clients ask about me and my background (within reason), because it generally is not therapeutic to come back with, "How will it help you to know that about me?" In addition, it is clear that Jill had a less-than-positive previous counseling experience, and I do not want to repeat that with her.

I fully admit to Jill that I am not completely knowledgeable about tennis and will need her help. Besides the fact that this is a true statement, it also is a way of establishing rapport and more equality in the relationship. I am making her the tennis expert. I might know more about psychological processes, but she is the teacher about tennis, and her experiences are valuable to me. By acknowledging and recognizing each other's expertise, we begin to set up a foundation for working together.

KC: Any other questions?

J: No, not right now.

KC: OK, then where would you like to start today?

J: Well, I guess my lack of motivation . . . I've been feeling so down . . . really depressed.

KC: Tell me more about what the depression is like for you.

J: [slow and quiet] I just don't feel like doing anything. I want to sleep all the time. I have no energy.

KC: When did you start feeling depressed?

J: I don't know. For a long time. Probably about my sophomore year in high school when I started really getting into tennis. I was doing pretty good, but the schedule was grueling, and I just started feeling worse and worse.

KC: So that's about four years . . . that's a long time you've been struggling with this.

J: Yeah. Well, I guess it comes and goes. Sometimes I don't feel as bad, but then other times I will.

KC: When's the last time you started feeling worse?

J: For about a month I've been feeling really depressed. Worse than usual.

KC: Where's the depression coming from?

J: Mostly tennis. I hate going on the court; it's always the same old stuff—working hard, being exhausted—and I'm tired of it. And my parents have put so much pressure on me. [We go on to talk about some of the information presented in the "Background Information" section.]

KC: Let me ask you about some of your symptoms. How has your appetite been?

J: I haven't had one. I'm trying to eat to keep up my energy, but I'm not too hungry.

KC: Have you lost weight?

J: Yeah, about 10 pounds.

KC: That's quite a bit.

J: I know, but I'm still doing OK.

KC: You mentioned wanting to sleep a lot. Tell me more about your sleeping patterns.

J: I want to sleep all the time. I just don't have much energy.

KC: How is your level of concentration?

J: Oh, it's gone. I can't study, and I'm worried about my classes.

KC: What's worrying you about your classes?

J: Oh, the usual: if I'm going to get high enough grades. But I'm not as worried about that right now as I am about this depression.

KC: OK. Is there anything you enjoy doing lately?

J: Um . . . [pause] . . . I don't know. I used to like to listen to music and talk to friends, but I just don't end up doing anything anymore.

KC: Have you thought about suicide?

J: Doesn't everybody? Yes, I've thought about it, but I wouldn't do it.

KC: Tell me more about those thoughts.

J: Sometimes I just wish I would go to bed and not wake up. It would be so much easier to leave all this behind me. Then I wouldn't have to worry about the pressure to always do well in tennis. You know, it's harder to win, because the only place to go is down and everyone wants to knock you out of the top spot. I feel my teammates are always trying to beat me. And then my parents only talk to me if I win or place. If I don't win, they want to know why not. Now I can't concentrate in school. I just have so many pressures that I want to get rid of. I don't like my life right now.

KC: Yes, you do have a lot of stress, and it sounds like sometimes you need a break, an escape.

J: Yes, that's it. Sometimes I don't know what to do. I just want to get away.

KC: Have you thought of any specific ways you would kill yourself?

J: Sometimes I think about taking pills. Or one time I was driving during bad weather and skidded. Normally I would have been scared but I thought, Oh well, I don't care if I crash. I wasn't even scared.

KC: If you think you might act on those thoughts, it will be important for us to talk more about them, all right?

J: Yeah, I know . . . I guess I should tell you I tried it once. [We go on to discuss her past suicide attempt.]

When someone complains of being depressed, I try to find out what is behind the depression and assess the symptoms. In this portion of the session, I have an outline of symptoms from the DSM-IV in my head, and I go down my mental list to determine where the client falls on each of these symptoms. She said yes to enough symptoms for me to consider a psychiatric consultation for antidepressant medication, but because she is an athlete, and is subject to drug testing in her athletic department, I may wish to pursue other options first. I also am concerned about the weight loss on an already lean athlete and her seeming unconcern. I will want to explore the possibility of an eating disorder or distorted body image, but I will come back to that later.

Her suicidal ideation seems more passive right now as opposed to her having an active plan. She shares with me that she has previously tried to commit suicide, so I will keep in mind that her depression has probably been quite severe in the past. I will continue to check on suicidal ideation in future sessions, but she does not currently appear to be a threat to herself.

KC: So, tell me what it is like to be a collegiate tennis player.

J: At the beginning of the school year, there is always a lot of tension when the freshmen come in and mess up the pecking order. Everyone is fighting for position and wanting that sixth spot. [In singles, only six women compete at any intercollegiate match, so if an athlete is number seven, she does not play unless a teammate is injured or ill.] But then when it gets to the season and the matches are close, everyone rallies together to win. All the parents are so screwed up, though. We [athletes] all look at each other and are embarrassed because of how our parents act.

KC: What do the parents do?

J: One time we all [parents and athletes] went out to eat after the tournament, and all the parents were getting wasted and buying their daughters drinks. The drink tab was $200. Many of the families have a lot of money and act selfishly. They just expect everything to be done for them and go their way, you know.

KC: Are there any positives about tennis?

J: There are some good things—I get to meet new people and see neat places. Sometimes traveling with the team is fun.

I want to get some idea of the environment in which Jill lives and trains. Even if I know a lot about the sport, the athlete's subjective interpretation of the environment is useful to me. She is able to recognize some of the positives involved but needs prompting. She focuses mostly on the competition and on family dynamics. I am filing away this information, because I believe it will be useful as I begin to understand her concerns. I will not, however, be doing any interventions to help her work on these issues at this point.

Second Session

First, we "warm up" with some general conversation about Jill's week, and then we move into therapy.

KC: So, how are you feeling today?

J: A little better. It helps to talk about it some.

KC: I'm glad to hear that. Where would you like to begin today?

J: I have a tournament coming up and I'm worried. I just don't care, but then I do poorly and my parents get on my case. Then I'm even more depressed.

KC: Sounds like there is a lot going on right now. Tell me what got you interested in tennis.

J: What does this have to do with my depression and the tournament?

KC: Good question. If you'll stay with me on this for a few minutes, I think you'll see how it is relevant.

J: OK [sounds skeptical]. I started when I was 8, and I played because my older cousin did.

KC: What kept you involved?

J: I won my first three tournaments and then won State at age 11. I got a lot of attention from my parents and became a person in their eyes.

KC: Then what happened?

J: Tennis was fun until I was 13. I was winning. Then I began to play more out of state, and the competition was more difficult. My parents would say I just didn't want it enough, and then they got overinvolved.

KC: What did they do?

J: My dad bought jump ropes so I could work on my endurance. He paid me to do sit-ups, and he would ride a bike alongside of me as I ran to make sure I did not stop halfway through. He would make me run the stands. Then tennis became a job. When I was a senior in high school I hated it, but they manipulated, no . . . yeah, manipulated me into playing.

KC: Manipulated you?

J: Yeah, they made me work in their business sweeping the floor and stuff and said, "This is what you'll do if you don't get a scholarship." They said, "You owe us because of all the money we've put into tennis." They just assume I'll turn pro after college.

KC: So it sounds like you don't feel it is your decision to continue playing tennis. You see it as your parents demanding your participation.

J: Yes. I can't quit or who knows what I'll be doing.

KC: Then I see why you aren't motivated for this tournament. You are not doing tennis for you right now.

J: No, I'm not, but I still have to play anyway.

K: So maybe we need to find meaning for you in tennis, find reasons that you want to play. Then maybe you can find some more motivation. If we can't find any reasons you want to stay with it, then you have a decision to make about possibly getting out.

J: Well, I have a hard time imagining myself not playing tennis. I think I want to do it, but I'm not sure. I'm just confused.

KC: Oh, it must be very confusing. This match, what does it mean to you? [We go on to explore this confusion in more depth.]

When I hear that Jill is not motivated for the tournament, I hypothesize that it is because of the parental pressures and lack of personal meaning for her in the game. Therefore, I ask her to review how she got started and what she liked about tennis. She does not understand why this is important at first, but as I guide her through the questions and give her some input, she begins to see that she is not playing tennis for herself anymore. I suspect that her lack of motivation (and potential to sabotage her performance) is a passive-aggressive way of getting back at her parents because she cannot find the words to express her displeasure about their involvement. I then will work with her on finding her own meaning in tennis. If she can find meaning and personal reasons to continue, then I will support her. If she determines that she really does not want to play, I will work with her toward that goal. The session continued on to explore these possibilities, but Jill was further into therapy before any clear decisions were made. She seems to be playing tennis because of her parents' expectations, and by bringing up the subject of finding her own meaning, I am planting the seeds for taking control over her life choices. Finding her own meaning involves reframing why she participates and competes; taking control is one step toward combating depression.

Later Sessions

J: [tearful] Things aren't good. I am really depressed. My parents are putting so much pressure on me, and they expect so much. I just can't live up to what they want. They keep telling me that they put all this money into tennis when I was in high school so I could get a college scholarship. Now they are thinking if I don't start doing better I might lose it [the scholarship]. Or maybe they think I will quit. Maybe I will quit [sounds irritated]. They told me if I lose it they won't pay for anything, and I'm on my own. It's just not worth it anymore. I'm miserable. I can't stand it.

KC: Jill, that's a lot for you to manage. No wonder you are feeling depressed. [I'm getting a funny feeling as I watch her and key in on the "it's not worth it" statement.] Are you thinking of harming yourself?

J: Why are you asking me that? I never said that. I have to say no, don't I?

KC: [gently] What do you mean you "have to"?

J: If I say yes, then you have to do something, right?

KC: Yes, if I feel you are in danger.

J: Well, I'm fine.

KC: [gently] I'm not sure I buy that.

J: I'm fine. . . . [pause] What would you do if I said yes?

KC: I know you are concerned that I might do something you won't like, and I'll be completely honest with you. If I thought you were intending to harm or kill yourself, and I couldn't get your assurance that you would stay safe until our next session, I would need to do something, maybe hospitalize you and let your parents know.

J: Oh, great. Well, I will not go to the hospital, and you can't tell my parents! They would be impossible. You said all this was confidential, and now you are going to tell my parents. I trusted you, and now you might hospitalize me. That's all I need. I think I better just leave now.

KC: I know you are tempted to walk out . . . and I don't blame you for being angry. This has to be frightening also. Let's first talk about what scares you.

J: There are all sorts of crazy people in the hospital, and I'm not crazy. I won't be locked up with a bunch of psychos. And my parents, they already have to know everything. I'd never hear the end of this. Isn't there anything that's mine, just mine?

KC: That's a good question. I am very torn about what to do right now. I can see why you feel like I would be breaking a confidence if I have to intervene in some way, and I see why it makes you angry. I know how important it is to you to keep your parents at a distance. At the same time, I am very concerned about you. I see you in all this pain, and I want to help you find another way out.

J: You're just concerned about your professional responsibility and covering yourself. Well, I absolve you of any responsibility.

KC: Of course I am concerned about my professional responsibility. But you are not just a patient to me. You are a real person who I care about, and I don't want to lose you. I want to work with you on this to get past your pain. But I'm still not sure what you are telling me—are you thinking about killing yourself?

J: I'm not going to say yes to that. I'll be fine.

KC: [I can see this line of questioning is not going to help, so I switch to a more hypothetical strategy.] If you were going to kill yourself, how would you do it?

J: Pills; I have lots of them saved up.

KC: What kinds?

J: Muscle relaxants, pain killers . . . I just want to go to sleep.

KC: How about if you give me the pills?

J: No, I'm not going to do anything with them.

KC: [gently] I think I understand what you are telling me. You are letting me know you are in pain but you don't want to present it in a way that I will have to act. I would like nothing more than to see you take responsibility for your own well-being. I don't want to hospitalize you. Can you commit to not harming yourself for the next 24 hours until we talk again tomorrow?

J: [pause] Yes.

KC: All right. Then I will not notify anyone, but you must make a commitment to me.

J: OK; do you promise not to tell my parents?

KC: I will not call them with what I know now. But you must agree to call me or the crisis hotline if you decide you want to kill yourself.

J: OK. Would you tell my parents then?

KC: It depends on the situation, but I will be completely honest with you and tell you what I am doing before I do anything.

J: So you won't tell my parents now?

KC: No. I am trusting you to take care of yourself. Will you agree to do that?

J: Yes.

KC: And you will call me if you are getting more suicidal?

J: I might.

KC: I need more of a commitment from you than that.

J: I'll make every effort.

KC: That still leaves you an out.

J: Yes, but don't worry about me.

KC: [gently] It will be impossible for me not to worry about you.

This was a particularly difficult session because I was so conflicted about what to do. I could not get a straight answer from Jill about whether she was an imminent danger to herself or if she was crying out for help. I knew that if I hospitalized her involuntarily, it would destroy the trust in our relationship. I wanted to believe that she would be "fine" but was aware that she was telling me what I needed to hear so I would allow her out of my office. I also knew she had attempted suicide in the past and wondered if this was a serious attempt or a cry for help. So as I shifted to more of a crisis intervention mode, the questions I struggled with were (a) Is she really suicidal (because she is clearly not telling me everything)? and (b) Do I risk the relationship to hospitalize her, or do I trust her tonight?

I also am aware of the dynamics that have evolved in the therapeutic relationship. She views me similarly to her parents (which I have been trying to avoid) and is angry at me for suggesting I could use my power to make her do something she does not want to do. I am uncomfortable with where the session is going because it no longer feels like we are on the same side. My usual approach is to support athletes and to help them make their own choices. At the same time, I have a responsibility to keep Jill safe, and involuntary hospitalization is an option I must consider.

As the session progressed, I decided that Jill was reaching out for help and needed me to hear her struggles and her hurt. This was the only way she knew to communicate the magnitude of it. She needed to have control in a world that felt very out of control to her. So she wanted to leave herself an out by not completely committing to a no-harm contract. At the same time, I wanted to avoid forcing her to do anything (if at all possible). I gave her my home phone number and insisted that she call if needed. She said she would not disturb me at home even though I insisted. I went home that night second guessing myself about how I had handled this situation. Through the night I ran over and over the conversation in my mind, looking for something I might have missed to give me a clue about what she would do. I wondered if I had made the right decision. At 5:00 a.m., she called me, apologizing for disturbing me at home (she had no idea how welcome a disturbance it was!). I was relieved to hear her voice and to know that she had made it through the night. She told me she had gone to a hotel and taken a few pills, but could not sleep. So in a daze she began cutting on herself, not to kill herself, but to feel something. We met the next day to further examine her feelings and actions. She chose life and decided to work through and with the pain. And I realized that I had done the best thing in trusting her to take care of herself.

Shortly after this session, therapy began to progress. We talked about how she could more directly tell me when she was hurting. She continued to struggle with many issues (parents, her future) but was not suicidal. This entire interaction seemed to be a turning point.

Exploring and Expressing Anger and Emotion

J: Today has been awful. If someone just looks at me funny, I start crying [tears up].

KC: What's the matter, Jill?

J: I don't know. I'll be fine, and then my coach will slightly raise his voice, and I'll just cry. And he doesn't understand.

KC: Give me some examples.

J: Well, this didn't happen today, but a while back when I hurt my ankle, I really needed my coach to help me. I couldn't drive, and I needed him to take me to the doctor. And he said he couldn't. He had some paperwork or something to do. I didn't understand because he always takes the other girls. I thought that he should have done his paperwork later, but I never said anything. I just got upset later. I felt so unimportant.

KC: When have you felt this way before?

J: Oh, with my parents, all the time. They expect me to do whatever they need at the drop of a hat. But God forbid I should ever ask for anything or need anything that gets in the way of their plans.

KC: What feelings go along with that?

J: Well, I am upset, sad [cries].

KC: You also seem angry.

J: I guess so. But I can't get angry with other people.

KC: You can't? What happens if you get angry?

J: I might look like my parents. They raged and tied each other up. It was scary. And if I get angry with my parents, they make my life miserable. So it's easier not to.

KC: So it seems there are two things you are saying here. Tell me if you think this is right. One is that your coach has done some things that remind you of your parents' behaviors. And your reactions toward him might be the same as you feel toward your parents. Two is that you have been keeping much of your anger inside.

J: Yes, my coach never understands why I get upset so easily. Actually, it is easier to get mad at my coach than my parents. But usually I don't tell him. Like with needing a ride to the doctor. I finally told him how much that upset me, and he said he didn't know it was so important to me to have him there. He thought the trainer was taking me. He said he would have changed things if he knew how important it was to me. I always just assume that I am unimportant to him and he doesn't care.

KC: So part of it is learning to ask for what you need.

J: Yes, and I've always been afraid to do that with my parents.

KC: It seems that a lot of unexpressed fear and anger toward your parents has built up and maybe some of it gets misdirected. How might you begin to express these feelings more?

J: I have to remember with my coach that I can explain myself more. He's pretty understanding as coaches go. I realize he doesn't know unless I tell him. I don't know about my parents. I can't imagine saying anything. It would be a nightmare.

KC: What about writing them a letter? You would not need to send it, but writing out your feelings as you would like to say them could be helpful. Maybe this would be a way to begin recognizing what you are angry about and directing it to them instead of someone else.

J: Yes, I can do that.

Jill often is unaware of her anger. She also is unaware that she expects the same motives and actions from her coach (or others) as she did from her parents. At home, she learned to hold on to and keep a lid on her anger because releasing it was chaotic and destructive. As she discussed examples of her interactions with her parents, it became clear to me that she did not always clearly communicate her needs and then felt slighted and unimportant. When she feels her coach is treating her similarly, her emotions and reactions to him are the same as to her parents. She interprets her coach's behaviors based on her parents' and then reacts strongly.

Freud's (1953/1917) conceptualization of depression as aggression and anger turned inward is useful for Jill because of her tendency to internalize much of her anger. She feels hurt and cries as opposed to saying, "That made me angry," and then discussing her feelings. She also is directing her anger toward a safer target—her coach. Her parents are really at the root of much of her anger, and she needs to begin directing it to them. She will be unable to do much direct confrontation because it is still too scary for her. Therefore, I suggested a letter that she does not send. This gives her the opportunity to freely express her emotions without repercussions. Later in our therapy, we might take a more cognitive-behavioral approach and begin to role-play how she could directly express anger to her parents. She also can work toward differentiating between inappropriate anger—anger that should really be directed at others—and anger that is left over from feelings towards her parents.

Reframing Parents' Involvement in Sport

J: I know I need to work more on my parents. I just can't seem to get away from them. They do such crazy things every time I try to get some distance from them. I have to talk to them at least every week, and they want to know every detail of my workouts, and then they have to talk about plans for the next tournament and how they will get there. If I try to talk less to them, my mom decides she has some catastrophic illness, and I have to talk with her more [we continue discussing her controlling and manipulative parents].

KC: So it feels like they are in control, and it is uncomfortable for you.

J: Yes.

KC: I wonder how you might begin to set some limits with them.

J: I don't know how. They always make me feel so guilty. If I stop talking to them, they say they have cancer or something. What if one day they really do? They just always know what to say to get me to do what they want.

KC: They seem manipulative and they know all the right buttons to push. How do you feel about trying something different with them? It would be difficult, and there would be pressure for you to fall back into your current role. But what do you think?

J: I don't know. I'll have to see. What is it?

KC: Let's start with something easy. How about telling them you will talk to them every other weekend?

J: Oh, I couldn't. I'd get the cold shoulder from my mom, and then she'd say things like "You never call anymore. You never tell us anything you do. I guess we just aren't important anymore after all we've done for you." Things like that. They would be so mad and make me feel guilty because I am their life.

KC: Hmm, well, you know, I'm thinking, it is not your responsibility to make your parents happy. They have made choices in their lives—to focus on you, not to develop other interests or friendships. I wonder if you do them any favors by continuing to be the dutiful daughter.

J: You don't understand how awful they can be.

KC: You're absolutely right. I haven't lived it as you have. But what I see in you right now is that your fear is preventing you from taking a risk. At first the risk will be challenging and uncomfortable, but it could ultimately make you happier.

J: [pause] Yes, I am afraid. I know what this will do to them. Is it really OK not to be so responsible for them?

KC: Of course; they are adults and must take responsibility for themselves.

J: I don't know . . . when I think about it enough, I know you are right, but when it comes right down to it, I get pulled in and end up doing what they want.

KC: So you know *logically* what the patterns are and what you need to do, and that's a good first step. But your emotional reactions seem to be directing your actions and haven't caught up with your head.

J: Yeah, that's it. Even though I figure it out and resolve myself to putting my foot down with them, I end up giving in. I know they need some help, some therapy. I keep suggesting it, and they refuse. I just can't give up on them.

KC: Try as you might, Jill, you cannot control what they decide to do. All you can do is offer support and suggestions, and they must make their choices.

J: I know. I just feel if I keep trying eventually they will agree.

The parents have had a strong influence on Jill and have invaded her life. She has no separation from them—what they feel, she feels. She has learned to be so in tune with them that she forgets to monitor her own emotions and needs. She feels they control everything and that her own control is limited. These dynamics have played a large role in her depression. My goal is to help her separate from her parents and to confront her on her irrational beliefs that she is responsible for her parents' feelings and well-being. This separation is a very difficult area for her because the patterns and the "dance" she and her parents do is so well choreographed and ingrained. Breaking out of that pattern will be uncomfortable for everyone, and she will feel pressure to maintain the status quo. I do not expect that after this session everything will change. I am planting a seed about how she can respond differently and take control of her life. Cutting down the time she talks with them about general things is a first step. Then we will work on setting more limits on how much they need to know about her tennis. We returned to the topic again and again throughout therapy.

Many of my comments in this session are directive and are geared toward problem solving. My style usually is to allow clients to take charge of devising solutions, but Jill requires more input from me. As a child, her parents did not teach her how to communicate effectively and work out problems. She did not learn how to be separate from her parents because of the enmeshed relationships between all of them. Much of the training in conducting consultations or therapy encourages the consultant or clinician to let clients make their own choices and to be less directive. I find that clients who have been inadequately parented do not always know where to start in solving their problems and they need more input from a therapist. Therefore, I have become more comfortable being directive when needed. I also am challenging her faulty thinking about her need to be responsible for her parents. I am encouraging Jill to take a different view. This change will not happen immediately, and she resists, but these initial challenges contribute to future changes.

Toward the end of therapy, Jill had made a clear shift in how she viewed her parents. She would report their behaviors and reactions and could easily distance herself from them. Instead of feeling guilty and responsible, she truly could say, "They make their own choices. I don't agree with how they have led their lives, and I think they could be happier, but I must let it go." It was such a relief for her to finally come to this conclusion, cognitively and emotionally. Then we worked on grieving the loss of the parents she always wished she'd had.

Termination Session

KC: As we agreed, this will be our last session. Will that still work for you?

J: Yes; things are much better for me.

KC: Let's spend some time reviewing where you are with the issues we've been discussing, then talk about your future goals and leave some time to say goodbye.

J: OK.

KC: First, let's look at your growth. Think about how things were for you when you first came to counseling, and then tell me where you are now.

J: Looking back, I can't believe I was the same person then. I was so depressed and hopeless. I wanted help from people but didn't know how to ask for it. Now, even though I am not always sure how to be most direct, I'm doing better at communicating and asking for what I need. Before, I was so tied in with my parents. I thought I could make them happy by excelling in tennis; I thought that was my duty. And when they weren't happy, I thought it was my responsibility. I would give them suggestions for improving their lives, and they wouldn't listen, and I still felt responsible. I didn't know how to separate my feelings from theirs or how to say no to them. So I was constantly angry and tried indirectly to make my points; then I'd feel guilty. Now I can see that they have chosen to focus on my tennis at the expense of having their own lives and making their own friends. They are so unhappy, but I know I can't be the one to make them happy. I've finally let go of the fantasy that I can ever have the type of relationship with my parents that I wished for.

KC: That is tremendous growth. You really have done a lot of work.

J: I also was thinking about tennis . . .

KC: Let me stop you a minute. I wanted to make sure you heard what I said.

J: Yes; you saw a lot of growth. It's always hard for me to hear the positives. I'm not used to it.

KC: That's why it's important to stay with this for a bit. Are you aware of the incredible growth that you have made happen for yourself?

J: Yes, I know I have worked hard to get better. Thank you for saying that to me.

KC: [pause] Now about tennis . . .

J: Yes. When I first came here, I wasn't doing tennis for me. In fact, I wished I could quit, and I really did want to die, but I guess I didn't have the guts to go through with it. I just couldn't see a way out, and then things were really bad when I came to your office that one day and wanted to overdose. I look back on that now, and I'm embarrassed to say that I was testing you. I desperately needed someone to listen to how much I was hurting. I guess I didn't know how to say it any other way. The fact that you didn't hospitalize me or call my parents made it easier to trust you.

KC: Thank you for telling me that. You know I agonized over what to do and finally decided that I would take the risk of allowing you to work this out yourself. I was relieved when you called me that morning.

J: Now I know better how to explain my pain and don't want to resort to that. Anyway, back to tennis; I've decided that I really don't want to be involved in the sport anymore. I used to hear about people I know winning tournaments. I'd be so envious because I'd think, I could do that, or, I was better than them; I should be doing that. But now I realize that I don't want that life. I don't want to train so many hours a week and travel every available weekend. I don't want to spend so much time with my teammates, who always have cliques or talk behind each other's backs. Most of all, I don't want to do the sport because it was for my parents, not me. They lived through me and made me hate tennis. Everything was so tied into tennis, and now it has a really negative association for me. So I have to be OK with stopping and making some other path for myself in my life. I know I can support myself financially in college if I have to.

KC: I know that is a decision you have struggled with. You now seem fairly comfortable with choosing a new direction.

J: Yes, I know I have to now . . . for me this time.

KC: You have done a wonderful job.

J: Do you really think I'm ready . . . I mean, to stop counseling?

KC: Oh, of course you are. You've been handling stress effectively now for the past few months. You have taken charge of your life. And you know where to find me if something comes up. But now you are ready to be on your own . . . so now we say goodbye.

J: I'm not really sure how to do this [pause]. I really want to tell you how appreciative I am of all your help. Words seem inadequate to express what it means that someone would take such an interest in me and believe in me. I wish there was something I could say.

KC: I understand, and I really appreciate your kind words. I want you to know that I also have truly valued our time together. It was so satisfying to see you learn about yourself and take charge of your life—to come away with confidence and direction. I was pleased to work with you for this past year and a half and to follow your progress. I feel privileged that you shared things with me that you have shared with no one else.

J: I just wish there was some way I could repay you for helping me find my life.

KC: [gently] There is no need. It's good for me to see you happy.

Termination sessions, especially for an athlete like Jill, with whom I have had an ongoing therapy relationship, are difficult for both of us. The athlete is not the only one who has formed an attachment; I have also. Jill planned when termination would occur, and I supported her choice. She wanted to end, yet still was questioning her ability to face challenges without the benefit of weekly or bimonthly therapy. She had come to rely on my input when she questioned herself. One of my goals was to give her my confidence in her so that she felt more comfortable making and standing by her choices in her life. I wanted her to know that she had grown enough and was healthy enough that she did not need me or therapy. So I was clear about knowing she was ready to terminate.

I like to have all clients, but especially those who doubt their "health," to review their progress verbally. And I like to hear them say it so that they listen to their own voices. Often they are surprised at the changes they see when they look over time. They may not see as many changes week-to-week, but over months the changes become apparent. Then I offer my observations as well, if I feel they have left out an important change. Jill could identify substantial changes, and as she reviewed her progress, I could see her confidence building.

She had difficulty accepting my compliment on her growth, an issue we faced frequently in therapy. I believe in recognizing clients' accomplishments whenever they happen and voicing the positive. Jill was not accustomed to hearing such positives growing up and often would not acknowledge that she had heard me. Earlier in therapy I had been confused about why she would ignore what I said. So I would ask her if she had understood my comment. She would say yes, but she was so unaccustomed to hearing positives, she did not know how to respond. Up to the end, I needed to stop her to be certain she could hear what I said.

Jill struggled to communicate her appreciation to me. I felt I understood her, even her unspoken words, but I allowed her to finish because I knew she wanted to verbalize her feelings. I also made a conscious effort to model appropriate and gracious acceptance of her compliments and at the same time to give her the credit for her own growth. It is tempting to take credit for an athlete's progress, but a sport psychology consultant who truly has the athlete's best interest in mind must be content being behind the scenes. Sport psychologists need to empower athletes to take credit for their accomplishments, both physically and mentally. My goal is for athletes to believe that even after sessions with a sport psychology consultant are terminated, they can manage any further challenges they will face.

Interestingly, Jill mentioned the suicide session. Because I had struggled with the best path to take, both to uphold my professional responsibility and to maintain a therapeutic relationship, it was helpful to hear Jill's impressions after being somewhat removed from that time. As I looked back, I could see her need to be heard, and she confirmed that I had adequately conveyed my understanding.

Sport psychology consultants must be prepared to treat more than behavioral performance enhancement concerns when helping athletes. Often more personal, clinical issues can interfere with performance, and the astute consultant must be prepared to treat these concerns or refer to a qualified mental health professional. This chapter illustrates some of the challenges of working with a depressed athlete and highlights some interventions over an 18-month therapy relationship. For another, and quite different, example of an athlete experiencing turmoil and making a suicidal gesture, please see chapter 10 in this volume.

REFERENCES

American Psychiatric Association. (1994). *Diagnostic and statistical manual of mental disorders* (4th ed.). Washington, DC: Author.

Bergandi, T.A., & Wittig, A.F. (1984). Availability of and attitudes toward counseling services for the college athlete. *Journal of College Student Personnel, 25,* 557-558.

Carson, R.C., Butcher, J.N., & Mineka, S. (1998). *Abnormal psychology and modern life* (10th ed.). New York: Longman.

Ellis, A. (1973). Rational-emotive therapy. In R. Corsini (Ed.), *Current psychotherapies* (pp. 167-206). Itasca, IL: F.E. Peacock.

Freud, S. (1953). Mourning and melancholia (J. Riviere, Trans.). In *Collected papers* (vol. 4, pp. 152-170). London: Hogarth Press and Institute of Psychoanalysis. (Original work published in 1917)

Hollon, S.D., & Beck, A.T. (1978). Cognitive and cognitive-behavioral therapies. In A.E. Bergin & S.L. Garfield (Eds.), *Handbook of psychotherapy and behavior change: An empirical analysis* (4th ed., pp. 428-466). New York: Wiley.

Parham, W.D. (1993). The intercollegiate athlete: A 1990s profile. *The Counseling Psychologist, 21,* 411-429.

Pinkerton, R.S., Hinz, L.D., & Barrow, J.C. (1989). The college student-athlete: Psychological considerations and interventions. *Journal of American College Health, 37,* 218-226.

CHAPTER 9

COUNSELING ATHLETES WITH EATING DISORDERS: A CASE EXAMPLE

Trent A. Petrie
University of North Texas
Roberta Trattner Sherman
Bloomington Hospital

Only a small percentage of women in the United States develop diagnosable eating disorders such as anorexia nervosa or bulimia nervosa (American Psychiatric Association [APA], 1994), yet large numbers of women experience a broad range of disordered eating attitudes and behaviors, including high levels of body dissatisfaction or body-image disturbance, excessive exercising to lose weight, binge eating, strict dieting and/or purging (e.g., vomiting), low self-esteem, depression, and unrealistic beliefs about their weight. Recent research suggests that as many as 60% of female undergraduates may experience some level of nondiagnosable eating disturbance (Mintz & Betz, 1988). Men also experience many of the same disordered eating problems, such as body dissatisfaction, restrictive dieting, and excessive exercising to lose weight, though they are less likely to develop a diagnosable eating disorder (APA, 1994). What is not clear about male prevalence rates is whether they accurately reflect the number of men who suffer from eating disorders or whether men underreport the extent to which they experience these problems, perhaps because of an unwillingness to admit to having a "female" problem (Thompson & Sherman, 1993).

The purpose of this chapter is to provide a case example of an athlete who has an eating disorder, specifically bulimia nervosa. The case begins with the initial identification and referral of the problem at the beginning-of-the-season medical evaluations. We then follow the athlete, Bonnie, through her first, second, third, fifth, eleventh, twelfth, and final sessions with the therapist, Dr. T. This case, although accurate in its presentation, does not represent a single, specific athlete. Instead, it illustrates the type of client who we see in our practices and exemplifies the kinds of problems that often arise in working with an athlete who has an eating disorder. Although this case example ends with a positive resolution for the client, it is not the only outcome we have experienced, nor should it suggest that therapists do not make mistakes in their work. In some situations, athletes may struggle for years with their eating disorders or require inpatient care that necessitates dropping out of school and their sports. In other cases, the therapist may fail to connect with the athlete in session, overlook important issues, focus too much on food intake and not enough on thoughts and feelings, try to assert too much control over the person, or set unrealistic expectations regarding treatment outcome (Thompson & Sherman, 1989). Before we discuss Bonnie, though, we provide an overview concerning the general etiology of eating disorders as well as our theoretical model for treating athletes with this disorder.

ETIOLOGY AND MODEL OF TREATMENT

Researchers have identified athletes as potentially at risk for the development of eating disorders (Burckes-Miller & Black, 1991; Petrie, 1993; Wilson & Eldredge, 1992). Athletes experience many of the same general sociocultural pressures as nonathletes, such as U.S. society's emphasis on thinness and unrealistic standards of beauty as portrayed through the media, which may influence people vulnerable to developing eating disorders. Moreover, athletes experience additional social demands and stressors from within the sport environment that may further increase their risk, including (a) coach expectations that the athlete reach and maintain a certain weight; (b) coach beliefs that reductions in weight will automatically lead to improvements in performance; (c) participation in sports that have specific weight requirements, demand a low percentage of body fat for performance, or value thin-body physiques; (d) peer pressure to use pathogenic weight control techniques, or seeing other athletes model such behaviors; and (e) participation in a sport whose culture normalizes pathogenic behaviors (e.g., excessive exercise) and conditions (e.g., amenorrhea) (Swoap & Murphy, 1995; Thompson & Sherman, 1999). In addition, the intense exercise, dietary restraint, and perfectionism common among high-performance athletes may be risk factors for the development of eating disorders (e.g., Davis et al., 1994; Wilson & Eldredge, 1992).

Reviews of eating disorder research with athletes have suggested prevalence rates of diagnosable and subclinical disorders comparable with, and in some cases greater than, those of nonathletes (e.g., Wilmore, 1991). Practitioner formulations of the causes and treatments of eating disorders vary widely depending on the theoretical orientations of the mental health professionals.

From a behavioral perspective, the therapist would evaluate the athlete's sport and social environments to determine what factors are playing roles in reinforcing and maintaining the disordered eating behaviors. Once identified, the therapist could develop a plan to alter the athlete's behaviors by extinguishing maladaptive, dysfunctional patterns and reinforcing new and healthier behaviors. A behavioral approach is useful in helping clients with eating disorders (particularly those who are severely underweight) gain, and then maintain, their weight and return to normal eating patterns (Halmi, 1985).

Psychodynamic approaches have been widely used to treat eating disorders, particularly anorexia nervosa. A psychodynamically oriented therapist who is working with an athlete might explore how the eating disorder symptoms reflect some type of intrapsychic conflict, how the disorder may be part of a power struggle with a parent or other authority figure, how the behaviors may indicate an out-of-control and unintegrated internal life, or how the disorder, particularly when it involves being severely underweight, may concern fears of sexual maturity/development and its impending ramifications. Obviously, in this approach, the focus is on helping athletes gain new understandings (insights) into their current behaviors and, as a result, providing the impetus for change.

Cognitive-behavioral approaches, with their focus on the pathogenic aspects of the sport and social environments and on people's emotional, cognitive, and behavioral responses to those environments, may offer the best match for treating athletes with eating disorders. From this perspective, the therapist works with athletes to identify the dysfunctional beliefs and values about their weight, body shape, worth, and esteem (Fairburn, 1985). The therapist then helps athletes determine the importance of the held beliefs and develop healthier, more functional cognitions about themselves, important others, and the environment. Throughout, the therapist takes an active stance in working with athletes. In addition, the therapist may at times shift into a psychoeducational approach. The purpose of using this approach is to educate athletes on normal and healthy ways of feeling, thinking, and behaving with regard to such issues as food, body size, relationships, and exercise/training.

Eating disorders are usually related to a combination of sociocultural, familial, personality, and biological factors. In essence, eating disorders are multidimensional and require professionals to intervene in multiple ways. In our work with clients who have eating disorders, we operate from a flexible cognitive-behavioral perspective that focuses on changing clients' behaviors and thoughts as they relate to the disorder. This approach includes modifying unhealthy eating and weight-related behaviors such as restrictive dieting, binge eating, purging (vomiting, laxative abuse), and excessive exercise. We also focus on helping clients change how they think about food, weight, their bodies, themselves, their relationships, and their lives. More specifically, we want to help them make their thoughts more rational, accurate, and positive. Clients' emotions affect, and are affected by, their behaviors and thoughts. Thus, we try to help them learn how to deal with their feelings without resorting to deleterious food- or weight-related thoughts or behaviors.

Most clients' treatments can be facilitated by involving significant others, such as parents, whenever possible. These significant others may come to therapy with the clients or the clients may talk to the person(s) on their own. Either way, clients benefit from sharing their thoughts and feelings with someone else and receiving support in return. We also recommend that clients work with a dietitian to receive nutritional information and guidance. By incorporating a dietitian into the treatment team, in-session time can be spent addressing inter- and intrapersonal aspects of the disorder and not simply managing food intake. In some cases, medication (typically antidepressants) may be a useful adjunct to this cognitive-behavioral approach. Receiving relief from depressive symptoms allows clients to focus on the dysfunctional thoughts, feelings, and behaviors that perpetuate the disorder. Finally, as central as all of the aforementioned components are in producing therapeutic change, how they are presented and implemented is perhaps more important. That is, the relationship between the therapist and the client and the processes that occur within that relationship can have a significant influence on the outcome of treatment (Thompson & Sherman, 1989). Thus, we always focus on developing an open, honest, genuine, and supportive relationship with our clients.

WEIGH-IN

At the beginning of each preseason, athletic trainers and the sports medicine physicians at the university Bonnie attends conduct medical evaluations for each team. First, athletic trainers see athletes individually to collect basic physical measurements. After this meeting, athletes are escorted to another room where the sports medicine physician conducts the physical exam. The case study begins with the interaction between a female athletic trainer, who is starting the physical evaluation, and Bonnie, a second-year swimmer for her NCAA Division I women's swim team.

Trainer: Bonnie, like we did at the beginning of last season, we're going to measure your height, weight, resting heart rate, and blood pressure to get baseline measurements for the year.

In our opinion, physical measurements such as height and particularly weight should be obtained only for necessary medical reasons (e.g., establishing baseline health data or determining hydration status after intense physical workouts). As illustrated by this case, weigh-ins should be done privately by a trusted and sensitive sports medicine staff member. In addition, because weight is a sensitive and personal issue for many people, it is important to let the athlete know why this information is being obtained and how it will be used.

Bonnie [appearing anxious and upset] Do I have to be weighed?

Trainer: Well, it is something we do as part of our physical exam [pause]. Is something bothering you about doing it?

B: I just don't like people knowing my weight, especially coach.

Coaches should not be involved in the weigh-in process, nor should weight be a central factor for making decisions regarding playing time or team selection (Thompson & Sherman, 1993). Although this hands-off approach may not reflect the current reality, in our opinion it represents the environmental ideal that we would like to see in all sport programs. Too many coaches are intimately involved in yearly, monthly, or even weekly weigh-ins. In a situation where a coach is concerned about a particular athlete's weight, we recommend that the coach relay that concern to the sports medicine staff. Sports medicine staff can then interact with the athlete regarding weight-related issues.

Trainer: I understand, and I want you to know that our general policy is to not share weight information with coaches unless there are extenuating circumstances, such as if the athlete's health were at risk [pause]. Is there something else bothering you that you want to talk about?

B: Well, I tried to drop some weight over the summer, but I couldn't. I'm heavier than I should be, and it's going to affect my times. Besides, I hate the way my body looks in a [swim]suit.

Trainer: I really do understand. A lot of the women athletes I've worked with over the years have expressed similar concerns. They feel really anxious about their weight and how they look. Some, too, are worried about how they might perform in the upcoming season, particularly if their coach told them they needed to lose weight.

B: I don't know what to do. I've been really worried about coming back to school and what would happen to me with my weight this high. I even tried to get out of this physical, but coach made it clear to us that we had to get it done now.

Trainer: Have you talked with anyone else about these concerns you've just shared with me?

B: No, not really. I was embarrassed, and I didn't want anyone else to know. Besides, I hoped I'd be able to lose the weight before I got to school [pause]. Do you think I should talk to someone?

Trainer: Yeah, it might be helpful. Trying to cope with weight issues can be hard. Sometimes talking with someone else can make things seem a little easier to handle.

B: Can I just talk with you?

Trainer: You can, but I also think it would be helpful to talk with someone else [pause]. I'm really glad that you told me all that you did, and I'd really like to help you. I just don't think I'd be the best person, because I don't have enough experience in this area. But there's someone else who I think could be really helpful. His name is Dr. Thomas, and he's a really nice man. He's helped a lot of our athletes who have had similar eating and weight concerns. Besides, meeting with him once won't hurt, and it might really help.

B: Do I have to?

Trainer: No, but I know I'd feel better if you talked with him.

B: [pause] How would I get in touch with him?

Trainer: I'd be happy to call him now to set up an appointment. Also, if you'd like, I can go with you to the first meeting and introduce you to him. I think you'll like him a lot and find him really helpful [pause]. Would you like me to make the call?

B: Yeah, I think so.

In this interview, the athletic trainer chose not to interrogate Bonnie about her specific eating behaviors. Instead, she paid attention to the anxiety that Bonnie was experiencing about being weighed and to the comments she made about her body. This athletic trainer was experienced enough to know that such anxiety and comments usually are red flags indicating a person at high risk for eating-related problems. Some trainers and sports medicine staff are comfortable discussing eating concerns in more detail and may ask about the length and severity of the eating problem, the extent to which the problem is interfering with the athlete's daily functioning (e.g., going to classes, practicing), and how the athlete has coped with the problem up to this point in time. Others, however, are not as comfortable or skilled and will focus primarily on making a referral to an eating disorder specialist. Whichever route the sports medicine staff takes, it is important that the issue be handled as sensitively and nonjudgmentally as possible, with the focus being on how athletes are feeling and not just on what they are eating or if they are purging.

Ideally, anyone working with athletes who have eating disorders should have expertise in the area. In addition, an understanding of sport and of the demands of high-level competition will facilitate the development of a therapeutic alliance. Without such knowledge, the eating disorder specialist may lack credibility and be less able to communicate effectively with the athlete. The athlete may then drop out of treatment prematurely. Thus, before beginning to work with athletes, therapists may find it profitable to develop an understanding of sport competition and athletes' experiences (Cogan & Petrie, 1996). Therapists who are less familiar with athletics and the sport culture can improve their understanding through personal participation in sports; by reading popular books written by athletes, coaches, and journalists; by talking directly with athletes and coaches; and by watching sporting events and talking with more knowledgeable spectators. Because athletics holds such a prominent position in so many cultures, gaining access to information about sport should not be too difficult.

In referring Bonnie, the trainer did three important things. First, she recommended a mental health professional who specializes in eating disorders. Because of the multidimensional nature of eating disorder problems, it is helpful for trainers and other health care providers to have good working relationships with professionals from other disciplines (such as psychology, medicine, or nutrition) who are trained in the treatment of eating disorders. Second, she normalized the situation by letting Bonnie know that this professional worked with other athletes at their school (but did so without revealing the names of the athletes). In addition, she created positive expectations for Bonnie through her description of the professional and her suggestion that Bonnie would like him. Third, the trainer helped Bonnie make an appointment by offering to call the professional at that moment. She also framed her statements as questions, including Bonnie in the decision-making process and providing her with support and validation. Although some may view this approach as taking too much responsibility for the athlete, we have found that athletes generally appreciate this kind of help and do not develop any unwanted dependencies. In addition, facilitating the referral in this manner increases the likelihood the athlete will follow through and receive the help she needs.

INITIAL MEETING

The initial meeting between the therapist and the client is a key moment. If a connection is not made, the likelihood of the client returning for a second session is significantly decreased. In Bonnie's case, as they had agreed, she and the athletic trainer went to the therapist's office together. This extra effort on the trainer's part greatly increased Bonnie's level of comfort and made her more willing, initially, to talk with the therapist. Because of the distance of Dr. Thomas' office from the university, the trainer drove Bonnie to this initial session and agreed to meet her after the session to take her back to the athletic facilities.

Dr. T: Hi, I'm Jim Thomas, and I'm happy to meet you. Please have a seat. When I talked with your trainer on the phone last week, she said that you might have some concerns that we could talk about [moment of silence]. Today is our chance to get to know one another and for me to better understand what's on your mind or what may be bothering you [pause]. To find out more about you, I'm going to ask you a lot of questions about a lot of different areas in your life. For instance, I'm interested in learning more about your sport performance, about your family, and about how you are doing at school. Although some of these questions may not seem directly related to what's been bothering you lately, they help me get to know you better and get a complete picture of who you are and how you are doing [moment of silence]. At the end of the session today, I want to spend a few minutes reviewing what we discussed and sharing my impressions. At that time we can decide how we want to continue to work together. Does that sound okay to you?

B: Yeah, I guess so. I mean, I've never been to a shrink before so I don't really know what to do in here.

Dr. T: Well, that's understandable. You can think of our time together as an opportunity for you to talk with someone who is not intimately involved in your sport environment. Sometimes, talking with someone outside of the athletic department can be helpful. By discussing any concerns you have, we can set some goals for how you can feel better, whether that is in school, your relationships, your sport, or in any other area of your life. We can then begin to work together to determine the best ways you can reach your goals and feel more satisfied with your life. What I'm most interested in is your health and happiness [pause]. Do you have any initial concerns about talking with me?

B: Well, I'm worried that my coach will not understand why I'm here and will be mad at me.

Dr. T: First, let me assure you that whatever we talk about is confidential. That means I won't share any information that you tell me without your written consent. I am here to help *you*. You are my concern, not your coach. If your coach does contact me, you and I will need to talk about what you would like me to say—if anything at all. Generally, all the coach wants to know is if you are attending your sessions and if, in general, you are making progress, but I can't even share that information without your consent. If a coach requests more detailed information, I would talk with you first. Would you be comfortable with my taking that approach in your situation?

B: Yeah, I think that sounds OK.

Dr. T: Good. Second, if you ever have any questions about what I'm thinking or what we're doing in here, I want you to know that it is OK to ask. I'll always tell you the truth and hope that you'll do the same with me.

In this initial segment, several important issues are covered. First, Dr. T provides Bonnie with a framework for how they will work together. In our opinion, the therapeutic process works best when it is not shrouded in mystery; instead, we always make the client-athlete aware of how therapy will proceed. Being up-front and honest about what is to transpire during sessions can go a long way toward establishing a strong working alliance. Second, Dr. T discusses the issue of confidentiality with Bonnie. In many situations, athletes are concerned about information getting back to their coaches or athletic department administrators. They often are scared of some form of retribution, such as being benched or even kicked off the team. Thus, spending sufficient time discussing how information shared in therapy will be handled can make the athlete feel more comfortable and increase the likelihood that he or she will open up. Athletes, however, function in complex systems, and some form of communication with coaches or the sports medicine staff, as outlined by Dr. T, may be necessary, particularly when treating an athlete with an eating disorder. Third, Dr. T established the expectation of honesty between Bonnie and himself. We want our clients to know that they can always ask us questions about their treatment and themselves and that we will always be honest with them. We also want them to realize that, without honest communication and disclosure, therapy will progress very slowly, if at all.

Dr. T: Bonnie, we've talked a lot about how we're going to work together, do you have any other questions before we discuss the concerns your athletic trainer mentioned?

B: No, I don't think so. I'm glad we talked about my coach and how to handle him. I feel better knowing that you aren't going to tell him the specific things I say.

Dr. T: I'm glad we cleared that up and you feel more comfortable. Remember, too, you can ask me anything at any time [moment of silence]. OK, so why don't we start by you telling me what you like about swimming.

Starting with easier topics, such as background information about the sport or his or her level of enjoyment, can help the athlete be more comfortable and ease into more emotionally challenging topics (see chapter 1 for more information on beginning relationships). As the practitioner explained to the athlete initially, the bulk of the session involves collecting a wide range of information. Because the presenting problem involves eating and weight concerns, obtaining information in those areas is necessary. Specifically, the following topics are covered during the intake:

- Personal History—family, issues growing up, current and past friendships and romantic relationships, current social networks, and levels of social support
- Medical Conditions and Medications—gastrointestinal problems, diarrhea, dizziness, menstrual status, and drug/alcohol use

- Eating and Weight History—history of fasting, bingeing and purging, current and past weight, exercise status (e.g., whether the athlete exercises beyond what is required by coaching staff), current appetite, what the relationship is between the athlete's eating and his or her sport performance, and what stressors may have precipitated the current binge-purge behaviors
- Sport Concerns—relationships with teammates and coaching staff, satisfaction with performance, training regimens, and practice and competitive schedules
- Other—academic/school performance and job/career status
- Current Symptoms (and severity of the symptoms)—levels of depression and anxiety, sleep patterns, level of focus/concentration, and memory

The preceding recommendations are only a summary. A more detailed discussion of how to obtain a complete assessment of someone with an eating disorder can be found in Crowther and Sherwood (1997).

Dr. T: Well, Bonnie, we're about out of time for today. As I said at the beginning of our session, I want to spend a few minutes summarizing what we discussed and talking about where to go from here. Okay?

B: Sure.

Dr. T: From what you told me today, it seems that the pressures of school and swimming have been really tough for you. Also, because you haven't made many friends here, there aren't too many people to talk with about the academic, athletic, and personal stressors you're experiencing. Does that seem accurate?

B: Yeah; I've felt really stressed and alone here.

Dr. T: You also mentioned how dissatisfied you are with your body shape and appearance and how your eating has gotten out of control. You said you've been bingeing since last spring and have been vomiting for the last couple of months. Clearly, the stress of being away from home, the academic pressures of school, and the higher level of athletic competition at the college level all have played a role. I know that this has been really upsetting to you and that you want to stop the bingeing and purging.

B: I feel so out of control that I sometimes just don't want to eat.

Dr. T: I know this is a scary time for you, but these are things we can talk about and hopefully resolve. I know we only touched on some of these areas, but we can pick up there next week if you want. Are you interested in rescheduling for next week?

B: I don't know. I feel a little better having talked with you, but I'm not sure if I have the time to come back every week.

Dr. T: Well, that's understandable. It's a tough time for you, and you aren't sure if meeting with me will help [pause]. Over the years, I've worked with many other athletes who have shared your concerns and been in similar positions. Getting started can be hard. But once they do, I've found that most of the athletes feel much happier and healthier by not having to keep all their thoughts and feelings to themselves. Having someone else to talk to and work through the problems with gives them a great sense of relief.

B: I'd like that, too, but I just don't know.

Dr. T: I'll tell you what, why don't we go ahead and schedule an appointment for next week at the same time. In the meantime, think about how you want to change to make yourself healthier and happier. If you decide to come back next week, you can bring these ideas to the session and we can talk further. If you want to cancel, just call me at the number on this card.

In this session, Dr. T has connected with Bonnie, though she still is reluctant to commit to once-a-week therapy. In order to commit to therapy, Bonnie must believe that Dr. T can help her as he has helped the other athletes with whom he has worked. Although Bonnie's sadness, pain, fear, and desire for things to be different are intense, her current condition also is very familiar, and thus, provides some psychological comfort. This comfort is a challenge for any therapist who tries to establish an alliance with a client. How do therapists help clients let go of their familiar and comfortable (yet dysfunctional) patterns so that clients can develop more functional, yet unknown (and thus, scary) behaviors?

In closing the intake, Dr. T did several things to strengthen the connection (and the future therapeutic alliance) between Bonnie and himself. First, he summarized the major points of the session, which allowed him to check how accurately he had understood Bonnie and her issues. This summary also enabled him to communicate that he had listened to and really cared about Bonnie. Second, he validated her feelings of being scared and unsure and normalized the process of therapy. He also gave her hope by mentioning the other athletes with whom he had worked and how talking had helped them feel happier and healthier. Third, when Bonnie was unsure if she wanted to return, he set up an appointment anyway. For us, handling appointments in this manner communicates to clients that we want to work with them and that we believe therapy can help while still giving them ultimate control over whether they return. Finally, he gave her something to think about until the next session. Providing clients with homework communicates that, in order to change, the client must be willing to work throughout each week and not just during the session. This out-of-session involvement helps clients stay more focused on their goals and more invested in the change process.

SESSION 2

Two days before the scheduled appointment, Bonnie called Dr. T's office to let him know that she would be there. That she is going to keep the appointment suggests that she believes therapy may be beneficial, though it is likely she still has some reluctance or ambivalence that will need to be addressed in future sessions. The athletic trainer will not accompany her to this session; Bonnie has made arrangements to get to Dr. T's office on her own.

Dr. T: So, how are you doing today, Bonnie?

B: Well, OK. I felt a little better after we talked last week.

Dr. T: I'm glad. I thought we had a good first meeting, too. You shared a lot of personal information that helped me get to know you better and understand your situation more clearly. Today, though, instead of my just asking you a lot of questions, I thought we could start by you telling me what you've been thinking about and doing since we last met.

B: [hesitating] Well, I was really bad over the weekend.

Dr. T: Bad? What do you mean, bad? Did you rob a bank or something?

B: [laughing] No. I just had a tough time over the weekend. My roommate had some friends in from out of town, but I really did not feel up to going out with them. I felt overwhelmed with school and ate a lot. I also threw up a few times.

Dr. T: [voice gentle and caring] So you felt lonely and had some trouble with your eating. Does that make you a bad person?

At the beginning of the second meeting, it is important for the therapist to affirm all the work that was done during the first meeting. It is not enough, however, just to say that the session was good. Dr. T also describes to Bonnie what made the session useful. In doing so, he communicates to Bonnie that certain behaviors are more beneficial to the therapy process than others. In addition, it is useful to begin sharing the responsibility of therapy with the client. Dr. T instructed Bonnie to begin the session and decide on the focus. Things may have happened to the client since the last meeting, and the only way to enter the client's phenomenological world is to let her experience and, in essence, talk about what is important to her. Thus, we refrain from putting too much structure on the client at the beginning of a session, that is, in defining the topic of the day. It can be much more informative to let clients begin and see what they bring up on their own.

When given the opportunity to begin a session on their own, it is not uncommon for clients with eating disorders to focus on their food intake and purging and let those behaviors define their self-worth. Through humor, Dr. T gently challenges Bonnie's notion of what is "bad." Humor in therapy has positive and negative aspects. Sometimes humor can be used (unconsciously) as a distancing defense. Bonnie just revealed some emotionally laden material, and then Dr. T made a joke, possibly because of his trepidations about diving into her emotionally precarious world. On the other hand, there are probably few better signs of a positively developing relationship than a therapist and client laughing together. Humor can be a valuable tool in therapy, but it can also serve the therapist's needs.

Dr. T uses Bonnie's feelings of being bad to introduce the idea that her worth and esteem as a person do not equal her eating behaviors. This separation of self-worth from external behaviors is often a theme throughout the treatment of clients with eating disorders.

Because the topic of the session is her eating difficulties, Dr. T addresses the issue of working with other eating disorder professionals, such as a dietitian and physician, in a team approach to treatment.

Dr. T: Since your eating is a problem that you want to change, I'd like you also to work with a dietitian. Have you ever worked with one or been on a meal plan?

B: No, I don't think so. What is it, some kind of special diet?

Dr. T: Actually it's quite different from a diet. Whereas the focus of a diet is to avoid certain foods, the focus of a meal plan is to figure out what nutrients are important for your health and to make a plan that ensures you'll get all of those nutrients each day. Having an eating plan puts the focus on health and can help you control your bingeing and purging. How does that sound to you?

B: OK, I guess, but this doesn't mean that I'm going to gain weight, does it?

Dr. T: Usually, it doesn't, unless your body is currently underweight. The focus of the meal plan is to provide you with the energy you need to function your best in all areas of your life, including your sport performance. Here is the name of a dietitian I work with. She really understands athletes and is very easy to talk to. I'm sure that she can answer any specific questions you have. Would you like to call her now to set up an appointment, or do you want to do it later when you are by yourself?

The team approach can be used effectively to address the multidimensional aspects of an eating disorder (Thompson & Sherman, 1993). In the preceding passage, Dr. T makes a referral to a dietitian who can help Bonnie establish regular, healthy eating patterns. By allowing the dietitian to focus on the specifics of food intake and energy output, the therapist is freed to focus more on the interpersonal and emotional aspects of the problem. This shift does not mean, though, that the therapist should not check in with the athlete about eating and purging behavior—he should. With the dietitian on the team, eating does not have to become the sole focus of each session (a situation that can be detrimental to the therapeutic process) (Thompson & Sherman, 1989).

In addition, because people with eating disorders often have concomitant physical complications, it is important for them to be evaluated medically. Ideally, this evaluation would be done by a physician who is trained to identify and treat eating disorders. Such evaluations may address gastrointestinal concerns, menstrual irregularities, blood chemistry, and electrolyte status. Dr. T makes a referral for Bonnie to see a physician because she complains of stomach pains and vomits regularly. If clients balk at seeing the physician, we take the time to explore their reluctance in session and try to help them feel more positive about the experience. We do not try to force them to go, but we do make them aware of the role a physical checkup plays in their improvement. If they are uncomfortable with a specific physician or (for college athletes) with the student health center in general, then we make a referral to another professional in the community.

The therapist can coordinate and maintain communication with the other professionals on a team. Before doing so, though, the therapist clearly explains to the client how the team will work and how communication will occur. Although clients may initially balk at the idea of several people talking about their problems, once we emphasize that coordinated treatment efforts facilitate recovery, they may feel more comfortable. We always tell our clients that they will be apprised of our communications with treatment team members and that they can ask us questions about what has been said at any time. This openness and honesty help them feel more in control of and involved in treatment. If clients agree with the team approach, we have them give consent to each professional involved so that communication can occur.

Dr T: When you see the dietitian, she'll ask you to keep a food log, which is like a diary where you record all that you eat each day. Although some people find them a bit tedious, it's important that you follow through and complete them. Doing so will help you identify problem areas so that we can develop the best strategies for eliminating your eating mistakes.

To increase the likelihood of treatment compliance, Dr. T prepares Bonnie for what she will experience when she works with the dietitian. He also offers a subtle reframing of her eating behaviors by referring to them as mistakes. This cognitive strategy helps normalize (somewhat) her actions and sets a nonjudgmental tone for future discussions regarding her feelings, her thoughts, and her eating behaviors.

Although clients may want to spend entire sessions focusing on their eating, the therapist can redirect them to the issues that likely underlie their disordered behaviors.

Dr. T: Bonnie, we've spent the first 20 minutes talking about your eating situation. I know that's a big part of your life right now, and I think working with the dietitian and physician will help [pause]. I'd like us to talk about other aspects of your life as well. Have you thought any more about the other problem areas that you identified last week?

B: Yeah; I thought a lot about my family and the expectations they have for me. I want to do so well in school and in swimming, yet when I don't, I feel like I'm letting them down. I think that's why I felt so depressed this weekend—I just don't know if I can handle all the pressures.

Throughout the remainder of the session, Dr. T guides Bonnie to discuss these more interpersonal issues as well as how she is coping with her school, sport, and family demands. By focusing on these issues, and on how Bonnie thinks about and feels about them, Dr. T is letting her know that he is interested in her as a person and is concerned about her overall happiness. He also is laying the groundwork for her to understand that her eating is really more a symptom of these other inter- and intrapersonal issues than the problem per se. To recover, she will need to address the underlying problem areas, learn new behaviors, and think and feel differently about herself and her relationships.

Dr. T: Bonnie, we're about out of time, but before we end, I wanted to let you know that I really appreciate all the work you're doing in here. You've shared a lot of personal information, some of which is very painful for you. I know it's not always easy to do, but being open and honest can only help us in our work together.

B: Thanks. I'm trying my best to tell you what's going on.

Dr. T: I know you are [silence]. Now, let's take a minute to summarize what we discussed today. We initially talked about your eating and how things had gone over the weekend. We agreed that you would go see the physician and begin working with the dietitian. Will you be able to make the appointments before our next meeting?

B: Yeah, I think so. I'll call tomorrow and see what's available.

Dr. T: Good. We also discussed a lot of nonfood-related issues, particularly your academics, your family, your coach, yourself, and your support network at school. Is that what you remember?

B: Yeah, that sounds about right.

Dr. T: OK. Over the next week I'd like you to think some more about these five areas and write down some goals you have. That is, how you would like to change in those areas and what things you can do to make those changes happen. OK?

B: Yeah, I think I understand.

Dr. T: Let me give you an example. You said you don't feel really close to your teammates or roommate, or to anybody else on campus for that matter. Maybe your goal could be to establish two or three friendships over the course of the semester. I'm not necessarily talking about becoming best friends, I just mean starting the process of getting to know some different people so you have someone to talk to. To do that, you might go to a party with some of your teammates, or eat meals with your roommate, or join a study group in one of your classes. How you do it is up to you. Does that make sense?

B: Yeah, thanks.

Dr. T: One last thing before we go. How you are feeling about working with me? Are we moving in the directions you see as important?

B: [pauses] I'm comfortable with you, though I'm a little overwhelmed by all that we've discussed. I know this is going to help, but I wish it weren't so hard.

As in the first session, Dr. T reinforces Bonnie's openness and honesty and communicates that the process of change is not always easy. Again, he summarizes the major issues that have been discussed and asks Bonnie to work on them during the upcoming week. Her homework assignments for the week will keep her treatment and the changes that she wants to make in the forefront of her mind, which can be helpful for clients with eating disorders because they often have the tendency to deny and delay what is painful or anxiety producing. By asking Bonnie how she feels about working with him, he communicates that he values the relationship and that he wants her to feel free to tell him if something is not going well. For us, the therapeutic relationship is the primary mechanism for change (see Petitpas, Danish, & Giges, 1999).

SESSION 3

During the week between sessions, the dietitian called to let Dr. T know that Bonnie had been in to see her and that they were working on the food logs for the first week. Bonnie began the session, talking without being prompted by Dr. T.

B: I saw the dietitian already, and I've begun to do the food logs. It's a pain, but she said doing them would help me make positive changes in my eating. You were right; she's really nice.

Dr. T: I'm glad you've started. She called to tell me that you'd been in but that you still had a few more days to go on the logs before she could give you anything concrete about your intake and energy expenditures.

B: I go back in a couple of days to talk about all that stuff then.

Dr. T: [nods]

B: Oh yeah, I also have an appointment with the physician. I couldn't get in until tomorrow, but I did call last week. I didn't want you to think I was blowing it off.

Dr. T: I didn't think you would. I trust that you'll be honest with me and let me know what's going on.

It is clear that Bonnie is learning the "rules" of therapy. That is, she coming to realize that the session is her time and that she does not have to wait for Dr. T to ask her questions before she can begin talking about what has been happening to her. In addition, she appears to not want to let her therapist down, which may signal her increasing commitment to therapy and trust in Dr. T. He affirms the importance of trust and honesty as the foundation of good therapeutic work.

Dr. T: Have you been thinking about anything else over the past week?

B: Yeah, I thought a lot about my eating and swimming. I realized that I feel a lot of pressure to lose weight for swimming.

Dr. T: Tell me more about the pressure.

B: Well, I don't like how I look in my suit. I feel fat, like my butt's just hanging out there and everyone is looking at it.

Dr. T: Do you feel this way in other situations?

B: Yeah, all the time; it's just worse when I'm wearing a suit and others are around.

Dr. T: Has anyone ever said you were fat or overweight?

B: No, most people tell me I'm in good shape and they wish they could look like me. But, they're probably just being nice and trying to make me feel better.

Dr. T: Sounds like your perception of your body size and shape is quite different from others'. Do you think you can see yourself accurately?

Body dissatisfaction and body image disturbance are primary characteristics of people with eating disorders. For athletes, these problems are often exacerbated by the environment and attire in which they must compete. In addition, the bodies of those in athletes' closest comparison groups (other athletes) are much closer to the societal ideal than most other people's bodies are. This may increase the pressures athletes feel to be thin and may explain their tendency to evaluate their bodies negatively. To be successful, body image treatments must (a) help clients achieve a more accurate view of their actual body size, (b) challenge society's unrealistic expectations about body shape and diet, and (c) help clients separate their self-worth from how they look and what they eat.

To address Bonnie's negative body image, Dr. T used an intervention that would provide Bonnie with concrete and visual information on how big she actually is versus how big she thinks she is (Sherman & Thompson, 1997). For this intervention, Dr. T placed a four-foot-long section of rope on the table and asked Bonnie to estimate the circumference of her hips by moving the rope into a circle that she believed reflected her current size. Dr. T marked this spot on the rope. Dr. T then had Bonnie wrap the rope around her hips so he could mark her actual size. As is the case with most eating disordered people, Bonnie significantly overestimated the size of her hips. This powerful visual feedback brought to light how inaccurate her own perceptions and self-statements about her body were. It also gave her and Dr. T ammunition to refute the belief that she was fat.

After this intervention, Dr. T and Bonnie discuss the other ways in which swimming is a stressor for her concerning weight.

Dr. T: You mentioned pressures; what other ones are there?

B: Well, I think I'd swim faster if I weighed less and were thinner.

Dr. T: Are the fastest swimmers on your team the thinnest?

B: No, but coach said my times would drop if I were in better shape.

Dr. T: What do you think he meant by that?

B: If I lost weight, I'd be faster.

Dr. T: Really? When you said that, I thought about other areas of your training, like strength and conditioning. Also, you just told me that being the thinnest does not always translate into being the fastest. There are a lot of individual differences that affect athletic performance [pause]. Could you be using your weight as an excuse?

B: What do you mean?

Dr. T: Some athletes find it easier to blame their weight when they aren't competing well instead of looking at other factors that might be affecting their performances [pause]. Does that hold true for you in any way?

B: [Pause as she looks down at her feet] Yeah, it does. It's hard for me to admit, but one of the first things I think of when I don't perform well is, If only I weren't so damn fat. It's only later that I might consider how I'd been training and practicing or whether my technique was any good that race.

For athletes with eating disorders, another ingrained belief is that weight loss automatically translates into improved performance. Thinner is better! Unfortunately, this belief creates additional pressure on people who are struggling with eating problems. Thus, therapists can introduce the idea that physical performance generally is the result of many interacting factors, only one of which may be weight. Athletes who hold irrational beliefs about weight and performance can be challenged to look at their performance more broadly and to focus on other aspects of training, such as strength and conditioning or mental skill building—areas that do not carry the same risks as dieting.

At the conclusion of this session, Dr. T introduces the emotion log to Bonnie.

Dr. T: We've talked a lot today about your feelings and how they're related to your eating, your sport, and the way you see your body. To help you become more aware of the relationship between your emotions and these other situations, I'd like you to begin keeping an emotion log. During the next week, I'd like you to use this handout to record how you are feeling, what you are thinking, and where you are whenever you eat. This could mean a full-blown binge and purge or just a time when you've eaten normally. I'm interested in learning more about what is going on for you when you eat, and the best way to do that is to record your thoughts, feelings, and behaviors in the moment. Does this make sense to you?

B: I think so. You want me to write down what I'm feeling when I eat, whether it's a binge or not.

Dr. T: Right, but not just what you feel. I'd also like you to record where you were when you ate and what you were thinking before, during, and after. There are places on the handout where you can record all that I've mentioned. I'd like you to do this each day for the next week and then to bring the logs to our next meeting. Can you do that?

B: Yeah, I think so.

Dr. T: [supportively] I'm not concerned with whether or not you binge or purge. You probably still will at this point in time. What I'm concerned with is that you begin to record your thoughts, feelings, and behaviors—the important point is for us to learn from any eating mistakes.

An emotion log (see table 9.1 for an example) can help increase clients' awareness about what does and does not trigger problematic eating and what is going on when they eat normally. We try to introduce this intervention relatively early in the treatment process. Clients with eating disorders generally feel out of control during a binge and purge—as if they are being compelled into the behaviors by external forces. Yet, the reality is that there are many environmental, emotional, and cognitive triggers that are within their control and likely contribute to the problematic behaviors. By becoming aware of what these triggers are—be they feelings, thoughts, behaviors, or physical environments—clients increase their chances of coping in different ways and making alternative behavioral choices.

SESSION 4

During the fourth session, Bonnie and Dr. T reviewed her emotion logs. They discovered that her binges appeared to be tied to her stress level. Whenever she became overwhelmed, which was usually in conjunction with having lots of homework or having bad workouts, she would get down on herself about her abilities and, ultimately, about how she looked. The more negatively she thought about herself, the sadder she became and the more she withdrew from others. This withdrawal generally coincided with her bingeing, which acted as a salve

Table 9.1 Emotion Log—Monitoring of Eating and Related Feelings, Thoughts, Behaviors, and Environments

Date :

Time of Day	Food/Liquid Consumed	Binge	Purge	Emotions/Thoughts/Behaviors/Context

1. Time of Day—indicate when you ate/drank.
2. Food/Liquid Consumed—indicate what you ate/drank (be as specific as possible in terms of amount and what was eaten).
3. Binge—place a check here if you considered what you ate/drank to be a binge.
4. Purge—place a check if you purged following what you ate/drank.
5. Emotions/Thoughts/Behaviors/Context—describe your emotions, thoughts, and behaviors before, during, and after eating. Also, describe the context (or environment) you were in when you ate.

against the loneliness and low self-regard. Unfortunately, the relief she felt was short-lived, as she would soon begin to worry about what she had just eaten and how she was going to become fatter than she already was. As her anxiety about weight gain increased, so did her need to purge the now unwanted food, which she did either through vomiting or additional exercising. Following the purge, she would feel disgusted with herself and would vow to restrict her food intake and not overeat..

As Dr. T and Bonnie identified this clear pattern, they discussed other ways to cope when feeling stressed. The different approaches they explored included talking more realistically about the situation (e.g., "I am feeling stressed now because I have a lot of schoolwork to do. I just need to get started and get through some of the assignments; then I'll feel better") and more positively about her athletic performance (e.g., "I really can do this. I just had an off day of practice, so I'll come back tomorrow and do the best I can. Everyone has an off day once in a while"). They also discussed how she tended to isolate herself from others and how this likely amplified her feelings of loneliness. Instead of pulling away from others when stressed or feeling down, she could reach out to her friends to get support and caring. Finally, they talked about how she could handle situations if she did binge eat; she did not have to purge automatically as she previously had. Dr. T further educated her about the realities of good nutrition and about the effects of vomiting and reminded her that she had concrete, visual proof that she was not as big as she had previously thought. He encouraged her to talk with others when she was feeling anxious about having overeaten and to practice talking more positively and humanely to herself about her situation. He also recommended that she use her emotion log to express the feelings she was experiencing.

By the fifth session, Bonnie had worked with the dietitian for a little over two weeks and had seen the physician. The physician had called Dr. T about Bonnie's exam and blood work; there were no medical problems. Bonnie also had started following the meal plans that she and the dietitian developed. As a result, she was beginning to feel more in control of her eating. Nevertheless, she still was feeling stressed about swimming and was beginning to realize that she might not want to compete anymore.

B: This has been a good week.

Dr. T: Good? How so?

B: Well, I mean I've been feeling more in control of my eating. I've been using the food plans pretty regularly, and I only binged and purged once this last week.

Dr. T: [nods supportively]

B: [pause] I was feeling down after practice one day, but other than that I've been more positive with myself.

Dr. T: What happened after practice?

B: Coach told me my swimming was below his expectations and that I needed to pick my training up a notch or I wouldn't be competing much this year. When he said it, I got really down on myself, thinking that if I weren't so fat I would be swimming better and stuff like that. By the time I got home I was pretty upset, and I didn't want to go to dinner with my teammates or be with anyone. Instead I went to my room and pigged out on some of the junk food my roommate keeps around. After I threw up, I was so angry and disgusted with myself. When I looked in the mirror, I didn't know it was me. My face was white, my hair all over the place, there were dark circles under my eyes and my throat hurt from sticking my finger down there. At that moment I just knew I had to stop!

Dr. T: You sound determined.

B: I am. When I was writing in my log, I realized how stupid it was to do this to my body because my coach made a comment to me. And you know what? He was right. My training has been poor this fall. I'm just not that excited about swimming this year.

Dr. T: Do you know why?

B: Yeah. I'm just tired, and it's not as much fun as it used to be. I've been swimming since I was seven.

Dr. T: [supportively] That's a long time to devote to one thing.

B: It is! I always liked swimming, but sometimes I thought I did it more for my parents than for myself. When I got my scholarship, my parents were thrilled. Don't get me wrong, I was excited too, but it seemed to mean more to them than to me. Last year was pretty fun, but now I just don't know.

Dr. T: What do you think you want to do?

B: I don't know. I do like swimming and being a part of a team, but I don't know if I want the daily grind that comes along with competing in college. It takes so much time that I'm stressed about school and don't have much time to do anything else. This last weekend a guy asked me out, but I turned him down because I was behind in my schoolwork and needed to spend the time catching up. We're going to try and get together this week, but it would be nice not to feel under so much time pressure all the time.

Dr. T: You're right; being an athlete takes an incredible amount of time and energy, and there are certainly trade-offs that have to be made. For some athletes, the trade-offs are not worth it; you have to decide what's most important to you and not just focus on what your coach or your family wants you to do. I think talking about this issue may help you decide what you want to do.

For many athletes who perform below their expectations, the issue of whether or not to continue in their sport may arise. Although this internal conflict, as well as external factors (such as family expectations), may have been present for many years, an eating disorder may distract the athlete from directly acknowledging it. As Bonnie began to work with her emotion logs, the reality that she might not be competing for herself came to light. In the remainder of this session, Dr. T and Bonnie discussed in more depth her motivations for swimming competitively. Because Bonnie was experiencing a strong need to relieve this conflict, and thus, might impulsively leave her sport, Dr. T purposefully gave her permission to take the necessary time to reach a thoughtful decision. Although Bonnie and Dr. T discussed this issue at length during this session, because of its magnitude and the desire not to rush to any conclusions, they revisited it as Bonnie worked through what she wanted to do.

Although not an issue for Bonnie, many athletes with eating disorders confront the reality that continuing to train and compete while symptomatic and in treatment is counterproductive and detrimental to their health. Because many athletes' self-esteem and identity are tied strongly to sport participation, they may have difficulty admitting that training is potentially deleterious, and they may be unable to pull themselves away from competition voluntarily. Thus, the therapist, in conjunction with the eating disorder team (e.g., dietitian, physician), may have to remove the athlete from training as a protective measure. Again, the athlete's physical and psychological health is of primary concern when any decision regarding limiting sport participation is considered. In addition, any such move should be made in a sensitive, caring manner. If athletes would like to remain involved with the team even though they are not training, every effort should be made to allow that to occur. Athletes could attend practices (but not train) or travel with the team to competitions (but not compete). If athletes gain support and esteem from remaining a part of the team, then keeping contact is probably therapeutic and a good thing to allow.

When an athlete is going to take time away from training and competing to recover, then the issue of what (and how) to tell coaches and teammates arises. Even if the athlete chooses to remain involved with the team, some reason must be provided for the change in training and absence from competition. We always discuss this issue directly with the athletes and encourage them to be the ones who decide how the information about their condition will be handled and what will be shared with the team. We encourage them to be honest in their communications but let them know that they also have a right to keep private the details of what they are experiencing. We also have them consider how others might respond to them (e.g., teammates being supportive, the media reporting on their situation) before they decide what to do. Once a decision is made, we offer them the opportunity to role-play in session what they will say to their coaches, teammates, and family (if they have not already told them). Such practice can help athletes feel more comfortable about, and prepared for, what they are going to do. Despite our support, some athletes will choose not to say anything at all about their absences (and just leave the team) or will request that their coaches tell the team. In such situations, we respect their choices and try to help them implement whatever decisions they have made in as positive a manner as possible. Through this decision-making process, we try to help athletes take control of their lives and make their own choices. Our role is simply to make sure they have thoroughly considered all their options and the possible consequences of their behaviors and are prepared to implement their decisions.

SESSION 11

In sessions 6-10, Bonnie and Dr. T continued to discuss the issues that were identified early in treatment. In particular, a focus of therapy had been Bonnie determining what *she* really wanted during her time in college. She came to understand that many of her decisions and actions were based on what others, particularly her family, expected her to do. As she talked through her choices with Dr. T, she became more confident in herself and her decision-making ability. In addition to this in-therapy focus, she made progress in addressing some of her other concerns, including the following:

- Academics—For her difficult classes, she had tutors and worked in study groups with classmates. She also spoke with some of her professors to let them know more about her time constraints with swimming and to determine ways in which she could meet the class requirements.
- Social Support—She realized how important spending time with other people was and made efforts to establish friendships with teammates and other students. She went to parties when she had time and felt happier and more satisfied with her social life.
- Sport—Although Bonnie had not a made a decision about whether she would ultimately continue to compete, she felt less pressure about swimming. As a result, she had more fun and noticed some improvements in her performances.
- Eating—She followed her meal plans and used her emotion logs and had not binged or purged for the preceding three weeks. She was proud of this accomplishment but knew that she was not completely stable with her eating. She still struggled when she became anxious.

The one area that Bonnie did not directly address was her family's expectations. She wanted to talk with them about her ambivalence toward swimming, but she did not want to let them down. At the end of the tenth session, Bonnie made the decision to call her parents to let them know that she wanted to talk about school and swimming when she was home over Thanksgiving. She entered the eleventh session visibly anxious and upset.

Dr. T: You seem really upset today.

B: Yeah, I've been feeling stressed since I spoke with my parents last week. When I called them, I wanted to tell them how things were really going with swimming and school, but they seemed so excited about those things that I just downplayed everything and told them I was fine. I told them we would talk more when I was home during the break. When I got off the phone, I was so upset that I just wanted to binge. Thankfully, my roommate and her friends were around so I was able to get through it by just hanging out with them. This really scared me, though, because I haven't had such an urge to binge in a long time—I didn't like feeling out of control again.

Dr. T: I know you felt overwhelmed when this happened, but did you notice how differently you handled it this time?

B: Yeah; when I look back on it I'm glad I didn't give in.

Dr. T: How do you feel about yourself?

B: Proud, I guess.

Dr. T: I'm proud of you, too. I think you've made a lot of wonderful changes for yourself [silence].

Dr. T: Have you thought about what you want to say to your parents when you go home?

B: That's about all I've thought about since I called them. I want to tell them what we've been talking about; you know, that I'm not sure I want to swim competitively after this year. But they've been so supportive of my swimming throughout the years that I don't want to let them down by quitting. I just don't know what to do.

Dr. T: You seem pretty sure that you would be letting them down. How do you know they'd feel that way?

B: Well, they've spent so much time and money on my swimming, and they were so happy when I got a scholarship. How else would they feel?

Dr. T: Maybe what has made them so excited over the years is that you've seemed happy with swimming. Maybe their focus was on your happiness and not your swimming or your getting a scholarship. In my work with other athletes, I've come to see that parents generally are most concerned with their children's happiness regardless of whether or not they are still competing.

B: I wish that was the case, but you don't know my parents. My dad is just so proud of me being here. He has all my swimming trophies in his office and tells all his friends that I have an athletic scholarship here. My mom is quieter, but I can tell she's also excited. I sometimes wonder if the only reason they care about me is because I've been successful.

Dr. T: It seems you have a lot of assumptions about how your parents feel about you. Have you ever asked them how they really feel and what they value in you as a person?

B: No; I don't think I could do that.

Dr. T: Yeah, it would be scary, but I'm confident you can do it. Besides, by asking them, you have the chance to test out your assumptions. I imagine your parents are very proud of you, and I just can't believe that the only reason they care about you is because you've been successful as a swimmer. Are you willing to take the opportunity to talk with them and find out?

B: [pause] I think so.

Athletes who question their involvement in sport often have to face the issue of their parents' acceptance and whether that acceptance and love is based solely on their sport performance. In this session, Bonnie is doing just that. She has been involved in sport since she was very young, and her parents have made choices and sacrifices to facilitate her participation. Because of the role swimming has played in this family, most of their interactions and discussions have centered on her sport performance. As a result, Bonnie has developed the idea that her parents' love and caring are directly tied to her continued participation and performance in swimming. Although such assumptions may be objectively invalid, they often are influential for athletes. When the issue of why (and how) they are valued arises, clients have the opportunity to move beyond untested assumptions to determine the true basis of the parent-child relationship. Because this relationship will likely be more long-term than an athlete's sport participation, it is an especially salient topic to address.

In this session, Bonnie realized how important her relationship with her parents is, which is what makes talking with them so scary. To help Bonnie, Dr. T acknowledged and normalized her fear and anxiety and encouraged her to work with him to find an effective yet comfortable way to talk with her parents. In session, they wrote down all the areas she wanted to cover with her parents. They then determined the best way for Bonnie to bring up the subject—which day during break, when, where in the house, and how she would ask them to talk. By considering options in this way, Bonnie was able to develop a plan of action that she believed would work for her. Once that plan was decided, Bonnie practiced what she was going to say with her parents. Although Bonnie was hesitant at first, Dr. T used the analogy of preparing for competition and how practice determines level of success. With Dr. T playing the role of Bonnie's parents, they practiced the various reactions Bonnie might face. Her parents might immediately accept her decision and communicate their support and love; they might communicate their love and support but let her know they do not understand her decision; or they might be disappointed in her for quitting. By the end of the session, Bonnie was feeling more secure in her decision to talk with her parents. She continued to practice on her own how to bring up the issue with them, which would increase the likelihood of her following through. Although Dr. T was confident that Bonnie would be able to talk with her parents, he gave her a number where he could be reached over the break should she want any support.

SESSION 12

Bonnie returned to this session after spending the Thanksgiving break at home with her parents. Bonnie had not contacted him since their last session.

B: [smiling] Well, I did it. I talked with my parents.

Dr. T: If your smile is any indication, it must have gone well.

B: It did. I was really scared when I got home, so I didn't talk with them that first night. I almost put it off even more, but I wanted to get it done before we went to my grandmother's for Thanksgiving. So, the morning before we were to leave, I asked them to sit down with me because I had some important things I wanted to say.

Dr. T: [nods affirmatively]

B: When they sat down, they were looking at me strangely, and I got really, really anxious. I remembered, though, what we had practiced, so I took a deep breath and just started talking. I know I didn't make much sense at first because I was going so fast, but once I got it out I was able to slow down and just talk with them.

Dr. T: That's great. You did what you planned even though you were scared.

B: Yeah, and you know what, they were really supportive. They told me that they loved me no matter what I did, that their excitement about my swimming was because they were proud of me and happy that I was doing something I enjoyed. My dad looked like he was going to cry, but he didn't, you know [chuckling].

Dr. T: How do you feel knowing your parents love you like they do?

B: [eyes tearing] Really special. I just didn't know.

Dr. T: [after a few moments of silence] How was the rest of your time with your family?

B: Really good, though a little surreal, like I was seeing them for the first time—different but good [silence]. I did pretty well with my eating, too. As we talked about last time, I was a bit nervous about eating at my grandmother's because she always has so much food and everybody just makes pigs of themselves [laughs]. I ate breakfast that morning, which helped, but I also ate more than I wanted at dinner. Even so, I was able to keep it all down, which felt good to do. When the weekend came, I was actually sad about leaving—usually I can't wait to get out of there.

By talking with her parents, Bonnie took a critical step to affirm the basis of their relationship and to establish honest, open communication as she moves into adulthood. She did this by discussing her feelings, which has always been a source of difficulty and discomfort for her. The remainder of the session was spent reviewing the progress Bonnie had made, particularly how she was becoming more self-confident, how she was talking more positively to herself, how she was feeling more in-control of her eating, how she was reaching out to family and friends for support (and receiving it), and how she was taking the time to make her own decision about swimming competitively. Dr. T and Bonnie also did some planning for how she would effectively cope with finals, which were just two weeks away. Given this progress, Dr. T asked whether she wanted to come back in one or two weeks. Bonnie chose to return in two weeks, though she knew that Dr. T was available in between should she want to talk.

As clients with eating disorders make improvements, particularly in their eating and emotional well-being, one strategy for continued treatment is to begin to space out appointments to give them the opportunity to depend more on themselves and the support networks they have established. Although some clients may initially balk at the idea of having less-frequent contact, communicating confidence in them can aid in this transition. As therapists move to less-frequent meetings, they can begin the process of preparing their clients and themselves for termination, making sure they spend sufficient time discussing the issue of saying goodbye and reviewing the progress they have made.

SESSION 13

During the two weeks since their last meeting, Dr. T had not heard from Bonnie. She came to this session knowing it would be the last one before the winter holiday break, during which she would go home for about a week and a half before she returned to school to resume her athletic training.

B: [smiling] Well, I'm done with finals!

Dr. T: Congratulations. How did they go?

B: I think well. Don't get me wrong, it was stressful. But this time, I seemed to go with the flow and get done what I needed to do.

Dr. T: How has your eating been over the last two weeks, particularly given the stress of finals?

B: I've been doing well. I'm not following my food plan every day, but I'm always eating regular meals. I sometimes snack and eat more than I want, but I'm able to get through those times without throwing up or having to go out and exercise. I'm really happy with how I'm handling myself and how I'm back to eating like a normal person.

Dr. T: I'm glad to hear that. I know you're still checking in with the dietitian, but I wanted to ask since you're going to be away for a while.

From a multidimensional treatment perspective, one hopes a client with an eating disorder will work continuously with a dietitian. Even so, it is useful for the therapist to at least check in with the client from session to session. When doing so, the therapist can ask about more than just bingeing and purging, because some eating disorder clients move from bulimia to more restrictive eating behaviors. Because this was the last session before Bonnie left for the winter break, Dr. T switched the conversation to going home to see her parents.

Dr. T: How are you feeling about going home?

B: Excited, though a little scared. I've been talking with my mom and dad pretty regularly since Thanksgiving, and I'm looking forward to seeing them. With the holidays and all the food that my family has around, though, I'm a little worried about my eating. I think I'll be all right if I just keep doing what I've learned in here and with the dietitian.

Dr. T: I think you're right. You've made a lot of important changes for yourself, and if you just continue with your plan you should be fine [silence]. I was wondering, in all your recent conversations with your parents, have you told them about your eating?

B: No, not yet. I wanted to tell them at Thanksgiving, but I was a little embarrassed and I didn't want everyone watching me when I ate.

Dr. T: Would it be helpful at this point to tell them?

B: I don't know; what do you think?

Dr. T: Well, from what you've said, they're very supportive and they care about you deeply. When you go home you'll probably need some support, and this could be a way to get that and to bring you even closer to them. How does that sound?

Another issue for adults who have eating disorders is whether or not to tell their parents about their situation. Obviously, such a decision should not be made lightly. Before proceeding, the therapist would be wise to consider thoroughly all the potential advantages and disadvantages with the client. Although many clients will tell their parents, it is a clinical decision that must be made on a case-by-case basis. In this case, Bonnie decided that telling her parents would provide the support she wanted. In session with Dr. T, she again planned out how she would tell them and then practiced handling different scenarios.

At the end of the session, Dr. T reviewed with Bonnie the progress she had made over the course of the semester.

Dr. T: You've accomplished a lot for yourself this semester and have reached most of the goals that you laid out when we first met. This holiday break might be a good opportunity for you to think more about your decision regarding swimming and to determine if there are any other issues you would like to address with me. Let's schedule an appointment for sometime after you return. What sounds good for you?

B: I don't know; I won't be back for a couple of weeks, and then we start swimming, so I'll be pretty busy. After that, classes start. I guess a month would be okay.

Dr. T: That sounds about right to me, too. At that time, we can review where you are and what you want to do from there. How does that sound?

B: Okay . . . but a month is a long time. Can I call you if there's a problem?

Dr. T: Of course. The number I gave at Thanksgiving still works.

FINAL SESSIONS

Bonnie returned for her next appointment and reported that she was doing quite well. Over the holiday break, she told her parents about her eating problem. Although they were initially taken aback, they listened to her and then offered the support she wanted. In addition, she had maintained regular eating patterns (with no purging) since about the sixth session (about three months prior). She felt more in control of her eating and better able to handle the stressors she faces as a college student-athlete.

Regarding her decision about swimming competitively, she decided to remain with the team. Talking with her parents relieved a lot of the pressure she was feeling about her performance. Her times were improving and she was having fun again—all without having lost any weight. What provided this new sense of freedom was the knowledge that *she* had made the decision to stay in swimming and that she could change that decision in the future if she wanted.

Bonnie saw Dr. T for one final session about the sixth week of the spring semester. She reported continuing to do well in school and in her sport, though each were stressful at times. Her eating behaviors remained stable, with no purging. Her support network at school continued to develop. She was dating someone and feeling satisfied with that relationship. At the end of the final session, Bonnie decided that she did not need to set up another appointment but would keep Dr. T's number in case she wanted to talk at some time in the future. Before concluding their last session, Dr. T discussed relapse prevention strategies with Bonnie and also gave her information about a local eating disorder support group that she might find useful to help her maintain the progress she had made in treatment.

CONCLUSION

In this chapter, we purposefully presented a case with a successful resolution and positive therapist-client interactions because it represents, in many ways, what typically transpires in therapy. In addition, this type of case represented the best way to illustrate how to work effectively with an athlete who has an eating disorder and to discuss the many issues that arise during treatment. We acknowledge, though, that therapy does not always unfold this smoothly. Complications can arise, and therapists, particularly those who are unfamiliar with athletes and eating disorders, can make mistakes that undermine the treatment process (see Thompson & Sherman [1989] for a detailed discussion on therapist errors).

Thus, our positive presentation and generalization in this case has been primarily for heuristic purposes. Generalizing too much, though, can be misleading and even a bit precarious when speaking of people with eating disorders. Each individual is just that—an individual. Although there are certainly similarities that many, if not most, persons with eating disorders share, each person's uniqueness requires special attention if treatment is to be maximally effective. In addition, cases of athletes with eating disorders can be quite complex, and managing such cases in the sport environment can require considerable time, personnel, and resources. For more information on eating behavior and athletes, we recommend that the reader review Thompson & Sherman (1993).

REFERENCES

American Psychiatric Association. (1994). *Diagnostic and statistical manual of mental disorders* (4th ed.). Washington, DC: Author.

Burckes-Miller, M., & Black, D. (1991). College athletes and eating disorders: A theoretical context. In D. Black (Ed.), *Eating disorders among athletes: Theory, issues, and research* (pp. 11-26). Reston, VA: American Alliance for Health, Physical Education, Recreation and Dance.

Cogan, K.D., & Petrie, T.A. (1996). Consultation with college student-athletes. *College Student Journal, 30,* 9-16.

Crowther, J., & Sherwood, N.E. (1997). Assessment. In D.M. Garner & P.E. Garfinkel (Eds.), *Handbook of treatment for eating disorders* (2nd ed., pp. 34-49). New York: Guilford Press.

Davis, C., Kennedy, S.H., Ravelski, E., & Dionne, M. (1994). The role of physical activity in the development and maintenance of eating disorders. *Psychological Medicine, 24,* 957-967.

Fairburn, C.G. (1985). Cognitive-behavioral treatment for bulimia. In D.M. Gardner & P.E. Garfinkel (Eds.), *Handbook of psychotherapy for anorexia nervosa and bulimia* (pp. 160-192). New York: Guilford.

Halmi, K.A. (1985). Behavioral management for anorexia nervosa. In D.M. Gardner & P.E. Garfinkel (Eds.), *Handbook of psychotherapy for anorexia nervosa and bulimia* (pp. 147-159). New York: Guilford.

Mintz, L.B., & Betz, N.E. (1988). Prevalence and correlates of eating disordered behaviors among undergraduate women. *Journal of Counseling Psychology, 35,* 463-471.

Petitpas, A.J., Danish, S.J., & Giges, B. (1999). The sport psychologist-athlete relationship: Implications for training. *The Sport Psychologist, 13,* 344-357.

Petrie, T. (1993). Disordered eating in female collegiate gymnasts: Prevalence and personality/attitudinal correlates. *Journal of Sport and Exercise Psychology, 15,* 424-436.

Sherman, R.T., & Thompson, R.A. (1997). *Bulimia: A guide for family and friends.* San Francisco: Jossey-Bass.

Swoap, R.A., & Murphy, S.M. (1995). Eating disorders and weight management in athletes. In S.M. Murphy (Ed.), *Sport psychology interventions* (pp. 307-330). Champaign, IL: Human Kinetics.

Thompson, R.A., & Sherman, R.T. (1989). Therapist errors in treating eating disorders: Relationships and process. *Psychotherapy, 26,* 62-68.

Thompson, R.A., & Sherman, R.T. (1993). *Helping athletes with eating disorders.* Champaign, IL: Human Kinetics.

Thompson, R.A., & Sherman, R.T. (1999). Athletes, athletic performance, and eating disorders: Healthier alternatives. *Journal of Social Issues, 55,* 317-337.

Wilmore, J.H. (1991). Eating and weight disorders in the female athlete. *International Journal of Sport Nutrition, 1,* 104-117.

Wilson, G.T., & Eldredge, K.L. (1992). Pathology and development of eating disorders: Implications for athletes. In K. Brownell, J. Rodin, & J. Wilmore (Eds.), *Eating, body weight, and performance in athletes* (pp. 115-127). Philadelphia: Lea & Febiger.

CHAPTER 10

LOOKING FOR HELP, GRIEVING LOVE LOST: THE CASE OF C

Steve T. Barney
Southern Utah University
Mark B. Andersen
Victoria University

Many of us struggle with the issues of coping and of adjusting to the demands of our social and physical environments. Some people cope remarkably well, whereas others are troubled with difficulties. Carson, Butcher, and Mineka (1998) reviewed research suggesting that approximately 20% of people in the United States will, at some point in their lives, experience difficulties that are diagnosable as mental health disorders. Depression, anxiety disorders, adjustment disorders, thought disorders, and substance abuses and addictions are all problems encountered frequently by those in the clinical or counseling professions, and occasionally by those in the sport psychology field.

Athletes are subject to the same types of struggles and problems as most other people. One may even say that athlete-specific pressures such as practice and workout demands, academic eligibility requirements (for those at universities), continual performance evaluations, and other factors may place more stresses on them than are usually found among their nonathlete peers. Because of the potential for personal and social difficulties among athletes, those who work with them can benefit from knowing how to recognize and help manage such conditions as depression, anxiety, problems with adjustment, and crisis situations.

The following is a case history of the first author's work with an athlete who experienced disruptions in many areas of his life. He had significant losses in his family, struggled with close relationships, lived incongruently with his core values, and even grappled with the idea of taking his own life in the course of our counseling relationship. Despite his struggles and problems, we made great strides in helping him become a better athlete and feel better about his competence to handle his life. We hope that with this case history as a springboard, others can learn more about how to use basic counseling skills to support athletes who are struggling. Such support can help foster a solid therapeutic relationship and can elicit the trust necessary to help athletes tackle some of life's most important and personal issues.

This case history traces the sport psychologist's work with a track athlete. It starts with the emotionally charged first session and chronicles the tests of trust and relationship building, the significant crises that arose and the resolutions of those crises, and the way life competence issues were handled. The case history also shows how the countertransferential needs (the needs of the psychologist) were met through the relationship and how, once the relationship was solidified and the crises were resolved, sport-specific concerns (i.e., performance enhancement) were addressed on a deeper level.

This chapter will focus on four major issues: (a) the structure of the relationship between the sport psychologist and the athlete, (b) the process of the relationship and the counseling skills used to enhance that relationship, (c) the deepening of the relationship through tests of trust and resolution of crises, and (d) the outcome of the relationship and the final work that was done.

THE BEGINNING

As in many sport psychology relationships, the athlete and the psychologist begin their work in the realm of performance enhancement. As time goes by and comfort levels increase, C starts to talk about deeper needs from his encounters with the psychologist.

C was a track athlete at a medium-sized Midwestern state-funded university. He responded to an announcement made in his undergraduate sport psychology course offering any university athlete a chance to meet with a sport psychologist in training for help honing athletic and life skills. C was eager to take advantage of such an opportunity and signed up almost immediately.

The sport psychologist in training (the first author) was a doctoral student in clinical psychology who was participating in an advanced practicum in applied sport psychology service delivery. The practicum students met weekly to practice and refine their skills. These weekly meetings provided a forum for group supervision of each student's work with athlete-clients. Issues and problems encountered in the practicum students' work were discussed openly and supportively with the other students and the instructor. In addition to the group meetings, individual supervision with the practicum instructor was also scheduled, weekly and on an as-needed basis.

The practicum class covered different approaches to working with athletes, from the psychological skills training viewpoint (primarily cognitive-behavioral), to psycho-educational approaches, to dynamic interpretations. The approaches that were taken with athlete-clients depended on the clients' individual needs (often a changing phenomenon) and the strengths of the practicum students. It was not uncommon for students to switch approaches (or augment approaches) as new material arose over the course of the practicum.

Once each athlete-client provided the practicum instructor with some pertinent personal and athletic information, the practicum class met and decided which athlete-clients best fit each practicum student's strengths, sport knowledge, and interests. After assignments were made, initial meetings between the practicum students and the athlete-clients were set up. Discussion in practicum class regarding this first meeting made a potentially unnerving situation more comfortable for both parties (see chapter 1 in this volume for a more detailed look at first interviews). The case history in this chapter is not only a study of C; it is also a study of a clinical psychology student and his first major encounter with an athlete in an applied sport psychology setting.

When the sport psychologist is a student in training, introductions are a bit different than they would be for someone established in a private practice. Although seemingly simple, formal introductions are actually complex and can have a significant influence on the developing relationship. Telling the athlete-client about the trainee's frame of reference and educational/sport background clarifies the relationship.

The initial meeting with C went something like this:

S: Hi! Come on in. Sit down and make yourself comfortable.

C: Thanks.

S: I'm Steve Barney, a graduate student in clinical psychology, and I've been taking a sport psychology practicum class. I understand you volunteered to come in and do some things you have been learning about in your sport psychology class.

C: Yeah. The instructor said this might be an interesting thing for me to try.

S: I'm glad you did. Before we start, I want to talk about a few things and let you know something about what this program is all about. Fair enough?

C: Fair enough.

Because the practicum student's work with athlete-clients was to be supervised by the practicum instructor and by fellow students in the class, informing the athlete-client of this arrangement was a priority. Provisions were made with the athlete-clients that everything would be discussed with the supervisor individually. If there was anything in the sessions that the athlete did not want shared with the class, that information would not be divulged in group supervision. Although each athlete-client had been informed of this structure, reminding C seemed important.

S: I am in a practicum class with six other graduate students here at the university. Each of us is working with an athlete and will be sharing some of the things we do in here. I want you to know that none of the other students in the class know who it is that I am seeing, and I will not use your name in class. Also, I will be meeting with my supervisor at least every week talking about what we do. He knows that I am seeing you, and his role is to help me learn to be a better sport psychologist so that my work with you will be effective. If we talk about things in our sessions that you would prefer I not share with the class, just tell me and they will not be brought up. I can talk about these types of issues with my supervisor individually. Does that sound okay with you?

C: Yeah; that's how my instructor explained it.

S: Do you have any questions about that?

C: Not right now.

S: Feel free to bring this up again if you need to.

C: Okay!

Telling the athlete-client about the parameters of the practicum class seemed to help ease any tensions or uncertainties he might have about the experience. In addition, discussing the confidential nature of the relationship made the athlete-client feel even more comfortable.

After a discussion of the ethical principles and code of conduct of the American Psychological Association (APA, 1992) in practicum class, it was deemed appropriate to share the following information with athlete-clients.

S: I also want you to know that apart from what we have just talked about, our relationship is strictly confidential. The only time I would ever break confidentiality with you would be if I felt, from what you told me, that there was a danger of harm to you or to someone else. And even then I would talk about the problem with you and let you know what I needed to do and who I needed to talk to. Do you have any questions?

C: Yeah; what about my coach?

S: If you choose to tell your coach that you are seeing me, that is up to you. Also, if you want me to talk with your coach about what we are doing, that is up to you as well. As far as I'm concerned, I won't say a word to him. But I would encourage you to let your coach know you are working on sharpening the mental aspects of your sport. I think most coaches like to be informed.

C: That sounds good.

At this point, C and I agreed about how the relationship would be structured, but little had been discussed regarding the content of the relationship or what the focus of our work together was going to be. We had yet to hammer out what would be OK to talk about, what our goals might be, and what each person might expect during the course of the relationship. Rarely do two parties begin a relationship with these questions answered. Broaching them, however, can lead to an informative discussion of the expectations each party brings to the table. Also, as stated in chapter 1 of this text, one of the purposes of the initial interview is to establish a good working relationship.

S: Now C, I want you to know that this is your time; we can discuss just about anything you want in here. We can focus on how to help you become a better athlete, or we can talk about school, studying, tests, relationships, family—anything. I also want you to know my perspective on a few things. I see people as people first. You may be an athlete, but to me you are a person who happens to be an athlete. Because I feel this way, I want you to know that we are not limited to just things that have to do with athletics. If there is anything affecting you as a person, it might affect you as an athlete as well. Maybe you have noticed something like that before.

C: Yeah, there have been a few times when I was stressed about a test, and I didn't do so well in practice . . . or times I was really concentrating on a meet and bombed a test. You mean you can help me with that, too?

S: We can certainly talk about it and see what we can do together.

I wanted C to feel comfortable discussing anything he wanted to, and I did this in a way that connected other aspects of his life to sport performance. Couching personal issues in sport contexts can make talking about them less threatening. At this early point, I could see that a working relationship was forming when C said, in a hopeful manner, "You mean you can help me with that, too?" The question shows that C is moving into a working relationship. He was saying to me, I am ready to work, and I am ready for you to help me. One cannot ask for too much more on a first meeting.

Once we had discussed the structure and potential content of the relationship, I wanted to get a better picture of C and elicit background information that I would use to put things into perspective and to set up a working plan. Reflective and empathic listening skills helped C feel he was being heard and understood.

S: So, C, tell me a little about yourself.

C: What do you want to know?

C seemed a bit slow to start, and I wanted to let him know that whatever he could tell me would help me out. Clients often seem eager to help the process along, but they may not know how to proceed. Letting C know that anything he could tell me would be helpful seemed to get him going.

S: Well, anything you feel would be helpful for me to get to know you better.

C: OK. I grew up in ______, a small town just north of here a couple of hours.

S: What was it like growing up there?

C: It was kind of rough.

This was a good sign; C was already willing to tell me about problems in his life by mentioning that growing up was rough for him. It appeared that a measure of trust had already developed, perhaps in part due to the "laying it out on the table" introduction. By telling me that his youth had been "rough," C was letting me in on his world. Using what is known as an *additive reflection,* or a *one-word prompt* (Egan, 1986), I ask him in a nonthreatening way to tell me more. With a simple question about what he meant by *rough,* I encouraged C to keep talking.

S: Rough?

C: Yeah; my dad died when I was young, and I was the oldest kid. I kind of had to help my mom raise my little brother and sisters. [I noticed a little shakiness in his voice and a slight quiver of the lip.]

Attending to nonverbal cues is one way to understand a client's underlying meaning and actual feelings, even if he is not presenting himself in a congruent way (Raskin & Rogers, 1989). It certainly seemed to help me detect things C had been battling for a long time.

S: That sounds like it might have been hard for you.

C: [recomposed] Nah, it was okay. We all got along pretty good, but then my mom died too, just a few years ago, and then we all lived for a while with my aunt and uncle.

In talking with and observing C, I was beginning to feel a great loss and a pervasive sadness. My suspicion was that there were some unresolved issues here (grief, loss, possibly guilt and anger), but I decided that encouraging C to disclose them in the first session might be too much for him. On the other hand, I wanted him to know that I empathized and that I was attending to his feelings and emotions. I decided to gently reflect my own feelings and perceptions and then allow C to go where he needed to go with his emotions.

S: I'm really sorry, C. I can only imagine that it must have been really difficult for you to get along, losing your dad and then your mom.

C: [obviously close to tears] It's been really hard, but I'm doing OK now. [He moves to safer ground.] I was always a pretty good athlete in school.

S: [allowing him to move away to that safer ground] Can you tell me a little about your sporting career?

Although C, in this instance, began to tell of significant events in his life, he appeared to find some unexpected and powerful emotions coming through. It was important to him to regroup and move to less emotionally valent topics. Recognizing that it was still much too early in the relationship to explore some of these difficult issues, I encouraged C to talk about whatever was most comfortable for him. C continued to talk about his sport history and the process of becoming an outstanding high school track star. He talked about the recruiting process and about some of the difficulties he encountered trying to decide where to go to college. Finally, he spoke about feeling a need to stay close to home (the reason he opted for the local state university).

As the scheduled time (50 minutes) drew to a close, I wanted to get a feel for how C was viewing the interaction. Because this was our first session, and because I recognized that C was not accustomed to discussing such personal issues and showing emotion as he had, I was concerned that the session might have been more than he could tolerate.

S: We've covered a lot of things in our session today, and it seemed as though you were able to talk about some things that were maybe a little difficult or sad. Sometimes that tends to be hard for people. I wanted to check with you and make sure you were OK with how things went today.

C: Yeah; I guess there are some things I don't really talk about much.

Referring to emotional reactions and identifying them as part of everyday life was my attempt to normalize his experience in the session. From here, acknowledging that C's struggles might have some impact on his current life would give him food for thought and allow him to return to these issues if he chose. We ended the first session with this message.

S: I want you to know that talking about things like that are OK if you want to. Sometimes things that we hold inside can really affect us as people, as students, and as athletes. Our conversations are confidential and we can discuss whatever you feel you might want to in here.

C: OK; thanks.

S: Was there anything that felt uncomfortable or disagreeable to you?

C: No; it was OK.

S: Do you have any questions or anything?

C: No, I don't think so. What time next week?

S: How about the same time? And when you come back, we will start by talking about whatever you want.

C: OK.

RELATIONSHIP BUILDING

By the end of the first session, C and I had begun to form a working therapeutic relationship. Allowing C to move at his own pace, normalizing his emotional reactions, and checking with him to see how he was feeling about what had transpired sent a message that he was an important part of the partnership. C's spontaneously seeking a return appointment appeared to be a message that he was invested in the process, that the session had gone well for him, and that he was willing to risk coming back. From our first encounter, I saw C as a sincere and honest yet guarded person who had a need to present himself in a controlled and competent way. Allowing him to control the tempo and content of our interaction gave him the flexibility he needed to feel in control of the relationship and able to express himself as he felt comfortable.

Apart from the initial meeting, it makes intuitive sense that the beginning of the second session may be one of the most important times in a therapeutic relationship. Both parties have had time to digest what had happened in the first session. Regardless of the actual verbal content, the emotions an athlete-client feels during the first session and immediately after are what are commonly recalled. Exploring these feelings can help the sport psychologist get a sense for where the relationship stands

S: Hi, C! Glad you could make it. Sit down; make yourself comfortable. [C opts for the cushioned sofa in the room.]

C: Hey, Doc! [Although I had introduced myself as Steve and as a graduate student, C spontaneously began calling me "Doc."]

The nickname or sobriquet "Doc" is usually one of familiarity and affection but is also one of respect. Calling me "Doc" may have indicated that C was comfortable with me and wanted to let me know he liked me and respected me. I probably should have dissuaded him from calling me that, but, for the sake of the growing relationship, I let it go. Correcting him would have served no purpose and could have been seen as a rebuke. And to be honest, I kind of liked the sound of it coming from C. This reflected my own positive countertransference to someone who had evoked strong emotions in me and whom I really wanted to help.

S: How's your week been?

C: Pretty hectic. We have been practicing hard, and I already have tests in most of my classes.

S: Sounds busy!

C: Not too bad. What are we going to do today?

With this last question, C may have been relating some uncertainty and seemed to be looking for some guidance regarding the nature of the relationship and the direction of future sessions. He was testing the waters, so to speak. Rather than directly answering his question, I felt it was important to gather more information about what he was really asking and what he needed by discussing his thoughts and feelings about the last session.

S: Before we decide what to do today, I'm wondering how you felt about our last session.

C: I thought it was good. [Notice that the query was about how he felt, and he responded with what he thought.] I kind of got off base a little talking about my parents, but it was pretty good.

At this point in the relationship, I made a therapeutic decision. I could have pursued the family issue, which might have served to deepen the relationship from the outset. Yet without sufficient therapeutic trust established, guiding C into another emotional encounter might have been too much for him to handle. Sensitively assessing a person's ego strength—his ability to adaptively deal with difficult issues—in a therapeutic relationship is crucial, particularly in the formative stages of that relationship. That C had quickly broached emotionally difficult issues in the first session suggested that they were particularly salient for him. Because he had so quickly retreated to the safer ground of athletics, I speculated that he might not have been prepared to deal with them in an adaptive fashion at that time. I opted to not bring up the family issues and to allow C to guide the discussion in hopes that a safer and more trusting relationship would be established and that when he felt more comfortable, these issues would resurface.

S: Like I said in the first session, we can talk about anything you want in here. Now then, I'm wondering if you had something in mind for today. [C had been taking an undergraduate applied sport psychology class and had been exposed to several performance enhancement techniques.]

In general, keeping an open format for discussion during a second session may help athletes feel that the course of the session is in their control. In this instance, C chose to direct the session into an action-oriented activity, probably in part to prevent broaching the emotional issues that had emerged during the first session. As previously discussed, allowing C to dictate in this manner ensured that he would not have to talk about personal issues until he was ready. Pushing athletes to discuss things for which they are not ready can impair the relationship that has begun. C came to me for performance enhancement, not for the treatment of parental loss. We would come around to his parents again, but it would take some time.

C: Yeah. My sport psychology instructor has been teaching us about relaxation and this autogenic training stuff. Can we do some of that?

S: Sure! What have you learned about autogenic training in class so far?

From here, a discussion ensued about autogenic training. We explored C's perceptions of autogenics and discussed his expectations. Although he had already experienced a modified autogenic induction in his class (feelings of heaviness), we reviewed the general procedure and talked about what he might experience physically and psychologically. I encouraged C to ask any questions he had about the procedure and then guided him in an initial autogenic induction.

C was a good student of autogenic training and experienced a very relaxed state in his initial trial. After several minutes on his own, he decided to end the autogenic-initiated relaxed state. A debriefing occurred, and the session ended (see chapter 2 of this volume for more details on relaxation inductions, preparations, and debriefings).

C enjoyed relaxation and autogenic training, and several forms of relaxation inductions were introduced and practiced over the next several sessions. Athletic performance enhancement through relaxation exercises and the use of imagery was the main focus of the following few sessions. Helping C use these skills in other areas of his life—for example, while studying, preparing for tests, or talking to professors—became the focus of our sessions for a time. During this psychological skills training period, C and I became more comfortable with each other and were both open to bringing new ideas and goals to the sessions.

TESTS OF TRUST

As C's comfort level increased, his interest turned from performance enhancement and relaxation skills to some more emotionally laden personal issues. Some of these issues were identified in one particularly intense session. C entered my office obviously distressed and anxious.

S: Hi, C. You look distressed today; is something wrong?

C: No, not really . . . well, I guess there is something.

S: Do you want to talk about it?

C: It's just my brother; he has been getting into trouble, and it's got me a little upset.

This was the first time since the intake that C had initiated a more personal discussion. Two things might have motivated him to talk about personal issues at this point: emotional distress, which can reduce reticence and interpersonal barriers, or the fact that he had gained sufficient trust in me as a psychology professional to have brought his struggles with his family into the conversation. In all likelihood, a combination of both factors was involved in this instance.

When an athlete begins to disclose personally distressing information, particularly for the first time, it is important that he feels heard and understood. This is not a time for advice giving or problem solving, but rather for reflective listening skills. Reflective responses tend to help the person express difficult thoughts, feelings, and experiences more easily. Simply repeating the most emotionally valent word from the athlete-client's sentence can help him continue his train of thought. Such a response can also signal that the sport psychologist is attending, understanding, and empathizing (Rogers, 1961).

S: Your brother's gotten into some trouble, and you're a little upset about it?

C: Yeah; he's been out drinking and causing trouble, and I am supposed to be taking care of him. You see, we are _______ [members of a conservative and abstemious Christian religion], and we don't believe in drinking. Do you know anything about _______s?

This question seemed to be sort of a "checking in." C was about to take a gamble in front of the psychologist and wanted to make sure the psychologist would understand. I reassured him that I was with him.

S: Yes, I know something about _______ s.

C: Well, after my mom died, I sort of took over raising my brother and sisters, and I feel kind of responsible for them [beginning to have an emotional crack in his voice].

S: Kind of like you are the parent to them?

C: [regaining composure] Yeah; it's been kind of rough. Anyway, he's out drinking and causing trouble, and I don't know what to do. My aunt and uncle are watching out for him right now, but I feel I should be doing more.

Instead of using "thinking" words as he had before, C was now using "emotion" or "feeling" words. Such a subtle transition may signal movement from the safety of thinking about things to the potentially painful feeling of them.

S: [reflecting C's feeling] It sounds like you feel rather helpless that your brother is drinking, and you might be feeling kind of responsible for it. After your parents died, you sort of became a parent to them, and maybe you feel you're not doing as good a job as you should.

C: That's exactly it!

C's reaction was emphatic, as if he were saying, "My psychologist understands me. Doc knows what I'm going through and I can really talk to him. I've found someone who understands me, cares for me, and will try to help me!" This exclamation and C's request in the following dialogue speak volumes about the relationship between C and myself. He seemed to put me in a parental role, and he did what some children do to parent figures when they are experiencing difficulties—he asked me for advice.

C: What do you think I ought to do?

S: It sounds like you would sure like me to tell you what you should do. Not knowing everything about the situation I can't really tell you how to solve your problem. What I can do is talk with you about things and maybe together we can help you decide for yourself.

Stemming from C's question, discussion ensued about C's family and the dynamics involved. Although the advice C sought was not expressly given, we discussed and explored his legal and moral responsibility to his siblings, the pressures he felt from his religious upbringing to maintain a strong and stable family, and his feelings of not wanting to disappoint his parents. We also discussed how difficult it is to make other people do what we think they should do, no matter how hard we try. Although I gave C no specific answers in this discussion, he seemed to appreciate being able to explore some of his feelings and thoughts about his family. Toward the end of the discussion, C's mood was significantly improved. He expressed, animatedly, that he had gained some new insights and ideas about how to handle the situation with his brother. I pointed out this improvement and insight in order to help C associate feeling better with talking about problems with a trusted resource. Another appointment was scheduled for the following week.

C: Hey, Doc! You remember my brother?

S: Yeah. What happened?

C: Well, I did a lot of thinking after the last session. I decided that all I could do was let him know I was worried about him and that I didn't think drinking was a good idea but that he was old enough to make his own decisions.

S: And how did that go?

C: It went really well. He told me he appreciated the fact that I was worried about him, and we left it at that. Then we played around the rest of the weekend and had a great time.

S: Good for you! It sounds like you handled things pretty well.

C: Yeah, I guess I just let them sort of take care of themselves [silence for a short time].

S: Apart from that, how are things going?

C: Pretty good. I have all these tests and stuff coming up; can we do some of that relaxation stuff that always seems to help me get ready for tests?

S: Sure!

It appeared that C had drawn information from the previous session to help him decide how he might best handle the situation with his brother. That the interaction with his brother was somewhat successful seemed to provide reinforcement for talking about personal problems within the athlete-psychologist relationship. C learned, from the relationship model he had with me, that talking things through, listening, and showing concern and care were important, and he seemed to have applied these skills in talking with his brother. This talking things out with his brother may have been the beginning of the internalization of the sport psychologist. See chapter 15 in this volume for more about internalization of sport psychologists and supervisors.

C had come back quite proud of his accomplishment with his brother and wanted to let his "good father" know about it. It seemed as though he was also saying, "I have had quite enough of pushing the limits for now—so let's get back to what we do so well together; let's relax." C was confident enough to ask specifically for what he needed to help him with pressing needs in his life at that time (i.e., mental preparation for tests). For the rest of the session, C walked himself through a series of autogenic training and relaxation exercises in which he imagined himself both studying for the tests and taking them as calmly and confidently as possible. C reported that he was able to achieve a deep state of relaxation and vivid imagery without external guidance. I gave him some positive feedback for his work and encouraged him to continue practicing at home on his own. Another appointment was scheduled for the following week.

THE CRISIS

C had revealed some powerful emotions (grief, sadness) in the first session. After that, time had been spent in relatively nonthreatening activities such as relaxation training. Through these activities, a considerable relationship had developed, and C had grown to trust me. Later, he had taken the relationship a step further and had reintroduced me to some emotions he felt about problems in his family (his brother causing trouble, leading to feelings of hurt, failure, not living up to his responsibilities, and guilt). That session, having turned out reasonably well, left C better prepared to discuss more freely even deeper issues with me.

C: Hey, Doc!

S: Hey, C; how are you?

C: Not too bad; I think I did well on my tests last week.

S: Good. Were you able to relax a little?

C: I was. In fact, all my roommates were wondering what I was doing while I was doing the autogenic exercises on my own, so I kind of showed them, and they all tried it. We had a bunch of relaxed guys sort of laying all over the place.

S: How did that go?

C: It was kind of hard at first, but it seemed to work OK. . . . [silence]

S: [C looked as though he wanted to say something, but then he hesitated. I pointed this out to him.] It looks as though there was something else you wanted to talk to me about.

C: Well, nothing really . . . except I kind of got into a fight with my girlfriend; you know, we haven't really been getting along very well lately.

S: No? You feel like talking about it?

C: Well . . . yeah, I think so.

C proceeded to recount how he and his girlfriend of the past two years had been struggling lately. He described her as a good person but "not a great influence on me." C's girlfriend was not of his faith and enjoyed going out to bars and drinking on occasion, a practice C joined her in sometimes. Moreover, C and his girlfriend had become sexually active, a practice that C's religion prohibits until after marriage. Although she appeared to have no problem with the current arrangement, C seemed to be struggling with his behavioral choices of late. The relationship between C and his girlfriend became the focus of our sessions for the next several weeks. In each session, he reported feeling confused and conflicted, and he discussed feeling spiritually torn because of his actions. I encouraged C to talk about these feelings and to see a local spiritual leader in his church.

The next week C reported that he and his girlfriend had broken up and that they had decided to see other people. His mood became sullen, and a dramatic change was readily noticeable.

S: Hi, C. Come on in; sit down.

C: Hey, Doc. [C's mood was visibly a depressed one, and he made limited eye contact.]

S: C, how are you? You don't look so good today.

C: I'm not. We broke up, and I don't think I can handle it anymore. I saw her in a restaurant here in town the other night with some other guy . . . I felt like crushing him. I got so angry that I went over and said something to her. This guy told me to leave her alone; he was so small I could have killed him, but I just left and went driving around for a while, and then I went home.

S: It sounds like seeing her with someone else was really hard for you and that it brought out some pretty angry feelings.

C: You know, I got so mad it kind of scared me. I really didn't know what I was going to do.

S: So what *did* you do?

C: Well, I just drove around thinking about things, ya know?

S: Like what?

C: Just like how crappy my life has been with all that's happened to me . . . my girlfriend, and my parents, and stuff.

I noted the juxtaposition of lost girlfriend and lost parents. Again, reflective listening and additive responses helped C feel that he was being heard and understood and that I was with him.

S: You're feeling badly about your parents passing away and these problems with your girlfriend and things having been pretty crappy?

C: Yeah, all that stuff [eyes watering and lip trembling] . . . all that stuff [openly weeping now].

S: [I repositioned so as to lean closer to him and maintained the silence for a time.] It's okay. [I spoke only when C glanced up as if to see how I was reacting to his expression of emotion; I handed him some tissues.] That's what we have these in here for.

This was the first time since the initial interview and his worry about his brother that C had really showed much negative emotion. He had wavered in his stoic appearance several times but had never broken down as he did in this session. Once he regained himself and dried his tears, he looked at me as if expecting me to laugh at him or to deride him. Guessing at C's emotions and reactions to his display might have been a risk to the relationship, but sensitively discerning his turmoil helped him feel that I was with him physically and emotionally.

S: It seems like maybe feelings for all of these things came out at once.

C: Yeah. I guess I never really cry; I didn't even cry when my dad or my mom died. I feel kind of stupid.

S: Stupid?

C: Yeah, that I sit here and cry like a baby in front of you.

S: You kind of wonder what I might be thinking of you now that I have seen you cry?

C: I guess so.

During an intensely emotional experience such as the one described, people who do not normally show a lot of emotions can become confused, uncertain, and even distressed about how the display may have affected those close to them. In this instance, the sport psychologist may find it helpful to divulge his own reactions to the emotion. If done honestly and supportively, this type of sharing can strengthen a relationship remarkably.

S: Well, I feel sad that there is so much hurt and sadness in you. I have come to feel a connection with you and it kind of hurts to see you so torn up like this. At the same time, I feel privileged that you felt comfortable enough with me to allow yourself to cry like that. Sometimes it takes a lot of trust between two people to express how you feel. I suppose that there might be a lot of hurt or even anger inside of you that you may have been keeping covered up for quite some time.

C: Yeah, I guess so.

C seemed to be hearing what I said, but the "I guess so" probably reflected his still being unsure of all that had just occurred. Clarifying the usefulness of emotional expression can help an athlete experience this type of situation as beneficial.

S: The key is to let it out as you are able. It seems to me like this may have been a starting place for doing that very thing. How do you feel now?

C: Well, after getting over feeling stupid, I guess I feel sort of better.

S: Now maybe we can talk about where these feelings come from.

C: OK!

C and I spoke at length about feelings he had about the events that had transpired in his youth. He was able to identify feeling disappointed in not having a father as most of the other boys in his town did. He processed feeling hurt and emotionally overwhelmed when his mother died.

I bungled an attempt to engage C in a discussion about perhaps feeling cheated or somehow angry that his parents had died and left him with so much responsibility. C did not recognize these kinds of feelings in himself. It might have been that admitting anger, especially at his parents for "leaving" him, was just a bit too much for C at that time. Anger against his parents would also have been a serious transgression of C's religious convictions. I was kind of overwhelmed with all the new emotional information, and I forgot to consider how my suggestion about anger would be taken by C. In retrospect, I probably should not have brought it up, but luckily, I did not push the point, and we moved past it quickly.

From clinical experience, we know that when a person begins to feel negative emotions openly, there may be significant residual emotion that has been brought closer to the surface of consciousness, making future emotional upheavals more likely. Helping prepare the person for this possibility is important. In addition, exploring a plan on which the person can rely for social support during these times can prove helpful. This preparation and planning was the next step I took with C.

S: Now, things aren't going to be fixed just because you allowed yourself to feel these emotions—you might feel like this several times during the week as well. If this happens, it might be best to talk with someone you feel comfortable with. Who do you think you can talk with that might be able to help you feel better?

C: I used to just talk with my girlfriend, but I guess I can't do that anymore. There is my aunt or a few guys on the team, but really nobody I know very well that way.

C's social support network appeared very limited. He had built most of his friendships and emotional attachments around his girlfriend. Supportive parents might have been an outlet for him during this time in his life, but since they had died, he was left with his aunt (with whom he got along reasonably well). Recognizing the lack of available support, I provided C the telephone number of the local student counseling center on-call service. In addition, I gave C my home telephone number and encouraged him to call if he needed to talk. I also suggested he could talk to a spiritual leader in his church. We scheduled an appointment for the following week.

Although I felt confident that I had covered all of the bases pretty well, in retrospect, there was a potentially dangerous omission in my interaction with C. Carson et al. (1998) suggested that among college students, those who have recently lost a relationship and those who manifest signs of depression (e.g., sad mood, tearfulness, insomnia, trouble concentrating) are at especially high risk for suicide. C struggled with both loss and depressed mood. A complete assessment for suicidal thinking or intent would have been beneficial at this time.

Typically, suicide is a topic that is difficult for people to discuss with each other. In the helping professions, however, it should be discussed openly, particularly with people who are experiencing major life stressors or relationship problems and are manifesting warning signs like depressed mood (Vidal, 1989). Vidal suggested that asking someone about suicidal thoughts does not "put the idea into their heads" as some might believe. Simply saying something like the following can be helpful:

> You know, sometimes when people feel this way or are troubled with these kinds of problems they begin to feel kind of hopeless about things. Have you been having trouble keeping hope or seeing the light at the end of the tunnel? Sometimes people who feel kind of hopeless think about ending it all, taking their own lives. Have you had any of these kinds of feelings lately?

Even if the answer is no, providing support and resources, such as a crisis line telephone number, is often a good idea. If the person acknowledges active suicidal thoughts or intent, obtaining details about the nature of these thoughts is important. To assess the severity of suicidal thinking, some helping professionals use the acronym *PAL*. Does the person have a plan (P) for committing suicide? If a plan is present, how available (A) are the components of the plan? Finally, if carried out, how lethal (L) might the plan be? If a person feels suicidal or has suicidal ideation, but has no plan, the intent to carry out the thoughts is likely to be less. Similarly, if a plan is in place, but the resources to carry out the plan are not available, the risk of imminent danger may be lower. Finally, if a person has a plan that is readily available, but it is not likely to be lethal (e.g., "overdosing on four Tylenol #3's"), the threat of actual suicide may be less than if the plan is clearly lethal (e.g., "shooting myself in the head with my pistol"). Regardless of the presence or absence of a specific, available, and lethal plan for suicide, thinking about ending one's life usually stems from feelings of intense hopelessness, pain, or guilt, and the expression of these feelings should never be taken lightly.

On the other hand, if a person is having active suicidal thoughts and has a specific plan that is readily available and potentially lethal, immediate preventative actions should be considered. Professional clinical and counseling psychologists might choose to do a crisis intervention themselves, or they may seek outside assistance. Nonclinical or counseling psychologists might feel more confident if a professional in these types of situations is consulted. In most communities, a person can phone 911 and be connected with suicide intervention teams or local psychiatric hospitals where he can be cared for and supported. (See chapter 8 in this volume for another example of a depressed and suicidal athlete.)

Had I performed some of these extremely important tasks, future difficulty might have been avoided. Three days prior to C's next regularly scheduled session, he called me.

S: Hello?

C: Hey Doc; this is C.

S: Hi, C.

C: Hey, I'm really sorry . . . but is there any way I could meet with you? I really need to talk with someone, and I can't think of who else to call.

S: Sure, C. Let me take care of what I am in the middle of and I can meet with you in half an hour. Is that OK, or do you need me to come right now?

C: No, no, a half hour will be fine. I'll see you there.

During this meeting, C revealed that the night before he had been feeling particularly despondent about his life. He had again seen his girlfriend with another man and again had a strong reaction. C had gathered some garden hose and some duct tape and had driven outside of town and tied the hose into his exhaust pipe and taped the other end in the window with the intent to asphyxiate himself. As he began feeling sleepy, he suddenly began to realize that he really did not want to die, and he turned off the car motor. After he had disconnected the hose and had gotten some fresh air, C slowly drove home and went to bed.

S: [somewhat shocked] C, why didn't you call me?

C: I just thought you would be busy, and I really didn't want to talk to anyone. Besides, at the time I guess I wasn't thinking too well.

Although it is important to support the person who has made a suicide attempt and to try to avoid comments that could contribute additional guilt, my reaction was one of helplessness and fear that I had almost lost someone with whom I had formed a close and emotional relationship. In addition, a certain amount of guilt and a sense of incompetence for not having discussed suicide with C was painfully present. In the heat of the moment, it is sometimes hard to think rationally and therapeutically. A supportive supervisor can help student practitioners sort out the jumble of emotions they experience when they hear of a client's suicidal behavior.

CRISIS RESOLUTION

An important first intervention following a serious suicidal gesture is to explore the resources upon which the client relied to help him opt for a different path (see Carson et al., 1998). Asking what stopped the person from carrying through their intent is one way of gathering information about such resources.

S: C, you don't know how happy I am that you stopped; what was it that made you stop?

Apparently, C had done some pretty deep, existential thinking during his suicidal crisis. He contemplated family, friends, and spirituality, and he was even able to consider the potential feelings and thoughts of others should he have completed the suicide.

C: I dunno, I guess I just started thinking about things differently. I know how my parents would have felt if I had killed myself. I think I know how my family would feel; I didn't want my girlfriend to have that guilt on her shoulders, and I knew God wouldn't want me to die that way.

S: [somewhat more composed] How are you feeling now?

C: A little better. I guess you could say I've been to hell, and now I'm kind of on my way back.

Once a person has attempted suicide, statistics suggest that there is a significant chance he or she will attempt it again (Hawton, 1992). Assessing current suicidal thoughts or intent in C was an important part of determining whether or not he was safe.

S: Are you having any more suicidal thoughts?

C: No. I don't think I will ever put myself in that position again.

S: I'm glad! Welcome back; now let's talk about what's been going on with you and where this all came from so we can make sure it won't happen again.

Although a suicide gesture as serious as C's should never be taken lightly, for him it seemed to be the ultimate test of trust. Trust in himself, in his God, in his memory of his parents, in his will to live, and in the therapeutic relationship we had established and nurtured over the course of our sessions thus far. After this event, difficult issues were much easier to discuss. In retrospect, my "why didn't you call me?" response was probably the shocked and stunned "parent" in me. I was confused and in turmoil, and I directed some frustration out at C. But that "why didn't you call me?" also contained the much more benevolent message, *I would have dropped everything to help you!* The other messages I sent, showing how happy I was that he was safe and was not thinking of suicide, also communicated that he was cared for.

DEALING WITH LIFE COMPETENCE AND CONFLICTS

After this episode, we began to explore in depth the conflict C felt over some of his behaviors and the strict moral code taught by his conservative religion. Although he remained committed to the church and to its teachings, in the past the peer pressure from friends and his girlfriend had persuaded him to do things he believed were immoral and sinful. He discussed how his religion was essentially a way of life for him, a culture from which he drew strength and purpose in life. C's religion focused on the eternal, and the belief in the possibility of seeing his parents again after this life was a critical factor in his coping with their deaths. So much a part of him were his religious beliefs that he became very distressed at not living his life according to this moral code. Guilt feelings over the rebelliousness of his brother combined with the distress he felt in his relationship with his girlfriend almost seemed to force him to begin reassessing his own life. The internal conflicts between what he believed to be right and his own behaviors became unbearably conscious, as did the emotions accompanying those conflicts. Our relationship after his taking the car out on that lonely road had developed to the point that talking and working out his conflicts began to seem like just something that we did together.

MEETING MY NEEDS

C and I were able to discuss openly the relationship we had built, and he related feeling as though our sessions had become a forum for him to experience the mentoring he never received from his father as a child. Meanwhile, I became acutely aware that I had deep emotional feelings for C as well. My relationship with C met my needs on several levels. Because I wanted to become a sport psychologist, having a meaningful and successful experience with C was important to me. Our work helped me feel competent as a fledgling professional. Moreover, graduate school was filled with assignments, lectures, readings, and performance evaluations of every kind, but very few opportunities to acknowledge one's human side and just be with someone without fear of evaluation or reprisal. Working with C became so comfortable, I came to see our sessions as a refuge against the storm of academic demands I often faced in graduate school. In assisting C develop life skills to help him relax, manage stress, and cope with the rigors of school, I was, in essence, helping myself with these same issues. On a deeper level, I saw a lot of myself in C. Although I had never experienced the life situations that C had endured, I painfully empathized with his need to contain his emotions and maintain a controlled façade. Moral and religious dilemmas were also not strangers to me, nor were the pains of seeing a romantic partner with a rival. I had relived a lot of my own personal issues as a result of my relationship with C, and experiencing him doing so well in coping with those issues strengthened me as well. I knew I had grown professionally and personally as a result of my relationship with C.

RETURN TO PERFORMANCE ENHANCEMENT

In remaining sessions, the focus was left almost entirely up to C. As he began preparing for the beginning of his season, he brought in tough issues such as his desire to be successful as a track athlete and his wishes to make the U.S. Olympic team after graduation. He struggled with the decision to use, or not to use, steroids. C had committed to himself several years previously that he would "perform clean" and that steroid use was not to be a part of his training regimen. Nevertheless, his association with athletes who did use steroids, and their improvements in performance, instigated some conflict in him. After weighing the pros and cons of steroid use both as an athlete, a student, a brother, and a faithful member of his conservative religion, C decided to remain clean.

C also came to the sessions complaining of some "hitches in my technique" that we addressed in psychological skill building sessions (e.g., imagery for technique alteration and consolidation). We engaged in complex performance enhancement activities and psychological skill building as we continued to explore deeply personal issues. Talking about problems and fears, in and out of competition, was no longer a problem for C.

TERMINATION

Toward the latter part of the academic year, the need to discuss termination of the relationship arose. I was planning to move away and begin a career elsewhere, and C had another year of college eligibility. The termination process, in a situation in which both parties have been touched so deeply, can be difficult and emotionally charged. With C, however, the loss of the sport psychologist, with whom he had shared his most intimate secrets and with whom he had developed a parent-like relationship, could have easily been reflective of the death of his parents. Discussion to this effect was open and occurred nearly every week of our last sessions together.

During our last meeting, the tone of the session was one of gladness and satisfaction. We reviewed some of the things we had accomplished and some of the struggles we had endured. We both agreed that although keeping in touch would be difficult, if either felt the need to seek out the other the contact would be welcomed. Although I never made personal contact with C after that semester we spent together, I did keep tabs on his athletic performances, which were covered by my local newspaper and other resources. The last report I received was from an athletic counselor at C's university who informed me that C was a fifth-year senior who had completed his athletic eligibility and was finishing up his degree.

CONCLUSION

My work with C reaffirmed for me that serving athletes can be a challenging, complex, and personally difficult undertaking for many sport psychologists. Successful work with athletes requires sensitivity to their athletic, academic, social, and psychological needs while simultaneously maintaining awareness of one's own prejudices, issues, values, and needs. Despite these difficulties, working with athletes can be a richly rewarding experience for the psychologist. Athletes can be highly motivated, competitive, dedicated, and successful, yet still have many of the frailties and problems endured by everyone else. Delivering sport psychology services designed to assist athletes overcome frailties and problems can help them become more successful athletes, but more important, such services, as was the case with C, can help them become happier, more successful, and more competent people as well.

Through my work with C, and my supervision, I believe I became a more competent sport psychologist. C helped me learn significant lessons, both personal and professional, and I left our relationship with a sense of having been privileged to be a part of this young man's life.

REFERENCES

American Psychological Association. (1992). Ethical principles of psychologists and code of conduct. *American Psychologist, 46,* 1597-1611.

Carson, R.C., Butcher, J N., & Mineka, S. (1998). *Abnormal psychology and modern life.* (10th ed.). New York: Longman.

Egan, G. (1986). *The skilled helper: A systematic approach to effective helping.* (3rd ed.). Monterey, CA: Brooks/Cole.

Hawton, K. (1992). Suicide and attempted suicide. In E.S. Paykel (Ed.), *Handbook of affective disorders.* (4th ed., pp. 635-650). New York: Guilford.

Raskin, N.J., & Rogers, C.R. (1989). Person-centered therapy. In R.J. Corsini & D. Wedding (Eds.), *Current psychotherapies.* (4th ed., pp. 155-193). Itaska, IL: F.E. Peacock.

Rogers, C.R. (1961). *On becoming a person.* Boston: Houghton Mifflin.

Vidal, J.A. (1989). *Student suicide: A guide for intervention.* Washington, DC: National Educators Association of the United States of America.

PART IV

THE STUDY OF SERVICE: FROM SUPERVISION TO COMPLEX DELIVERY

CHAPTER 11

SUPERVISION I: FROM MODELS TO DOING

Judy L. Van Raalte
Springfield College
Mark B. Andersen
Victoria University

WHAT SPORT PSYCHOLOGY SUPERVISION IS

Supervision, as a topic of investigation and discussion, is a new area on the academic and professional sport psychology scene. The first published works in supervision appeared in sport psychology journals only within the last six years (e.g., Andersen, 1994; Andersen, Van Raalte, & Brewer, 1994; Anderson, Van Raalte, & Brewer, in press; Andersen & Williams-Rice, 1996; Barney, Andersen, & Riggs, 1996; Van Raalte & Andersen, 1993). Supervision is the central concern in the training of applied sport psychologists, and interest in supervision is growing. Recently, at the 1998 Association for the Advancement of Applied Sport Psychology (AAASP) meeting, more than 20 presentations had something to do with supervision and the training of applied sport psychologists (see the *Journal of Applied Sport Psychology,* volume 10, 1998 [Supplement]).

Supervision of applied sport psychology practice is (or should be) a relatively long-term interpersonal relationship. As such, the supervisory relationship is fraught with some of the same joys, interests, conflicts, and frustrations that many long-term intimate relationships have. One ideal outcome of intimate relationships is the growth and development of self-knowledge and understanding (by the trainee) through close contact, feedback, and communication with another person.

Supervision's primary purpose in applied sport psychology is to ensure the care of the athlete-client. The secondary, but still important, purpose is the development of the sport psychology trainee as a competent, knowledgeable, and ethical practitioner. Ideally, supervision helps trainees understand themselves, their strengths and weaknesses, and their needs. This understanding helps trainees appreciate what they bring to the consulting relationship that aids (and possibly hinders) their work with athletes.

In other helping professions, in and out of sport, extensive supervision is an integral part of the training process. For example, athletic trainers are required to have 1,500 hours of supervised practical experience before they are considered eligible for certification. Clinical psychologists undergo anywhere from 3,000 to 4,000 hours of supervised predoctoral practica and internship training before sitting for national boards. Clearly, supervision is central to the development of the trainee and the protection of clients in a variety of helping professions.

In sport psychology, however, no clear-cut guidelines exist for trainee supervision in most countries. Barney et al. (1996) have suggested a model of training sport psychologists in supervision, and Andersen and Williams-Rice (1996) have discussed the role of supervision in applied practice, but to date, professional organizations have formally adopted nothing more than rudimentary suggestions. The Association for the Advancement of Applied Sport Psychology (AAASP) makes specific sport psychology supervision recommendations for those applying for certified consultant status, requiring just 400 hours of supervised experience for certification. What those 400 hours should consist of is not clear.

In Australia, however, specific guidelines have been laid out for the education and training of people who wish to call themselves sport psychologists. For example, for a master's in applied psychology with a specialization in working with athletes, the Australian Psychological Society (APS) requires that students have 1,000 hours of supervised practicum experience in generalist and specialist placements. Registration (licensure) as a sport psychologist in the state of Victoria requires a master's degree from an APS-accredited program in sport psychology and documentation of two additional years of supervision after graduation. Australia is probably ahead of most countries in establishing guidelines for training and statutory bodies to register sport psychologists. Antipodean sport psychology is also unique in that the accreditation of programs and the registration of professionals all take place within the parent discipline's professional body (the APS) and relevant board (e.g., Psychologists' Registration Board of Victoria).

Research on the current state of affairs of supervision in sport psychology highlights the limited supervised experience trainees receive (data mainly from North American samples). For example, Andersen, Van Raalte, and Brewer (1994) found that graduate students in sport psychology had a median of less than 100 hours of supervised practicum experience. More recently, in a study of doctoral graduates of sport psychology programs, the median of supervised practical hours was less than 400 (Andersen, Williams, Aldridge, & Taylor, 1997). This increase in supervision appears to be an improvement over previous findings, but it probably just reflects the fact that the people who were examined had either completed their doctoral degrees or had actually had a practicum or internship experience (no scores of "0" entered the calculations). Also, many sport psychology graduate students are not in the field to become practitioners, so they do not take practica; or, if they are required to take practica, they complete the minimum. The median amount of supervision reported, however, is less than the minimal AAASP requirements and far less than the standards met by trainees in other similar professions. The numbers imply that over half the students completing doctoral degrees do not have, at least upon graduation, the number of supervised hours necessary to apply for certification from AAASP. Thus, although supervised experience is essential for both the care of the athlete-client and the development of the trainee, it has not received the attention it deserves in the field of applied sport psychology.

GOALS

As stated earlier, the object of supervision is to develop competent and ethical practitioners as well as to ensure the care and welfare of athlete-clients. But supervision is also a career-long process, and even though this chapter focuses on supervising graduate students, we fervently believe supervision is something sport psychologists need to be giving *and* receiving as long as they practice. So the goal of supervision, in the long run, is, as always, the care of clients; but it is also the continued growth and development of practitioners throughout their careers.

At the beginning of a supervisory relationship, the first order of business is assessing the supervisee's needs, skills, deficits, orientation, knowledge, anxieties, and so forth. Well, that is not exactly true. The first goal of the supervision intake interview is usually to help the trainee relax and start talking freely and to build rapport. An example of a supervision first meeting is presented in chapter 12 of this volume.

Some see supervision, from the very beginning, as a parallel process (Doehrman, 1976; Friedlander, Siegal, & Brenock, 1989) in that what occurs in supervision is similar to what is happening in the athlete-trainee relationship (cf. Frances & Clarkin, 1981; McNeil & Worthen, 1989). Thus, beginning sport psychologists, when starting service delivery with an athlete, also make assessments of athlete needs, strengths, and anxieties. There are, however, differences between supervision and working with athletes, and they will be discussed in the concluding section of this chapter on supervision versus treatment.

Supervisors have a weighty role to play in supervision because they become models of professional behavior for supervisees. In the intimate learning experience of supervision, trainees often internalize the supervisor. That is, they take the supervisor's ethics, attitudes, and even to some extent interpersonal style, and make them their own (Barnat, 1974; Schneider, 1992). This internalization process highlights the powerful role supervisors have in the education and training of future sport psychologists. It is also a warning to supervisors about their own behavior: Be careful about how you behave; you may begin to see all your good, and bad, behavior reflected in your students. We know that loving, caring parents often produce loving, caring children. We also know what happens when parenting is authoritarian, distant, cold, and abusive. Supervision is a great place to be a good parent.

Assessment of supervisee needs begins at the first meeting of supervisor and supervisee. Regardless of the theoretical orientations of those involved, supervisors and supervisees should have conversations about the supervisees' history in sport psychology; what they feel competent delivering; what skills they would like to hone or even acquire (e.g., hypnosis, autogenics); what types of clients they have successfully worked with; and what they see as their strengths and weaknesses. Supervisors should help supervisees make honest assessments of their skills and determine what they need from supervision. In addition, supervisors can help supervisees articulate their theoretical orientations. Often, supervisees do not espouse a formal theoretical orientation, but theoretical roots can be gleaned from what supervisees say about techniques and change processes they have used (e.g., the typical cognitive-behavioral techniques frequently used by sport psychologists). A wise plan for supervisors is to express their own theoretical orientations clearly and even to describe how they typically work with athletes, so that supervisor and supervisee understand how each views athletes, interprets athlete behaviors, and understands sport psychologist-athlete relationships. This airing of theoretical orientations clarifies approaches and can reduce conflicts and misunderstandings later in the supervisory relationship.

Baird (1999) has identified three major approaches to dealing with the theoretical orientations of supervisors and supervisees, two of which will be discussed here. The first approach is the single-model (or one-theory) approach. The supervisor espouses one way of looking at service and behavior change (e.g., cognitive-behavioral) and believes the intern or practicum student should learn that approach and become committed to it. The second approach is where supervisors have a model that works for them, and the supervisee may choose to work within that framework or to experiment with other models. This latter approach is a laissez-faire one; the supervisee can choose any orientation he or she prefers, and the supervisor will try to help.

The advantage to the one-theory approach is that the student receives in-depth instruction and has a chance to learn one approach thoroughly. Also, it is difficult for supervisors to be well versed in several approaches, and the one-theory approach lets them work within their strongest areas of expertise. The disadvantages are that the student's orientation (e.g., behavioral) might not mesh well with the supervisor's (e.g., psychodynamic), and that the one-theory approach can give students the impression that there is only one way of doing sport psychology, and thus foreclose future professional growth.

The second approach—letting supervisees choose other models besides the supervisor's—gives the supervisee more latitude to explore other orientations, but it may not be the best approach for a beginning practicum student who needs plenty of structure in order to feel secure. For trainees with more background and experience in service delivery, this approach can provide opportunities to expand repertoires and case formulations.

The process of meeting the needs of supervisees is similar to a common sport psychology intervention, goal setting, in that the plan to meet supervisee needs is a mutually agreed-upon process. Supervisors and supervisees enter into negotiations aimed at delineating the responsibilities and duties they each have in a working alliance. This alliance is designed to ensure that athletes receive competent service and to help supervisees grow into competent practitioners. For example, a supervisee may wish to acquire skills in hypnosis. If the supervisor is competent in that area, readings and discussion of work in hypnosis, instruction in induction techniques, and applications of hypnosis to sport may become part of the supervision process.

Supervision as a mutually agreed-upon process, however, does not imply equality. Supervisors, with their wider range of experience and knowledge, may see something within the athlete or supervisee that warrants immediate attention. It is common for beginning sport psychologists to exhibit salvation needs in that they want to save or help athletes. Supervisees may therefore take on the role of problem solver for athletes rather than helping athletes learn to solve problems for themselves. Supervisees may not recognize their own investment or over-involvement in the lives of their athletes, but supervisors should point out to supervisees that such needs require constant monitoring. At a more serious level, supervisees may have a strong desire to work with a particular group, such as eating-disordered athletes. Supervisees may not recognize that this need stems from unresolved issues about weight and eating in their past athletic careers. Supervisors must be careful that supervisees are not using athlete sessions to work out their own unresolved issues. Although supervision may be a therapeutic process, it is not meant to be therapy, and another important role of the supervisor is to refer supervisees for counseling or psychotherapy to resolve serious personal issues that may interfere with service delivery to athletes. See the section Supervision Versus Treatment for further discussion.

MODELS OF SUPERVISION

Supervision of trainees is the process; competence and better care of athletes are the outcomes. Various models of supervision share the common outcome goal of increased competence. Through the following supervision processes, the supervisee develops into a competent professional:

- formulating athlete cases
- learning cognitive-behavioral techniques
- internalizing the supervisor
- making mistakes
- learning from mistakes
- learning limits
- comprehending one's own needs
- understanding oneself in relational contexts with athletes, coaches, and supervisors

Different approaches to supervision in clinical and counseling psychology reflect different approaches to behavior change and psychotherapy. Below, we present the most common models of supervision along with a developmental model of how supervisory relationships evolve over time.

Behavioral Models

Behavioral models of supervision are based on classical and operant learning theories (Boyd, 1978; Delaney, 1972). These models place the least emphasis on relationships between supervisors and supervisees. Rather, attention is paid to supervisee skill development (e.g., relaxation induction, guided imagery), and the supervisor's role is directive and instructional. The supervisor reinforces desirable trainee behaviors and corrects inappropriate actions. Behavioral models can be appealing, especially to beginning sport psychology trainees, because they are relatively straightforward, offer recipes for action, and provide structure.

Cognitive-Behavioral Models

Cognitive-behavioral models of supervision (Blocher, 1983; Kurpius & Morran, 1988) have a great deal in common with many techniques and processes used in the delivery of sport psychology services. Kurpius and Morran's model also has a distinct parallel-process aspect to it. That is, what happens between sport psychologists and athletes (e.g., relaxation, imagery, goal setting, cognitive restructuring, mental rehearsal) also occurs in supervision. For example, if a trainee is going to introduce relaxation to an athlete, the supervisor may instruct the supervisee to mentally rehearse the upcoming session. This approach to supervision can be attractive to sport psychology students, because they are often already familiar with the techniques used in service delivery, which are the same as the techniques used in supervision. Thus, practicum students are practicing what they preach; they are using on themselves the techniques that they teach athletes.

As Ken Ravizza (quoted in Simons & Andersen, 1995) has pointed out, one should not be using these powerful techniques (e.g., relaxation, imagery) with athletes until one has worked with them oneself for a substantial period of time. Supervisor behavior in this model can also have therapeutic features. Just as trainees may challenge athletes' irrational belief systems, supervisors may also address trainee faulty thinking (e.g., I must be a perfect sport psychologist).

Phenomenological Models

Phenomenological models of supervision stem from research and theory in humanistic and existential psychology. Carl Rogers' work (1957, 1961) is probably the best example of humanistic psychology applied to the supervisory experience. In phenomenological supervision, the supervisor's role is to create an environment that is conducive to trainee growth and development. Supervisors provide empathy and unconditional positive regard for supervisees and encourage supervisees to direct their own learning at their own pace. This approach provides a safe and threat-free environment, something all supervisors may wish to strive for. However, for some supervisees this model may be anxiety-provoking, because it does not provide sufficient structure and direction, especially for the beginning practicum student. Advanced trainees, however, may welcome such a model as they become comfortable with more independent sport psychology service delivery.

Psychodynamic Models

Psychodynamic models of supervision (Mueller & Kell, 1972) have their roots in Freud's work. The central issue in psychodynamic supervision (as in psychodynamic psychotherapy) is the relationship; in this case, the one between the supervisor and the supervisee. The basic assumption of this model is that understanding how supervisees relate to supervisors is intimately and directly connected to how supervisees relate to athletes in their care. Awareness of what supervisees bring to their relationships with supervisors provides insight into their ongoing relationships with athletes and helps supervisees understand the dynamics of their interactions with athlete-clients. Often in psychodynamic supervision, the emphasis is not on supervisor-supervisee relationships but involves discussion of how athletes and supervisees are relating to each other. Central to that relationship are issues of transference and countertransference, which are discussed in more detail later in the chapter.

A strength of psychodynamic models of supervision is that they involve thorough examination of trainees' motivations for being in the field as well as their needs and wants. A difficulty with this approach is that it is predominantly process focused and may be foreign to sport psychologists with an outcome-based focus (e.g., improved performance). By process focus, we mean an analysis of the inter- and intrapersonal dynamics that are occurring in service delivery and how those processes help or hinder the goals of service delivery and the behavioral outcomes. Psychodynamic supervision is not a place to start supervisory work with a new graduate student. If this type of supervision is to be used extensively, it is probably best for advanced doctoral trainees, and it can be an enlightening approach to use in peer or collegial supervision.

Developmental Models

Developmental models of supervision (e.g., Hogan, 1964; Littrell, Lee-Borden, & Lorenz, 1979; Stoltenberg, 1981; Stoltenberg & Delworth, 1987) have more to do with the evolution of the supervisory relationship over time than what actually happens *in* the supervision work. Stoltenberg's work was based on Hogan's and involves a description of four stages of trainee growth. These stages of growth are applicable to all the models previously discussed.

The first stage describes neophyte trainees starting out in their first practica or internships. Such trainees are understandably anxious, often have a need to know the right thing to do, may have a low tolerance for ambiguity, and can, at times, be quite concrete. This stage is the most dependent period, with the trainee often clinging to the supervisor. The supervisor at this time might wish to provide a fair amount of structure but also leave room for the development of some autonomy. The behavioral models of supervision might be better fits of supervisee needs at this point rather than the supervisee-directed (phenomenological models) or the ambiguous and potentially personally threatening psychodynamic models.

In stage two, supervisees begin to feel more competent in their abilities and start to develop their own individual approaches to service delivery. This stage marks the beginning of independence from the supervisor, but the individuation and separation process involves ambivalence, with vacillations between dependence and autonomy. Supervisors at this point might wish to loosen structure and let supervisees have more control of supervision sessions, thus further increasing autonomy. This might also be an appropriate time to move to phenomenological models of supervision, which by their nature are more supervisee directed.

Stage three involves a resolution of the separation/individuation conflict of stage two, because supervisees are close to becoming independent practitioners. Supervisees are now the primary source of structure for supervision, and their relationships with supervisors are nearly collegial. At this advanced stage of training, supervisees may be ready for in-depth exploration of their relationships with clients. Psychodynamic approaches to supervision may be particularly effective and instructive at this time.

In the fourth stage, supervision has become a mutually beneficial interchange between peers and can be considered a part of continuing education and training. Ideally, collegial supervision continues throughout the professional lives of sport psychology service providers.

COMMON ISSUES

Supervision shares many common issues with psychotherapy, counseling, and sport psychology service. Many of those issues have to do with communication difficulties, developing relationships, and ego defenses of the parties involved. One of the most fascinating and complex issues in supervision is the developing working alliance and the evolving relationship between the supervisee and supervisor

Transference and Countertransference

Even though transference and countertransference are concepts developed within psychoanalytic psychotherapy (Cook & Buirski, 1990), they have heuristic value regardless of which supervision model one assumes. In a dynamic sense, *transference* is the phenomenon whereby clients begin to relate and respond to sport psychologists/therapists in a similar manner to the ways in which they have related to significant others in their pasts (e.g., parents, siblings, or grandparents). The past significant other need not even be a real person. For example, athletes may relate to a coach as the "good" father or mother they had always wanted. In supervision, transference might involve a supervisee who had overbearing, authoritative parents, and, when confronted with the power differential of supervision, related to the supervisor either with undue deference and obsequiousness or with resistance and hostility. Thus, patterns of interactions with parents may be repeated in supervision. *Countertransference* is where the sport psychologist begins to relate to the athlete in a similar way. The sport psychologist, for example, may relate to the athlete as a younger sibling and become overprotective and possibly controlling. Thus, some countertransference phenomena can lead to trainee behavior that is not in the best interest of the athlete.

In a less-dynamic accounting, positive transference and countertransference are essentially about how athletes and sport psychologists get along with each other. Do they like each other? Has a working alliance formed between them? Paying attention to the quality of the interpersonal relationship between trainees and athletes is an essential part of effective supervision. Even if one espouses a behavioral model for service delivery and supervision, behavioral interventions are probably more effective if positive transference and countertransference exist between the trainee and the athlete.

Studying the phenomena of negative transference and countertransference can be quite useful in both supervision and service delivery. If an athlete begins to respond to the sport psychologist in a similarly negative way as she has responded to her stifling and authoritative father, there may be two major reasons why this is occurring. The athlete may be projecting her parent onto the authoritative figure of the sport psychologist, or the sport psychologist may actually be doing things—subtly, or not so subtly—that are similar to what the parent has done in the past (e.g., being authoritarian, engendering guilt, or telling her what she should be doing). The sport psychologist's own behavior may contribute to the negative transference. Powerful questions for sport psychologists to learn how to ask (and to keep on asking) when confronted with an athlete's negative personal response is, What did I do? What was there about my behavior that contributed to this negative reaction? The willingness to ask these questions and to seek honest answers goes a long way to understanding negative transference phenomena.

Negative countertransference is also a powerful source for understanding oneself in a relational context. Sport psychologists' negative reactions to athletes may stem from the athletes' unpleasant personalities, but the questions of interest for supervisors and supervisees are, What are the possible sources of this negative reaction to the athlete? Are any sources from within the supervisee? How much of my dislike of the athlete is really *my* stuff? Negative transference and countertransference can be powerful and informative teachers. They can highlight what supervisees bring to their work with athletes and also what supervisees and supervisors bring to the work of supervision.

Dependence and Autonomy

Dependency and autonomy/individuation issues are also part of the developmental process in supervision. Lack of dependence early in supervision might be a sign that something is seriously wrong. Beginning trainees who know it all are worrisome students. These trainees may not reveal all their behaviors to their supervisors for fear of criticism; they may also engage in behaviors that are not in the best interest of their athlete-clients.

In contrast (and more commonly), beginning trainees are quite dependent on their supervisors for guidance and support. This natural early dependent state should evolve (Stoltenberg, 1981) into autonomy. If, over time, trainees do not develop autonomy and confidence in their own decisions and interactions with clients, then supervisors might wish to look at their own behavior for clues to how their actions may contribute to the maintenance of dependency. For example, a supervisor's own need to help the supervisee become a good sport psychologist may lead the supervisor to offer lots of advice and help in problem solving that undermine trainee confidence. Instead, supervisors should be helping trainees to solve problems for themselves.

RIGHTS AND RESPONSIBILITIES

In the supervisory relationship, both supervisor and supervisee have rights and responsibilities to each other and to their athlete-clients (Andersen, Van Raalte, & Brewer, 1994). Supervisors' responsibilities include, but are not limited to, the following:

- Provide clear delineations of the trainees' and supervisors' roles
- Remain current with trainees' cases and provide an adequate amount of direct supervision
- Convey opinions regarding trainees' weaknesses and strengths
- Appropriately discuss nonfulfillment of practicum requirements when necessary
- Display empathy, listen attentively, and encourage trainees' expressions of feelings and opinions
- Encourage trainee feedback regarding the supervisory process
- Foster trainee autonomy and independence
- Maintain ethical responsibility to trainees and to the athletes served
- Keep information about trainees' progress confidential
- Provide appropriate models of professional behavior

Trainees also have specific responsibilities:

- Prepare for supervision sessions
- Keep up-to-date progress notes on individual athlete meetings and group presentations
- Critically examine their strengths and weaknesses as sport psychologists
- Continually seek clarification of roles and expectations
- Do not conceal any information about athlete sessions or group meetings from supervisors
- Provide feedback to supervisors on the supervisory process
- Maintain ethical responsibilities to their athlete-clients
- Seek to emulate a model of ethical and professional behavior in interactions with athletes and supervisors

Obviously, supervisors and trainees have additional rights and responsibilities to each other and to the athletes they serve. For further elaboration on the rights and responsibilities of athlete-clients, trainees, and supervisors, consult the ethical principles of psychologists and code of conduct (APA, 1992).

The supervisory process can be assessed by using an instrument such as the one presented in the appendix. This instrument can be completed by both supervisor and trainee and then discussed by both parties. Continued assessment and reassessment of how supervision is progressing can enhance the trainee's development. This assessment can obviate potential conflicts that arise because of inattention to discrepancies between how supervisors and trainees view the process.

PRACTICAL ISSUES

Although the rights and responsibilities of supervisors and trainees are clear, difficulties can arise in implementing appropriate supervision. The purpose of this section is to identify some of the factors that make ideal supervision difficult and to suggest some means of overcoming these challenges.

Time Constraints

Supervision is a time-consuming process. Both supervisors and trainees must prepare and set aside significant blocks of time for supervision. The pressures of other academic demands, such as class assignments and jobs for trainees and teaching and publication pressures for supervisors, can make scheduling particularly difficult. In some cases, such as clinical psychology graduate programs, supervision is a requirement for training. In other situations, however, time for supervision must be found in already busy schedules.

Some supervisors find group supervision to be a useful adjunct to individual supervision (Hayes, 1990; Wilbur et al., 1991). Group supervision, however, brings up the question of confidentiality. Supervisees can be advised not to reveal enough information for other students to identify the athletes they are working with, but often that tactic is difficult and awkward. Another solution is to explain to the athlete-client that the student would like to discuss the case with other students and with an expert in order to better serve the athlete. Accompanying this request would be assurances that the details of the athlete's situation would not go beyond the group.

Group supervision allows several trainees to meet with the supervisor at the same time. Trainees can benefit from interactions with the supervisor and can also learn from their peers. Some neophyte trainees find group supervision less threatening than individual meetings, because they see that other trainees also make and learn from mistakes. Others, however, may be hesitant to fully discuss sticky situations in a public setting or may find revealing their own weaknesses in a group threatening. A combination of both group and individual supervision is probably ideal. Later, as supervisees progress through their developmental stages, one-on-one collegial supervision and peer-group supervision become viable and time-saving alternatives (Benshoff, 1993; Borders, 1991; Remley, Benshoff, & Mowbray, 1987).

Financial Considerations

In master's and doctoral programs with internships and practica, students rarely pay supervisors for their time. It is all part of the educational degree package. Graduates of programs that did not provide enough supervision for AAASP certification, however, will have to find supervisors for their work with athletes. Unless they are incredibly lucky, they will have to pay for those services.

What is an hour of supervision worth? Probably whatever the supervisor and the supervisee decide. In most clinical and counseling psychology practices, a supervision hour is billed at the same rate as a therapy hour. Many clinicians and sport psychologists have sliding scales for their fees, and such a system for billing also seems appropriate for sport psychology supervision. For example, there is no reason why a well-established sport psychologist who seeks supervision on some particularly complex cases should not pay another psychologist full fees. In contrast, a new doctoral graduate, just scraping by, may not be able to afford a hundred dollars or more an hour for supervision. A reduced rate for the recent doctoral graduate seems fitting. Also, in the APA ethical principles of psychologists and code of conduct (APA, 1992) there is the strong suggestion that psychologists offer a portion of their time pro bono as a service to the field. More senior sport psychologists might want to consider offering some supervision pro bono, or at a drastically reduced rate, for new sport psychologists coming up in the field. In the next chapter, we present, as part of a case study, an example of how to determine payment for supervisory services.

Availability

Finding time for supervision can be difficult while one is a student but may become even more challenging for neophyte sport psychologists once they have completed their formal educational requirements. Sachs (1993) highlighted the need for both novice and experienced sport psychologists to remain involved in supervision of their work. He suggested that sport psychologists might want to consider using peer supervision, consulting with colleagues to discuss difficult cases. As with other forms of supervision, these discussions may reinforce the approach/analysis currently being used or may lead to more effective alternative strategies. In some cases, peer supervision may consist of face-to-face meetings or telephone discussions. In other situations, sport psychologists may choose to have regular peer-supervision group meetings to provide greater consistency and time for discussion. Some sport psychologists have sought supervisory input from their colleagues on Internet listserves (e.g., SPORTPSY). The specific form of supervision selected depends on a variety of factors (e.g., geography, finances, time). The important thing is for sport psychologists to continue to be involved in sport psychology supervision.

COMMON PROBLEMS

When supervisor and trainee mutually agree on the process and content of supervision, problems are minimized. Nevertheless, a number of challenges can arise. Typical sport psychology trainee problems related to supervision have to do with an over-eagerness to provide services and to become good sport psychology professionals. The solution to this type of problem is generally for trainees to become more aware of their own behaviors and of their need to help too much (see chapter 12 for a specific example), as described in more detail in the following text. For trainees with more serious troubles, direct discussion, remedial course work, and referral for counseling may be warranted.

Supervisee Wants to Help and Befriend Athlete

Sport psychology trainees often work in classrooms, locker rooms, and stadiums. In addition to individual meetings, they observe athlete reactions to teammates, to coaches, and to practice- and competition-related situations. Thus, the sport milieu requires significantly more involvement and less formality than do traditional psychotherapy office settings (see chapter 1).

In an effort to build rapport, or in response to reduced formality, some neophyte sport psychologists become chummy with their athlete-clients. Some beginning sport psychologists are not quite comfortable with the role of counselor and, thus, fall into the more familiar role of friend. Unfortunately, being the team buddy can lead to helping too much and can foster athlete dependency. Clearly, dependency is not in and of itself problematic. Athletes are dependent on sport psychologists to help them learn mental skills. However, trainees must learn to let athletes develop their own strengths with the goal of functioning effectively and independently.

When confronted with situations in which trainees seem overly tied to their clients, supervisors can ask trainees to consider the question, "Do sport psychologists serve the athlete by making themselves indispensable?" (Andersen & Williams-Rice, 1996). Most trainees understand that some psychological distance between sport psychologist and athlete can help athletes feel more comfortable about sharing personal information. If athletes see the team psychologist as just that—the team mental trainer rather than the person with a bunch of different roles, from training-table dinner companion to ice fetcher for the athletic trainer—then maybe the sport psychologist will be viewed as the person to talk to about "what is on your mind." Also, discussing the idea with trainees that one of the goals of effective sport psychology should be to put oneself out of a job might also be warranted (Henschen, 1991).

Supervisee Feels Threatened by Supervisor

Some trainees may leave discussions of the proper delivery of sport psychology services with the feeling that they are performing inadequately or letting their athlete-clients or supervisors down. If trainees discuss their fears and anxieties about how they are doing with their supervisors, then problems can be resolved. If, however, they feel too threatened to have candid discussions, then more serious problems can result, because trainees are working without complete feedback and supervisors are dispensing advice based on incomplete or distorted information. The problem here may not be primarily the supervisee's. Supervisors also need to examine their own behaviors to determine how they may be contributing to the supervisees' feelings. Many practitioners can recall a supervisor whose words, or even looks, could put the fear of some deity in them.

Interestingly, similar problems can result with trainees who idealize their supervisors. In both cases, threatened or idealizing trainees may decide to hide the whole truth from their supervisors and discuss only the things that they feel will impress. These trainees may hope that they will receive supervisor approval for doing everything just right.

Supervisors should be aware of trainees' tendencies to edit sessions and present themselves favorably and should encourage trainees to discuss both their successes and failures. Involvement in group supervision and frank discussions about the importance of taking well-thought-out risks and learning from mistakes can be useful. Trainees who are unwilling to address their shortcomings are likely to limit their skill development and, possibly, put their athlete-clients at risk.

Supervisor Does Not Confront Problematic Supervisees

Some trainees are simply not prepared to serve as sport psychologists (e.g., trainees who are academically unprepared, have major emotional challenges, are abusing substances, or have manifest psychopathologies). Whether the trainee purposely resists supervisor suggestions because of a personality disorder or is incapable of addressing the demands of the practicum because of a substance-abuse issue, it is incumbent upon the supervisor to handle the situation.

Supervisors should begin with direct discussion and possibly confrontation. It may be necessary to arrange for remedial course work for those who are academically deficient and do not have a firm grasp of theory and practice. Referral for counseling should also be considered when appropriate (e.g., for substance abuse and for some forms of psychopathology). The more extreme path of dismissal from a program is an uncomfortable option at best but sometimes a necessary one for the protection of athletes (and the reputation of the field). For a more detailed discussion of the legal, ethical, and supervisory issues around impaired graduate students and sport psychology practitioners please see Andersen, Van Raalte, and Brewer (in press).

CONCLUSIONS AND SOME WORDS ON SUPERVISION VERSUS TREATMENT

The mainstream applied psychology literature includes extensive discussions on preparation for becoming a supervisee (Baird, 1999; Berger & Buchholz, 1993), structure and training models in supervision (Freeman, 1993; Hess, 1980; Loganbill, Hardy, & Delworth, 1982), and ethical issues in the supervisory process (Bartell & Rubin, 1990; Harrar, Vandecreek, & Knapp, 1990; Sherry, 1991; Upchurch, 1985). Although applied sport psychology is just beginning to examine this central mentoring aspect of training, we believe that the goals of sport psychology supervision are clear. First, supervision protects the welfare of the athlete-clients, and second, it provides for the development of competent, ethical sport psychology practitioners.

We have discussed parallel processes in supervision (Frances & Clarkin, 1981; McNeil & Worthen, 1989), and briefly, how supervision has therapeutic aspects to it (Burns & Holloway, 1989; Rubenstein, 1992). Both supervision and working with athletes have as goals enhancing competence, whether it is on the playing field or as a practitioner. But what are the differences between supervision and treatment or therapy? If one looks at Kurpius and Morran's (1988) cognitive-behavioral model of supervision, what occurs in supervision (e.g., mental rehearsal, cognitive restructuring) appears almost identical to what cognitive-behavioral sport psychologists do with athletes.

There are several models of supervision (e.g., behavioral, phenomenological, psychodynamic) that may be appropriate for sport psychology. Regardless of the model of supervision espoused, supervision almost always has some parallel-process features. Both supervision and treatment of athletes involve assessments of needs, strengths, and weaknesses. There are, however, significant differences between supervision and treatment or therapy.

Choice is the first distinction between athletes working with sport psychologists and trainees working with supervisors. Athletes have a great deal of choice and freedom to participate, or not participate, in receiving sport psychology services. Initiation and termination of services can occur at almost any time the athletes wish. In the supervision of practica and internships, especially in sport psychology, there is often little choice. Supervision begins with the start of the semester, finishes at the school year's end, and there may be only one supervisor available. Thus, no choice is possible. Also, the supervisee cannot terminate a supervisory relationship without academic or professional consequences. Even in post-degree situations, there may be little choice in supervisors because of geography, finances, and time. Athletes face no such pressures when they seek sport psychology services.

The primary task of supervision is to protect the welfare of the client. The primary task of service delivery to athletes is the athletic and personal development of the client. Thus, the supervisee is always second banana to the athlete. Trainees may grow and develop through supervision, but that is a secondary focus of the activity. Also, sport psychologists are rarely in an evaluative position over their clients, except in cases where sport psychologists are consulted about team selections (an extremely rare event). Thus, sport psychologists are not often asked to make decisions that may affect athlete careers. In contrast, supervisors, especially those in academic institutions supervising graduate students, are in evaluative positions, and what they say or put in writing can have an effect on a trainee's future.

A final difference between supervision and treatment is the preponderance of dual roles in sport psychology supervision. In many sport psychology training programs, the practicum supervisor might also be the dissertation advisor, a classroom instructor for an advanced course, and a collaborator on a research paper for publication. Handling these multiple roles does not have to be a problem, but such complicated relationships are usually not present in athlete-sport psychologist interactions. An open and honest discussion of the issues of choice, freedom, evaluation, and multiple roles and how all of these features of supervision might affect the supervisory process can only help a complex relationship develop in a healthy manner.

If a trainee has a good experience with supervision, he or she will likely have positive attitudes toward and respect for supervision and for service delivery. Being aware of the obstacles to obtaining and maintaining satisfactory supervisory relationships helps sport psychologists figure out ways to provide and receive quality supervision over the course of their careers. We hope this chapter has provided a background for the next chapter, which concerns the actual delivery of supervision services. Supervision lies at the heart of both the professional and the personal development of sport psychologists. Through supervision, we hope sport and exercise psychologists will hone their skills, learn about themselves, and better serve the needs of their athlete-clients.

REFERENCES

American Psychological Association. (1992). Ethical principles of psychologists and code of conduct. *American Psychologist, 46,* 1597-1611.

Andersen, M.B. (1994). Ethical considerations in the supervision of applied sport psychology graduate students. *Journal of Applied Sport Psychology, 6,* 152-167.

Andersen, M.B., Van Raalte, J.L., & Brewer, B.W. (1994). Assessing the skills of sport psychology supervisors. *The Sport Psychologist, 8,* 238–247.

Andersen, M.B., Van Raalte, J.L., & Brewer, B.W. (in press). When applied sport psychology graduate students are impaired: Legal and ethical issues in supervision. *Journal of Applied Sport Psychology, 12.*

Andersen, M.B., Williams, J.M., Aldridge, T., & Taylor, J. (1997). Tracking graduates of advanced degree programs in sport psychology, 1989-1994. *The Sport Psychologist, 11,* 326-344.

Andersen, M.B., & Williams-Rice, B.T. (1996). Supervision in the education and training of sport psychology service providers. *The Sport Psychologist, 10,* 278-290.

Baird, B.N. (1999). *The internship, practicum, and field placement handbook: A guide for the helping professions.* Upper Saddle River, NJ: Prentice Hall.

Barnat, M. (1974). Some characteristics of supervisory identification in psychotherapy. *Psychotherapy: Theory, Research, and Practice, 11,* 189-192.

Barney, S.T., Andersen, M.B., & Riggs, C.A. (1996). Supervision in sport psychology: Some recommendations for practicum training. *Journal of Applied Sport Psychology, 8,* 200-217.

Bartell, P.A., & Rubin, L.J. (1990). Dangerous liaisons: Sexual intimacies in supervision. *Professional Psychology: Research and Practice, 21,* 442-450.

Benshoff, J.M. (1993). Peer supervision in counselor training. *The Clinical Supervisor, 11,* 89-102.

Berger, S.S., & Buchholz, E.S. (1993). On becoming a supervisee: Preparation for learning in a supervisory relationship. *Psychotherapy, 30,* 86-92.

Blocher, D.H. (1983). Toward a cognitive developmental approach to counseling supervision. *The Counseling Psychologist, 11,* 27-34.

Borders, L.D. (1991). A systematic approach to peer group supervision. *Journal of Counseling and Development, 19,* 248-252.

Boyd, J.D. (1978). *Counselor supervision: Approaches, preparation, and practices.* Muncie, IN: Accelerated Development.

Burns, C.I., & Holloway, E.L. (1989). Therapy in supervision: An unresolved issue. *The Clinical Supervisor,* 7 (4), 47-60.

Cook, H., & Buirski, P. (1990). Countertransference in psychoanalytic supervision: An heuristic model. *Psychoanalysis and Psychotherapy, 8,* 77-87.

Delaney, D.J. (1972). A behavioral model for the practicum supervision of counselor candidates. *Counselor Education and Supervision, 12,* 46-50.

Doehrman, M.J.G. (1976). Parallel processes in supervision and psychotherapy. *Bulletin of the Meninger Clinic, 40,* 3-104.

Frances, A., & Clarkin, J. (1981). Parallel techniques in supervision and treatment. *Psychiatric Quarterly, 53,* 242-248.

Freeman, S.C. (1993). Structure in counseling supervision. *The Clinical Supervisor, 11,* 245-252.

Friedlander, M.L., Siegal, S.M., & Brenock, K. (1989). Parallel processes in counseling and supervision: A case study. *Journal of Counseling Psychology, 36,* 149-157.

Harrar, W.R., Vandecreek, L., & Knapp, S. (1990). Ethical and legal aspects of clinical supervision. *Professional Psychology: Research and Practice, 21,* 37-41.

Hayes, R L. (1990). Developmental group supervision. *Journal for Specialists in Group Work, 15,* 225-238.

Henschen, K. (1991). Critical issues involving male consultants and female athletes. *The Sport Psychologist,* 5, 313-321.

Hess, A.K. (1980). Training models and the nature of psychotherapy supervision. In A.K. Hess (Ed.), *Psychotherapy supervision: Theory, research, and practice.* New York: Wiley.

Hogan, R.A. (1964). Issues and approaches in supervision. *Psychotherapy: Theory, Research, and Practice, 1,* 1739-1741.

Kurpius, D.J., & Morran, D.K. (1988). Cognitive-behavioral techniques and interventions for application in counselor supervision. *Counselor Education and Supervision, 27,* 368-376.

Littrell, J.M., Lee-Borden, N., & Lorenz, J. (1979). A developmental framework for counseling supervision. *Counselor Education and Supervision, 19,* 129-136.

Loganbill, C., Hardy, E., & Delworth, U. (1982). Supervision: A conceptual model. *The Counseling Psychologist, 10,* 3-42.

McNeil, B.W., & Worthen, V. (1989). The parallel process in psychotherapy supervision. *Professional Psychology: Research and Practice, 20,* 329-333.

Mueller, W.J., and Kell, B.L. (1972). *Coping with conflict: Supervising counselors and psychotherapists.* New York: Appelton-Century-Crofts.

Remley, T.P., Jr., Benshoff, J.M., & Mowbray, C.A. (1987). A proposed model for peer supervision. *Counselor Education and Supervision, 27,* 53-60.

Rogers, C.R. (1957). Training individuals to engage in the therapeutic process. In C.R. Strother (Ed.), *Psychology and mental health.* Washington, DC: American Psychological Association.

Rogers, C.R. (1961). *On becoming a person.* Boston: Houghton Mifflin.

Rubenstein, G. (1992). Supervision and psychotherapy: Toward redefining the differences. *The Clinical Supervisor, 10,* 97-116.

Sachs, M.L. (1993). Professional ethics in sport psychology. In R.N. Singer, M. Murphey, & L.K. Tennant (Eds.). *Handbook of research on sport psychology* (pp. 921-932). New York: Macmillan.

Schneider, S. (1992). Transference, counter-transference, projective identification, and role responsiveness in the supervisory process. *The Clinical Supervisor, 10,* 71-84.

Sherry, P. (1991). Ethical issues in the conduct of supervision. *The Counseling Psychologist, 19,* 566-584.

Simons, J., & Andersen, M.B. (1995). The development of consulting practice in applied sport psychology: Some personal perspectives. *The Sport Psychologist, 9,* 449-468.

Stoltenberg, C. (1981). Approaching supervision from a developmental perspective: The counselor complexity model. *Journal of Counseling Psychology, 28,* 59-65.

Stoltenberg, C., & Delworth, U. (1987). *Supervising counselors and therapists: A developmental approach.* San Francisco: Jossey-Bass.

Upchurch, D.W. (1985). Ethical standards in the supervisory process. *Counselor Education and Supervision, 25,* 90-98.

Van Raalte, J.L., & Andersen, M.B. (1993). *Special problems in sport psychology: Supervising the trainee.* In S. Serpa, J. Alves, V. Ferreira, & A. Paulo-Brito (Eds.), *Proceedings of the VII World Congress of Sport Psychology* (pp. 773-776). Lisbon: International Society of Sport Psychology.

Wilbur, M.P., Roberts-Wilbur, J., Morris, J.R., Betz, R.L., & Hart, G.M. (1991). Structured group supervision: Theory into practice. *Journal for Specialists in Group Work, 16,* 91-100.

APPENDIX

SPORT PSYCHOLOGY SUPERVISORY SKILLS INVENTORY

For the following sections, evaluate your supervisor (or if you are a supervisor, evaluate yourself) on each of the items by circling the number that best represents your opinion of your supervisor. Circle NA only if the item is in no way applicable to you or your supervisory experience; otherwise, use the following 5-point scale.

1 = unsatisfactory
2 = marginally satisfactory
3 = satisfactory
4 = very satisfactory
5 = outstanding

I. Providing Information and Technical Support

1.	Conveys practicum requirements to students	1	2	3	4	5	NA
2.	Conveys understanding of the sport psychology supervisor's role to students	1	2	3	4	5	NA
3.	Provides information to supplement the students' theoretical knowledge	1	2	3	4	5	NA
4.	Communicates knowledge effectively	1	2	3	4	5	NA
5.	Suggests appropriate outside reading material	1	2	3	4	5	NA
6.	Demonstrates sufficient sport psychology expertise with the presenting concerns of athletes	1	2	3	4	5	NA
7.	Provides direct suggestions for interventions when needed or requested	1	2	3	4	5	NA
8.	Demonstrates intervention techniques when needed or requested	1	2	3	4	5	NA
9.	Provides guidance in implementing diagnostic procedures	1	2	3	4	5	NA
10.	Provides guidance for maintaining records and report-writing tasks	1	2	3	4	5	NA

II. Fulfilling Supervisory Responsibilities

11.	Remains up to date regarding graduate students' ongoing cases	1	2	3	4	5	NA
12.	Provides adequate amount of direct supervision	1	2	3	4	5	NA
13.	Conveys opinions regarding graduate students' specific consulting/counseling strengths	1	2	3	4	5	NA
14.	Conveys opinions regarding graduate students' specific consulting/counseling weaknesses	1	2	3	4	5	NA
15.	Suggests ways for students to improve areas of weakness	1	2	3	4	5	NA
16.	Appropriately confronts students for not fulfilling practicum/internship requirements	1	2	3	4	5	NA
17.	Provides opportunities for sufficient number of supervisory conferences	1	2	3	4	5	NA
18.	Provides comprehensive supervisory evaluations periodically	1	2	3	4	5	NA
19.	Evaluates students' performance fairly	1	2	3	4	5	NA

III. Facilitating Interpersonal Communication

20.	Encourages students' expression of feelings and opinions relevant to their development as sport psychologists/counselors	1	2	3	4	5	NA

21. Listens attentively to students	1	2	3	4	5	NA
22. Demonstrates empathy and respect toward students	1	2	3	4	5	NA
23. Communicates at a level consistent with the students' professional development	1	2	3	4	5	NA
24. Maintains emotional stability during supervisory encounters	1	2	3	4	5	NA
25. Exhibits an appropriate sense of humor	1	2	3	4	5	NA
26. Allows students sufficient opportunity to interact during the supervisory conferences	1	2	3	4	5	NA
27. Encourages students' feedback concerning the supervisory process	1	2	3	4	5	NA

IV. Fostering Student Autonomy

28. Remains receptive to students' ideas concerning intervention strategies	1	2	3	4	5	NA
29. Shows flexibility in permitting a variety of valid procedures for psychological intervention	1	2	3	4	5	NA
30. Motivates students to develop consulting and/or counseling skills	1	2	3	4	5	NA
31. Encourages self-appraisals of students' consulting and/or counseling skills	1	2	3	4	5	NA
32. Encourages students to become increasingly more independent and autonomous professionals	1	2	3	4	5	NA

V. Providing Professional Model

33. Maintains an appropriate ethical responsibility to the athletes served	1	2	3	4	5	NA
34. Maintains confidentiality regarding the students' performance in practicum/internship	1	2	3	4	5	NA
35. Discusses with the students the ethical standards regarding interactions with clients	1	2	3	4	5	NA
36. Discusses with the students ethical behavior regarding supervisor and supervisee interactions	1	2	3	4	5	NA
37. Demonstrates interest and enthusiasm regarding the profession	1	2	3	4	5	NA
38. Provides an appropriate model of speech and language	1	2	3	4	5	NA
39. Maintains an appropriate professional appearance	1	2	3	4	5	NA
40. Provides an appropriate professional model overall	1	2	3	4	5	NA
41. Overall rating of supervisory effectiveness	1	2	3	4	5	NA

From Andersen, Van Raalte, & Brewer, 1994.

CHAPTER 12

SUPERVISION II: A CASE STUDY

Mark B. Andersen
Victoria University
Judy L. Van Raalte
Springfield College
Greg Harris
Victoria University

In this chapter, we will trace the development of a supervisory relationship over the course of a year. The supervisee was an apprentice sport psychologist who had completed an advanced degree in psychology (in Australia) with an emphasis in sport psychology. He had been asked by an Australian rules football farm team (young men under 19 years of age) to work with their players and staff. The apprentice's university advisor gave him the first author's name as someone to contact about receiving supervision. Our case study will start with the first phone contact.

Supervisor (S): [answering the phone] Hello.

Trainee (K): My name is K, and Dr. Fawkner gave me your name as someone to talk to about supervision.

S: What can I do for you?

K: I completed my degree at Ballarat University working with Dr. Fawkner in sport psychology, and now I am starting to do some work with an under-19 footy team [slang for Australian rules football]. Dr. Fawkner said I needed to get supervision, and I need supervised hours for registration later. She said I should give you a call.

At the time of this encounter, one could become registered as a psychologist in Australia with a four-year psychology degree plus two years of supervision. A master's degree is now becoming the standard degree for registered (Australian equivalent of licensed) practitioners.

S: So what did you have in mind?

K: Well, I am not sure; I am kind of new at this. I guess what I wanted to know is if you would be willing to supervise my sport psychology work. I got a very part-time job working for the Chargers.

S: I rarely do supervision outside our own graduate students, so I think it would probably be best if you and I sat down face-to-face and got to know each other a bit. That way we can see if we want to do supervision together. I might not be a good match for you, and vice versa. Some people click with each other; some don't. We may have entirely different orientations . . . we'll see. If it works out that we think we should do this, then we can talk about time commitment, scheduling, and payment.

K: Payment?

S: Yeah; I don't work for free, and I am not cheap.

K: Oh.

S: Don't worry about payment for now, we'll deal with it later, when and if we decide we want to do supervision together. So how is Thursday or Friday afternoon this week?

K: Thursday would be OK; how about 2:00 P.M.?

S: That would be fine. You know where my office is? City Campus, 11th floor.

K: Got it; see you Thursday.

Two events in the beginning of supervision have occurred in this initial phone conversation. Besides introducing myself, I have tried to communicate that supervision is something we decide on together and that it is a mutually approached (aside from the obvious authority differential) and agreed-upon process. I have let K know that we will be looking for a fit between him and me and that it is OK if a fit is not there. As in working with athletes, supervising sport psychologists is about forming a working alliance. How much parallel process actually occurs in supervision depends on the orientation of the supervisor and the needs of the supervisee (Frances & Clarkin, 1981; McNeil & Worthen, 1989).

The next major exchange of interest was the mention of money, something that seemed to take K by surprise. I sensed his discomfort and, possibly, was a bit too flippant with my joke about not being cheap. I probably increased his anxiety about meeting me with such an unthinking comment. To counteract my poor phone etiquette, I tried to place payment on a back burner and minimize, for now, its importance. I was probably not completely successful at undoing my unsympathetic response.

Payment for services, however, is not unimportant. Research in counseling and clinical psychology has shown that paying for services has an impact on attendance at sessions, satisfaction with services, and outcome (Callahan, 1994; Conolley & Bonner, 1991; Herron & Sitkowski, 1986; Herron & Welt, 1992). In general, people value what they pay for, and I anticipated that payment for services was going to be an issue. Supervision is time-consuming; it is often intellectually and emotionally taxing and warrants remuneration. Like sport psychology work, supervision is a (paid) service designed to help people get better and become more competent at what they do. Supervisees coming from university programs and university placements where supervision was a part of the curriculum have not had to pay for services. Thus, K's being a bit taken aback at the prospect of having to fork out some money was not surprising.

THE SUPERVISION INTAKE

The initial meeting with a potential supervisee has much in common with sport psychologists meeting athletes for the first time. In academic institutions, especially in North America, the supervisee and the supervisor will already know each other, because often the supervisor of graduate student practica is also the instructor for graduate seminars in sport psychology and may even be the student's thesis or dissertation advisor. Psychologists try to avoid dual roles, but dual roles are almost unavoidable in sport psychology graduate programs. One person in a department may be the research mentor, practicum supervisor, and classroom instructor for a graduate student, and all those roles have distinct power relationships and different methods of student evaluation. Keeping all those roles well defined, and the evaluations well encapsulated, can be challenging. For practicum supervisors who are already well known to supervisees, a conversation about multiple roles, when to wear different hats, and how to keep the roles as well delineated as possible would probably be a good place to start a supervision relationship.

In the case of K, however, we did not know each other, and our only connection was through a colleague at another university. As with seeing athletes, the first order of business with new supervisees at the initial meeting is to help them start talking about themselves. Asking questions like, "What would you like to get out of supervision?" is probably not the best way to start, especially with a neophyte like K. Such a question assumes the supervisee knows what he wants, or knows what he needs—an often unwarranted assumption. That type of question also may put the supervisee on the defensive and make him feel that he is being quizzed and has to come up with the right answer in order to please the supervisor. I had already communicated the idea that this first meeting was to see if we wanted to work together. The supervisee, knowing this supposition of the first meeting, may try to perform in order to please me, get on my good side, and have me take him on as a supervisee. Thus, as much as I want this encounter to be nonthreatening, there is a strong evaluative component to it right from the beginning, and quizzing the supervisee could have the unwanted result of exacerbating his anxieties about the encounter.

So supervisors need to stack the deck in favor of supervisees. We can do so by asking questions the supervisee can easily answer and that allow the supervisee to showcase himself and his accomplishments. I usually start out with a question about educational background, such as, "Tell me about yourself; what have you been doing in school for the last four years?" I prefer to start with an area a bit distant from sport and service delivery, get the supervisee talking, ask follow-up questions I know he can answer about his education, and then slowly move into sport and sporting experiences (usually another area the supervisee can easily talk about). I do all this easy stuff in order to help dissipate some of the jitters a supervisee may have in this early encounter and to show the supervisee that my office is a relaxed, comfortable, and nonjudgmental place to be. That is how I started with K.

In contrast to my work with athletes, I have a distinct agenda in a first meeting with a potential supervisee. With athletes, my job is to follow them and help them tell their stories (see chapter 1). With new supervisees, I do want to hear their stories, but I also want to find out rather specific things about them: their educational backgrounds, their theoretical orientations (if they have one), how they see themselves as deliverers of service, how candid or armored they are about themselves and their strengths and weaknesses, what sort of sense of humor they have, whether any psychopathology red flags fly at the first meeting, and so forth. My agenda is in place because supervision is a huge investment of time and resources, and I do not want to make such an investment unless I can get excited about the potential for the person I am dealing with to develop into a fine practitioner. Typically, when supervising graduate students, we often do not have the choice. We have to supervise the good ones and the not-so-good ones. In a private supervision, as with K, I had a choice to say yes or no.

S: Come on in, K; nice to meet you. Have a seat in the comfy chair. [I have a very comfortable chair that I use for seeing clients in my office. It is also the supervisee chair for my students.]

K: [sitting down] This is nice [the chair]; I think I need one of these.

From a psychodynamic viewpoint, that first line of K's is a gem. I often ask students to notice the first thing athletes talk about when they start a session. Those first utterances may be signposts as to what athletes have on their minds and may indicate what the content of the sessions will be. Sometimes first comments are prophetic, and sometimes they are not, but it does not hurt to notice them and keep them for future reference in the session and in supervision. So what does K's comment, "This is nice; I think I need one of these" say about K, about me, and about our supervision intake? At the very least, it suggests that he is comfortable being here. The "this is nice" may be about more than the comfortable chair. I did not know what his expectations were, but he could have easily had some trepidation about meeting me because of my insensitive comment about money. The "this is nice" could be about a feeling of relief, and that once K saw my comfortable office and chair, some of his concerns went away and he felt a sense of, Hey, this could be all right. If the first statement was about K and how he was feeling, the second statement (i.e., "I think I need one of these") was about K and me. He might have been saying, I want (or need) something you have (knowledge, comfort). I want to be able to see clients and put them in a comfy chair; I need what I hope is about to happen. In chapter 2, Burt Giges discussed a central tenet of psychodynamic theory: that all behavior (in this case, verbal behavior) has meaning. My tentative interpretations of the meaning of K's words were, of course, speculative, but probably not far from the mark (pun intended).

Overanalysis? Possibly, but these are the sorts of ideas that go through my head as I start this very interesting dance of getting to know a new supervisee. In any case, on a less-dynamic note, K sure sounded like he was comfortable to begin with.

S: Well, K, what I like to begin with is you telling me about yourself, your interests, sports, and so forth; but first, I guess I would like to hear about your educational background. I know you went to Ballarat University, so why don't you tell me about getting your degree there?

K: Okay; I started out there in physical education 'cause I just love sports, and then I found out that I could get a double degree in PE and psychology, so I went that route. And then in my fourth year, I did a special project in sport psychology and actually did some stuff with a team.

It looked like K was ready to jump right in and start talking about sport psychology service and his experiences. So much for my concerns about getting him comfortable and getting him rolling. He was there. That last line about doing "stuff with a team" is just begging for me to ask, "And what did you do with them?" Instead of jumping right in and letting him run with his sport psychology experience with a team, I wanted to hold off a bit. I had a feeling I had a galloping supervisee who was just waiting to get out of the gate. I could just see his enthusiasm starting to boil (please excuse the mixing of metaphors, but I do a lot of metaphorical thinking as I listen to clients and supervisees), and I thought, This kid really wants to be a sport psychologist in the worst way (already I was having some paternal feelings for him). I decided to redirect him away from his work with a team back to his education. I did this redirection to get a picture of how he saw his education, how it influenced how he thought, and how connected his education was to his wanting to be a sport psychologist. I have found, with some graduate students in our applied program at Victoria University, that formal education (theories, models, research, and so forth) is viewed as something to get through in order to get the degree so that they can go out and work with athletes. I had found similar attitudes also common among clinical and counseling psychology graduate students I worked with in the United States. We do our best to pound that attitude out of our graduate students (and pound in the importance of theory and research), but we are not always successful. By steering K back to my agenda, I was trying to let him know that I thought educational background was important; at least as important as his work with a team.

S: Ballarat is certainly one of the schools that provide a good undergraduate basis for sport psychology with their double degree. So before we talk about your work with the team, why don't you tell me about the highlights of your double degree, such as favorite courses, teachers, what you learned that was valuable . . . stuff like that.

K: Sure, but then I'll tell you about the basketball team; it was cool. [I was going to need some reins.] I really liked the two sport psych courses I took. The first one was a lot of research, which was OK, but in the other one we did a lot of performance enhancement stuff like relaxation and that was great. The other course I really liked was exercise physiology. I wasn't too keen on all the papers we had to write for sport psych and some other classes. I am not a good paper writer, and I had a hard time with them. I did OK, and got decent marks, but the papers were a pain.

S: How about different courses and teachers in the psychology department?

K: Well, Dr. Fawkner was really good, she did the sport psych classes and supervised the work with the basketball team, and she was in the psych department. I also liked my personality theory class. All those different theories were fun, like Freud and Jung. I didn't see much relevance to sport psych, but I enjoyed reading about them.

There are some major demand characteristics inherent in a sport psychology supervision intake interview. K probably thinks I want to hear about his views of sport psychology service and his experiences, and even though I try to direct him away from those experiences to other aspects of his education, he brings the conversation right back. Nevertheless, I was a bit concerned that his interest in theories and models in psychology seemed limited and that his primary focus had been to get to a point of doing work with athletes. I did feel that K was someone who really, really wanted to help athletes, and I had a suspicion that if we were to enter into formal supervision, his strong need to help and be involved would become a focus of our work together.

A positive note was that K seemed quite willing and comfortable talking about his academic weaknesses (i.e., writing papers), and that forthrightness augured well for our working together. I next wanted to find out a little about K's sport background (e.g., sport of choice, coaching experience).

S: Sounds like the university gave you some good foundations. Tell me a bit about your sport background—what you competed in and if you have any coaching experience.

K: Well, I played footy all through college [Australian rules football played at the high school level], but my real love is basketball, and I do some basketball coaching of an under-16 team.

S: So what about your sport background and your university studies led you to want to do sport psychology?

K: I think one of the biggest problems I had in footy, and later in basketball, was my mental game. Sometimes I would get so pissed off at myself for mistakes that my game would just go to hell. I wasn't cool on the court or the field. I wanted to be, but something just got in the way. I used to get almost physically sick before games with worry and excitement. I guess I really wanted to do so well, but I think I got in my own way. When I took that class in sport psychology, I kind of had one of those déjà vu things. I was reading about myself on the court with all that stuff about relaxation and anxiety and performance. Dr. Fawkner used to tease me about wanting to study myself, so please don't you do it, too. [I was tempted, but didn't say a word.] Anyway, I think things really clicked for me when I started studying the mental side of sport, and I said to myself, That is what I want to do . . . I want to help people with their mental games. But even more than that I want to help athletes and coaches get along together; some of my coaches were great, but some were bastards. I think I would be good at being a sport psychologist.

There was no doubt about K's enthusiasm and desire to become a good sport psychologist. It was another positive sign that he could see some humor in studying himself and felt comfortable enough with me to warn me off teasing him about it. The phenomenon of studying oneself appears again and again in graduate students (and practitioners) and probably has roots in wanting to go back and, at least vicariously, fix inequities, injustices, or poor decisions one made that were the sources of anxiety, emotional turmoil, and loss. K's motivations about becoming a sport psychologist and the needs he was bringing to the table were not topics for in-depth discussions in a supervision intake, but they would form a substantial part of future supervision. Another good sign about K's comfort in the intake encounter was his use of colorful language to express himself. Someone more guarded would probably not have used words like *hell* and *bastards,* but then again, this interview did take place in Australia, where colorful language is common. My impression of K up to this point was one of an open, enthusiastic, self-deprecating, and quite guileless young man.

I tried to phrase the next questions I asked in a way that would not make K feel defensive. First, I would ask him about his applied experience working with the basketball team, and then I would ask about the theoretical framework or the models he used in working with the basketball players. This latter question was couched in terms of his academic preparation and the material he was assigned.

S: You certainly have the drive and enthusiasm for the work. That's good. Why don't you tell me about your applied work with that basketball team?

K: It was really great. The Ballarat Bombers are this under-16 team, and my job was to observe practice, help out occasionally on court with drills, and talk with the coaches and players . . . like that. But my main sport psych job was to give these team presentations once a week on performance enhancement. I did one on relaxation, one on confidence, one on imagery, and a few others. I made relaxation tapes for the guys who wanted them, and a couple of the guys would just sort of pull me over after practice and talk to me about staying cool for the game or whatever.

S: How did those group sessions go?

K: To tell you the truth, they were kind of mixed. Sometimes the guys seemed real involved and asked a lot of questions. Other times it seemed like a bunch of the guys weren't interested. Maybe you and I could work on some group presentation stuff, like you could watch one of mine and give me some feedback.

S: That is certainly a possibility. Tell me, when you were out there with the guys doing the group presentations and talking to them courtside, what sort of frameworks or models that you might have gotten from your Ballarat Uni course work were you using to guide what you presented or how you talked to the guys?

K: Sorry, I am not sure what you mean. But like for the goal-setting talk, I just took the stuff out of the goal-setting chapter, kind of modified it for basketball, and used that as a foundation for the talk.

S: Yeah, that's sort of what I mean. If we work together, we will be talking a lot more about frameworks and models and how they get translated into sport psychology service. Tell me a bit about the supervision you received for that work.

K: Dr. Fawkner was my practicum supervisor. She gave me lots of material and lots of really good ideas about group presentations. She watched me present and gave great feedback. She also taught me how to ask what she called elaborative questions, ones that got people to elaborate—not just yes/no questions. That was really helpful.

S: And what was your favorite part of that whole applied experience?

K: That has got to be the guys coming over and talking to me. We would sit down and talk about performance, or what they were doing in school, and I would sometimes give them some tips like some cue words, or taking a deep breath, or staying in the present. Later, after a game, occasionally a guy would say, "those breaths helped," or something like that, and it really made me feel good, like I was doing something for them. I think that is what I want to do for a job—talk to athletes. I know I have a long way to go and that I am just starting out, but I really think that this is what I want to do. So that's why I am talking to you, to get some more training and help.

The sheer force of K's desire to be a sport psychologist was a bit overwhelming, but the passion seemed genuine and, at least as far as I could see at this early stage, relatively free from any psychopathology. His need to help athletes was expressed much more strongly than in most students I had encountered, and I knew that discussing that need would occupy more than a small chunk of our work together. Again, K showed how candid and honest he could be when assessing his own work. He unabashedly reported that some of his group presentations just did not seem to gel. He was showing a lot of traits that are desirable in a supervisee: being honest, self-reflective, passionate, and wanting to learn. Major markers of the developing working alliance came up in this last interchange. He specifically asked me if I could help him on his group presentations, and later, he stated, "that's why I am talking to you, to get more training and help." He was ready to jump in; for him, the working alliance was already there. I, however, was a bit hesitant. Despite all his fine qualities, I had a feeling this supervision was going to be a lot of work. There was a deficit apparent in his background on theory and models of service delivery. I would be doing a fair amount of work helping him get up to speed on why one does the things one does in service delivery and getting him to have a coherent framework in his work with athletes. He would have quite a bit of reading to do, and a substantial portion of supervision would involve reading and discussing models and approaches (bibliotherapy for supervisees). It did appear he had received some quality supervision about group psycho-educational presentations, and that was a plus.

At this point, I was thinking it was about time to ask that quiz question I mentioned earlier in this chapter. I sensed he already had several ideas about what he wanted out of supervision.

S: I think we might be able to do some work together, so I tell you what, why don't you tell me about what you would like to get out of supervision, what you would like to work on, and so forth, and then I'll tell you about how I generally go about supervising—my theoretical orientation, etc.; OK?

K: OK. [He pauses, and I think I misjudged his readiness for the quiz. I reframe the question.]

S: So what would you like to learn?

K: [exhales] I'd really like to get good at my group presentations. I don't think I am entertaining enough. Sometimes when I am talking to the guys, it's just going great, and we're laughing and bringing up good examples, like of choking and stuff. But other times it seems they are bored, and I am bored, too. Maybe you could help me spice up those group talks.

S: We could work on helping you really grab your audience, get them involved, and get them to be a part of the presentation. Group talks are not easy; they require a lot of preparation and a lot of thinking on your feet. We could definitely work on that. What else?

K: I love doing relaxation, and I really got into autogenics, but I could use some help in getting my inductions down, like my voice and pacing. I hate my voice; I want to make it a real relaxing one. I have a tape that I use almost every day, and the woman's voice on it puts me right under in about a minute. [I was pleased he was doing what he does with athletes on himself.] I want to be able to do that.

S: That's also something we could work on together. We might even grab some graduate students around here for you to practice on. What else?

K: I am not real sure. I really want to be a good sport psychologist. What do you think I need to work on?

S: I know we don't have to work on your passion and enthusiasm for the field; you have bucket loads of that. I'd like to tell you how I work in supervision—what I think is important—and that may give you some more ideas about what you might like to work on. Supervision to me is something you and I have to come to some agreement on. I have a few nonnegotiables, but a lot of what we do together comes from you and me sitting down and mutually agreeing on what it is that we are going to do.

What followed was a relatively long monologue in which I explained my approach to supervision, how training (e.g., learning autogenic inductions) could also be part of supervision, how the primary object of supervision was the care of athletes, how my major theoretical orientations revolved around cognitive-behavioral and psychodynamic principles, and how, after the care of athletes, the focus of the supervision would be K himself. I talked with K about learning the cognitive-behavioral canon (e.g., relaxation, imagery, goal setting, self-talk, cognitive restructuring) of sport psychology backward and forward and about how to make cognitive-behavioral formulations of athletes in order to apply appropriate interventions. I also discussed a more dynamically oriented approach, in that I would want us to look at relationships.

S: So I guess what I am saying is that I will want you to work on the cognitive-behavioral interventions both on yourself and with your athletes, and then I will want you to look at yourself in relation to your athletes and coaches, and even me at times. I am convinced that the main propellant behind sport psychology work is the quality of the relationships between sport psychologists and athletes. So, K, you are going to be a big focus of our work together—your needs, your personality, how you relate to athletes, how athletes relate to you, your fears, your responses to athletes' successes and failures, your strengths, and your weaknesses. That is how I think people become good psychologists, by learning about themselves and understanding themselves in relation to the people they serve. It will be a lot of work. It could get ugly, but I have a feeling it won't remain so for long. It could be painful, but a lot of learning is. I remember learning how to snowboard. That has to be a whole lot more painful than supervision. But I can guarantee you that if you stick with it, it will be endlessly fascinating. So that's my spiel. Kind of longwinded, huh? So what do you say?

K: Whoa! That's a load of stuff to think about, but you know, you, too, sound kind of enthusiastic about supervision. I'm game. I say we do it. When do we start?

S: Well, we already have by starting to set the groundwork. I think we need to talk in more detail about the content of supervision, such as how much training in techniques and presentations you want versus how much athlete case formulation, and so forth, and we can do that later today or in our next session. But I now think we need to talk about money.

K: Oh, yeah . . . how much is this going to cost?

S: This is kind of like the rest of supervision; the price is a mutually agreed upon figure. If you were an established sport psychologist looking for supervision on tough cases I would charge you a whole bunch. If you were a student in our program you would get supervision for no extra charge. Your figure will need to lie somewhere between those two extremes; the pay scale slides. It really depends on what you can afford out of your pocket and what I am willing to work for.

K: [hesitating] I am not real sure; I don't want to insult you. If we meet once a week for an hour I could maybe afford $40. To tell you the truth, my wife and I are kind of poor.

I knew, from conversations with Dr. Fawkner at Ballarat University and from a few things I gathered while talking to K, that $40 a week was going to be a stretch, so I suggested a fee less than that amount. K seemed quite relieved, and I could feel righteous in that I was fulfilling my responsibilities to the profession. As suggested in Principle F of the American Psychological Association ethical principles of psychologists and code of conduct (1992), psychologists are "encouraged to contribute a portion of their professional time for little or no personal advantage" (p. 1600).

Another interesting interchange occurred that revealed how the relationship was developing. I had given K some mild, goodhearted ribbing about his enthusiasm for the field earlier. After my long talk about supervision, he gave that friendly ribbing right back to me with his statement, "you, too, sound kind of enthusiastic about supervision." K could take it, and he could dish it out and keep a sense of humor about himself and me. His comment showed just how far we had come in an hour in terms of getting comfortable with each other.

We ended our session with some logistics about times and dates, keeping progress notes, and scheduling his training sessions (e.g., learning relaxation inductions). So, what was accomplished in this first session? In many ways, this supervision intake session was not a difficult one because of K, his personality, and his passion. I did not have to expend time and energy drawing him out. The working alliance formed quickly, especially on K's part (I was a bit more cautious), and the relationship grew to the point of being comfortable joking about each other. We established a foundation for future work, came to agreements on finances and what would happen in supervision, and set up a schedule for future sessions. I knew there were a few issues that would feature prominently, one of which was his need to help, or possibly even save, athletes. Soon we would be talking about another need—his desire for recognition. The unraveling of that story came in our third session.

SESSION 3: NEEDING RECOGNITION

K quickly settled into the plan of supervision. We will not go into the details of the training exercises (e.g., learning autogenics) we covered in supervision. Other parts of the book, such as chapters 5 and 14, have details of relaxation inductions. Rather, we will focus on those supervision sessions that had more to do with K on a personal and professional level. K arrived for session three with an expression on his face that I could not read well. It looked like disappointment or confusion (or both). Before a supervision session, I like to go over my notes from the last session to make sure I refresh my memory about any homework assignments and anything that might spill over into the present session. I remembered that in session two we had gone over a relaxation induction. K had done all right, but I ended up making a lot of suggestions. In retrospect, I thought I might have overwhelmed him with so many suggestions, and my actions might have been interpreted as negative criticism. That possible look of disappointment on his face might have indicated that I was not quite sensitive enough to how he was taking my feedback. Early in supervision relationships, I sometimes misjudge how tough or how sensitive supervisees are, and I find that I need to make adjustments in my style. It was possible that all my feedback to him about his technique had caused him to become quite disappointed in himself. With that confused or disappointed look, he started right in with a story of his experiences at the end of a game.

> K: I want to talk to you about something I felt last night at the game. I have been working with these guys for about six weeks, and I think we have done some good stuff together. I am at training every night, and I felt like I was part of the team. But at the game last night, I did my little pregame talk about staying in present time, I was out there for the changes [breaks at the ends of quarters], and I talked to a few of the guys one-on-one during the half. We won, but when it was all over, everyone was all out there congratulating each other, and I was, like, all alone; nobody said a thing to me. I think I was part of that win, but it sure didn't feel like it to me. I guess I was just disappointed that no one said, "thanks for your help."

I was silent for awhile, as much from being surprised by his story as from wanting to give him time to go on. My surprise stemmed from the deeply personal quality of his story about being left behind. I was getting these rather dolorous mental images of a sad little waterboy being left behind at the ballpark while his victorious players and coaches forget about him and go off to celebrate. That K felt that he could tell me this story of his own hurt feelings and that he thought it important enough to bring to supervision indicated that we had progressed rapidly to the heart of the matter of supervision: supervisees' understanding of themselves, their needs, and their responses to the people they work with. His story was about disappointment for not receiving recognition for his contribution. With that picture of a 10-year-old waterboy in my head, I felt that this was also a long-standing hurt. Probably somewhere along the way, and maybe in his sport experience, K had been left out or unrecognized for what he had to give. And K was someone who needed to give in a big way and then needed to be recognized for what he had given. One worrisome phrase he used, "my little pregame talk," suggested that maybe K was even beginning to belittle his own contributions.

When I supervise sport psychology students and practitioners, I ask them to read the introduction to Basch's *Doing Psychotherapy* (pp. 3-6, 1980) titled "Listening Like a Psychotherapist." I tell them mentally to replace the word *psychotherapist* with the words *sport psychologist* every time it appears. Those few pages contain some of the best advice ever written on how to talk with people. Basch writes about using oneself as a barometer or source of information about what is going on with the client. Basch suggests that we should use our own reactions (e.g., the feelings we get when we hear the athlete's story or our emotional responses to the supervisee's plight) and in that way gain another level of understanding. I do the same thing with myself in supervision. I noticed that I was having two major responses. One was a complex feeling of sadness and confusion for this hurt little boy in front of me who so much wanted to please. This feeling was accompanied by a sense that some of his confusion had roots in the previous session, where I had not been sensitive enough to his need for recognition and had communicated (unwittingly) that he was not a good sport psychologist (my overwhelming feedback perceived as a message that he was incompetent). The other strong response I was having was, Yo, buddy! That's the way it is! Sport psychologists are in the background, and so they should be. We don't get the credit. Get over it. Athletes are not out on that field so at the end of the day they can stroke your ego. Grow up! I had the thought that both these responses reflected something useful for me as a supervisor. One was a response to K's past, and the other was a response to K's future. Unless K could get a handle on his reactions that were rooted in the past, he was not going to get to his future.

I decided to let the hurt child know, through empathic reflection, that I understood. This approach, I hoped, would allow the young man to look at that hurt and where it came from. He was already on the right track by bringing up the whole subject in supervision.

S: Kind of hurts, doesn't it?

K: Yeah; it left me kind of sad, and even a little angry.

S: You put in a lot of work, and then you're not recognized for it.

K: I wasn't asking for much.

S: But it is tough when you don't even get a pat on the back. Have you ever had these feelings before?

K: What do you mean?

S: Well, have you ever felt you contributed to something, like on a team or in school, and then got ignored and felt hurt?

K: Now that you mention it, I always tried really hard in footy and basketball and worked my ass off, but I was never that good a player. But God, I tried. I only remember a couple times that any of my coaches ever said, "good hustle," or, "nice effort" to me. I guess I left a lot of games feeling a little sad about not getting that pat on the back.

S: Is there a connection here to what happened last night?

K: I don't know, but now that you put them together, they do sound kind of similar. Have you ever felt that you weren't appreciated?

This last question is another marker of the developing relationship. K is confused by his responses, and he is looking to me for a model (a major step in the process of identification with the supervisor) of how to interpret and deal with disappointment. The question from K becomes, You're the sport psychologist, how would you handle this? and it really boils down to, Please help me understand this. There are other questions K is asking, such as, Is it OK to feel this way? and, Do other sport psychologists feel this way? It may also be that I hit quite close to something painful for K and he has turned the focus back on me (deflection) in order to take some of the heat off himself. It's likely that the questions, the deflection, and the nascent identification are all happening at once.

It was not the appropriate time in our relationship to offer a dynamic interpretation of what he was experiencing by explaining that his emotional reaction might be based, in part, on what had occurred in our last supervision (my suggestions interpreted as information that he was a not-so-hot sport psychologist). Nor did I believe he needed to hear that his response probably had deeper roots, going back even earlier than his hurt feelings in sport. I believed what would be most useful to him at this point was a talk about the role of the sport psychologist in the grand scheme of things.

K's response to being left out triggered reflections about times when I had had similar responses. One of the benefits of supervision is that it helps supervisors examine, and reexamine, their own past experiences. I had experienced something similar enough to what K had that I thought I could tell him a story that might help him put his experience in a different frame.

S: Let me tell you a story. It's not exactly like your story, but it's close enough. When I was at Arizona State, I was doing a lot of work with the swimming and diving teams, spending a significant amount of time on the pool deck, videotaping the divers or the swimmers underwater [videos of turns and backstroke starts] and doing a significant load of one-on-one sessions. I was spending a huge amount of time with these athletes, and I had begun to question what I was doing. Was I out there primarily because I had been a swimmer and was sort of living vicariously on the pool deck? Was I doing any good? Times and diving scores of the athletes I worked with weren't consistently getting better. Although I didn't exactly have feelings of being left out, I asked questions such as, Is what I am doing here really an important thing? Am I helping anyone? Because I, too, wasn't getting any major feedback that my work was appreciated. In talking with my supervisor about my feelings and questions, she reminded me that the work of a psychologist is often unnoticed. Service is appreciated, but that appreciation is not usually overtly acknowledged. She also reminded me that it actually is the sport psychologist's place to be in the background and that evidence of appreciation isn't a weekly or even monthly event, but that when it does come, it comes in some of the most gratifying and humbling ways. That little pep talk helped me continue. She was absolutely correct, because a month after graduation that year I received a card from a swimmer I had worked one-on-one with on a variety of issues including the end of her swimming career. It was a thank-you card, and she had written on it, "Dear Mark, I can't thank you enough for what you did for me. I would not have made it through the year without our talks. I am now ready to get on with my life. Thanks again, you were the best." That floored me, pleased me, and sent me thinking, Whoa! What a responsibility we have with our potential influence on athletes' lives. I hadn't realized how much a part of her life I had been that year and just how helpful our talks had been. One note like that from a client can keep you going for a good six months. I guess my point is that we are appreciated; it's just that the interval between reinforcements may be quite long. [I paused for a bit.] So . . . what are you thinking?

K: I am thinking I would like one of those thank-you cards . . .

S: [almost interrupting] Everyone would.

K: But I get what you are saying. I think maybe I need to put my own ego on hold and not worry so much about being appreciated, and that sometime down the line a thank-you will come.

S: Good, but don't put that ego completely in the background. When you get those twinges of, Where's my gold star for the day? they are telling you something about yourself. And bringing this issue up in supervision is exactly the right thing to do. It's precisely what we need to talk about. Because feeling sorry for yourself, sadness over a lack of recognition, and bits of anger over the whole thing can negatively affect how you deliver service to those athletes and coaches who don't seem to appreciate you. That is the sort of baggage you bring to your work that we need to look at, and I am so pleased that you brought it up today. A continuing lesson, which I still keep learning, too, and I hope you will continue to learn, is how not to step in your own crap.

K: That's what I need, a . . . PCD: a personal crap detector.

Self-disclosure by the supervisor can serve several purposes, many of them objectionable (e.g., supervisor gratification, supervisor aggrandizement, or supervisor over-identification with the supervisee). Before I self-disclose and tell a story about myself, I try to always ask the question, Who is being served by my disclosure? (the same question that appeared in chapter 1). Although it was quite pleasant for me to recall that particular incident with the swimmer, I told the story to K for a variety of reasons. First, it was an illustration of how helpful sport psychologists can be in athletes' lives, even though they rarely get feedback. That was something K probably needed to hear (recall his belittling comment about his pregame talk). Second, it was a useful story to tell in the service of continuing to build the working alliance, encouraging the positive transference and identification with the supervisor. That identification may sound like a pathological need on the supervisor's part, but I mean it in the sense that as supervisors we are role models for service delivery. I wanted K to take on and identify with the role of sport psychologist as the person in the background. Third, I wanted to give K a bit of encouragement and let him know that appreciation would come his way eventually.

My first reaction to K's response to my question, "So . . . what are you thinking?" was, Damn, he's not getting the point. But I was wrong, and I probably should have paused longer to let him go on. K had just heard a story of an athlete's appreciation, he had been emotionally affected by it, and he wanted the same thing for himself. When asked what he was thinking, he replied in a fashion that someone with more personal armor would never have. He replied forthrightly, and he got the point of the story, too.

My last mini-lecture to K about doing the right thing in bringing these feelings up in supervision served three main purposes. One, I think he needed a pat on the back (in many ways), so I gave him one he richly deserved. Two, I wanted to reinforce the behavior of bringing such experiences to supervision, and three, I wanted to make up for what might have been an overwhelming session for him the previous week. So I needed to tell him he was doing just fine (serving both his and my needs). His final comment on needing a personal crap detector showed just how far he had come with looking at a disturbing emotional reaction in a new light. He could now make a joke about it.

SESSION 7: NEEDING TO HELP

By this session, K had also picked up some work with a basketball team. Occasionally he would audiotape his one-on-one sessions with athletes, and we would listen to the tapes and discuss them during supervision. The following is from a session K had with a basketball player.

K: What's been happening?

Athlete (A): Coach won't give me enough court time. He keeps putting other players in ahead of me when I should be put in. I keep getting pushed back behind other players [sounds whiny].

K: What do you mean?

A: I've been on this team for four years now and another player who has come on the roster only in the past year is being pushed forward ahead of me [beginning to sound angry and frustrated]!

K: Why do you think that is?

A: Coach gets along with him better, joking around and stuff, and then gives him stacks more opportunity to play and succeed. If I had been given the opportunity he had when I first started, I'd be a much better player than I am right now [really pissed off].

K: But that player has a much different style than you and has different strengths in different parts of his game than what you do. There are parts of your game that you have developed better than he has, you know, like your field shooting. You need to focus on those areas so you can be the best around in that particular skill.

I asked K to stop the tape at this point so we could discuss what was going on between him and the athlete. K was asking questions that seemed to escalate the athlete's feelings of dissatisfaction with his court-time situation. Then he offered a rather unsatisfactory reframing of the situation that ignored the athlete's feelings of frustration and crossed dangerously close to giving some sort of coaching advice in telling the athlete which parts of his game he should concentrate on. For example, the coach might prefer that the athlete work on his weaknesses and not concentrate primarily on his strengths. I had a suspicion that the athlete did not receive this suggestion too well, because it did not really address his presenting concerns, which were (a) not getting enough court time and (b) his frustration and anger about being overlooked in preference to a newer player. One cardinal rule in working one-on-one with athletes is that if you miss or do not address directly something that is important to the athlete, don't worry too much, because the athlete will bring it up again (and again) until you do address the concern.

K: God, now that I hear that again, I gotta ask myself, What was I thinking?

S: Well, okay, that's a good question. What were you thinking?

K: I think I was trying to get this guy to calm down. You could hear from the tape how he was getting sort of all wound up. I guess I wanted to offer him a different way of looking at things, and how he needed to focus on things under his control.

S: When you're around people who are getting angry and upset, or starting to yell, what happens to K?

K: Excuse me?

S: It may sound off the track, but what is your usual reaction to being around angry people?

K: I would prefer to not be in the neighborhood.

S: But that is kind of hard to do, leave the scene, in a one-on-one session.

K: Do you think I was trying to calm him down so I wouldn't feel so uncomfortable?

S: How does that interpretation feel to you?

K: I don't know; he seemed like he was getting so upset, and I wanted to help him feel better, but my attempts to refocus him didn't work.

S: Why did you want to help him feel better?

K: I see where you're going . . . that I wanted to help him feel better so I could feel better. We talked about this before, how I always want to make things right and help anyone who is in trouble.

S: I think it is one of the strongest needs you bring to your work with athletes. I am not sure where it comes from, but it is one that I think you need to be vigilant about. I am not too surprised that your refocusing didn't work. What is it we always say about not addressing issues important for the athlete?

K: Yeah, yeah [mock quoting], "If you don't address an important issue the athlete brings up, it will come up again and again until you do."

S: So what was the real issue here, do you think?

K: I think I needed to address all his hurt and anger and let him get it out, because after my attempt to refocus him, he almost looked like he was going to cry, and he said, "I'm thinking of telling them all to piss off and say I quit."

S: You know, sometimes people don't need to feel better; sometimes they need to feel worse. You might have been the only one he could blow off steam to and you tried to put a cork in it. So what happened after that?

K: After he got kind of teary and said he was thinking of quitting, I said it sure sounded like he was upset and unhappy and kind of angry about how he was being treated, and that opened the floodgates. He then went on about how frustrated he was, how he was trying to go somewhere with his basketball, how hard he worked, how basketball was the only thing he was really good at, how he was having doubts about his skill, and I just let him go. I think he felt better getting all that out.

S: Perfect! See how that worked? You asked him what was happening, and he told you a story of hurt and frustration. You didn't address it and asked him another question. He comes back with more hurt. You ask another question. He gets even more upset. You try to redirect him, and now he's moving into crisis. You finally address all his hurt, frustration, and anger, and out comes a huge release of emotion, anxiety, doubts about competency, self-esteem, and what have you. You kind of took the long way around to get there, but it is good that you finally did. I think we have two related things here that make you end up going the long way around. One, your discomfort with strong negative emotions, and two, your need to help people feel better or help fix things.

K: Why do I always want to make things nice?

S: Watching ourselves in service and relationship to others is just endlessly fascinating, but I am not sure why you need to make nice. Maybe you can explore that with your counselor. [K was seeing a counselor for his own personal growth.] I'd bet, however, that you were also the peacekeeper in your family. What I do think is real important is recognizing aversions and needs and making sure they don't interfere with service.

K: I can see how my needing to help can just get in the way. Like we've talked about before, it's not my job to solve the athlete's problems, and if there are strong emotions coming out, don't run from them. Run *with* them. Oh, and before you jump on me about my trying to reframe and refocus the player . . . that was so off-base; I can't believe I told him to concentrate on his strengths. That was moving into the coach's territory, and I just about smacked myself when I heard what I said.

I did not quite know how to take K's line about being jumped on. Had the session so far been a bit much for him? Or was it that he was just making a lighthearted jest at me? When a supervisor deals with sensitive issues that get in the way of service (like K being uncomfortable with displays of negative emotions and his need to make everyone happy), the supervisee may feel threatened, or even attacked, no matter how gingerly the supervisor tries to address them. Supervision can be threatening, and what may seem like a gentle push by the supervisor can be perceived as a violent shove by the supervisee. K's second reference to violence, ". . . just about smacked myself," could have been about him wanting to punish himself before I had a chance to punish him and thus avoid my retribution. And then I thought to myself, Jeez, Mark, give it a rest. K is doing fine in supervision; he's comfortable joking with you.

A strong need to help coupled with an aversion to negative emotions were probably K's biggest hindrances to his service. One goal of supervision is to discover the supervisee's impediments, recognize them when they pop up in their many and protean forms, and hold them at bay while we help the athlete tell a story, solve a problem, or deal with an overwhelming event. Although there is no doubt that supervision can be therapeutic and that personal growth and understanding occur in both supervision and in therapy, supervision differs markedly from psychotherapy or counseling (see chapter 11 for some of those differences). K's question, "Why do I always want to make things nice?" is moving into the realm of counseling or psychotherapy. I really could not answer that question, nor would it have been appropriate for me to speculate any more than I did. K was in counseling (something every sport psychologist should experience), so I made a suggestion that he might want to look, with his counselor's help, at his family dynamics to see if it was his job in the family to make things nice. I have often found that the supervisees with the strongest needs to help, to save, and to protect also had the role of family peacekeeper or protector. But this material was something for K and his counselor to work through.

My comment about how looking at ourselves in relationship to others is "endlessly fascinating" became the viewpoint from which we approached examining K, his relationships with his athletes, and his formulations of their concerns. K was developing a sense of wonder and enchantment about his and others' behavior, something I hoped he would carry all through his career. Often a supervision session would end with one of us saying, "Well, that was endlessly fascinating." Helping the supervisee develop a sense of deep interest in his athletes' behaviors, his own behaviors, and his relationships with others is one of my main goals in supervision. Beginning sport psychologists are often concrete and overly worried about judgments of right or wrong or good and bad concerning their service delivery. Becoming fascinated helps them transcend such dichotomous thinking. When what they do with an athlete works really well (or completely backfires), I want my supervisees to become enthralled and to learn more about why it worked or why it failed. Naive moral judgments tend to stifle development, whereas fascination promotes learning and deeper understanding. If students leave supervision fascinated by themselves and the athletes they work with, then I feel I have done my job.

TEN MONTHS LATER: CHANGING HATS

K and I had been doing supervision for almost a year, and I felt he was developing into a fine practitioner. His concerns about recognition, his aversion to negative emotions, and his strong need to help did not disappear completely. Nor did I expect them to; such needs and aversions are usually the result of a lifetime of experiences. But he was getting better at recognizing when his stuff was coming up and interfering in his service delivery. Our supervision had wound down to once every two to three weeks, and then in one session K started talking about the next stage of his education. He was interested in an advanced graduate degree by research. (Here in Australia, we follow a British educational model where many master's and doctoral degrees are primarily research degrees requiring very little course work. The major focus of the degree is the thesis or dissertation).

SESSION 31

K: I have been thinking lately that I want an advanced degree in sport psychology.

S: Well, that's something new; where did that come from?

K: I've been thinking about it for a while and thought today I would run it by you.

S: Okay; so, why do you want to get a graduate degree?

K: This may sound silly, but I would like the letters after my name on my business cards.

S: I don't think that's silly, but why do you want the letters?

K: I think if I have those letters, then I will be seen as more of a professional. Maybe they will help my credibility with future coaches and athletes. I think about it as an investment for my future livelihood. Those letters may help with first impressions.

S: That's a perfectly good reason to pursue a graduate degree. So, you know how it works around here; the degree is primarily your thesis. My first warning to students starting a research degree is that they have to be fascinated [that word again] with the research question. There is little worse than trying to complete a thesis that doesn't really interest you. Have you thought of any topic that really grabs you and that you want to look into?

K: Yeah; like I said, I've been going over this for some time. You know how we talked about how coaches and athletes see sport psychologists? I would like to look into how athletes and coaches here in Australia view sport psychologists and sport psychology services, something like those articles you gave me.

A month or two previously I had given K some articles on how athletes view sport psychologists (e.g., Martin, Wrisberg, Beitel, & Lounsbury, 1997; Orlick & Partington, 1987), because the way K was seen by others, such as coaches and players, was a recurrent theme in supervision. Athletes' and coaches' impressions of sport psychology and sport psychologists are interesting, and some might say crucial, areas of inquiry for applied practitioners and the field in general. Athletes and coaches are the consumers of services, and their attitudes can have a direct impact on how service develops, not to mention on the future earnings of applied sport psychologists. K's research interests were intimately tied to his need for recognition and his concerns about how he was viewed. I just had to tease him about it (probably because I felt close to him).

S: Let's see, you want some letters after your name for recognition, and you want to find out how people view what you do. I do believe Dr. Fawkner was right. You *do* want to study yourself [we both start laughing].

K: I'm just trying to be like you. [I supervise and write about supervision.]

S: [We are both still chuckling.] You got me there. It makes you think this whole bloody profession is deeply and hopelessly narcissistic.

K: But seriously, I would like to do the degree with you.

S: I'm flattered, and we would really need to talk some more about it, because it will change our relationship.

K: How so?

S: Well, now you are essentially a private client of mine paying for services. If you were to be my student, it wouldn't be right for me to also have you as a client and have you pay me money. So we would need to terminate supervision before you enrolled in graduate school.

K: Bummer, but I understand. It's kind of like wearing two hats, or the problem of dual roles, isn't it?

S: Exactly. Why don't we spend some time talking about what you want to do in graduate school?

The teasing, and K throwing it back at me, shows that we really had come far in our relationship. His line about wanting to be like me is not only a very funny and pointed "back atcha" about my own narcissistic tendencies, it also contains some truths about the relationship. As supervisees identify with and internalize their supervisors, they do, in a way, become like them. Just as I have internalized my mentors and can still hear their voices, K had internalized me. In K's case, his research interests in the consumer side of service delivery paralleled my work in the education and training of service delivery providers. K's new interests, however, would change our relationship.

In many cases during the training of sport psychologists in graduate school, the practicum supervisor is also the thesis or dissertation advisor and the classroom instructor. Those multiple roles need not necessarily pose a problem (see the first part of this chapter), because they are all still teacher-student roles. Moving from paying consumer to student is a large jump to make without losing something. In paying tuition at university, he would essentially be paying for my time as his research advisor. Adding an additional paying role (service supervisor) would make both roles awkward.

K and I talked about his project and my expectations of a graduate student, and we agreed to work together on his research degree. We also talked about him getting a new supervisor, and I gave him the names of a couple of people outside the university. The next session was our last as applied practice supervisee and supervisor.

SESSION 32

K and I talked about what was going on with his athletes, and eventually, near the end of the session, we came around to talking about ending this aspect of our relationship.

K: I am going to miss our sessions.

S: They have been very interesting to me. This is sort of like when things end with a client. It stirs up stuff in both the psychologist and the athlete.

K: So what's it stir up with you?

K's reflection back to me looks suspiciously like he is now the supervisor who is trying to help me deal with an emotionally complex time. His question probably has more than one source. He has strongly identified with his supervisor, and he is asking a question that could easily have come from me. Also, just like with his athletes (and himself), he wants to know what makes people tick, and that keen interest in human behavior extends to his supervisor.

S: It reminds me of my first experiences in long-term supervision and how I felt when that ended. And I wonder about what's happening with you.

K: Well, it's not really goodbye. We're just changing a few things, but I did want to let you know how much I appreciate all the time and effort. When I look back over the past year, it's kind of shocking how naive I was. I just want to say thanks for all you did; I literally learned heaps.

S: I learned a lot, too, and I think we'll both learn a lot as you head down the research route. So far the trip's been endlessly fascinating.

K: Yeah, you're right . . . endlessly fascinating . . .

REFERENCES

American Psychological Association (1992). Ethical principles of psychologists and code of conduct. *American Psychologist, 47,* 1597-1611.

Basch, M.F. (1980). *Doing psychotherapy.* New York: Basic Books.

Callahan, T.R. (1994). Being paid for what you do. *The Independent Practitioner (Bulletin of the Division of Independent Practice, Division 42 of the American Psychological Association), 14* (1), 25-26.

Conolley, J.C., & Bonner, M. (1991). The effects of counselor fee and title on perceptions of counselor behavior. *Journal of Counseling and Development, 69,* 356-358.

Frances, A., & Clarkin, J. (1981). Parallel techniques in supervision and treatment. *Psychiatric Quarterly, 53,* 242-248.

Herron, W.G., & Sitkowski, S. (1986). Effect of fees on psychotherapy: What is the evidence? *Professional Psychology: Research and Practice, 17,* 347-351.

Herron, W.G., & Welt, S.R. (1992). *Money matters: The fee in psychotherapy and psychoanalysis.* New York: Guilford Press.

Martin, S.B., Wrisberg, C.A., Beitel, P.A., & Lounsbury, J. (1997). NCAA Division I athletes' attitudes toward seeking sport psychology consultation: The development of an objective instrument. *The Sport Psychologist, 11,* 201-218.

McNeil, B.W., & Worthen, V. (1989). Parallel process in psychotherapy supervision. *Professional Psychology: Research and Practice, 20,* 329-333.

Orlick, T., & Partington, J. (1987). The sport psychology consultant: Analysis of critical components as viewed by Canadian Olympic athletes. *The Sport Psychologist, 1,* 4-17.

CHAPTER 13

FIRST INTERNSHIP EXPERIENCES—OR, WHAT I DID ON HOLIDAY

Vance V. Tammen
Ball State University

This chapter recounts my first internship experience at the United States Olympic Training Center (OTC), and that is how this chapter should be read—as the experiences and knowledge of one beginner learning about doing applied sport psychology. So this chapter may be more useful for graduate students and practitioners just starting out than for seasoned professionals. This chapter also has a wide-eyed, gee-whiz flavor that probably reflects the combination of naiveté, wonder, and enthusiasm many of us experienced early in our work with athletes. In keeping with the themes of the previous two chapters, a central feature of this chapter is my relationship with my supervisor at the OTC and how knowing you have a net really helps you spread some wings.

I write about my educational background to show how training influences one's views of doing applied sport psychology. I also write about three specific experiences at the OTC and how those experiences shaped my views and my philosophy of doing applied sport psychology. The chapter includes a supervision dialogue—some of it my best attempt at reconstruction—and although some dialogue is edited for illustrative purposes, the meaning and essence are what I remember.

How we do applied sport psychology is usually in a state of flux. Because doing applied sport psychology is a dynamic process, we change and adapt our helping strategies as we gain new knowledge and have new experiences. I am still learning and developing as a practitioner, even though I have been doing applied sport psychology for almost a decade now. These stories are some of my early experiences, and I hope students and practitioners can use them to demonstrate what should (or maybe should not) be done during internship experiences.

EDUCATIONAL BACKGROUND

To understand my experiences at the OTC, it is helpful to have some idea about how my educational experiences shaped my initial views of the sport psychology world and my philosophy about doing applied sport psychology. I have a bachelor of science in physical education (PE), with an area of emphasis in the social science of sport. While I was earning a baccalaureate degree in PE,

I was also taking undergraduate psychology classes. In retrospect, my university seemed like one of the last bastions of entrenched behaviorism in America. My cognitive psychology class was almost entirely based on association learning, and my motivation and emotion class also had a strong behaviorist, reward-contingency flavor. I ended up taking 35 hours of psychology, and I found out later that purely by chance I had taken the hours in sequence. That meant that if I transferred to the College of Liberal Arts and Sciences and took four semesters of a foreign language, I would have a major in psychology as well as physical education. Well, I was in the final semester of my senior year, and the last thing I wanted to do was try to learn a foreign language. I grew up in rural Midwestern America, and some have argued that just learning formal English was a pretty good accomplishment for me.

I continued on in a master's degree program in sport psychology in another exercise science department at a different university. My advisor was (and is) a consummate scientist; his philosophy and orientation to sport psychology was different from my undergraduate education, but not remarkably so. He was dedicated to the understanding and application of theory, but we rarely discussed or talked about applied issues. His philosophy was that most master's students should not work with athletes because they did not have enough training or understanding of the issues involved. His point of view was, and I paraphrase, that master's students often have enough information to be dangerous. I now tend to agree with him. Of course at the time, I thought I knew it all. My master's program taught me a great deal about how to think like a sport scientist, how to be a critical thinker, and how to question theory. Although I still wanted to do applied sport psychology, I knew that I really wanted to be a researcher as well as a practitioner.

I then applied to some PhD programs in physical education/sport science/kinesiology. After seeking advice and meeting with some of the people with whom I thought I might like to study, I was fortunate enough to be accepted at one of the top schools in the nation for sport psychology. My advisor there taught me a great deal about doing sport psychology, about doing science, and about myself. He allowed to me start working with athletes and teams, under strict supervision at first, and then more and more independently. The approach to working with athletes was an educational one with formal educational presentations and follow-up on individual one-on-one psychological skills work. I learned about being a scientist and planning research as well as using research and theory and applying them to the practice of sport psychology. Later, I was to learn even more about research, but that took place after I came back from the Olympic Training Center.

SHAPING OF VIEWS, BIASES, AND PHILOSOPHY

My experiences in graduate school shaped my views about sport psychology service and planted in me a number of biases that became ingrained. Because I came from a PE background, I thought that the model of sport psychology service, and doing sport psychology, boiled down to psychological skills training. My view was that psychological skills are like physical skills; they must be practiced to be learned. Most of my early training focused on learning psychological skills (e.g., relaxation, imagery, goal setting, self-talk) and then learning how to teach those skills to others. Thus, I worked with coaches and athletes as an educator; I did not have clients. In many ways, attending psychology classes in the last bastion of behaviorism was not the worst thing I could have done, because most of my interventions were cognitive-behavioral (CB) in orientation (e.g., relaxation, goal setting). Today, I still have a strong CB philosophy, but my paradigm has shifted, and new viewpoints about service have opened for me.

While going to graduate school I also took electives in psychology, educational psychology, and counseling. I took graduate classes in personality, abnormal psychology, motivation, cognition, and principles of counseling, and I quickly learned that not all people in psychology are interested in sport or athletes. This was an eye-opening experience, because so much of my formal education had revolved around sport and athletes. The fortunate thing was that I had some theoretical knowledge about areas of psychology other than psychological skills. I believe having that extensive background in both PE and psychology put me at an advantage when I applied to the United States Olympic Training Center for a research assistant position.

With that as a rather lengthy introduction to my background, it should be apparent how my training as an undergraduate in PE (cognate in psychology), my master's in PE, and my PhD work in kinesiology shaped my biases. To me, doing sport psychology consisted primarily of teaching psychological skills, which of course I felt pretty competent to do. The mode of operation I learned was that applied sport psychology practitioners do a formal psycho-educational presentation to teams and then work one-on-one with individual athletes. The athletes approach the practitioner after the formal educational presentations and ask if the sport psychologist can help them with some psychological skills. The practitioner then teaches those skills. I remember attending a talk where the presenter said that sport psychologists often preach to the converted. He said that about one-third of athletes reject what sport psychologists say unequivocally, one-third accept it, and one-third waver, so we should teach skills to the third that accept what we say in hopes that they will do well and convert the wavering third. After many years of service delivery, this axiom still rings true to me. To some extent we all preach to the converted when we practice applied sport psychology, and it was a great guide for me when I landed at the OTC.

OLYMPIC TRAINING CENTER EXPERIENCE

I went to the OTC, and I was given a number of prescribed duties and a few assumed ones. I was hired as a research assistant, so my prescribed duties including doing research, and I participated in several projects. I was also expected to interact with coaches and athletes when they came into our labs or when athletes attending camps came in for testing. These were tasks that I felt comfortable and competent doing. I also had some assumed duties because of the training I had in applied sport psychology. I was told that I could see athletes as clients, teach mental/psychological skills to teams and individuals, and work with coaches on psychological skills training. I asked my supervisor, Shane Murphy (head of sport psychology at that time), what was the most important thing for me to do. He told me, in his Australian brogue, "Just don't do any harm." I was later to learn that this is one of the main axioms of psychology, but at the time I thought it was a word of warning about working at the Center, which of course in many ways it was.

THE FIRST ATHLETE

I had been at the OTC for a total of one day, and I was still trying to figure out how interoffice mail on the computer worked, when my supervisor approached me and asked if I would like to work with an athlete. He knew I had done psychological skills training while at Illinois, and he thought this athlete would be a good starter for me. Not being one to back away from a challenge, I hopped to and said, "You bet." The athlete was a 21-year-old Olympic weight lifter who wanted to develop his psychological skills and begin formal psychological skills training. The first session was spent doing an intake interview and building rapport. I had some formal training in doing intakes and in rapport building, but for the most part I was flying by the seat of my pants. I was doing all the best attentive listing, active listening, following, acknowledging, reflecting, head nodding, and open body positioning I could. It seemed to be working. We were having a good time, with him talking and me listening, and he started talking about psychological skills. He said he was feeling nervous at meets and sometimes in the weight room; he had never felt like that before, and he felt he needed to do some relaxation skills. I said to myself, Hey, you can do that, and I started talking about potential relaxation techniques. We decided on Jacobsonian relaxation. I took him through a relaxation session and helped him associate relaxed muscles with cue words like *calm, loose,* and *easy.* This first session went well, and he scheduled an appointment for the next day.

After that first session, I went to speak with my supervisor, basically to tell him what I did and to get a pat on the back. Supervision of course, is rarely that easy.

Vance Tammen (VT): [after telling the story about the first session] So that was what I did.

Shane Murphy (SM): What other impressions did you get from him?

VT: Well, you know, I got the feeling that he really wanted to tell me some more stuff, but he just didn't know where to begin.

SM: What I would like you to do, Vance, is to open to door and let the athlete talk about anything that might be bothering him. Don't push your agenda. Just follow the athlete and act as a sounding board. Sometimes people just want to talk about their problems, and who better to talk to than a perfect stranger . . . a trained perfect stranger.

VT: Okay; I won't push any agenda, and I'll let him talk about whatever is bothering him. But what if it is about something I don't know how to deal with?

SM: Vance, you seem to have a good personality; people seem to want to open up to you. You have a good head on your shoulders and good training. Just asking about what you should do if you don't know what to do shows you know something about professionalism in psychology. When and if you feel out of your depths, you probably are; I then will help you out. But until you have experienced the depths, you'll never know if you can swim.

That supervision session really made me feel good about what I was doing. First of all, it showed that my supervisor was going to be there to catch me if anything went wrong. It also showed me that he had enough belief in what I was doing to let me continue. I might have felt a bit paranoid about boundaries of practice when I got to the OTC, but that session showed me that I was going to be allowed to push those boundaries as much as possible.

The athlete came in the next day right on time.

Athlete/client (AC): I feel really comfortable talking with you.

This comment made me feel incredibly proud and reassured, because it showed that rapport was building and that an alliance, or bond, was forming. I was still a bit unsure of my skills, and his comment helped my anxieties.

What I did not see at the time, because I was more focused on my relief than on his processes, was that his telling me about his comfort with me was exactly what helped him talk about what was really troubling him. Also, I might have been thinking that he might talk to others about working with me; word of mouth is a powerful line for referral.

VT: Thank you; I am glad you feel comfortable talking with me. Is there something more you would like talk about concerning your weight lifting?

AC: Yes, I don't know if I want to do weight lifting anymore.

At that point some alarm bells went off. I knew how to do psychological skills; this was career termination stuff, stuff that I had a few doubts about handling well. But we had just started, and I did not want to pawn him off without giving listening a try. I heard my supervisor's voice in my head saying, "sometimes people just want to talk about their problems." So I thought, Just let him talk.

VT: Why do you feel like you don't want to lift anymore?

AC: I've been lifting for five years; it's my whole life, you know. I really like . . . I love it, but I just don't know if I want to do it anymore. I have no social life, and I don't feel I am going anywhere. . . .

VT: What do you mean?

AC: I haven't been on a date in two years; I put off my last year at college so I could lift. I'm now behind, and I don't know when I will graduate.

VT: Is there anything else?

AC: Yeah; I don't really see any future beyond weight lifting. I mean, I can't become a professional weight lifter, and I ain't large enough to become a pro wrestler. Just what do I do after I am done being a lifter? I need to do other things. I guess I need to have a life.

I began to plug his responses into some of the theoretical information I had stored in my brain, trying to see patterns. I could see goal theory, retirement issues, perhaps some career crisis issues, and perhaps even burnout. My brain was working overtime, and then he said something that brought me back from my thoughts.

AC: I don't know if I'm burned out or just really tired of lifting all the time. [He started crying.] I'm sorry [about crying].

Now I was really flying by the seat of my pants, because all the male athletes I had ever met, including myself, were macho types who often kept their feelings inside. But I could see this boy (and at this point he seemed like a young boy to me) was really hurting.

VT: It's OK to cry. I can see you are really hurting, and crying is normal. Go ahead and cry. It's nothing to be ashamed about.

In a way, for this athlete to even consider the thought of burnout or retirement was like starting a grieving process. He had been lifting for over five years with intense dedication to his training, and now he had just vocalized to a total stranger that he thought he might be burned out or tired of lifting and that maybe it was time to walk away from his sport. This realization is hard for any athlete to make, and he had just made it at the ripe old age of twenty-one. He continued to talk about retirement from lifting, and I continued listening. At this point I was a sounding board, not giving any advice, only listening and empathizing with him. We ended the session with me asking if he still wanted to work on relaxation, or if he would rather explore the issues of burnout and retirement. He seemed to be emotionally OK (at least he had stopped crying, much to my relief), and he said that he would like to do both. I agreed, I think because relaxation training gave me something solid to grasp. I was a bit shaken by what had happened. One part of me was thinking, Wow, the kid really opened up to you, that has to be a good thing, and the other part of me was thinking, Is this an area I should even get into? Do I have the required skills to help him? With these thoughts in my mind, I went to supervision.

VT: So I told him it was OK to cry, and I just let him cry.

SM: That was probably the best thing you could have done. When people are feeling really sad and blue, sometimes the best thing they can do is cry.

VT: Yeah, but he is an athlete. No athlete . . . no guy has ever cried in front of me before.

SM: That showed you had opened a door for him. Your presence and personality allowed him to express his true feelings. That is what a psychologist should do.

VT: But I am not a psychologist. I am not even a psychologist in training.

SM: But you are now filling that role. How do you feel about continuing to work with him?

VT: Well, it's clear this is no longer a question of psychological skills, and I don't know if I have the competence to go into retirement issues.

SM: Yes, but how do you feel about working with him?

VT: At least he trusts me enough to tell me about his problems.

SM: And that's the most important thing. He trusts you and he is talking to you. As long as he trusts you and keeps talking, you should probably continue working with him. You have already established rapport, and I don't think you should disrupt that.

VT: But this could go into areas that I don't have any expertise in.

SM: He trusts you, and you seem to be doing OK with him. If you start to feel really uncomfortable and out of your league, I will be there to help or for referral. Once you begin to feel uncomfortable and in over your head, as I said before, you probably are. That is when you may need to refer. Until then, even with your level of training, you don't have enough experiences to know what you can and can't handle. At this time, it is important to keep the client talking. As long as he is talking to you, he is comfortable with you, and you don't want to disrupt the rapport.

Supervision gave me the faith to keep working with the athlete-client and to get a feel for what my comfort levels were. This opportunity is something that is not stressed enough in many current applied sport psychology programs. We are often so afraid of stepping over boundaries that we do not allow our students to push the limits of their skills. My supervisor's confidence in me meant a great deal, because I was not operating from a straight psychology or counseling background. I do not think he would have given me the reins, however, without a good feel for my training, my skills, and my knowledge base.

I continued to meet with the athlete for the next week while he was at the weight lifting camp. As we went through the sessions, I learned a great deal about listening skills and guarded advice giving, and the athlete still wanted to work on relaxation skills training. He kept asking me what he should do, and I kept saying, "What would you like to do?" At the time I did not know what to make of his repeated requests for advice. In retrospect, however, I think he was seeing me as an advisor or perhaps as a parental figure who could tell him what to do (I was only a few years older than he, so at that point I wouldn't have considered the idea that I might be a parental figure). The connection I made with the weight lifter showed me that I did have skills to offer other than relaxation, imagery, or goal setting, skills that I did not think I had developed in any formal classroom. The easy path would have been to play the role of advisor and solve his problem for him. Our job, however, is to help athletes solve their problems for themselves.

The athlete continued to lift at the camp, and I think having someone to talk with helped him feel better about his life choices. I opened our last session with a question.

VT: What are you going to do when you go back home?

AC: I think for a while I'll keep lifting. I still don't know myself what I want to do. I love lifting, but I have a feeling in my guts that I might . . . should go do other things. I sure would like to go out on a date.

VT: Perhaps you could use the relaxation skills we worked on to make yourself feel comfortable enough to ask a girl out. [I started laughing.]

AC: Hey! Good idea. [He started laughing too.] Some of the rehearsal things we did couldn't hurt, could they? I could do the belly breathing before I pick up the phone [and he laughed some more].

VT: Yeah; breathe away, dude [more laughter, moving toward belly laughing for the two of us]. OK, OK . . . now what about the lifting?

AC: I feel good about it now, but who knows what I'll feel once I get back home? All I can do is try.

VT: Well, I wish you good luck and skill. I've enjoyed working with you. Thanks for giving me such a pleasant experience.

AC: I've enjoyed working with you, too. We talked about so much more than I thought we would. Thanks for being there. I'll keep you posted on what I do.

The athlete and the sport psychologist making fun of themselves and laughing shows how far we had come in our short time together. He went back to his hometown, and like many athletes who would come through the training center, I never saw him again, nor did I ever hear what became of him. I once again went to supervision.

VT: So we had a good laugh, and then he said he would keep me posted about his training.

SM: We'll see if he keeps in contact. Many times we never see the clients again. That is just the way it works out—other things become more important to them, and we lose contact. I wish we wouldn't, but we do.

VT: Well, I really learned a lot about myself by working with this weight lifter.

SM: Really? What are some of those things?

VT: I do have something other than psychological skills to offer to athletes. The athlete opened up and let his feelings out. I know not everyone will do that, but this week showed me that doing sport psychology is more than relaxation and imagery.

SM: Yes, sport psychology is much more than relaxation and imagery; it's goal setting, too [he laughs]. Seriously, I think you were able to get a firsthand view of your own skills for working with people. You handled yourself well, and you appeared to do many things that helped your athlete.

VT: Thanks. I think I also learned to push the boundaries of comfort and practice. But I felt uncomfortable doing that. I am sure there are people somewhere who would say I should have bailed out and referred once the retirement issue came up.

SM: You did push your own competence boundaries, but not too much. You never really strayed far beyond your training. You didn't dive into terra incognita. You stuck with your cognitive-behavioral skills, and you still kept the relaxation training going. You allowed the client to explore the burnout and retirement issues while still doing psychological skills. You stuck with what you knew, and you learned about dealing with other issues. I think it was a good start. Those who might say you should have bailed out would gloss over the fact that you continually came to me for debriefing sessions and for advice. You did the right thing and allowed yourself to explore your competencies. Besides, you were being supervised by a very competent psychologist [self-mockingly laughs].

My first OTC athlete experience did teach me some valuable lessons. First off, if an athlete is talking with you, you are doing something right. All the active listening skills in the world are not going to get people to open up. You have to build genuine rapport. Some people have that ability as a innate gift, others have to work on it, but it is a skill that can be developed (there the PE philosophy comes through again). Once an athlete is talking with you, it is important to keep the person talking by not giving your views, opinions, or advice. As my supervisor pointed out many times while I was working with this weight lifter, "He knows what he wants to do, he just wants to bounce it off another person. You can offer up differing perspectives to the issues, and you can tell him about your view, but don't tell him what to do. He must make his own decision."

I also learned that one should keep working with an athlete even if the comfort zone is breached. I have now done this stretching of the comfort level for over 10 years, and I have a good idea about what I can competently deal with and what I cannot handle. I needed experience, however, to find those comfort levels and push them. It is up to professionals to know their limits. My experience under a competent supervisor showed me that backed with the training I had in graduate school, I could explore and expand the boundaries of my competence (for more about training, see Sachs, 1999).

AN ASPIRING OLYMPIAN

This case has some twists that also taught me a great deal about doing applied sport psychology. The athlete was a male field hockey player in his mid-twenties. His age was quite advanced for the USA field hockey team, so he was one of the "old men" of the team. Another intern and I had been doing educational sessions with the team for about three months. The athlete approached me and asked if we could meet. I said, "sure," and we set a time to talk later.

I started doing an intake interview, building rapport with the athlete, and we talked about many of the topics we had covered in the group sessions. Then he said the following:

AC: My father doesn't want me to be here anymore. He feels it is time that I got a real job.

The presenting problem seemed to be psychological skills, but the real issue was something else entirely. I could hear my supervisor's voice again: "He is talking; just keep him talking. He may only want a sounding board to bounce things off." So I asked the athlete to tell me about his father (my comfort level was stretching) and why his father wanted him to get a real job.

AC: My father played in the Olympic Games and won an Olympic medal in field hockey. He was born in [a Middle Eastern country], and he and my uncle played on the same team. They both won medals. He came to the United States in the late 1960s to build a better life for himself and for us. I want to compete in the Olympics like he and my uncle did. I really want an Olympic medal of my own.

VT: I can understand that. What else is going on with your dad?

AC: Well, my father thinks success is money, and you can't be a success unless you have a job. He wants me to come home and start working in the family business. My older brother works there, and it's expected that I will work there, too. I think he wants us to take over in a few years.

VT: I can see where he would like to leave the family business to his sons, but it is interesting that he doesn't want you to try for the Olympics like he did. Why do you think that is so?

AC: He thinks that sport is something you do when you are young, and now that I am in my mid-twenties he feels it's time I get to work—quit playing a kid's games and start earning a living.

Of course, the athlete's story brought a number of possibilities to mind about parent/child conflict, emulation of the parent, trying to please the parent, and other developmental and psychological issues. I thought about which theory to apply, and I could tell I was getting lost, because I was thinking primarily about what course of action would cause the least harm rather than what would be good for the athlete. In supervision, we talked about a number of potential issues, including the surface and subsurface issues. Once again, comfort was the topic.

SM: How comfortable do you feel working with this athlete?

VT: Well, he approached me rather than one of the other staff members. We are all doing the educational sessions, but he chose me. I would guess he must feel comfortable with me, because he opened up about the issue right away. I feel I owe it to him not to refer him to you or to someone else. He pointed out to me that he really only wanted to talk with me. I think I need to keep seeing him.

SM: I agree with you. You have already referred out a few people you didn't feel comfortable with. I trust your judgment. What are your other impressions?

VT: Well, I think there is a lot more going on than just this parent-wanting-him-to-get-a-job thing. I think there is the possibility of other types of family conflict and the potential of even some cultural conflict.

SM: What do you mean?

VT: His father is from ______; perhaps he has some old-world views. He [the athlete] was reared here in America. I would bet that he has a more liberal view about work and living than his father does. I think there is a distinct possibility of that.

SM: You could be right, but at this time we don't know that.

VT: Right, and I don't know if that is something I should get into. I read *The Family Crucible* [Napier & Whitaker, 1978], but I don't know if I can do any work in family conflict issues. Just reading that book is a pretty limited training. I don't know if I want to go into any cultural conflict issues. It might help him understand what is going on, but it might not ease his discomfort.

SM: I agree. What do you think you could do?

VT: Well, he said he is going home in a week or two to talk with the family. Maybe we could do some psych skills like imagery, relaxation, and role-playing to get him ready for the conversation.

SM: Great idea! Keep the work with him at the psychological skills level. You really don't have that much time to go any deeper into cultural issues or father/son conflict issues. Just as you get to the meat of the issue, he is going to have to leave. Let's only focus on what you can help him accomplish. I would bet you are right that there are other things operating here, but we just don't have time to approach those issues. Keep him talking about his relationship with his father; that is important, but I like the idea of using the psych skills to get him ready for the conversation with his dad.

I continued meeting with the athlete for about two weeks prior to his heading home for a meeting with the family. He spoke a great deal about his problems in communicating with his father, especially about pleasing his father. He believed he owed his father a great deal for moving the family out of the home country and allowing him to grow up in America. He also had some conflicts because his father was from the old world, and he was more American in his orientation.

There were many conflicts operating here, and there were a variety of viewpoints about what intervention might work best. Athletes are often at the OTC for only a short time, so the sport psychologist may not be able to explore issues as thoroughly as he or she wants to.

In supervision, I started to question whether I should explore some of the other issues floating out there rather than only take an approach that focused on developing skills for his upcoming conversation.

VT: If he comes back to the program, do you think we should explore more of the father-son conflict and the cultural conflict?

SM: If he comes back and he wants to talk about it . . . maybe. Having seen you work these past few months, I have confidence that you could explore those issues and do a good job with it. Remember, though, he might not come back, and if he does, he might not want to discuss these issues. Let's just see what happens for right now.

VT: I really wouldn't mind trying my hand at a more cognitive intervention at this stage. You know, maybe some rational-emotive therapy [RET] to attack some of his irrational thoughts.

SM: I think you could do a good job with that, but time is short, and we don't know if he will come back or not. Just keep him talking and working on the psychological skills. Besides, RET might not be the best approach at this time. Too many other things could affect whether RET will work or not. Stick with the psychological skills for now.

We would do imagery, relaxation, and role-play sessions so that the athlete could act out a number of scenarios of how to talk with his father and discuss his desires to play for the U.S. Olympic Team. The athlete then went home to talk with the family. He returned and told me that all went pretty well, but his father still wanted him to get a real job. One of the role-plays we did included this discussion. One of the strategies we explored was for the athlete to tell his family that he would try out for the team, and if he made it he would stay at the OTC. If not, he would return home to get that real job. This scenario is almost exactly what played out, and the athlete said he was glad we had rehearsed that scene in practice sessions. He also believed that the relaxation sessions and imagery session had helped to prepare him for the confrontation about his sporting career. In the end, the athlete did make the U.S. team, but the USA did not qualify to compete in the Olympic Games until 1996, and I know this athlete never did compete in any Olympic Games.

The following is an excerpt from a later supervision session.

VT: It appears that he did use some of the skills we worked on.

SM: That's great.

VT: This was the first time I had really used psychological skills in any situation other than the playing fields. It was really cool to have him use these skills in a situation that was not performance oriented.

SM: But you're wrong. The discussion with his father was a performance situation, just like hitting a penalty shot. The pressure was on, and you know what pressure and nervousness can do to performance. Anytime nervousness gets in the way of a goal, you can have a poor performance. It sounds like he used the psychological skills to rehearse and control his emotions for his performance with his father. Perhaps he even felt more confident going into his conversation with his father due to what you did in the lab with him.

VT: I never really thought of it that way. Yeah, it was a performance piece. I hope what he learned in the lab carries over to the field. In my biased view it should, but that is not always the case, is it?

SM: No, not usually. What is good for one situation doesn't always transfer to other situations. I do think it was a great idea to take what you know about applied sport psychology and apply it to this situation. It should have also taught you that you can apply psychological skills to situations other than sport.

VT: Like I said, it was the first time I had applied the skills outside the playing field. That was really cool. But one thing . . . he was only the second athlete to come to me about a psychological skills issue and then talk about a personal problem. Does this often happen?

SM: For me, more than 30% of the time, but for you, I would guess it will not happen as much. Much of it has to do with our professional training and the questions we ask. Much of it depends on the situation we are in as well. If you're seen as being there to do primarily psych skills, then I would guess personal issues would not come up too often. If you are seen as a general psychologist at a site, you will have many more clients coming in for personal problems.

The 30% figure is a little larger than the numbers Kirschenbaum, Parham, and Murphy (1993) reported for services delivered at an Olympic Festival. The breakdown for the 1991 festival was about 66% performance-related concerns, 18% for personal issues, and 18% for injury-related problems.

Looking back at the field hockey player case, there were many ways we could have approached his issues. I took one way that fit within my biases and comfort zone of doing sport psychology: keep the client talking and work on developing psychological skills that he could use in his confrontation with his father. Based on my training at the time, this CB approach was perhaps the best path to take. We could have explored issues related to family conflict, cultural conflict, or even doubts about his ability and competence, but would it have led to a better conclusion? The answer is, probably not. Given the short time span and the issues involved, we did the best we could, and the athlete felt happy about what we did together.

This case opened my eyes to one major issue about working with athletes. For the most part, my time at the OTC was spent doing educational and psychological skills sessions, but every once in a while an athlete would come in, ostensibly for performance enhancement, and then would switch the topic to personal psychological or relationship issues. These instances were rare for me. I think I have dealt with 7 such cases in 10 years, and 4 happened in the 7 months at the OTC, but they did occur, and it is important that budding sport psychologists know how to deal with these situations. I believe that training in graduate schools and practica should cover material for how to recognize and help athletes deal with the personal psychological issues that can and will crop up from time to time.

I was once at a conference in Australia where a sport psychologist at the Australian Institute of Sport said that only psychologists should work with athletes, because less than 20% of all issues that come up are related to performance enhancement. From my experiences, data would not support the 20% figure, but for this person, 20% is obviously the case. Perhaps one way to get a full picture of what is an apparent discrepancy can be found in our training. Most people who are based in training centers in Australia (the national and state institutes) and the United States (OTCs) are trained as clinicians or counselors, and because training shapes our biases, people tend to look for things that confirm their biases. People trained in clinical or counseling programs might be more likely to explore, probe, or ask questions related to issues other than performance enhancement. Also, in a national training center environment, where high-level performance is linked to so many human behaviors other than psychological skills, perhaps the staff do see more non-performance-based issues.

So, who is right? My gut reaction is that no one is wrong. Issues come up, bombs are dropped, and everyone had better have training to recognize the situation and help the client to the best of their ability. If there is one caveat, it is that the questions we ask will lead us to answers that will most likely confirm our biases. It would behoove practitioners to know their biases so they are more likely to ask neutral questions that lead to the heart of the clients' problems, not their own. Because I was trained as a scientist as well as a practitioner, I can identify and assess my own biases and try not to let my scientific biases affect my research. I have tried to carry this understanding over to my practice of sport psychology, and for the most part I believe I have succeeded. From what I can see of sport psychology graduate programs and from talking to others about their educational experiences, I think we do not do enough bias-awareness training.

As my time passed at the OTC, my supervisory relationship grew and evolved. My supervisor became more comfortable with my work with athletes, and he was more willing to let me work independently. He was still there to offer advice and to guide my thinking, but he was also becoming more willing to trust my judgments and my own views about each case. This relationship had grown over an intense seven months. We had gone from a supervisor-subordinate relationship to a collegial relationship. These developments are important transitions in any supervisory relationship, and ones that are crucial to effective learning. The supervisory sessions were not always smooth sailing, but we both felt comfortable enough to voice our views.

TOP OF HIS GAME

This last case is interesting to me because of its end result. It was, perhaps, one of my most casual meetings with an athlete, but it stuck in my mind as having the potential for negative consequences. The athlete was 21 years old and was one of the top persons in his sport. He and the entire USA squad were at the OTC for a week-long camp of physiological, biomechanical, and psychological testing. I had been dealing with the coaches to set up much of the itinerary, and I had worked overtime in the lab to get the fitness reports out to coaches. The coaches really appreciated when any staff member worked overtime to get things done and ready for them, especially because their sport was considered a minor one. I have always remembered that, and I always try to go the extra mile when working with all coaches and athletes. One day, the athlete just described came to my door.

AC: I've been told you are a sport psychologist.

VT: Well, I like to think I am . . . among other things. What can I do for you today?

AC: I think I need to talk to someone.

VT: Come on in, have a seat. About what?

AC: Did you get my test reports done?

VT: Yes, I did; we can look at them if you want.

We looked at the reports, and I noticed he was kind of fidgety and not paying much attention. I decided to do a little exploring

VT: Are the reports the only reason you came here?

AC: No, I guess the reports can wait. I'm thinking about taking a break from my sport.

VT: Really? What brought this on? Usually at these camps athletes get fired up.

AC: Oh, it has nothing to do with the camp. This is lots of fun. I've been pissed off with the administration of our sport for some time, and I think it's reached a head. Since I am pissed with them, I don't really want to compete anymore. They have taken my passion away.

VT: Tell me more about what's going on.

The athlete proceeded to tell me about his run-in with the sport administrators at the 1988 Winter Olympics at Calgary and how this was hurting his preparations for the upcoming winter season. I decided I needed more background, so I asked him to tell me about his history. Without giving too many details, he started his sport when he was 11 or 12 years old, right after the 1980 Olympics in Lake Placid. He had been competing since then and had slowly risen through the ranks, so that at the age of 21 he was one of the best the Americans had ever produced. He said he was willing to give it up and leave his sport altogether. He said he felt he was going through a rebellion-against-authority stage, and it was easy to rebel, especially because the sport administration was such a mess.

In some ways this case is similar to the first case in this chapter—an athlete contemplating retirement. The case was unique for me, because I only met the athlete once, for less than one hour, and the presenting problem had nothing to do with performance enhancement. It was related to his own feelings of rebellion and frustration with the sport administrators. He continued to tell me more about his feeling for his sport as well.

AC: I really love my sport—the wind, the speed. It is a great adrenaline rush. Have you ever seen it?

VT: Yes, I have. It looks like a lot of fun. That is one sport I have always wanted to do, but I really don't have the facilities or the opportunity where I live.

AC: You come to Lake Placid, and I'll teach you myself. If not me, I am sure one of the coaches will. They are really happy with all the work you have done with us this week.

VT: Well thanks, I appreciate that, but let's get back to you wanting to leave the sport.

AC: Maybe it's not the administration; maybe I am just tired of doing this all the time.

VT: What do you mean? The travel, the training?

AC: Yeah, all those things. I like going to other countries, but I hate living out of a suitcase. Most of the time we don't even do any sight-seeing. I like the training, especially weight training. I've been told I need to cut back on the lifting, but I think they are all wrong. I don't like training all the time, though. There are times when I just want time to myself. All these things make me tired, but I still love my sport.

VT: Yes, but why do you want to leave the sport?

AC: Maybe I don't. Like I said, it is my passion, my obsession. Maybe I need a break. You know, time away from it.

The athlete was jumping around from topic to topic and point to point. I think a great deal of that had to do with him getting a feel for me. His comment, "I'll teach you myself," suggested he might have already developed some positive feelings for me. He did not quite want to attack the issue directly, and I think he was still exploring and bouncing his ideas off me.

VT: Breaks can sometimes work, but what about losing training time to your competitors and team members?

AC: There is that to think about, but I think I really need a break.

And then I said something that at the time I believed was pretty benign, but as I thought about it later, I knew it might have been wrong.

VT: True, sometimes breaks can be good things, especially if you did it during the summer rather than during the season.

AC: Yeah, we really don't do much during the summer, anyway.

VT: If your sport truly is your passion, your obsession, a break might be just what you need to recharge your batteries.

In retrospect, it is that last comment where I think I might have crossed the line from helper to advisor. We continued to talk for about another 15 minutes about what was bothering him. Almost all of the talk revolved around his desire to take a break from what he was doing, and we went around that topic the whole time. He thanked me for listening to him, and I never saw or heard from him again. I discussed the athlete briefly in supervision, and my supervisor asked how I felt. I told him I was somewhat concerned about my advice to the athlete. He said that the advice sounded harmless enough and that I should not worry about it.

Three years later I read about this athlete in *Sports Illustrated,* and he was talking about his break from sport. He talked about how he quit the team for one season to snowboard (not his competitive sport). He also took the summer off to surf and skateboard. He talked about how at that stage he was not having any fun in his sport. The article stressed how his break had showed him how much he loved his sport and how much he missed it. The article also chronicled how he came back the following winter and started his rise in the international ranks. As I was reading, I found myself worrying that the athlete would say, "I talked to a sport psychologist, and he told me to take a break." I called my supervisor.

VT: [after pleasantries about family and school] Did you read the *SI* article on AC?

SM: No, I haven't got to it yet. Who is he?

VT: He is someone I met with back at the OTC; you remember, when the ______ team came in for the camp. It looks like he is talking about something I may have had a hand in.

SM: What are you talking about? Are you mentioned in *SI?*

VT: No, he didn't mention me by name. Well, to refresh your memory, you might recall I met with an athlete, and I suggested he take a break to recharge his batteries. It looks like he did just that.

SM: For how long?

VT: Looks like a whole season.

SM: You think he did that because of you?!

VT: He doesn't say it in the article, but that is exactly what we had talked about.

SM: Doesn't mean that you had anything to do with his decision.

VT: True, but I could have planted a seed.

SM: Well, you didn't make his decision for him. Why didn't you tell me more about him wanting to leave the sport while you were at the OTC?

VT: Well, we were doing the reports for the coaches, and I think that was occupying both our minds. I tried to talk with you about it right after our session, but you said what I did was pretty benign.

SM: Well, I think I still feel that way. I don't think your advice had much to do with his decision, and the end result was good. He came back to his sport, and it looks like he has a good chance to medal at Albertville. I wouldn't lose too much sleep over it.

VT: But it could have had serious consequences. Next time I'll keep my big mouth shut.

SM: Well, we all say things we wish later that we hadn't said. Take this as a lesson learned. No harm, no foul. And either way, the decision is still his. Now, let's talk about the Mets and the Cubs this summer. You know the Cubs will stink again, as usual. . . .

My supervisor took the incident in stride; I was more upset. Looking back, I should not have said anything, but all in all, the end result was a good one. The athlete obviously reached his decision on his own, but I still could not help but feel a little guilty about our session together. We all reach points where we wish we had not said something during a session. I think that is something we tend to gloss over in our educational settings. We tend to talk about all the good cases, but there are times where negative cases can also be enlightening. For me, the lesson that sometimes the most benign comment can be the message that the client latches onto the strongest took three years to sink in. We need to be aware that an athlete may take what we say to heart. Sometime athletes come to us when they are vulnerable; they are often looking for someone to tell them what they should do. We can give our views and our opinions, offer up contradictory views to theirs, or play devil's advocate, but the decision to act (or not act) should come from the athlete. This case was interesting to me, because something I said could have ended in a negative result. But maybe I am overestimating my influence on the athlete. It could have been that the athlete had already made a decision to take a break, but that decision felt a little lonely, and he was looking for friendly confirmation. If he had not gotten confirmation from me, he probably would have found someone else to give him the go-ahead. Perhaps I was nothing more than a friendly and convenient green light. The incident did teach me to watch carefully what I say and to think critically about the advice I give to athletes.

LESSONS LEARNED

My journey at the OTC had come to an end. I estimate that I worked with well over 60 athletes during my time there. For the most part, my work with the athletes consisted of standard psychological skills training (PST) and education. During most of the sessions, we focused on goal setting, relaxation training, imagery, attention/concentration training, and the usual skills in the sport psychology canon. Because these cases involved important issues in addition to PST, I think they highlight what graduate training and internship experiences can and should be like.

The first lesson learned is that the internship experience should allow students to focus on finding their own boundaries of comfort and expertise, and then stretch them. Students should be allowed to explore what they know and how to apply what they know (and what they are learning) under competent supervision. The internship experience should be one where students are constantly testing their comfort levels while being backed up by a supervisor. If students are given the comfort of a safety net (the supervisor) and a push to test their limits and become uncomfortable, then they should be able to grow as practitioners of applied sport psychology. If they are too closely guarded, it is possible that they will never push their comfort levels to discover what they can competently do or even find out where their comfort levels are. As advice to future interns: Jump into the deep end, but make sure a really good lifeguard (what a perfect synonym for supervisor) is watching out for you.

A second lesson learned from my first internship experience is to be open and honest with your supervisor. Doing so will help you push the envelope of competence and comfort. I had an open relationship with my supervisor where I was not afraid to say whatever was on my mind. Not all supervision sessions went smoothly; there were times where we would both question each other's theory, opinions, and techniques, but we did not let those arguments interfere with the bigger picture of giving a good product to the athletes, coaches, and clients. Attempting to develop that open relationship, where there is a free flow of ideas and opinions, was a core feature of the internship process. I felt the supervisory relationship was one of the best teaching tools we had while I was at the OTC.

The third lesson from my OTC experience is that we should be scientific in our practice. I once heard Dan Gould say, "Nothing is more practical than good theory," and I would like to add, "and nothing is more theoretical than good practice." This mantra has always guided my practice since the OTC experience. During my entire time at the OTC, I attempted to relate what I was hearing to theoretical constructs. I would guess that comes from my training as a scientist, but it is an invaluable tool for practicing in the real world. We all need something to hang our hats on when it comes to our practice of applied sport psychology, and for me, that something is a strong theoretical background in social psychology. Too often, naive people think that CB techniques are all that one needs to do sport psychology. That is, we sprinkle around some goal setting, some relaxation, some imagery, some attention training, and poof! we are doing sport psychology. Or, some people believe that theory is for scientists, but to practice one only needs a good personality. I once met a student who said that he did not need theory to practice; he only needed a good personality. He absolutely refused to learn theory no matter how hard we tried. Well, to paraphrase Shakespeare, when this person started to practice, he was a lot of sound and fury with little substance, and he never kept clients for very long. His problem was that he had nothing to hang his practice on but his personality. Once the athletes and coaches figured out the personality only carried limited information, and there was no depth to his practice, they quickly found competent others to work with. On the other hand, I had another student who came in believing that technique *and* personality would carry him as a sport psychologist, and I kept stressing the theory part. He finally started to learn theory, and to this day he thanks me for making him put theory into his practice. He feels this approach has made him an effective and successful practitioner.

The fourth lesson I learned is the importance of having a varied practicum experience. Not everyone is lucky enough to do their first internship at a place like the OTC, but other venues are opening up. Some universities have internship experiences in athletic programs with eminently qualified supervisors. The main rationale I can give for varied experiences is that it follows one of the main themes for this chapter—testing and stretching boundaries and competencies. Learn where you are competent and where you need to improve. Don't be afraid to go into untried and untested areas to get the experience. Be willing to take on challenges, and be willing to give service for free in order to get experience.

I guess an overall lesson is to know more and do more than what is required of you. Do not be content to finish the degree and internship experiences with the minimum credits to graduate. By knowing more than what is required of you, you should be a better practitioner, and all athletes, clients, and coaches with whom you work will thank you. If you are in a psychology program, get experience in the sport sciences. If you are in a sport science program, get experience in psychology.

Coaches and athletes expect to give 110%. For sport psychologists to be respected and effective, they, too, must be willing to give that much. When working with teams, go to their training sessions and experience what the athletes experience. I have gone as far as to play the sport with the athletes just to get a feel for what they do. I once played as goalie with the USA handball team just to see what their training was like. Yes, I wore the team's logo on my forehead for a while, but it showed the team members that I was not afraid to put myself in their shoes.

I gained their respect, and I would not have been able to do that if I had been content to only sit in my office and talk. From that time on, I have always made it a point to be with the athletes on the field at some time during training in addition to meeting with them in the office.

ENDINGS

Thanks for coming on my first internship journey. It is my hope that this chapter has illustrated what to do, or in some cases what not to do, in a first internship. In all ways, the internship was the most rewarding experience I have ever had as a sport psychology professional. It helped that I had good training in graduate school, a great supervisor, and an excellent environment in which to work. This experience, which I had almost a decade ago, shaped my views about how sport psychology should be done, and I can share it with my own students, both here at Ball State and in Australia. Because I can share the experience now, as a university professor, I am having my second-most rewarding experience as a professional—that of teacher and supervisor.

REFERENCES

Kirschenbaum, D.S., Parham, W.D., & Murphy, S.M. (1993). Provision of sport psychology services at Olympic events: The 1991 Olympic Festival and beyond. *The Sport Psychologist, 7,* 419-440.

Napier, A.Y., & Whitaker, C.A. (1978). *The family crucible.* New York: Bantam Books.

Sachs, M. (1999). The sport psychologist-athlete relationship: Implications for training: Comment on Petitpas, Danish, & Giges. *The Sport Psychologist, 13,* 344-357.

CHAPTER 14

INTO THE MAELSTROM: A FIVE-YEAR RELATIONSHIP FROM COLLEGE BALL TO THE NFL

Frances L. Price
University of Wyoming
Mark B. Andersen
Victoria University

This is the story of a young man who moved from college football to a beginning career in the National Football League (NFL). It covers his senior year in college and the first four years of his NFL career. This is also the story of the evolution of a counseling relationship that spanned five years and continues to this day. As noted in chapter 1, sport psychology service delivery begins from a wide variety of referral sources, occurs in myriad physical locations, and covers a range of issues far beyond classic performance enhancement.

The maelstrom in the chapter title refers to the turbulence of being in the NFL and to the phenomenon of progressing and relapsing, going around and around. A central feature of this chapter is regression to old, maladaptive patterns of behavior. The athlete I (first author) worked with learned new and healthier patterns of behavior through our interactions. Repeatedly, however, when he experienced stressful times, he would slip back into old behaviors, which actually made his stressful times even more disruptive. This cycling back and forth between new and old patterns of behavior is a common occurrence in psychological service. It appears that we do not just learn a new behavior once; we tend to learn, forget, relearn, and revisit those new behaviors over and over again before they become consolidated. Another theme in this chapter is the development of strong transference and countertransference phenomena in the relationship between the sport psychologist and the athlete.

Two major theoretical orientations form the bases of service and the understanding of what is happening in service delivery in this chapter. All of the interventions—the relaxation, the goal setting, the challenging of irrational thoughts—have as their foundation cognitive-behavioral therapy. The understanding of the relationship between the athlete and me, however, has its roots in psychodynamic theory.

The football player in this chapter, James, and I developed a relationship in various ways—through face-to-face meetings, my attendance at practices and camps, electronic mail communication, and long-distance phone consultation. I also spent some Sundays in a sports bar watching him play on satellite TV, and I traveled to attend his professional games. The chapter covers the years James and I worked together, and I will present the critical issues, conversations, and events for those years along with commentary on James and on our growing relationship. The first critical issue, which half the chapter is dedicated to, was a hamstring injury James sustained shortly before NFL scouts were due on campus.

PEER REFERRAL

One evening, getting home from work, I received a phone call from one of the collegiate football players I was seeing for sport psychology consultation. He was calling to say that a teammate of his had pulled a hamstring. He wondered if I would be willing to do some healing imagery with his teammate, because he and I had used such imagery several times during the past two years, and he had found it helpful. He said that the NFL scouts were coming to work out (essentially do skills and strength tests) both him and his teammate in ten days. He thought his teammate had great potential, but because he had not received much media attention and exposure, this upcoming tryout might make or break his NFL chances.

Several athletes I work with do not mention to others that they are seeing a sport psychologist. This silence may have to do with the stigma of seeing a "shrink" (cf. Linder, Brewer, Van Raalte, & DeLange, 1991; Linder, Pillow, & Reno, 1989), so I was pleased that the football player had confided in a fellow athlete in order to help him. I have found that this word-of-mouth teammate referral has been one of the most important sources of gaining new clients. If someone believes you have been helpful, then your name is going to be mentioned.

FIRST MEETING

I conducted a thorough intake interview with James, and I gathered background information relative to athletics, academics, and personal issues. We discussed prior injuries as well as his present situation and hamstring injury. I also attempted to assess current stressors and to determine how he related to others and to his environment, in order to assess strengths and skills that might influence our work. James appeared to be a young man who was mentally healthy with substantial personal resources to help him cope with school and sport. The main area of concern (besides the injury), which James himself brought up, involved difficulty being in touch with his emotions and expressing himself emotionally.

James (J): You know, my father isn't very emotional. I don't want to be like that.

Frances Price (F): I'm not sure what you mean.

J: Don't get me wrong. My father's a good man, but you know, he's one of those men who provide for their families and everything, and just don't show much emotion. I don't want to go through life like that.

F: And how would you rather be?

J: Oh, I don't know. . . . I think I would just like to be able to feel. . . . Yeah, you know . . . I want to be able to express my feelings, to be more open . . . I think.

James may have felt cut off from his emotions, but he had enough insight to recognize what was missing, and he wanted to do something about it. James came into my office, ostensibly, to work on a specific issue (his injury) in order to accomplish a specific goal (be in good enough physical condition to impress some NFL scouts). But with only mild prompting from me, he brought up a psychological life concern that had ramifications far beyond his potential professional football career. That James brought this issue up in our first meeting, with the strong implication that his feeling and showing emotion were facets of himself he wanted to work on with me in the future, suggested that a solid working alliance between the two of us was already forming. Also, depending on where our work would take us, I felt James' ability to be in touch with his emotions could be critical in terms of establishing that psychological link to how one actually performs on the playing field, which is a fundamental component of most of the athletic performance enhancement work I do. Experiencing emotion and passion would become one of the themes of our five-year counseling relationship. For the time being, though, we focused on his injury.

F: What are you doing in terms of rehabilitation?

J: Ice and stim so far. I think they're planning on doing some massage today, though. You know, to break up the bad blood in there or something.

F: I see. How have you felt since you got hurt? How do you feel about this injury and your situation?

J: Well, to tell you the truth, I was kinda down at first. I thought that would be it for me. I really want to be able to run for the scouts, but I can't do it with a pulled hamstring. I don't know. Should I even tell the scouts that I'm hurt? Do you think it will hurt my chances? But back to what you asked me at first; I'm feeling a little better because Robert [the referring teammate] said that he had injuries, and whatever you did with him helped. He's so positive, too, and I know he's done well. When he told me about some of the work you two did, I started feeling more optimistic. Know what I mean?

James certainly seemed motivated and receptive to trying the intervention I had used with Robert (a healing intervention of autogenic induction with imagery directed at increasing blood flow to the injured area). I wanted to assess his feelings and any attributions he was making as a result of this injury. He seemed a bit down, but hopeful. His questions to me, "Should I tell the scouts? . . . Will it hurt my chances?" indicated that James was looking to me for advice in this rather confusing time. His injury was nearly 24 hours old, and I thought that getting started as soon as possible would probably help James feel that something was getting done. I made copies of pictures of the muscles involved for him to study. I find that a basic anatomy book is a useful resource when working with injured athletes.

F: James, I am not sure exactly what we will end up doing yet, but it's important that you become an active participant in the healing process. One of the first things we'll do is get a good mental picture of the injured area. Please study these pictures. They are the superficial muscles of the back of the thigh and leg, the lateral rotators and hamstring muscles, and the deep muscles of the back of the thigh. Your ability to visualize this and to know your injury is going to be helpful.

J: OK. You want me to take these with me?

F: Please. One other thing I would like you to think about before we begin our work tomorrow is that there's nothing like maintaining a positive mental attitude. It can only help the task at hand and any other work we do together.

J: OK, but I'm not sure what it is you want me to do.

F: For example, if someone asks how you're doing, or how your hamstring's doing, respond by saying something positive and affirming like, "It's coming along," or, "It's getting better."

J: OK.

F: Also, in case we go the autogenic route as we talked about, please do not eat within an hour and a half of our meeting. There is a small chance that you might feel uncomfortable doing it soon after eating. Also, please wear some comfortable, loose-fitting clothing.

J: OK. I'll see you tomorrow. Thanks so much for taking the time to talk to me today.

After even a brief encounter, I like to give athletes a little homework to do, something to take away from the meeting. This homework can serve a couple of purposes. First, the athletes may begin to feel they are actually starting to do something about whatever it is they came to talk to me about, and second, when I next see them I can ask how things went with the homework task, did they actually do it, and if so, how often. If an athlete does not take to heart the advice or homework and does not perform the task between visits, then there may be a serious question of motivation and commitment.

My assessment of James was that he was highly motivated and extremely receptive. He was much more open to the mental aspects of rehabilitation (cf. Ievleva & Orlick, 1991) than I anticipated. He seemed ready to work even with the stressful NFL tryouts being near, and my impression was that he wanted to make some personal changes as well. He was also pleasant and polite, and I was looking forward to working with him. There was not much time to get him ready for the NFL scouts, but I hoped our work would be a positive experience as well as help him achieve his personal and professional goals.

THE WORK BEGINS

We met Saturday afternoon as scheduled. James was on time and ready to begin. Because the NFL tryout was soon, I decided to try autogenic training and healing imagery. I consider autogenic techniques, for some athletes, to be much more powerful than progressive muscle relaxation (PMR), and the effects seem to be more profound. With practice, a relaxed state can be achieved quite rapidly. In terms of imagery, Ievleva and Orlick (1991) found, in a retrospective study, that positive images of healing and/or performance imagery were related to better recovery.

There are a variety of reasons why relaxation and imagery might be helpful in the healing process. Injured people often brace the injured area to immobilize the muscle or joint so as to limit pain. That bracing may actually restrict blood flow. Learning to relax may help reduce the bracing and promote blood flow to the injured area. Imagery and relaxation may also aid immune system function. The immune system is intimately involved in inflammation and the removal of damaged or necrotic tissue. A thorough discussion of relaxation, imagery, and healing can be found in Graham's (1995) informative book *Mental Imagery in Health Care: An Introduction to Therapeutic Practice*.

F: Have you ever done anything like where you tense a group of muscles, then relax, tense another group of muscles, then relax? [I demonstrate.]

J: [shakes his head] No, I've never done anything like that.

F: OK. Well, sometimes I use that technique to help people relax and get to know their bodies better. Once people are comfortable with that technique, I often introduce autogenic training, which is a more mental technique. It's the one your teammate Robert told you about, with the feelings of heaviness and warmth in your arms and legs. Personally, I think autogenics is more helpful for rehabilitation. We don't want to tense up muscles close to injured areas. Many of the people I have worked with who have done both techniques prefer autogenics. The only problem is, like with almost anything else, in order to be good at it, you have to practice, and it does seem to take a while to get good at it. Therein lies our dilemma. Since our time is so short, with the scouts coming . . . is it next week?

J: It's on the 17th, which is next Friday. Then there will probably be a couple of other workouts after that.

F: Well, I don't think we have the time to begin with progressive muscle relaxation. I suggest that we try autogenics instead. Would you be willing to give it a shot? If we can do it, I think that technique might be our best bet right now. Let me tell you a little more about it, and what you can expect.

J: OK.

F: What will happen is you will get comfortable. You're tall, so we will have to figure out how best to do that, maybe on the floor with a cushion. Then you will close your eyes, breathe easily and regularly, and I will start by doing what is known as a body scan. I will briefly talk to you about your different muscle groups. I will make some suggestions of relaxing and you will try to get rid of any tension in your body. Then I will give you more suggestions, such as, "My right arm is heavy. My left arm is heavy," which you will repeat inside your head [see chapter 4 for more detail on autogenic training]. Then, once you are sufficiently relaxed, we will try some imagery. Many people believe that the combination of autogenics and imagery may actually accelerate healing. There are stories in the literature of world-class athletes who were injured and felt that imagery helped them heal faster and perform better afterward, and much sooner than they would have ordinarily. What I had in mind for today will not be related to athletics, your athletic performance, or your injury. I just want to see what you do with all of this. Then we'll know where we are and how to proceed. How does that sound?

J: Fine. I'm excited! Robert told me you helped him, and if he has confidence in you, then my only question is, When can we get started?

F: In a few minutes. I need to make sure that you know what to expect and that you're comfortable with everything.

J: I'm very comfortable, and I'm ready to get to work.

Autogenic Training

Most of the autogenic scripts and healing imagery scripts I use are modified from Shultz and Luthe (1969), Harris and Harris (1984), and Porter and Foster (1990). I modify standard autogenic statements by giving suggestions of sinking and the spreading of heaviness and warmth. For example, between the statements, "My right arm is heavy," I would occasionally interject, "Feel your right arm comfortably sinking."

This induction was his first experience with autogenics, and I was curious about James' ability to do imagery. When we had completed the relaxation phase of the induction, I guided James through some basic imagery, which involved a safe place and seeing colors. There were no sport or athletic performance suggestions. Once the imagery was over, I told James to take his time and sit up slowly when he was ready. He remained on the couch for quite some time. I thought he might have fallen asleep, but his breathing pattern did not seem like sleep. I left him alone, and several minutes later James sat up very slowly.

F: Are you all right?

J: Yeah . . . wow . . . that was somethin' else. I ended up in . . . like a mineshaft . . . and I felt so good I didn't want to come back. That was . . . unbelievable.

F: Were you able to get heavy and warm?

J: Yeah . . . but it took a while. Heaviness was easier for me than warmth. And when you said somethin' about my arms and legs being so heavy that I sink into the couch, I actually did! Unbelievable . . . I really never thought it would feel this good . . . wow.

F: This stuff gets easier and quicker, and you will get better at it the more you do it. Congratulations on getting so far on your first try. Were you able to do the colors?

J: Yeah . . . that was kind of exciting . . . but it's interesting . . . the mineshaft, or whatever it was . . . it was like an old abandoned mine . . . that was in black and white.

F: That's OK. I think you did very well, especially since this is your first time. You must have also maintained a passive attitude like we talked about, which is often difficult to do, and that's really positive. That's what we want. I'm really interested in what this was like for you. There is no good or bad, or right or wrong here. All that matters is what happened and what it was like for you. Did you experience any floating or numbness or anything unusual or scary? Anything not feel good?

J: Not really. I did notice my right arm tingling once, but I remembered what you said, and I didn't worry about it.

F: So, how do you feel overall?

J: Real good. I can't believe how good I feel . . . how relaxed I feel. And you know what? I don't know if this was supposed to happen, but when I came in here, my hamstring was sore. It doesn't feel as sore now. I thought I felt OK when I came in here, but I feel noticeably better now. This is unbelievable. Thank you.

F: You're welcome. We'll take time to talk about the relaxation after each session. That way I can know what it was like for you. If something was working or not working, where we are, where we go from here, stuff like that. Does that make sense?

J: Perfect sense.

F: So it is important for you to be totally honest with me. No matter if something worked or not, I need to know. That way I can do my best for you, and we can build on the good things, work on other things, and hopefully get you healthy and to a better place.

J: Sounds good.

We took the time to debrief after every induction session. Getting feedback from the athlete is critical, because it helps me modify later inductions. His responses and reactions following this initial induction helped me develop a better sense of what his strengths and weaknesses were and where we might go from here. The induction proved to be very powerful for James. That he had a positive experience and felt good reinforced his confidence in me, and helped build trust, which significantly enhanced our working relationship.

Before he left, we spent time looking at the anatomy pictures. We determined where the injury was and what it might look like. Having familiarity with what the muscles look like can be helpful in generating an image for the subsequent healing exercise.

Healing Imagery

It is highly unusual to see a client as often as I saw James. In that first week, I saw James almost every day and sometimes twice a day. With NFL tryouts fast approaching, and the draft six weeks away, I felt that it was reasonable to accelerate treatment. I wanted James to quickly develop good psychological skills, especially with respect to relaxation and imagery, and I felt this could best be accomplished through a more aggressive, intensive approach.

After examining color pictures of the superficial and deep muscles, arteries, and veins of the injured area, we began our first healing imagery induction. The script went something like the following:

F: Settle back comfortably. Close your eyes and stretch your entire body as you take a deep breath . . . in through your nose, and out through your mouth. Just breathe easily and regularly, as you would ordinarily . . . naturally, easily, and regularly. [I gave him a couple of minutes.] Check in with your body now, starting with your head and face. Notice if there are any areas of tightness or pain. Allow your face to relax, to soften. Allow your forehead to become smooth. Let all concerns, cares, and frustrations fade away, and leave you. Shift your attention slowly from your neck to your shoulders, letting go of any tension there. Gently lower your shoulders as you allow warmth to flow from your shoulders into your upper back and chest . . . down through your solar plexus, relaxing it. . . . Feel at peace in body and in mind. . . . Allow the warmth of relaxation to spread down from your upper back into your lower back . . . your stomach . . . your abdomen. . . . Allow those areas to become warm. Slowly shift your attention to your hips and buttocks. Allow the muscles to relax . . . let go. Now shift your attention down to your legs, your hamstrings . . . quads . . . knees . . . calves . . . ankles . . . feet, and toes. Send all of the tension—any tightness, any stiffness, soreness, or pain—out the bottoms of your feet. See if you can send a wave of relaxation through your body . . . from your head down through your feet . . . leaving only peace, warmth, and softness. [I gave him some time here.] And once again, allow a wave of relaxation to flow throughout your body, from your head down through your feet [I gave him some time] . . . and continue breathing easily and regularly, as you let go more and more. Allow yourself to feel relaxed, and at peace, and enjoy the way that feels. [I waited a few seconds.]

What followed were the warmth and heaviness cycles we had done earlier.

F: The heaviness and warmth will continue to grow and spread, as you now focus your attention on the injured area, on your left hamstring. Take an internal view. Become fully aware of the depth, size, and shape of the injured area. Connect with this injury. See it . . . feel it . . . center on it . . . focus on it . . . acknowledge its presence within you. Get to know it . . . totally and completely. Become aware of the superficial muscle fibers as well as those that are deep, deep inside. Let yourself see and feel the area . . . become aware of the injury and the surrounding area. Notice any discoloration, any bruising, any bleeding, any inelastic, fibrous scar tissue . . . be aware of the entire area . . . and know it thoroughly. When you are fully aware of the injured area, determine what you need to do in order for it to heal. [I waited a few seconds.] Remain connected with the injured area as you let go of any anger, frustration, or anxiety you may have felt as a result of this injury. Let it all go. Release any and all negative energy or thoughts you may have had as a result of this injury. Let go of any resistance you have felt as a result of this injury. Soften . . . release, and disperse any negativity by allowing it to take the shape of a small ball . . . and see it roll away . . . out of your sight. [I gave him several seconds.] Also release any tightness and resistance in your body as you slowly begin to send positive, healing warmth to the injured area. Imagine the tissue around your injured left hamstring relaxing . . . softening . . . releasing. Imagine the blood coursing through your arteries . . . bringing nutrients and oxygen to the injured area. Imagine the veins taking away the injured cells, and imagine new, healthy cells taking their place . . . revitalizing the sore, tender, and stiff areas. The new blood is healing your left hamstring and the surrounding area. Feel the new blood as it circulates . . . bathing and nourishing the injured area. . . . Feel the warmth as the new blood helps builds new tissue and heals your left hamstring. Feel the warmth of the new blood. Feel the nutrients. Feel the muscle fibers, and see them growing together, aligned, as healthy, pliant, flexible tissue grows. See the hamstring muscles and the surrounding area healing. See the muscle fibers mending, and coming together. [I gave him several seconds.] And once again . . . [I repeated the guided imagery.]

And continue to imagine your left hamstring and the surrounding area becoming stronger and stronger . . . more and more supple . . . more and more flexible. Continue to see the blood flowing . . . bathing your left hamstring and the surrounding area until it is healthy, flexible, and strong again. It's a good, pleasant, warm feeling . . . and you enjoy the way that feels. [I waited several seconds.] But be patient James, with yourself, and the injured area. Know that it needs more time to heal completely. And continue to release any anxiety, fear, or frustration you might still feel as a result of this injury. And let yourself release any stiffness or pain you might still feel around the injured area . . . softly . . . gently . . . let your body soften and let it heal. [I waited several seconds.] And begin to focus again on the soft, warm, peaceful area of your body, your left hamstring that is now healing. Send it strength . . . send it energy. And imagine a warm, pale-gold color surrounding the injured area. See it and feel it expanding from the injured area into all parts of your body. The warm golden color beginning at the top of your head . . . flowing down through your facial area . . . neck and shoulders . . . arms . . . upper back . . . chest . . . abdomen and stomach . . . lower back . . . hips . . . thighs . . . hamstrings . . . quads . . . knees . . . calves . . . ankles . . . feet . . . and toes. See and feel yourself filled with a warm, golden-yellow glow like a summer sunset. . . . The color is healing your left hamstring and filling it with strength and energy. You are healing, and it feels good to know that you're an integral part of the healing process. It feels good to know that you're engaged in the repair of your left hamstring . . . of your body. [I waited a few seconds.] Now slowly, allow the image of golden yellow light to disappear. [I waited several seconds.]

And see and feel your left hamstring and the surrounding area becoming more supple . . . more flexible . . . stronger . . . and more resilient. Remember the healing, and know that your body will come through for you again. Know that you will be restored to good health . . . in an energetic, vibrant state . . . full of strength and power, and endurance.

And say affirmations of healing to yourself: I am healing. I will get healthier every day. I am healing quickly. My left hamstring is becoming stronger, more flexible, and more resilient. I will heal completely. My body is quick, strong, and powerful. I will be healthy and pain free. And see and feel yourself . . . healthy and pain free . . . your mind and body harmonious . . . and at peace. And enjoy how it feels to be quick, strong, powerful, healthy, and at peace. [I waited several seconds between each affirmation and several more seconds when finished with the affirmations.]

Now begin to reconnect with your present environment. Notice any sounds in the room or outside. Notice any smells. Notice how your body feels against the couch. And remember that you are relaxed, centered, healing, and at peace. And when you're ready, take five deep breaths. On the count of five, move your feet and legs. On four, move your abdomen and torso. On three, move your arms and shoulders. On two, move your neck and head. On one, open your eyes, and sit up slowly when you're ready. You will feel refreshed . . . relaxed . . . alert . . . healthy, and at peace. [I waited several seconds.] Now, James, we'll count backward . . . five . . . four . . . three . . . two . . . and one.

As was the case with the initial autogenic induction, healing imagery went much better than expected. Once he collected himself, we debriefed, as usual.

F: So, how was it?

J: You know, I could actually see the injured area. I believe that it was gray in color, whereas the healthy area was more pink. I also got heavy and warm more quickly than I did earlier today.

F: It sure seemed like you let go quickly. You know, I think the theory behind the electrical stimulation you receive in the training room is analogous to what you just did mentally; that is, to get more blood to flow to the injured area. You know, you might try to connect with the injured area, as you just did, when you undergo stim treatments.

J: That's a good idea. With practice, I bet I can get more blood to my hamstring easier and more deeply than the stim machine can alone. If I can do that, that might speed up the healing process even more.

F: Let's try that and see how you feel. Let's see if you notice a difference.

J: Sounds good.

James seemed to enjoy being an active participant in the healing process. His openness and his facility with mental skills were impressive. I felt the relationship was developing nicely when James began referring to me as his "head coach." The working alliance had formed quickly, and it appeared James' transference to me was one of respect and affection. I had become a coach. Freud loved word play, and I could not help but wonder about the depth of transference, because *head coach* means both mental coach and number-one coach.

The next day was Sunday. We did healing imagery after James got back from church. We also went to the training room for treatment, and I discreetly guided James through imagery designed to help him connect with the injured area while he was undergoing electrical stimulation. He reported being satisfied with his efforts to connect with the injured area during stim treatments. After lunch we did performance imagery, and that night we did another session involving healing imagery. Following our last session that day, James reported "definitely feeling better."

The primary difference between the healing and performance imagery inductions at this point was that the performance imagery did not include suggestions of heaviness. The performance imagery served two purposes. One was to help keep James connected to his sport until he was able to participate more fully, and two, I also planned to combine healing and performance imagery in the near future.

PREPARING FOR THE DRAFT

I made healing imagery and performance tapes for use outside our sessions. James practiced his mental skills that Monday by listening to a tape at home. He noted that the sensations of heaviness and warmth were coming easier, and he wanted to try to get to that point in our session on his own. We decided that he would raise his right index finger when he had completed a body scan and was sufficiently heavy and warm and ready for guided imagery. On this particular day, that took approximately two minutes. Following our session, James went to the training room for treatment to connect with the injury himself. Following treatment, he reported that his hamstring felt "tired, but good tired." He also continued working with one of the strength coaches. Rather than dwell on James' limitations, we focused on what he could do. A colleague, and sport psychology supervisor, passed through the Field House one day and noticed that James was conversing with someone who inquired about the status of his injury. He replied, "It's coming along." She was impressed at how positive he was in the face of such an untimely injury.

James and I were unable to meet the next day, but we talked on the phone. The following day, Wednesday, James received an unexpected phone call from an NFL defensive coordinator who wanted to work him out that afternoon (two days before he thought he might get a call). James was able to perform quickness drills (e.g., box drill) but no 40-yard dash. His hamstring felt "a little tired" afterward, and he kept it wrapped. That evening, he reported that he "did a little blood flow on my own" while lying in bed with no audio tape.

We met the next day, a Thursday. We talked about precompetition/preperformance routines and about remaining in present time. James usually reported feeling better after our sessions. On this particular day, he noted that he felt more focused on his goal of healing completely. Several NFL scouts were scheduled to be in town the next day. James was not sure whether or not he would try out. He had to see how he felt.

That Friday, James debated about running for the scouts. He decided to be honest and did what he could comfortably, without risking further injury. He was able to perform the box drill and the 5-10-5 drill as he had two days before. He was also able to do the L-drill but decided not to do more explosive exercises such as the standing long jump, the vertical jump, and the 40-yard dash. He was satisfied with the lifting (225-pound max) and position drills and reported feeling good about his effort over all. Incidentally, the player who introduced me to James popped his ankle during that same tryout. He called my office from the training room requesting services. This period turned out to be a very busy time.

James and I did not meet the next day, Saturday, but he practiced mental skills on his own. The next week we met at least once on four days. During the following two weeks we met for imagery sessions most days, and we scheduled times to talk in order to make sure that he stayed on top of any personal issues as well as any potential problems that might adversely affect his athletic performance. James continued to heal and performed better and better each time out. His mental skills improved substantially, and he was able to get ready for guided imagery almost instantly by the end of the third week.

James must have performed well enough to impress the scouts. Several teams flew him to their facilities for tryouts. Unfortunately, taking these trips caused James to miss school and get behind. A full-time student, James had a demanding science major and was enrolled in several labs. In addition to athletic performance concerns, we addressed time-management and academic issues. As an athletic academic counselor, providing academic support was an integral part of my job description. James felt supported athletically and academically, and he continued to get healthier and to do well in school. We also continued to work on personal issues such as showing his emotions. James' relationship with his girlfriend was a bit rocky, and we often discussed the problems they were having.

The NFL draft occurred nearly six weeks after James and I met. His performances for the scouts had commanded some media attention, which was another area we addressed. James did not know what the future would bring, but he wanted to continue our relationship. James felt comfortable bringing virtually anything to our sessions. He felt good about our working relationship, and he looked forward to the future. His attitude toward the draft was that he had worked hard and had done everything he could. He seemed prepared to accept the outcome, good or bad. I feel closely connected to many of the athletes I work with, but my reactions to James were stronger than usual. I could see I was becoming an important part of his world. I found myself really caring for this football player who worked so hard and was just so damned nice. I was beginning to feel like some proud big sister (but I kept my countertransferential responses in check).

An NFL team that had not even flown James out for a tryout drafted him. The player who introduced James to me was also drafted. It was an exciting time. Even though James was not a high draft pick, he was ecstatic. The next three weeks involved trips to mini-camp and finals. The hamstring was still not 100 percent. We continued to address the injury, but we tended to focus more on helping James complete his senior year and get prepared mentally and physically for the challenges of the NFL. James was going to have to relocate, and there were still unresolved issues with respect to his girlfriend.

One day James called and asked to speak to me. This was an unscheduled appointment. Concerned, I asked if everything was all right. He said we would talk when he got there. James arrived a few minutes later and burst into my office.

F: James, are you okay?

J: No! My girlfriend and I just broke up.

F: I'm sorry to hear that. It might help to talk about it.

J: This is all your fault!

F: [a bit taken aback] What do you mean?

J: This is all your fault! Before I started working with you, I would not have felt all this pain. We had different values and probably would have broken up anyway, but it wouldn't have hurt this much.

I let his comment about me go, and we discussed his feelings further. He decided that he would rather fully experience life, including the pain, than be as numb as he had been previously. I had mixed feelings about James' disclosure. On the one hand, I felt badly because he was in so much pain. I knew he really cared about his girlfriend, and I was sorry that things had not worked out. On the other hand, I felt good because James was already making progress toward his goal of getting more in touch with his emotions. Even though he had burst into my office, it felt good that he was comfortable and secure enough in our relationship to confront me. He not only shared difficult material but also allowed himself to be vulnerable. I felt that he trusted me, and I hoped that he felt accepted.

That session proved to be a turning point in our relationship, taking it to another level. James' "this is all your fault" was at one level an accusation. At another level, it was a thank-you. The strength of his transference, my influence on him, and my responses to his connection with me were all topics I discussed in lively supervision sessions (see chapters 11 and 12). My supervision had a strong psychodynamic flavor. I worried at first that James' attachment to me was a type of dependency, and the last thing I wanted was for him to become dependent on me. I grew to see that transference and countertransference are ubiquitous phenomena in almost all human relationships (e.g., teacher and student, lovers, supervisor and supervisee). Understanding transference and countertransference is something that helps us avoid fostering dependency because of our own countertransferential needs. In a true sense, athletes do become dependent on sport psychologists; they are dependent on them to learn new skills. James was dependent on me to help him get back on track as he went around and around in the whirlpool of the NFL. The goal, however, is to minimize those dependencies as the athlete learns new ways of behaving and thinking and becomes more and more independent.

James was in mini-camp for the next three weeks. He took tapes I had made for him, and we communicated by phone regularly. His hamstring was nearly 100%, and athletic trainers at the NFL facility monitored his progress and continued treatments. James' biggest problems at this point involved dealing with being evaluated and handling the mental and physical demands of professional athletic competition. The following dialogue is from one of our telephone conversations.

J: We're just getting started, and I'm already tired. This is tough.

F: What's the toughest part so far?

J: All of it. We practice in the morning, eat lunch, practice in the afternoon, and eat dinner. When we're not practicing, we're in meetings. There's so much to learn, and the competition is fierce. Everybody is good athletically, but some people seem tougher mentally than others. They videotape and evaluate everything. It's really stressful. It's hard too, 'cause you don't know exactly what they're looking for. Even though I am a rookie and know I have a lot to learn, sometimes I feel like I can't make a mistake.

Following mini-camp, James returned home for less than a week. He had to move. He bought a car and was excited about the prospect of not being in debt. We met twice when James was in town, and he wanted to continue to work with me. We decided to work long distance and scheduled weekly telephone appointments, speaking more often if necessary. Although we talked regularly on the phone, James felt that we could work more effectively if I developed a greater appreciation for his situation.

During his time as a student, James had not had to pay for athletic counseling services. Now that he had an income, he told me he wanted to start paying. I did not feel comfortable charging him after he turned pro (I was still a graduate student in clinical psychology), but we struck a deal. He would pay for my transportation and lodging to visit him and watch him in camps (and later in home games). This arrangement gave me a break from my normal work schedule, allowed me to see my client work out and play, and gave me time to visit some close relatives who live in the city where James plays. Those trips seemed like plenty of compensation for psychological services.

Many graduate students receive payment for psychological services in terms other than money (tracksuits, a trip with the team). Quite often, this type of remuneration is all the teams can afford. I am still in school and under supervision, and working with James is part of my applied sport psychology training. Once I become a fully licensed practitioner, we will have to adjust payment for services along more traditional lines. Long-distance consultation does need to be compensated for in a reasonable manner. If one talks long distance for an hour, that is still an hour's worth of service. If one observes a practice or a game, one is still working. Our arrangement actually obviated all the issues of charging for each hour of each separate activity, but the details of payment for long-term, long-distance, multimodal delivery should be worked out. Watching a game on TV should be paid for, but maybe not at the same rate as a one-on-one session. Figuring out what my time is worth for each activity will be an awkward process, but it is one James and I will be doing in the near future when I become licensed.

James flew me out so that I could see firsthand what training camp and his environments were like. I also attended two preseason games. This experience was invaluable; it let me see what he was going through and gave me a much greater appreciation for the stresses and situations that he encountered. I observed practices and became familiar with players' and coaches' personalities, and I developed a greater appreciation for what intra-team competition was like. At training camp, sessions with James involved phone calls, conversations that took place while he was walking from the practice facility to the hotel for lunch, or brief talks in a car (players could not have people in their rooms). Dealing with physical fatigue, remaining healthy, and staying mentally fresh became the most pressing challenges.

James made the team, and he was excited but also grateful, humble, and relieved. I was too, and my response to James' news showed me just how connected I had become to this young man. Because players can be released at any time, we attempted to determine what James needed to do in order to maintain the level of play that would keep him in the NFL. We also monitored personal concerns and maintained the connection between what he was thinking and feeling and how he was performing.

ROOKIE SEASON

Shortly after his first regular season began, James seemed lonely. He had to learn what he needed to do in order to remain centered and to function and perform optimally. Occasionally, I sent him encouraging postcards with pictures of home. He also subscribed to his college town's newspaper. He flew his girlfriend out a couple of times, but they were never able to reconcile.

James and I communicated by phone at least once a week throughout this adjustment phase. An example of one conversation follows:

F: How's it going?

J: All right, I guess. Thanks for the postcards. I appreciate that.

F: I'm glad you enjoy them. So how are you?

J: OK. Football's going OK, but we're not even halfway through the season and we've played almost as many games as we did in an entire season in college. I'm really busy, too.

F: Are you sure you're OK? You sound kind of sad.

J: Yeah, I get kind of lonely sometimes.

F: What's the matter?

J: I don't know. Mary [his ex-girlfriend] just left. It's over. I don't know a lot of people here, and I don't have anyone to do things with. I'm trying to find a church and meet people, but it hasn't been easy. I'm also tired. Traveling so much is really hard. I'm trying to remain positive, but I'm not playing much, and sometimes I get discouraged. I haven't been sleeping well lately, either, and the other day, I tweaked my good hamstring.

In addition to the daily rigors of professional athletics, other challenges included finding a church, making new friends, and accepting his role on the team. Traveling to away games was grueling, and mental and physical fatigue were constant concerns. Halfway through the season, James became tired and seemed discouraged. He had already played in nearly as many games as he would have in a regular college season, and he still had at least six games remaining. He was also not playing as much as he had hoped, and he began to lose confidence. At about the same time, he started having trouble sleeping and injured his hamstring.

I sent him another healing imagery tape, with a deep relaxation/sleep induction on the other side. We continued to process a variety of issues weekly, and his attitude improved. James' mental skills also improved. He had drifted a bit from his mental practice, and the new tapes helped bring him back. James had learned to use relaxation, imagery, daily practice goals, and positive self-talk, but as the stressfulness of the season wore on, James began to slip back into old patterns of behavior and thinking. This relapsing pattern would emerge again and again. Fortunately, he also relearned what he needed in order to stay fresh mentally, remain centered, and enhance his chances of optimal performance. It seemed that the better he felt personally, the better he played. To feel better, he needed an occasional break from football, especially on his day off. He put time out from football (reading, playing his guitar, going to movies, eating out with friends) into part of his weekly schedule. He also discovered that the more passionately he played, the better he played. Getting in touch with and expressing his emotions on the field was a key to his improved performance. He began playing more near the end of the season.

His team went to the first round of the playoffs that year, which made his season even longer, but he made it through that first year.

We were able to spend a little time together when James passed through town during the off-season. We evaluated the past season. James expressed satisfaction with our work, so we decided to stick with what we were doing. Although we did not have a schedule, we planned on keeping the lines of communication open.

YEAR TWO

Prior to reporting for his second mini-camp, James bought a computer. Electronic mail opened up another avenue for service delivery and facilitated communication if something came up between scheduled phone calls, or if we were unable to reach each other by phone.

The major issues during year two involved lack of playing time and balancing his career, his civic/religious speaking obligations, and his personal life. Lack of playing time continued to be a source of great frustration. Although he played more than he had the previous year, he longed to make more of a contribution. Scheduling conflicts during this time made regular telephone communication difficult, so we e-mailed often. We agreed to talk on Wednesday evenings. What follows is an example of the type of communication that took place about halfway into the regular season:

J: Hey, Frances! How are you doing?

F: All right, and thanks for the e-mail. I appreciate knowing what's going on. So what's up with you?

J: Well, I guess I'm mostly frustrated. It kills me to be on the sidelines when we're getting beat like we do. I just don't know what to do. I am feeling kind of down.

F: I understand your frustration about playing time, but I'm also interested in what that down feeling is about.

J: I'm not sure.

F: Can you tell me more about what's happening at practices and games? How are you being treated?

J: I don't know. This is kinda hard. I don't like the way my position coach treats me. I'm doing the best I can. No matter how hard I try, if I make a mistake, he gets in my face and screams, and stuff like that.

F: Like what?

J: You know . . . [James proceeds to tell me things I would not care to see in print.]

F: I see . . . and how does all of this make you feel?

J: [silence] Like crap. I don't like it. I'm working harder and playing better than some of the other guys who play, and they aren't treated like that. You know what I mean?

F: I think so. Sounds like you're being demeaned and degraded, and you don't like how that feels.

J: Exactly.

F: So when you feel like this, how does it affect you?

J: You know, I never thought about it like that, but I think I have been too worried about what the coaches are thinking and if I'm going to get to play or not, even at practice. I stand there on the sidelines, knowing that I am just as good as some of the older guys, and wonder why I'm not playing more.

F: So in other words, you're not focused on your real job . . . on your play?

J: Right. And you know what else? I find myself getting down even at practice.

F: And what is that about?

J: I'm not sure. Do you have any thoughts?

F: A few. It seems like you are doing a lot of negative thinking about yourself and your play. I wonder if you're losing confidence. I wonder how much you're personalizing what's going on, and what, if anything, you're afraid of. I also wonder if not playing hurts, and if you're shutting down emotionally to a certain extent, so you won't feel the pain, and if that might not also be affecting the quality of your play . . . and as you discovered last year, when you play with passion, and really feel, that is when you play best.

J: I think you could be onto something here. You know, I think I got a little sidetracked.

F: Well, maybe we can get things back in perspective.

J: I think you're right. So what do I need to do?

F: Well, what can you do? Do you decide who plays?

J: No.

F: Then perhaps you need to let that go. What can you do something about?

J: I can do something about how I practice and play.

F: OK. So, what can you do about practice? What needs to happen? We haven't talked about daily practice goals in a while.

J: Well . . . now that you mention it, I think I've kind of gotten away from that a little bit.

F: OK. So, let's set some goals. What might you work and improve on in practice?

James had an oscillating pattern of mental training and negative thinking. Each season he would start out with a positive attitude and faithfully practice his mental skills. As a season would wear on, he would practice his mental skills less and begin to slip into negative thinking. In working with athletes over several years, I have found that the need for recycling, or getting back on track, is common. In this case, I challenged James' negative thinking by helping him see the futility of worrying about things that he could not control and shifting his focus to the features of his play that he could control.

YEAR THREE

James seemed to be doing well this year, and I watched him each Sunday in a sports bar so that when we spoke I would have seen him play that week. Although James appeared to be exceeding many of his performance goals, we had not communicated for a few weeks. I had no idea that he was becoming frustrated once again with the lack of playing time and the differential/negative treatment by his position coach. On one particular Sunday, James' play seemed tense. He also appeared to be experiencing minor performance decrements, and it seemed as if he was having difficulty maintaining his focus. When he came out of the game, his coach yelled at him, and he hung his head. I was concerned, because these behaviors were uncharacteristic.

F: James, it seems like you end up in a slump about the same time every year. We really need to do better about staying on top of things.

J: I agree. I thought things were going well, and I hate to bother you if nothing's wrong.

This last comment suggests that also he might be embarrassed or ashamed to admit to me that things are not going well, and that he, once again, is getting off track. Transference brings with it some problems. Clients who have strong positive transferences to their counselors often want to please them, and admitting that one has again gotten off track may be perceived as disappointing the counselor.

F: But that's the whole point. It's never a bother. If things are going well, you can build on that, and if we don't have as much to talk about, then maybe we can talk less, but I think we should still touch base.

J: Yeah, you're probably right. I do seem to do better when we talk, don't I?

F: I think you play better when *you're* on track, and maybe talking helps you stay on track. So what's up? It looked like you were having a rough day Sunday. What's going on?

J: I'm frustrated again.

F: With?

J: I'm tired of playing on the scout team and hardly playing in games. I'm tired of the double standard. I work hard, and I don't ever ask to be taken out. I do everything I'm asked to do, even beat people out in practice, and I still don't get to play. I haven't missed a practice or a regular-season game. They're starting a guy who doesn't even practice. He's undisciplined and still starts. I'm playing better than one of the guys who plays ahead of me that's making a million dollars, and I still don't get to play. Plus, I'm tired of being demeaned and degraded if I do make a mistake. I'm just tired of it. I don't mean to complain or be negative, but . . .

F: I don't think you're being negative. I think you're being honest, and it's important for me to understand your experience and perception of the situation. It sounds like you feel used.

J: I do, and I don't like how I'm being treated, and I am not sure what to do about it. I feel like I have nothing to lose, and I feel like confronting my position coach, but I am afraid that I might not be able to control my anger.

F: Well, it sounds as if you've done all you can. You cannot control your position coach's behavior, but you can control how you react or respond to it.

J: Yeah, but that response is what I'm worried about. I could end up losing everything . . . but you know what? At this point, I almost don't care. I have done everything the best I can. I have no regrets. I've almost had it! [We proceeded to problem-solve ways in which James might approach his coach, assert himself in an effective, appropriate manner, and still feel good about himself.] I will look him in the eye when he yells at me and be more assertive. I might even go and talk to him, and ask him just what I need to do. I will let you know how it goes.

F: James, is anything else bothering you?

J: I don't think so. Why do you ask?

F: I don't know. You still don't sound right. How are *you?*

J: OK. I've been really busy, though. I get up early and go to the facility around 9:00, work out, go to meetings, and practice until 2:00 or 3:00, run errands or come home and eat, and lately I've had more speaking engagements than usual.

F: So, are you taking care of yourself? What are you doing for you, the person, not the football player? Do you have any off time to relax or get rejuvenated? Are you taking any time for yourself on your day off?

J: Not really. I try to go to the movies every once in a while, but I haven't been lately.

F: You sound lonely again. Are you?

J: Yeah, I think I am. Sometimes it's really difficult. You know, I just moved into a new place. It would be nice to have some company sometimes . . . to have someone to do things with.

F: I understand. I thought you were getting out and meeting more people.

J: I guess I am, but those opportunities are really limited during the season.

F: I know they are, and your situation is far from ideal, but you might try to take some time and do something you enjoy, do something for yourself on your day off and at other times during the week, if possible. For example, I know you like to read. When's the last time you picked up a book?

J: You know, it's been a while, and by the time I get around to reading, I'm usually too tired, and I fall asleep. But you're right. I miss that.

F: And dinners. I know you like to go out to eat. There isn't anyone you can ask to join you for a meal?

J: As a matter of fact, there is this woman I met at church. It might be fun to ask her out for dinner, and maybe even a movie.

F: Stuff like that. Things to help you keep balanced and maintain perspective. Remember, the better you feel, the better you seem to do.

J: You're right, and I feel better already, just talking about it. I do need to do better about taking care of myself. I eat right and get enough sleep and do all of these things so that I can play football.

F: I know, but if you're not right, none of it matters.

J: You're right. Thanks; I feel so much better. I'm glad we talked, and we should do this more often. It really helps. Whenever I get off track, I probably need to talk about it.

This conversation was fairly typical with respect to the levels on which James and I communicated. Except for the times when he was injured, he rarely had a situation involving performance decrements that did not involve something personal. Once we figured out what was going on, he was always responsive and willing to make positive changes. Professional athletes may appear to lead glamorous and enviable lives. For many athletes, their lives are full, but also lacking, in that they have little time for themselves. Making time for himself was key to playing to his fullest, but as the demands and stresses of football wore on through the season, time for self began slipping away, and James would, once again, get off track.

Two weeks later, I flew out to another game. James was playing a little more than before and played a great game. Interestingly, I noticed things about his position coach's behavior that I had not noticed before and could not see on television. Even though I heard James and understood his frustration, actually seeing this coach's behavior firsthand put several things in perspective. Sharing my perceptions of his coach's behavior (which clearly had nothing to do with James personally) seemed to put things in perspective for James, too. The issue with this coach never came up again.

YEAR FOUR

Unusually busy schedules resulted in an increase in e-mail consultation during the fourth year. By this time, I had also met nearly everyone who meant anything to James. I met most of the members of his family, his financial advisors and accountant, martial arts instructors, women he dated, several close friends, acquaintances, and people from his church. James referred to him and me as a team, and it is obvious from the story I am telling here that James' transference with me was deep. My own countertransferential responses felt maybe like an aunt with her favorite nephew. I did not quite feel maternal toward him (my supervisor has suggested that I am just resistant to recognizing the mothering I do), but I did feel intimately connected. A five-year relationship that covers the deeply personal details of an athlete's emotional and professional life has to be an intimate one. The picture of a cool and detached psychologist is a false, and even dangerous, image. We are affected by, and invested in, the athletes we work with. Our investment in them, our connection with them, and our faith in them are what fuel the working alliance and help the athletes grow and get better. Monitoring our investment in our athletes (through supervision) helps us make sure our countertransferential feelings, emotions, and behaviors do not get in the way of what is best for them. The athletes we work with are also invested in us. James' transference really stands out in the following exchange:

F: The last couple of times I've seen you play in person, you had good games.

J: I can't help but be motivated when you come to see me play. There's just something about knowing that you've been there for me since the beginning. I always want to play my best when you come to town.

F: OK, James, you know how you played today? You were fired up, you played with passion. Now remember those feelings and those thoughts you had today and how great it felt to be playing so well. That is your mental model; that is the whole picture I want you to bring to every game. If you can play that way when I am in the stands, you can play that way any Sunday. You've just showed yourself you're a great player. Keep on showing yourself every week until the end of the season how good you are.

My role in James' life was, in terms of time, minimal. In terms of influence, it was humbling. Some of the fuel behind James' performance was his relationship with me. I tried to use his play on the days I was in the stands in order to show him that great play was something *he* did, something he was capable of accomplishing any day of the season. He thought he played better because I was in the stands, and I am sure there is some truth in what he said. I made a cognitive intervention based on his transference to show him that if he can have a great day once, he is capable of having it again and again.

James really seemed to be coming into his own during this fourth year. He played well, his play was consistent, and he continued to gain confidence and improve. The passion was there, and he was excited about football again. He also seemed happier, and he had more of a social life.

THE BIG PARTY

James' team did so well that they made it to the Super Bowl. I was going to go watch my client play in the Super Bowl. I thought to myself, Now, this is extraordinary.

J: The media has been unbelievable. I just want to get out of here and play some football. You know, I've really been blessed. Some guys never get this opportunity. This is unbelievable!

F: Isn't it? James, I'm really happy for you. I know you're excited. You've worked long and hard, but there's still work to do. Your challenge is going to be to maintain your balance, focus, and the quality of your play. Now, as with that great playoff game, it's a matter of maintenance. Anything we haven't done isn't going to get done. Just keep doing the things that got you there.

J: You're right. I'll be OK.

I spoke to James in a manner that communicated, You've done all the work, stick with what you know and have fun. I was trying to be an island of calm and reason in a truly wild and stormy sea. James arranged for me to experience the Super Bowl firsthand, and I was able to appreciate some of the pressures and stresses he was experiencing. I spent most of my time with members of his family. On game day, his father was especially emotional. Other members of his family seemed overwhelmed and became tearful at times. In the midst of all of the excitement and emotion, I had to make a conscious effort to remain focused, because I had a whole new set of informal clients: James' family. The only time James and I talked before the game was after brunch on game day. James was especially peaceful, calm, and focused.

F: How are you holding up?

J: OK. I just want to play football. How are you? How's everybody else doing?

F: We're OK. Your family's rather emotional, but everything's under control. Are you ready?

J: I'm ready!

F: You've really worked hard. You've handled the distractions of the week really well, too. There's really not a whole lot to say. Now it's just a matter of maintaining. It's all about the quality of your play.

J: You're right. I'm ready to roll! Thank you for everything. I'm glad you're here.

James played very well and achieved all of his goals for the game. His team, however, did not play well and lost. We agreed to talk in a couple of weeks, after he got home. Several teams expressed interest in James after the Super Bowl. He ended up signing a multimillion-dollar contract with another team.

CONCLUSION

This case illustrates several of the complexities involved in long-distance, long-term service delivery. One of those complexities is the multiple modes of service delivery. James and I communicated by telephone, e-mail, fax, in person, and while traveling from place to place, and I watched him play on television. Communication via telephone and e-mail was often difficult, and it was most challenging during the height of the season. Sometimes we played phone tag for several hours or even days. We also found ourselves talking on cell phones while James was traveling. James believed that he felt and performed better when we talked. Nonetheless, communicating regularly by long distance was problematic.

In James' case, one of the most negative consequences of infrequent communication was his relapses, his regression to old patterns of maladaptive thinking and behavior. When James and I communicated regularly, he stayed on top of several recurrent themes: stresses associated with football and travel, fatigue, frustration, loneliness, and other personal issues. James still does not tend to phone as often when he is feeling good and playing well. As a result, several weeks may elapse between telephone conversations, and some sort of relapse might be expected. Monitoring those relapses and communicating regularly are areas we continue to try to improve upon.

Work with other long-distance clients raises another issue. I never work with athletes long distance unless I feel I know them reasonably well. James had good psychological skills, and we had a strong working alliance before he went to the NFL. Having a good sense of James psychologically, cognitively, and biomechanically enabled me to "read" him well from a distance.

Another striking feature of this case was the transference and countertransference. James and I have a special relationship. My supervisor maintains that James' transference and my countertransference have strong parent-child qualities. He believes that James sees me as a stable, guiding force in his life and as a source of unconditional love and caring. Part of James' work in football has motivational roots in pleasing me and making me proud of him. I now tend to agree, and I am proud of James. I have finally become the idealized good mom. It has been very rewarding for me to see how far James has come athletically, personally, and professionally. I am also humbled that the quality of our relationship might have helped him maximize his gifts and opportunities. I learned a great deal and also grew personally and professionally during this time. I am grateful to James for the opportunities that working with him provided, and I look forward to continuing work with James and the challenges he will face.

REFERENCES

Graham, H. (1995). *Mental imagery in health care: An introduction to therapeutic practice.* London: Chapman & Hall.

Harris, D.V., & Harris, B.L. (1984). *The athlete's guide to sports psychology: Mental skills for physical people.* Champaign, IL: Leisure Press.

Ievleva, L., & Orlick, T. (1991). Mental links to enhanced healing: An exploratory study. *The Sport Psychologist, 5,* 25-40.

Linder, D.E., Brewer, B.W., Van Raalte, J.L., & DeLange, N. (1991). A negative halo for athletes who consult sport psychologists: Replication and extension. *Journal of Sport and Exercise Psychology, 13,* 133-148.

Linder, D.E., Pillow, D.R., & Reno, R.R. (1989). Shrinking jocks: Derogation of athletes who consult a sport psychologist. *Journal of Sport and Exercise Psychology, 11,* 270-280.

Porter, K., & Foster, J. (1990). *Visual athletics: Visualizations for peak sports performance.* Dubuque, IA: William C. Brown.

Shultz, J.H., & Luthe, W. (1969). *Autogenic therapy* (Vol. 1). New York: Grune & Stratton.

PART V

BRANCHING OUT: OTHER PRACTITIONERS, OTHER SETTINGS

CHAPTER 15

DOING SPORT PSYCHOLOGY AT THE REALLY BIG SHOW

Sean C. McCann
United States Olympic Committee

Doing sport psychology at a competition, big or small, is an extension of doing sport psychology in an office or practice facility. Although the environmental context is certainly different, the structure created by theoretical underpinnings, basic philosophy, and ethical concerns remains a consistent guide to practice in the stressful environment of high-pressure competitions.

THEORETICAL UNDERPINNINGS

Nearly all of my supervisors and mentors in clinical and sport psychology have had a cognitive-behavioral (CB) orientation, and this has no doubt influenced my strongly CB approach to sport psychology. A CB framework fits comfortably in the world where I practice, because it is practical, can be flexibly modified for long-term and short-term consultation, and is optimistic about the influence of cognition on overt behavior. As I hope to show in the examples from the Olympics, practicality, flexibility, and optimism are critical factors when doing sport psychology at major competitions.

The general tenets of the CB approach should be well known to readers of this volume from the work of Mahoney (1991), Meichenbaum (1977), Ellis (1962), Beck, Rush, Shaw, & Emery (1979) and others (see also chapters 1, 10, and 11). CB theory has been a mainstay of sport psychology service delivery, and most sport psychology interventions have come directly from behavior therapy or from cognitive-behavioral therapies.

To describe CB sport psychology in the most general terms, I tell athletes that until they have consistent control of their thoughts and imagination (self-talk, imagery), they will not have consistent control of their behaviors. I emphasize that sport psychology is all about gaining consistent control of behavior in the demanding environment of sport. This demanding environment (especially at elite competitive levels) creates the need for athletes to increase awareness and control of their thought processes, because the behavior (athletic performance) resulting from or influenced by these thoughts is measured so precisely, objectively, and immediately.

BASIC PHILOSOPHY

My basic sport psychology philosophy flows directly from my CB orientation. Thus, the focus of my work with athletes and coaches centers on specific behavioral goals, education as part of interventions, and skill development. Other aspects, such as partnerships with clients, encouraging independence, and a coaching approach, grew out of the CB orientation and have been repeatedly reinforced by the daily realities of working with elite Olympic athletes.

Focus on Specific Behavioral Goals

Starting a sport psychology intervention with the idea that the athlete will develop specific behavioral goals is a practical framework for shaping interventions. From a theoretical standpoint, this framework suggests that insight is not sufficient for a successful intervention, that all interventions can be evaluated, and that behavioral change is the ultimate measure of success. From a practical standpoint, measuring behavior is familiar to athletes, can appeal to an athlete's desire for demonstrable progress, and can provide a simple focus for solving complex problems in a highly stressful environment.

For example, a wrestler who has been too cautious and passive might decide that to win, he needs to be more active and aggressive. This planned change is a good start, but in a sport psychology session, I will typically try to help him get more specific. For example, we might define active and aggressive as starting the first 30 seconds of the match with high energy, forward movement, and perhaps a specific takedown attempt. These specifics would come from a list generated by the athlete or perhaps the athlete and coach together.

Education as Part of Intervention

Using education as an integral part of an intervention helps ease the transition from group lectures and workshops to individual sessions, the two primary components of my work. In addition, an educational approach models the kind of thinking and self-analysis that is necessary for athletes to modify and apply insights gained with the sport psychologist. For example, when working with a gymnast who has developed a specific anxiety about a certain dangerous move on the high bar, I typically teach the athlete the theory of fear and anxiety development (from a CB perspective) as a prelude to beginning an intervention. Armed with a basic knowledge of anxiety, the athlete can become a true partner in changing unproductive thoughts and behavior.

Skill Building

Many writers have described sport psychology as the teaching of a set of mental skills. Although this description may be limiting, there is no doubt that the concept of mental skills building has greatly contributed to the acceptance and growth of the field of sport psychology. The common lexicon of terms such as imagery, goal setting, self-talk, and relaxation training provide a very useful way to communicate about many CB ideas and interventions. In addition, athletes and coaches share a comfort with a skill-oriented approach. Finally, general skill sets can be modified to deal with specific challenges, and the modification and refinement of general skills form a large part of my consultation at the Olympics and other major competitions.

For example, when working with a cyclist at the Olympic trials, I might observe new heights of competitive anxiety. Based on prior skill building in the areas of relaxation and self-talk, we can expand and modify these skills for the present intense situation. We may decide on a 10-second relaxation exercise paired with a cue word to help the athlete feel confident, in control, and ready to perform in the 2 minutes before her trials race.

Partnerships With Athlete-Clients

Although educating the athlete regarding the theory, the process, and the goals of an intervention in a fairly directive manner is critical to intervention success, this educational interaction should not be confused with a master-disciple relationship. The CB orientation's focus on partnerships with clients is much less viable if the consultant has been set on a pedestal in the athlete's mind. Being seen as warm, knowledgeable, and trustworthy can greatly help a consultant in his or her work, yet the relationship needs to be balanced.

A partnership approach allows for give-and-take feedback to the sport psychology consultant, and plenty of flexibility when dealing with an athlete (the actual "expert") who may well be the "senior partner" in the relationship. As an international star in the Olympic sport of shooting recently said to me, "I doubt there are many sport psychologists who know more about the mental aspects of shooting than the top 20 shooters in the world." Respecting and learning from this practical knowledge is facilitated by a partnership approach. I have found that quality experiences and increased confidence have been facilitated by the sport psychologist admitting that "I don't have a solution to your problem. Perhaps we can work together and think of one?" The partnership I am referring to here is another name for the *working alliance* that has been a central feature of this book.

Encouraging Independence

Although many athletes naturally avoid dependence on sport psychologists or on other people generally, some athletes can quickly develop a dependent relationship with a sport psychologist. The reasons for such attachments can vary from a good performance following a brief intervention (which can create the appearance of a "magic wand" effect) to a sense that the sport psychologist "is the only one who cares about me as a person" to the vulnerability that can occur when an athlete openly talks about insecurities and fears in sport.

Whatever the cause of the dependence, my approach is to handle it gently (especially for the vulnerable athletes who have confided deeply personal concerns) and actively foster athlete independence. The case of an athlete who had a breakthrough race the day after I worked with him provides an example of the way I encourage independence. "You did this!" he said excitedly in the finish area. I responded by saying, "Thanks, but this was all your work. I was just a happy spectator like everybody else. Now make sure you remember what you did today."

Encouraging independence stems from both philosophical and practical concerns. On a philosophical level, I am opposed to what I call the *guru-fication* of sport psychologists. Guru status can benefit the guru, but is bad for the field and, almost invariably, bad for the client. The field is harmed by a perception that sport psychologists are only effective through unique, secret, or magical techniques. The guru-dependent athlete is harmed by the guru's tendency to take credit for the successes of the athlete (but never the blame for the failures). The dependent athlete is also harmed by the lack of opportunities to develop problem-solving skills independently and the lack of opportunities to develop the confidence that he or she can solve performance problems.

On a practical level, unless one works with only a few athletes, it is impossible to be always available for the athletes at critical performance moments. Most of the teams and athletes I work with travel constantly, often competing on the other side of the world. Even with cellular phones, faxes, and e-mails, education and skill building to foster athlete independence is the only functional strategy when one may see an athlete just a few times a year.

WORKING AT THE OLYMPICS AND OTHER HIGH-PRESSURE COMPETITIONS

In many ways, working with athletes at the Olympic Games is no different from working with athletes in any other competitive setting. A sport psychologist working at a competition needs to understand the logistics of the particular sport, including practical issues such as scheduling, access, and team routines. He or she also needs what is perhaps the most critical yet underappreciated skill a sport psychologist can develop—knowing how to be accessible without being in the way.

How to achieve this accessible state varies from sport to sport and often depends on the personality of the consultant. The consultant who wears anxiety on his or her sleeve or who needs to keep busy should avoid the start area of a ski race, for example, because athletes will see the nervous behavior and learn to avoid the consultant. On the other hand, a loose, relaxed consultant may be a useful presence at the start. In many sport situations, the consultant can stay close to the coach, who may appreciate the opportunity to talk. In all cases, however, the consultant must respect the routines, the habits, and even the superstitious behaviors that are the standard operating procedure of a team. For example, in one sport I made the mistake of saying "have a good one" to an athlete just before he performed at an international competition. I was told by a team member that my comment was a mistake, because the head coach had just said something to the athlete, and the head coach on that team "always" says the last thing an athlete hears.

The best way to learn these unwritten rules is through making mistakes, attending practices, receiving feedback from coaches and athletes, and having regular exposure to competitive environments. Therefore, before a sport psychologist arrives at "The Big Show," a great deal of work needs to be done so that he or she is already seen as a functional part of the competition team by the coaches and athletes.

One basic strategy that a sport psychologist learns from working with a team at a competition is that he or she must adapt to the team's schedule and procedures. Many standard clinical and educational practices do not fit in competitive environments. For example, the consultant should not expect to have access to official team meeting rooms. There may not be time for scheduled team-building sessions, and the consultant may not have access to all team members at once. He or she also may not be able to reserve private, comfortable spaces for one-on-one sessions.

Practitioners learn to perfect the ski-lift consult, the bus-ride consult, the 10-minute breakfast table team-building session, and the confidential session in public places such as hotel lobbies, parking lots, and trainers' tables. These catch-as-catch-can consulting encounters are realities for a sport psychologist in most competition settings. I have had to console a crying athlete 10 feet from the coach whose outburst caused the tears, motivate an athlete over a walkie-talkie radio listened to by teammates, and answer critical questions about a coach while driving a minivan full of team members.

In addition to these unusual consulting circumstances for sport psychologists at typical competitions, events such as the Olympics have their own rules. Increased pressure, media attention, and performance consequences are combined with different schedules, a host of new logistics challenges, and generally frayed nerves. Athletes and coaches, who are normally unflappable, suddenly start flapping. For example, one older athlete told me to be prepared to notice how the head coach "freaks out" at the Olympics. Sure enough, the coach steadily grew more anxious and compulsive in her checking and rechecking of situations. Although the older athlete had seen this before, some of the younger team members were initially quite distracted by this new Olympic pathology. Although a sport psychologist may also be feeling nervous, one of the keys to performing well as a consultant in these situations is to handle the pressure effectively and to bring a confident, upbeat, and optimistic manner to interactions with athletes and coaches.

AN OLYMPIC STORY

The characters in the following vignette are composites from my Olympic Games consulting with a number of athletes; they do not represent any specific Olympian or coach I have counseled.

Heidi is a 23-year-old alpine ski racer for the U.S. ski team and a member of the U.S. Olympic Team. She has been skiing since age 4 and racing since age 12. Heidi's parents are originally from Austria, where they both raced for the Austrian national team before immigrating to America to work as ski instructors. Heidi's parents remain in the ski industry, both working for a large ski resort in Colorado. I met Heidi at a ski team training camp four years ago, when she first made the international traveling team for the United States. At that time, Heidi sat in on a group workshop on goal setting. In other group sport psychology settings, Heidi remained friendly but made no individual contact until last year, during her first season on the World Cup circuit.

Heidi approached me in Europe, two days before a World Cup giant slalom race in which she was entered. She had noticed a pattern of racing poorly on icy courses such as the one she was about to race on, and a teammate who had overcome a similar problem suggested that she talk to the sport psychologist. At that time, she indicated that although her parents thought sport psychology was mumbo jumbo and something for whiners, she respected the advice of her Olympic medal-winning teammate, who worked regularly with me. After two individual sessions and good success working on the specific race behaviors Heidi wanted to change, Heidi and I began to work regularly at training camps, races, and through e-mail.

By the time of the Olympics, I had met ten or so times in individual sessions with Heidi, mostly at camps, but three times at races. Heidi also sent me e-mail updates from Europe during the race season. One month prior to the Olympics, I accompanied Heidi's team to a World Cup, where Heidi won one race and got a second place in another. These results were typical of the year she had been having, winning or placing in almost every big race and becoming the star of the U.S. team and a favorite for an Olympic medal.

At the Olympics, I first saw Heidi at the finish area of the giant slalom race course, during training two days before the opening ceremonies.

Sean McCann (SM): Hey there, Heidi!

Heidi (H): [skiing into the finish area, then taking off her skis] Hi, Sean! I heard you were here, and I wondered when I would see you. How long have you been here?

SM: Ten days; right when the Olympic village first opened. I've been working with a couple of teams that got here then.

H: Oh, wow, you'll be here a while then; what, like a month?

SM: Yep, a little longer than a month.

H: God, it already seems like a couple of weeks, and I've only been here three days.

SM: Oh yeah?

H: Yeah, all the running around to get stuff done, like sponsors and interviews and clothing and stuff. Crazy!

SM: Like we talked about last month, the Olympics *are* crazy. How has the last month been?

H: Funny you should ask! A little intense; there's been some stuff with Thomas [Heidi's coach], my folks, and Bob [Heidi's boyfriend]. Can we talk later?

SM: Sure; you want to hook up at your hotel after training?

H: Yeah. I've got to get worked on at 1:00 [massage and physical therapy], and we have dry land at 2:30 to 4:00 [strength and conditioning training]. How about 5:30, so I can take a nap first?

SM: Sounds good, I'll see you in the lobby at 5:30. Hey, if something changes in your schedule, here is a card with my cell phone number.

H: OK, great. I'm glad you are here. [Heidi puts her skis on and goes to take another run.]

Frequently at the Olympics, a consultant must travel two hours or more in order to make a one-minute contact like this one. Although it may seem like a great deal of time and effort for little gain, this apparently casual contact with Heidi accomplished a great deal. First, the athlete sees the consultant at her training site, which sends a reminder that he is part of the performance team at the Games. Being at that location also indicates the sport psychologist's ability to get through the maze of logistics at the Olympics in order to be accessible. In addition, the consultant is relaxed and casual in conversation but is able to quickly check in with Heidi on her recent history. Heidi is brief, but direct, in stating the first issues she wants to talk about, giving an early indication that issues off the ski slopes may have a bearing on her ski performance.

By agreeing to meet later at the hotel and not asking follow-up questions, the consultant shows an understanding of the importance of the training runs, the realties of a ski racer's schedule, and an awareness of the need to expect schedule changes. Giving the cell phone number may be the only way to ensure communication, in case Heidi has an unexpected conflict. In addition, a consultant at the Olympics must be accessible 24 hours a day before, during, and after the Games.

At the Hotel

Although the majority of Olympians stay in the Olympic Village (special housing built to house the thousands of athletes attending the Games), many teams also have hotel space or other housing near their competition venues. Such arrangements are often made for winter sports (e.g., alpine skiing) when the venues are far from the central Olympic Village. What this arrangement means is that, in some ways, skiers have less disruption of their normal competitive environment. During the greater part of the World Cup ski-racing season, athletes live out of duffel bags, moving from one alpine hotel to another. Thus, in this respect at least, the Olympic environment is not as disruptive for skiing as it is for some sports.

I am in the hotel lobby, 30 minutes before my appointment with Heidi, when Thomas Andersen, the head downhill coach, comes in and sees me. Thomas is a Norwegian who lives in Europe but coaches the U.S. women's speed team. Thomas was a good ski racer in his native country, making it as far as the Junior World Championships for Norway, before specializing in coaching. Thomas is a quiet, methodical coach, excellent with technical details, preparation, planning, and teaching one-on-one. Although Thomas' strengths have helped Heidi and her teammates move up rapidly in international rankings, his style has drawbacks at times. Thomas is not a motivator, and he lacks charisma and easy social skills. At times, athletes complain that Thomas does not seem to care about them as people, although they admit that he is always fair and never plays favorites. Usually seen as cool or even unemotional, Thomas tends to get anxious at the biggest events, or at other times during the season when the schedule changes, interfering with the team's training plan.

Thomas (T): Hello, Sean.

SM: [rising from the couch] Hi there, Thomas!

T: How are you?

SM: Good, thanks. How are things going?

T: Well, to be honest, pretty nuts.

SM: Oh yeah?

T: We have been fighting to get decent training time, and athletes are worried about going to parties, getting tickets for their families, and going to other events. Last night we had a team meeting, and Heidi was late because her agent had scheduled an interview at the same time. This whole scene is out of control. I am going to address some of these issues tonight. Will you be at our team meeting?

SM: I certainly can be.

T: Good, I would like to have you there.

SM: No problem [brief silence]. How are *you* doing, Thomas?

T: I'm OK. I'm pretty good. It's just a little crazy here. I'll be OK.

This interchange points out a few of the exceptional aspects of the environment at an Olympic Games and other high-pressure events. There certainly are more distractions, less familiar schedules and surroundings, and potentially a significant loss of control for a coach. One of the lesser known truths of major sports events is that the pressure is worse for the coach than for the athlete. At the Olympics, for example, you almost never hear mention of a coach unless something goes wrong. Many coaches have been focused for four years on this moment, only to find that all of their normal systems are disrupted at this crucial time. For coaches, especially those with Thomas' detail focus and long-term planning approach, these disruptions can be incredibly stressful. Some coaches do not do well in the Olympic situation and can actually have a negative impact on their athletes' performances.

I was aware of this possibility and knew that I could play three primary roles at the Games for a coach with whom I had worked extensively in the past: confidant, reality tester, and pressure reliever. From this interchange with the coach, I already knew that Thomas was not at his best. When he talked about things being out of control, I knew that he might try to increase structure with the athletes, perhaps through harsh directives (his typical reaction to his *own* feelings of being out of control). What might have been more useful was for Thomas to feel more in control of his own anxiety. What I first attempted to do was listen to Thomas' description of the situation. Then I began to raise his awareness that his own emotional state was an important performance factor. Although I usually wait for Thomas to tell me when he needs to talk, I decided it might be useful to be more direct than usual.

SM: Do you have some time to talk today?

T: Uh, sure, tonight after our team meeting. What are you doing for dinner?

SM: Eating with you, I guess.

T: OK, good. Yeah, I really wouldn't mind talking a bit. Are you meeting somebody now?

SM: Yes, Heidi wanted to meet.

T: Oh boy, you have some work today! She is on a roll.

SM: Oh yeah?

T: Yes, all the other skiers are pissed off at her, all the coaches are pissed off at her agent, and she appears to be pissed off at her boyfriend! I would like to get rid of everybody, but it is too late for that. I'm worried that all this nonsense could cost us a medal. Well, I'm glad you are seeing her. See you tonight?

Handling issues of confidentiality can be problematic in a team setting on the road. Because many competition consults are in public view (e.g., in a hotel lobby), it can be difficult to prevent public knowledge of a session, and an agreed-on system or policy must be developed in order to handle questions such as Thomas'. In my work at the Olympic Training Center, I have gone as far as to not answer a question about whether or not an athlete is coming in to see me in order to protect privacy. My typical policy is to agree with athletes and coaches that I will share the fact of having had a session with an athlete, but I will not talk about the specifics of the session unless the athlete asks me to.

A consultant is often asked to be a go-between in order to translate athlete concerns for the coaches, but I nearly always refuse to play that role, instead pushing the athletes to talk to the coaches directly. I see that as a necessary communication skill athletes need in order to advance. I will sometimes spend a session in a role-play, working through potentially difficult conversations between athlete and coach. Included in these communication skill-building exercises are attempts to increase athletes' awareness of how a coach's comment can cause them to have an emotional response.

A sport psychologist can facilitate this investigation of the internal response process by having athletes keep thought and emotion logs that track their thoughts, feelings, and behaviors. In this way they can begin to understand how cognitions lead to behavior. For example, a young gymnast may find that she repeatedly gets frustrated, angry, and tearful in response to a coach who tells her that she is not as good as another competitor. She may find that her powerful reaction begins with her belief that she is not talented at all and works very hard to prevent other people from seeing her lack of talent. If that were the case, a role-play of discussions with her coach would require awareness of internal cognitions as well as external behavior. Obviously, this type of cognitive behavioral logging of thoughts takes time and is rarely possible in a competitive setting such as the Olympics.

Work with Heidi on these issues took place very early on in our consulting relationship. In her case, we had worked to minimize her self-destructive response to Thomas' critical comments in training. The key to changing her behavior had been her awareness that Thomas' direct, uncensored style mirrored her father's approach during her early racing career. She became aware that her internal thought process led her to say to herself, Piss off, Thomas. I won't do anything for you! Of course, Heidi had to learn that she was doing the training for herself (which she learned to say to herself when she started to get angry at Thomas). Heidi walked into the lobby five minutes after Thomas left.

H: Hey.

SM: Hi, how are you doing?

H: Not bad.

My question was intentional, not a simple conversational transition. A colleague of mine at the Olympics was once told by a coach not to say "how are you doing?" because a few athletes were interpreting this phrase, and a concerned look, to mean that something seemed wrong. In Heidi's case, I was guessing that she was not doing as well as usual, but given her response, I decided to hold off on follow-up questions for the moment.

SM: Is this time still good for you?

H: Yep, I'm all set. Where do you want to meet?

SM: I noticed a quiet table over in the corner, out of the view of the lobby. Will that work?

H: Yeah, great.

As previously mentioned, meeting locations on the road are rarely perfect. The hotel consult is a good example of the awkwardness. Even when meeting rooms are available, they are usually filled with athletes reviewing videotape or with coaches or other team personnel. I virtually always rule out hotel rooms as meeting places as well. Athletes and coaches often double up, meaning that a session may interrupt a nap, a shower, or a phone call from home. In addition, when working with female athletes, I am not comfortable working in a hotel room. My primary discomfort arises from the potential cues that working in a bedroom and talking about very personal issues may create for some athletes. In addition, the potential for legal liability associated with meeting an athlete in a hotel room also makes me anxious, so I err on the safe side.

Given the limitations, I most frequently end up in a quiet corner of a lobby, a restaurant, or even a hotel bar on its off hours. Athletes rarely object, but I have found myself strongly wishing for a better alternative when an athlete breaks down crying in this fairly public setting. If I have an option, I typically face outward, with my back against the wall, so that the athlete is less aware of teammates, coaches, or other people who may be walking through the lobby.

SM: So, do you want to give me a three-minute summary of what's going on?

H: Three minutes, huh? I think I need more time!

SM: Well, we have 90 minutes until the team meeting, so use all the time you need.

I have found that infrequent contact sometimes results in athletes feeling overwhelmed when we first sit down, because of the amount of material they have to review (competitions, personal life, training, and so forth). To make their task as historians more manageable, I often ask for a short summary, which helps them go fairly rapidly into many issues. The summary request also helps me when I work with an athlete who jumps right into an issue, neglecting an important environmental factor until the end of the session (e.g., "Oh yeah, I forgot to tell you, my wife moved back to San Francisco with our baby . . ."). On the other hand, as Heidi's comment illustrates, it is important to give athletes as much time as they need to tell their stories.

H: OK, so you remember how Thomas and I were going back and forth in Chile last summer?

SM: Quite well.

H: Well, after you and I talked that time, and then I talked to Thomas about stuff, things got better for pretty much the whole season, but lately it feels like the same stuff is happening. And in the past two weeks, it seems like it is happening in three directions!

SM: What do you mean?

H: Well, Bob [the boyfriend] is traveling with me. My mom and dad are here, and Andre [Heidi's agent] is here, too. It's like I'm having the same interaction with all of them. I'm constantly irritated and stressed, and I feel like I'm not doing anything well. Bob thinks I should look out for myself more, Dad thinks Bob should keep his nose out of things, Andre keeps saying how I need to take advantage of opportunities, and Thomas says I am too distracted. I think he may be right, but the way he says it is so annoying that I just get really mad. Even my mom is bugging me about hooking her up with some figure skating tickets! Oh, and my teammates all hate me. So basically, I am skiing great and can win a medal, and everybody thinks I am a jerk and screwing things up.

SM: Ohhh-kaaay—so what do you think?

H: Actually, I was hoping you could tell me what I should think! No, seriously, I know this is not what you and I talked about at the end of last season and the beginning of this season. Keeping loose and keeping things focused works best for me, and that's not where I am right now. This whole season has gone great—three wins, five top 10's—and it's mainly because my head has been so confident and focused, and I have stopped thinking so much about winning and losing. In the past month I have totally lost control of my thinking, my feelings, my environment, and it feels like I am at a really dangerous point right now.

At this point, I am consciously fighting impulses to dig into all these important issues. There are times, when I am working with athletes who begin to have great insights and observations about their situations, that I feel myself getting completely charged up and excited to get to work. I know that I have ideas, strategies, experiences, examples, and metaphors than can suggest a new cognition, a new way of thinking about the situation, that may help the athlete. I believe that these ideas can help the athlete behave in a more productive way, and I start to prepare a mini-lecture in my head until I am only thinking about what *I* want to say as opposed to what the athlete is saying. It is moments like these with Heidi when I rein in my impulse to talk, I concentrate on listening, and I ask neutral questions. That way I can see where she is, check out my hunches, and let her talk.

SM: Oh yeah? Why's that?

H: Well, I kind of feel that I have been doing everything right, and now I am just losing it.

SM: Losing it how?

H: Well, like all the people, and feeling pulled in conflicting directions, and starting to think about *what ifs?* It's like one of those scenes in a movie or TV show, where you see a coil of rope is wrapped around the foot of the character, and something is pulling the rope underwater, and you know the guy is about to be pulled underwater, but the guy doesn't realize it yet.

SM: So, things are going OK on the surface, but you feel in trouble and about to get pulled off the boat?

H: Exactly! But I don't know how to stop it all and get my training and racing focus back.

SM: Well, I have a few ideas that I think will help, but before we dive into solving specific problems, I want to make sure I understand the big picture. I guess I need to understand the "rope" that is wrapped around your foot. Is it OK if we spend some time on some of the stuff you talked about earlier, with your family, teammates, agent, and boyfriend?

H: Actually, that would be great, because I haven't been able to explain it all to anybody.

This interchange has a few important components. It highlights the importance of questions. In many ways, the choice and timing of specific questions is the central mechanism a consultant uses to direct a sport psychology session. Although I could have jumped into one or another specific issue, I chose to stay in a "wide-angle view" by asking a few more broad questions. Although this did not generate any new information, I had a clearer sense of how Heidi felt, and I got to hear her interesting and powerful metaphor about the rope. With the questions, I am also able to test my hunch that Heidi needs to talk about all the environmental pressures before she can effectively focus on specific racing issues. Of course, in this situation, I knew we had two days before Heidi's Olympic race and that we would be able to meet again. If we could have met only once, and our meeting was the night before the race, I might have decided to narrow in on performance issues immediately and hope that the other issues wouldn't intrude in the subsequent 12 hours.

In the 40 minutes before the team meeting, Heidi filled me in on the state of her relationships; her conflicts with the coach; jealousy within the team regarding the media attention she was getting; the demands of her agent, who wanted to maximize media time; and the subtle pressure of her family, who wanted to support her. At the end of the session, I agreed with Heidi that the rope was wrapped around her ankle and was moving fast. We stayed with the metaphor and discussed whether it made sense to try to untangle herself or to take a more aggressive approach by grabbing an axe and chopping off the rope (i.e., by isolating Heidi from her environment). As Heidi talked about the variety of pressures, she realized that the primary step she needed to take was to set some clear limits with the people around her.

Although setting limits sounds like a simple and easy idea, overwhelmed Olympians often have difficulty in doing that. Based on work with other Olympic athletes, I suggested to Heidi that she consider the pre-event and post-event time periods as two completely different situations that called for two completely different sets of behavior. This tactic has proven helpful in guiding family members and other people who do not understand the mental and physical demands of performing in a high-pressure situation. By setting specific post-event dates for socializing, shopping, or attending other events, the athlete can then declare the pre-event time period off-limits to distractions. With this general guideline, Heidi quickly came up with her own people-management plan and ended the session with a great deal of relief.

H: Yes, this will definitely work. It's amazing how easy it seems now that I have talked it out.

SM: Well, it is hard to admit that people you care about can actually be obstacles to performance. If you had no emotional or social ties to these guys, we wouldn't even be talking about this stuff.

H: Yeah, it's especially weird with family, because without them I wouldn't even have a ski-racing career.

SM: True, but most families are relieved to be told how to act at the Olympics. You are giving them a specific plan and making them a true part of your support team.

H: It's kind of new, though, me telling them how to act.

SM: Well, let's face it, you are the expert in high performance now. Speaking of which, can we get together tomorrow to talk more about performance issues?

H: Definitely. Same time tomorrow?

SM: Sounds good to me. Just phone me if your schedule changes.

With that, Heidi and I walked together to the pre-dinner team meeting in the coaches' hotel suite. The group of 15 consisted of athletes, coaches, ski technicians, and the team leader for skiing (an Olympics-only position handling logistics and interfacing between the USOC and the ski team). One of the first things that struck me when I began attending team meetings for various individual sport national governing bodies is how short these meetings are. The meetings nearly always focus on logistics and plans for the next day. There are rarely any motivational speeches or general messages to the entire team. Recognizing this, I have rarely asked to speak at these meetings, and when I do speak, I almost always keep my comments brief (less than a minute in length). As the meeting was finishing up, Thomas made note of my presence.

T: As you all can see, Sean is here. Sean is busy with a lot of other teams here at the Games, but has graced us with his presence tonight. Anything you want to say, Sean?

SM: Thanks, Thomas. Yes, I am busy like all of you, but there is no place I would rather be right now than here. Don't have a lot to say except to remind folks what we talked about a few months ago. For you first-timers, the Olympics is a bit of a circus, and I expect you have already discovered that. You need to find a way to perform as if there wasn't a circus going on. Sometimes that is easier to say than do, but I know you all have the skills and resources to do it effectively. If anybody wants to talk about specific issues, or just wants to talk, I'm going to be around, so catch me after the meeting to set up an appointment. Other than that, great to see everybody, and good luck over the next two weeks or so. It's going to be fun.

As the meeting breaks up, three athletes come up to make appointments for that night or the next day. Two of the athletes are no surprise, because they regularly schedule individual sessions with me, but my contact with the third had primarily consisted of team meetings and casual on-hill discussions. At the Olympics, I find that even the few first-time appointments are generally with athletes who have had exposure to me at some camp at the Olympic Training Center. For this reason, it is difficult to argue for bringing sport psychologists to the Games who do not have any prior experience with the athletes.

At dinner with Thomas, I found that he was trying, in vain, to control many uncontrollable factors. His worries ranged from the weather to the bedtimes and social life of his athletes to how other nations were training in less-than-ideal conditions. Although I had seen Thomas anxious at other competitions, I had not seen him in such a state before.

T: This whole scene is ridiculous. Everyone expects us to win medals, then they take away my ability to do things the way I always do. When I was at my last Olympics, as an assistant coach, I didn't realize how disruptive this environment was. We know how to put on ski races, but they don't let us do it. There is an Olympic person in charge of everything.

SM: How are folks handling things?

T: I don't think the athletes realize how messed up things are, so they seem fine. The coaches and I are probably handling things the worst.

SM: What do you think you aren't handling well?

T: Well, the weather has been bad, and training has been limited. That is pretty frustrating. I've snapped at Eric [assistant coach] a few times over things that aren't his fault. He hasn't said anything, but I know he is upset with me.

SM: How have things been going between the coaches and athletes?

T: I think pretty well, except I am in conflict with Heidi about her decision making. How did your meeting go with her?

SM: It was a good meeting.

T: Good. I know you can't tell me details, but do you think she is handling the pressure well?

SM: Well, I think a lot of folks are in the same boat, feeling pressure and not sure what to do, or not sure if what they normally do is good enough. I was having a similar discussion yesterday over at speed skating with an athlete who was also a favorite to win a medal. There is a special challenge for favorites at the Olympics. When the fact that you can really win an Olympic medal becomes concrete in your mind, it is so hard not to think about screwing up your chance.

T: Oh yeah, I can feel that as a coach.

SM: Well, as I was working with the speed skater, I tried to emphasize that worrying about failure or messing up was not how he got to be a favorite. You need to go for it at the Olympics even more than at other events. Athletes who go into events trying to defend against mistakes make the biggest mistake of all. They change what they normally do and take themselves out of their preferred performance state. I think the same is true of coaches.

T: What do you mean?

SM: It is easy to get so worried about the coaching errors you want to prevent that you start to become defensive, negative, and doubtful. Athletes pick up on that. It can be contagious.

T: Oh great, something else to worry about! No, seriously, I think that might be happening to us. This is the most important week of my coaching career, and I am having a hard time sleeping because I worry about the things that can go wrong.

SM: So what would you tell an athlete who told you the same thing?

T: Well, athletes are different. Somebody has to worry about stuff, and that is me!

SM: Humor me, Thomas. What would you tell an athlete who told you he couldn't sleep because he was worried about things that might go wrong?

T: OK, OK. I would tell him to focus on his strengths, on what he needed to do to ski fast, and stay positive and confident.

SM: Anything else?

T: I would tell him that it is normal to feel worried, and not to worry about worrying.

SM: My work here is done.

T: Wait a minute, it is different for the coach. I do have to worry about everything!

SM: Well, I think the main reason it feels that way is because coaches at the Olympics don't know what their jobs are. After the last Summer and Winter Olympics, I did an exercise with the head coaches asking them how they knew they had done a good job at the Olympics. It was amazing how many of them based their answers only on whether their athletes had medaled or not. I had them come up with a list of behaviors that great Olympic coaches must display. They came up with a long list of specific behaviors and then rated themselves on each. It was pretty useful.

T: What kinds of things did they come up with?

SM: All kinds of things, from taking time to reduce your own stress by running or working out, to keeping a sense of humor, to delegating well, to trusting your plans, to planning well, to staying flexible. I have the form if you would like to do it.

T: I think that would be great.

SM: I will give you one right after dinner, and if you fill it out, I bet you will sleep better tonight. Because I know you are doing an amazing job. I think you just need to believe that a little bit more. Just focus on doing a good job coaching, staying positive and confident, and . . . what was that last thing you said you would tell the worried athlete?

T: Don't worry about worrying, it is normal! OK, OK. I will try to take my own advice. Thanks.

This interaction with Thomas had more of my "sermonette" style, in which I tell stories and cite anecdotes or research in order to make a point. One reason I slipped into this style was to deflect specific questions about Heidi by using the story of the speed skater. With this example, I could get across some broad themes that are true for Heidi (and Thomas!) without revealing specifics of my session with her. When I do get in sermonette or lecture mode, I need to balance my own desire to tell a story with the needs of my audience. I have occasionally found myself launching into an anecdote triggered by a client's comment, and three minutes later, at the end of the story, forgetting what connection the story has with the person in front of me. As I said earlier, restraining the impulse to tell rather than listen is usually a good idea.

The specific issues raised in the anecdote about Olympic coaches following the Games are true. The mistake of evaluating a coaching performance based only on the outcome of the competition is, not surprisingly, common among Olympic coaches. Helping coaches focus on good coaching rather than good outcomes reduces anxiety and increases consistently good coaching. After raising this issue for further thought, I spent about 20 minutes discussing the impact of coaches' frustration and anxiety on the athletes. Thomas agreed it might be useful for the coaches to meet to discuss how they were coming across to athletes.

Two Days Later

The night before Heidi's race, I was eating in the Olympic Village dining hall when I received a phone call from her. She was in the Village but was heading back up to the team's hotel in the mountains. She wondered if we could talk together on the bus. I agreed and we met a few minutes later in the line for the bus.

SM: Hey there!

H: Hi, Sean; thanks for meeting. Do you have something else to do up at the mountain?

SM: No, I'll just stay on the bus and come back down.

H: Oh, are you sure that's OK? I mean, I know you are busy.

SM: Heidi, meeting with athletes is my job. It's no problem; in fact, it's great to get out of that office. I've got a newspaper to read on the ride down. [Getting on the bus now, I look around at the other riders, mostly Scandinavian Nordic skiers. They probably understand English, but none are Heidi's competitors, and they will probably not be interested in our conversation. Nonetheless, I walk with Heidi to the last row of the bus, a few rows behind anyone else.]

SM: So, from reading the training results, I see that you are skiing fast.

H: I know. That's the problem.

SM: Oh yeah? Why's that?

H: Well, I won training today, and I almost always race well when I train fast. Other racers are coming up to me and saying things like, "This is your race," and stuff like that. My folks have been a lot better since I talked to them; thanks, by the way. It really was easy, like you said. But today my mom started talking about how all the U.S. medal winners are appearing on late-night TV shows, and I started thinking about it, and that's about all I can think of, how my life can change if I win. I have been thinking about sponsorships, and commercials, and money to buy a house and a car and to pay for college. I know this is exactly the wrong stuff to think about, and that's why I called you. I need you to hypnotize me, or shut off my brain or something! No, seriously . . . I am worried because I know this is wrong, and it can make me get into the "don't screw it up" thinking we talked about the other day. I have been really good, but all of a sudden, it is like 12 years of imagining myself hearing the "Star Spangled Banner" are over and I have a really good chance to have it happen.

SM: Funny, isn't it, how it all changes when things go from a fantasy or abstract idea to something real and concrete?

H: Yeah. The feeling that I have something to lose is hard to shake.

SM: Well, that is something we need to work on before you race tomorrow.

H: I know!

SM: OK, so give me more details. You had a great training run today. Were you distracted today before or during the training run?

H: Not really. Riding the lift up before inspection, Marie [a French competitor] said that she thought I would win tomorrow. That made me a little nervous, but during inspection I was really pretty focused, and I was very focused during the training run. The day before I had made a few mistakes, and I knew I could do better today. It really wasn't till after I won the training that I really started to think so much about stuff. But over the past 6 hours or so, I haven't gone 20 minutes without seeing myself on TV or on the podium. I feel a little crazy.

SM: Well, as kind of an expert in that area, I can say for sure that you aren't crazy. On the other hand, it is worth trying to get better control of your thoughts so you don't worry so much about your lack of control. Does that make sense?

H: Yes.

As Heidi described her situation, I realized that this bus ride was a critical opportunity. In all likelihood, it would be my last chance to work with Heidi, and the next 16 hours could have an enormous impact on her race performance. I had seen this exact phenomenon in other Olympics, and I had seen athletes perform terribly in response to the sudden realization that they were very close to their dreams. The combination of my knowledge of Heidi and my experience in dealing with her situation led me to be more directive than usual.

SM: Well, why do you think that these thoughts about seeing yourself after the race are dangerous?

H: It's not the thoughts so much as my worry that they are distracting me, and that I can't seem to stop them no matter how hard I try.

SM: Well, I haven't met too many athletes who could successfully push away thoughts so real and powerful. It takes a lot of energy, and maybe you need that energy for other things right now. How about an alternative to pushing the thoughts away?

H: Sure.

SM: You know how we talked about compartmentalizing some of your thoughts about your family?

H: Yeah.

SM: Well, remember how we talked about how you treat the thoughts as real and important and needing to be dealt with, but maybe not on the morning of the race? The same thing is true of these really positive thoughts of victory. By thoroughly considering all the great stuff that can happen for a specific period of time, like 30 minutes or an hour, however much time you need to really consider it, you can then set those thoughts aside and focus instead on seeing yourself skiing well. I first heard of that idea from another sport psychologist, and I later talked to an athlete who had done that in the Olympics, and the athlete felt it was a key for her winning a medal. I have seen it work a number of other times at really big events. I know it sounds simple, but are you willing to try it?

H: Yeah, but what exactly should I do?

SM: Well, after the bus ride, can you get 20-60 minutes by yourself?

H: Sure.

SM: Okay, then use that time to let your fantasies run wild. See yourself doing whatever you think might happen if you have success, in real detail. Then, once you have played it out, let go of those thoughts, knowing that you have already had those thoughts and that you will think more about them after the race. By really letting yourself concentrate on the thoughts that are coming in, you will use less energy than you would to push the thoughts away, and you can then use the extra energy tomorrow, before and during the race.

H: Okay; I'll try it. I think that will work for me.

SM: Good. I think it will, too. Now, once your mind is a little less occupied with those thoughts, do you have a clear, simple performance plan for tomorrow?

H: Do you have one of your handy-dandy race goal sheets?

SM: As a matter of fact, I do!

H: What a surprise!

Heidi is sarcastically referring to a pre-race ritual we have developed. When I am at competitions, I go over the forms with her, but when she is on her own, she fills out her own sheets. The form is one page, large print, and says the following:

TO SKI FAST, I WILL

1.
2.
3.

This is a process-oriented, or behavior-based, goal sheet. The goals will change depending on the race-hill terrain, what Heidi is working on in terms of technique, and other factors. In the past, she has filled in things such as "stay relaxed," "attack the course," "hands down the hill," and "have fun." If the concepts seem too vague or too complicated, I ask for an explanation or a simpler idea. My goal in using this sheet is threefold. First, I want the athletes to keep things simple. Second, I want the athletes to focus on controllable factors, and third, I want the athletes to feel increased confidence by the act of completing this exercise. To this end, I ask the athletes to rate how much confidence they have that they will achieve each of these goals. If the confidence is less than 70%, I ask them to rework the goals into something they are more confident about achieving. For example, if an athlete believes that a relaxation exercise is critical, but she is only 50% sure she will do it, I ask her if she can instead set a goal of doing her relaxation exercise before the competition. I always ask athletes what their jobs are, and in Heidi's case her job is to ski fast. For other athletes, it can be to wrestle well or to ski well.

H: All right; number one is "keep my hands forward." I did that today, and it made a big difference. Number two is "visualize myself at speed during course inspection." This course is a little icy, and it is easy to see yourself scrubbing speed on some of the turns. I need to really see an aggressive line when I go through inspection. Number three is "have fun!" Today, I was skiing without fear and totally loving this course. I need to try to keep it up.

SM: Those sound good, a lot like the goals for the World Cup in Italy.

H: Yeah, well that was a big event for me, and the hills are almost identical.

SM: How is your confidence on each of these goals?

H: Numbers one and two are 90-95%. I just need to make them a priority. Number three is more like a 70 or 80%, because I am a little stressed out. I think I should do an extra free-ski training run before the race, totally focused on how I love this hill and the thrill of being here. That should help. Will you be there tomorrow?

SM: Yep.

H: Well, maybe you could remind me, too. Just in case.

SM: It's a deal. So, what's your job?

H: To ski fast!

SM: Can you do it?

H: Yes, I already have.

SM: Will you do it?

H: YES!

SM: How will you do it?

H: Hands forward, visualize speed, have fun.

SM: Great. Well, here's your stop. See you on the hill in the morning.

H: OK. Thanks a lot, Sean. I really appreciate it.

SM: As always, Heidi, it's great to work with you.

CLOSINGS

Sometimes, an athlete like Heidi has a great result in the hours following your sport psychology intervention. At times like those, it is seductive to see yourself as the agent of a wonderful victory. The athlete you work with often comes up to you and thanks you for your help. As she leaves to do interviews and as the television cameras close in on her in her moment of glory, you realize that her life is forever changed. This is powerful and heady stuff, and a few of these moments can last a whole career (or so I hope!).

On the other hand, Heidi might have failed miserably following an almost identical scenario. One experience of this other scenario, the one in which a talented athlete you have just worked with fails miserably in the Olympics, reminds you why people get nervous in sports. It really *is* better when you win, and losing can be pretty miserable. This truism holds for athletes, for coaches, and for sport psychologists. I have experienced both situations and have learned that the agony of defeat for a sport psychologist is not at the finish area, when you see the tears and perhaps comfort the unsuccessful athlete. For me, at least, the hard part is being by myself afterward and wondering what I could have done differently.

Given this reality in sports and in sport psychology consulting, it is useful to apply the advice I gave Thomas in this chapter, in which I suggested that coaches need to define what a good coaching job is and to pay attention to that above all. To evaluate a consulting performance properly, sport psychologists must understand what they can control and what they cannot. Consultants need to define what an excellent big-event sport psychologist does and work toward that goal.

Closure for the Sport Psychologist

Until a consultant is able to get distance from an athlete's performance and to shift the focus back to the actual job he or she has done, the consultant will be prey to a number of potential sport psychology evils. Like coaches who evaluate themselves solely upon an athlete's performance on the field, a sport psychologist can begin to believe that an athlete loss equals a bad job, whereas an athlete victory equals a good job. This simplistic and rather dichotomous evaluation contains dangerously egocentric reasoning.

For example, I am lucky enough to have traveled to three Olympic Games as a sport psychologist. In each case, I have worked with a large number of athletes who won no medals and set no records. In each case, I have also worked with a small number of athletes who have won medals and have set records. What kind of job did I do? The answer, of course, is that wins and losses are not a relevant measuring stick.

Every Olympic medal is the product of genetics; family background; fortuitous exposure to a sport that suits the athlete; dozens of coaches, significant others, and sponsors; sport science; proper nutrition; sports medicine; good timing; and big doses of luck. The role of a sport psychologist is sometimes highlighted, because it is a service that can make a difference at the last minute, but it is simply one very small piece of a very big puzzle.

To get back to the task of evaluating a sport psychology consulting performance—I believe that I must take my job very seriously and take myself much less seriously. What I mean is that when I self-evaluate, I start from the premise that I have no unique gifts or traits that have resulted in my current position. On the other hand, I treat my position as a great responsibility deserving my best effort. If I know where to apply that effort and how to do my job, I will be successful more often than not. During the brief period of the Olympic Games, I focus my effort on a few key behaviors and the personal skills I need to draw on to carry out those behaviors:

1. Was I accessible at key moments? (planning)
2. Did I behave in a way that never added stress and usually reduced stress? (arousal control, personal stress-management)
3. Did I adapt to the schedules and needs of coaches and athletes? (flexibility)
4. Did I listen well? (effective communication)
5. Did I project a caring, approachable image? (empathy)
6. Did I pitch in on nonpsychological tasks? (team building)
7. Did I avoid negativity and retain a sense of humor? (positive self-talk, personal stress management)
8. Did I always remember how much fun this is and how lucky I am? (reality testing)
9. Was I creative and intuitive when working on performance challenges? (listening skills, anxiety control, self-confidence)
10. Was I able to develop a performance plan, commit to it without needless second-guessing, and communicate this plan in a positive, useful way? (self-confidence, anxiety control, communication skills)

Closure for the Athlete

Post-Olympic let-down, sometimes leading to depression in severe cases, is remarkably common among athletes. It makes sense when one compares the situation for Olympians to other sport and nonsport events. Imagine an all-encompassing career project that rewarded all your skills, structured your life and daily schedule, and gave you the opportunity for tremendous accomplishment (knowing you are among the best in the world) but that ended abruptly, early in your life, and forced you to take a completely new direction. At the very least, such an end to a career project would pose an emotional challenge. Despite whether the Olympics end in personal victory or in personal defeat (however an athlete measures the outcomes), there is remarkably little attention paid to the psychological concept of closure with athletes and coaches.

Part of the difficulty is timing. Olympians often leave the Olympics to go onto other events. The whirlwind travel schedule of the elite athlete continues unabated, despite the emotional roller coaster of the previous few Olympic weeks. Even when an athlete ends a competitive career at an Olympics, the rush of people, media, and obligations gives the athlete very little time to gain perspective, catch a breath, or deal with strong emotions. Some sport organizations structure and schedule a wrap-up meeting to get closure. A great many others scatter and leave closure to chance. I have found that taking a few minutes to talk about the events and the likely future, as I do in the following exchange with Heidi, is a great investment of time.

SM: Hi.

H: Hi.

SM: How's life as an Olympic medalist?

H: Busy.

SM: What have you been doing?

H: Business, media, family, watching other events—definitely not sleeping!

SM: Has it been fun?

H: Yeah, a blast really. A little unsettling, though.

SM: Why's that?

H: I told myself I would figure out the rest of my life after the Olympics. I had the idea it would be so easy once I got this out of my system. I am less sure now than ever.

SM: Less sure about what? What's next?

H: Exactly. I'm not nervous about performing now; now I'm nervous about life! I know I should be so happy. I mean this is my dream, and I am happy, but . . . I don't know. I just feel . . . I don't know, so unclear about stuff. Am I crazy, or do I always need something to make me crazy all the time? Do you know what I mean?

SM: You are completely typical, not crazy at all. Sometimes it is worse when you do poorly at the Olympics, because you are also in mourning, but the issues are still the same. Life changes. Your life changes, and you need to change in some real ways, too.

H: Like how?

SM: Well, it depends. We said we would talk about future stuff, like retirement decisions and other choices, at the end of the season. I want to make sure we keep that appointment. Next month, right? [Heidi nods.] Good, because depending on some of these competitive and business choices, you will have lots of other choices. For now, however, it is safe to say that your emotional roller coaster will continue for a while. Expect it, and it will bother you a little less. Of course, call or e-mail whenever you need to talk about it. These feelings tend not to follow a set schedule.

H: You mean I can't expect elation every morning and anxiety every night?!

SM: You want a training schedule?

H: Sure. That's something I'm good at.

SM: You are good—no, *great*—at *a lot* of things. Having lots of skills often means having a lot of good options. This is stressful; get used to it! It's the burden of success. I'm not worried about you at all. Anyone who can do the work you have done the past three years will do just fine.

H: Thanks.

SM: Yes, this might be an appropriate time for me to tell you how proud I am of the work you have done. I know the medal is a concrete symbol of your success, but I'm not nearly as impressed with the medal as with how far you have come, how much sacrifice you have made, and how you have juggled 10 different things in your life through the Olympics. I wouldn't have believed it possible. The past three years has been an amazing effort, and you should be very proud of that effort most of all.

H: Here comes the roller coaster! You'll have me crying again. Thanks, Sean. I appreciate all you have done.

SM: Thanks for letting me a part of your team. It has been a blast. See you next month?

H: You bet.

SM: Have fun at closing ceremonies, Heidi. You've earned it.

Closing ceremonies, as the name implies, do offer a measure of closure. I also attended the ceremonies, and as exhausted as I was, I did have a lot of fun. As previously noted, sport psychologists need closure, too.

REFERENCES

Beck, A., Rush, J., Shaw, B., & Emery, G. (1979). *Cognitive theory of depression.* New York: Guilford Press.

Ellis, A. (1962). *Reason and emotion in psychotherapy.* New York: Lyle Stuart.

Mahoney, M.J. (1991). *Human change processes: The scientific foundations of psychotherapy.* New York: Basic Books.

Meichenbaum, D. (1977). *Cognitive behavior modification.* New York: Plenum.

APPENDIX

Coaching Behaviors: Self Rating Form

Step One: Make a list of coaching behaviors that are critical for your best performance as a coach in competition (These are your behaviors, not the behaviors of your athletes. For example, Olympic coaches have listed behaviors such as "delegating less vital jobs to assistants," "maintaining composure under stress," "maintaining a personal exercise program," "taking risks at big competitions when appropriate, "effectively motivating each athlete," as critical to success as an Olympic coach.)

1. ______________________________
2. ______________________________
3. ______________________________
4. ______________________________
5. ______________________________
6. ______________________________
7. ______________________________
8. ______________________________
9. ______________________________
10. ______________________________
11. ______________________________
12. ______________________________
13. ______________________________
14. ______________________________
15. ______________________________

Step Two: Choose the 10 most important behaviors for coaching success in your sport. Put a checkmark next to these items and rate yourself on each, using a 1-10 scale (1 = I never behave this way; this is a tremendously underdeveloped skill. 10 = I consistently behave this way; this is a very well-developed, almost automatic skill for me.)

Step Three: Based on your personal results, write down two behaviors you are skilled in using but normally don't give yourself credit for (coaching strengths to maintain) and two behaviors that are a personal challenge for you (coaching behaviors to develop.)

Coaching strengths to maintain:

1) ______________________________

2) ______________________________

Coaching behaviors to develop:

1) ______________________________

2) ______________________________

CHAPTER 16

DOING SPORT PSYCHOLOGY WITH INJURED ATHLETES

Gregory S. Kolt
Auckland University of Technology

Rehabilitation of injured athletes is increasingly becoming a multifaceted process. Injured athletes are seeking rehabilitation input not only from physicians and physical therapists but also from other health care providers (e.g., podiatrists, dietitians, sport psychologists, masseurs, exercise scientists, and athletic trainers). It is not uncommon for a variety of rehabilitation providers to work with professional or elite sports teams, allowing injured athletes access to a range and combination of services to facilitate their rehabilitation. The majority of athletes, however, do not fall into the professional or elite category and have restricted access to a variety of health care personnel—including sport psychologists. For this reason, it is important to evaluate the role that nonpsychologist rehabilitation personnel (e.g., physical therapists, athletic therapists, athletic trainers, and sports physicians) can play in addressing the psychological aftereffects of injury.

The purpose of this chapter is to outline the type and extent of psychological and counseling interactions that physical therapists can undertake with injured athletes, to discuss athletes' and physical therapists' perceptions of the role of physical therapists in dealing with psychosocial aspects of injury, and to outline briefly the use of cognitive-behavioral techniques that can be integrated into rehabilitation programs. Also, I have included a short section dealing with the relationship between physical therapists and athletes, with particular reference to touch. Finally, the majority of the chapter will be dedicated to the dialogue between a physical therapist and an athlete who was undergoing extensive long-term rehabilitation for a knee injury. The issues raised in this case study, and the commentary on the dialogue, illustrate the integration of sport psychology with other aspects of the rehabilitation process. The case study also highlights the point that sport psychology should not be viewed as something separate from physical therapy but rather as part of the overall delivery of rehabilitation services. See Shaffer and Wiese-Bjornstal (1999) and Wiese-Bjornstal, Gardetto, and Shaffer (1999) for further discussion of the integration of psychological and physical care of athletes in sports medicine settings.

ROLE OF THE PHYSICAL THERAPIST

Athletic trainers may be the primary health care professionals who deal with injured athletes in North America (Larson, Starkey, & Zaichkowsky, 1996). Further, according to several researchers (e.g., Tuffey, 1991; Wiese & Weiss, 1987; Wiese, Weiss, & Yukelson, 1991), sports medicine professionals and athletic trainers are in the best position to address the psychological aspects of injury with athletes. In other regions of the world (e.g., Australia, the United Kingdom), where an athletic trainer is a relatively unknown entity, physical therapists (called *physiotherapists* in British Commonwealth countries) are seen as the primary caregivers to injured athletes (Francis, Andersen, & Maley, 2000; Gordon, Milios, & Grove, 1991). For the purpose of this chapter, references made to the role of physical therapists in dealing with the psychosocial aspects of injury rehabilitation also apply to other similar groups of rehabilitation providers. For example, if athletic trainers read this chapter, they should mentally substitute the words *athletic trainer* every time they read *physical therapist.*

Rehabilitation researchers have suggested that physical therapists and athletic trainers can use psychological techniques with athletes to facilitate recovery and rehabilitation from injury (Gordon, Potter, & Ford, 1998; Kolt, 1996, 1998; Kolt & Kirkby, 1996; Shaffer & Wiese-Bjornstal, 1999; Wiese-Bjornstal & Smith, 1993). For example, Gordon et al. (1998) reported that those sport injury rehabilitation personnel "in regular contact with athletes during treatment are in an ideal position to inform, educate, and assist with the psychological as well as physical sequelae of injury" (p. 141). Gordon et al. further recommended that such rehabilitation providers receive specific education to prepare them for these tasks, a suggestion Wiese-Bjornstal and Smith also supported.

Gordon et al. (1991) found, in a study of physical therapists, that most of them could see the importance of addressing the psychological aspects of injury. A large majority of therapists, however, reported that they were limited in their ability to deal with the psychosocial aspects of the recovery process and desired further practical training in this area. In a related study, Pearson and Jones (1992) reported that injured athletes believed physical therapists and other health care providers had not consciously considered the emotional effects of their injuries. Despite that fact, Pearson and Jones' findings also suggested that physical therapists are the members of the health care team best equipped to help with the emotional aspects of sport-related injury.

In some circumstances, however, athletes are reluctant to seek counseling to help them cope with injury. Some athletes may view help seeking as a sign of weakness and would rather suffer the consequences of a problematic rehabilitation than request formal psychological assistance. It therefore appears logical to combine aspects of psychological counseling with the physical modalities of rehabilitation. This suggestion was supported by one of the athletes interviewed by Pearson and Jones (1992): "If you could combine the two skills [physical therapy and psychology] and, while treating, actually talk to them [athletes] and explain the psychological situation, it would put their mind a lot more at rest." (p. 767). In summary, it appears that both physical therapists and athletes feel that psychological interventions alongside the physical aspects of rehabilitation would be of benefit to the overall rehabilitation process.

PHYSICAL THERAPISTS' PERCEPTIONS

In the last decade, four studies examined physical therapists' and athletic trainers' perceptions of their roles in providing psychological intervention as part of rehabilitation programs (Francis et al., 2000; Larson et al., 1996; Ninedek, 1998; Wiese et al., 1991). The two studies that focused on physical therapists (Francis et al., 2000; Ninedek, 1998) used the survey instrument Wiese et al. (1991) developed. The studies had similar findings.

Physical therapists distinguished athletes who were coping well with their injuries from those who were coping less successfully by the following characteristics: willingness to listen to the physical therapist, positive attitude, intrinsic motivation, and willingness to learn about injury mechanisms and rehabilitation techniques. In addition, physical therapists indicated that the most effective tools for helping athletes cope psychologically with injury were good interpersonal/communication skills, a realistic timeline to full recovery, an understanding of rehabilitation strategies on the athlete's part, and coach support. The most important strategies for physical therapists in dealing with injured athletes were setting realistic goals, having a positive and sincere communication style, understanding individual motivation, and understanding stress and anxiety.

Much of what these results come down to is having a good bedside manner (e.g., solid communication skills, informing the athlete of procedures, sensitivity to what the athlete is going through). The National Athletic Trainers' Association (NATA) supports physical therapists and athletic trainers in providing basic counseling and psychological intervention. In North America, any athletic trainer who is certified by the NATA is expected to possess certain Athletic Training Educational Competencies (NATA, 1999), one category of which relates to psychosocial intervention and referral (see end of chapter). Reading the competencies, it is apparent that athletic trainers in North America are expected to be quite sophisticated in matters concerning psychological interventions (they should be capable of delivering motivational, stress-reducing, and imagery techniques to rehabilitating athletes), recognition of psychological disturbances (e.g., eating disorders, substance abuse, depression), and referral processes. Ideally, athletic trainers (and physical therapists) would meet all the NATA competencies, but currently, it is questionable how well such competencies are met.

Physical therapists need to recognize what their limitations are, and they should be aware of the boundaries of practice when providing psychological help to athletes during rehabilitation. It is important that physical therapists evaluate their experience and formal qualifications and be able to identify situations in which it would be appropriate to refer athletes to other suitably qualified professionals (e.g., clinical or sport psychologists).

ATHLETE–PHYSICAL THERAPIST RELATIONSHIP

Touch is a very powerful means of communication, and in physical therapy it is a central feature of many modes of treatment (MacWhannell, 1992). It would be extremely difficult to provide certain types of rehabilitation therapy (e.g., soft-tissue techniques, mobilization, manipulation, stretching) from a distance. Using touch for communication (and treatment) is commonplace in sport. For example, wrestling involves direct bodily contact between participants for prolonged periods of time. Further, it is not uncommon for coaches to use touch with athletes in the form of manual guidance of body parts to either teach new skills or to refine existing techniques (e.g., gymnastics, figure skating, ballet). Several other sports (e.g., football, rugby) involve body contact with opponents through tackling. Some people may feel inhibited by being touched in physical treatment, whereas touch helps others relax and frees up emotions (Nathan, 1999). It is likely that for most athletes touch is caring and comforting and is seen as an integral part of the culture of sport. Touch places the physical therapist and the client in a potentially closer relationship than that established in some psychotherapies.

Injured athletes, already in an intimate situation during physical treatment, may open up more to physical therapists than to some other health care providers. Several techniques used in physical therapy (e.g., craniosacral therapy) often result in emotional release (Upledger, 1990). As just mentioned, given the intimacy of physical therapy, athletes may feel that the relationship between themselves and their physical therapists allows self-disclosure of their thoughts and feelings. These self-disclosures may be directly related to the injury itself (e.g., concerns regarding returning to their former sporting level, fear of reinjury), or they may stem from other personal factors that could be affecting the athletes' progress in rehabilitation (e.g., relationship issues, school issues). Such factors arise routinely in physical therapy and need to be addressed, discussed, and possibly resolved by the athlete with the help of the treating practitioner. Being equipped and prepared to work with the emotional and cognitive issues of athletes in rehabilitation is a question of education, experience, and a sober appraisal of one's competencies. Books such as *Psychology of Sport Injury* (Heil, 1993), *Psychological Bases of Sport Injuries* (Pargman, 1998) and *Psychological Approaches to Sports Injury Rehabilitation* (Taylor & Taylor, 1997) are useful sources of information for practitioners wishing to expand their understanding of injury and rehabilitation.

Confidentiality in counseling injured athletes deserves a special mention. There is no reason for physical therapists to treat psychological issues any differently from other aspects of rehabilitation. Physical therapists have essentially the same standards of confidentiality as psychologists. In sport rehabilitation settings, however, the physical environment in which interaction takes place may be quite open and public. Physical therapists commonly work with athletes in team training or warm-up rooms. Even when athletes are being treated one-on-one by a physical therapist in a clinic setting, often a number of people will be in the same rehabilitation area at that time. If athletes do raise issues in discussion that require a further level of confidentiality, physical therapists might suggest that discussion continue in a different location (e.g., "If you'd like, we could talk about this further in my office when you've finished your exercises").

In summary, it appears that there are four main factors indicating reasons for physical therapists to use basic counseling and psychological techniques when dealing with injured athletes. First, because physical therapists generally spend longer periods of time with injured athletes than many other members of the health care team, athletes may be more likely to raise psychological issues with them during the rehabilitation period than with other health care professionals. Second, the level of relationship established between athletes and their physical therapists (with the use of touch) is conducive to athletes opening up about other psychosocial issues, so it would be beneficial to deal with these concerns at the time of rehabilitation, particularly if the issues are affecting the recovery progress. Third, because of the psychological aftereffects of athletic injury, it appears reasonable that such issues are discussed concurrently with the physical aspects of rehabilitation so as to maximize both the psychological and physical rehabilitation processes. Finally, according to the research reviewed in the preceding text, injured athletes believe that physical therapists are in an ideal position to provide them with basic psychological services. This belief merits attention because of the reluctance of some athletes to seek formal psychological help during injury rehabilitation.

In some circumstances (e.g., elite sports programs, professional sports teams), however, sport psychologists are part of the support staff for athletes. In these cases, physical therapists and sport psychologists should work coherently as a team. With the athlete's consent, the physical therapist can discuss rehabilitation progress issues (e.g., difficulties in goal setting, concerns about the athlete's ability to step up to the next level of rehabilitation) with the psychologist so that appropriate counseling and psychological interventions can be implemented. Sport psychologists can also help teach cognitive rehearsal when athletes are retraining movement patterns for sport skills. Physical therapists, therefore, should be aware that if sport psychologists are available, and if athletes are willing to involve them in the rehabilitation process, all parties can work together toward the best possible outcome.

A final note before the case study: I am both a state-registered psychologist and a physical therapist (in Australia). Thus, I am *not* typical of most physical therapists who treat athletes. In the following case study, I delivered both psychological and physical treatment to the gymnast under my care. Please read the case study as an example of the most efficient marriage of physical treatment and psychological care. Keep in mind, however, that in many cases the types of services presented would be delivered by two professionals working in close cooperation.

CASE STUDY

This case study highlights the relationship between an injured athlete and her physical therapist. The physical therapist provides counseling as part of the rehabilitation program, and the athlete is not seeking any psychological intervention outside of her professional relationship with the physical therapist.

SESSION 4

Rebecca is a 16-year-old gymnast who is seeing a physical therapist for rehabilitation of an anterior cruciate ligament reconstruction. Her injury occurred when she landed awkwardly from the uneven bars in a training session two weeks prior to the National Championships (a selection meet for national team places). Rebecca is on the state team, and she had been training 30 hours per week prior to the injury.

Rebecca underwent reconstructive surgery of her knee two days after the injury. Immediately following the injury, she had been seen by a physician at a sports medicine clinic who had referred her on the same day to see an orthopedic surgeon. Both medical practitioners had clearly diagnosed an isolated anterior cruciate ligament rupture and had recommended immediate arthroscopic reconstruction surgery. After an overnight stay in the hospital following the surgery, Rebecca was discharged with crutches to use and was referred for physical therapy rehabilitation. The physical therapy was to begin four days after the operation. Her physical therapist worked closely with other members of the state and national gymnastics team and had treated Rebecca on several occasions for relatively minor injuries.

Rebecca had already attended three physical therapy sessions over the preceding 10 days. It was not until the third session (two days before) that Rebecca began to hint to the physical therapist that there were psychological issues that were concerning her. It was also at this session that the physical therapist had identified certain potential behavioral or psychological aftereffects that he felt could affect Rebecca's rehabilitation process and eventual return to sport.

Physical Therapist (PT): Good morning, Rebecca. How are you going with all those exercises we went through a couple of days ago?

Rebecca (R): Well, I have been doing them as regularly as possible. It hasn't quite been the three times each day that you recommended, but I've just found it difficult with all my teammates visiting at home all the time to see how I am getting along. I haven't been able to find the time with all of that and trying to keep up with the schoolwork that I'm meant to finish before I go back [to school] next week.

PT: That's quite thoughtful of all your gym buddies to keep an eye on you. They obviously have been thinking about you a lot.

R: Well, they really are good friends, but in a way it does get a bit annoying. I suppose that they mean well by visiting, but in some ways it just keeps on reminding me about the injury and the fact that I can't do gym like them at the moment. Also, some of them have just gone to nationals, which also hurts me. I really wish that I could be back in training again.

PT: How does it annoy you?

R: All of them are quite curious about my knee. They keep asking whether I am in pain, how far I can move the knee, and when I can start back at the gym again, and they think that I was quite lucky because I had a week off school after the operation. I just get really sick of all the questions they keep asking. I feel that in some ways I just want to be at home by myself and forget that the injury ever happened.

PT: I'm not surprised that you think that. I've seen a lot of people in your situation, including some gymnasts, who also in this early stage of rehabilitation just want to stop thinking about the injury. Your teammates probably haven't been in your situation and don't realize that. Would you have preferred that they didn't come to see you?

R: No, not really.

PT: Why do you say that?

R: I don't know. It's hard to say. I think that if they hadn't come to see me, I'd probably be quite annoyed that they weren't thinking about me and that they'd forgotten that I even exist.

It is clear that Rebecca is concerned about certain aspects of her injury, and in particular, the continued focus that she is being encouraged to have on her knee. It is also evident that she is quite at ease talking about these issues with the physical therapist. Their relationship is at the point where Rebecca feels the physical therapist is a safe person to talk to, first about her annoyances, and possibly later about more serious personal concerns. To avoid losing the momentum of the initial dialogue, but also to ensure that Rebecca does not see this session as simply an attempt on his part to dabble in the psychological aspects of the injury, the physical therapist starts the physical aspects of the rehabilitation session while continuing to talk to Rebecca about her concerns.

PT: Kind of leaves you with mixed feelings . . . so let's start with a look at how your knee is progressing, and we'll keep on chatting as I start mobilizing it.

At this point, when the athlete is beginning to question some of the psychological consequences of her injury, the physical therapist's careful use of language helps to both build Rebecca's self-confidence and establish the working alliance. Note the use of the phrase "let's start with a look at how your knee is progressing," which indicates to the athlete that the physical therapist believes the rehabilitation is progressing, not stagnating. Also, the physical therapist's transition from talking to the patient to getting on with other aspects of the rehabilitation session (i.e., "and we'll keep on chatting as I start mobilizing it") indicates that he places importance on both talking and rehabilitation. The expressions "let's" and "we" are hallmarks of working alliance language and let the athlete know that what is going on is a collaborative effort, both physically and psychologically. The session does not simply change from counseling to the physical aspects of rehabilitation; the physical therapist's language indicates to the athlete that he is willing to take on a counseling role and that it will be incorporated into the normal physical therapy rehabilitation.

The physical therapist has now begun to assess and treat Rebecca's knee and recommences the dialogue that they had left off with a few minutes previously.

PT: So, how you are feeling about your knee?

R: Well, I suppose that I'm a bit annoyed at myself for hurting the knee. I didn't realize it until one of my closest friends from my team said that it was a pity that I hurt my knee on a trick I usually do so well. I mean, I always land that dismount well. It would have made more sense if it had happened on a skill that I was just learning or a move that I wasn't confident about. Bars is usually my best event.

PT: Yes, I remember you got a third place on bars at nationals last year. I think you were just coming off a sprained ankle at the time and hadn't done any dismounts for about a week before that meet. I remember you telling me that you were really concerned that you wouldn't even be allowed to compete at nationals because you hadn't done any dismounts or tumbling for two weeks.

R: You've got a good memory!

PT: Thanks. You've got a history of bouncing back. You proved that to yourself last year, didn't you?

R: I can see what you mean, but there is a bit of a difference between an ankle sprain and a knee job. People always get better from ankle sprains, but I know of two other gymnasts who quit because of their knees. One tried to get back into it about a year later, but blew her knee out again. The other moved on to diving.

A few critical issues have come out here. The first point is that by talking to the athlete about her concerns while working on her knee, the physical therapist is able to distract her from feeling the discomfort associated with some of the mobilizing techniques. This distraction approach is quite useful in managing pain during rehabilitation. It is often not until the physical therapist stops talking that the athlete notices any major discomfort from the treatment techniques. This distraction, however, should be used carefully, because quite often we require feedback on pain from the athlete to monitor and modify the techniques we are using. The second point is that the physical therapist attempted to use the outcomes of the athlete's past experience (i.e., the ankle sprain) to build up her feelings of self-efficacy in relation to the current situation. In this case, the athlete outlined the disparity between the two injuries and chose to focus on other knee injuries that fellow gymnasts had incurred and the perceived less-than-desirable outcomes that she remembered. In this situation, the physical therapist should remind the athlete of other gymnasts who did have a successful return to gymnastics after major knee injuries.

In this section of dialogue, the physical therapist has, in several ways, contributed again to building the working alliance with Rebecca: First, he has shown Rebecca that she is viewed as more than an injured knee; second, he has indicated that he knows her history well (a message that he cares about her enough to follow her career, not just her injuries); and finally, he has shown a sincere interest in her injury and future return to sport. This feeling of being cared for and having someone concerned about her is itself therapeutic for Rebecca. The physical therapist, also, in this case, is being a bit of a cheerleader, saying that he thinks she can do it. Rebecca's focus on the negative, however, may be indicativ1e of a substantial fear for her future as a gymnast.

PT: I can understand your worries about getting back into gymnastics. I've seen a lot of these injuries, but with the advances in surgery in the past 10 years, most athletes are now getting back to their sports. A number of years ago, you would have been in a plaster cast for a few weeks following this type of injury. But you'll be off those crutches by the end of this week and riding an exercise bike and getting a good workout within two more weeks. All you have to do is watch footy [Australian rules football] on TV, and you'll see a bunch of players who have had similar operations. I know several gymnasts who have had successful returns to elite-level competition. You remember Jacqui W., who was on the national team a couple of years ago? Well, she had a similar injury to yours, and after 10 months she was back into full training and on the state team.

R: I know, I know . . . It's just that I had so much hope of making the national team this year, and my coach was all for it. If I had made it, she probably would have been selected as [national] assistant coach. Usually, when a coach has a gymnast on the team, they get to be an assistant to the head coach. In a way, I may have been her only chance of making it to nationals.

Here, the athlete acknowledges that she should be able to get back into her sport, but she is also negating the effects of this positive point by expressing guilt regarding her coach. It is important to keep the momentum going on the positive outcome and not to deal with too many issues at one time. After all, the physical therapist should be primarily focusing on the physical aspects of rehabilitation while helping the athlete cope with the injury and rehabilitation. Dealing with Rebecca's guilt may take some further thought and a discussion with a psychologist supervisor. The rehabilitation will be a long one, and discussing her guilt may or may not be necessary. For now the physical therapist will keep Rebecca's relationship with her coach in the back of his mind.

At this point in the session, the physical therapist gets the athlete to go through her exercise routine, and no further direct dialogue on behavioral or psychological aspects of the injury takes place. As the athlete is leaving the clinic, the physical therapist briefly summarizes what Rebecca has achieved today.

PT: Well, I'll see you again in three days. You really have done well today. Both your strength and range of movement are improving ahead of plan. When you're doing your exercises over the next few days, just think about some of the things that we talked about today, as I really feel that you're the type of person who has the ability to get back into gymnastics at the same level you were.

Leaving the session on this note has achieved several goals. First, it has encouraged the self-efficacy of the athlete. Second, it has indicated to the athlete that it has been her hard work and efforts that have got her to improve so well to date. Third, it has indicated to the athlete that she has the ability to rehabilitate the injury successfully and return to gymnastics. These comments to the athlete also encourage an internal locus of control, placing less emphasis on the role of the physical therapist (dependency fostering), a problem common in the rehabilitation of long-term athletic injuries. The athlete in this session was fairly negative at times but was challenged by the therapist through reframing (regarding the other athletes' visits; would she really not want them to care so much?) and giving positive examples (countering her examples of athletes who did not come back after surgery with many athletes who have). Each time the athlete was brought around. If negative thinking is recalcitrant to change, however, and reframing does not move the athlete to a more positive attitude, then the negative outlook will need to be addressed and processed. For Rebecca, reframing/reconstructing was all that was needed. With a more negative or depressed athlete, reframing may not work, and the negative emotional reactions would probably need attention and exploration before the athlete could move on to a more positive outlook.

SESSION 5

During the assessment of Rebecca's knee strength and range of movement, the physical therapist noted that she was in more pain than she had been three days previously and that there was slightly more swelling than had been evident in her last session.

PT: How have you been going with your work at home, Rebecca?

R: I've generally been going well, but I have noticed it hurts more when I do the exercises. It could be that I am doing extra exercises.

PT: What do you mean by "extra"?

R: Well, I thought a lot about what we were talking about last time and got really fired up. I decided that I would give it everything I have and work as hard as I can to get back. I suppose I came to my senses and decided that the only way to get over this knee thing is to work as hard as I can. I've been doing the exercises a couple more times each day, and I think that it was this extra work that made it a bit worse.

At this point, the physical therapist should chastise himself for not having made crystal clear to Rebecca that she was to do *only* the amount of home exercise prescribed, and no more. Aside from that omission, some significant changes have taken place with the athlete since their last session. On the positive side, Rebecca has come to terms with the injury and feels she is the one who can control its outcome by the amount of effort she puts into her rehabilitation. Further, she has set herself an important long-term goal of getting back to her former level of gymnastics. Although these decisions augur well for Rebecca's progress, there are also some negative aspects to her strong resolve. First, she appears to have misinterpreted the way in which to progress with her rehabilitation. This misunderstanding is seen in her statement, "I've been doing the exercises a couple more times each day." It must be made clear to the athlete at this stage that she should be working hard, but within the guidelines that the physical therapist has given her. It is not uncommon for some athletes to overadhere to rehabilitation protocols and to perform too much work and exercise at different stages of the rehabilitation process. Many athletes subscribe to the "no gain without pain" edict. Rebecca's views on rehabilitation should also be corrected at this stage because pain can indicate worsening or aggravation of signs and symptoms. Omitting some ground rules and lessons about rehabilitation was the physical therapist's error. Fortunately, Rebecca's misconceptions were caught early.

PT: Well, you really have to be careful about how much you do with the knee at the moment. Being so early on, the knee is still at a great risk of being aggravated. What you have to focus on is doing the exercises as best you can but within the guidelines that I give you, exactly as you have been doing until now. If you perform the exercises correctly, you will get the maximum benefit from them. There is no real need to do them a greater number of times than on your rehabilitation sheet, and your increase in exercise might have caused that extra swelling and pain. You will find that the pain will probably settle down within a day or two, so don't be too worried about it. We're going to move to the next stage of the rehabilitation program at the start of next week anyway, so you'll have a lot more to do at home then.

R: Sorry, it's just I'm getting so bored. I'm used to spending 30 hours a week in the gym, and all of a sudden I'm not there anymore. I need to do something with that time, so I thought increasing my rehab would be a good idea.

PT: I can understand what you're saying, and a lot of athletes I treat for the same injury tell me exactly the same thing. What I usually get them to do at your stage is go into the gym to do their exercises. It's a bit more interesting than doing them at home. I know you've got most of the equipment that you need in there, and by doing it that way you might feel more part of the team. How does that sound?

R: I'm not really sure. I haven't actually been back there since I blew my knee out. I don't really know how that would feel, but it would be nice to see all the girls again.

PT: Next week I'm going to get you going on some more dynamic rehab such as the exercise bike and some wobble board work; you could quite easily do that in the gym and at the same time get back into your upper-body conditioning and stretching program. Do you want to talk to the coach about it?

R: I'd like it if you could talk to her about it first, because I want to make sure that I'm not going to be in the way. You know, I don't just want to be hanging around.

PT: I'd be happy to give her a call and organize it all with her. I might even see if she can come down to the clinic with you at some stage so that all of us together can go through the work that you can be doing in the gym. In a way, she could supervise that part of the rehab you do in the gym, and I can keep an eye on you here. She can always call me here if she is unsure of what you are meant to be doing. What do you think of that?

R: It'll be kinda weird going back to the gym, but it would be great being back with the team.

An important part of rehabilitation from long-term injuries has now been established in the dialogue; that is, the support of team members and the coach. In the past few weeks, Rebecca has gone from training in the gym with teammates and coaches for up to 30 hours per week to a situation where she has had only minimal contact. This change in contact can be a difficult adjustment for injured athletes. Encouraging Rebecca to return to the gym and agreeing to involve the coach as an integral assistant to the rehabilitation process may give her a sense of returning to normality.

Rebecca's comment about talking to her coach, "I'd like it if you could talk to her . . . make sure I am not going to be in the way" probably indicates that her guilt about disappointing the coach is still strong and that she is reluctant about even talking to her. The physical therapist recognized that and was willing to help her out of an anxiety-provoking task.

At this stage in the session, the physical therapist returned to dealing with the physical aspects of the rehabilitation session using communication aimed to enhance self-efficacy and to give the athlete a better sense of control over the outcome of her injury.

SESSION 10

This rehabilitation session took place approximately two weeks after Rebecca had increased her rehabilitation program. She had been carrying out aspects of her program three times per week in the gym.

PT: Hi Rebecca; how are you feeling today?

R: I'm going really well, and I can really feel my knee getting stronger. I think I trust it more. I don't even feel that I am limping or favoring it anymore.

PT: That's great. Let's start by putting the muscle stims machine on the leg to get that medial quadricep contracting a bit better, and then I want to hear how you've been going with your workouts at the gym.

Note that the physical therapist has referred to Rebecca's rehabilitation (under the supervision of her coach) at the gym as a *workout*. The word has been used intentionally to equate it (in terminology) to the gymnastic workouts that others are doing. This simple choice of words can serve the purpose of suggesting to the gymnast that the type of work she is doing at the gym is equally as important as a usual gymnastics workout, and it is preferable to referring to the athlete's work as rehabilitation exercises, injury exercises, or alternate training tasks.

In usual physical therapy rehabilitation, there is ample time to discuss psychosocial issues with athletes. At various times, the physical therapist may be applying soft-tissue massage techniques to the athlete, or the athlete may be receiving some form of treatment from an electromedical machine. These times should not be wasted but rather used to open the door for the athlete to talk about whatever is on her mind. It can also be a time to present cognitive-behavioral skills.

R: Things have been going really well. Some of my gym buddies have commented that if they saw me walking down the street or riding the bike they wouldn't even know that I had recently had a knee operation.

The moving of some of the rehabilitation program to the gym has been beneficial for Rebecca in her outlook to getting back on track.

R: I'm getting so into the bike work, the wobble board, and my sport-tube stuff that I find my mind just wandering. Before I know it, I'm sweatin' and feel like I've worked really hard.

At this stage, the physical therapist should note that the physical exercises are going well, and that Rebecca is seeing the benefit from them. One approach that the physical therapist (in combination with the coach) might take would be to encourage Rebecca to use the time when her mind is "just wandering" for some form of cognitive rehearsal of skills. Rebecca will need these skills when she returns to her usual gymnastics training. It is helpful to introduce such skills in a way that helps the athlete see their benefits and potential and to involve the coach further in this aspect of rehabilitation. After all, the coach should have input into which skills would be most appropriate to rehearse cognitively.

PT: I'm really pleased to hear that you're getting so much out of your gym workouts. It is very important that those sessions support the work that we are doing together here in the clinic. Generally speaking, one without the other is not the best recipe for a successful rehab. Your coach actually rang me this morning and mentioned how pleased she was with your progress. I told her that I also think you are going really well. We decided that you could use your time even better if we got you to start to practice some of your skills mentally by visualizing them. In a way, it's an approach that you can use to prepare yourself for when you start doing some of your gymnastic tricks again. How does that sound?

R: I used to do that before competition, but I don't know whether I was doing it correctly.

PT: It's great that you have used it before. Your coach and I were thinking that the ideal time for you to do it would be when you are doing long sets of exercises, riding the exercise bike, or doing your stretching and conditioning on the floor. You know, those times when you mentioned that your mind just wanders. We might as well use that time for something that prepares you for later.

R: Yeah, sounds great to me. I'm kind of worried about being able to do all the stuff I did before. What's the best way to do visualization?

PT: Well, as I'm working out some of that tightness in your hamstring muscles in a few minutes, I'll talk to you about it. I can also give you a videotape to take home that talks about visualization and mental practice as well. That should start you off, but make sure you talk to your coach about it next time you're at the gym. She told me that she has used this technique with quite a few other gymnasts and was going to work out the best skills for you to start on. I know that when I used to do gymnastics I found visualization really useful.

If the physical therapist is to sell the techniques of visualization and mental rehearsal to the athlete as important parts of the rehabilitation program, he must give them credibility. This credibility has been established in three ways. First, the athlete reported that she had used the technique before. Second, the coach believes in the value of using this technique with other athletes. Finally, the physical therapist, by using some self-disclosure regarding his own prior gymnastic career, identified with Rebecca and also suggested to her that the technique had been helpful for him. The latter two of these ways might convince the gymnast that if powerful others (i.e., the coach and the physical therapist) have personally used the technique before, then it must be a useful skill to try. Many physical therapists may not know about, or value, imagery (cf. Francis et al., 2000). Consultation with (or referral to) a sport psychologist to help the athlete develop imagery exercises and hone imagery skills might be the best way to proceed.

SESSION 25

At this stage, Rebecca was four months post-injury and had been progressing with the physical aspects of her rehabilitation at a rate slightly quicker than expected. Her orthopedic surgeon and physical therapist were happy with her strength, range of motion, and other knee functions. It had been decided that Rebecca could now begin some light weight-bearing gymnastic elements and work on her bars skills (avoiding any dismounts) as well. This decision was made in a four-way meeting with Rebecca, the coach, the physical therapist, and the orthopedic surgeon. Specific guidelines were given as to the extent of work allowed.

Further, in the past two months, in addition to Rebecca's physical therapy rehabilitation, she had been focusing on her mental rehearsal skills (see chapter 6 on imagery in this volume for more information on working with mental rehearsal), improving her self-efficacy regarding returning to gymnastics (through the general communication between herself and the physical therapist), and goal setting. Specifically, the goal setting incorporated a series of weekly rehabilitation and workout goals, goals in relation to beginning some actual gymnastics training, and her major goals of returning to competitive gymnastics at the state team level. Physical therapy rehabilitation decreased to once a week (her progress was assessed at these sessions), and exercise and physical activity routines gradually increased. This decreased contact between the physical therapist and the athlete meant that the athlete had to take on further responsibility, in combination with her coach, for her own rehabilitation.

PT: How's it all going at the moment, Rebecca, now that you have begun to swing a bit on bars and work out on some of your floor routines?

R: I tell you what, it was certainly a bit scary when I first started on bars again. I really felt tight and rigid. I couldn't relax even on the simple stuff. All I could think about was dismounting and blowing my knee out again. And I'm not even doing dismounts at the moment.

PT: What was it like when you were up on the bars?

R: Well, I can't really lie. I have actually swung a bit on bars in the past month, when the coach was out of the gym, but just really simple stuff. It didn't worry me at all then. But now that I know I can start training some of my old tricks again, I feel that the pressure is suddenly on. I just keep thinking of falling off onto that darn knee of mine. Last night when I was training, one of my hands actually slipped off when I was swinging. I was lucky that I managed to save the fall and didn't put any pressure on my knee. My heart wouldn't stop racing, and I found it really difficult to get back on there.

PT: I can understand how difficult that must have been for you. Did you manage to do more bars in that training session?

R: I did some more, but not as much as I had set out to do. In one way, I didn't really know whether the coach was angry with me or not. She just didn't say anything about it. I felt she was angry with me for doing such a stupid thing.

PT: Why do you think your coach would have been angry with you?

R: I don't know. It's just that she didn't say anything. I keep blaming myself and imagining that she thought I was a loser because I fell off on such a simple trick. I have seen her get angry sometimes when we mess up easy moves.

At this point, the physical therapist realizes that the athlete is having trouble focusing on gymnastic skills. In a sport such as gymnastics, where concentration and focus are central features of safety (particularly with the athlete's knee at the stage it is), it is useful to address skills that can help the gymnast to improve her ability to concentrate on the task at hand. In addition, the gymnast has interpreted the coach's reaction to her fall from the bars in a negative way. That is, the gymnast has given herself some negative self-talk with the statement, "I keep blaming myself and imagining that she thought I was a loser because I fell off on such a simple trick." It could be that Rebecca is projecting her fear and guilt about disappointing the coach by interpreting her coach's reaction as a uncaring one. It is probable that the athlete has misinterpreted the coach's reaction and that there were a number of reasons for the coach's response.

PT: Let me take a look at that knee while we're talking just to check that it is all right. The fact that you're walking well and that there doesn't appear to be any swelling probably means that you've done no damage, anyway. Getting back to what you said a moment ago—knowing your coach, I don't believe that she'd think you were a loser for falling off. Are there any other reasons you can think of for why she might have just ignored the incident?

R: I don't really know. She would normally comment on something like that. I just think that she is losing interest in me as a gymnast. Maybe she doesn't believe that I'm good enough to get back into full training again or to make it onto the state team. Maybe she thinks that I'm too old to give it a good go at this stage.

It is clear that the athlete has not answered the question, "Are there any other reasons you can think of for why she might have just ignored the incident?" Instead, the athlete has further catastrophized (or overinterpreted) the incident and has immediately started to cast doubts over her abilities to achieve her goals. To bring the session back on track, the physical therapist tries to focus the gymnast on the question that was originally asked.

PT: Rebecca, tell me more about why you believe your coach ignored your fall. What makes you think she believes you're a loser?

R: Well, I suppose that one reason could be that she was thinking of other things at the time. Knowing her, she may have chosen not to make a big thing of it so that I wouldn't worry too much about it and so that the other girls wouldn't get concerned.

PT: By the sound of it, it was probably a pretty minor incident, something that happens all the time in a sport like gymnastics.

R: Yeah, I agree with you. Now that I think about it, people are having those minor slip-ups every day at training. I was just really worried about my knee, and I wanted her to comment in some way, at least to say that she saw it.

It appears that Rebecca really wants and needs the attention from her coach, particularly in light of her feelings that she has been a disappointment and is the reason the coach did not get an assistant's job with the national team.

PT: Maybe she is trying to give you a bit more independence in what you do at training and not look over you all the time as she did when you got back to the gym.

R: She normally does trust us older girls a lot. Quite often she'll ask us to coach the younger kids on some of the skills that they're learning, particularly the ones that we're good at. I'm probably just overreacting a bit because I'm really worried about my knee.

PT: What about your comments a few minutes ago about your coach not thinking you're good enough any more? It seemed she was really supportive of you returning to competition when we had that meeting with the orthopedic surgeon last week.

R: She *has* been really great. She could have just ignored me right throughout the knee injury like what happened to my friend who does figure skating. She had an awful time and really struggled to start training again. I always do this to myself. Whenever I get upset about something, I tell myself the worst and I just can't concentrate on anything. These negative things just stay in my head.

At this stage, the physical therapist has helped the athlete identify that she has some irrational beliefs regarding her coach's treatment of the falling incident. Further, with some guidance, the athlete was able to generate more rational beliefs or alternatives to the coach's response (or lack of response). The issue of Rebecca's guilt over disappointing her coach was never directly addressed but seemed to begin to resolve itself with her more rational approach to interpreting her coach's behavior. The positive thing was that Rebecca at least realized that she seemed to develop some negative self-talk and irrational beliefs about worrisome incidents. At this stage, the physical therapist wanted to get the athlete to use positive self-talk, coping statements, and self-instruction to achieve better concentration so she could focus on her gymnastic skills during training.

PT: It seems you're finding it hard to concentrate on your gymnastics tricks as you're practicing them. It's quite common for many of us to tell ourselves negative things in our heads, or use *negative self-talk* as we call it, when we're a bit uncertain of what we are doing. You're making some big steps here in getting back to gymnastics so soon after your knee reconstruction, and I can understand it if you are a bit anxious. One of the ways to approach it is that if you can focus your concentration onto the skill that you are about to perform, it usually distracts you from the anxiety you may be having. Sometimes things won't be all smooth sailing, and there are going to be some difficulties along the way to reaching your goals. For example, you interpreted that minor fall you had quite negatively. A different way of approaching that would have been to use what we call a *coping statement*. That is, you give yourself a message that says that you can cope with a particular problem. For example, you could have said to yourself, This fall was only a minor slip-up; I didn't hurt myself, and in the larger picture it's fairly insignificant. What do you think of that?

R: I've tried something like that, but the "you could have wrecked your knee" thoughts keep coming back.

PT: And they probably will for a while. It's mainly a question of practice, but I think a combination of your mental rehearsal and positive self-talk will eventually help your negative thinking.

R: I found that visualization worked well when I wasn't really training yet, but I've let it go in the past few weeks.

PT: Well, let's get back to it then. Probably the best way to do it is this: Before you get up on the bars, go through a couple of mental rehearsals of the skill you are about to do. It can certainly help you focus and block out the other thoughts trying to get into your mind. Another method that many other athletes use when they're having trouble concentrating is to give themselves a specific instruction to follow when they are about to do the skill. For example, what is one instruction that you could use if you were about to do a giant swing on the bars?

R: Oh, I don't know. I can't think of specific things like that.

PT: Well, what would be the instruction that your coach would normally give you before doing that trick? Why don't you shrink your coach down and imagine her sitting on your shoulder. What sort of instruction would she give you?

R: She would probably tell me to open my shoulder angle up as I reach the bottom of the swing.

PT: Perfect! There you go. There is the self-instruction that you have to concentrate on when doing that skill. Generally, by focusing on that instruction, you're less likely to get the unwanted thoughts distracting you during that skill.

R: I'll give it a shot.

In the course of this rehabilitation session, the physical therapist introduced the athlete to some methods of developing concentration to deal with the anxiety-related distractions that she was experiencing. Lapses in concentration, at this stage, could easily have led to reinjury of the knee. The orthopedic surgeon, the physical therapist, the coach, and Rebecca herself had agreed that she would return to gymnastics training activities slightly ahead of schedule. Thus, even more than usual, all measures to prevent reinjury were considered. In relation to the use of mental rehearsal, the physical therapist had the athlete apply the strategies she had used earlier in rehabilitation (for maintenance of skill level and building of self-efficacy) to a setting where it could help her focus and concentration.

In addition, using an imaginary miniature coach, as the therapist suggested, to help develop an appropriate self-instruction worked well for Rebecca. In many circumstances, particularly those that involve athletes who have elevated anxiety levels, distracting negative thoughts make it difficult for them to generate appropriate self-instructions. Without these appropriate self-instructions, anxiety can elevate further, making appropriate concentration elusive.

A further technique that may be useful to help an athlete concentrate when returning to sport is called *moment-for-moment,* sometimes referred to as *staying in present time*. This strategy encourages the athlete to focus only on the one task that she has to do at that point in time. That is, not to worry about things that she has already done (successfully or unsuccessfully) and not to worry about things that she has to do in the future.

PT: There is one more approach that I want to have a quick chat to you about that you may find useful in your training now. It is actually something that we used a lot of in the earlier stages of your knee rehabilitation. Do you remember back to when you were doing all those sets of ten quadriceps contractions? Initially, you told me that you found it really hard to get through them all, and you suggested that if you thought about doing only one set at a time it was more manageable than worrying about all the other sets you had to do after that. That's a great skill to use now that you're back at gym again. Just take one moment at a time.

R: I suppose that that would work pretty well for me, because last night I was specifically thinking about the fall on the bars when I was trying to swing later.

PT: So instead of thinking about what you don't want to do, like fall, you're thinking about what you need to do to perform well right now. It can work for you if you practice it and use it consistently. As we've discussed before, all of these mental skills are similar to physical skills that you learn. Once you've been introduced to them, they need practice before you get good at them. Then, if you want to use them in the more difficult times, you must be really good at them. Think back to when you were learning some of your harder gymnastics tricks. You tend to practice them to a level that allows you to do them consistently under the pressure situations such as competitions. If you aren't proficient at them, you may be able to perform them well in training, but in competition, they are harder. Does that make sense?

R: Yes, it does.

PT: And the bonus is that most of these skills you have developed over the past four months can be used for many aspects of your life. For example, it's not uncommon for people to get a bit anxious about exams at school. There's no reason why you couldn't use techniques such as the moment-for-moment at that stage and just take one question in the exam at the time. Or you could use the mental rehearsal to practice a presentation that you have to give in front of the class. It could certainly help you to focus on the talk and enhance your confidence in giving the presentation. It would actually be a good idea to practice these skills outside of your sport as well. That would make you more able to adapt the skills to a variety of situations.

R: I've got a big bio exam coming up; maybe I'll try some of these things for that.

The critical point just made to the athlete is that mental skills require just as much practice as physical skills. Many athletes have the misconception that because mental skills take place in the head, they should come naturally, and that practice is not necessary. It was also of value to expand the use of the mental skills to other areas of life. This expansion allowed the athlete to see wider applications, and therefore, greater reason to practice the skills to a high level. Given that many elite-level gymnasts are quite goal-driven, they are likely to take on a skill that they believe will give them an added edge and one that they can use to improve performance.

CONCLUSIONS

The foregoing dialogue and commentary illustrate that there are number of ways in which a physical therapist can begin to deal with some of the psychosocial aspects of the injury and rehabilitation process. Throughout the dialogue, one can see a gradual buildup of the athlete's trust in the physical therapist. This trust is an important factor if the athlete is to adhere to the advice on psychosocial issues touched upon in rehabilitation sessions. Also highlighted was the efficient use of time in rehabilitation sessions (especially in the earlier stages) to discuss concerns that the athlete may have and to put into action some of the basic cognitive-behavioral skills that can facilitate the overall recovery process and the return to sport.

The main emphasis of this case has been the importance of dealing with the psychosocial sequelae of injury at an early stage (or even proactively, prior to detection) and concurrently with the physical aspects of rehabilitation.

Discussing psychological concerns is a natural progression from the relationships built up between athletes and their physical therapists. Because of the long periods of time spent together, and with the use of touch as an integral part of physical rehabilitation, athletes may be more likely to self-disclose the psychological and behavioral concerns they have about their rehabilitation with their physical therapists than with some other rehabilitation providers. Physical therapists who feel they are not qualified to discuss personal psychological issues with their clients may wish to acquire some basic knowledge (see Heil, 1993; Pargman, 1998; Taylor & Taylor, 1997) and counseling skills through workshops, continuing education programs, and professional development seminars. Specifically, the Association for the Advancement of Applied Sport Psychology and Division 47 of the American Psychological Association offer seminars and workshops on aspects of mental skills every year. Physical therapy professional groups, along with athletic training associations, are becoming more and more sensitized to psychological issues in rehabilitation. It is likely that greater opportunities for education and training in mental skills for rehabilitation will appear at annual association meetings.

REFERENCES

Francis, S.R., Andersen, M.B., & Maley, P. (2000). Physiotherapists' and male professional athletes' views of psychological skills for rehabilitation. *Journal of Science and Medicine in Sport, 3,* 17-29.

Gordon, S., Milios, D., & Grove, J.R. (1991). Psychological aspects of the recovery process from sport injury: The perspective of sport physiotherapists. *Australian Journal of Science and Medicine in Sport, 23,* 53-60.

Gordon, S., Potter, M., & Ford, I.W. (1998). Toward a psychoeducational curriculum for training sport-injury rehabilitation personnel. *Journal of Applied Sport Psychology, 10,* 140-156.

Heil, J. (Ed.). (1993). *Psychology of sport injury.* Champaign, IL: Human Kinetics.

Kolt, G.S. (1996). Psychosocial factors and sports injury rehabilitation. *Australian Journal of Psychology, 48 (Suppl.),* 114.

Kolt, G.S. (1998). Psychological aspects of sports injury: Practical applications for rehabilitation. In S. Hniat (Ed.), *The scene through their eyes: Proceedings of the Fifth International Congress of the Australian Physiotherapy Association* (pp. 266-267). Hobart, Australia: Australian Physiotherapy Association (Tasmanian Branch).

Kolt, G.S., & Kirkby, R.J. (1996). Injury in Australian female gymnasts: A psychological perspective. *Australian Journal of Physiotherapy, 42,* 121-126.

Larson, G.A., Starkey, C., & Zaichkowsky, L.D. (1996). Psychological aspects of athletic injuries as perceived by athletic trainers. *The Sport Psychologist, 10,* 37-47.

MacWhannell, D.E. (1992). Communication in physiotherapy practice, I. In S. French (Ed.), *Physiotherapy: A psychosocial approach* (pp. 98-112). Oxford, England: Butterworth-Heinemann.

Nathan, B. (1999). *Touch and emotion in manual therapy.* London: Churchill Livingstone.

National Athletic Trainers' Association. (1999). *Athletic training educational competencies.* Dallas, TX: Author

Ninedek, A. (1998). *An investigation of sports physiotherapists' perceptions of the importance of psychological strategies in sports injury rehabilitation.* Unpublished honour's thesis, La Trobe University, Melbourne, Australia.

Pargman, D. (Ed.). (1998). *Psychological bases of sport injuries* (2nd ed.). Morgantown, WV: Fitness Information Technologies.

Pearson, L., & Jones, G. (1992). Emotional effects of sports injuries: Implications for physiotherapists. *Physiotherapy, 78,* 762-770.

Shaffer, S.M., & Wiese-Bjornstal, D.M. (1999). Psychosocial intervention strategies in sports medicine. In R. Ray & D.M. Wiese-Bjornstal (Eds.), *Counseling in sports medicine* (pp. 41-54). Champaign, IL: Human Kinetics.

Taylor, J., & Taylor, S. (1997). *Psychological approaches to sports injury rehabilitation.* Gaithersburg, MD: Aspen.

Tuffey, S. (1991). The role of athletic trainers in facilitating psychological recovery from athletic injury. *Athletic Training, 26,* 346-351.

Upledger, J.E. (1990). *SomatoEmotional release and beyond.* Palm Beach Gardens, FL: UI.

Wiese, D.M., & Weiss, M.R. (1987). Psychological rehabilitation and physical injury: Implications for the sportsmedicine team. *The Sport Psychologist, 1,* 318-330.

Wiese, D.M., Weiss, M.R., & Yukelson, D.P. (1991). Sport psychology in the training room: A survey of athletic trainers. *The Sport Psychologist, 5,* 25-40.

Wiese-Bjornstal, D.M., Gardetto, D.M., & Shaffer, S.M. (1999). Effective interaction skills for sports medicine professionals. In R. Ray & D.M. Wiese-Bjornstal (Eds.), *Counseling in sports medicine* (pp. 55-74). Champaign, IL: Human Kinetics.

Wiese-Bjornstal, D.M., & Smith, A.N. (1993). Counseling strategies for enhanced recovery of injured athletes within a team approach. In D. Pargman (Ed.), *Psychological bases of sport injury* (pp. 149-182). Morgantown, WV: Fitness Information Technology.

APPENDIX

NATIONAL ATHLETIC TRAINERS' ASSOCIATION ATHLETIC TRAINING EDUCATIONAL COMPETENCIES FOR PSYCHOSOCIAL INTERVENTION AND REFERRAL (NATA, 1999)

This content area is a collection of the knowledge, skills, and values that the entry-level certified athletic trainer must possess to recognize, intervene in, and refer when appropriate, the sociocultural, mental, emotional, and physical behaviors of athletes and others involved in physical activity.

Cognitive Domain

1. Describes the current psychosocial and sociocultural issues and problems confronting athletic training and sports medicine and identifies their effects on athletes and others involved in physical activity.
2. Compares the psychosocial requirements of various sports activities to the readiness of the injured and ill individual to resume physical participation.
3. Understands the psychological and emotional responses (motivation, anxiety, apprehension) to trauma and forced physical inactivity as they relate to the rehabilitation and reconditioning process.
4. Describes the basic principles of mental preparation, relaxation and visualization techniques, general personality traits, associated trait anxiety, locus of control, and athlete and social environment interactions.
5. Provides health care information to patients, parents/guardians, athletic personnel, and others regarding the psychological and emotional well being of athletes and others involved in physical activity.
6. Disseminates information regarding the roles and functions of various community-based health care providers (sport psychologists, counselors, social workers).
7. Describes the accepted protocols that govern the referral of athletes and other physically active individuals to psychological, community health, or social services.
8. Describes the theories and techniques of interpersonal and cross-cultural communication among certified athletic trainers, athletes, athletic personnel, patients, administrators, health care professionals, parents/guardians, and others.
9. Employs the basic principles of counseling, including discussion, active listening, and resolution.
10. Describes the various strategies that certified athletic trainers may employ to avoid and resolve conflict among superiors, peers, and subordinates.
11. Identifies the symptoms and clinical signs of common disordered eating (anorexia nervosa, bulimia) and the psychological and sociocultural factors associated with these disorders.
12. Identifies the psychological issues that relate to physically active women of childbearing years.
13. Identifies the medical and community-based resources that disseminate information regarding safe sexual activity and the health risk factors associated with sexually transmitted diseases.
14. Describes commonly abused substances (e.g., alcohol, tobacco, stimulants, nutritional supplements, steroids, marijuana, and narcotics) and their impact on an individual's health and physical performance.
15. Recognizes the signs and symptoms of drug abuse and the use of ergogenic aids and other substances.
16. Identifies the societal influences toward substance abuse in the athletic and physically active population.

17. Contrasts psychological and physical dependence, tolerance, and withdrawal syndromes that may be seen in individuals addicted to alcohol, prescription and nonprescription medications, and/or "street" drugs.
18. Describes the basic signs and symptoms of mental disorders (psychoses), emotional disorders (neuroses, depression), or personal/social conflict (family problems, academic or emotional stress, personal assault or abuse, sexual assault, sexual harassment) and the appropriate referral.
19. Identifies contemporary personal, school, and community health service agencies, such as community-based psychological and social support services.
20. Formulates a plan for appropriate psychological intervention and referral with all involved parties when confronted with a catastrophic event.
21. Describes the acceptance and grieving processes following a catastrophic event.
22. Identifies the stress-response model and how it may parallel an injury.
23. Defines seasonal affective disorder (SAD).
24. Cites the potential need for psychosocial intervention and referral when dealing with populations requiring special consideration (e.g., those with exercise-induced asthma, diabetes, seizure disorders, drug allergies and interactions, or unilateral organs).
25. Describes motivational techniques that the certified athletic trainer must use during rehabilitation and reconditioning.

Psychomotor Domain

1. Intervenes, when appropriate, with an individual with a suspected substance abuse problem.
2. Communicates with appropriate health care professionals in a confidential manner.
3. Uses appropriate community-based resources for psychosocial intervention.
4. Uses motivational techniques with athletes and others involved in physical activity.
5. Develops and implements stress reduction techniques for athletes and others involved in physical activity.
6. Develops and implements mental imagery techniques for athletes and others involved in physical activity.

Affective Domain

1. Accepts the professional, ethical, and legal parameters that define the proper role of the certified athletic trainer in providing health care information, intervention, and referral.
2. Accepts the responsibility to provide health care information, intervention, and referral consistent with the certified athletic trainer's professional training.
3. Recognizes the certified athletic trainer's role as a liaison between the physically active, athletic personnel, health care professionals, parents/guardians, and the public.
4. Accepts the need for appropriate interpersonal relationships between all of the parties involved with athletes and others involved in physical activity.
5. Accepts the moral and ethical responsibility to intervene in situations of suspected or known use and/or abuse of legal and illegal drugs and chemicals.
6. Accepts the moral and ethical responsibility to intervene in situations of mental, emotional, and/or personal/social conflict.
7. Recognizes athletes and other physically active individuals as deserving of quality professional health care.
8. Accepts the individual's physical complaint(s) without personal bias or prejudice.
9. Respects the various social and cultural attitudes, beliefs, and values regarding health care practices when caring for patients.
10. Accepts the role of social support during the injury rehabilitation process.

CHAPTER 17

DOING SPORT PSYCHOLOGY IN THE COACHING ROLE

Britton W. Brewer
Springfield College

"Not all the successful coaches I have known have been effective teachers of techniques, but with no exceptions, all have been effective on this human side of the coaching coin" (Doherty, 1976).

As illustrated by the quotation from Doherty, a noted scholar of track and field, coaching clearly involves more than educating athletes about the technical aspects of their sports. In attempting to elicit maximal performances from athletes under their tutelage, coaches must draw upon and develop in their athletes resources of a distinctly psychological character. Coaching tasks such as motivating athletes, building team cohesion, facilitating the setting of goals, and communicating effectively with athletes are clearly psychological in nature. Recognizing the relevance of psychology to the enhancement of sport performance, many coaches obtain graduate degrees in sport psychology (Burke & Johnson, 1992). Sport psychology is also commonly included as a unit in coach training programs such as the American Coaching Effectiveness Program (Bump & McKeighan, 1987).

This chapter is about the interface between coaching and sport psychology. Consistent with the mission of the book, the chapter deals more with the process than the content of applying sport psychology to coaching. Other excellent resources (e.g., Martens, 1987; Martin & Lumsden, 1987; Williams, 1998) are available for coaches who wish to learn about various psychological principles and techniques that can be applied in sport settings. Those efforts will not be duplicated here. Instead, the focus of this chapter is on issues associated with how sport psychology is applied by coaches. Before examining ways to incorporate sport psychology into coaching practice and discussing the referral of athletes for sport psychology and other support services, I will first address the appropriateness of coaches operating in the psychological realm and functioning as sport psychologists.

DUAL-ROLE ISSUES

In applying sport psychology to coaching, coaches run the risk of entering a dual-role relationship in which they serve concurrently as coach and sport psychologist to their athletes. Dual-role relationships, which should be examined carefully in situations involving work of a psychological nature (Ebert, 1997), can be problematic from both ethical and practical standpoints.

Ethical Considerations

Ethics codes in psychology have been developed to help maintain the public's trust by increasing the likelihood that psychologists will not harm their clients and will provide quality services (Koocher & Keith-Spiegel, 1998; Whelan, Meyers, & Elkin, 1996). Although there are no explicit ethical guidelines for coaches seeking to function as sport psychologists for athletes with whom they work, the following section of the *Ethical Principles and Code of Conduct of the American Psychological Association* (APA, 1992) deals with multiple relationships in general:

> Psychologists must always be sensitive to the potential harmful effects of other contacts on their work and on those persons with whom they deal. A psychologist refrains from entering into or promising another personal, scientific, professional, financial, or other relationship with such persons if it appears likely that such a relationship reasonably might impair the psychologist's objectivity or otherwise interfere with the psychologist's effectively performing his or her functions as a psychologist, or might harm or exploit the other party. (p. 1601)

In a recent survey of members of the Association for the Advancement of Applied Sport Psychology (AAASP) by Petitpas et al. (1994), responses to an item inquiring about whether serving concurrently as coach and sport psychologist for a team was ethical were highly variable. Consequently, Petitpas et al. labeled the dual-role behavior as controversial. Scholarly writing on the coach-sport psychologist dual role has also reflected the controversial nature of the topic.

Adopting a strict interpretation of APA ethical guidelines, Ellickson and Brown (1990) argued forcefully against coaches taking on the role of sport psychologist, citing a number of potential conflicts of interest in such a dual-role situation (e.g., defining who the client is, maintaining confidentiality versus making public statements about athletes, and keeping rigid versus flexible interpersonal boundaries between coaches and athletes). Rebuttals to the statements of Ellickson and Brown by Buceta (1993), Burke and Johnson (1992), and Smith (1992) emphasized the compatibility of the roles of coach and sport psychologist for educational (i.e., performance-oriented) issues but not for clinical (i.e., therapeutic) concerns.

Clearly, the functions performed by coaches with psychological training who use psychological performance enhancement techniques with their athletes may overlap with those of sport psychologists. Nevertheless, such coaches are acting as sport psychologists no more than coaches who teach their athletes stretching exercises and recommend cryotherapy for sore muscles are acting as physical therapists or athletic trainers. Almost by definition, coaching involves performing multiple tasks that cut across disciplines. Psychologically trained coaches merely have a larger behavioral repertoire from which to draw in helping athletes enhance their performance. Ethical constraints come into play when, as previously noted, serving simultaneously as coach and sport psychologist impairs the provision of psychological services to the athlete (because the coach is too busy with other coaching functions) or jeopardizes the athlete's sport standing (because of the nature of the information divulged to the coach). Such situations are most likely to occur when athletes have issues requiring clinical attention or other problems of sufficient magnitude to draw the coach beyond the coaching role into a role more typically occupied by a counseling or clinical psychologist. In these situations, the most appropriate course of action is generally to refer the athletes in question to another professional for psychological assistance.

Practical Considerations

Because coaching has multiple and extensive professional demands, it makes sense from a practical perspective that coaches with training in sport psychology can ethically deliver some interventions (e.g., psychoeducational programs) but not others (e.g., psychotherapy) to their athletes. In many cases, coaches clearly cannot do it all—that is, provide a full range of coaching and psychological services for their athletes—without reducing their competency in either the coach or the psychologist role (Buceta, 1993).

In addition to the issue of competence, functioning jointly as coach and sport psychologist (as opposed to being a coach who applies knowledge of sport psychology) can have an adverse effect on other pragmatic concerns. Being compelled to adhere to the ethical obligations of sport psychologists can, in some situations, handcuff coaches and actually hamper their effectiveness and their relationships with athletes. For example, requiring athletes to furnish written consent for coaches to release information about them, however trivial that information may be, to others (e.g., the media, medical practitioners) could introduce a cumbersome level of formality to coach-athlete interactions that erodes rather than protects the bonds that coaches have with their athletes.

Beyond the ethical barriers and practical disadvantages to coaches serving concurrently as coach and sport psychologist, there may be pragmatic advantages (even for coaches with training in sport psychology) to enlisting a person who is not the coach to serve as sport psychologist. Such a practice may help coaches gain a fresh, unbiased perspective on the athletes with whom they work (Gardner, 1995; Smith, 1992) and devote greater attention to overall coaching objectives (Buceta, 1993). It can also provide athletes with additional reinforcement for mental training procedures taught by coaches.

INCORPORATING SPORT PSYCHOLOGY INTO COACHING PRACTICE

Excepting those sport psychology activities that produce potential ethical and practical conflicts, there are a number of ways that coaches can incorporate sport psychology into their coaching practice. In particular, coaches can use knowledge of sport psychology principles and techniques with their athletes in the following ways: to foster a team environment conducive to the pursuit of optimal sport performance, to teach sport skills, to teach general psychological skills, to practice sport-specific psychological skills, and to prepare for competition.

Fostering an Optimal Team Environment

As noted at the outset of the chapter, most successful coaches are adept in using psychology, often implicitly rather than explicitly, to get the most out of their athletes. The use of psychology in coaching is perhaps most apparent in the team environment that coaches help create. By fostering an environment characterized by clear communication, team cohesion, and motivation toward a common goal (Carron & Hausenblas, 1998), coaches can facilitate the pursuit of optimal sport performance. Coaches can establish a favorable team environment at their first team meeting, as evidenced by the monologue from this collegiate swim coach.

Coach (C): Welcome, newcomers, and welcome back, returners! For those of you who don't know me, I'm Coach Smith, but you can call me Smitty if you want. I'm real glad you're all here. It's going to be a great season. Before we get into all the mumbo-jumbo paperwork and physical examinations and other BS that the powers that be say we've got to do, I'd like us to get to know each other a bit better. Why don't we go around the room and have each person give your name—or at least what you would like to be called—hometown, year in school, major, and best swimming story—assuming you did any swimming—from the off-season.

In his introductory remarks, the coach communicated that he is approachable, interested in the athletes becoming acquainted with their teammates, and focused on swimming. The comment about the powers that be helped to instill group unity against a vaguely specified entity of others (i.e., the intercollegiate athletics department). Following the icebreaker activity, the coach continued his attempt to set the tone for the season to follow.

Athlete #1 (A #1): What about you, Smitty?

C: You would have to ask me that, wouldn't you? Who came up with those questions anyway? [winks] Oh, all right. As you know, I'm Smitty. I was born and raised in Kansas City, Missouri. And I'm in about my 35th year of school, give or take a few. I guess you could call me a PE major. And my swimming story from the off-season is that I actually hauled my ass back in the pool over the summer and swam some laps. Hence the near-return of my boyish figure.

Team: [laughs]

C: Now, let's move on. I'd like to say a bit about my coaching philosophy. First of all, I coach for fun and assume you are all out here to have fun, too. Believe me, I wouldn't coach if coaching weren't fun for me—I don't get paid enough! Sure, I like to win as much as the next guy, and you have more fun when you're winning, but basically I'm out here to have fun. That doesn't mean, however, that I don't take swimming seriously. I do. You can ask the upperclassmen about that. Secondly, I want to emphasize that we are a swim team. We're made up of individuals, but the team is where it's at. Individual successes are great, but there's something about the electricity of a big team win that just can't be topped. Those of you who've been around here a while will remember how great it felt to beat Southwestern to win the conference title. I think I'm still trying to get the chlorine out of my boots from when you chucked me in the diving pool!

Athlete #2 (A #2): The Smitman's getting wet again this year!

C: I hope so, but there's a lot of work that needs to be done before that happens. Now, our program here is what you might call holistic. We like to emphasize all the things we can do to succeed as a team. Yes, swimming plays a big part. We swim hard, and swim long, too, at least early on, and then when we taper, we taper hard and rest hard, meaning that when we're supposed to be resting, we do just that—rest. Strength and flexibility training are also a big part of our program. They get you swimming faster and prevent injuries. We work on technique and strategy, and the mental part of the sport, too. We'll do goal setting, imagery, concentration training, the whole nine yards. Nutrition is important, also. We work on eating the right foods at the right times. No, we're not going to keep track of what we eat like Richard Simmons, but we will see that cheese fries are not the ideal prerace snack!

We'll work on all these things throughout the season. I will do everything I can to help you to become the best swimmers you can, and for us to become the best team we can. If there's something bothering you, please come to me to talk about it. I rarely bite. I've been doing this long enough to know that th ere's no one right way to do things, and I'm open to your feedback. If you don't feel comfortable speaking with me, please talk to your captain, Manny. He's been here almost as long as I have, give or take 10 or 15 years, and he's a good guy—he can swim pretty fast, too.

In his speech to the team and his occasional dialogue with team members, the coach provided a set of expectations for what the team would do throughout the season, used humor to engage the team's attention, and asserted his role as a benevolent leader.

Coaches should be aware that each interaction they have with their athletes can influence the team environment. In general, there is much to be said for coaches adopting a positive approach that involves providing reinforcement for desired athlete behaviors (Martin & Lumsden, 1987; Smith, 1998). Regardless of the particular approach coaches take to create a team environment, it is important that they select an approach that is consistent with their personal style and coaching philosophy (Yukelson, 1998). Coach Smith's salty, humor-laden demeanor might not work for all coaches, although most would accept the general messages that he conveyed.

Teaching Sport Skills

Instruction and physical practice are the tried-and-true methods coaches use to teach sport skills to athletes. Coaches with training in sport psychology can use their advanced knowledge to enhance teaching of sport skills through traditional means by adding a psychological component. In the following example, a tennis coach instructs team members, waiting in line during a drill in which a sport skill is practiced, to rehearse mentally the skill that they are about to practice physically.

C: OK, crew, let's gather 'round. In the next drill, we're going to work on overheads. Giles, Trixie, [assistant coaches] and I have noticed recently that, on the whole, we can stand to improve our execution of overheads in practices and matches. You work all point to get short balls and overheads, so it's important to finish the point when you get the chance. There are only a few key fundamentals to keep in mind when hitting overheads. You need to turn your shoulder toward the net and take small steps to get into position. Turn your shoulder and take small steps. Some of you also need to work on keeping your heads up as you hit the ball. In this drill, we're going to have you break up into three groups of four. We're going to have you start with your racquet touching the net. We'll feed you three lobs each. The person who is first in line will hit the overheads, the person who is second in line will shadow the overheads from behind the service line, and the third person in line will mentally image hitting the overheads from behind the baseline while the fourth person jogs back to the end of the line. So, you'll be hitting, jogging, imaging, and shadowing. When you image the overhead, make sure that you feel your shoulder turning to the net and feel your feet taking small steps to get into position. Image having your head up and swinging loose as you put your overheads away. Is that clear?

A #1: We're going to do *what?!* I don't get it!

A #2: We did this last year for volleys, Darlene. Just stand in line behind me, and you'll figure it out.

Coach: Any more questions? OK, let's break into groups and get this thing going! Remember, turn your shoulder and take small steps. Keep your head up!

In situations such as this, where the coach presumably had taught team members about imagery procedures at an earlier time, coaches can use sport psychology techniques to maximize practice time, keep team members involved throughout drills, and facilitate additional practice of sport skills.

Practicing Sport-Specific Psychological Skills

Coaches can readily apply specialized knowledge of sport psychology to help athletes develop and practice psychological skills that pertain directly to involvement in particular sports. Sport-specific psychological skills include such behaviors as maintaining concentration over an extended period of time in endurance sports, developing preperformance routines, identifying opponent weaknesses, and recognizing patterns in sports where athletes are face-to-face with their opposition (e.g., football, tennis, wrestling). Rather than simply engaging athletes in physical practice and hoping that they will pick up the requisite psychological skills along the way, coaches can adopt a proactive stance in which they actively help athletes acquire and maintain sport-specific psychological skills. By describing explicitly the skills they want athletes to develop and by structuring physical practice in ways that allow athletes to rehearse the skills, coaches can increase both awareness and retention of the skills. The following distance-running example shows how sport-specific psychological skills can be honed in practice.

C: OK, now that you've run over here to the golf course and gotten some stretching and strides in, we'll begin today's workout. What we're going to do is essentially two mini-tempo runs separated by four minutes of jogging. But there's a slight twist to it . . .

A #1: I knew it! Shadow runs!

C: Yes, Toby's right. We're going to do shadow runs. What these involve is pairing up with a partner—of *my* choosing—and having one of you run on the other guy's shoulder—not five yards behind, right on his shoulder—for the first five minutes and then having the guy who was in the lead run on the shoulder of the guy who was following for the last five minutes. Then, after four minutes of easy jogging, switch the order around and do it again on the second ten-minute stint. They should be done at tempo-run pace. The goal is not to lose the guy behind you but rather to practice maintaining contact with the guy in front of you. In races, it is essential for you to be able to stay with guys in front of you, when you're not moving through the pack, of course. Today we'll work on shadowing the guy in front of you. That's why they are called *shadow runs.* Any questions?

After doing such a workout, the coach inquired how each pair of runners did. The discussion with one pair went as follows:

C: How'd it go?

A #1: That was tough! The first one wasn't too bad, but the second one was a bear.

A #2: He went by me like a bat out of hell on the first one when it was his turn to lead! I stayed right with him, though. I think he paid the price a bit when it was my turn to lead on the second one.

A #1: Yeah, but I was with you until the last 30 seconds.

C: So, you made all but 30 seconds out of 20 minutes in contact?

Athletes #1 and #2: [nod affirmatively]

C: Great! Now, how did you manage it when it got tough?

A #1: I just told myself that I would stick to him like glue and not even let the slightest of gaps open up.

C: Excellent! And you, Hank?

A #2: I'm not sure exactly, but you said to maintain contact, so I maintained contact!

C: Well, nice workout, guys! I appreciate your efforts. Now, why don't you keep moving and get a cooldown in before you tighten up.

In this example, the coach prefaced the workout with a description of the sport-specific psychological skill to be practiced and concluded with an affirmation of the intent of the workout. Sometimes, as with shadow runs, training sessions in which sport-specific psychological skills are practiced can benefit athletes both physically and psychologically. Shadow runs enable athletes to both obtain vigorous physical practice and rehearse the psychological skills of staying alert, regulating effort, and maintaining concentration under duress.

Teaching General Psychological Skills

Coaches can also adopt an educational role to teach their athletes psychological skills that may have applicability within and outside of sport. As long as they are able to draw a connection between learning such life skills and important sport-related processes or outcomes (e.g., getting along with teammates, getting enough rest, maintaining academic eligibility, staying motivated), coaches can devote practice or meeting time to presenting information on a variety of topics, including effective communication, time management, stress management, and goal setting. The volleyball coach in the following example appealed to the importance of arousal-regulation for effective sport performance in presenting a progressive relaxation exercise to her squad.

C: OK, gang, today we're going to spend some time on mental skills. We're going to work on learning how to relax. Can anyone tell me why it might be useful to learn how to relax for volleyball?

A #1: So you don't choke!

C: Right! One thing that players tend to do is to tighten up when the match gets tight. How many times have you seen someone serve it into the bleachers when it's crunch time?! This can happen because the player's muscles are actually tighter than they are when the match is not at such a crucial point. The exercise that we're going to do will help you get your level of muscular tension under your control. Now, why don't you find a place on the mats and get yourselves in a comfortable position . . .

Following the exercise and a brief discussion of how the athletes responded to it, the coach attempted to enhance the transfer of the skill to other domains.

C: Relaxation is a skill just like any other. You get better with practice. And we'll continue to devote some practice time to working on it, but you've really got to practice it on your own for it to be most effective. Being able to regulate your muscle tension is certain to help you on the court. It may help you other places, too. Can you think of how else it might help you?

A #1: It'll help me fall asleep when I'm stressed. I practically fell asleep here today!

A #2: I can use it to keep cool when I'm taking exams. Like A and P, for example.

C: Good! Learning how to relax can be useful for coping with stress, falling asleep at night, dealing with traffic, and many other situations you may encounter.

By teaching general psychological skills, coaches can contribute both directly and indirectly to the sport performance and quality of life of their athletes.

Preparing for Competition

Competitive situations, often a primary focus for both coaches and athletes, provide an excellent opportunity for coaches to apply sport psychology principles and techniques. Many coaches introduce elements of sport psychology into their precompetitive coaching behavior without even realizing it. Common coaching practices such as providing athletes with scouting reports on opponents, conducting training sessions in conditions simulating those likely to be encountered during competition (e.g., crowd noise, field surface, course topography), and standardizing precompetitive warm-up routines facilitate athletes' mental preparation for competition. More directly, psychological methods can also be used by coaches toward the same end. For example, coaches can help figure skaters develop imagery to mentally rehearse their routines off the ice. Similar interventions can be implemented by coaches with athletes in other sports in which significant details of the competitive experience are known in advance, as in Alpine skiing, bowling, golf (teeing off), gymnastics, ski jumping, and track and field.

Because of the vital importance athletes typically ascribe to competition, coaches can hook athletes into using sport psychology techniques by actively involving them in the process of mental preparation for competitive events. Several years ago, I encouraged members of the intercollegiate cross-country team that I coach to mentally collect details of a course where both an early season invitational and the regional championships were being hosted. After competing in the invitational, my assistant coach and I asked the runners to pool their collected memories of the course and helped them generate an imagery script for use prior to the conference championship. The resulting script served the dual function of having the athletes become invested in the use of sport psychology techniques and facilitating mental preparation for the conference championship. A sample of the sort of imagery script created by the team follows.

> The start is in an open area. You go slightly downhill the first 50 m, then up a steeper upgrade (dead grass and dusty). There's a big rock in the middle where the trail narrows. Go around the cornfield loop. Stay wide on the tough 90-degree turns. Go along another straight section (passing the mile mark) with the road on your left. Wind behind the starting line and head down a long downhill. Watch the uneven terrain, ruts, and pricker bushes. Hug the field line (on the right) as you run downhill toward the railroad tracks. Begin another straight section. There are railroad tracks and bushes on your left and big hay bales on your right. Spot the Tufts billboard on your left. Go along another straight section. Stay alert; don't fall asleep. The straight section ends coming up on a steep but short incline and going through a gated rusty fence. Go on the right-hand side of the big rock three-fourths of the way up the hill. Go down a gradual downhill (a great place to change your rhythm), wind alongside the tree line and pass the two-mile mark. Be careful of any soft dirt spots. Head slightly uphill and into the woods with the cornfield loop to your right. Go down an uneven 25-m downhill through the woods. Watch for the broken-up stone wall. There are continual rolling hills for 400 m. Go around one last 90-degree right-hand turn and continue up the slight upgrade out of the woods. Break into a cornfield. There's a 90-degree left turn. Then wind right (toward the road). Pass by fire hydrants, the cornfield loop to your right, the initial mile mark, and then (50 m later) the three-mile mark. Continue on this straight stretch as you did during the first loop. Continue back behind the starting line, down the hill, along the railroad tracks, up the steep hill, through the gate, into the woods, past mile four, out of the woods, alongside the road (800 m to go). As you near the cornfield loop, wind to your right and head toward the finish (400 m to go). Pick up your pace. Make a gradual left turn. Run alongside a hill on your left. Kick now!
>
> The footing is very rough from here to the finish. Be aware that the finish comes up quickly as you dart down a hill and head toward the finish line.

After the script was developed, I used it in two imagery sessions with the team prior to the regional championships, once approximately a week before the meet and once the night before the competition. The role of the imagery intervention in mental preparation for the big race is apparent from the dialogue that occurred the night before the championships.

> C: Well, as always, the coaches' meeting was interesting, but I learned nothing revolutionary. How was your dinner?
>
> A #1: Great, we got lots of carbos!
>
> A #2: We're well hydrated, too!
>
> A #3: Yeah, speaking of hydrated, I've got to use the facilities.
>
> C: OK, while Chico attends to his bladder, let me pass out the numbers for tomorrow. Make sure you get enough safety pins. Four should do the trick.
>
> A #2: Do they go on the front or on the back?
>
> C: On the front, as with every meet for which we've worn numbers this season.
>
> A #2: Well, you never know.
>
> A #4: Get with the program, Shaw!
>
> C: All right, I've got just a few quick announcements. The course is going to be exactly like it was when we raced on it last time. They are going to put wood chips down on some of the damp areas on the trail near the two-mile mark.
>
> A #2: What about that big rock on the hill? In a big race like this one, someone could get impaled on it or something.
>
> C: The race director said that they would wrap an orange cone around it as best they can and that it should not be a problem. We'll be in box 23 on the starting line.
>
> A #1: Is that from the left or the right facing the starting line?
>
> C: I'm not sure, but it's right in the middle, regardless. Our big rivals will be two boxes away in number 25. Now, we'll

meet tomorrow at 8:00 A.M. for breakfast and leave for the meet at 9:00 A.M. Please try to be on time so that you give yourself ample time to digest your meal before the race. What time will we be meeting for breakfast?

Team: 8:00 A.M.!

C: Good! I just want to make sure that we're all on the same page. We now have the option of doing some imagery or retiring for the evening. It's up to you. We did it earlier in the week and ran over the course this afternoon. What do you say?

A #1: Imagery! Let's do it.

A #2: I think I'm going to hit the sack. I'd probably just fall asleep anyway.

C: No problem. Sleep well. So the rest of you are staying?

A #3: You got it!

Others: [nod affirmatively]

After I led the team through the course one final time through imagery, I asked the athletes how they felt about the approaching competition and received the following responses.

A #1: I'm definitely ready for the race. I could see the course more clearly than ever and could even hear you yelling for me.

A #4: Chico's snoring aside . . .

A #3: Hey, c'mon . . . I haven't slept well lately . . . I had a lot of exams this week!

A #4: I stayed alert throughout the whole race, even the part I kind of zoned out on last time.

C: Good! Anyone else? No? OK, well, thanks for your attention and let's get some sleep. Tomorrow's going to be a good day for us!

The athletes' decision to participate in the nighttime imagery session (with the exception of one athlete) and their reactions to the imagery itself suggested that they valued the imagery as part of the mental preparation process. That the content of the imagery session was essentially theirs to begin with might have increased the team members' enthusiasm for including the exercise in their prerace routine.

The applications discussed in this section are only some of the ways that coaches can incorporate sport psychology into their coaching practice. Other applications of sport psychology to coaching are limited only by the characteristics of the sport and the imagination, creativity, and experience of the coach. Also, it need not be the coaches who implement sport psychology applications with the athletes under their tutelage. Coaches, even those with training and competence in sport psychology interventions, may wish to enlist an outside consultant to perform specialized sport psychology functions for their teams.

REFERRAL FOR SPORT PSYCHOLOGY AND OTHER SUPPORT SERVICES

As shown in the previous section of the chapter, there are numerous options available for coaches with some training in sport psychology who wish to incorporate sport psychology principles and techniques into their coaching. Nevertheless, for many coaches, doing sport psychology may mean making a referral to a sport psychologist or other support service provider. In this section of the chapter, reasons for referral and the referral process are examined.

Reasons for Referral

Coaches may seek referrals for their athletes to receive sport psychology and other support services for a variety of reasons. Ethical and professional constraints (e.g., lacking competence to deal with the issue presented by the athlete), practical limitations (e.g., lacking sufficient time to work with the athlete on a particular issue), and personal preference (e.g., choosing not to work with an athlete on a given issue) may prompt coaches to look to other practitioners to help their athletes address issues of concern.

Referral situations arise frequently when athletes report or display behavior warranting clinical attention, such as issues pertaining to identity, sexuality, eating disorders, emotional adjustment, relationships, and substance abuse (Heyman & Andersen, 1998). Because of the trusting relationships that coaches often have with their athletes, they can be in an excellent position to identify situations of a clinical nature for athletes under their direction. As exemplified by the following exchange that occurred between a coach and an intercollegiate athlete when school was not in session, athletes may decide to tell their coaches directly about issues of concern, especially when the athletes are aware that the coaches have training in sport psychology.

Tessa: Coach, do you have a few minutes? There's something that I'd like to talk with you about.

C: Sure, come on in. What's going on? How's your training going?

Tessa: Training for the fall is going pretty well. The injury hasn't come back . . . No, that's not it . . . I just haven't been feeling right lately.

C: Not feeling right; how do you mean?

Tessa went on to describe symptoms resembling those of a depressive disorder, although of insufficient duration and magnitude to be diagnosable according to the *Diagnostic and Statistical Manual of Mental Disorders* (American Psychiatric Association, 1994). It appeared that regular, job-related contact with a former romantic partner was the trigger for the emotional disturbance. Because of the number of depressive symptoms Tessa reported, the coach followed with a probe for suicidal ideation and introduced the idea of referral.

C: Have you been having any thoughts about hurting yourself?

Tessa: I'm not sure I'd mind if something happened to me right now, but, no, I wouldn't do anything to hurt myself intentionally.

C: So, you're not thinking about suicide or anything?

Tessa: No, not really.

C: I'm glad that you came and talked with me about this. It definitely sounds as though you're going through some tough times and you're not your usual self right now.

Tessa: Yeah.

C: Would you be interested in talking with someone about this?

Tessa: Yeah, maybe.

C: Well, I think the Counseling Center is closed for the summer, but would you mind if I called in to find out who might be available locally to work with you?

Tessa: OK, but I can't pay very much. Money's kind of tight right now.

C: OK, let's call in and see. Many counselors have sliding fee scales, which might make it affordable for you.

Tessa: Good.

The coach then contacted an on-call mental health practitioner to find out about high-quality, low-cost referral possibilities for Tessa. The coach gave the referral information obtained from the mental health practitioner to Tessa. When the coach next saw Tessa 10 days later, Tessa thanked him for talking with her and informed him that she had not followed up on the referral because "things are getting better already." Tessa returned to school in the fall with no evidence of the problem that had caused her to seek her coach's assistance and, incidentally, had the best competitive season of her career. Even though Tessa never went to see a counselor, the contact with her coach may have been therapeutic in itself. In listening to Tessa and giving her a referral, the coach conveyed that she cared for Tessa, a response that might have helped Tessa begin lifting herself out of the doldrums. The coach used her psychological training to identify Tessa's level of distress and to plot an appropriate course of action, recognizing that it was inappropriate for her to function as clinician.

Although Tessa did not meet with her coach with the intention of requesting a referral for mental health services, some athletes seek out their coaches for just that reason. For example, a male intercollegiate lacrosse player named Emmett took his coach aside after a disappointing competitive performance:

Emmett: Look, I gotta talk with you about something.

C: OK.

Emmett: I'm not where I should be. I'm not even close to the player I was my freshman year, and last year was, well, a waste, if you know what I mean.

C: Uh huh.

Emmett: Can you get me into rehab or something? I want to quit getting high all the time. I do it, like, every day, and I want to be good again. Can you help me?

C: What I can do is call the substance abuse specialist on campus and find out what the options are. I'll get back to you as soon as I know anything. Sound okay?

Emmett: Aw, you know it!

In this case, the athlete made an overt request for a referral and the coach helped facilitate the athlete's request. In most cases, however, athletes with issues warranting clinical attention are unlikely to be as direct as Emmett (and even Tessa), especially when they perceive the possibility that acknowledging the presence of such issues may adversely affect their opportunities to compete. Coaches need to be observant of the psychological status of their athletes in order to detect behavioral disturbances that make referral a likely course of action. Coaches can also obtain information about the well-being of their athletes from teammates and family members, as illustrated in the case of Adam (discussed later in the chapter). When coaches identify reasons for referral to a clinical practitioner by means other than direct contact with the athlete in question, referral is an even more delicate process than usual. Coaches must assess the situation carefully and pose the possibility of referral to the athlete tactfully.

It is also appropriate for coaches to make referrals for performance-related issues (which may, as in Emmett's case, be wrapped up in a clinical issue). Performance-related reasons for referral vary widely across coaches, athletes, and sports but have the common core of being an issue on which the coach does not feel competent, capable, or comfortable working with the athlete as a function of ethical, practical, or personal considerations.

Derrick, a triathlete, was referred to a sport psychologist for a performance-related issue. Derrick had been a successful competitor for five years at the time of referral. He frequently finished in the money and often was victorious in low-key competitions. Nevertheless, he had a tendency to tighten up and perform well below his expectations in important, high-pressure races. Derrick's coach hypothesized that Derrick's subpar performances in big races was due to an excessive concern over race outcome that resulted in increased muscle tension (sometimes to the point of actual cramping). Even though Derrick's coach was well trained in sport psychology methods, he recognized that adding a psychologically based performance enhancement regimen to the coach-athlete relationship might increase Derrick's already high level of performance anxiety. Consequently, the coach referred Derrick to an athletic counselor. This counselor worked with Derrick on stress management and other performance issues to help him gain a fresh perspective and to reduce any coach-generated pressure to excel. Later, once Derrick had worked extensively with the athletic counselor, the coach agreed to help Derrick make an imagery tape, using the coach's voice to enhance the contextual validity.

Referral Process

Once coaches have identified a reason for referring an athlete to a sport psychologist or another type of practitioner, the referral process begins in earnest. When coaches are uncertain as to whether a particular athlete might benefit from referral, they should contact a professional whom they know for consultation. Indeed, because no single practitioner is likely to be capable of dealing optimally with the wide range of reasons for referral that may occur, it is useful for coaches to have one or two such "point persons" (perhaps one sport psychologist and one mental health professional) available as a matter of standard practice to help them direct referrals to qualified professionals. Most mental health practitioners and many sport psychologists have referral networks that enable them to contact colleagues who have expertise in addressing the various concerns presented by their clients (Van Raalte & Andersen, 1996).

The ultimate success of a referral can be strongly influenced by how the referral is presented to the athlete (Bobele & Conran, 1988). As illustrated by the case of Emmett, some athletes may actively seek out referrals from coaches. For situations such as that experienced by Tessa, a direct referral from the coach is appropriate. Coaches can help prepare athletes for the possibility of referral by explaining the reasons for referral (if necessary), describing what is likely to be involved in working with a sport psychologist or support service provider, and being sensitive to athletes' concerns about referral (Bobele & Conran, 1988; Heil, 1993; Van Raalte & Andersen, 1996).

In circumstances where potential reasons for referral are less overt (e.g., known to the coach by careful observation or by comments from teammates or family members) or less urgent, coaches may wish to take an indirect approach to referral. An example of the indirect approach is inviting a sport psychologist to meet with the team for a series of educational (ostensibly performance-related) workshops, during or after which the sport psychologist is made available to athletes for individual consultations. Such an approach gives tacit support from the coach for athletes to pursue issues of concern with a professional. In an effort not to place athletes under undue pressure to meet with a sport psychologist or support service provider, coaches should not single out athletes publicly as needing individual consultation. Regrettably, I have heard several coaches point to an athlete in front of her teammates and say "she needs to work with you [sport psychologist] because she's a real basket case." Referral is best handled as a private matter between coaches and athletes.

A common misconception about referrals is that once they are made, coaches are not involved in the athletes' treatment (whatever it may be) and that coaches have essentially washed their hands of the athletes. Coaches may feel relief once one of their athletes has been directed toward the help they need, but they do not have to be alienated from what occurs after the referral takes place. Although some athletes (e.g., Emmett) may prefer to meet on their own with the target of the referral, other athletes may respond well to *referring in,* which involves having the coach join the athlete in the meeting (Andersen, 1992). After being referred in, athletes may later decide to meet individually with the sport psychologist or other support service provider. Nevertheless, having the coach present at the initial meeting(s) can minimize potential feelings of abandonment in the athlete and make smoother the athlete's transition into work with another professional. Referring in demonstrates the coach's commitment to helping the athlete and shows that the coach unequivocally supports the referral.

The case of Adam shows how a coach might go about referring in. Adam was a freshman intercollegiate cross-country runner in his first year of participating in the sport (although he had run track and field in high school, where he had excelled in the 800m run and the decathlon). More mesomorphic than most distance runners, Adam appeared highly motivated and eager to please his coaches and teammates with his work ethic as the season began. Despite admonitions from his coaches and teammates, he displayed a consistent tendency to overdo his training in terms of both volume and intensity. Shortly after the first meet in which Adam competed (and performed exceptionally), teammates expressed concern that Adam appeared to be eating insufficient quantities of food to sustain his training load. A day or two later, Adam's father called the head coach from out of state to voice his concern over his son's possibly excessive weight loss. Because the coaching staff had no immediately observable justification (in terms of Adam's appearance or performance) to act on the situation, the coaches decided to monitor Adam closely before adopting a plan of action. Several days later, Adam had a notably substandard performance in his second race. The following conversation occurred after the race, when the head coach approached Adam.

C: Tough one today, huh?

Adam: I felt fat out there.

C: Fat? What do you mean?

Adam: I don't know . . . you know, like a chunky monkey.

C: What do you think made you feel that way? Have you gained weight?

Adam: [shakes head and shrugs shoulders]

The coach viewed Adam's mention of feeling fat as a thinly veiled invitation to discussion Adam's eating. Consequently, the coach was able to pursue Adam's diet in conversation without revealing the concerns of his father and teammates. In response to a question about what he had been eating lately, Adam described a diet high in carbohydrates and fruits, but little else (virtually no fat and no protein). The coach used Adam's response as an opportunity to introduce the possibility of referral.

C: I'm no nutritionist or dietitian, but it sounds like you're missing some ingredients essential for optimal performance. Would you be interested in learning more about your eating?

Adam: If it will help me perform better, yeah, sure.

C: We could call Student Health to set something up with the dietitian on Monday. I think she's available once a week, but I'm not sure what day. Would you want me to come along with you to see what's going on and maybe learn something in the process?

Adam: Yeah, that'd be cool.

The coach then scheduled an appointment at a time mutually convenient to Adam and himself. The coach discussed Adam's situation with the dietitian prior to the appointment. At the appointment, the coach said little while the dietitian assessed Adam's diet and body composition (Adam had an atypically high percentage of muscle weight) and discussed with Adam a rationale for changing his diet. A follow-up appointment, which Adam attended, was scheduled without the coach. The outcome of the intervention was striking. Adam's eating habits changed immediately and dramatically and persisted for the remainder of the season despite ever-worsening competitive performance, due most likely to staleness or overtraining. Although Adam's subsequent track and field season later in the school year was substandard in relation to his high school accomplishments, his eating and training behaviors did not appear to hamper his performance on the track.

Once successful referrals have been made, the referral process is not over. Rather, the next step is follow-up, where coaches ask the athletes who have been referred about how their work with the sport psychologist or other support service provider is going (Brewer, Petitpas, & Van Raalte, 1999). Follow-up enables coaches to show their support for the referral and to evaluate the success of their referral. When referrals do not work out, coaches learn this through follow-up and make alternative arrangements when necessary. Coaches may wish to confer directly with the professionals to whom they have referred athletes, but they should recognize that the professionals may be able to provide only limited information about the athletes because of confidentiality restrictions.

In each of the case examples presented in this chapter, the athletes accepted the referrals made by their coaches. Such acceptance may not always be the case. When athletes decline a referral at one point, it can always be reintroduced at a later time (Heil, 1993).

PREPARING TO DO SPORT PSYCHOLOGY

Specialized training is essential for coaches seeking to incorporate sport psychology into their professional practice. At a minimum, coaches hoping to do sport psychology should become familiar with the field, its issues, and its techniques through reading books and journals and attending workshops and conferences on sport psychology. Additional knowledge and skills can be gained through course work and supervised field experience in applied sport psychology. Some coaches, believing in the value of sport psychology for their coaching, or pursuing an academic specialization of interest, undertake courses of graduate study and earn master's or doctoral degrees in sport psychology, counseling, or related fields. In general, gaining advanced training in sport psychology can increase coaches' behavioral repertoires and leave them better prepared to do sport psychology in the coaching role.

Another form of preparation for coaches wishing to do sport psychology is less formal, involving discussions with sport psychology consultants (and other practitioners) whom coaches may seek out to refer athletes experiencing difficulties. In developing a network of potential referral targets, coaches can ask sport psychologists about their preferences and specialties with respect to presenting concerns, client populations, and methods of intervention. Coaches can also inquire about *how* the sport psychology professionals generally work in terms of referral practices (e.g., referring in); communication with the coach; and number, frequency, and location of sessions. Conversations of this kind with sport psychologists not only provide coaches with information about how sport psychology is done but also enable coaches to make referrals more appropriately and effectively.

SUMMARY AND CONCLUSIONS

Coaches are in a unique position to apply sport psychology principles and techniques with athletes. They can incorporate sport psychology into their coaching practice to foster an optimal team environment, teach sport skills, practice sport-specific psychological skills, teach general psychological skills, and prepare athletes for competition. For ethical and practical reasons, it is appropriate for coaches to refer athletes to sport psychologists and other support service providers in certain situations. Referrals are typically made for clinical issues or performance issues outside of the coach's purview. Referral is a delicate process that can be enhanced by having coaches demonstrate their support before, during, and after the referral. Formal training in sport psychology and informal interaction with sport psychology consultants can help coaches prepare to do sport psychology more effectively and, ultimately, better serve the athletes with whom they work.

REFERENCES

American Psychiatric Association. (1994). *Diagnostic and statistical manual of mental disorders* (4th ed.). Washington, DC: Author.

American Psychological Association. (1992). Ethical principles of psychologists and code of conduct. *American Psychologist, 47,* 1597-1611.

Andersen, M.B. (1992). Sport psychology and procrustean categories: An appeal for synthesis and expansion of service. *Association for the Advancement of Applied Sport Psychology Newsletter, 7* (3), 8-9.

Bobele, M., & Conran, T.J. (1988). Referrals for family therapy: Pitfalls and guidelines. *Elementary School Guidance, 22,* 192-198.

Buceta, J.M. (1993). The sport psychologist/athletic coach dual role: Advantages, difficulties, and ethical considerations. *Journal of Applied Sport Psychology, 5,* 64-77.

Brewer, B.W., Petitpas, A.J., & Van Raalte, J.L. (1999). Referral of injured athletes for counseling and psychotherapy. In R.R. Ray & D.M. Wiese-Bjornstal (Eds.), *Counseling in sports medicine* (pp. 127-141). Champaign, IL: Human Kinetics.

Bump, L., & McKeighan, J. (1987). *American Coaching Effectiveness Program: Sport psychology.* [Videocassette]. Champaign, IL: Human Kinetics.

Burke, K.L., & Johnson, J.J. (1992). The sport psychologist-coach dual role position: A rebuttal to Ellickson & Brown (1990). *Journal of Applied Sport Psychology, 4,* 51-55.

Carron, A.V., & Hausenblas, H.A. (1998). Group dynamics in sport (2nd ed.). Morgantown, WV: Fitness Information Technology.

Doherty, J.K. (1976). *Track and field omnibook* (2nd ed.). Los Altos, CA: Tafnews Press.

Ebert, B.W. (1997). Dual-relationship prohibitions: A concept whose time never should have come. *Applied and Preventive Psychology, 6,* 137-156.

Ellickson, K.A., & Brown, D.R. (1990). Ethical considerations in dual relationships: The sport psychologist-coach. *Journal of Applied Sport Psychology, 2,* 186-190.

Gardner, F. (1995). The coach and the team psychologist: An integrated organizational model. In S.M. Murphy (Ed.), *Sport psychology interventions* (pp. 147-175). Champaign, IL: Human Kinetics.

Heil, J. (1993). Referral and coordination of care. In J. Heil (Ed.), *Psychology of sport injury* (pp. 251-266). Champaign, IL: Human Kinetics.

Heyman, S., & Andersen, M.B. (1998). When to refer athletes for counseling or psychotherapy. In J.M. Williams (Ed.), *Applied sport psychology: Personal growth to peak performance* (3rd ed., pp. 359-371). Mountain View, CA: Mayfield.

Koocher, G.P., & Keith-Spiegel, P. (1998). *Ethics in psychology: Professional standards and cases* (2nd ed.). New York: Oxford University Press.

Martens, R. (1987). *Coaches guide to sport psychology.* Champaign, IL: Human Kinetics.

Martin, G.L., & Lumsden, J. (1987). *Coaching: An effective behavioral approach.* St. Louis: Times Mirror Mosby.

Petitpas, A.J., Brewer, B.W., Rivera, P.M., & Van Raalte, J.L. (1994). Ethical beliefs and behaviors in applied sport psychology: The AAASP Ethics Survey. *Journal of Applied Sport Psychology, 6,* 135-151.

Smith, D. (1992). The coach as sport psychologist: An alternate view. *Journal of Applied Sport Psychology, 2,* 56-62.

Smith, R.E. (1998). A positive approach to sport performance enhancement: Principles of reinforcement and performance feedback. In J.M. Williams (Ed.), *Applied sport psychology: Personal growth to peak performance* (3rd ed., pp. 28-40). Mountain View, CA: Mayfield.

Van Raalte, J.L., & Andersen, M.B. (1996). Referral processes in sport psychology. In J.L. Van Raalte & B.W. Brewer (Eds.), *Exploring sport and exercise psychology* (pp. 275-284). Washington, DC: American Psychological Association.

Whelan, J.P., Meyers, A.W., & Elkin, T.D. (1996). Ethics in sport and exercise psychology. In J.L. Van Raalte & B.W. Brewer (Eds.), *Exploring sport and exercise psychology* (pp. 431-447). Washington, DC: American Psychological Association.

Williams, J.M. (Ed.). (1998). *Applied sport psychology: Personal growth to peak performance* (3rd ed.). Mountain View, CA: Mayfield.

Yukelson, D.P. (1998). Communicating effectively. In J.M. Williams (Ed.), *Applied sport psychology: Personal growth to peak performance* (3rd ed., pp. 142-157). Mountain View, CA: Mayfield.

CHAPTER 18

LEAVING SPORT: EASING CAREER TRANSITIONS

David Lavallee
University of Teesside
Mark B. Andersen
Victoria University

Sport psychology practitioners commonly find themselves helping competitive athletes cope with career transitions (Murphy, 1995). Although one of the only inevitabilities in high-performance sport is that all elite-level competitors will have to terminate their sporting careers, some athletes experience adjustment problems when faced with retirement. For this reason, practitioners have suggested that, in some cases, psychological interventions may be useful for athletes pre-transition and post-transition (Baillie, 1993; Danish, Petitpas, & Hale, 1993; Petitpas, Brewer, & Van Raalte, 1996).

The purpose of this chapter is to provide an overview of intervention strategies for practitioners who are working (or who are interested in working) with athletes in transition. First, we present background on the theoretical frameworks sport psychologists have employed when consulting with this population. We then illustrate counseling an athlete in pre-transition; in this case, an adolescent male who is contemplating leaving his sport. The following case example involves post-transition group work with three athletes who precipitously exited their sports. The chapter concludes with an overview of additional resources and interventions to consider in the psychological care of athletes in transition.

THEORETICAL FRAMEWORKS

A growing body of literature has emerged within the sport psychology community on the topic of career transitions (e.g., Baillie, 1993; Taylor & Ogilvie, 1998). Following Bookbinder's (1955) pioneering examination of post-retirement careers of professional baseball players, researchers have established that high-performance athletes are confronted with a wide range of psychological, interpersonal, and financial adjustments when they end their careers. The earliest studies concentrated almost exclusively on the psychological difficulties experienced by retired athletes (e.g., Haerle, 1975; Hallden, 1965; Miholvilovic, 1968), and this focus led to the development of a number of explanatory models to guide practice.

The initial conceptualizations, stemming primarily from social gerontological theories of aging (e.g.,

Cummings & Henry, 1961), roughly equated athletic career termination with retirement from the work force. Practitioners have also used stage models (e.g., Kubler-Ross, 1969) to compare the experience of retirement from sport with the psychological patterns associated with death and dying. Despite the intuitive appeal of some of these perspectives, they eventually proved to be limited in practice, because they were unable to characterize the nature and dynamics of the career transition process in an adequate fashion (Taylor & Ogilvie, 1994). For example, it is difficult to compare occupational retirement with retirement from sport, because athletes generally end their sporting careers at an age which biologically and chronologically occurs at a much earlier time in their lives (Murphy, 1995). Stage models, in a similar fashion, propose that participants in elite-level sport are universally overwhelmed by transition-induced stress.

Erikson's (1950, 1968) dynamic psychosocial model of the challenges and conflicts people face through the life span has been proposed as a framework practitioners can use when working with student-athletes (Andersen, 1996). Three of Erikson's stages (i.e., identity, intimacy, generativity) are often connected to transition processes and can ease (or exacerbate) transition turmoil. In addition, many North American athletes end their careers when they graduate from college. This period, the early 20s, is also the time of establishing intimacy or facing isolation. Erikson's concept of *generativity*—of giving back something, of guiding the next generation versus stagnating in a midlife crisis—occurs during a stage of life when most athletes have finally retired. Giving back to the sport through teaching, coaching, or writing may be ways to ensure a healthy retirement and fulfill the needs of generativity. When studying the phenomena of career transitions, practitioners may find it useful to examine the psychosocial-developmental transitions or tasks athletes may also be facing (e.g., establishing identity, forming intimate relationships, giving back). This approach gives a dynamic and more holistic picture of the changes and challenges athletes encounter in their sports and in their lives. Erikson's model also supplies a framework for the types of interventions sport psychologists can use (e.g., helping athletes explore who they are).

More recently, developmental models of transition (e.g., Schlossberg, 1981) have also been adopted as alternative frameworks for working with athletes in transition. These models characterize retirement from sport as a process and propose that the attributes of the athlete, cognitive appraisals of the career termination, and characteristics of the post-retirement environment all interact throughout a sports career transition (Brewer, Van Raalte, & Petitpas, in press). Although developmental models have been instrumental in stimulating research in the area (e.g., Parker, 1994; Sinclair & Orlick, 1993), they do not indicate the specific factors that influence the quality of adjustment post-retirement (Ogilvie & Taylor, 1993). Moreover, the developmental models of transition that have been applied to retirement lack clinical utility, because they do not provide a framework in which interventions can be employed (Taylor & Ogilvie, 1994).

With these criticisms in mind, sport psychologists have developed conceptual models of sports career transitions to guide post-transition professional practice (e.g., Gordon, 1995; Taylor and Ogilvie, 1994, 1998). These models examine the entire course of the career transition process and focus on how the quality of an athlete's adjustment is influenced by three things: the causal factors that initiate the career termination process, developmental factors that differentiate positive and negative adaptation, and coping resources that affect the career transition response. The strength of these frameworks is that once specific career transition difficulties appear, appropriate psychological interventions can be recommended (Taylor & Ogilvie, 1994).

ATHLETES IN TRANSITION

In this section, we present two case studies to illustrate the ways in which career transition theory is put into practice. The first focuses on an adolescent swimmer contemplating leaving his sport. The second case is based on a group session conducted with three target pistol shooters who experienced unanticipated career terminations.

Thinking of Quitting: Transitions in Sport and Youth

Joel was a very talented 16-year-old swimmer whose father first contacted the second author (Mark) by phone. In that conversation, the father expressed concern about Joel, because he felt Joel had not been quite himself. His father thought that Joel might be thinking about quitting swimming. He stated that all he wanted for his son was for him to be happy, and if he wanted to quit swimming, that was fine. He also let me know that it was Joel who had brought up the idea of talking to a sport psychologist. Joel's father seemed to be a concerned and loving parent, but there appeared to be some communication difficulties between Joel and his folks. His father said, "Joel doesn't talk much to us about what's going on with him. Maybe we pester him too much. He's having some difficulties, and I would like him to talk to someone." I suggested he have Joel call me, and we would set up an appointment. Joel did so later that day, mentioning that he wanted to talk about his swimming. We'll jump past introductions.

Sport Psychologist (SP): Joel, you said on the phone you wanted to talk about your swimming. So tell me, what's happening there?

Joel (J): I don't know. It's just that swimming is not really fun anymore, and I am losing to people I should be able to beat. I'm just not making the improvements I should. Sometimes it's such a chore to get to the pool, and once I get there, I just want it over with. My coach is trying to get me to change my stroke, and I do it for awhile, but then I just fall back into my old pattern.

As Joel was talking, I noticed he was not really whining about what was going on for him in swimming; rather, I got a strong feeling of sadness and confusion. I suspected some of the sadness might have come not only from his getting beaten more lately but also from his contemplating quitting swimming altogether (as his dad suggested might be the case). In working with adolescents, I find useful Erikson's (1950, 1968) formulation that the central psychosocial developmental task of Joel's age group is meeting and resolving the conflicts and challenges of forming an ego identity (an integrated self-image of who we are and what we want to become). I thought the confusion I sensed might have been coming from a more general confusion many adolescents have about who they are during their identity development. Joel's poor competition performance and his not having fun any more were coming at exactly the wrong time. Just as his main task, according to Erikson, was to form an identity, part of what he had identified strongly with for many years (Joel as swimmer) appeared to be slipping away. I needed a big picture of how Joel got to this unhappy place he was in, and I explained it to him in just those terms. Asking him to construct a picture of himself might help him (and me) hear how far he had come in establishing a sense of who he is.

SP: It sounds like you're not in a real happy situation right now.

J: You're right there. I don't know . . . I know I am not having fun much anymore.

SP: Joel, what we need to do is get a big picture of Joel. If we can get a picture of who Joel is, what's happened in his life, and how he got to where he is now, then maybe we can start to change some things for the better. I don't know what those changes would be right now, but as we paint the big picture of Joel we'll have a better idea. So I'll be asking questions about you, your swimming, your past, your family and friends, school, plans for the future, all sorts of things that will help us paint a better picture of you. OK?

J: Sure . . . what do you want to know?

SP: Well, you've mentioned twice now that swimming is not much fun anymore. Tell you what—I want you to go back now to a time when swimming was a lot of fun.

J: That would be the year I was 13.

SP: OK, so tell me all about that time. What you were doing; what was fun?

J: Back then, it was great. I was one of the best swimmers in my age group. I had some best mates and we did stuff together, went to movies together, and we just had a good time in the pool. Everyone told me I was going to be this great swimmer. I was tall for my age [at 16 he was over six feet] and had these long arms. But I guess I'm not living up to my potential. I just don't seem to be getting better now as I should, and I'm tired all the time. It would be great if it was like it was when I was 13, but things don't work that way.

Joel's train of thought moved him from, at first, a happy memory of friends and swimming to thinking about what people had said about his potential, to present-day feelings of sadness and regret. It was a bit of an emotional ride. He went from a big smile to a flat affect in less than 30 seconds. I asked the question about when swimming was fun to see if there was something we could use from that time and pull it into the present. But the question kind of backfired in that bringing up the past, although at first pleasant, triggered associations and comparisons with the present state of affairs and actually seemed to make Joel feel even a bit more lost. His acknowledgment that he wanted to regress (go back to being 13 again) but that that was not a solution was a sign that I was working with an insightful and mature 16-year-old.

Joel's sabotaging of his own good memories with negative present comparisons was a pattern that would repeat itself in a variety of ways. For example, later in our sessions I would ask him to tell me a good feature about himself, and he would say something like, "I'm an easygoing bloke, but sometimes I get angry." There was always a "but" followed by something negative. He had been training himself for the past year or two to be a champion of self-deprecation.

Joel made a couple of remarks that I needed to hear more about. His being tired all the time could be a product of training (or overtraining), and his reference to having had "some best mates" led me to wonder about his circle of friends now. Much of one's identity development is often constructed with the help of one's peer group. If Joel felt relatively isolated, then his task of figuring out who he was would be even more challenging than usual.

I asked him about his training schedule and any other symptoms that might indicate overtraining. He reported that his energy levels were low, that he had a chronic low-grade problem with his left rotator cuff, and that he would sometimes "get real mad" at a teacher or a fellow swimmer. His training did not seem excessive, but his other physical and psychological symptoms suggested that he might be developing overtraining syndrome. He told me he had an appointment in the near future with a sports medicine physician to look into his fatigue, so I felt those complaints were being handled in the most appropriate way at that time. I wanted to find out about his getting mad, but I chose first to go with the issue of his relationships with peers. So, I inquired about his best mates back when he was 13 and his current friends now.

SP: You mentioned you had some good friends back then; what were they like?

J: There were four of us; we all swam together, and we would ski together too and do a lot of stuff. One of my friends I could talk to about anything. And we pushed each other and yelled and screamed for each other at meets. I was happy back then; I guess I really miss those times [again a happy memory followed by sadness].

A simple dynamic interpretation of the statement, "One of my friends I could talk to about anything" is that it is a question about Joel's and my developing relationship. Joel may be asking, on an unconscious level, "Can I talk to *you* about anything?" I decided not to address his "question" for the time being, knowing that if it really were an important question for him, it would come up again.

SP: It sounds like it was a good time, but something has changed, and you don't seem too happy now. What happened to those friends?

J: Well, two of them dropped out of swimming, and my best friend moved away.

SP: And what is your circle of friends like now?

J: I wouldn't call it a circle, maybe more like a short arc. I don't really have any close friends. There's a guy I joke around with at practice, and we have this friendly rivalry in the pool, but we don't go out and do anything together beyond swimming.

SP: Any friends who are girls?

J: There's this one girl in swimming who I kind of like, but she can also irritate the heck out of me. I haven't gone out on any dates, but right now I really don't want to, either.

The picture of Joel I was forming seemed almost paradoxical. Despite the fairly sad and lonely story Joel was telling, I was seeing a very intelligent, self-effacing, honest, sincere, polite, and good-looking kid. He seemed like just the kind of boy parents hope their daughters will bring home to meet the family. But despite all his fine qualities, which I knew he could, in time, recognize and appreciate, I was getting this overwhelming sense of isolation, loss, and confusion. His task of identity construction, during a period that for many of us is a turbulent time, was made doubly tough because a source of aid in the construction of identity, his best mates, disappeared. In recalling the times with his friends, he would light up, only to sink back down in a small moment of grief. It seemed Joel was stuck in those halcyon days and was having some trouble getting over their loss.

Joel was in the limbo of transition on several fronts. He was leaving childhood behind, and he was potentially leaving swimming (and with it a large chunk of his current limited identity) behind as well. I was concerned that Joel was vulnerable, even with all his positive traits, to developing depression. I needed to ask about suicidal ideation.

SP: Joel, I'm getting a picture here of a bright guy with a whole lot going for him, but he is unhappy, really misses the good old days, feels rather isolated from others, and is confused about what he wants to become. With that picture, I get a bit worried, and I need to ask you about any thoughts or plans you've had about harming yourself.

J: You mean kill myself? Sure, I've thought about it; I would guess most people have had those thoughts, but I would never do it; don't worry. It's kind of a final solution to problems, isn't it? I think I would rather have my problems than that sort of solution.

SP: That's good to hear. I like your attitude, but if at any time you start to get those types of thoughts, promise to call me or at least talk to someone else about it.

J: It's a promise.

SP: OK, good. Now, while we're in the "painting a picture of Joel" mode, let's expand that picture out a bit more. Tell me about school—the good, the bad, and the ugly.

J: Well, the good is math and the sciences. I really like that stuff. The bad is English, and the ugly is Spanish. That may be because they are so difficult for me. I have moderate dyslexia, so spelling and reading and understanding, and even worse, writing English is a pain. I just don't want to have anything to do with it. Then when it comes to Spanish, I am hopeless. They do all those tests [achievement tests] everyone takes in school to determine what level you're operating at. Well, the conclusion on me is that I can work at this really high level, but that it's not showing up in my performance in school. As they say, "there's an apparent disparity" [he may have trouble with English, but his vocabulary is much larger than that of most 16-year-olds I know]. Sort of like my swimming; I've been told so many times that I have all this "potential," but I don't seem to be realizing it now. I'd like to concentrate on math and science, maybe become an engineer, and not have to worry about all that English stuff.

Joel has filled in a lot of the picture with his story about school. From his class work, he is getting mixed messages. He apparently does quite well in the sciences and math but then gets the message that he is not so bright when it comes to language. Also, the test results send the message, "you are bright, but you are not achieving," an echo of what is happening in swimming. It is no wonder there is some confusion in his life. His comment about becoming an engineer is a welcome one. It indicates that he is having some thoughts about the future. I want to pursue that potential future part of his identity, but I first want to explore his dyslexia and difficulties with language.

SP: An engineer, huh? That sounds pretty interesting, and I want us to talk some more about that, but before we do I'd like to get back to Spanish and English. They seem to be a big pain.

J: Yeah; I go into class, and I just hate it. I try and I never get better than a B and sometimes get a C+.

SP: And you are used to getting As?

J: Yeah; I am supposedly this "gifted" student, but I just get by in English.

SP: Are you often this hard on yourself?

J: What do you mean?

SP: Here's what I am seeing: a bright student who is also dyslexic, who finds English difficult, probably in part due to the dyslexia, but who manages to sometimes get Bs. Sounds to me like you are doing great in English given the circumstances, yet it seems like you are beating yourself up for not excelling in an area in which you have a disadvantage. You might want to be a little nicer to Joel; he's not a bad guy.

J: You sound just like my parents and my coach. It's like there's a conspiracy going on here [he smiles and then laughs].

SP: Oh no, paranoia! You got in to see me just in time! [we both start laughing].

Joel's joking about a conspiracy was a very good sign about the developing working relationship. It suggested that Joel was becoming comfortable with me. His comment opened the door for me to make a humorous response. A psychologist and an athlete laughing together about themselves is a solid indicator that the working alliance is progressing well. Also, seeing his laughter was a relief for me. I thought, this lost and confused kid can still laugh at himself; he probably has a lot more resources than I suspected that will help him find his way. I returned to the theme of him being tough on himself.

SP: From your mention of the coach, it sounds like he's noticed you beat yourself up. What do you say to yourself at meets and in the pool?

J: I guess I do put myself down a lot, especially lately, when I haven't been swimming well.

SP: So give me an example of what you would say to yourself after you lost a race to someone you could have beaten a year or two ago.

J: I don't know; I try to say something like, You're a better swimmer than that, but what I am doing lately is saying, You're not even a swimmer at all. And that's what I would like to talk about with you. I think I want to quit swimming, but I want to get a scholarship to college. I think I can do it with my swimming, but not the way I am going now, so maybe that won't work out anyway. I used to just love swimming, but now . . . I don't know. If I quit, I'd no longer be a swimmer; then I don't know what I would be.

SP: Sounds like you're in a bit of a bind. What you used to love is now an often unpleasant experience, but if you leave it behind you'll be losing a big chunk of yourself.

J: I think you're right; I am feeling kind of lost.

SP: And kind of alone?

J: Yeah, but I don't care too much about friends right now.

SP: Joel, I am going to have to disagree with you on this one. You should have seen yourself when you were talking about the good times with your mates. You had a big smile, and your face lit up. And then it seemed you got sad because of how much you missed those friends. Am I off base here?

J: No, I guess you're right. It's just that I don't know how to make friends. Those guys I swam with, I'd been swimming with for years. It's like we'd always been friends. And my best friend I could talk to about anything.

There are Joel's implicit questions again: Can I talk to *you* about anything? Can you replace something I have lost? These questions now need to be addressed.

SP: It's kind of tough to lose someone like that, and I am no substitute for a best friend, but when you're in here we can talk about anything you want—anything at all—swimming, parents, school, feelings, dreams, friends—you name it. Speaking of friends, making new friends is awkward, at times even a bit scary. Nobody likes rejection. But helping you with the job of making some new friends could be something you and I do together. We can talk about some ways to go about getting connected with people a little later. What I would like to go back to is the question you seem to be struggling with, and that is, If I quit swimming, then what am I? So quitting swimming is like losing yourself.

J: I've been a swimmer for so long, it's hard to think of me as anything else. Without swimming, I guess I really don't know who I am.

SP: Well wake up and smell the teenage years!

J: What?

SP: Sorry, Joel, I didn't mean to be flippant, but finding out who you are and who you want to become is your job at this time in your life. It's the job of all young people as they move into adulthood. Most people your age are going through something similar to you. You may have a bit rougher time of it because often some of the people who help us figure out who we are, are our best mates, and your best mates kind of disappeared on you. In one sense it is really good that you are thinking about quitting swimming, because it brings up the whole question of who you are outside of swimming. Many athletes develop what is called an *athletic identity,* and they see themselves almost exclusively as athletes. For example, many swimmers' careers end in their mid-twenties. Those who identified themselves as swimmers exclusively end up going through what you're going through, but it's possibly worse because they are already 24 years old and are trying to cope with a problem that 14- to 18-year-olds usually deal with. Some day, sooner or later, you won't be swimming. When that time comes, I hope you'll have a strong sense of who you are beyond your swimming. By asking and trying to answer the "who am I?" question, you are completing the job of adolescence. Congratulations; you are on exactly the right path.

J: I think I understand what you mean. It's sort of like I'll have to quit sometime, and then what?

SP: Exactly! Leaving sport is a whole lot easier if you don't also leave behind a whole chunk of yourself.

J: But right now this "job" of mine doesn't feel very good.

SP: And you probably won't feel too much better for awhile, and you will feel lost, and you will feel alone, and you will get frustrated with yourself and others. It will be a bumpy ride.

J: Great! And I don't even know where to begin [looks a little hopeless].

SP: Well, Joel, I think you have begun. You've asked the question. I would be more than happy to help you figure out some of the many answers to the question, Who is Joel?

J: [smiling now] I'd like that.

My verbal glass of cold water in the face and the following didactic intervention were aimed at reinterpreting Joel's sense of being lost. I was trying to help him see that not knowing who he is does not mean he is really lost; rather, he is in the exact place he should be for this time in his life. I also did not sweeten the reframe. I let him know that his confusion and feeling lost were not going to go away soon but that they also were part of a normal process. Joel got my message that if the answer to "who am I?" was only "a swimmer," then sooner or later he was truly going to be lost. The sealing of our working alliance came with my offer to help and his acceptance of that help.

I worked with Joel for another year on a variety of issues. When he began to examine his life and his relationships (family, teachers, coaches, new friends), he started to appreciate how much more there was to him than his swimming. Joel made significant progress in getting a handle on his negative thinking about himself and about his English "problem." He was able to restructure his thinking about English as not something he hated but as something that really taxed his resources and was a challenge. His getting mad at others had more to do with frustrations with himself that he projected outward. Also, many of his problems in the pool slowly resolved as Joel began to see himself as more than a swimmer and as he measured his self-worth by other yardsticks than swimming performance. Paradoxically, as swimming became less central to Joel's sense of self, the potential he had not realized slowly became a reality. We worked on his social skills and his feeling awkward trying to make friends. Through goal setting, positive thinking, log keeping, and other cognitive-behavioral interventions, Joel's short arc did become a small circle of good friends. Joel ended up getting a scholarship and going to a big swimming university that also had a well-known engineering school.

A foreclosed athletic identity and developmental arrest do occur among athletes, but the majority of athletes progress through their psychosocial stages quite competently. For some athletes, however, leaving sport brings up questions of identity outside of sport. Most pre-transition counseling should touch on issues of, Who am I outside this thing I do three hours a day? From Brewer, Van Raalte, and Linder (1993) and Brewer et al. (in press) we know that athletic identity, especially a foreclosed one, can lead to adjustment difficulties. Helping athletes establish a sense of who they are beyond sport is a useful intervention that can occur anytime in an athlete's career, even several years before retirement, as in Joel's case.

The last I heard from Joel was that he was having a good freshman year in the pool and that he had a steady girlfriend. His retirement from swimming would probably be a few years away, but he now had tools and a sense of who he was that would serve him well when he finally left his sport. Joel had made a big transition from knowing himself as a swimmer to knowing so much more about who he really is.

Shot Down: Counseling Athletes Post-Transition

Based on a synthesis of 12 studies, which specifically examined psychological adjustment to retirement from sport, Grove et al. (1998) documented that nearly 20% of the (more than 2,000) athletes studied experienced psychological adjustment difficulties when they ended their careers. As illustrated in Joel's case, practitioners can play a vital role in helping athletes pre-transition. When working with athletes post-transition, sport psychologists have advocated that an approach is needed that helps athletes develop an understanding of what they are going through at that moment in time (Baillie, 1993; Petitpas et al., 1996). Based on the existing theoretical, empirical, and practical knowledge in the area, here are some examples of the questions we have in mind when providing interventions to athletes following their career termination:

1. Is the athlete terminating his or her sporting career voluntarily or involuntarily, and what is his or her locus of control?

2. To what extent does the athlete identify with the athlete role (Brewer et al. 1993)?
3. To what extent has the athlete foreclosed on areas of his or her life outside of sport (Murphy, Petitpas, & Brewer, 1996)?
4. To what extent are coping resources (e.g., social support) available to the athlete?
5. Does the athlete have previous experience with transitions (Pearson & Petitpas, 1990)?
6. To what extent has the athlete continued his or her involvement in sport-related activities since career termination?
7. To what extent did the athlete plan for a post-sporting career?
8. Does the athlete possess and understand transferable skills (Mayocchi & Hanrahan, in press)?
9. To what extent did the athlete use transferable skills for the transition, and what is currently used?
10. To what extent did the athlete achieve his or her sport-related goals?
11. Has the athlete had access to career-transition support services, and if so, to what extent has he or she used these services?
12. To what extent does the athlete have a new focus after retirement?

Geoff, Phoebe, and Tony are competitive target pistol shooters who experienced unanticipated career terminations six weeks prior to the following consultation. As a result of sudden changes in firearm legislation in their home country, all shooting associations and clubs were prevented by law from staging and participating in domestic competitions. People who retained funding after this decision was passed were also required to train outside the country if they intended to try to qualify for international shooting competitions. Unfortunately, the majority of shooters could not afford to continue training on a full-time basis and were forced to retire from their sport.

Geoff, Phoebe, and Tony attended a one-day career transition workshop organized for competitive shooters six weeks after their collective forced retirement. The following excerpts are taken from a small group session conducted by the first author (David) with the three shooters during the workshop. Although working with transitional athletes on an individual basis is a recommended method of delivery (Grove et al., 1998), sport psychology practice is more than a dyadic activity. To supplement the material presented in this case study, the reader is directed to the literature that reviews group counseling principles and techniques (e.g., Corey, 1994; Gazda, 1989).

SP: Hello, everyone. Please come in and have a seat.

Tony (T): Thanks. It's been a while since you've seen us, hasn't it?

Phoebe (P): Yeah, it's been about three months for me.

SP: It has been quite some time. I am pleased to see that you could all make it today.

Geoff (G): I only wish we were coming to see you today to talk about our performance in shooting . . . like we used to.

Helping athletes make successful transitions out of sport is not a simple process. Sport psychologists are sometimes approached months (and occasionally years) after athletes have ended their competitive careers. In some instances, athletes seek a sport psychologist's help for the first time after their playing careers are over. In this case, however, I had the advantage of having previously worked individually with each of the shooters on a range of performance enhancement issues up until the end of their shooting careers. Therefore, developing rapport was not as complicated as it might have been if we were meeting for the first time. The challenge here was how we could build on our existing relationships and address the athletes' concerns, whatever they might be. Because they were reflecting on and longing for the past, I already suspected, at this early point in the session, that Tony, Phoebe, and Geoff were stuck someplace about six weeks back in time.

SP: I thought we could use our time together today to share our thoughts and feelings about what has happened over the past six weeks. If we have time, I was also hoping we could discuss what your initial reactions were upon hearing the actual decision [to abruptly terminate competitive shooting], as well as what your future plans are. If you have any other issues that you would like to talk about at any time, then we can do that as well. I would really like this to be an open forum. Would anyone like to begin?

Tony, Geoff, and Phoebe had been teammates at one time or another in their careers, so I thought it would be best to begin the session by opening it up for discussion (rather than by starting with an exercise to help the group participants get to know one another). Just as in individual counseling, it is important for small discussion groups to have a number of explicit aims. Although these may fluctuate as the session progresses, it is the role of the group facilitator to clarify the group's objective(s) from the outset. In this case, I initially tried to create an environment in which everyone was encouraged to contribute.

T: I'll start. Could you tell us how long are we going to feel this way?

SP: That is a great place to start, as I'm sure we would all like to know the answer to that question. As we all may not be feeling the same way, could you share with us how you are feeling, Tony?

T: Well, it's really hard to express it in words . . . I guess I'm just angry at what has happened. I had dreams of going to the Olympics, and now they are all gone. I feel as if I have nothing to show for it at the moment.

SP: Thank you, Tony. If it is okay, we'll come back to what you have said in a minute. I would just like to give Phoebe and Geoff an opportunity to share with us how they have been going.

P: Well . . . I was really worrying about my future until today. The [career transition] workshop sessions this morning have helped explain some of the things that have been going through my mind.

SP: Could you tell us, Phoebe, what you feel has specifically changed in your mind, in terms of how you are feeling now compared to how you were feeling in the weeks leading up today?

P: I was just really confused about everything before today. In seeing everyone who is in the same boat I am, I have realized that I am not alone.

SP: And how about you, Geoff?

G: Personally, I have come to recognize that I need to start concentrating on finding a job real soon. I just don't know where to start.

Athletes in transition tend to respond well to small-group sessions, because they are provided with an opportunity to share their feelings about the transition (Petitpas et al., 1990). Tony elected to make the first contribution and subsequently followed my use of the word *we* by suggesting that everyone in the group is feeling the same way he is. Indeed, this state of affairs may be true. What I did, however, was assume that this universal condition was not the case and ask him to share his own feelings with the group. I used this tactic not only to encourage Tony to be the first to voice his thoughts about his career transition but also to give the others an opportunity to consider their own feelings. Geoff and Phoebe were then invited to provide their views so that comparisons could be made.

After listening to everyone's first contributions, I had high expectations for the group. Overall, I had the feeling that all three members were interested in interacting with each other and honestly sharing their experiences. It appeared that Phoebe was coping better with her transition than the others were. Her comments about not being alone reflected feelings of universality, which is one of the most significant learning experiences members of a group can have (Yalom, 1995). It was my hope that Geoff and Tony would come to the same experience during the course of our meeting. Tony expressed some bitterness but seemed enthusiastic about being able to share his feelings. Geoff appeared somewhat concerned about his future career path.

After all three people had had further opportunities in the session to express their experiences and emotions in greater detail, I returned to Tony's original question of how long the group members might feel the way they do.

SP: So, in response to Tony's first question about what you all may be feeling—I wish there was a formula that could tell you how long you should expect to feel angry, confused, and concerned about your future. Unfortunately, there isn't. What I can tell you, however, is that all of these feelings are normal. It is normal to be concerned about your future. It is normal to be angry. It is also normal to be confused. You have all been so committed to your shooting that there really isn't any other way you could feel right now.

In order to reach the elite level in their chosen sport, people like Geoff, Phoebe, and Tony have to make considerable sacrifices in their lives. Once a certain level is reached, these same people also often enter into a kind of Faustian bargain with themselves in order to maintain their sporting abilities. As discussed by Gardner (1993), the Faust legend exemplifies the notion that accomplished people often feel that they must compulsively adhere to the development of their talent in order to preserve their level of attainment. Many people who become embedded in an arrangement in which they are exclusively committed to their sports also feel that their ability will be compromised or even irretrievably lost if the dedication is relaxed. Although such a strong commitment to the athlete role can have positive effects on sporting performance, people who highly value the athletic component of the self are at risk of experiencing adjustment problems when they end their careers (Brewer et al., 1993). When working with athletes post-transition, sport psychology practitioners need to consider that self-identity can also be adversely influenced by the transition itself (Brewer et al., in press; Lavallee et al., 1998), and post-transition athletes may feel lost and uncertain of who they are.

T: But I just don't think it's fair that some people just suddenly decided that we could no longer do what we have trained so long and hard for!

SP: We were all aware for a few years that this was a possibility, weren't we? I recall us all talking about this during one of our squad meetings last year.

T: Sure, we knew it was a possibility that we might be forced to retire. I, for one, didn't think that it would come to this . . . a situation where we have to physically move out of the country in order to train.

Research has identified that personal choice, injury, deselection, and chronological age are the most prevalent reasons for retirement from sport (Ogilvie & Taylor, 1993). An involuntary sports career transition such as the one presented here often proves to be difficult to handle because it is something for which the athlete is seldom prepared (Fortunato, 1998). There is an inconsistency in Tony's perception of why his shooting career ended, however, because he also mentioned that the group members have the opportunity to continue to train and compete abroad. I was unsure if the group had similar views to Tony's, so I rephrased what I thought he meant.

SP: As we both know, all professional shooters have to end their careers at some point. For some, this may happen early as a result of problems with their vision. Others may simply decide that the time is right . . . and that they want to spend more time with their families. In this case, you've said that you were forced to retire from shooting. You have also just suggested that you have the option of moving abroad to continue training. There seems to be an inconsistency here, and I think it is something we should try and clarify before moving on. OK?

In addition to helping people understand and appreciate the complex issues surrounding the career transition process, sport psychologists can work more directly with athletes to help them develop feelings of control over the situation (Murphy, 1995). Researchers have found that athletes who experience the greatest adjustment difficulties do not have an internal locus of control over the cause of their career terminations (e.g., Lavallee, Grove, & Gordon, 1997). My planned purpose here was to address Tony's discrepancy directly about why he felt his career ended in order to alter the group's perception of their career termination. Such an approach is consistent with Glasser's (1965, 1989) model of reality therapy, which suggests that the practitioner's fundamental task is to challenge the client to take effective control. Although I was speaking to the entire group, my comments were directed to Tony because I sensed some hostility from his earlier remarks.

P: Given the options we had at the time, it just wasn't financially possible.

SP: What did you see as your other options at the time, Phoebe?

P: Well, it was either to retire then and there or look for a sponsorship . . . and getting an international sponsor at that point did not look very promising for us.

SP: From everything that you have said, it sounds as if you felt that it was in your best interest to retire. Would that be right?

T: I don't know about best interest, but it was either retire or go into huge debt training abroad. I guess I could have chosen a financial nightmare, but I preferred not to [his anger seems to be fading].

SP: [looking at Geoff] It certainly doesn't make it any easier, does it?

G: No, it doesn't.

SP: In some cases, it's actually more difficult when you consciously decide to make a clean break from your sport. You were all given two rather bad choices, retirement or serious financial difficulties, and you had to choose. That choice was under your control, but unfortunately, all the options were bad. Maybe if we look at your retirement in that light we can move ahead and consider your next step.

G: Well, that is just it . . . my problem is that I really did not start seriously considering what I wanted to do as a career until recently. And even now, I am still unsure.

While observing the group's behavior and listening to what they were saying, I did not detect any deep-seated feelings of despair or apathy. Phoebe's remark about the likelihood of obtaining sponsorship was said with notable confidence. Tony's anger was still there, but it seemed to be mellowing. It was Geoff's response to my comment about making a clean break from the team that led me to shift the group's focus for the remainder of the session to career exploration and planning issues.

A recurring theme among elite-level athletes is their resistance to planning for their career termination (Murphy, 1995). Although sport psychologists often do not receive formal training in career counseling techniques, they can help people cope with the transition out of sport. Coping has been identified as a complex and dynamic process for athletes in transition (Grove, Lavallee, & Gordon, 1997), and research suggests that the presence or absence of coping resources for athletes upon career termination influences the overall quality of adjustment (Taylor & Ogilvie, 1998). Planning for a career prior to retirement from sport has been found to be one of the most effective transition-related coping strategies (Wylleman et al., 1993). In some instances, pre-retirement preparation can moderate concerns about the career transition process and can subsequently allow athletes to concentrate more fully on their sport (Murphy, 1995). During their sporting careers, Geoff, Phoebe, and Tony did not develop post-shooting plans, and as a result, they were now apprehensive and uncertain about their futures. I, therefore, tried to communicate an understanding of Geoff's situation and to validate any feelings of inadequacy that group members may have been experiencing.

SP: I understand and appreciate what you are going through. Given the nature of elite-level shooting, competitors are left with little time to consider, while they're competing, what they would like to do in the future. Has this been the case with you, Geoff?

G: It has. I really haven't had time to do anything since I started training full-time. You know . . . our coach always said that we shouldn't concentrate on anything else [other than shooting] if we wanted to retain our place on the squad.

The career development of athletes is often influenced by the sporting environment in which they participate. As Petitpas et al. (1990) have suggested, some coaches have fears that encouraging athletes to engage in career transition planning will distract them from their focus on high-level achievement and will subsequently detract from their sport performance. This old-school philosophy is becoming increasingly uncommon in contemporary sport, because coaches are recognizing that career transition planning can contribute to enhanced performance (Crook & Robertson, 1991). It is, however, an issue that practitioners need to be aware of, because athletes who are encouraged to invest strongly in sport to the exclusion of other activities often have a maladaptive orientation to career planning prior to retirement (Brewer et al., in press; Murphy et al., 1996; Pearson & Petitpas, 1990).

SP: Geoff, you also mentioned, at the start of this session, that you are not sure where to begin looking for a career.

G: Well, I actually have been thinking about a few different things over the past few years, but I have not done much about it. I did try looking for a part-time job last year . . . but I was not able find one that offered enough flexibility for me to maintain my training and competition schedule. My shooting always seemed to get in the way. I guess I don't have that problem now.

SP: So you have [said emphatically] been thinking about your career for some time now. It shows that you are further along than you might think. I recall [in one of our sessions the previous year] you once mentioning to me an interest in teaching. Is this something you are still interested in?

G: To be honest, I really haven't given it much thought since then. I could see myself teaching. I just don't know if it is what I want to do in the long term.

SP: One of the biggest myths about jobs is that you have to start planning today for a career that will last the rest of your life. If any of you are unsure about what you would like to do at this stage, you may want to consider taking a more short-term approach. This would allow you to explore all of your options. I'm always here if you want to come in and spend some time talking through any particular career options you might be interested in. After doing that, we could work on setting some goals for your career . . . just like we used to do in terms of your shooting performance.

Counseling athletes in transition can be successful only if the athlete and the sport psychologist work together to identify common objectives. Geoff's neglect to engage in career transition planning led him to assume that a decision about a career needs to be a permanent one. Because this belief lies at the heart of much of the anxiety people feel in selecting an occupation (Krumboltz, 1992), I addressed his comments with a person-centered, nondirective approach in the hope of encouraging the group members to explore their career options in a more short-term light. When people are ready to begin planning a career outside of their sports, the practitioner can provide support by using vocational interest inventories and suggesting a number of areas to explore. As I often do in cases where an athlete is uncertain about where to begin, I recommended, as this session was ending, that each of the shooters spend time formulating a number of career goals in order to help them retain control over their career transitions.

Geoff, Phoebe, Tony, and I continued to work together intermittently over the next five months. In that time, we examined as a group how they could maximize their sporting experiences by learning how to transfer skills they developed in shooting to other areas of their lives. I also worked individually with each of them on a wide range of career transition issues. In between our sessions, I recommended that they regularly consult the book *Athlete's Guide to Career Planning: Keys to Success from the Playing Field to Professional Life* (Petitpas et al., 1997). This self-help book is an exceptional resource for athletes at all competitive levels, and it contains numerous career exploration and planning exercises as well as useful reference material on sport-related careers and other job search guides.

Geoff and Phoebe both went on to make successful career transitions. Geoff ultimately enrolled in an undergraduate program in teacher education. Phoebe now works for a local newspaper, in the hopes of one day becoming a sports journalist. Tony, however, continued to experience difficulties in coping with his life after shooting. As I worked with him individually, he eventually was able to identify a number of interests outside of shooting. After this had occurred, I referred Tony to a career counselor who has helped him begin to shape a satisfying career path for himself.

PAST, PRESENT, AND FUTURE

As the demands associated with competitive sport have increased over the years, so has the importance of career transition issues in sport psychology practice. In 1980, McPherson reported that an extensive literature search generated 20 references pertaining to this topic. In 1998, over 200 references were identified on career transitions in sport, including 93 citations that highlighted professional practice issues (Lavallee, Sinclair, & Wylleman, 1998; Lavallee, Wylleman, & Sinclair, 1998). During this time, an international special-interest group has been developed in association with the European Federation of Sports Psychology (FEPSAC) to exchange information on applied and investigative work in the area (Alfermann et al., 1999). Several career transition intervention programs have also been developed by governing bodies and sport institutes around the world to help athletes prepare for their career termination (Anderson & Morris, in press; Gordon, 1995; United States Olympic Committee, 1988). Many of these programs employ the services of sport psychologists to provide pre-transition and post-transition counseling services to athletes. Moreover, the Australian Institute of Sport provides training opportunities and supervised practice through a graduate certificate in athlete career and education management (Anderson & Morris, in press).

Along with the psychological interventions discussed in this chapter, sport psychologists may also want to consider a number of other behavioral, cognitive, emotional, and social approaches that have been offered in the literature. For example, Wolff and Lester (1989) recommend using Meichenbaum's (1985) stress inoculation therapy as a technique to facilitate career transition adjustment among elite athletes by addressing the career termination before it actually occurs. Emotional expression (Yalom, 1980) and cognitive restructuring (Beck, 1979) are also methods that can be used to help athletes generate alternative interpretations associated with distressing reactions to retirement from sport (Gordon, 1995; Taylor & Ogilvie, 1994). In addition, Shapiro's (1995) eye movement desensitization and reprocessing has been suggested as a psychomotor technique that can ameliorate the effects of undesirable beliefs and images associated with career-ending injuries (Sime, 1998). The beneficial role of Harvey, Weber, and Orbuch's (1990) social psychological coping approach has also been illustrated with samples of elite athletes who experienced greater post-retirement adjustment to the extent that they engaged in productive confiding activity (Grove et al., 1998; Lavallee, Gordon, & Grove, 1997).

The topic of helping athletes leave their sports has grown tremendously, and sport psychologists are often the ones who supply service to retiring and retired athletes. Researchers have helped us understand a great deal about athletes in transition. What we need now is solid training in applied sport psychology programs at the master's and doctoral levels that teaches budding sport psychologists how to work effectively with athletes in transition.

REFERENCES

Alfermann, D., Bardaxoglou, N., Chamalidis, P., Lavallee, D., Stambulova, N., Menkehorst, H., Petitpas, A., Salmela, J., Schilling, G., van den Berg, F., & Wylleman, P. (1999). *Career transitions in competitive sports.* Biel, Switzerland: European Federation of Sports Psychology.

Andersen, M.B. (1996). Working with college student-athletes. In J.L. Van Raalte & B.E. Brewer (Ed.), *Exploring sport and exercise psychology* (pp. 317-334). Washington, DC: American Psychological Association.

Anderson, D., & Morris, T. (in press). Athlete lifestyle programs. In D. Lavallee & P. Wylleman (Eds.), *Career transitions in sport: International perspectives.* Morgantown, WV: Fitness Information Technology.

Baillie, P.H.F. (1993). Understanding retirement from sports: Therapeutic ideas for helping athletes in transition. *The Counseling Psychologist, 21,* 399-410.

Beck, A. T. (1979). *Cognitive therapy and emotional disorders.* New York: New American Library.

Bookbinder, H. (1955). Work histories of men leaving a short life span occupation. *Personnel and Guidance Journal, 34,* 164-167.

Brewer, B.W., Van Raalte, J.L., & Linder, D.E. (1993). Athletic identity: Hercules' muscles or Achilles' heel? *International Journal of Sport Psychology, 24,* 237-254.

Brewer, B.W., Van Raalte, J.L., & Petitpas, A.J. (in press). Self-identity issues in sport career transitions. In D. Lavallee & P. Wylleman (Eds.), *Career transitions in sport: International perspectives.* Morgantown, WV: Fitness Information Technology.

Corey, G. (1994). *Theory and practice of group counseling* (4th ed.). Pacific Grove, CA: Brooks/Cole.

Crook, J.M., & Robertson, S.E. (1991). Transitions out of elite sport. *International Journal of Sport Psychology, 22,* 115-127.

Cummings, E., & Henry, W.E. (1961). *Growing old and the process of disengagement.* New York: Basic Books.

Danish, S.J., Petitpas, A.J., & Hale, B.D. (1993). Life development intervention for athletes: Life skills through sports. *The Counseling Psychologist, 21,* 352-385.

Erikson, E.H. (1950). *Childhood and society.* New York: Norton.

Erikson, E.H. (1968). *Identity: Youth and crisis.* New York: Norton.

Fortunato, V. (1998). Getting the axe: Adjustment process of delisted Australian rules footballers. *Journal of Applied Sport Psychology, 10, (Suppl.),* S119.

Gardner, H. (1993). *Creating minds.* New York: Basic Books.

Gazda, G.M. (1989). *Group counseling: A developmental approach* (4th ed.). Needham Heights, MA: Allyn & Bacon.

Glasser, W. (1965). *Reality therapy.* New York: Harper & Row.

Glasser, W. (1989). Control theory. In N. Glasser (Ed.), *Control theory in the practice of reality therapy: Case studies* (pp. 1-15). New York: Harper & Row.

Gordon, S. (1995). Career transitions in competitive sport. In T. Morris & J. Summers (Eds.), *Sport psychology: Theory, applications and issues* (pp. 474-501). Brisbane, Australia: Jacaranda Wiley.

Grove, J.R., Lavallee, D., & Gordon, S. (1997). Coping with retirement from sport: The influence of athletic identity. *Journal of Applied Sport Psychology, 9,* 191-203.

Grove, J.R., Lavallee, D., Gordon, S., & Harvey, J.H. (1998). Account-making: A model for understanding and resolving distressful reactions to retirement from sport. *The Sport Psychologist, 12,* 52-67.

Haerle, R.K. (1975). Career patterns and career contingencies of professional baseball players: An occupational analysis. In D.W. Ball & J.W. Loy (Eds.), *Sport and social order* (pp. 461-519). Reading, MA: Addison-Wesley.

Hallden, O. (1965). The adjustment of athletes after retiring from sport. In F. Antonelli (Ed.), *Proceedings of the 1st International Congress of Sport Psychology* (pp. 730-733). Rome: International Society of Sport Psychology.

Harvey, J.H., Weber, A.L., & Orbuch, T.L. (1990). Interpersonal accounts. Oxford: Basil Blackwell.

Krumboltz, J.D. (1992). The wisdom of indecision. *Journal of Vocational Behavior, 41,* 239-244.

Kübler-Ross, E. (1969). *On death and dying.* New York: Macmillan.

Lavallee, D., Gordon, S., & Grove, J.R. (1997). Retirement from sport and the loss of athletic identity. *Journal of Personal and Interpersonal Loss, 2,* 129-147.

Lavallee, D., Grove, J.R., & Gordon, S. (1997). The causes of career termination from sport and their relationship to post-retirement adjustment among elite-amateur athletes in Australia. *The Australian Psychologist, 32,* 131-135.

Lavallee, D., Grove, J.R., Gordon, S., & Ford, I.W. (1998). The experience of loss in sport. In J.H. Harvey (Ed.), *Perspectives on loss: A sourcebook* (pp. 241-252). Philadelphia: Brunner/Mazel.

Lavallee, D., Sinclair, D.A., & Wylleman, P. (1998). An annotated bibliography on career transitions in sport: I. Counselling-based references. *Australian Journal of Career Development, 7,* (2), 34-42.

Lavallee, D., Wylleman, P., & Sinclair, D.A. (1998). An annotated bibliography on career transitions in sport: II. Empirical references. *Australian Journal of Career Development, 7,* (3), 32-44.

Mayocchi, L., & Hanrahan, S.J. (in press). Transferable skills for career change. In D. Lavallee & P. Wylleman (Eds.), *Career transitions in sport: International perspectives.* Morgantown, WV: Fitness Information Technology.

McPherson, B.D. (1980). Retirement from professional sport: The process and problems of occupational and psychological adjustment. *Sociological Symposium, 30,* 126-143.

Meichenbaum, D. (1985). *Stress inoculation training.* New York: Plenum.

Mihovilovic, M. (1968). The status of former sportsmen. *International Review of Sport Sociology, 3,* 73-93.

Murphy, S.M. (1995). Transitions in competitive sport: Maximizing individual potential. In S.M. Murphy (Ed.), *Sport psychology interventions* (pp. 331-346). Champaign, IL: Human Kinetics.

Murphy, G.M., Petitpas, A.J., & Brewer, B.W. (1996). Identity foreclosure, athletic identity, and career maturity in intercollegiate athletes. *The Sport Psychologist, 10,* 239-246.

Ogilvie, B.C., & Taylor, J. (1993). Career termination issues among elite athletes. In R.N. Singer, M. Murphey, & L.K. Tennant (Eds.), *Handbook of research on sport psychology* (pp. 761-775). New York: Macmillan.

Parker, K.B. (1994). "Has-beens" and "wanna-bes": Transition experiences of former major college football players. *The Sport Psychologist, 8,* 287-304.

Pearson, R., & Petitpas, A. (1990). Transitions of athletes: Developmental and preventive perspectives. *Journal of Counseling and Development, 69,* 7-10.

Petitpas, A.J., Brewer, B.W., & Van Raalte, J.L. (1996). Transitions of the student-athlete: Theoretical, empirical, and practical perspectives. In E.F. Etzel, A.P. Ferrante, & J.W. Pinkney (Eds.), *Counseling college student-athletes: Issues and interventions* (2nd ed., pp. 137-156). Morgantown, WV: Fitness Information Technology.

Petitpas, A., Champagne, D., Chartrand, J., Danish, S., & Murphy, S. (1997). *Athlete's guide to career planning: Keys to success from the playing field to professional life.* Champaign, IL: Human Kinetics.

Petitpas, A., Danish, S., McKelvain, R., & Murphy, S.M. (1990). A career assistance program for elite athletes. *Journal of Counseling and Development, 70,* 383-386.

Schlossberg, N.K. (1981). A model for analyzing human adaptation to transition. *The Counseling Psychologist, 9,* 2-18.

Shapiro, F. (1995). *Eye movement desensitization and reprocessing: Basic principles, protocols, and procedures.* New York: Guilford Press.

Sime, W.E. (1998). Injury and career termination issues. In M.A. Thompson, R.A. Vernacchia, & W.E. Moore (Eds.), *Case studies in applied sport psychology: An educational approach* (pp. 195-226). Dubuque, IA: Kendall/Hunt.

Sinclair, D.A., & Orlick, T. (1993). Positive transitions from high-performance sport. *The Sport Psychologist, 7,* 138-150.

Taylor, J., & Ogilvie, B.C. (1994). A conceptual model of adaptation to retirement among athletes. *Journal of Applied Sport Psychology, 6,* 1-20.

Taylor, J., & Ogilvie, B.C. (1998). Career transition among elite athletes: Is there life after sports? In J.M. Williams (Ed.), *Applied sport psychology: Personal growth to peak performance* (3rd ed., pp. 429-444). Mountain View, CA: Mayfield.

United States Olympic Committee (1988). *Career assessment program for athletes: 1988-1989 seminar workbook.* Colorado Springs, CO: Author.

Wolff, R., & Lester, D. (1989). A theoretical basis for counseling the retired professional athlete. *Psychological Reports, 64,* 1043-1046.

Wylleman, P., De Knop, P., Menkehorst, H., Theeboom, M., & Annerel, J. (1993). Career termination and social integration among elite athletes. In S. Serpa, J. Alves, V. Ferreira, & A. Paula-Brito (Eds.), *Proceedings of the 8th World Congress of Sport Psychology* (pp. 902-906). Lisbon: Universidade Tecnica de Lisboa.

Yalom, I.D. (1980). *Existential psychotherapy.* New York: Harper Collins.

Yalom, I.D. (1995). *The theory and practice of group psychotherapy* (4th ed.). New York: Basic Books.

CHAPTER 19

BREAKING OUT: DOING SPORT PSYCHOLOGY WITH PERFORMING ARTISTS

Kate F. Hays
The Performing Edge

All of life, in some ways, is about performance. Whatever our construction of the world—that is, our thoughts and feelings—our behavior is directly linked to that understanding. From this admittedly over-inclusive perspective, applied psychology can then be described as designed to enhance performance. Practitioners help elaborate and support those aspects of clients' lives that work most effectively, facilitating an increased sense of competence.

Even if one adopts a somewhat less grandiose stance, it is nonetheless possible to regard performance as encompassing more than sport performance alone. The practitioner who understands performance issues in relation to athletes is in an excellent position to transfer that knowledge base to other performance domains (Heil, Sagal, & Nideffer, 1997), those areas where a person needs to present some aspect of him- or herself to others in a public manner. Likewise, sport psychology principles can be generalized to other aspects of life (Gallwey, 1997).

In particular, the concepts, techniques, and skills applicable to sport performance can be readily transferred to our understanding of, and work with, performing artists. Both psychological skills training and the resolution of performance-related problems are relevant to "getting up on stage." Performing artists respond well to techniques focusing on performance enhancement (Hamilton, 1997). Likewise, they may experience both physical and psychological problems relating to performance. Among the most frequent difficulties encountered by performing artists are repetitive strain (overuse) injuries and performance anxiety (Clark, 1989). Although the latter issue may in some ways seem an obvious comparison with sport, the parallels in regard to the physical sequelae of overuse are striking as well. "The artist's counterparts of tennis elbow or swimmer's shoulder are clarinetist's thumb, cymbalist's shoulder, flutist's forearm, and violinist's neck" (Lubell, 1987, p. 253).

In the sections that follow, I describe psychological and performance issues that musicians may face. Performing artists may approach psychological interventions in ways both similar to and different from athletes, and I discuss these approaches next. After a description of my personal treatment philosophy, the rest of the chapter illustrates the brief treatment of an adolescent musician.

MUSIC PERFORMANCE ISSUES

Internal and external demands are the hallmarks of performance. Even in the face of elements outside of a musician's control, the emphasis on flawless technique and performance places an extraordinary level of expectation on the musician. As with competitive athletics, the level of competition among musicians can be intense. The job market for professional musicians is a tough one, and fewer than 30% of musicians are employed full-time in their profession (Hamilton, Kella, & Hamilton, 1995). A juror at a prestigious performing arts school, by way of illustration, observed the palpable tension during student auditions and commented, "I hate audition time at Juilliard. The whole building shakes" (Kogan, 1989, p. 14).

Many athletes begin sports training as young children; musicians also begin instrumental training in early childhood. As with athletes, social and emotional development can be affected. Focus and discipline, hours dedicated to practice, and single-minded concentration on a goal—all have costs along with rewards. In adulthood, musicians confront the reality that jobs are scarce and pay is low. These realities can set the groundwork for a pervasive, continuous anxiety and an amalgam of psychological, societal, and economic concerns layered in with performance issues (Nagel, 1992).

If applied sport psychology can be said to be in its adolescence, the treatment of performance issues in other disciplines is still in its infancy (Clark, 1989). Despite the numerous parallels with sport, concerns in performing arts medicine began receiving systematic attention only in the late 1970s and early 1980s (Lederman, 1989). Because orchestras do not rely on star players in the same way that sports teams do, there is less financial risk to organizations if a player needs replacing (e.g., potential loss of advertising revenue, lower fan attendance). Compounding the disregard by management, medical specialists who treat musicians have traditionally considered psychological performance issues as too minor to require direct medical intervention (Clark, 1989).

Performance practice in the arts can, however, result in a variety of medical and psychiatric difficulties. Repetitive strain injury, also referred to as overuse syndrome, is a "common disorder characterized by pain and loss of function in muscles and ligaments used in instrumental performance" (Clark, 1989, p. 29). Overuse syndrome tends to be associated with abrupt changes in performance practice, such as altering one's technical style or a marked increase in playing intensity. Although students may not frequently experience this problem, the rate may be as high as 70-80% among members of professional orchestras. Only minimal attention has been drawn to the etiology, prevention, or effective treatment of musician overuse injuries, even though such problems have been recognized for a considerable time and obviously affect many musicians (Clark, 1989). As with athletes (Williams & Andersen, 1998), stress responsivity and generalized muscle tension may be precursors to injury. Improved self-monitoring, relaxation training, and reduction in performance anxiety might all be helpful preventatives (Clark, 1989).

More recognized, although equally likely to be dismissed, is performance anxiety itself, also referred to as stage fright, "a state of nervousness or apprehension concerning performing before an audience" (Clark, 1989, p. 30). Amateur musicians and students may experience more performance anxiety than professionals. "One must perform to get in [to Juilliard], and one must perform to make the grade there" (Kogan, 1989, p. 11).

> Although a certain amount of stress and anxiety focuses attention and is necessary for optimal performance, excessive levels are clearly detrimental. Performers describe themselves as being under constant stress, with notable increases at the time of auditions, contests, solo performances, and performances before panels of experts, or juries (a word that implies stress) as a degree requirement in conservatories. . . . The consequences of even minor mistakes are perceived as potential disasters. (Lockwood, 1989, p. 225)

In addition to being emotionally difficult to manage, the somatic components of stage-fright tension can directly affect performance. For example, tremors interfere with bow control and fingering for string players; shortness of breath affects wind players and singers (Lockwood, 1989). In addition, tension and concern about these symptoms can not only exacerbate the symptoms themselves but can also directly affect concentration and memory (Clark, 1989; Hamilton, 1997; Lockwood, 1989). Negative internal preoccupation (e.g., negative self-talk) can also increase. Self-confidence can be undermined. A downward spiral may develop, in which self-criticism and performance tension negatively and synergistically interact. Performance progressively deteriorates in the resulting positive feedback loop.

TREATMENT OF PERFORMING ARTISTS

In contrast to sports, there is a long-standing tradition of, and connection between, the arts and psychotherapy, and that tradition has been interconnected with psychoanalysis. Starting with Freud, both psychoanalytic theory and practice have incorporated and studied art and artists. In psychodynamic terms, for example, Nagel (1992) suggested that stage fright relates to conflicts around exhibitionism or fear of parental aggression and that the need both to succeed and to avoid failure can be stirred in regard to performance. (Despite the parallels drawn in this chapter between the arts and sport, if you say "exhibitionism" or "fear of daddy's disapproval" to a hockey team, you will no doubt lose them forever.)

In contrast to athletes, it is accepted, and at times expected, that performing artists will seek treatment, often using psychodynamic forms of psychotherapy. Despite the popularity of psychodynamic therapy among performing artists, Clark (1989) noted that systematic desensitization, exposure therapy, and cognitive restructuring are especially helpful with musicians. In a recent book on performing arts psychology, Hamilton (1997) cites numerous examples of behavioral and cognitive-behavioral treatment with performing artists. Harris (1985) found that brief cognitive-behavioral group counseling was effective for musical performance anxiety. Other cognitive techniques, such as worry time, cognitive reframing, visualization, concentration training, and "inner game" training for musicians have proven useful (Green & Gallwey, 1986; Lehrer, 1993).

Perhaps because of the traditional psychotherapeutic link, it is important when artists come to sport psychologists for help to clarify the type of service being sought as well as proffered. Although some performers choose or anticipate an intrapsychic, reparative focus, others are interested in a consultative, behaviorally-based perspective. In the latter instance, whether described as consultation or coaching, the practitioner working on performance issues with clients may receive a mandate quite different from that of psychotherapy. As with other consultative experiences, a number of implications may be present: a fairly short-term focus, an acknowledgment of the client's skill and knowledge with regard to her or his own area of expertise, and limitations concerning deeper work on old issues.

Before presenting the case history of a young musician, I will outline the philosophical background and training that I bring to working with performing artists. Issues regarding competence to work with a musician are embedded in the case description.

TREATMENT PHILOSOPHY AND PERSPECTIVE

My initial training in clinical psychology was psychodynamic, my philosophy existential and humanist. Over the years, I have found that cognitive-behavioral perspectives and techniques have fit both my personally pragmatic style and my attitude toward clients. I have come to see the psychotherapeutic interchange as an opportunity for internal or interpersonal education within an interpersonal context. Kelly's client-as-scientist (Maher, 1969), subsequently developed as *collaborative empiricism* (Beck et al., 1979), also complements the perspectives implicit within a feminist philosophy of therapy (Brown, 1994). An egalitarian relationship forms a foundation and supports the client's internal power and striving for increased competence. I find that whether I am working on clinical issues or those of sport or performance, my goals are to understand and respect my clients' understanding of the world so that I can help them elaborate and grow. My ultimate goal, ironically, is to become obsolete.

I have brought these same beliefs and approaches to my training and work in sport psychology, and, more recently, to consultation and therapy in regard to performance issues. In solo and group practice, rural and urban settings, whether in clinical practice or at a sports medicine facility, this fundamental attitude imbues my interactions with others.

SETTING THE STAGE

Not all cases start out with as much complexity in the referral process as did this one. As in sport performance enhancement, however, I immediately needed to clarify and address a number of referral issues, whether actively or reflectively.

I received a phone message that the physician-director of a low-income child health clinic in a nearby city had called. I returned her call at my next break between clients. In her abrupt and rapid-fire, yet warm manner, Dr. Moore gave me the following information and requested my help:

> I've got a girl I want you to see. She's 15. Her family's had a difficult time of it. Her father is out of work because of a disability, and they're really struggling. But they're all hard working and a really nice family. I've known Martha for years, and she's really talented. She sings, and sings well. But she breaks out in hives. Is that something you can work with?

With these few comments and questions, a number of concerns immediately became apparent. Issues that I addressed directly with Dr. Moore included appropriate service, competence to perform such a service, motivation issues with indirect referrals, and finances. I was also aware of other thoughts, ranging from the pragmatic (did I have time in my schedule?) to the generic (marketing a specialized service; relationships with referral sources).

Most directly, Dr. Moore was asking whether I could see an adolescent who was presenting with a psychogenically induced skin disorder. I needed to make an immediate decision about my competence and comfort in seeing (a) an adolescent (b) apparently dealing with a psychophysiological reaction to stress in relation to (c) music performance issues.

When a child or adolescent is being referred, the practitioner is always confronted with the question of who should be seen. Is this a family issue or a personal one? What does the adolescent him- or herself want? Who is really interested in addressing the presenting issues? Is this issue primarily of concern to the referring person, the adolescent, or someone else altogether? Although my background includes extensive training and work with children and adolescents, as well as adults, I may not be the most appropriate person for the situation if family therapy is necessary.

At a broader level, the question of competence presented itself—whether competence to conduct the appropriate intervention or competence with regard to the particular performance area. The first general principle of the American Psychological Association's *Ethical Principles and Code of Conduct* states that psychologists "provide only those services and use only those techniques for which they are qualified by education, training, or experience" (American Psychological Association, 1992, p. 1600).

Minimal direct education or training appears available in regard to working with performers (Hamilton, 1997). I have long had an interest in the application of sport psychology principles to the performing arts, having found that these principles and techniques effectively address many of the same performance concerns. In general, in delivering sport psychology services, knowledge of the specific sport one is working with is a considerable advantage (Gould & Damarjian, 1998). This type of knowledge is likewise valuable in other performance areas. The preceding definition of competence suggests that competence consists of specific training plus the application of one's knowledge to other areas. As an amateur musician myself, I brought to this work my own direct experience of the performance issues faced by musicians.

Over the years, I have worked with musicians and have applied some of the same performance enhancement techniques that I use with athletes. Although I have worked most in applied sport psychology, I have marketed a generic performance perspective. I have placed ads in program books for music performances, for example, describing my consulting practice, The Performing Edge, as involving "performance enhancement training for the performing artist, athlete, or business person." In this referral, Dr. Moore herself may have intuitively understood the connection between one type of psychological skills training and another, or her way may have been paved by some of my marketing activity.

Speaking with Dr. Moore, I weighed a number of competing issues. I was at the moment over-booked and needed to limit new cases. And yet, having this person make this kind of referral felt like a real coup. Dr. Moore was someone whose positive perception of my capability mattered to me. Working with performing artists was, also, a direction in which I wanted to steer my practice, and besides, I could not think of anyone else to whom I would refer this young woman. Interest aside, however, it was important to make an initial judgment as to the appropriateness of individual, compared with family, intervention. I responded and inquired further.

> KFH: She sounds really interesting. Do you think that Martha is receptive to seeing me? And do you think that there are family issues I might need to address?
>
> Dr. Moore: It was Martha herself who talked with me about the hives the last time she was in for a check-up. She's eager to talk with someone. I think her father has had some major difficulties. He was actually hospitalized a few times. But Martha is a mature kid, and I think she'd really like to work on these issues by herself.

In conducting performance-related work, a variety of intertwined assessment and financial considerations arise. In addition to issues regarding the marketing of, and the market for, such services, there are a number of aspects of diagnosis to consider, and these relate to philosophy, credentialing, and preference.

For some, *diagnosis* implies a medical model and a psychopathological perception of both the client and the client's problem. Although diagnosis can be at odds with a developmental perspective, diagnosis can, alternatively, be a shorthand description of the problem. In many jurisdictions, financial reimbursement based on diagnosis is reserved for certain types of licensed practitioners. In the United States, psychologists licensed to practice independently can be reimbursed by third parties (e.g., insurance companies) for relevant treatment of specifically diagnosed problems, whereas educational sport psychologists conducting sport counseling might well not be. Thus, even though some practitioners might consider making a diagnosis, if it is not reimbursable through a third party, assigning a diagnosis may be moot. In working with clients on performance issues, there is also the question of client preference and financial capacity. Although the practitioner might be able to make a reimbursable diagnosis and see doing so as useful, the client may prefer to pay directly rather than be limited by health care regulations or feel concerned about issues of breach of privacy.

In the instance described here, it appeared, sight unseen, that Martha's hives could be diagnosed as a result of anxiety, in which physical symptoms were manifested for psychological reasons. I assumed that the family's income was fairly low. Because the case sounded intriguing and potentially short-term, I was prepared to adjust my fees if necessary.

> KFH: What's the family's financial situation?
>
> Dr. Moore: They're on Medicaid [low-income health care]. Mother's working but father's disabled.

Unless the family objected or Martha herself wanted to make a symbolic gesture of payment, it seemed most practicable to assume that with the combination of diagnosis, provider credential, and likely intervention, it would be appropriate to bill Medicaid for such services.

With these clarifications, I became practical.

> KFH: I would be glad to take her on. Is there a way that she can get here after school?

Dr. Moore assured me that the family kept appointments that they made. She wrote down the relevant appointment information and said that she would let the family know.

I, in turn, sent standard forms to the family, including a confirmation letter that detailed our clinic's policies and practices and a health and insurance information form to be filled out and returned at the first appointment.

FIRST SESSION

Anticipating the usual mother and daughter pairing, when I went to the waiting room I was startled to see a teenager sitting with her father and a young girl. They were the only people in the waiting room. When working with children and adolescents, there is always the question of who to greet first, the therapist's chronological peer, that is, the parent, or the identified patient. I make it a practice to start with the client.

"Martha?" I asked, as I approached an unprepossessing young woman, my hand outstretched. She appeared younger than 15, in that amorphous stage of puberty wherein layers of fat compete with secondary sex characteristics. She took my hand, limply, and said yes with her face slightly averted.

Are we going to get anywhere? flashed through my mind. With some dread, I wondered whether I was going to have to deal with a sluggish and sullen adolescent from whom I would attempt to pry information.

"I am Kate Hays," I said. I would leave it to her whether to think of me as "Dr. Hays" or "Kate" or some indeterminately named person (see chapter 1 about introductions, the avoidance of titles, and the use of first names).

I turned next to her father, dressed in casual workmen's clothes. I introduced myself to him, and briefly squatted down to be at eye level with Martha's younger sister, Sarah, engrossed in tidying her doll's clothing. Returning to Martha's father, I made small talk about the ease or difficulty of finding our office. He said that he had had no difficulty—he had been here before for organizational meetings. We were meeting at a feminist practice with a visibly feminist name, and I was surprised at his level of comfort and apparent social activism. I reminded myself, yet again, not to make assumptions based on appearance, gender, or class.

My next task was to determine whom I would see. Typically, I ask clients, particularly adolescents, to decide how we will start. With the particular constellation in front of me, I was already weighing whether enough toys were available to occupy Sarah if the father joined us. On the other hand, if Sarah were also present, she might, as many young children do, add some useful information concerning the family's dynamics.

> KFH: Martha, would you like to meet just with me, or would you like your father to join us today?

Still appearing diffident, Martha responded that she would like to meet with me on her own. I let her father know that we would be finished in about 50 minutes, and he in turn told Martha that they would be going down the street for a while but would meet her back in the waiting room.

INTAKE GOALS AND PROCESS

The goals of a performance intake are multiple (Taylor & Schneider, 1992). The practitioner wants, at the very least, to begin a number of processes: obtain relevant performance history, gather pertinent social and developmental history, develop an initial formulation of the issues (whether a formal diagnosis or a less rigidly defined understanding), design a preliminary treatment plan and homework assignment(s), and set expectations around the intervention. One can effectively meet these goals only if they occur within the broader context of the tasks of an initial interview, not as static and discrete objectives. The process should be designed to enhance rapport building and client-practitioner regard.

My initial concerns about Martha's interpersonal awkwardness or shyness immediately appeared unfounded.

Once in my office, Martha settled into a deep chair and responded easily to my questions in measured and thoughtful tones. I began in the traditional, open-ended manner.

KFH: What brings you here?

Martha's reply was direct and to the point. This response, I thought, boded well:

Martha (M): I'm breaking out in hives. It's happening all the time.

KFH: *All* the time?

M: Well, especially when I'm singing. I know that I get nervous. And after I'm done singing, I break out in hives for 10 or 15 minutes. My chest, arms, and face turn this awful blotchy, itchy red. Everybody can see it.

KFH: Does this happen every time that you sing?

M: Well, no, it happens especially in class, when we have voice exams. And sometimes at concerts, too.

KFH: How long has it been going on?

M: It started in eighth grade a bit. Then in ninth grade, I sang some solos. It happened some then. Our choir had 50 kids. Now there are just 16 of us, and it's happening more.

In this brief interchange, Martha had given me a considerable amount of information, both about her concerns and her functioning. Her somatic reaction had been in existence for a few years now and had gradually increased. It appeared to be related to increased attention to herself and her own performance, and its source seemed to be heightened self-consciousness and self-criticism or a maturing awareness of others' response to her. I recognized that Martha was a good informant; that is, someone who was self-reflective. I was also impressed at Martha's capacity for self-observation.

Martha described her family situation. She was the second of five girls; her older sister, Laurie, was in college. Martha spoke with a certain distaste of Jodie, a year her junior, who had recently become rebellious. Martha said that she enjoyed being the oldest at home: "I like having all the responsibility—being in charge." She was generally an A student, although recently she had been receiving Cs in geometry. She was planning to become a music teacher. Her parents, she commented, were proud of her musicianship, and freely praised her performances with no implied criticism or undue expectation.

Martha's comment about her parents' attitude brought me back to a confusion I wished to clear up.

KFH: Martha, there are a couple of reasons people feel self-conscious about performing. Sometimes it's because they're criticizing themselves, and sometimes it's that they're worried about what other people think about their performance. Do you have an idea which it might be for you?

M: I don't know. Maybe it's both things. The music is harder. We sing in parts all the time. And I hear it more when I don't get the sound I'm supposed to. And sometimes I think about what people are hearing, too, and what they think of me.

Having obtained some basic information, my approach at this point was very much one of collaborative empiricism. I was assuming, and acting as if, together, she and I would be able to sort out this hives mystery. At times, I will explicate this perspective with clients. At this moment, however, I continued asking questions to help clarify patterns and exceptions, in a style that was intended to imply, Let's see if together we can figure out what is going on.

KFH: I'm wondering, Martha, about the times when you *don't* get hives. Can you think of times and places where it *doesn't* occur?

M: Last year, I sang at my church, and nothing happened there. I think I felt more comfortable.

Again, I was receiving two kinds of information. Martha was telling me the facts. In addition, I was aware that she had not only been experiencing the symptoms but also reflecting on them, trying to make sense of them, and developing her own hypotheses. Here, she was tying anxiety, discomfort, and self-consciousness to the hives. It was clear that she had already made the psychosomatic link. I thought it useful to underscore that connection before moving in a new direction.

KFH: Mm-hmm. I think you're making an important point, Martha. When you feel more comfortable, maybe you're not as likely to break out in hives. And on the other hand, when you feel singled out in some way, it makes you more nervous, and your body reacts. Our job [not *my* job as the expert, or *her* job as the person burdened with this problem, but the collaboration of two people in search of the solution to a puzzle] will be to see if we can figure out how that got started and what it's about—and most important—what we can do to help change it. So let's go back to when it started. Tell me more about your eighth-grade year.

M: It was a hard year. My father was having problems. He had flashbacks from when he was abused by his parents and was in the hospital a few times. Mom lets me and Laurie know everything. Dad's family is pretty messed up. Both his brothers drink and take drugs. Dad doesn't talk to them and we've stopped seeing them, even at Christmas.

Martha, again, was giving me a tremendous amount of information. She was describing a family that had experienced major psychiatric upset, yet one that seemed able to make constructive use of some of their difficulties, maintaining communication, connection, and differentiation. On the assumption that Martha and her older sister were able to handle difficult information, their parents kept them informed about the true family situation, and thus, they were reinforced for their maturity. In some ways, "knowing everything" might be a burden. Martha's comments, however, suggested a sense of pride that her parents trusted her emotional competence.

Martha also was recognizing that interpersonal issues can have a direct impact on people's functioning. I began thinking about this family as one that was resilient, even in the face of adversity. I could appreciate Dr. Moore's sense of attachment to this family through the challenges that they had faced.

Empathic silence, when it does not make the other person too anxious, can be an excellent vacuum into which a client will pour more information. I waited. Martha made the connection between symptoms and performance more explicit.

> M: I think maybe I started getting nervous three years ago, because of all the problems my father was having and the way that I worried about him.

This reflection was obviously significant. At the same time, her comment presented an explicit choice point: regardless of whether or not I placed a diagnostic label on her, in working with her I could either focus on the etiology of her symptom or I could focus on symptom management. There are not many moments in performance work when the practitioner is confronted with such a clear contrast between the clinical and the educational perspectives. The decision that one makes is a matter of timing, of client, and of sequencing (as well as of practitioner training, orientation, and preference). If I were going to teach Martha any performance enhancement techniques today, I needed to start soon, because we were about halfway through the session. If, on the other hand, we embarked on dealing with Martha's experience three years ago, I would need to give this discussion the time it deserved. If I began our encounter from a psychopathological perspective, a later shift to performance enhancement might become difficult. If, on the other hand, I started the intervention by focusing on performance enhancement, yet noted little effective change or heard more complex family pathology, I could then begin exploring root causes (Hays, 1995).

I decided to acknowledge Martha's insight, reinforce her family's assessment of her maturity, and keep track of the information she had shared thus far. I let her know my plan and invited her to modify it as she saw fit.

> KFH: It sounds like that was a very difficult time for your whole family, and for you, as one of the older daughters. The connection that you're making may be absolutely on target. I tell you what: we've got a while left today, and I'd like to use it to show you some things you can do to deal with the hives. But I'd like you to let me know next time we meet if you think we're skipping over some things that feel important to you—or any time, if there are some memories of that time in your life that you'd like to talk about. How would that be?

My question to her was not pro forma but rather a genuine check that she had understood the choice I was suggesting and that she found it acceptable. I had also inserted into this statement an expectation that she would return.

> M: That's OK. I'd just like not to have hives.

Interventions

At this point, although I knew I would continue to gather material, I felt that I had enough information to make some initial suggestions. Adolescents, with their current and tangible focus, appreciate learning specific techniques. So do performers. If Martha left here feeling more competent and with an increased sense of control, she might be more likely to return.

I needed to decide which of the myriad performance enhancement techniques I would use. The decision was based on what I thought the central issue was (in this instance, performance anxiety); how I thought this particular person would be likely to absorb information (very easily); and a sense of sequence—that is, which techniques to start with in this session that could serve as building blocks for future sessions.

I used a pad of paper with carbon paper underneath the first page so that I could retain a copy and give Martha the top copy to take home with her. I wrote down four phrases—relaxation, self-talk/affirmations, attention, and imagery—so that I would remember to address each topic.

> KFH: Martha, you've recognized for quite a while that even though these hives are showing up on your body, they're really a signal you are giving to yourself about some of your thoughts. How about if I show you some ways to calm down your nervous thinking and worrying? Then perhaps your body won't feel it has to do you the "favor" of letting you know that you're nervous.
>
> Now, because you've been taking voice lessons, you've probably learned a lot about the right way to breathe, but just to make sure, I want you to show me how you breathe. As you're sitting there, would you put your hands together over your tummy, like this, [demonstrating] with your fingers just barely touching. Now breathe in and out, slowly and deeply. Pay attention to when your fingers separate and when they come back together again.

When I do not instruct people in proper breathing technique but assume that they know how to breathe properly, I have found that a number return with the comment that deep breathing was not effective. Of course not. They were breathing from high in their chests, not in their diaphragms. I have learned that if I am going to encourage breathing techniques, I need to make certain that clients have experienced diaphragmatic breathing before they leave the office.

As Martha contemplated her breathing, I gained further confirmation that she was a good student. I observed that she was following my instructions. As her fingers separated and came together, I could see, clearly, that she had learned diaphragmatic breathing, perhaps through her music instruction. It was important, nonetheless, that she articulate the rhythm of her breathing. After a few minutes she redirected her gaze toward me.

KFH: What did you find out?

M: When I breathe in, my stomach goes out, and when I breathe out, my stomach goes in.

KFH: That's exactly right. You'd be amazed how many people haven't figured that out and don't know how to breathe. Now, maybe it will help if I give you a picture of what's going on when you breathe. You know, your hands pulled apart as you were breathing in, not because your belly was really filling up with air but because your lungs were. What happens when you inhale is that your lungs are like a balloon. As you start putting air in the balloon [I gestured a rounding, expanding balloon], your diaphragm [I arced one hand in a crescent, below the "balloon" and as I spoke, flattened the arc], which is just below your lungs, flattens out. And when it does that, it puts pressure on your internal organs. They have nowhere to go but out. And so that is why it seems like your belly is expanding. Then as you exhale, the diaphragm pulls back up into its resting spot, making room for your organs, as your lungs lose air.

Nodding comfortably, Martha rested her hands on her stomach. Elaborating slightly, I also suggested to Martha that she develop a rhythm of breathing in through her nose and out through her mouth. Each time she exhaled, she could think to herself the word *calm.* I asked her to practice that.

M: You know, I feel less tense already.

Her comment made me realize that in my enthusiasm to explain diaphragmatic breathing to her, I had neglected to give her the "punch line," the reason for doing this breathing! Sometimes a bit of self-deprecating humor helps. I made a wry face:

KFH: Thanks for getting me back on track. That was the whole point of this! Exactly! What you're learning how to do is to be the one in charge of how tense—or relaxed or calm—your body is going to be. Because your body can't be tense and relaxed at the same time. So if you get it calm, the hives are less likely to show up.

I handed Martha the paper on which I had written the four phrases.

KFH: You might want to write some things down about what we've just been doing, so you'll be able to remember them.

Martha wrote: "Calm, breathe in through nose and out through mouth."

KFH: Okay, here's one other thing you can do with your breathing. Sometimes it helps to have something specific to look at, so that you can concentrate and focus on your breathing. One very handy thing is to use your thumb, because it's always with you. You don't need to pick it up or be obvious about it; you can just look down in your lap at your thumb while you're breathing and saying *calm* to yourself. Why don't you try that, now?

Martha followed these instructions, and added "focus on thumb" on the piece of paper. She looked up at me, expectantly.

There was still a bit of time left, and Martha appeared to be eagerly and actively absorbing these suggestions. At the same time, I did not want to overwhelm her with too much. I decided to just make a start on teaching her techniques in relation to the other issues I had noted. I spoke about the ways in which we sometimes say negative and self-critical things to ourselves, and how that undermines our confidence. Rather than elaborate the complexity of cognitive restructuring, the homework I suggested was designed to help her focus on (and thereby reinforce) the positive.

KFH: Let me give you another idea, and we can do more with it next time. It's basically that there's a part of you that wants to keep doing better, and the best way to do that is to think positive thoughts to yourself. So during this next week, when you are feeling good about yourself, see if you can notice those moments and kind of tune in to see what you're saying to yourself about yourself.

Under "self-talk/affirmations," Martha wrote "good things I say."

KFH: That actually reminds me of something else, Martha. Along with listening to the good things you're saying to yourself, you might try noticing the positive things that Mr. Jones says, as well.

She added a new category: "Other tips," and wrote, "Listen to positive things Mr. Jones says."

KFH: Okay. There are just a few other ideas I have that you might get started on. And remember—this is sort of like a cafeteria. I don't expect you to eat everything that's here—or even want to. Instead, I'm giving you some ideas, and you're welcome to pick and choose among them.

Martha smiled and shook her head.

M: Oh, I really like having all these different ideas. It will be fun to try them out.

Through gestures and words, Martha seemed to be confirming my observation that she was easily absorbing these techniques, at least at a preliminary level. At the same time, I recognized that she might be merely being compliant, a "good student" without the initiative to truly shape these to her own life. With the cafeteria image, I intended to convey my recognition of the potential for overload as well as offer her a method for handling so much material. I was also expressing an awareness that different techniques appeal to different people. I noted to myself that I would need to assess what use she was able to make of the techniques I was suggesting.

There is something enormously seductive about working with an avid, comprehending student. The teacher, consultant, or therapist can become distracted from appropriate pacing by the satisfaction and reward of being seen as knowledgeable, helpful, and instructive. Despite her reassurances, in retrospect I now think that it would have made more sense to discontinue further suggestions and instead, to review in considerable detail what we had already discussed. Martha needed the time to practice, absorb, and sort among the information she already had. Rather than do that, however, in my enthusiasm I added more ideas. The irony is that as I spoke about attention, I probably lost some degree of focus.

> KFH: Well, good. I think they are fun. And the whole point of this, again, is that it helps you to feel more in charge of yourself. Okay, two more. One is that thinking about hives and worrying and wondering about them probably gets you more worried, and that increases the likelihood that in fact you will get hives. But you've got a lot of choices about where to direct your attention. You can worry about whether the hives will break out, and that can start a kind of snowball effect. Instead, you could make an "unsnowball" effect. You can change the direction of your attention. Instead of thinking about how you're reacting, you can focus on other things. For instance, you could decide to pay attention to what's going on around you, or what the music is about, or hitting the next note dead on, or breathing fully.

Martha wrote: "Shift attention focus. Don't pay attention to hives. Unsnowball effect. Pay attention to singing and breathing."

> KFH: I have one other suggestion. This is one where you can use your imagination. When you're in that very calm space after you've done some focused breathing, I'd like you to picture a giant hand that can just gently but firmly push those hives back down under your skin so that you don't need to have them showing.

On reflection, if I were going to offer these further suggestions, the imagery could have been consistent. I could have tied the imagery suggestion to attentional focus. I could, for example, have had Martha play with the notion of individual flakes of snow cooling the heat of her skin, soothing or melting the hives. Instead, I introduced both a new technique and a new image to her. I did not subsequently hear her discuss the giant hand, perhaps because it was not tied to the other images. Perhaps it was not an image that resonated for her. Possibly by then she really was in overload.

Martha wrote: "Slow breathing pushing it down with hands."

> KFH: Well, we're just about out of time for today. I'd like to see you in about a week and see how things are going. Would that work for you?

Martha said that she thought so. Commending and summarizing, I concluded and reiterated for her.

> KFH: Wow! We've done a lot in the past hour. I'm glad we've gotten a start on dealing with those hives. And remember, the things to really focus on this week are the breathing, and the positive thoughts, and directing your attention, and the big hand that can smooth away the hives. And also remember the fun you've had in learning these ideas. Play with them and do whatever works best for you.

Looking lighter, Martha went back to the waiting room to meet up with her father and sister.

SECOND SESSION

As it happened, Martha's mother called to postpone the next session. A post-first-session cancellation frequently means an unintended one-session treatment, and so I was a bit concerned. The cancellation appeared, however, to be a legitimate postponement, and we made an appointment three weeks hence. This time, I found Martha sitting by herself in the waiting room, comfortable in these surroundings.

She was, as well, clearly more comfortable in herself. She now had some new ways to direct her attention and understand herself. Eagerly, when we got to the office, she began.

> M: I've done the breathing a lot. And it helps each time I do it. I just get calm. The hives still show up sometimes, but it's not bothering me as much anymore. I also noticed, when I really listened, that my music teacher isn't *picking on* me. He's correcting me. He corrects other people, too. Maybe that's how he has to do his job. Otherwise, how would I learn to sing?

Once again, I was struck with this young woman's insightfulness and her general psychological-mindedness. She had been able to make use of a number of the suggestions. In addition, she had used the framework of observation as an opportunity, a green light. She could begin redirecting her attention from the self-conscious and self-sabotaging toward attending to others' motives and actions. And further, she was demonstrating that she was capable of moving beyond the assignment to begin drawing her own conclusions.

My impulse was to do the emotional equivalent of scooping her up into my arms and yelling, "Eureka! You've got it!" Anticipating that she would be startled, and perhaps shamed, silenced, or overwhelmed if I were so demonstrative, I instead decided to tone down my reaction and to start where she had ended, gradually working in comments about her responsiveness and hard work. Part of what was fueling the hives was self-consciousness, so I chose to pick up on her last remark.

KFH: It *is* interesting, isn't it, when you notice what other people are doing? I think it takes your mind off yourself a bit, and lets you really see the big picture more clearly. Maybe even helps give you more information about what it's like to be a music teacher.

Here, I was validating her observation and linking the positive intent imputed to her teacher to a beneficence that she might experience in regard to her own self-assessment. On her way to becoming a teacher of others, she could instruct herself. I continued:

KFH: And it sounds like you've really been working on this stuff the past few weeks. You've found that doing the breathing helps. Maybe you've found that it becomes easier and more automatic, too, the more you do it. Your mind and body are just getting more comfortable making that connection between deep breathing and decreased tension. And the hives just aren't showing up as much any more. Are there other things you've noticed or thought about during this time?

M: Well, I thought some more about when Dad was in the hospital three years ago. It was really scary at first. When he was in the hospital, I missed him, but he was so quiet when he was home that sometimes it was like he wasn't there, and that was scary, too. I don't know . . . maybe it does have something to do with how the hives got started, but right now I don't care all that much about *why* it started; I just want to do something about it. Dad's doing pretty well these days, anyway.

I noted to myself that Martha had again raised the issue of her history. She was *saying,* however, that she did not see the need to discuss that experience further. I decided, at least for the moment, to go along with her assessment. I did not assume that the experience was not important. Rather, I again recognized that further exploration might become relevant at some future time, especially if her anxiety seemed more pervasive or unresponsive to the current interventions. I also did not want to minimize the value of retrospective review.

KFH: Well, I'm glad you had the chance to think about it some more—and to talk with me about what happened in the past in the first place. It's funny how symptoms start. Sometimes the beginning matters a whole lot, and sometimes what's much more important is how you handle things right now. And as I said before, if at any time you want to come back to talking about your dad, or your worries three years ago, that would be fine with me. So what would you like us to be focusing on today?

M: Well, I did notice some of the things I say to myself to encourage myself.

Martha was asking here that I acknowledge what a good student she had been in doing her homework. She was also moving to the direct content of her affirmations. I decided to recognize both.

KFH: You really have been busy these three weeks. What did you notice?

M: What I say to myself is, I can do it, or, sometimes, I'll do fine.

Once again, I had paper and carbon ready so that we could emphasize the main points and develop homework ideas. This time, I wrote: "Affirmations: I can do it. I'll do fine."

KFH: Those are great, Martha! What you're doing, in a few words, is really comforting and encouraging yourself. And you said them positively. And they focus on the present and the future. Those are really helpful affirmations to have.

I was supporting and at the same time giving her information about the content of constructive affirmations. I noted Martha moving a bit restlessly in her seat.

M: Yeah, well . . .

I immediately wondered if I had responded with more enthusiasm than Martha could tolerate. I heard her next comment from that perspective.

M: I don't know, I mean, sometimes I can *say* that to myself, but I don't necessarily believe it. What if I don't do fine? What if I mess up? I keep thinking about that, and then it gets me more nervous.

KFH: That's hard, isn't it? There you are, wanting to support yourself, but you are wondering whether being too positive makes the whole thing sound and feel false. You're asking me some really interesting questions. And I agree with you. It would be great if all we had to do was think positively and then everything would be fine. And I know that it doesn't work to just pretend those worries aren't there. So here's an idea. Think of it as two different pieces. First, recognize what you're feeling, and *then* give yourself the affirmation. If all you do is stay with the feeling, you'll probably end up more nervous. On the other hand, if all you do is give yourself affirmations, the part of you that is worried will feel ignored and may need to get "louder" or more obvious. This way, your worried self feels heard, and your practical side helps resolve it. I call this a "1-2 approach." So what you could do [and here I wrote down: "1-2 approach: (1) acknowledge the feeling,

(2) affirmation"] is say something to yourself like: "Yes, of course I'm worried. This is a big performance. But I've done other big performances. I'll do fine."

Martha smiled. Feeling that she had been heard, reassured, and given new tools, she became comfortable divulging more information about her musical self.

M: You know, that reminds me of something else I thought about. When I play the violin, I don't get worried—and I don't get hives. So it's not like it's everything about music.

KFH: You're right. Isn't that an interesting observation! I wonder what *is* different for you about playing the violin than singing.

M: Well, usually, when I play it's in the orchestra . . . but no, even when I've played at family events it doesn't get me so nervous.

Not only had Martha done considerable reflection in the intervening weeks, she also had the spontaneity to assess and revise those observations as she was reporting them in session.

KFH: So it's sort of about not standing out. But it's also about being with people you know. One thing may cancel out the other. But even more, it sounds like it's about the value that you put on your singing. It really means a lot to you, doesn't it?

Even if it doesn't totally make sense yet, Martha, I think you're on the right track. You know, you're showing me at least three different things right now. One is that you're discovering that if you stand back from your music and look at it, you start to understand patterns and notice what goes together. Then you can start to understand what the specific things are that worry you, and that means you can figure out how to respond to those worries. Also, when you break the music down, it's not just everything about music. Seeing that makes music-making feel less scary. And the other thing is a bit harder to explain. I don't quite "get" why it works, but I know that it does: Even if you're not totally aware of it, you've figured out some ways to respond differently to some of the same kinds of thoughts for violin as compared with singing. So you may be able to learn from what works in violin playing and then apply it to your singing self.

To direct her attention and contemplation, I wrote down: "What is different about my violin performance compared with vocal performance?"

KFH: I also want to go back to something we were talking about earlier, with the affirmations, and that has to do with perfection. That's a tough one, because I think that part of being a musician includes working on performing perfectly. Sometimes, expecting perfection can help us do things just right. But sometimes it feels so much like a judgment that we end up feeling more nervous. That can mean even more mistakes, and then the expectation really interferes with our performance.

We're going to be finishing up soon today [I wanted to cue her in case there was other material for us to get to], but as I think back over what we've talked about [I was beginning to summarize themes], it seems to me that we've spent a lot of time discussing those ways in which we [here, I was normalizing her experience] have two voices in our heads—the negative and worried, and the positive and excited. There's a book I have that I think does a good job of describing those voices and gives some techniques that you can use in music. It's called *The Inner Game of Music*. I wonder if you'd like to borrow it.

Bibliotherapy can be a powerful tool for behavior change; an alternate method for clients to absorb information from others. Along with thinking that she might find the book useful, this gesture implied that Martha was competent to direct some of her own learning.

She seemed pleased and said that she would like to look at the book. Then, as a kind of throwaway, she began talking about an entirely new subject. Like Columbo, the Peter Falk detective who mentioned the most crucial information as if it were a last thought or a minor aside, she said:

M: There's one other thing I thought of. I haven't been dating much yet, but this boy in my class might ask me out, and I was wondering if some of these ideas would work well with dating, too.

KFH: Absolutely, Martha. You know, one thing I find when working with people [again, I was normalizing her experience and reinforcing her cognitive processing] is that those who benefit most from these ideas are the ones who see that they really are just tools. They really are ways of thinking about and handling your worries. So these methods can be used for music performance, or taking tests, or figuring out how to handle your nervousness about dating. So, yes, I think that could work real well. Let me know how it goes.

Does it make sense to you to come back again?

Again, I designed my question to include her as coparticipant in the decision. Martha agreed to another session.

KFH: I was thinking if you have a bit of time to practice and then come back, it might work well.

Rather than assume the traditional psychotherapy weekly time frame, I had taken a cue from the way in which she had made good use of the intervening time between the first two appointments. We set a time to meet two weeks hence.

TERMINATION

Again, Martha was enthusiastic and engaging as we settled into our now-familiar seats. To see where she would like to start the session, I asked:

KFH: How's it been going?

M: Really well. We're getting into concert season, so we've been rehearsing something at least every day, and we've already done one of our holiday performances. And I only broke out in hives once during all those times! It's great. I'm not so afraid anymore, because it feels like it's going away.

Matching and mirroring her enthusiasm this time, I responded:

KFH: I'm delighted to hear that, Martha! What good work you've done.

As in athletic coaching, it really *was* the work that *she* had done. My role had been to make an accurate assessment of her needs, gear my interventions in a way that increased the likelihood that she could absorb and use them—and then watch, support, and shape as the consequences began to unfold. In crediting her, furthermore, I was reinforcing her competence regarding both the techniques and the increased sense of self-confidence.

I followed up on her comment, in the previous session, about the possibility of dating, choosing to bring the topic up early in case there was a fair amount to discuss.

KFH: Last time you mentioned toward the end that you were interested in dating but also maybe nervous about it. I thought I'd ask you about it today at the beginning, in case you wanted to spend some time talking about it.

M: Well, I did do some of the breathing just before lunch period, when I knew I was going to see Brendan. And I think maybe that helped me to talk with him, and not just smile and pick my nails. But I've heard he's going out with somebody else, so I guess I won't get to try these ideas with him right now.

KFH: Well, you *sound* like it's OK with you. Is it?

M: Yes, it is. I mean, I'd like to go out with somebody, I think. But I guess I'm not sure I really want to go out with just one person. Besides, most of the boys in my class are kind of jerks.

Martha spoke with a sense of dismissiveness, perhaps about boys or about our continuing this line of discussion. I returned to our earlier focus. Knowing adolescents' short spans of willingness for treatment, I sensed that this might be our final session. I began gearing the session toward the tools she would want to have to continue this work on her own.

KFH: You know by now that I go about these things systematically, so let's see if we can figure out both what has gone right all those times, and also what happened that one time you broke out, so we can minimize the hives even further.

M: OK. Well, like we talked about, I don't get bothered by Mr. Jones' comments anymore. It's like he's giving me information and that's helpful. Also, I've been remembering to breathe deeply. I do it before rehearsals and when we're working on something difficult. I've been doing it before my solos. I think the thing that's different about the violin playing—I did think about that a lot—is that usually I'm with other people, so my part doesn't stand out as much. Or other times, it's with my family, or at church, and so I think that people won't be so critical of my performance. But it's really more about how I've been getting myself scared. I've been thinking that playing the violin is just something I do, but that singing is *me*.

But you know, I'm still me, whatever kind of performing I'm doing. So, maybe I could get more comfortable about singing. I could tell myself that I know how to sing and enjoy it.

Her observations were not new, but the conclusions she had drawn were. I reflected:

KFH: I think those are very important points. Sometimes singing does seem more personal, because there's nothing in between you and your audience. But after all, your voice *is* an instrument. And you're getting so much more confidence as you're learning. You know, what I hear is that you are both more conscious of yourself and yet less self-conscious.

Martha looked—appropriately—puzzled. I had given her a paradox to contemplate and remember. At the same time, explaining it, I acknowledged the mystification.

KFH: Maybe I wasn't very clear. What I meant was this: When you were self-conscious, everything revolved around you, and the more you thought about your performance, the more self-critical you became, and this made you more anxious, and it all tended to spiral down. You've broadened your thinking. You are paying attention to yourself, but you're seeing yourself in the bigger picture, too. Sometimes it's that you're one person in the performing group. Sometimes you take your feeling of nervousness as a reminder to respond differently. I think you *are* solving the problem. Your skin is telling you that, isn't it? But speaking of hives—what do you think did happen that one time that was different?

I had waited until this moment—having emphasized what had gone right—to come back to the time when the symptom reappeared. My assumption was that now, as compared with earlier in the session, Martha would feel less shame and have a greater capacity to observe herself objectively.

M: Oh, it was something that I just didn't expect. At the last minute, Briana—she's the other good singer in our choir—got sick, so Mr. Jones asked me to sing her part. I knew the music, it wasn't that; I think it was just that I was surprised. I forgot all about breathing. I forgot about everything I learned.

KFH: OK, so what you're saying is that when the ducks are more or less lined up in order, you're now feeling pretty comfortable, even if there's some performance tension. And of course there always will be. In a way, that's how you know that you're performing. But maybe there are times when things happen that are a surprise, and those may throw you off. That's the moment when you're likely to start worrying, or criticizing yourself; all those things that make the hives likely to show up. Right now, when you're in performance season, you mostly want to spend time imagining everything going perfectly. But when you're thinking about your concerts, a few times, say a few days before your next performance, you might just take some quiet time to imagine things going differently.

By describing "things going differently," I was offering Martha an alternate perspective. I was suggesting to her that she could view surprises as alterations in an anticipated pattern rather than as catastrophes.

KFH: Perhaps you're not where you thought you'd be on stage, or Mr. Jones misses a cue, or one of your friends gets nervous. . . . Just allow yourself to imagine that, and picture what you could do to handle it. And then always remember your affirmations, so that you can conclude each image with "I can do it," or "I can do this one—and other things if they happen, too."

So, why don't we start making a list of things that you can do to handle unexpected situations.

I titled this page "Handling Unforeseen Situations."

"#1. [I wrote] Affirmations. Go with the flow."
"#2. When all else fails, BREATHE. Use thumb and forefinger pressed together as cue."

Here I explained to Martha that if she put all her tension into her thumb and forefinger, she could use the tactile sensation to remind herself to take deep breaths and at the same time relax the rest of her body.

"#3. Do an 'attention-scan': Find the right spot–break the loop.
a. Mr. Jones
b. music (external or internal)"

KFH: There are times when you want to focus on Mr. Jones and what he's saying or how he's conducting. That will get you off of thinking about yourself. At other times, it may make sense to focus on the music. And there are so many things you can direct your attention to. That's one of the great things about making music. It might be technical, like remembering to breathe so that you will be able to sustain a long phrase two measures farther along, or translating the words of a song in another language so that you can give a sense of meaning to the audience. You might enjoy a particular harmony, the way you're pushing against someone else's sound. Each of these is useful and productive. And the reason I'm mentioning them is because they move you out of feeling self-conscious and second-guessing yourself.

"#4. Remember to be myself, at ease, having fun."

M: I think those ideas will work really well. I can already picture myself doing them.

I sensed the finality in her vocal tone, and decided to initiate the question of termination as well as leave the door open for further contact.

KFH: You know, we've done a lot of work in the past month, Martha. And you've picked up these ideas and put them to very good use very quickly. I'm glad it's worked so well. And I'm wondering, do you feel like you want to go practice these ideas on your own now?

M: Well, yes I do. It's been great. I'm surprised that it was so easy. But I think mostly what I need to do now is just do these things, just practice.

KFH: You've maybe heard the old story of the person in New York who hails a taxicab and says, "How do I get to Carnegie Hall?" and the cab driver says, "Practice, practice, practice."

Here, I was linking psychological practice, which was new to her, with performance practice, with which she was already familiar and comfortable. There was also the message of the joke itself: that if one practices, all things are possible. In addition, this is a standard music joke. By telling it, I was intimating that I considered Martha a musician.

KFH: I think you're right. At this point, you have a number of basic tools to help you perform better mentally. You just—as if it were so easy!—need to practice them, to keep putting them to use. So maybe it does make sense for you to work on them on your own.

At the same time, you know, if you feel like you're slipping or want to understand a bit more, you're welcome to call me at any time. Lots of times, people do come back in. It's sort of like going to Dr. Moore's and getting a booster shot. You don't necessarily need to do the whole thing all over again, but being reminded helps strengthen what you already know.

The other thing is, if there ever is family stuff you want to talk about, whether it's from the past or the way that things are going, you know that I'd be glad to talk with you about those things, too. We decided not to do that this time, and that seems fine, but sometimes it helps to have someone outside your family to talk to. And by now, you kind of know what my style is.

Martha nodded her head in assent.

EPILOGUE

Martha had agreed to write to me in three months to let me know how things were going, but I did not hear from her. Likewise, it took a few calls to the family before the book I had loaned her showed up at my door one day. Whether Martha had read it or not, I do not know. After the intensity of our brief connection, I felt frustrated. I wished to have the reinforcement of confirmation that the work we had done had had a positive impact. Also, hearing from her could provide information for future interventions, whether with her or someone else. Yet with Martha, as with other clients, the contractual relationship meant that I would know only a small part of her story.

I did receive some information two years later. Dr. Moore sent me a photocopy of a newspaper clipping. In the photo accompanying the story, Martha, now a high school senior, looked relaxed and comfortable. She was shown playing the guitar to an attentive audience at a dinner-concert.

REFLECTIONS

What is it that constitutes doing sport psychology when one is doing it with other performance populations? This chapter has described some of those characteristics, within the frame of a particular case example. In part, it involves the application of a number of standard performance-related techniques, here illustrated with relaxation training, breathing techniques, affirmations, attentional focus, imagery, reframing, and associative and dissociative thinking. As with sport performance, the work with Martha was also rooted in the performance practice itself; in this case, music. More broadly, this case example illustrates a number of the interpersonal issues and methods endemic to any counseling or consultative situation, including engagement, timing, and the use of verbal and nonverbal cues. I deliberately retained description of some of the choice points as well as interventions that might have worked better if done differently. It is, after all, not only our clients' growth, but our own learning that helps us continue, endlessly fascinated by the people we encounter and the work that we do.

REFERENCES

American Psychological Association. (1992). Ethical principles of psychologists and code of conduct. *American Psychologist, 47,* 1597-1611.

Beck, A., Rush, J., Hollon, S., & Shaw, B. (1979). *Cognitive therapy of depression.* New York: Guilford.

Brown, L.S. (1994). *Subversive dialogues: Theory in feminist therapy.* New York: Basic Books.

Clark, D.B. (1989). Performance-related medical and psychological disorders in instrumental musicians. *Annals of Behavioral Medicine, 11,* 28-34.

Gallwey, W.T. (1997). *The inner game of tennis* (Rev. ed.). New York: Random House.

Gould, D., & Damarjian, N. (1998). Insights into effective sport psychology consulting. In K.F. Hays (Ed.), *Integrating exercise, sports, movement, and mind: Therapeutic unity* (pp. 111-130). Binghamton, NY: Haworth.

Green, B., & Gallwey, W.T. (1986). *The inner game of music.* Garden City, NY: Anchor.

Hamilton, L.H. (1997). *The person behind the mask: A guide to performing arts psychology.* Greenwich, CT: Ablex.

Hamilton, L.H., Kella, J.J., & Hamilton, W.G. (1995). Personality and occupational stress in elite performers. *Medical Problems of Performing Artists, 10,* 86-89.

Harris, S.R. (1985, August). *Brief cognitive-behavioral group counseling for musical performance anxiety.* Paper presented at the annual convention of the American Psychological Association, Los Angeles.

Hays, K.F. (1995). Putting sport psychology into (your) practice. *Professional Psychology: Research and Practice, 26,* 33-40.

Heil, J., Sagal, M., & Nideffer, R. (1997). The business of sport psychology consulting. *Journal of Applied Sport Psychology, 9 (Suppl.),* S109.

Kogan, J. (1989). *Nothing but the best: The struggle for perfection at the Juilliard School.* New York: Limelight.

Lederman, R.J. (1989). Performing arts medicine. *New England Journal of Medicine, 320,* 246-248.

Lehrer, P. (1993, May). *Tension in performance.* Paper presented at Concord Community Music School, Concord, NH.

Lockwood, A.H. (1989). Medical problems of musicians. *New England Journal of Medicine, 320,* 221-227.

Lubell, A. (1987). Physicians get in tune with performing artists. *The Physician and Sportsmedicine, 15,* 246-256.

Maher, B. (1969). *Clinical psychology and personality: The selected papers of George Kelly.* New York: Wiley.

Nagel, J.J. (1992, August). *Stage fright and the performing classical musician: Psychological and career issues.* Paper presented at the annual convention of the American Psychological Association, Washington, DC.

Taylor, J., & Schneider, B.A. (1992). The sport-clinical intake protocol: A comprehensive interviewing instrument for applied sport psychology. *Professional Psychology: Research and Practice, 23,* 318-325.

Williams, J.M., & Andersen, M.B. (1998). Psychosocial antecedents of sport injury: Review and critique of the stress and injury model. *Journal of Applied Sport Psychology, 10,* 5-25.

AFTERWORD

Shane M. Murphy
Gold Medal Consultants

I am privileged to have been the first person other than the editor to read this remarkable book. It is the first book to accurately depict the complex and dynamic work of everyday sport psychology. I found it a fascinating read, and I am sure you will, too. I have a strong belief in the possibilities for psychology to help people, in all walks of life, tackle difficult performance challenges, and this book shows both how exhilarating and how challenging that struggle is.

The most impressive quality of this book is that it focuses on the *process* of sport psychology interventions. The sport psychology literature is filled with texts that describe techniques and interventions. Although many of these works are excellent, they leave the lingering impression that sport psychology is the sum of such interventions as goal setting, visualization, and attention-control training. Yet the practicing sport psychologist realizes that knowledge of such techniques is but the first step in a long journey toward gaining proficiency in actually being able to help athletes manage their performances successfully.

If you have worked with athletes who come to you with questions about their psychological approaches to sports, you know that the practitioner's role is accompanied by continual questions. When do I know enough to make an intervention? Which performance issue should I tackle first? Are some of these performance issues related to each other? Which intervention strategy is most likely to prove beneficial over the long term? Should I suggest changes directly or encourage the athlete to discover the necessity for changes herself? How long should our relationship continue? When does it make sense for me to withdraw from the consulting relationship? Such questions are rarely discussed, even briefly, in texts that focus on the variety of intervention strategies available to sport psychologists. The beauty of *Doing Sport Psychology* is that these questions, and many others, are the heart and soul of the book.

The chapters address these internal dialogue questions—the puzzle of how to do sport psychology—by the simple yet elegant method of describing the actual encounters that take place between sport psychologist and athlete. This method has so much to recommend it; it is a wonder that no one else has used this form of education before. When the back-and-forth between athlete and sport psychologist is set down on paper, there is no escape available by hiding behind theoretical discussions or by citing reams of supporting research. The reader is free to judge the interaction for him- or herself. The author may propose various interpretations of the encounter, but when the actual words of the athlete and sport psychologist are set down in print, I am free to make up my own mind concerning the nature of what happened during the consultation experience. I had this experience on many occasions while reading these chapters: Yes, I see what the author is saying, but that's not what I think is happening here; or, I would have done something quite different in that situation. I think it's wonderful when a book challenges our thinking in this way. I am looking forward to many thought-provoking discussions with graduate students and other learners in our field based on our joint readings of the materials contained herein.

Reading this book has caused me to reflect on my own work with elite athletes and to observe how infrequently I ever do straightforward interventions such as those we see studied so often in our journals. It's important that sport psychologists acknowledge how difficult applied work is and try to understand what we are doing when we make an effective intervention. In the spirit of this book, I offer my own transcripts of some work I have been doing recently with an elite middle-distance runner, Leanne. I hope I can provide a final nugget to ponder for those who have made it through the preceding chapters. I have been seeing Leanne as part of an ongoing consultation with a professional track team. In the following transcripts, you can analyze the type of interventions I am performing.

Leanne first came to see me during a training camp for the pro team for which I consult. An accomplished 800-meter runner with a background of some strong international performances, she described a history of "losing focus" during races. She frequently performed below her own expectations. During our initial session, I asked about her pre-race energy level, and she commented that sometimes she seems to perform well when she is relaxed, but at other times being too relaxed seems to result in poor performances. I gave her some awareness-building instructions, and we planned to meet again at a subsequent camp.

I met Leanne twice more over the course of the next six months, once at a meet in which she was competing. At this race she expressed considerable frustration with her performances during the past season, but she subsequently had one of her best races of the season and finished third in the final. Our joint focus when we met was on helping her develop a consistent psychological approach to competitions and big races.

The following transcript is taken from the session following her third-place finish. It took place about three months later at a preseason conditioning camp.

Shane Murphy (SM): What would you like to work on in your mental game plan for the coming season?

Leanne (LO): I just want to be able to take the confidence I have now and have that same confidence when I start competing this year. I'm running well, I'm not thinking about it, and I feel great.

SM: What do you think you need to do to have that confidence during track season?

LO: I don't want to do anything! I'm sick of thinking about it. I just don't want to be so confident and work so hard and then have another shitty season like last year. [Leanne's voice raised in pitch while she was saying this, and a lot of tension was present in her face.]

SM: It seems that even talking about the possibility of having a bad season is pretty distressing for you.

LO: No, it's not. I'm OK about it, I just don't want to do all this, work on the mental training and everything, and then have a bad season again. [Leanne seemed short of breath as she continued to talk.]

SM: It seems to be important to know what to do if you do have some bad results. If you're confident and running well, that's great. But if you lose confidence and start racing poorly, how do you handle that?

LO: [breaking down into racking sobs] I don't! None of this is working. The more I think about this, the worse I do. I just want to stay confident. When I work with you I start thinking about all this again. It's too much [continues crying].

SM: [getting up and grabbing a tissue box and giving it to Leanne] I think you're the expert on you, Leanne. You know yourself much better than I do. Maybe you don't need to think about this stuff.

LO: I don't want to do a pre-race routine and then have a terrible race. All this doesn't work for me. I just don't want to hold myself back.

SM: How do you hold yourself back?

LO: [still sobbing occasionally] I'm confident now, and I'm running great. But what if I'm confident before a race and I run like crap?

SM: But isn't that the great thing about competing, that keeps it exciting? You can be confident and do great, but sometimes you seem to do everything right, and you're very confident, and you have a bad finish. You don't have control over the results.

LO: But I do the visualization, and the goal setting, and I relax before a race and do the deep breathing, and it's no good; I still run like crap.

SM: Leanne, those are all bells and whistles. You're way beyond that. You're such a great runner. You don't need shortcuts to race well. You just have to focus on the important things.

LO: But everything I read says all that stuff is important. I read that book that says I should do positive affirmations every day and everything. That's what sport psychology is about, isn't it?

SM: Sport psychology is about learning to do your best even when the pressure is on. Things like visualization and positive self-affirmations are good learning tools to help athletes learn how to do their best. But those aren't the things that make you run great. You and your excellence and your hard work make you a great runner.

LO: [Breathing deeply, she slumps back in her chair like the tension has been drained out of her.] But why do I hold myself back? It's like I went in a mountain bike race last week, just for fun and to keep me in shape in the off-season. The first race I raced against all guys and I was screaming down the hill in practice, but then in the race I was forcing it way too much, I wanted to do well so badly. I messed up my line and I wasn't fast and I raced like crap. Then in the second race I was against all these girls and I knew I could beat them, not that I'm a better rider, but I just knew I could beat them in the race, and I won by like 15 seconds, but it should have been like 45 seconds. I get so frustrated when

I do that. Why do I just coast enough to beat them? I should have raced so much better. There must be a happy medium, in between trying too hard and just coasting.

SM: When I saw you race at the end of last season, you were doing very well. You got that silver medal in Lake Bejoun, and you ran great.

LO: But even there, I raced so well in the heats and in the first run, and I was leading, and I wanted it so bad, I tried so hard on that last run, but if I had just stuck to my game plan and raced smart, I would have won.

SM: So you know what to do.

LO: But I don't do it. I hold myself back. Why can't I just go for it?

SM: It sounds like you feel that you get in your own way.

LO: Exactly. It's as if I'm afraid of failing. If I really go for it this year, and race like I know I can, I might have a really incredible year. But I might also have a disaster of a year. I don't know. And I don't let myself try. I don't go for it.

SM: Twenty years from now, if you look back on your running career, which would you rather be able to say about yourself? Would you rather have been conservative and not risked it all, made the Olympics and finished 20th? Or would you rather have risked it all and really gone hard, and perhaps not even have made the team, but at least have known you gave it everything you had?

LO: Of course I want to be able to say I gave it everything. It's not about making the Olympics. So what am I afraid of?

SM: Now we're talking about the really important stuff. That's what's important, isn't it, Leanne? To take the risks and really go for it? But it's really scary. If you let it all hang out and don't succeed, you have no excuses.

LO: [Long pause; she sits quietly.] I seem to keep getting in my own way, but it's really up to me. If I really go for it and let it all hang out, at least I'll be able to look at myself in the mirror. I hate the thought of losing it all, though.

SM: I think every athlete has that fear. At least all the athletes I've spoken to. But you don't have to spend much time thinking about that. If you concentrate on what you need to do to run well, you won't have time to think about failures that may never happen.

LO: But I don't want to screw myself up by over-analyzing every race like I did last season.

SM: Then don't. Keep it simple. You don't need to meet with me at every camp. You're the expert on you.

LO: I think that would help me stop obsessing about what a mental wreck I am. You don't mind?

SM: I'm here to help. If talking to me doesn't help you race well, then don't meet with me.

LO: But today talking to you was helpful.

SM: I'm always here to talk. If you want to talk to me about risking it all and going for it, pedal to the metal, you know where to find me.

LO: OK; we'll leave it at that.

SM: Great. I enjoyed meeting with you. Good luck this season. I'll tell Chuck [LO's coach] that we may not need to meet again for a while.

LO: Thanks, I really appreciate that.

Looking over this session with Leanne, I find that I'm not employing any imagery or relaxation techniques, but I am making an intervention. First, I gently help Leanne confront her own fears. The tension is obvious in every muscle of her being, but for a time she resists facing it. When she does, the anxiety bursts out in tears—but rather than backing off, getting upset, or changing the topic, I stay with the source of the anxiety. This tactic helps Leanne identify her major fears, and when she does so, the relief of confronting the hidden fear is obvious. I even discount the importance of typical sport psychology interventions in order to reinforce Leanne's self-image as a successful competitor—after all, she has been successful and has reached the top of her sport without my help. My hope is that she will again take responsibility for her own achievements, her successes, and her failures and stop over-analyzing every mistake. Her response pattern is typical of many high-achieving athletes with a tendency toward perfectionism. I end the session by giving her the permission to decide when, and if, she wants to see me again.

At another training camp, four months later, she asks if she can meet with me again. We go to the coach's office and sit down.

SM: Last time we met, we ended by saying that we would meet only if you really needed to talk to me again. What's going on?

LO: Well, my last two meets haven't gone well. I didn't make finals on either occasion. Coach says that if I don't improve my ranking, he won't take me with the team to Europe for the race season.

SM: That must be a worry.

LO: Totally. If I don't go, I won't improve my rankings. My sponsors might drop me. I might have to stop competing [tears appear in her eyes].

SM: What do you have to do to make the European trip?

LO: I need to reach finals in our last race here this weekend. I have to reach finals.

SM: How do you feel about the way you are racing?

LO: Pretty good, surprisingly. I've had some bad luck with poor starts and poor lanes the last two races, but I still feel very competitive with the runners who are here.

SM: How are practices going?

LO: Great. I'm right there with the times I need to have.

SM: How confident do you feel?

LO: Not very. It's screwed up. I'm running well, but I keep thinking of my poor performances, and I can't let that happen to me again. What do you think I should be doing before races? Should I be relaxing? Psyching myself up?

SM: Remember last time we talked, you decided that you need to keep it very simple, not think too much, if you are going to race well?

LO: I remember.

SM: How are you doing with that?

LO: I've had some problems. My mind starts racing. I doubt myself.

SM: What do you need to do to keep it simple, to stay focused?

LO: You know, I need a reminder to do that. I forget. It's silly, but when the shit starts hitting the fan, everything goes out of my head.

SM: Is there anyone at the races who can remind you to stay focused?

LO: Chuck, but he makes me nervous.

SM: Why?

LO: Because he's looking at me, deciding if I'm going to go to Europe or not.

SM: Is there anyone else?

LO: Hines [the assistant coach]; he's good. He's calm.

SM: Have you asked him to remind you to focus on your race plan 10 minutes before the race?

LO: No.

SM: [remains silent]

LO: I could do that. Hines would do that for me. He needs to grab me right before I go out on the track, about 15 minutes before the race.

SM: When he reminds you, can you focus on that plan?

LO: Oh, yeah. I know I can. If he talks to me for a minute or two, I can put that other stuff out of my mind.

SM: Sounds like you need to talk to Hines.

LO: I will. I'll do it tomorrow.

SM: Good luck. Keep it simple and have fun.

LO: I'm going to try.

In this session I build on my previous experiences with Leanne, reinforcing to her my belief that she is the expert, that she needs little guidance from me. When she identifies her pre-race confusion as a stumbling point in her performance, I face a choice. Do I try to teach her some focusing method? But I know from our previous conversations that she knows focusing strategies and that she has been able to focus and succeed in the past. So I ask if she needs some help focusing. She then identifies a strategy that has good potential for success, and I reinforce her decision. The session is very short. By actions as well as words, I am emphasizing the message, "keep it simple, don't over-analyze." Leanne achieved a podium result in her next race, and she went to Europe with the team, where she won enough prize money to support her running for the next year. As with most of my interventions, I judge my effectiveness by a combination of the athlete's subsequent ability to manage her performance and the satisfaction and sense of meaning she derives from the performance process.

Even this brief vignette was a challenge to write, because I am aware that readers will be able to look at my work and pass judgment. I had to resist the temptation to edit my own sessions. This book would not have succeeded had not its contributing authors shared a critical quality—honesty. I am full of admiration for these authors, who opened up their work to such critical analysis. It takes courage to expose one's work (not one's thinking) to open critique by anyone who reads these pages. The one thing that I thought many of the chapters shared was what I would call a fierce honesty about describing the nature of sport psychology consulting. You get a real feel for what it's like to do sport psychology consulting when you read these chapters. This is not an easy task. As editor of my own volume on the subject, I know how hard it is to convey what actually occurs during athlete-sport psychologist interactions. The authors here show you both their successes and failures—not only the satisfaction to be had in successful consulting but also the pain of failed attempts to make a difference. You won't read a better chapter anywhere on the challenges of doing elite-level sport psychology consulting than the one written by Sean McCann. It is a chapter that makes me envious, not just because I wish I had written it, but mainly because I wish I had been able to generate these insights into the consulting process myself.

I shouldn't point to any one chapter, because all the chapters herein have so much to offer, but I can't help emphasizing a few. The chapter by Frances Price and Mark Andersen offers a fascinating look at a developing relationship with an athlete-client over a long time period. Daryl Marchant gives us a unique view of a consulting relationship with a professional team while focusing on goal setting. Kate Hays, in her inimitable style, not only illustrates how sport psychology principles can be applied to working with a musician but also shows the challenges of working with the young performer. The chapter by Vance Tammen raised my blood pressure several notches, because I was the supervisor whose work Vance discussed, but in the end I was able to let go of my impulse to call Vance and tell him, "Hey, that's not the way I remember it," and instead admire his honesty in confronting his challenges and perceived failures. Burt Giges, in a series of brief portraits, highlights key principles he has learned from years of performance consulting while showing how remarkably brief some effective interventions can be. These chapters made a lasting impression, but every chapter here makes a strong contribution, and for that I must also thank Mark Andersen.

A final question, which is raised indirectly by this book and has often been discussed in the sport psychology literature, is whether sport psychology will ever be a viable profession. Simply put, will there be jobs in the future for those wishing to pursue careers in sport psychology? Given the always limited number of opportunities in the world of sport, it is difficult to be optimistic in answering this question. Let me, however, ask a different question. What sort of demand will exist in the future for experts specializing in helping individuals, groups, and organizations achieve high-level performance? Groups and teams in fields as diverse as business, health care, education, the performing arts, and finance are under tremendous pressure to achieve excellent bottom-line results. I believe there is already, and will continue to be, tremendous demand for experts who can help teams achieve high performance. In order to help individuals and teams achieve excellence, professionals will need expertise in a variety of areas such as

- leadership
- teamwork
- stress management
- burnout
- career satisfaction and meaning
- flow and happiness
- life management
- coaching effectiveness
- emotional intelligence

This book convincingly demonstrates that sport psychology is a field with a considerable database of information in all these, and many more, areas. No other field I can think of covers the psychology of performance excellence as broadly as sport psychology does. If sport psychology continues to broaden its scope and to study high performance across a variety of areas, I believe that its future is very bright. I must admit that I have modified my thinking on this topic over the years. In some of my earlier writings I advocated that sport psychology should maintain a narrow focus on the study of sport. I now believe that no other field uses the variety of perspectives offered within sport psychology to understand the process of high achievement. Sport psychologists must continue to develop the theory and practice of performance excellence in order to meet the growing needs of society. This book represents a significant step forward in that process. I believe it will be a catalyst for progress within our field, and I hope that it inspires everyone who reads it to *do* sport psychology.

INDEX

The italicized *f* and *t* following page numbers refer to figures and tables, respectively.

ABOUT THE EDITOR

Mark B. Andersen is a registered psychologist and associate professor at Victoria University in Melbourne, Australia. He has served as the head of graduate research studies in the School of Human Movement, Recreation, and Performance and coordinates the master's of applied psychology degree (sport and exercise psychology emphasis) in the department of psychology. He received his doctorate from the University of Arizona in 1988 and immigrated to Australia in 1994, but he is still listed on the U.S. Olympic Committee Sport Psychology Registry. His teaching includes statistics, research design, psychology of rehabilitation, and the professional practice of psychology. His areas of research interest include the psychology of injury and rehabilitation; the role of exercise in mental health, well-being, and quality of life; the training and supervision of graduate students; and the practice of sport psychology service delivery. He is the first and current editor of the Professional Practice section of the international journal *The Sport Psychologist.* In 1994 he received the Dorothy V. Harris Memorial Award for excellence as a young scholar/practitioner from the Association for the Advancement of Applied Sport Psychology (AAASP) and is an AAASP-certified consultant. Dr. Andersen has worked for many years counseling athletes ranging from 12-year-old juniors to American and Australian Olympians.

CONTRIBUTING AUTHORS

Steve T. Barney is an assistant professor in the department of psychology at Southern Utah University (SUU). He received his PhD in clinical psychology from the University of Wyoming. Currently, he teaches courses in abnormal psychology, group dynamics, psychological testing and assessment, psychotherapy, and applications of psychological principles to sport. His research interests include clinical training processes, posttraumatic adjustment, personality assessment, and pedagogical effectiveness. Dr. Barney maintains an active clinical practice working with student athletes, the general student population, and the faculty and staff at SUU. Issues of particular interest in his work with student athletes include end-of-career adjustment, coping with injury, athletic identity concerns, building self-esteem, and enhancing life skills.

Britton W. Brewer is an associate professor of psychology at Springfield College in Springfield, Massachusetts, where he teaches undergraduate and graduate psychology subjects, conducts research on psychological aspects of sport injury, and coaches the men's cross country team. He received his doctorate in clinical psychology from Arizona State University in 1991. Dr. Brewer is listed in the United States Olympic Committee Sport Psychology Registry, 1996-2000, and is a certified consultant for the Association for the Advancement of Applied Sport Psychology (AAASP). In recognition of his early career accomplishments in sport psychology, Dr. Brewer received the Dorothy V. Harris Memorial Award from AAASP and the Developing Scholar Award from the International Society of Sport Psychology in 1997. He currently serves on the editorial boards of the *Academic Athletic Journal,* the *Journal of Applied Sport Psychology,* and *The Sport Psychologist.* He was voted Northeast 10 Conference Men's Cross Country Coach of the Year in 1994. Dr. Brewer is chief executive officer of Virtual Brands, a company that develops multimedia products for promotion of excellence and well-being in sport, health, and life.

Karen D. Cogan is a counseling center psychologist and assistant professor at the University of North Texas (UNT). She also is the coordinator for practicum and outreach at the UNT Center for Sport Psychology and Performance Excellence. She has authored or coauthored several articles, book chapters, and books including *Sport Psychology Library: Gymnastics.* She is a licensed psychologist, an AAASP-certified consultant, a member of the United States Olympic Committee Sport Psychology Registry, and member of the USA Gymnastics Health Care Providers Network. She consults with athletes in a variety of sports and currently is a consultant for the United States Ski and Snowboard Association. Dr. Cogan's professional leadership experience includes serving on the American Psychological Association's Division 47 Executive Committee as member at large and secretary-treasurer.

Burt Giges is a clinical professor in the athletic counseling program in the department of psychology at Springfield College in Springfield, Massachusetts, where he also serves as consultant to the women's track and field team. He is special consultant to the USA Track and Field sport psychology program and provides consultation to the Westchester Track Club in New York. He has given workshops on self-awareness for sport psychologists at numerous universities around the country. He is a member of the editorial board of *The Sport Psychologist* and was on the executive board of the Gestalt Center of Long Island. While in college, he was on the fencing team, and after graduating from medical school, he conducted research at the Army Medical Research and Graduate School in Washington, DC, and at the Rockefeller Institute for Medical Research in New York. He later served as team physician to a high school football team. For many years, Dr. Giges was a member of the faculty in the department of psychiatry of the Albert Einstein College of Medicine.

Greg Harris is completing his master's degree in the school of human movement, recreation, and performance at Victoria University in Melbourne, Australia. His current research involves the perceptions athletes hold of sport psychologists and sport psychology service delivery. He is also an associate member of the Australian Psychological Society. In addition to his research, Mr. Harris consults with numerous state and national teams, providing psychological skills training aimed at increasing coping resources, expanding stress management strategies, and enhancing sport performance. Mr. Harris is a former basketball player who competed at the state level in Australia. He has also coached junior and senior regional teams in the sport.

Kate F. Hays is a clinical psychologist specializing in sport and performance psychology. She received her doctoral degree from Boston University. After 25 years of working with athletes and performing artists in New Hampshire, she moved her practice, The Performing Edge, to Toronto. Dr. Hays has taught and published widely for both general and professional audiences on performance and practice issues in both sport and the performing arts. She edited *Integrating Exercise, Sports, Movement, and Mind: Therapeutic Unity* and wrote *Working It Out: Using Exercise in Psychotherapy.* Dr. Hays is a fellow of the American Psychological Association and a certified consultant for the Association for the Advancement of Applied Sport Psychology (AAASP). She is listed in the United States Olympic Committee Sport Psychology Registry, 1996-2000, and is currently president-elect of Division 47, Exercise and Sport Psychology of the American Psychological Association. She is a committed, noncompetitive runner, swimmer, and singer.

Gregory S. Kolt is an associate dean for research and professor of health science at Auckland University of Technology in New Zealand. His PhD from La Trobe University focused on the psychological aspects of gymnastics injury, performance, and participation. Dr. Kolt is a registered psychologist and physical therapist and has worked with national sport teams and many individual athletes. He teaches sport physiotherapy and sport and exercise psychology in several graduate programs and at various sports medicine courses run by the International Olympic Committee throughout the Oceania region. Dr Kolt is the associate editor of *Physical Therapy in Sport,* and his research interests include the psychology of injury and rehabilitation and participation motivation in sport and exercise. He is a former nationally ranked gymnast.

David Lavallee is a principal lecturer in the school of social sciences at the University of Teesside, England, where he teaches courses in psychology and directs the Centre for Sport Performance and Applied Research. As a chartered psychologist with the British Psychological Society, he has research and applied interests in counseling in sport and exercise settings. He received his master's degree in counseling psychology from Harvard University and his PhD in sport psychology from the University of Western Australia. Dr. Lavallee serves on the editorial board of the *Journal of Personal and Interpersonal Loss.* He is also a former All-American soccer player.

Daryl B. Marchant is a lecturer at Victoria University in Melbourne, Australia, where he teaches undergraduate and graduate applied sport psychology subjects. He received his master's degree from the University of Alberta and his PhD from Victoria University. Dr. Marchant consults extensively for professional Australian rules football teams and with athletes from a range of sports including golf, rifle shooting, horse racing, basketball, rugby union, soccer, cricket, and tennis. He is a member of the Australian Psychological Society and the College of Sport Psychologists. Dr. Marchant's research interests are primarily in competitive anxiety, psychometrics, and applied sport psychology service delivery.

Herb Marsh is dean of graduate research studies and founding director of the Self-Concept Enhancement and Learning Facilitation (SELF) research centre at the University of Western Sydney in Australia. He obtained his PhD in psychology from UCLA in 1974 and has worked in many areas of psychology including sport, education, social, personality, developmental, and quantitative, and was recognized as the 11th most productive psychological researcher in the world across all psychological disciplines. He is the author of psychological tests that measure self-concept, motivation, and teaching effectiveness. Dr. Marsh has published more than 200 articles in international journals, has reviewed articles for more than 50 journals, and has been on the editorial board of eight international journals including the *International Journal of Sport Psychology* and the *Journal of Sport & Exercise Psychology.* His interests in sport psychology include self-concept and motivation of both elite and non-elite athletes and outcomes associated with participation in sport.

Sean C. McCann is the head of sport psychology for the U.S. Olympic Committee at the Olympic Training Center (OTC) in Colorado Springs. Dr. McCann received a PhD in clinical psychology from the University of Hawaii. Currently, he works directly with Olympic athletes and coaches, supervises a team of USOC sport psychology staff, and writes and speaks on sport psychology issues. Dr. McCann worked as a sport psychologist for the 1994 U.S. Winter Olympic team in Lillehammer, Norway; the 1996 Summer Olympic team in Atlanta; and with the 1998 Winter Olympic team in Nagano, Japan. Dr. McCann is a licensed psychologist in Colorado, and he is on the editorial board of the journal *The Sport Psychologist.*

Shane M. Murphy became the first full-time sport psychologist at the Olympic Training Center (OTC) in Colorado Springs in 1987. In 1992 he became the first psychologist to head a multidisciplinary sport science team at the OTC. He was the U.S. team sport psychologist at the 1988 Summer Olympics in Seoul and at the 1992 Winter Olympics in Albertville. In 1996 he was the sport psychology consultant for the U.S. canoeing and kayaking team at the Summer Olympics in Atlanta. He has worked with Olympic athletes in figure skating, track and field, men's gymnastics, swimming, fencing, skiing, and many other sports. He is currently a sport psychologist for the U.S. snowboarding team. Dr. Murphy has written more than 40 research articles and papers and is the author of the books *The Achievement Zone* and *The Cheers and the Tears.* He is also the editor of *Sport Psychology Interventions* (Human Kinetics). Dr. Murphy is former president of Division 47, Sport and Exercise Psychology of the American Psychological Association. He is the cofounder of Gold Medal Consultants, a consulting firm that helps athletes achieve their highest performance potential. He has a BS, MS, and PhD in clinical psychology. Dr. Murphy's research interests are in mental imagery and performance and the measurement of mental performance skills. He teaches sport psychology at Sacred Heart University in Fairfield, Connecticut.

Clark Perry, Jr. is a registered psychologist employed at the Australian Institute of Sport in Canberra. He received his BA in psychology from Trenton State College and his MEd in psychology of human movement from Temple University. He is currently completing his doctorate at the University of Western Sydney. In 1990, he moved to Australia to take up an applied position working with elite athletes. As a sport psychologist, Clark has provided services to the Australian swimming, cycling, baseball, and triathlon teams at the 1992 and 1996 Olympic Games. He has also counseled athletes at eight world championships, two Commonwealth Games, and numerous national and international competitions. He has published articles covering the topics of self-concept, immune function, performance enhancement, sport psychology practice, flotation REST, and imagery. Clark is a founding member of the Australian Psychological Society's College of Sport Psychologists, a member of the Australian College of Clinical Psychologists, and an accredited Level II baseball coach.

Albert J. Petitpas is a professor in the psychology department at Springfield College in Springfield, Massachusetts, where he directs the graduate training program in athletic counseling. He is a fellow and certified consultant of the Association for the Advancement of Applied Sport Psychology (AAASP). His research and applied work focus on developmental concerns of athletes, such as managing transitions and coping with injuries. Dr. Petitpas has provided consulting services to a wide range of sport organizations including the U.S. ski team, the Career Assistance Program for athletes of the U.S. Olympic Committee, the National Football Foundation's Play It Smart Program, and the First Tee.

Trent A. Petrie is an associate professor in the department of psychology and the director of the Center for Sport Psychology and Performance Excellence at the University of North Texas. Through the center, Dr. Petrie and his colleagues have developed an interdisciplinary training program for master's and doctoral students in psychology and kinesiology. As a licensed psychologist and certified consultant for the Association for the Advancement of Applied Sport Psychology (AAASP), Dr. Petrie has worked extensively with athletes of all ages and competitive levels. His research interests have focused on eating disorders, academic and life skills, and the psychological antecedents of and reactions to athletic injury. With his coauthor, Dr. Eric Denson, he recently published *A Student Athlete's Guide to College Success: Peak Performance in School and Life.* A former collegiate athlete, Dr. Petrie remains physically active and involved in sport.

Artur Poczwardowski is an assistant professor in the department of psychology at St. Lawrence University. For over a decade he has consulted with athletes and teams in a number of sports including soccer, diving, air pistol shooting, speed skating, and figure skating. At the elite level, he worked with the 1992 Olympic Polish men's and women's judo teams. In addition, he taught relaxation to approximately 1,400 students while conducting courses in psychoregulation strategies at the Academy of Physical Education in Gdansk, Poland. He was involved in competitive judo for 14 years. He represented his university in a Division I team competing on national and international levels. Dr. Poczwardowski received his PhD in exercise and sport science from the University of Utah. He has published articles and book chapters on sport psychology practice and has more than 30 national and international presentations to his credit. His professional interests include coach-athlete relationships, fear of failure and fear of success in various performance domains, psychological skills training, and sport psychology consulting models.

Frances L. Price recently completed her doctorate in clinical psychology at the University of Wyoming. While working on her PhD she served as an academic athletic advisor in the intercollegiate athletics department. Dr. Price, herself a former collegiate athlete, has been working with athletes on performance enhancement and personal counseling for over eight years. She has also served as a clinical psychologist for the general student population. Dr. Price has recently expanded her services to include advising rodeo athletes.

Clay P. Sherman is an assistant professor in the division of kinesiology and health promotion at California State University at Fullerton. He received his PhD in exercise and sport science from the University of Utah. His major research interests relate to the development and application of educational approaches for teaching life skills to children and youth through the medium of sport and physical activity. Dr. Sherman has published in physical education, coaching, and sport psychology journals. Before beginning his graduate studies, Dr. Sherman was head coach for a swim team, an alpine ski instructor, and a caseworker/counselor for youths on probation. Dr. Sherman competed in college as an alpine skier and was a Triathlon Federation professional member from 1986 to 1988, racing both nationally and internationally. Currently, Dr. Sherman enjoys water polo, scuba, hiking, and mountain biking with his wife, Debbie.

Roberta Trattner Sherman received her doctorate in counseling psychology from Indiana University in 1982. She is codirector of the eating disorders program at Bloomington Hospital in Bloomington, Indiana, a program she cofounded in 1988. Dr. Sherman also serves as clinician and consultant to the Indiana University Department of Intercollegiate Athletics. In addition to her clinical and consulting work, she conducts research, writes, and provides professional workshops on eating disorders. Dr. Sherman also serves on the editorial board of *Eating Disorders: The Journal of Treatment and Prevention.* Included in her publications are two books she has coauthored titled *Helping Athletes With Eating Disorders* and *Bulimia: A Guide for Family and Friends.*

Jeff Simons is a registered sport psychologist and the director of Optimal Performance Consulting in Melbourne, Australia. Dr. Simons received his PhD from the University of Illinois at Urbana-Champaign and has 12 years of university teaching experience at the University of Southern California, UCLA, University of Colorado at Boulder, and Victoria University. He has more than 16 years of experience working with coaches and athletes in more than 35 sports, specializing in performance enhancement for youth to elite competition. Dr. Simons has been a sport psychology consultant to USA Wrestling, USA Track and Field, and numerous university and elite athletes in the U.S. He served as a sport psychologist for the 1996 Australian Olympic team for track and field and diving. He has been a consultant to the Victorian Institute of Sport since 1995, working with a wide variety of state, national, and Olympic-level athletes. He is the sport psychology coordinator for Athletics Australia and will serve as the psychologist for the Australian track and field and taekwondo teams during the 2000 Sydney Olympics.

Vance V. Tammen is currently an assistant professor at Ball State University. He was a lecturer in sport psychology at Victoria University in Melbourne, Australia, from 1994 to 1998, where he was also a registered sport psychologist. He completed his PhD in kinesiology at the University of Illinois at Urbana-Champaign, with a specialization in sport and exercise psychology. He has taught undergraduate and graduate classes in sport psychology, exercise psychology, psychology of coaching, group processes in sport and exercise, applied sport psychology, as well as NCAA Champs life skills, and a wide variety of physical activity classes. Dr. Tammen's research specialty is the social psychology of sport, exercise, and physical activity. He has worked as an applied sport psychology consultant with numerous athletes, teams, coaches, umpires, and referees ranging from youth sport to collegiate and Olympic levels.

Judy L. Van Raalte is an associate professor of psychology at Springfield College in Springfield, Massachusetts, where she teaches undergraduate and graduate psychology subjects and conducts research on self-talk and sport performance. She is listed in the United States Olympic Committee Sport Psychology Registry, 1996-2000, and is a certified consultant for the Association for the Advancement of Applied Sport Psychology (AAASP). Dr. Van Raalte was the recipient of the Developing Scholar Award from the International Society of Sport Psychology in 1997 and the Dorothy V. Harris memorial award for excellence as a young scholar/practitioner from AAASP in 1996. She is president of Virtual Brands, a company that produces multimedia applications for promotion of excellence and well-being in sport, health, and life.